341 BRL.

THE BRITISH YEAR BOOK OF
INTERNATIONAL LAW

THE
BRITISH YEAR BOOK OF
INTERNATIONAL LAW

1990

SIXTY-FIRST YEAR OF ISSUE

OXFORD
AT THE CLARENDON PRESS
1991

Oxford University Press, Walton Street, Oxford OX2 6DP

Oxford New York Toronto
Delhi Bombay Calcutta Madras Karachi
Petaling Jaya Singapore Hong Kong Tokyo
Nairobi Dar es Salaam Cape Town
Melbourne Auckland

ad associated companies in
Berlin Ibadan

Oxford is a trade mark of Oxford University Press

The British Year Book of International Law is an annual
publication, starting with Volume 52 (1981). Orders for
subscriptions or for individual volumes can be placed through
a bookseller or subscription agent. In case of difficulty please
write to the Retail Services Dept., Oxford University Press
Distribution Services, Saxon Way West, Corby, Northants
NN18 9ES, UK

British Library Cataloguing in Publication Data
The British year book of international law.
1990; sixty-first year of international law
1. International law—Periodicals
341'.05 JX1
ISBN 0-19-825726-0

Computerset by
Promenade Graphics Ltd., Cheltenham, Glos.

Printed in Great Britain
by Biddles Ltd.
Guildford and King's Lynn

Editorial Communications should be addressed as follows:

Articles and Notes:
PROFESSOR IAN BROWNLIE
All Souls College, Oxford, OX1 4AL.
Books for Review:
PROFESSOR J. G. MERRILLS
University of Sheffield Faculty of Law,
Crookesmoor Building, Conduit Road,
Sheffield, S10 1FL.

The Editors and members of the Editorial Committee do not make themselves in any way responsible for the views expressed by contributors, whether the contributions are signed or not.

The British Year Book of International Law is indexed in *Current Law Index*, published by Information Access Company.

CONTENTS

R. H. GRAVESON

PROFESSOR Ronald Harry Graveson, CBE, QC, Professor Emeritus of Private International Law at King's College, University of London, died on 5 January 1991 aged 79.

He was born in Sheffield and educated at King Edward VII School, Sheffield and at Sheffield University, where he graduated LL B in 1932 and LL M in 1934. He was awarded the degree of LL D of that University in 1955. He then studied at Harvard, gaining his SJD in 1936. By London University he was awarded the Ph.D in 1941 and became LL D in 1951. He was admitted as Solicitor in 1934 and after war service was called to the Bar in 1945 and served his year as Treasurer of Gray's Inn in 1983. He became QC in 1966.

Graveson's distinguished career as a law teacher began in 1946 and ended with his retirement in 1978. He was Reader in English Law at University College, London from 1946–7, when he moved to King's College as Professor of Law. Thenceforth his energies were devoted to that College, where he was Head of Department and for much of the time Dean of the Faculty of Law. In 1972–3 he was President of the Society of Public Teachers of Law. Graveson was closely connected with many academic bodies in the fields of international and comparative law. He was a member of the Institute of International Law and the International Academy of Comparative Law and of the Council of the British Institute of International and Comparative Law, being Joint Editor of the *International and Comparative Law Quarterly* from 1955 to 1961. He was Chairman of the UK National Committee of Comparative Law from 1955–7 and President of the International Association of Legal Science from 1960 to 1962.

Graveson was very active in establishing links between this country and foreign institutions and universities and this was fully recognized in Europe. He held honours from Belgium, France, the Netherlands and Germany and was awarded honorary degrees by the Universities of Ghent, Uppsala, Leuven and Freiburg.

Graveson built up the Faculty of Law of King's College as a leading centre for the study of International Law and Comparative Law. His own main interest was Private International Law, particularly in its comparative aspects. He was perhaps the only person ever to have held a Chair of Private International Law in any university in the United Kingdom. Graveson published several scholarly works in this field, including *The Comparative Evolution of Principles of the Conflict of Laws in England and the USA* (1960); *General Principles of Private International Law* (1964); and *Comparative Conflict of Laws* (1976). All of these are significant contributions to learning. He was perhaps best known as the author of his textbook, *Conflict of Laws*, first published in 1948, which reached a seventh edition in 1974. This provided a clear and comprehensible account of the subject for students and contained much good sense; it was, unfortunately, rather overshadowed by Geoffrey Cheshire's *Private International Law*, against which it must have been difficult for any jurist to compete.

Graveson was a thorough and careful scholar. He was a rather quiet and gentle-mannered person with, however, a blunt manner of speaking, and a sharp sense of humour. He was astute to advance the interests and careers of his students and his staff and the institutions of learning to which he belonged. Many have enjoyed his kindness. He enhanced the reputation of this country in the wider legal world.

J. G. COLLIER

THE LAW AND PROCEDURE OF THE INTERNATIONAL COURT OF JUSTICE
1960–1989*

PART TWO

By HUGH THIRLWAY‡

I. GENERAL PRINCIPLES AND SOURCES OF LAW

(continued)
Division B: Sources of Law

* © Hugh Thirlway, 1991.
‡ Principal Legal Secretary, International Court of Justice.

INTRODUCTION

Perhaps the most striking feature of the use made by the Court, in its decisions during the period considered, of the various sources of international law, and indeed of the concept of sources, is its fidelity to the traditional approaches to the matter. For many observers, the developments in what are regarded as law-making activities in the United Nations and through other international bodies, the use of consensus, and increasing reference to ideas of equity or equitable principles, have rendered obsolete the enumeration of sources found in Article 38 of the Statute of the Court.

Thus to quote the conclusions of a recent paper by a distinguished internationalist:

(1) The erstwhile emphasis on formal 'Sources' of International Law belongs to the earlier, 'classical' era of International Law and is no longer particularly relevant, and certainly in no way controlling, in the present era of transition and large-scale change in International Law and in the international society it is supposed to reflect.

(2) The emphasis today has shifted from the old neo-positivist insistence on closed, *a priori*, formal categories of 'sources', to a neo-Realist, Law-as-Fact approach in which the enquiry, as to a claimed principle or rule of law, is directed to whether the parties involved, expressly or by their conduct, regard the proposition concerned as normative and legally binding upon them . . . [1]

However true these views may be of the approach to law found among the representatives of States at international conferences and in international organizations, or indeed in Foreign Ministries, it does not correspond, or no longer corresponds, to the International Court's view of its role.[2] Specifically with respect to the philosophy underlying the decisions of the Court, a less radical assessment made in 1985 was that the Court's judgments revealed

la tendance à rechercher la solution qui s'adapte le mieux aux exigences du cas concret, en évitant, dans la mesure du possible, toute prise de position de caractère général et abstrait. D'où la partie prépondérante faite à la *pratique* des Etats parties au différend, une 'pratique' qui interprète la règle de droit et qui pourrait, le cas échéant, faire ressortir aussi l'existence d'une coutume interprétative à portée réduite, liante ces Etats et ces Etats seulement.[3]

But only a year later, in 1986, on the subject of international customary law, for example, the Court had this to say:

The Court notes that there is in fact evidence, to be examined below, of a considerable degree of agreement between the Parties as to the content of the customary international law relating to the non-use of force and non-intervention. This concurrence of their views does not however dispense the Court from having itself

---

[1] McWhinney, ' "Classical" Sources and International Law-Making Process of Contemporary International Law', *International Law at the Time of its Codification* (1987), p. 341. For a fuller exposition of these views, see the same author's *The International Court of Justice and the Western Tradition of International Law* (Nijhoff, 1987), chapter II, *passim*.

[2] This is not to say that the Judges have accepted with unanimous satisfaction the system of Article 38: in the *Fisheries Jurisdiction* cases, for example, Judge de Castro found difficulty in fitting 'the concepts of special rights, preferential rights and historic rights' into the traditional categories:

'It is not easy to prove the existence of a general practice accepted as law, nor would these concepts appear to form part of the general principles of law recognized by civilized nations. But it does appear possible to overcome the difficulty resulting from the unfortunate drafting of Article 38 of the Statute with the assistance of the teachings of the most highly qualified writers. One cannot make a sharp division between customary law and the principles of law.' (*ICJ Reports*, 1974, p. 100.)

This is, however, very far from saying that the traditional system of sources had become outdated.

[3] Ferrari Bravo, 'Méthodes de recherche de la coutume internationale dans la pratique des Etats', *Recueil des cours*, 192 (1985–III), p. 315.

to ascertain what rules of customary international law are applicable. The mere fact that States declare their recognition of certain rules is not sufficient for the Court to consider these as being part of customary international law, and as applicable as such to those States.[4]

It is of course possible to regard the Court as shackled by the requirements of Article 38 of its Statute, and therefore unable to respond to or participate in the progressive development which international law may be said to be undergoing in this respect. Indeed, in the judgment quoted, the Court continued:

> Bound as it is by Article 38 of its Statute to apply, *inter alia*, international custom 'as evidence of a general practice accepted as law', the Court may not disregard the essential role played by general practice.[4]

Neither the Court nor parties before it have however found reason to chafe against the constraints imposed by the Statute; and other judicial or arbitral instances have found it appropriate to be guided by Article 38 on the basis, as observed recently by Judge Mosler, of a consensus that no better definition exists of the norms of international law.[5] Nor do the decisions of the Court—with one notable exception—appear to have prompted criticism grounded on any theory of the outmoded character of the law it has to apply. In fact the dissatisfaction engendered by the *South West Africa* judgment of 1966 should not be attributed primarily to problems of the *sources* of law applied by the Court, but rather to its handling of such questions as the proper interpretation of the Mandate for South West Africa, and the significance of the 1962 decision on the preliminary objections in the case. Even if, as is arguably the case, the Court was insufficiently aware in 1966 of a general recognition of an impact on law of certain transformations in international society, a greater awareness was surely demonstrated sufficiently in its advisory opinion of 1971 on Namibia.

It will therefore be possible in the present article to take each of the sources of law referred to in Article 38 of the Statute (with the exception of the 'views of publicists'—a source the influence of which, however great in fact, is never avowed), and to consider what reference to it the Court has made during the period under consideration. The plan of the present article is based, in accordance with the policy declared at the outset of this series,[6] on the structure of Sir Gerald Fitzmaurice's articles. As chance would have it, the decisions examined by him during the period to 1959 were not such as to prompt much reflection on the question of sources of international

---

[4] *Military and Paramilitary Activities in and against Nicaragua (Nicaragua v. United States of America), ICJ Reports*, 1986, p. 97, para. 84.

[5] 'Bedeutungswandel in der Anwendung "der von den zivilisierten Staaten anerkannten allgemeinen Rechtsgrundsätze"?', *Pensamiento jurídico y sociedad internacional (Mélanges Truyol Serra)* (Madrid, 1986), vol. 2, p. 816.

[6] This *Year Book*, 60 (1989), pp. 6–7.

law, though Sir Gerald had much to say on the subject elsewhere.[7] Where such questions arose, he chose to deal first with certain concepts outside the traditional enumeration of Article 38, paragraph 1, of the Statute, before turning to custom; treaties as sources of law were not dealt with independently of the general section on 'Treaty Interpretation and other Treaty Points'.

In the present article, the pretenders to the title of sources which do not find recognition in Article 38—humanitarian considerations and economic and other interests—will be examined first, followed by treaties, custom and the general principles of law; and finally the subsidiary sources, specifically judicial decisions.

<h2 align="center">CHAPTER I:</h2>

<h3 align="center">MISCELLANEOUS MINOR SOURCES OR PSEUDO-SOURCES</h3>

1. *Considerations of Humanity*

In the first of his articles, Fitzmaurice included considerations of humanity among the sources of law,[8] basing his view on the *Corfu Channel* case where the Court referred to 'elementary considerations of humanity' as an element contributing to the establishment of Albania's obligation to notify shipping of the existence of a minefield in its territorial waters.[9] He noted however that 'all the implications of this view . . . remain to be worked out'.[10] Subsequently, he appears to have resiled from the position that considerations of humanity could be a separate source of law: in his paper 'Judicial Innovation—Its Uses and Perils' published in 1965,[11] he considered the humanitarian provisions of the various Hague Conventions as 'special applications of a much more general principle of universal applicability'[12] or as a 'principle, originally expressed only in conventional form, [which] had received such general recognition . . . as to have become a received rule of customary international law'.[13]

A resounding statement on the relationship between considerations of a humanitarian character and rules of law was made by the Court in the 1966 judgment in the *South West Africa* cases:

---

[7] See for example his Academy lectures, 'The General Principles of International Law considered from the Standpoint of the Rule of Law', *Recueil des cours*, 92 (1957-II), p. 5; 'Some Problems regarding the Formal Sources of International Law', *Symbolae Verzijl* (1958), pp. 153 ff.; 'The Future of Public International Law and the International Legal System in the Circumstances of Today' (Institut de droit international, Special Report, 1973).

[8] This *Year Book*, 27 (1950), p. 17; *Collected Edition*, I, p. 17.

[9] *ICJ Reports*, 1949, p. 22.

[10] Loc. cit. above (n. 8), footnote 4.

[11] *Cambridge Essays in Honour of Lord McNair* (Oceana, 1965), p. 24.

[12] Ibid., p. 29.

[13] Ibid., p. 30.

Throughout this case it has been suggested, directly or indirectly, that humanitarian considerations are sufficient in themselves to generate legal rights and obligations, and that the Court can and should proceed accordingly. The Court does not think so. It is a court of law, and can take account of moral principles only in so far as these are given a sufficient expression in legal form. Law exists, it is said, to serve a social need; but precisely for that reason it can do so only through and within the limits of its own discipline. Otherwise, it is not a legal service that would be rendered.[14]

To some extent this impressive statement should in fact be regarded as *obiter*; the question with which the Court was dealing was not one of the possibility of the direct generation of rules of law by humanitarian considerations. The point at issue was whether the applicants had standing to seek to enforce the obligations of South Africa under the Mandate—whether they had 'a legal right or interest in the subject-matter of their claim'. Thus the suggestion was not that humanitarian considerations acted to impose on South Africa obligations other than those imposed by the Mandate, but that it was legitimate, on the basis of humanitarian considerations, to regard those obligations as owed to, and enforceable by, all States of the international community.

The Court referred to this argument as

what is perhaps the most important contention of a general character that has been advanced in connection with this aspect of the case, namely the contention by which it is sought to derive a legal right or interest in the conduct of the mandate from the simple existence, or principle, of the 'sacred trust'.[15]

It examined it in the light of a statement of principle, as follows:

Humanitarian considerations may constitute the inspirational basis for rules of law, just as, for instance, the preambular parts of the United Nations Charter constitute the moral and political basis for the specific legal provisions thereafter set out. Such considerations do not, however, in themselves amount to rules of law. All States are interested—have an interest—in such matters. But the existence of an 'interest' does not of itself entail that this interest is specifically juridical in character.[16]

On this basis, the Court refused to see the 'sacred trust' as a source of legal right or interest for the applicants:

The sacred trust, it is said, is a 'sacred trust of civilization'. Hence all civilized nations have an interest in seeing that it is carried out. An interest, no doubt;—but in order that this interest may take on a specifically legal character, the sacred trust itself must be or become something more than a moral or humanitarian ideal. In order to generate legal rights and obligations, it must be given juridical expression and be clothed in legal form . . .[17]

---

[14] *ICJ Reports*, 1966, p. 34, para. 49.
[15] Ibid., p. 34, para. 51.
[16] Ibid., p. 34, para. 50.
[17] Ibid., p. 34, para. 51.

In the present case, the principle of the sacred trust has as its sole juridical expression the mandates system. As such, it constitutes a moral ideal given form as a juridical régime in the shape of that system. But it is necessary not to confuse the moral ideal with the legal rules intended to give it effect. For the purpose of realizing the aims of the trust in the particular form of any given mandate, its legal rights and obligations were those, and those alone, which resulted from the relevant instruments creating the system, and the mandate itself, within the framework of the League of Nations.[18]

The Mandate was drawn up to give, so far as thought necessary, juridical expression to the principle of the sacred trust. Whether the compromissory clause was to be read as entitling individual League of Nations members to enforce performance of all the Mandatory's obligations was a question of interpretation of the Mandate; and the humanitarian considerations underlying the Mandate were certainly a material element. But that was its only relevance: the nature of the relevant legal obligations was defined, and the entity upon which those obligations rested was identified, the only question being the identity of the beneficiaries of the obligation, in the sense of 'those entitled to enforce it'.

In the passage quoted, the Court was responding less to the arguments of the applicants—who probably regarded the question of 'legal interest' as having been definitively settled by the 1982 judgment—than to the views of dissenting judges, particularly Judge Tanaka.

In his dissenting opinion, Judge Tanaka stated:

The historical development of law demonstrates the continual process of the cultural enrichment of the legal order by taking into consideration values or interests which had previously been excluded from the sphere of law. In particular, the extension of the object of rights to cultural, and therefore intangible, matters and the legalization of social justice and of humanitarian ideas which cannot be separated from the gradual realization of world peace, are worthy of our attention . . .

As outstanding examples of the recognition of the legal interests of States in general humanitarian causes, the international efforts to suppress the slave trade, the minorities treaties, the Genocide Convention and the Constitution of the International Labour Organisation are cited.

We consider that in these treaties and organizations common and humanitarian interests are incorporated. By being given organizational form, these interests take the nature of 'legal interest' and require to be protected by specific procedural means.

The mandates system which was created under the League, presents itself as nothing other than an historical manifestation of the trend of thought which contributed to establish the above-mentioned treaties and organizations. The mandates system as a whole, by incorporating humanitarian and other interests, can be said to be a 'legal interest'.[19]

---

[18] Ibid., pp. 34–5, para. 52.
[19] Ibid., p. 252.

Judge Tanaka was, however, addressing himself to the true question in issue:

However, what is in question is not whether the Mandate is a legal interest or not. What we are considering is not legal interest in itself, but its relationship with persons who possess it, that is to say, the question of the existence of a legal interest as a condition on which the Applicants, as Members of the League, possess the right to have recourse to the International Court.

Each member of a human society—whether domestic or international—is interested in the realization of social justice and humanitarian ideas. The State which belongs as a member to an international organization incorporating such ideas must necessarily be interested. So far as the interest in this case affects the rights and obligations of a State, it may be called a legal interest. The State may become the subject or holder of a legal interest regarding social justice and humanitarian matters, but this interest includes its profound concern with the attitude of other States, particularly member States belonging to the same treaty or organization. In short, each State may possess a legal interest in the observance of the obligations by other States.[20]

In the case of *Military and Paramilitary Activities in and against Nicaragua (Nicaragua* v. *United States of America)* the Court had some opportunity to press further the question of the relationship between humanitarian considerations and positive law. It there found that mines were laid close to Nicaraguan ports without any warning or notification being given either to Nicaragua or to shipping of other countries. It referred to the duty of notification of minelaying imposed in time of war by Hague Convention No. VIII of 1907, and continued:

It has already been made clear above that in peacetime for one State to lay mines in the internal or territorial waters of another is an unlawful act; but in addition, if a State lays mines in any waters whatever in which the vessels of another State have rights of access or passage, and fails to give any warning or notification whatsoever, in disregard of the security of peaceful shipping, it commits a breach of the principles of humanitarian law underlying the specific provisions of Convention No. VIII of 1907. Those principles were expressed by the Court in the *Corfu Channel* case as follows:
  'certain general and well recognized principles, namely: elementary considerations of humanity, even more exacting in peace than in war' (*I.C.J. Reports 1949*, p. 22).[21]

The wording of this passage suggests an interpretation more in line with Fitzmaurice's original assessment of the *Corfu Channel* decision than with his later views: the Court here appears to be regarding 'principles of humanitarian law' as a self-sufficient source of law, rather than either part of general customary law or one of the general principles of law in the sense of Article 38, paragraph 1(c), of the Statute of the Court. There is no examination of the State practice, and it does not seem to be suggested that a rule

---

[20] Ibid., pp. 252–3.
[21] *ICJ Reports*, 1986, p. 112, para. 215.

of customary law has crystallized round the provisions of Hague Convention No. VIII—which, in any event, refers only to practice in time of war.

However, the operative clause of the same judgment puts matters in an entirely different light: the Court there finds that

> the United States of America, by failing to make known the existence and location of the mines laid by it . . . , has acted in breach of its obligations *under customary international law* in this respect.[22]

The Court's thinking, in the course of this single judgment, seems to have followed a course parallel to that of Fitzmaurice: initially an assertion of humanitarian considerations as a fundamental and independent principle, followed by an assignment of that principle to the corpus of customary law. In the specific case of non-notified mining, it is difficult to see upon what actual practice of States the Court was entitled to base a finding of the existence of 'obligations under customary law'.

Further light on the Court's attitude to humanitarian law is thrown by its reference, in a different section of the same judgment, to the Geneva Conventions of 12 August 1949, which, as the Court noted, Nicaragua had not invoked in support of its claim for breach of obligation not to kill, wound, or kidnap citizens of Nicaragua. The Court put aside any question of application of the 'multilateral treaty reservation':

> The Court however sees no need to take a position on that matter, since in its view the conduct of the United States may be judged according to the fundamental general principles of humanitarian law; in its view, the Geneva Conventions are in some respects a development, and in other respects no more than the expression, of such principles. It is significant in this respect that, according to the terms of the Conventions, the denunciation of one of them
> > 'shall in no way impair the obligations which the Parties to the conflict shall remain bound to fulfil by virtue of the principles of the law of nations, as they result from the usages established among civilized peoples, from the laws of humanity and the dictates of the public conscience' (Convention I, Art. 63; Convention II, Art. 62; Convention III, Art. 142; Convention IV, Art. 158).[23]

The Court referred to the rules defined in Article 3 of each of the four Conventions, and stated:

> There is no doubt that, in the event of international armed conflicts, these rules also constitute a minimum yardstick, in addition to the more elaborate rules which are also to apply to international conflicts; and they are rules which, in the Court's opinion, reflect what the Court in 1949 called 'elementary considerations of humanity' (*Corfu Channel, Merits, I.C.J. Reports 1949*, p. 22; paragraph 215 above). The Court may therefore find them applicable to the present dispute, and is thus not required to decide what role the United States multilateral treaty reservation might otherwise play in regard to the treaties in question.[24]

---

[22] Ibid., pp. 147–8, para. 292(8), emphasis added.
[23] Ibid., pp. 113–14, para. 218.
[24] Ibid., p. 114.

The reference to the Geneva Conventions as 'in some respects a development, and in other respects no more than the expression of such principles' recalls the approach of the Court to the relationship between custom and multinational treaties in the *North Sea Continental Shelf* cases. The resemblance is, however, superficial; there was no question in 1949 of the crystallization,[25] in Article 3 of the Conventions, of a norm of customary law. As an expert in the field has observed:

> Comme bien de publicistes l'ont reconnu, l'article 3 des Conventions de Genève de 1949 marque un changement fondamental dans la situation et la protection de la personne humaine en cas de conflit interne.[26]

It appears therefore that what the Court had in mind were principles which did not require translation into customary law, through practice and *opinio juris*, for their effective application. The obligation which the Court found rested on the United States Government 'does not derive only from the Conventions themselves, but from the general principles of humanitarian law to which the Conventions merely give specific expression'.[27] At a later point in the judgment, however, the Court refers back to its finding as having been

> that general principles of humanitarian law include a particular prohibition, *accepted by States*, and extending to activities which occur in the context of armed conflicts, whether international in character or not.[28]

The cryptic words 'accepted by States' could be taken as indicating that the prohibition in question was a 'general practice accepted as law', i.e., an international custom; but it seems more consistent with the Court's approach to read it as referring to the embodiment of the prohibition in question in the Geneva Conventions.

There is a further important distinction to be made between the section of the judgment dealing with the mining of Nicaraguan ports and that dealing with the conduct of the *contras* seen from the standpoint of humanitarian law. The mining of the Nicaraguan ports was, as the Court found, an act directly attributable to the United States Government, which therefore was held to have committed a breach of international law—customary law. In the case of the elements of humanitarian law reflected in the Geneva Conventions, however, the Court rejected the submission that the acts committed by the *contras* could be attributed to the United States.[29] The

---

[25] See the discussion of this concept below, Chapter II, section 3.

[26] Wilhelm, 'Problèmes relatifs à la protection de la personne humaine par le droit international dans les conflits armées ne présentant pas un caractère international', *Recueil des cours*, 137 (1972–III), p. 332. See also Meron, 'The Geneva Conventions as Customary Law', *American Journal of International Law*, 81 (1987), pp. 356–7.

[27] *ICJ Reports*, 1986, p. 114, para. 220. On the other hand Judge Jennings, in his dissenting opinion, expressed doubt 'whether those conventions could be regarded as embodying *customary law*' (ibid., p. 537, emphasis added). Judge Ago also reads the judgment as finding the general principles of humanitarian law to be part of customary law: ibid., p. 184, para. 6.

[28] Ibid., p. 129, para. 255, emphasis added.

[29] Ibid., p. 113, para. 216.

finding against the United States in this respect was, in the terms of the operative clause, that by disseminating a terrorist manual to the *contra* forces, it had 'encouraged the commission by them of acts contrary to general principles of humanitarian law',[30] with the clear implication that by doing so the United States had committed a breach of its own obligations under an international law.

This obligation, not spelled out in the operative clause, is explained in the body of the judgment. Having, as noted above, referred to Article 3 common to the four Geneva Conventions, which lays down rules 'to be applied in the armed conflicts of non-international character', but which, 'in the event of international armed conflict, . . . also constitute a minimum yardstick . . . ', the Court continues:

> The conflict between the *contras'* forces and those of the Government of Nicaragua is an armed conflict which is 'not of an international character'. The acts of the *contras* towards the Nicaraguan Government are therefore governed by the law applicable to conflicts of that character; whereas the actions of the United States in and against Nicaragua fall under the legal rules relating to international conflicts. Because the minimum rules applicable to international and to non-international conflicts are identical, there is no need to address the question whether those actions must be looked at in the context of the rules which operate for the one or for the other category of conflict.[31]

At this point, the Court has thus established that there are obligations, resulting from the Conventions themselves, resting on the United States, in relation to the conflict in Nicaragua. It then turns to Article 1 of the Convention:

> The Court considers that there is an obligation on the United States Government, in the terms of Article 1 of the Geneva Conventions, to 'respect' the Conventions and even 'to ensure respect' for them 'in all circumstances', since such an obligation does not derive only from the Conventions themselves, but from the general principles of humanitarian law to which the Conventions merely give specific expression. The United States is thus under an obligation not to encourage persons or groups engaged in the conflict in Nicaragua to act in violation of the provisions of Article 3 common to the four 1949 Geneva Conventions.[32]

The finding is thus that there is an international obligation, deriving not from the Conventions themselves, but from general principles of humanitarian law, to ensure respect for the provisions of the Conventions. This time there is not only no enquiry into practice and *opinio juris*: there is no mention of custom or customary law, either in the body of the judgment or in the operative clause. The Court's approach may therefore be regarded as a finding on the basis of customary law, which is inadequately reasoned and

---

[30] Ibid., p. 148, para. 292(9).
[31] Ibid., p. 114, paras. 218–19.
[32] Ibid., pp. 388–9, para. 259. Judge Schwebel cites in this context Ago's Seventh Report to the ILC on State Responsibility (*Yearbook of the ILC*, 1978, vol. 2, part 1, p. 55, paras. 62, 63).

explained,[33] or as a finding based simply on general principles of humanitarian law, having, and requiring, no basis in custom.

It may be significant that Judge Schwebel, in his dissenting opinion, has no doubt that the Court's finding could not be supported by customary law:

> Customary international law does not know the delict of 'encouragement'. There appears to be no precedent for holding a State responsible for breach of the Geneva Conventions for the Protection of War Victims of 1949 by reason of its advocacy of violations of humanitarian law, though it may reasonably be maintained that a State which encourages violations of that law fails to 'ensure respect' for the Geneva Conventions, as by their terms it is obliged to do.[34]

Yet Judge Schwebel was able to vote for the relevant paragraph of the operative clause, because

> Whether or not the Government of the United States may be held responsible under international law for the publication of the manual on the ground of 'encouragement', what is beyond discussion is that no government can justify official advocacy of acts in violation of the law of war.[35]

One must conclude that the contest between general principles and customary law for possession of the field of general humanitarian law ended, in the *Nicaragua* v. *United States* case, in a draw. The obligation to give notice of mines is, it seems, one of customary law: but there may be a noncustomary general principle forbidding encouragement of breaches of the laws of war.

2. *Legal Interests, Legitimate Interests, Economic Interests*

In the series of articles devoted to the work of the Court in 1951–1954, Fitzmaurice included, under the general heading 'Sources of Law', a section on 'So-called legitimate interests. Economic interests'.[36] This categorization was something of a *lucus a non lucendo*, since the argument of the section was that the Court had in fact not sanctioned so-called legitimate, or economic, interests as being *per se* sources of law and of State rights. The observations there made however afford a useful framework for examining a number of cases during the period now under consideration in which the Court has had to weigh the legal implications of 'interests' appertaining to, or asserted by, States.

An apparent exception to the principle that interests may not be in themselves sources of rights under international law is suggested by the notorious dictum of the Court in the *Barcelona Traction* case concerning obligations *erga omnes*:

> an essential distinction should be drawn between the obligations of a State towards

[33] This is the view of Meron, 'The Geneva Conventions as Customary Law', *American Journal of International Law*, 81 (1987), pp. 353 ff.
[34] *ICJ Reports*, 1986, pp. 388–9, para. 259.
[35] Ibid., p. 389, para. 260.
[36] This *Year Book*, 30 (1953), pp. 69–70; *Collected Edition*, I, pp. 199–200.

the international community as a whole, and those arising vis-à-vis another State in the field of diplomatic protection. By their very nature the former are the concern of all States. In view of the importance of the rights involved, all States can be held to have a legal interest in their protection; they are obligations *erga omnes*.

Such obligations derive, for example, in contemporary international law, from the outlawing of acts of aggression, and of genocide, as also from the principles and rules concerning the basic rights of the human person, including protection from slavery and racial discrimination.[37]

The concept of obligations *erga omnes* has already been discussed in the first article of this series, where it was noted that the practical implication is that

a claim may be brought by any State against any State alleging a breach of an obligation towards the international community as a whole, without the applicant State having to show that it has itself, directly or through its nationals, suffered injury from the alleged breach.[38]

It was also there shown that the possibility of such an *intérêt d'agir* in the absence of a substantive interest may be very much more limited than the 1970 dictum suggests, and may in fact depend on participation in a multilateral treaty.[39] Furthermore, while the Court did not indicate the basis of its assertion, it appears that the existence of 'obligations *erga omnes*' can only derive from developments in customary law.[40] If this is so, the principle of the essential jurisprudential infertility of legal interests remains intact.

(1) *The distinction between rights and interests: the* Barcelona Traction *case*

In its judgment in the *Barcelona Traction* case, the Court rejected a contention that the measures in the Spanish courts complained of, although taken with respect to Barcelona Traction and causing it direct damage, constituted an unlawful act *vis-à-vis* Belgium because they also, though indirectly, caused damage to the Belgian shareholders in Barcelona Traction. The Court stated:

This again is merely a different way of presenting the distinction between injury in respect of a right and injury to a simple interest. But, as the Court has indicated, evidence that damage was suffered does not *ipso facto* justify a diplomatic claim. Persons suffer damage or harm in most varied circumstances. This in itself does not involve the obligation to make reparation. Not a mere interest affected, but solely a right infringed involves responsibility, so that an act directed against and infringing only the company's rights does not involve responsibility towards the shareholders, even if their interests are affected.[41]

This part of the reasoning of the judgment is rendered less satisfactory by

[37] *ICJ Reports*, 1970, p. 32, paras. 33–4.
[38] This *Year Book*, 60 (1989), p. 94.
[39] Ibid., pp. 101–2.
[40] The reference to '*contemporary* international law' points in this direction.
[41] *ICJ Reports*, 1970, p. 36, para. 46.

a certain confusion, already examined, as to the identification of the legal system within and by virtue of which the 'rights' referred to by the Court existed. Nevertheless, on its own terms, the distinction is clear; an interest is something which is valuable to its holder, like a right; but the loss of, or action prejudicially affecting, an interest is *damnum sine injuria*, and the party responsible (in the causative sense) cannot be made to pay for it. Put another way, a right entails the existence of an obligation to respect the right; there is no obligation to respect mere interests.[42]

(2) *Interests as the inspiration of a practice producing a customary right: the* Fisheries Jurisdiction *cases*

As Fitzmaurice points out,

Legitimate interests may be the *inspiration*, motive power or force behind certain practices of States leading to the evolution of a customary rule of general international law. But of course the *source* of the eventual rule is the custom or practice: the interests involved are only the reason for it.[43]

An excellent example of this is afforded by the preferential fishing rights of the coastal State, the genesis and nature of which were examined in the judgments in the *Fisheries Jurisdiction* cases in 1974.

The question of the enforcement against the United Kingdom and the Federal Republic of Germany of the Icelandic fishery regulations was approached by the Court on the basis of opposability of those regulations to the applicant States, not that of the inherent validity of the regulations as a matter of general international law. Thus the question was left open whether the additional areas claimed by Iceland as part of its fishery zone were or were not still part of the high seas.[44] In the high seas, it was generally recognized, every State has the right to fish as an aspect of the freedom of the seas, subject, according to Article 2 of the 1958 Geneva Convention, to a requirement that such freedoms be exercised 'with reasonable regard to the interests of other States in their exercise of the freedom of the high seas'.

The Court found that a development of this comparatively simple system had occurred, one which was contingent in the sense that there was no change in the position of States unless a certain condition was fulfilled, and then only in the sea areas where such condition was fulfilled. A convenient

[42] Such an obligation may be created by treaty: cf. 1958 Geneva Convention on the High Seas, Article 2. This however concerns interests directly belonging to States, the existence of which (as something less than rights) must be taken to be recognized by international law. In *Elettronica Sicula* Judge Oda doubted whether anything short of a specific provision in a treaty could provide for diplomatic protection of shareholders' interests: *ICJ Reports*, 1989, p. 86.

[43] Loc. cit. above (n. 36).

[44] This is in fact something of an over-simplification. It is arguable that the whole discussion of the preferential rights of Iceland as coastal State in a situation of exceptional dependence on fisheries, and the established rights of the applicants, is only consistent with the view that Iceland's unilateral extension was invalid, despite the clear disclaimer on this point in the joint separate opinion (*ICJ Reports*, 1974, p. 45); but the point is not material to the present discussion.

definition of the condition was quoted by the Court from a proposal made
at the 1960 Law of the Sea Conference:

> A special situation or condition may be deemed to exist when:
> (a) The fisheries and the economic development of the coastal State or the feed-
>   ing of its population are so manifestly interrelated that, in consequence, that
>   State is greatly dependent on the living resources of the high seas in the area in
>   respect of which preferential fishing is being claimed;
> (b) It becomes necessary to limit the total catch of a stock or stocks of fish in such
>   areas . . . [45]

Once this condition is met, as the Court found, 'the preferential rights of
the coastal State come into play'.[46] The justification for these rights is the
consideration defined in (a) quoted above—the economic and human interests of the coastal State. Yet it is not these interests themselves which
create, or are transformed into, preferential fishing rights; the rights are the
creature of customary international law, through practice:

> State practice on the subject of fisheries reveals an increasing and widespread
> acceptance of the concept of preferential rights for coastal States, particularly in
> favour of countries or territories in a situation of special dependence on coastal
> fisheries . . . [46]

Nor are the economic interests of the coastal State the only interests to
have an impact on the legal position: the preferential rights of that State

> cannot imply the extinction of the concurrent rights of other States, and particu-
> larly of a State which, like the Applicant, has for many years been engaged in fish-
> ing in the waters in question, such fishing activity being important to the economy
> of the country concerned.[47]

Like the preferential rights of the coastal State, the 'concurrent rights'
derived their status as rights from State practice, not from their economic
basis.

(3) *Interests underlying the establishment of prescriptive or historic rights:
the* Tunisia/Libya *case*

To quote Fitzmaurice once again:

> State interest may be the reason or motive for the building up by prescriptive
> means of a historic title or special right not normally accorded by law. But again, it
> is the usage or custom, acquiesced in by other States, that constitutes the legal
> foundation or source of the right.[48]

In the case concerning the *Continental Shelf (Tunisia/Libyan Arab
Jamahiriya)*, Tunisia claimed the existence of historic rights of exploitation

---

[45] *Second United Nations Conference on the Law of the Sea*, Summary Records, pp. 13, 14, 15, 173,
quoted in *ICJ Reports*, 1974, p. 25, para. 57.

[46] *ICJ Reports*, 1974, p. 26, para. 58.

[47] Ibid., pp. 27–8, para. 62. For details of the economic impact on the British fishing industry of an
exclusion from the Icelandic fishing grounds, see the UK Memorial, *Pleadings*, vol. 1, pp. 312–15.

[48] This *Year Book*, 30 (1953), p. 70; *Collected Edition*, I, p. 200.

of fixed fisheries and the collection of sedentary species (sponges) over a considerable area of the shallow Gulf of Gabès. The Court declared that:

> The historic rights claimed by Tunisia derive from the long-established interests and activities of its population in exploiting the fisheries of the bed and waters of the Mediterranean off its coasts . . . [49]

The Court in fact made no finding as to the validity or opposability to Libya of the historic rights claimed, since it found it unnecessary to do so. It did however deal with the basis on which a claim to such rights might be justified:

> It is clearly the case that, basically, the notion of historic rights or waters and that of the continental shelf are governed by distinct legal régimes in customary international law. The first régime is based on acquisition and occupation, while the second is based on the existence of rights '*ipso facto* and *ab initio*'.[50]

It is thus clearly stated that historic rights are a matter of customary international law, that if they are 'based on acquisition and occupation' it is because custom recognizes that acquisition and occupation may have this effect. Such acquisition and occupation occurs in order to advance or preserve the interests of the coastal State; but those interests themselves are extra-legal in character.

(4) *Economic and other interests as 'relevant circumstances' for purposes of an equitable delimitation of maritime spaces*

The precise legal status of the various considerations which may be taken into account for a judicial delimitation of maritime spaces is somewhat obscure, in view of the interpretation of the concepts of 'equitable criteria', 'equitable methods' and the need to achieve an 'equitable result'. Something has already been said on this in the first of these articles;[51] and the matter will be given further consideration in a later article in the specific context of the law of the sea. On the basis, however, that reference to equity is not to an unstructured, random or individualized equity, so that it does not act as a cut-out between the requirements of law and the considerations taken into account, or capable of being taken into account, something may be said of the Court's treatment in this context of claims based on economic or socio-economic interests.

In the *Continental Shelf (Tunisia/Libya)* case, the Court declined to attach any significance whatever to the interests of this kind relied on by either party. Tunisia had relied on, *inter alia*, 'its relative poverty vis-à-vis Libya in terms of absence of natural resources like agriculture and minerals'; Libya had referred to 'the presence or absence of oil or gas in the oil wells in the continental shelf areas appertaining to either Party', but rather

---

[49] *ICJ Reports*, 1982, p. 72, para. 98.
[50] Ibid., p. 74, para. 100.
[51] This *Year Book*, 60 (1989), pp. 51–62.

in relation to its reliance on arguments drawn from geology.[52] The Court was prepared to recognize the possible geological relevance of oil or gas deposits, but on comparative economic poverty, its ruling was terse:

> The Court is, however, of the view that these economic considerations cannot be taken into account for the delimitation of the continental shelf areas appertaining to each Party. They are virtually extraneous factors since they are variables which unpredictable national fortune or calamity, as the case may be, might at any time cause to tilt the scale one way or the other. A country might be poor today and become rich tomorrow as a result of an event such as the discovery of a valuable economic resource.[53]

The reason given is not entirely convincing: the presence and extent of agricultural resources, relied on by Tunisia, was a stable and predictable factor. As to the possible economic transformation as a result of a windfall benefit from hydrocarbon resources, in effect what Tunisia was saying was that it ought to be put in a position where the *likelihood* of this on Tunisian territory or sea-bed areas would be nearer equality with its likelihood on the Libyan side.

A somewhat similar *argumentum ad misericordiam* was used, also against Libya, by Malta, which relied on, as relevant circumstances, 'the absence of energy resources on the island of Malta, its requirements as an island developing country, and the range of its established fishing activity'.[54] The Court's rejection of this contention was in this case more solidly reasoned:

> The Court does not however consider that a delimitation should be influenced by the relative economic position of the two States in question, in such a way that the area of continental shelf regarded as appertaining to the less rich of the two States would be somewhat increased in order to compensate for its inferiority in economic resources. Such considerations are totally unrelated to the underlying intention of the applicable rules of international law. It is clear that neither the rules determining the validity of legal entitlement to the continental shelf, nor those concerning delimitation between neighbouring countries, leave room for any considerations of economic development of the States in question.[55]

Malta had also referred to defence and security interests; the Court did state in this respect that 'Security considerations are of course not unrelated to the concept of the continental shelf', having been, for example, referred to in the Truman Proclamation.[56] The Court, however, left the question open whether they could or should be taken into account for delimitation, though in a later passage in its judgment it referred to the possibility of a delimitation line being placed 'so near to one coast as to bring into play other

---

[52] *ICJ Reports*, 1982, p. 77, para. 106.

[53] Ibid., p. 77, para. 107.

[54] *ICJ Reports*, 1985, p. 41, para. 50.

[55] Ibid. See also the interesting comments in the dissenting opinion of Judge Oda on the irrelevance of considerations of world social justice: ibid., p. 159, para. 66.

[56] Ibid., p. 42, para. 51.

factors such as security',[57] which implies that security would be regarded as a material factor.

In the meantime, the Chamber formed to deal with the *Gulf of Maine* case had been willing to attribute some role in the process of arriving at a delimitation to factors other than 'the factors provided by the geography of the Gulf itself', namely certain 'other circumstances' which 'ought properly to be taken into consideration in assessing the equitable character of the result produced by this portion of the delimitation line'.[58]

These other circumstances may be summed up by what the Parties have presented as the data provided by human and economic geography, and they are thus circumstances which, though in the Chamber's opinion ineligible for consideration as criteria to be applied in the delimitation process itself, may . . . be relevant to assessment of the equitable character of a delimitation first established on the basis of criteria borrowed from physical and political geography.[58]

Little practical impact was, however, in fact permitted to such circumstances. It was particularly on the Canadian side that 'the development of this country's fisheries'—and therefore any delimitation of its exclusive fishery zone—had 'an obvious socio-economic impact on the communities inhabiting certain counties of Nova Scotia'.[59] The Chamber however considered that

there is no reason to consider *de jure* that the delimitation which the Chamber has now to carry out within the areas of overlapping apparent as between the respective exclusive fishery zones must result in each Party's enjoying an access to the regional fishing resources which will be equal to the access it previously enjoyed *de facto*. Neither is there any reason why the delimitation should provide a Party in certain places with a compensation equivalent to what it loses elsewhere.[60]

While considering for this reason that

the respective scale of activities connected with fishing—or navigation, defence or, for that matter, petroleum exploration and exploitation—cannot be taken into account as a relevant circumstance or, if the term is preferred, as an equitable criterion to be applied in determining the delimitation line,[61]

the Chamber had still a fallback position:

What the Chamber would regard as a legitimate scruple lies rather in concern lest the overall result, even though achieved through the application of equitable criteria and the use of appropriate methods for giving them concrete effect, should unexpectedly be revealed as radically inequitable, that is to say, as likely to entail

---

[57] Ibid., p. 52, para. 73.
[58] *ICJ Reports*, 1984, p. 340, para. 232.
[59] Ibid., p. 342, para. 236.
[60] Ibid.
[61] Ibid., p. 342, para. 237.

catastrophic repercussions for the livelihood and economic well-being of the population of the countries concerned.[62]

For the Chamber, therefore, interests of this kind are, in the field of maritime delimitation, at least something to be kept an eye on: 'catastrophic repercussions for the livelihood and economic well-being of the population' might render inequitable what would, from all other points of view, have been a wholly equitable delimitation.

There is an evident resemblance between this approach to the interests of coastal populations in fishing grounds, and the conditions underlying the customary-law concept of preferential rights of the coastal State, dealt with in sub-section (2) above; but the juridical mechanism by which they affect the result is wholly different.

(5) *The special case of intervention under Article 62 of the Statute*

In two cases, both also relating to maritime delimitation,[63] the Court has been called upon to consider the interpretation to be given to Article 62, paragraph 1, of the Statute, whereby: 'Should a State consider that it has an interest of a legal nature which may be affected by the decision in the case, it may submit a request to the Court to be permitted to intervene.' Despite the requirement for permission, and the apparently wide terms of the second paragraph of the Article ('It shall be for the Court to decide upon this request'), it appears that the existence of the appropriate legal interest confers a procedural right.[64] This is of course no exception to Fitzmaurice's observations in 1953, since such right is created by the Statute, an international treaty.

Independently of this procedural right, the concept of 'legal interest' contemplated by Article 62 is elusive. At times the expression has been treated, by counsel and by the Court itself, as virtually equivalent to 'legal right'; at other times the two are distinguished. The *travaux préparatoires* only serve to convey the strong impression that the draftsmen of the Statute had not really thought the matter through, and had no very clear idea what a 'legal interest' should be, or—a more charitable supposition—that they wished to leave the Court a wide margin of appreciation.[65] Further examination of the matter will be reserved for a later article, on intervention in the context of the procedural law of the Court.

---

[62] Ibid.

[63] *Continental Shelf (Tunisia/Libyan Arab Jamahiriya), Application to Intervene*, judgment, *ICJ Reports*, 1981, p. 3; *Continental Shelf (Libyan Arab Jamahiriya/Malta), Application to Intervene, ICJ Reports*, 1984, p. 3.

[64] 'The Court . . . does not consider paragraph 2 to confer upon it any discretion to accept or reject a request for permission to intervene for reasons simply of policy' (*ICJ Reports*, 1981, p. 12, para. 17).

[65] The recent decision of the Chamber permitting Nicaragua to intervene in the *Land, Island and Maritime Frontier Dispute* between El Salvador and Honduras falls outside the period considered. That decision does not however throw much additional light on the distinguishing characteristics of an 'interest of a legal nature' as opposed to a right.

Chapter II:

Treaties and Conventions in Force

The present chapter deals only with such aspects of the Court's decisions as relate to the use of 'treaties and conventions in force' as a source of the law to be applied, and the theoretical considerations underlying the idea of a treaty as a 'source' of law; it is not concerned with the provisions of individual treaties, or with questions of treaty interpretation—matters to be examined later in this series.

For purposes of jurisprudential analysis, the classic concept of sources of law and the division of law into treaty law, customary law and general principles of law, presents considerable convenience. It is however a purely theoretical underpinning which does not normally require scrutiny in the course of decision of an individual case. During the period covered by Sir Gerald Fitzmaurice's series of articles in this *Year Book*, no aspect of a case, and no dictum of a judge, gave rise to any need to consider the matter, so that he had no occasion to consider treaties as sources.

1. *Source of Law or Source of Obligation? The* Gulf of Maine *case*

In a paper published in 1958, Fitzmaurice in fact advanced the view that treaties are not a source of law in the formal sense, but only sources of obligation, or sources purely in a material sense;[66] this distinction was also adverted to in his discussion in this *Year Book* of 'Status or Regime Creating International Instruments'.[67] The present writer has expressed doubts elsewhere[68] as to whether this distinction is a valid or useful one; but it had hitherto appeared to be a matter of purely academic interest. Aspects of a recent decision of a chamber of the Court make it appropriate to re-examine the idea.

The Chamber seised of the *Gulf of Maine* case made one somewhat curious dictum at the outset of its examination of the law applicable to the maritime delimitation it was asked to effect. At this stage of the judgment, it was engaged in 'consideration of the problem of ascertaining the rules of law, in the international legal order, which govern the matters in issue in the present case'.[69] After referring to the sources of law enumerated in Article 38 of the Court's Statute, it continued:

So far as conventions are concerned, only 'general conventions', including, *inter*

---

[66] 'Some Problems regarding the Formal Sources of International Law', *Symbolae Verzijl* (1958), pp. 153 ff. See also, for a rather similar approach, Arangio-Ruiz, 'The Normative Role of the General Assembly of the United Nations and the Declaration of Principles of Friendly Relations', *Recueil des cours*, 137 (1972–III), at pp. 724–6, paragraph 164.

[67] This *Year Book*, 35 (1959), p. 231: *Collected Edition*, II, p. 633.

[68] *International Customary Law and Codification* (1972), pp. 25–6.

[69] *ICJ Reports*, 1984, p. 288, para. 79.

alia, the conventions codifying the law of the sea to which the two States are parties, can be considered. This is not merely because no particular conventions bearing on the matter at issue . . . are in force between the Parties to the present dispute, but mainly because it is in codifying conventions that principles and rules of general application can be identified.[70]

The implication of the final clause seems to be that even if there had been a 'particular convention'—i.e., a bilateral treaty—in force between the parties and relevant to the subject of the dispute, the chamber would not have regarded it as a source of the 'rules of law . . . which govern the matter at issue'. It is of course perfectly true that such a treaty would not, indeed could not, lay down 'rules of general application', though it might reflect such rules as existed as part of general customary law. Nevertheless, such a treaty would have the force of law between the parties, and would indeed prevail, as *lex specialis*, over any contrary provisions in conventions, codifying or otherwise, of more general application.

It is suggested that this passage, if it is anything more than a *lapsus calami*, betrays at once a highly academic approach to judicial law-finding, and an unadmitted, and perhaps unconscious, distinction between treaties as sources of law and treaties as sources of obligation. For the purpose of resolving the dispute of which the Chamber was seised, a particular convention would have been most relevant; if it had committed the parties to a particular form of delimitation, it would have been necessary and sufficient to declare the obligation created by the treaty. The solution of the dispute so arrived at might have been irrelevant to the trend of general international law on the subject, or indeed contrary to it. A treaty which is thus a source of obligation may be quite uninteresting to the academic observer, as compared with the general convention, particularly the general codifying treaty, which can be regarded as something more than a source of obligation—a source of law.

The weakness of this approach is that it overlooks the fact that the effect of the two types of convention is identical *for the parties to them*: whether they are called sources of law or sources of obligation is unimportant. The general convention is more interesting for reasons extrinsic to its nature and effect as a treaty; it is, or may be, a 'source', in some sense, of law for States not parties to it.

Since, as the judgment states, there were no relevant 'particular conventions' in force between the United States and Canada, the observation quoted above is, in the strictest sense, *obiter*. Something of the same attitude of mind, deductive from general principles rather than inductive from directly applicable texts, seems to underlie the Chamber's handling of the problem of the applicability of the 1958 Geneva Convention on the Continental Shelf, to which both States were parties.

The problem arose from the requirement of the Special Agreement that

---

[70] Ibid., p. 291, para. 83.

the Chamber 'decide, in accordance with the principles and rules of international law applicable in the matter as between the Parties', the question: 'What is the course of the single maritime boundary that divides the continental shelf and fisheries zones of Canada and the United States of America . . . ?'[71] Given that, as the Chamber found, the question, taken in isolation, of the continental shelf boundary, was mandatorily governed by the 1958 Geneva Convention, while the question of the boundary of the fisheries zones was to be regulated by customary law, a possible answer to the question would have been that there was no such 'single maritime boundary'.[72] This would, however, have been a frustration of the Special Agreement and the judicial proceedings which it engendered.

The Chamber notes that

It is doubtful whether a treaty obligation which is in terms confined to the delimitation of the continental shelf can be extended . . . to a field which is evidently much greater, unquestionably heterogeneous, and accordingly fundamentally different.[73]

It rejects the Canadian argument that the provisions of Article 6 of the Continental Shelf Convention

apply directly, i.e., as treaty-law, 'to the continental shelf as a component of a single maritime boundary', and also, but as a 'particular expression of a general norm', to the superjacent fishery zone, as the other component.[74]

In the view of the Chamber 'there is no trace in international custom of . . . a transformation' of the 'equidistance-special circumstances rule' into a rule of general international law.[75]

The Chamber's conclusion was as follows:

In short, the Chamber does not believe that there is any argument to justify the attempt to turn the provisions of Article 6 of the 1958 Convention into a general rule applicable as such to every maritime delimitation. The treaty provisions in question, as the 1969 Judgment of the Court pointed out, can have no mandatory force as regards delimitation, even delimitation of the continental shelf alone, between States which are not parties to the 1958 Convention. Similarly [*d'une manière analogue*], they cannot have such mandatory force even between States which are parties to the Convention, as regards a maritime boundary concerning a much wider subject-matter than the continental shelf alone.[76]

The elegantly-stated analogy does not, it is suggested, advance the argument. Whether a State is bound by a particular convention is normally a straightforward question admitting only of a simple positive or negative answer; and the *North Sea* judgment in 1969 was dealing with the question

---

[71] Ibid., p. 253.
[72] This was the view of Judge Gros: ibid., pp. 362–77.
[73] Ibid., p. 301, para. 119.
[74] Ibid., p. 302, para. 121.
[75] Ibid., p. 302, para. 122.
[76] Ibid., p. 303, para. 124.

of the applicability to a non-party State not of the provisions of the Convention as such, but as (it was asserted) expression of a rule of customary law. Whether, between parties to a treaty, the treaty does or does not apply to a particular subject-matter is a question of interpretation of the treaty; the treaty is not deprived of any effect between the parties by reason of the fact that it cannot be interpreted as widely as one party may pretend. The Chamber in effect conjures away the difficulty; by refusing to accept that the 1958 Convention can apply to delimitation of the fisheries zones, it concludes that the Convention has no application at all, even to the element of the asserted single maritime boundary to which it is of immediate application—the continental shelf.

What is striking is the intellectual framework of the judgment into which this argument is integrated. After disposing further of the arguments of the parties based on estoppel, the Chamber introduces the next section of its judgment as follows:

> It has just been noted that the Parties to the present case, in the current state of the law governing relations between them, are not bound, under a rule of treaty-law or other rule, to apply certain criteria or to use certain particular methods for the establishment of a single maritime boundary for both the continental shelf and the exclusive maritime fishery zone, as in the present case. Consequently, the Chamber also is not so bound.[77]

In an earlier passage in the judgment, the Chamber had explained that it would examine 'special international law . . . as at present in force between the Parties' in order to ascertain whether that law might 'include some rule specifically requiring the parties, and consequently the Chamber, to apply certain criteria or certain specific practical methods to the delimitation that is requested'.[78] Before doing so, it had however already enquired into general customary law in the matter, and satisfied itself that there was a 'fundamental norm of customary law governing maritime delimitation', and that 'general customary international law is not the proper place in which to seek rules specifically prescribing the application of any particular equitable criteria, or the use of any particular practical methods'.[79] One cannot but feel that this order of proceeding indicates that it was neither expected nor desired that the enquiry into 'special international law' should produce any legal rule requiring the application of a particular delimitation criterion or method, or otherwise capable of operating to displace the application of the 'fundamental norm of customary law'.[80]

This in turn points to an approach which sees the specific treaty relation of the parties, as parties to the 1958 Geneva Convention, as no more than a

---

[77] Ibid., p. 312, para. 155. Note also that in the next paragraph the Chamber concludes that its approach does not have to be 'influenced by *predetermined preferences*'! (Emphasis added.)

[78] Ibid., p. 300, para. 114.

[79] Ibid., p. 300, paras. 113–14.

[80] The conclusion—that this was not the case—when arrived at recalls the phrase of Pascal: 'Console-toi, tu ne me chercherais pas si tu ne m'avais trouvé' (*Pensées*, vii, p. 553).

'source of obligation', rather than a source of the law governing relations between them—this despite the Chamber's use of the term 'special international law'. There are a number of revealing uses of language scattered throughout the judgment which point to a desire to seek the solution of the case in principles of wide general application, the stuff of which 'leading cases' are made, rather than in the particular treaty arrangements of the parties, which are equally 'sources of law'.[81]

2. *Applicability of Law derived from a Treaty Source: the* Nicaragua v. United States of America *case*

In the previous article in this series, attention has been drawn to the problems which arose in the case concerning *Military and Paramilitary Activities in and against Nicaragua* (*Nicaragua* v. *United States of America*) from the need to consider the possibility that rules of identical or substantively overlapping content might derive from two different sources—treaty law and customary law. That case should now be considered from a different standpoint: that of the severability of 'multilateral treaty law' from the corpus of a State's rights and obligations—the possibility of ignoring all that flows from a particular source of law while continuing to assess a State's conduct by reference to international law shorn of this element.

The reason why the Court found itself obliged to adopt an approach of this kind was of course the restrictions which it regarded as imposed upon it by the jurisdictional title relied on. The basis of jurisdiction as regards the respondent was the United States declaration under the Optional Clause, which contained the celebrated 'multilateral treaty reservation', excluding

disputes which arise under a multilateral treaty, unless (1) all parties to the treaty affected by the decision are also parties to the case before the Court, or (2) the United States of America specially agrees to jurisdiction.[82]

The Court considered that it had to

ascertain whether any third States, parties to multilateral treaties invoked by Nicaragua in support of its claims, would be 'affected' by the Judgment, and are not parties to the proceedings leading up to it,[83]

and concluded that such was the case as regards the United Nations Charter and the Charter of the Organization of American States. From this it followed, the Court held, that the United States declaration did not per-

---

[81] For example, the reference in paragraph 124 of the judgment to a Canadian contention as an 'attempt to turn the provisions of Article 6 of the 1958 Convention into a general rule applicable as such to *every maritime delimitation*' (emphasis added); the only question was whether it was applicable to that particular delimitation.

[82] *ICJ Year Book*, 1984/5, pp. 99–100.

[83] *ICJ Reports*, 1986, p. 34, para. 47.

mit the Court to entertain such claims of Nicaragua, based on those instruments, the decision on which would 'affect' third States. To this the Court added:

the effect of the reservation in question is confined to barring the applicability of the United Nations Charter and Organization of American States Charter as multilateral treaty law, and has no further impact on the sources of international law which Article 38 of the Statute requires the Court to apply.[84]

There is a certain ambiguity in the word 'applicability': what the Court must have meant was that it was itself debarred from applying the two Charters for the purpose of deciding the dispute, not that the Charters did not apply to the relations between the United States and Nicaragua, including those aspects of their relations which gave rise to the dispute. This ambiguity recurs later in the judgment:

even if a treaty norm and a customary norm relevant to the present dispute were to have exactly the same content, this would not be a reason for the Court to take the view that the operation of the treaty process must necessarily deprive the customary norm of its separate applicability. Nor can the multilateral treaty reservation be interpreted as meaning that, once applicable to a given dispute, it would exclude the application of any rule of customary international law the content of which was the same as, or analogous to, that of the treaty-law rule which had caused the reservation to become effective.[85]

In the previous article in this series,[86] attention was drawn to the problem whether customary rules can be regarded as applicable, in any real sense, to the relations between two States which have concluded a treaty governing precisely those relations. What is here more of interest is the treatment by the Court of 'multilateral treaty law' as a separate 'block' of law, capable of being applied or not applied independently of other law, simply because it derives from an independent 'source'.

The extent to which the Court's thinking in respect of the multilateral treaty reservation is dominated by the idea of 'multilateral treaty law' as a block of law which can be applied or not applied, independently of the other aspects of the legal relations between the parties, is thrown into relief by the dissenting opinion of Judge Oda; he points out that

the issue—which relates to the applicable law—of whether, *once* the Court assumes jurisdiction over a case, it can apply the rules of customary and general international law apart from any applicable treaty rules, is quite different from the other issue—which relates to the Court's jurisdiction—of *whether* a State's declaration excludes 'disputes arising under multilateral treat[ies]' . . .[87]

---

[84] Ibid., p. 38, para. 56.
[85] Ibid., p. 94, para. 175.
[86] This *Year Book*, 60 (1989), pp. 147 ff.
[87] *ICJ Reports*, 1986, p. 217, para. 10, original emphasis. The same criticism is made by Morelli, 'Giurisdizione della C.I.G. e diritto applicabile', *Rivista di diritto internazionale*, 70 (1987), p. 660.

Judge Oda therefore considered that

the Court should have proved, not that it can apply customary and general international law independently, but that the dispute referred to it . . . had *not* arisen under these multilateral treaties.[88]

The Court was in effect treating the dispute as divisible into two: a dispute as to the obligations of the United States under the multilateral treaties, and a dispute as to its obligations under customary international law; and only the former was to be treated as a dispute which 'arose under a multilateral treaty'.

3. *Status or Regime-creating Instruments: the* South-West Africa *and* Namibia *cases*

In his first article in the *Year Book* series Fitzmaurice mentioned the dicta of certain judges in the 1950 advisory case on the *International Status of South West Africa* as

authority for the proposition that certain types of international régimes or systems, while having their origin in instruments contractual in form, are not themselves of a contractual character, but rather have, or acquire, an essentially objective, self-contained character, a status independent of the instrument that created them, so that their existence is not affected by the lapse of that instrument, material changes in its terms, or the disappearance of one of the parties to it.[89]

At the very end of the last article he wrote in the original *Year Book* series, he returned to the point, in connection with certain remarks of Judge Lauterpacht in the *Petitioners* case;[90] Fitzmaurice then suggested that, for the reasons given by Judge Lauterpacht, 'such instruments are in the material sense sources of independent international law'.[91] It is the concept of an instrument of this kind as a source of independent law which will here be studied, in the light of the subsequent judicial developments in relation to the Mandate for South West Africa.

It is to be observed that Fitzmaurice, who was well known for his meticulous choice of words and use of language, refers to these instruments not as 'independent sources of international law', but as 'sources of independent international law'. What he was suggesting was not that such instruments constitute a source of law alongside and independent of the sources listed in Article 38, paragraph 1, of the Statute;[92] but that in certain circumstances consequences of an exceptional kind could flow from such instruments, going beyond what is normally regarded as treaty law. A well-established precedent, to which Fitzmaurice was clearly alluding, was the category of

[88] Ibid., p. 219, para. 14, original emphasis.

[89] This *Year Book*, 27 (1950), p. 8; *Collected Edition*, I, p. 8.

[90] *Admissibility of Hearing of Petitioners by the Committee on South West Africa*, *ICJ Reports*, 1956, pp. 48–9.

[91] This *Year Book*, 35 (1959), p. 231; *Collected Edition*, II, p. 633.

[92] If this were suggested, the question would arise how such a source could come into existence: see the present writer's *International Customary Law and Codification* (1972), pp. 39 ff.

dispositive treaties;[93] as the *Aaland Islands* case[94] showed, these may create an international regime which may be invoked for its own benefit by an 'interested State' which was not a party to the original treaty. There is however nothing in this in itself which is radically inconsistent with the concept of treaties as based on autonomy of will: the intention of the parties that third States shall benefit from the treaty is sufficient. As the Vienna Convention expressly provides,[95] such a *stipulation pour autrui* need not be merely in favour of one State or a group of States, but may be in favour of all States.

When the question of the status of the Mandate for South West Africa for purposes of Article 37 of the Statute came before the Court for decision in 1962, on the basis of the preliminary objections filed by South Africa, Sir Gerald Fitzmaurice filed a dissenting opinion jointly with Sir Percy Spender. Before considering what the Court had to say on the matter, it is enlightening to consult this dissent. Article 37 of the Statute, it will be recalled, is the transitional provision whereby

> Whenever a treaty or convention in force provides for reference of a matter to a tribunal to have been instituted by the League of Nations, or to the Permanent Court of International Justice, the matter shall, as between the parties to the present Statute, be referred to the International Court of Justice.

The authors of the joint dissent emphasized that for Article 37 to apply, it was essential that the Mandate should be not merely 'in force', but 'in force as a treaty or convention'. In their view, the Court in 1962 was merely following the 1950 advisory opinion (with which, in any event, they disagreed) in holding that the Mandate was still 'in force on an *institutional basis*'.[96] The main, if not the only, reason why the two dissenters did not consider that the Mandate was in force 'as a treaty or convention' was because, on the basis of any analysis of the identity of the original parties to it (Principal Allied and Associated Powers, members of the League, Council of the League, etc.), following the demise of the League 'the number of parties is less than two, and therefore, *as a treaty or convention*, the Mandate is no longer in force'.[97]

Fitzmaurice's view of the Mandate as the typical (if not the only) example of a 'status or regime-creating instrument' is thus consistent. For him a treaty could perish *as a treaty*, but leave behind, like the Cheshire Cat's grin, the status, regime or institution which it had embodied or created: 'their existence is not affected by the lapse of that instrument . . . or the disappearance of one of the parties to it'.[98]

---

[93] A term which, however, Fitzmaurice regarded as 'not a happy one': see 'The Future of Public International Law and the International Legal System in the Circumstances of Today' (Institut de droit international, Special Report, 1973), p. 30.

[94] *League of Nations Official Journal*, 1920, Special Supplement 3.

[95] Article 36, paragraph 1, of the Convention on the Law of Treaties.

[96] *ICJ Reports*, 1962, p. 495.

[97] Ibid., p. 503.

[98] Fitzmaurice, loc. cit. above (n. 89).

The view expressed in the 1962 joint dissenting opinion is however in some sense a refinement of the earlier view stated by Fitzmaurice in this *Year Book*. Even in 1950, the Court appears to have contemplated the survival of the Mandate as a treaty, not merely as an institution, since it expressly found in the 1940 opinion that 'Having regard to Article 37 of the Statute of the International Court of Justice', Article 7—the disputes settlement clause—of the Mandate 'is still in force'.[99]

This was also the view taken by the majority of the Court in 1962;[100] accordingly the question whether the institution of the Mandate could survive the disappearance of the treaty for lack of parties did not arise. The Court made no specific finding as to the identity of the parties; however, its ruling that the applicants were still 'members of the League' for the purposes of Article 7 of the Mandate, on the basis of the actions taken by the members at the time of the dissolution of the League, suggests that it regarded the surviving States which had been members of the League as the parties to the Mandate as a treaty.

The 1966 decision in the *South West Africa* cases, given after the pendulum-swing in the composition of the Court, did not, in view of the grounds on which it was based, have to deal with the question of the continued existence of the Mandate as a treaty or as an institution,[101] and therefore calls for no comment in the present context.

The question of survival of the Mandate as an institution or as a treaty was commented on in the advisory opinion given in 1971 on *Legal Consequences for States of the Continued Presence of South Africa in Namibia (South West Africa) notwithstanding Security Council Resolution 276 (1970)*—the *Namibia* opinion. In this case, the argument that the Mandate survived only as an institution was not presented by Fitzmaurice in his powerful dissenting opinion, which was based on other grounds. It was, however, put forward by South Africa in oral argument.[102]

When examining 'the situation which arose on the demise of the League and with the birth of the United Nations', the Court found that the League was the international organization entrusted with the supervisory functions which were an indispensable element of the Mandate. It continued:

But that does not mean that the mandates institution was to collapse with the disappearance of the original supervisory machinery. To the question whether the continuance of a mandate was inseparably linked with the existence of the League, the answer must be that an institution established for the fulfilment of a sacred trust cannot be presumed to lapse before the achievement of its purpose. The responsibilities of both mandatory and supervisor resulting from the mandates

[99] *ICJ Reports*, 1950, p. 138. For Fitzmaurice and Spender, this is apparently a finding *per incuriam*: cf. *ICJ Reports*, 1962, p. 472.

[100] *ICJ Reports*, 1962, p. 334.

[101] It is striking however that the judgment, for which Fitzmaurice voted, was stated to be given 'without pronouncing upon, and wholly without prejudice to, the question whether that Mandate is still in force'—whether as treaty or institution is not stated: *ICJ Reports*, 1966, p. 19, para. 7.

[102] *Namibia* case, *Pleadings*, vol. 2, p. 269.

institution were complementary, and the disappearance of one or the other could not affect the survival of the institution.[103]

The emphasis on the survival of the institution, rather than the continued existence of the treaty, will be noticed.

On the other hand, the Court also applied the technique which in the previous article in this series[104] has been referred to as 'intertemporal *renvoi*'—the attribution of the intention of parties to an instrument as being that it shall be interpreted in the future in the light of intervening developments of international law—and stated also that 'an international instrument has to be interpreted and applied within the framework of the entire legal system prevailing at the time of the interpretation'.[105] Generally speaking, a treaty falls to be interpreted: an institution does not. If the institution is capable of surviving the treaty which established it, one might suppose that it is also capable of developing 'within the framework of the entire legal system', without there being any need for interpretation or re-interpretation of the treaty.

The Court had then to examine the legal justification for the termination of the Mandate claimed to have been effected by General Assembly Resolution 2145 (XXI). It found that

with the entry into force of the Charter of the United Nations a relationship was established between all Members of the United Nations on the one side, and each mandatory Power on the other[106]

and that

One of the fundamental principles governing the international relationship thus established is that a party which disowns or does not fulfil its own obligations cannot be recognized as retaining the rights which it claims to derive from the relationship.[107]

The Court however found it necessary to buttress this argument also by reference to the law of treaties:

In examining this action of the General Assembly it is appropriate to have regard to the general principles of international law regulating termination of a treaty relationship on account of breach. For even if the mandate is viewed as having the character of an institution, as is maintained, it depends on those international agreements which created the system and regulated its application. As the Court indicated in 1962 'this Mandate, like practically all other similar Mandates' was 'a special type of instrument composite in nature and instituting a novel international régime. It incorporates a definite agreement . . . ' (*I.C.J. Reports*, 1962, p. 331). The Court stated conclusively in that Judgment that the Mandate ' . . . in fact and

---

[103] *ICJ Reports*, 1971, p. 32, para. 55.
[104] This *Year Book*, 60 (1989), pp. 135 ff.
[105] *ICJ Reports*, 1971, p. 31, para. 53.
[106] Ibid., p. 45, para. 90.
[107] Ibid., p. 46, para. 91.

in law, is an international agreement having the character of a treaty or convention' (*I.C.J. Reports*, 1962, p. 330).[108]

The Court thus appears to have oscillated between the view that the Mandate as a treaty was dead, but its 'soul went marching on' as an institution; and the view that the Mandate as a treaty had, thanks to the life-prolonging operations effected in 1946, continued to exist until terminated by General Assembly Resolution 2145 (XXI).

One further clue to the Court's thinking may be given by its treatment of the problem of the consequences for non-member States of the United Nations of the continued presence of South Africa in Namibia. It characterized that presence as an 'illegal situation': for member States, the precise significance of the term 'illegal' was probably not material. For non-member States, however, the Court found it necessary to specify that

In the view of the Court, the termination of the Mandate and the declaration of the illegality of South Africa's presence in Namibia are opposable to all States in the sense of barring *erga omnes* the legality of a situation which is maintained in violation of international law . . . [109]

This raises an interesting question: in what circumstances is a breach of treaty, however serious, a violation of international law *erga omnes*, and not merely *vis-à-vis* the other party or parties to the treaty? Admittedly a question of territory was involved, but is this the criterion?[110] The special, institutional, character of the Mandate has certainly a role to play in this finding.

The jurisprudence of the Court in relation to the Mandate for South West Africa does not permit of a firm conclusion as to the possibility of a regime-creating treaty being a 'source of independent international law', as suggested by Fitzmaurice. With the independence of Namibia, the whole historical chapter of the Mandates system has closed; and it is probably wise to treat that system as to such an extent *sui generis* as to be, at least in the aspect here considered, not capable of lending itself to any useful generalizations.

CHAPTER III:

CUSTOM

1. *The Relationship of 'General International Law' and Customary Law*

There is a temptation—to which, as we shall see, the Court itself is not immune—when discussing principles or rules of law either at a fairly high

---

[108] Ibid., pp. 46–7, para. 94.

[109] Ibid., p. 56, para. 126.

[110] If, for example, the United Kingdom were to retain the New Territories of Hong Kong beyond the date of expiration of the lease from the Government of China, it would be acting unlawfully *vis-à-vis* China, but would its occupation be illegal *erga omnes*?

level of abstraction or in a field in which little concrete practice can be referred to, to assert and rely on the dictates of 'general international law'. If, for reasons of convenience or of principle, one adopts the enumeration of sources in Article 38 of the Statute of the Court as being exhaustive, one may be somewhat at a loss as to where this 'general international law' is to be fitted in. It would seem by definition not to be treaty law: which leaves custom and the general principles of law. The content of the latter category is a question not free from controversy, which will be discussed further in the following chapter, but it does appear to have at least some element of universality or eclecticism, in the sense that the solutions adopted to analogous problems in the various systems of municipal law are pointers serving to help identify the 'general principles of law'.

(1) *The 'natural law of the continental shelf': the* North Sea *cases*

The first decision to be examined from this standpoint is the judgment in the *North Sea Continental Shelf* cases. That judgment is well known to furnish the *locus classicus* for a definition in traditional terms of the conditions for the establishment of a rule of customary international law, but it deals also with arguments presented to the Court, the relationship of which with the recognized sources of law is obscure or shifting. The main passage of the judgment of interest in this context is introduced as follows:

It is maintained by Denmark and the Netherlands that the Federal Republic, whatever its position may be in relation to the Geneva Convention, considered as such, is in any event bound to accept delimitation on an equidistance-special circumstances basis, because the use of this method is not in the nature of a merely conventional obligation, but is, or must now be regarded as involving, a rule that is part of the *corpus* of general international law;—and, like other rules of general or customary international law, is binding on the Federal Republic automatically and independently of any specific assent, direct or indirect, given by the latter.[111]

Attention is drawn to the phrase 'rules of general *or* customary international law', which appears to suggest that there are rules of general international law which are neither conventional nor customary in nature.

The judgment continues:

This contention has both a positive law and a more fundamentalist aspect. As a matter of positive law, it is based on the work done in this field by international legal bodies, on State practice and on the influence attributed to the Geneva Convention itself,—the claim being that these various factors have cumulatively evidenced or been creative of the *opinio juris sive necessitatis*, requisite for the formation of new rules of customary international law. In its fundamentalist aspect, the view put forward derives from what might be called the natural law of the continental shelf, in the sense that the equidistance principle is seen as a necessary expression in the field of delimitation of the accepted doctrine of the exclusive

---

[111] *ICJ Reports*, 1969, p. 28, para. 37.

appurtenance of the continental shelf to the nearby coastal State, and therefore as having an *a priori* character of so to speak juristic inevitability.[112]

The distinction is thus clearly spelled out: the 'fundamentalist' argument is independent of any demonstration of State practice and *opinio juris*, but—if correct—leads to the conclusion that there exists a rule of general international law. Since the Court is here stating the arguments of a party before examining them, it is necessary to anticipate the Court's conclusion, which was:

that the notion of equidistance as being logically necessary, in the sense of being an inescapable *a priori* accompaniment of basic continental shelf doctrine, is incorrect. It is said not to be possible to maintain that there is a rule of law ascribing certain areas to a State as a matter of inherent and original right . . . , without also admitting the existence of some rule by which those areas can be obligatorily delimited. The Court cannot accept the logic of this view. The problem arises only where there is a dispute and only in respect of the marginal areas involved. The appurtenance of a given area, considered as an entity, in no way governs the precise delimitation of its boundaries . . . [113]

The Court did not reject the contention of Denmark and the Netherlands on what would have been the more radical ground that the rule of law they contended for was not discernibly rooted in a recognized source of international law; that 'natural law', whether of the continental shelf or of some other context, is not a source of law.

Now it is of course not possible to argue in general that because the Court chooses to use argument A to reject a submission made to it, it follows that it would not have endorsed argument B which would also have led to such a rejection. Nonetheless, in this case the discussion of the 'natural law' argument in its own terms, with no precautionary reservation, does permit the inference that the Court did not regard as heretical the idea of a rule of law having 'an *a priori* character of so to speak juristic inevitability'.

The argument which the Court referred to as 'fundamentalist' and as based on the 'natural law' of the continental shelf was not described in precisely those terms by the two parties which put it forward. The kernel of that thesis was expressed in argument by Sir Humphrey Waldock as follows:

we rest upon what we . . . conceive to be a fundamental norm of maritime international law: the principle of proximity or of greater nearness to the coast. We contend that the principle is inherent in the very concept . . . of a State's being a coastal State with respect to a given maritime area, and also in the very concept of a coastal State's exclusive rights over areas adjacent to its coast.[114]

---

[112] Ibid., pp. 28–9, para. 37.
[113] Ibid., p. 32, para. 46.
[114] *Pleadings*, vol. 2, p. 95.

Summing up on the point, Waldock stated:

the Court is, in our opinion, fully warranted in having recourse to the fundamental norms of maritime law in order to find the principles applicable to the delimitation of the continental shelf in the present cases, and in then designating 'proximity' or 'contiguity' as the relevant norm calling for the application of the equidistance principle.[115]

Yet although Denmark and the Netherlands referred to 'the fundamental norms of maritime law', it is not clear that they did so in a natural-law spirit, on the basis that such norms were fundamental in the sense of not needing to derive from any recognized source. Just prior to the summing-up in the last passage just quoted, Sir Humphrey Waldock argued that:

whether the principles and rules embodied in Articles 1 and 2 [of the 1958 Geneva Convention] are viewed as treaty provisions or as an expression of customary rules, their interpretation and application must, we believe, take account of the *corpus* of principles and rules of which they form only a part.[116]

The reference to customary law may be significant.

At all events, whether or not the parties so conceived it, the contention as to the fundamental principle of proximity did not need to by-pass the recognized sources of law. It was, and is, generally recognized that the law of the continental shelf, as expressed in the opening articles of the 1958 Geneva Convention, was neither created by the Convention itself nor rooted in a norm of natural law, but had become established as customary international law, through the normal means for the generation of such law. Accordingly, the proximity principle could be presented as entailed in, or a necessary corollary of, what States had accepted by way of customary principle, namely the rights of States *ab initio* and *ipso facto* over shelf areas off their coasts. This is indeed a more logical construction than to say, in effect, that the rights enjoyed by States over the continental shelf derive from customary law, but that the extent of those rights is to be determined by reference to principles established not by customary law but by natural law.[117] In other words, while it is indeed a question of 'juristic inevitability', this refers to the process of derivation of one norm from another: and if the more fundamental norm is one of customary law, then the derived norm is equally one of customary law, even if there is no direct and specific State practice to support it.

The Court in fact, in its handling of this contention of the parties, rejected the idea that the equidistance rule was necessarily built into the

---

[115] Ibid., p. 99.

[116] Ibid.

[117] This is particularly evident in the contention, rejected by the Court in the passage quoted on p. 33 above, that the law which confers a right must also lay down rules for the determination of the extent of the right. Though dealt with by the Court as though it were an argument of the parties, it was most cogently put forward by Judge Morelli in his dissenting opinion (*ICJ Reports*, 1969, p. 200, para. 3).

continental shelf concept, without commenting on the nature which the rule would have had if it had been so built in.

Judge Tanaka, however, expressed the matter clearly in his dissenting opinion. He considered that the equidistance principle had been shown to be itself part of international customary law; but then added: 'In the event that the customary law character of the principle of equidistance cannot be proved, there exists another reason which seems more cogent for recognizing this character'.[118] For him the equidistance principle flowed from the fundamental concept of the continental shelf,[119] so that if that concept was established customary law binding on the Federal Republic, so was the equidistance principle:

The method of logical and teleological interpretation can be applied in the case of customary law as in the case of written law. Even if the Federal Republic recognizes the customary law character of only the fundamental concept incorporated in Articles 1–3 of the Convention, and denies it in respect of other matters, one cannot escape from the application of what is derived as a logical conclusion from the fundamental concept,—a conclusion which, in respect of the delimitation of the continental shelf, would reach the same result as Article 6, paragraph 2, of the Convention.[120]

Judge Morelli also regarded the one principle as the 'necessary consequence' of the other, and stated specifically that he therefore saw no need for State practice to show that 'a specific custom has come into existence in this connection'.[121]

The conclusion must be that the judgment in the *North Sea Continental Shelf* cases does not, contrary to appearances, lend support to any theory of the existence of a category of 'general international law' distinct from conventional and customary law, or of norms of 'natural law' requiring no ancestry in the recognized hierarchy of sources.

(2) 'General law': the Barcelona Traction case

The treatment of customary law in the *Barcelona Traction* judgment is remarkable for its lack of explicitness: this is one of the unsatisfactory features of this generally disappointing decision. There is in fact no specific reference to customary law as such in the judgment at all: the issues discussed are referred to in terms of 'international law',[122] 'general rules',[123] 'general law',[124] 'obligation' or 'international obligation'[125] or 'general international law'.[126] However, at the outset of the judgment, the Court defines

[118] *ICJ Reports*, 1969, p. 179.
[119] Ibid., p. 180.
[120] Ibid., p. 181.
[121] Ibid., p. 202, para. 6. It is however not entirely clear from Judge Morelli's terminology whether he regarded the 'general international law' of the continental shelf as customary in nature.
[122] Judgment, paras. 36, 37, 38, 50, 51, 52, 54, 58, 70, 78, 82, 93, 97, 98.
[123] Judgment, paras. 36, 54, 64, 88, 92, 93.
[124] Judgment, para. 37.
[125] Judgment, paras. 33, 34, 35, 86.
[126] Judgment, para. 87.

the question to be examined as 'the right of Belgium to exercise diplomatic protection',[127] and there can be no doubt that the law of international responsibility, of which the law governing the right to exercise diplomatic protection (for example, the rules as to nationality of claims) is part, is of customary-law origin. The matter had in fact been clearly expressed in terms of customary law, in the context of the Court's 1964 judgment on the preliminary objections in the case, by Judge Wellington Koo in his separate opinion:

> The salient issue of the whole question, from the point of view of international law, is the right of protection of a State of the legitimate interests of its nationals, shareholders in a foreign company, against a wrongdoing third State. In regard to the evolution of a rule of customary international law there always exists the possibility of a difference of opinion as to the degree of uniformity of the facts and the regularity of their occurrence necessary to warrant, on this basis of reasoning, an affirmation of its existence.[128]

Of the numerous judges who appended opinions to the 1970 judgment, only Judge Ammoun states the turning-point of the decision clearly and explicitly in terms of customary law:

> In short, since the right claimed by the national State of the shareholder, that of taking up his claim against a third country, does not constitute an exception to a legal rule, the extension of which to a new case is asked for, but such right can derive from the possible existence of an international custom, it is to be concluded that the elements which constitute the latter, to be drawn in various degrees from treaty or State practice, from international decisions or from legal literature, are not of such a nature as to lend support to this new case.[129]

For Judge Ammoun, 'diplomatic protection depends not on general principles of law recognized by nations but on international customary law';[130] this is not only correct, but also the unavowed basis of the Court's judgment. The references in that judgment to 'general international law', and similar expressions, must be taken to refer to the corpus of rules governing international responsibility and diplomatic protection, established as customary international law.

One might therefore have expected to find in the judgment of the Court an examination of what Judge Ammoun refers to as 'treaty or State practice, . . . international decisions or . . . legal literature'; but there is no such examination, save for the following passage, in the context, not of the general question whether a right of diplomatic protection of shareholders has become established by State practice, but of the more restricted question of the circumstances in which the corporate veil has been lifted:

---

[127] *ICJ Reports*, 1970, p. 32, para. 32.
[128] *ICJ Reports*, 1964, p. 63, para. 33.
[129] *ICJ Reports*, 1970, pp. 320–1, para. 27.
[130] Ibid., p. 321, para. 28. For the opposite view see Charpentier, 'Tendances de l'élaboration du droit international public coutumier', *L'Élaboration du droit international public* (Société française pour le droit international, 1975), p. 127.

The Parties have also relied on the general arbitral jurisprudence which has accumulated in the last half-century. However, in most cases the decisions cited rested upon the terms of instruments establishing the jurisdiction of the tribunal or claims commission and determining what rights might enjoy protection; they cannot therefore give rise to generalization going beyond the special circumstances of each case. Other decisions, allowing or disallowing claims by way of exception, are not, in view of the particular facts concerned, directly relevant to the present case.[131]

One explanation for this unexpected lacuna[132] may lie in the intellectual construction involving recourse to municipal law underlying the judgment. In its simplest form the argument is that international law (by which is to be understood, customary law) recognizes an entitlement to make an international claim only if the nationals of the plaintiff State have suffered injury to their 'rights' (as distinct from 'interests') for which the defendant State is responsible; and 'rights' in question are defined as rights by municipal law.[133] Thus since the question whether the Belgian nationals were injured by the acts of the Spanish authorities is governed not by customary international law but by municipal law, it would be inappropriate to refer, in order to answer this question, to State practice. It might nevertheless have been appropriate to refer to State practice or the practice of international tribunals to show that, for example, shareholders' rights against the company had never been treated as susceptible of injury attributable to action by a foreign State against the company.[134]

(3) 'General international law' of indeterminate origin: the WHO Agreement case

A case in which noteworthy use was made of the concept of 'general international law' was the advisory opinion requested on the *Interpretation of the Agreement of 25 March 1951 between the WHO and Egypt*. Before examining the opinion itself we may note that to ask the Court to interpret an international agreement is to ask it to apply a category of law which, as has been observed in the first article in this series, is neither itself treaty law (except to the extent that the Vienna Convention on the Law of Treaties may be applicable as a convention) nor, apparently, purely customary law. Had the Court confined itself to interpreting the 1951 Agreement, and in

---

[131] *ICJ Reports*, 1970, p. 40, para. 63. As noted above, an arbitral award may be regarded as State practice, or as a 'judicial decision' for purposes of Article 38(1)(d) of the Statute. On the latter aspect, see Chapter V, below.

[132] Akehurst interprets the judgment as a finding 'that there was no general custom giving Belgium *locus standi*' (this *Year Book*, 47 (1974–5), p. 28, n. 6), but the page reference he gives to the *Reports* is to the page (47) at which the Court employs the negative formulation that 'the protection of shareholders requires that recourse be had to treaty stipulations or special agreements'.

[133] But which municipal law? See the earlier article in this series, this *Year Book*, 60 (1989), pp. 117 ff.

[134] This might have been difficult: see Lillich, 'The Rigidity of Barcelona', *American Journal of International Law*, 65 (1971), p. 522; Lillich and Weston, *International Claims: Their Settlement by Lump Sum Agreements* (1975), p. 43; Lillich, 'Lump Sum Agreements: Their Continuing Contribution to the Law of International Claims', *American Journal of International Law*, 82 (1988), p. 69.

particular Article 37, in the light of the recognized canons of interpretation, the question whether in doing so it was applying customary law or some other category of law, though not without interest, would have been largely academic.

However, the Court redefined the question put to it for advisory opinion in the following terms: 'What are the legal principles and rules applicable to the question under what conditions and in accordance with what modalities a transfer of the [WHO] Regional Office from Egypt may be effected?'[135] The Court did not indicate specifically at any point what kind of legal principles and rules it was looking for, nor where it would look for them—in the practice of States or international organizations or otherwise. It did however make clear, as in a sense it had already done by re-defining the question put, that the relevant principles and rules were not to be found solely within the four corners of the 1951 Agreement, as a matter of treaty law:

> Whatever view may be held on the question whether the establishment and location of the Regional Office in Alexandria are embraced within the provisions of the 1951 Agreement, and whatever view may be held on the question whether the provisions of Section 37 are applicable to the case of a transfer of the Office from Egypt, the fact remains that certain legal principles and rules are applicable in the case of such a transfer.[136]

The Court then found that 'a contractual legal régime was created between Egypt and the Organization which remains the basis of their legal relations today.'[137] Such regime was presumably developed around the 1951 Agreement, and was purely conventional in nature unless it were the subject of a bilateral custom of the kind found to exist in the *Right of Passage* case, a conceivable but inappropriate interpretation. On that basis, the view could be taken, and was taken by individual Members of the Court, that the contractual regime contained within itself implied terms as to termination of the regime and the obligations of the parties in that event. This view is most clearly expressed by Judge Mosler:

> Since an implied rule by its very nature contains no provision concerning the modalities of its application, the parties must get in touch in order to enter into consultations and negotiations with respect to the time-limits and measures which may be appropriate for enabling the transfer to be effected in an orderly manner. The parties' obligation to reach an understanding with respect to the consequences of denunciation results from the contractual link between them, which requires them to work out in common a solution to the problems arising from the application of the Agreement where no express rules are laid down to govern the matter.[138]

---

[135] *ICJ Reports*, 1980, p. 89, para. 36.
[136] Ibid., p. 92, para. 42.
[137] Ibid., pp. 92–3, para. 43.
[138] Ibid., p. 129; cf. also Judge Gros, ibid., p. 107. Similarly, Judge Ago pertinently observed that 'being *lex specialis*, a treaty provision in force between two parties has inherent priority over such rules of a general nature as may also be applicable between them': ibid., p. 162.

The argument in the judgment, however, proceeds on a different basis: the Court proceeded to refer to 'a considerable number of host agreements of different kinds, concluded by States with various international organizations and containing varying provisions regarding the revision, termination or denunciation of the agreements'.[139] It regarded these as 'not without significance in the present connection':

> In the first place, they confirm the recognition by international organizations and host States of the existence of mutual obligations incumbent upon them to resolve the problems attendant upon a revision, termination or denunciation of a host agreement. But they do more, since they must be presumed to reflect the views of organizations and host States as to the implications of those obligations in the contexts in which the provisions are intended to apply. In the view of the Court, therefore, they provide certain general indications of what the mutual obligations of organizations and host States to co-operate in good faith may involve in situations such as the one with which the Court is here concerned.[140]

In other words, what is significant for the determination of the nature of the mutual obligations of Egypt and the WHO in the specific case is the attitude of 'international organizations and host States' as a category, or as two categories. Taking, for example, the definition of State practice, for the purposes of the identification of customary law, given by Akehurst,[141] that is, 'any act or statement by a State from which views can be inferred about international law',[142] it appears that what the Court was looking for and defining in the *WHO* case was the body of customary law applying to the revision, termination or denunciation of host agreements, underlying or supplementing the actual provisions of the host agreements themselves.

At the least, if it is not customary law which is here being applied, it is the body of law applicable to the interpretation of treaties, which may perhaps be formed from practice without the strict requirements of universality and *opinio juris*; this is indeed suggested by the Court's reference, in the next paragraph of its opinion, to the provisions of the Vienna Convention on the Law of Treaties and the (then) Draft Articles on Treaties between States and International Organizations, concerning the treaties in which a right of denunciation is implied by reason of their nature.[143] These international conventional instruments do not however extend so far as to supply the answer to the question which the Court found had been put to it; for that, reference to something more in the nature of customary law was needed.

Viewed in this light, the support in international practice for the obligations which the Court found to rest upon Egypt and the Organization is

[139] Ibid., p. 94, para. 45.
[140] Ibid., p. 94, para. 46.
[141] 'Custom as a Source of International Law', this *Year Book*, 47 (1974–5), p. 1.
[142] Ibid., at p. 10.
[143] *ICJ Reports*, 1980, pp. 94–5, para. 47. For Judge Sette Camara, the matter was regulated by 'general principles of the law of treaties': ibid., p. 189. Cf. Ferrari Bravo, 'Méthodes de recherche de la coutume internationale dans la pratique des Etats', *Recueil des cours*, 192 (1985–III), p. 313.

very sparse. Furthermore, reference to treaties as examples of State practice involves a well-known risk: the inclusion of a particular provision in successive treaties may be seen either as a recognition of an existing rule, or as a recognition that there is no such rule so that it is necessary to include a provision to cover the point. The intellectual process of the *WHO* advisory opinion appears to be the construction of a pattern of a model relationship between an international organization and a host State, on the basis of the host agreements in existence, and on that basis to outline a model procedure for the termination of the relationship as it might have been devised by a prescient draftsman. The Court, having put to itself the question which, it thought, *ought* to have been asked, gave the answer which *ought* to have followed from the host agreement which *ought* to have been entered into.

2. *The Elements Constitutive of Custom*

(1) *Introduction*

Even in a study of this kind devoted to the jurisprudence of the International Court, the definition given by the Court in the *North Sea Continental Shelf* cases of the elements necessary for establishing a rule of customary international law hardly needs to be quoted, so familiar has it become to every international lawyer as the *locus classicus* on the subject. Without going so far as to assert, with Macaulay, that 'every schoolboy knows'[144] the passage, it may at least be supposed that no first-year student of international law will be ignorant of the dictum:

Not only must the acts concerned amount to a settled practice, but they must also be such, or be carried out in such a way, as to be evidence of a belief that this practice is rendered obligatory by the existence of a rule of law requiring it. The need for such a belief, i.e., the existence of a subjective element, is implicit in the very notion of the *opinio juris sive necessitatis*. The States concerned must therefore feel that they are conforming to what amounts to a legal obligation.[145]

It should not of course be overlooked that at this point in the *North Sea* judgment the Court was dealing with the contention that a rule which had taken precise shape as a rule of treaty law, by inclusion in a multilateral convention, was

a norm-creating provision which has constituted the foundation of, or has generated a rule which, while only conventional or contractual in its origin, has since passed into the general *corpus* of international law, and is now accepted as such by the *opinio juris*, so as to have become binding even for countries which have never, and do not, become parties to the Convention[146]

and that this was a result 'not lightly to be regarded as having been

---

[144] See Macaulay, *Lord Clive* (1840): 'Every schoolboy knows who imprisoned Montezuma and who strangled Atahualpa'.

[145] *ICJ Reports*, 1969, p. 44, para. 77.

[146] Ibid., p. 41, para. 71: see section 3 below.

attained'.[146] Nevertheless, the passage may be taken as a general statement of the requirements of the formation of customary international law, with the reservation that some flexibility, particularly in the consistency of practice required, may be possible when the contours of the alleged rule have not been traced in advance by its inclusion in a treaty. The enquiry *what is* the rule (if any) of customary law is not an identical process with the enquiry *whether* a postulated rule has entered customary law.

It appears convenient to discuss the handling by the Court during the period under review of these two elements—State practice and *opinio juris*—in separate sections of this paper; but the distinction is not always easy to make, and sometimes indeed appears almost artificial.[147] Is it required that there be a 'settled practice' only because anything less will not be sufficient 'evidence of a belief that this practice is . . . obligatory'? If it is clear *aliunde* that the 'States concerned . . . feel that they are conforming to what amounts to a legal obligation', is it only by adding evidence of State practice that one can establish that that obligation is, and is regarded by the States concerned as, an obligation of customary law?[148]

There is much that could be said—and indeed much that has been said—on these questions. Our purpose here is however only to see to what extent the decisions of the Court, including the *North Sea* decision itself, throw light on theories of customary law. Before turning, however, to the *opinio juris*, we may observe that one area in which they tend to merge into each other to a particular degree is that of the law of international responsibility. If an international claim is brought by one State against another, and admitted by the defendant State, this is evidently an act of State practice. The same may, it is submitted, be said if the claim is upheld by an international judicial or arbitral tribunal.[149] At the same time, it is difficult to deny that the State which admits a claim does so because it is conscious of an obligation to do so, thus affording 'evidence of a belief that the practice is rendered obligatory by the existence of a rule of law requiring it'.[150] Evidently account may have to be taken of all the circumstances, including any disclaimer of legal liability or insistence on the *ex gratia* nature of any reparation made,[151] but in general the practice is not severable from a state of mind amounting to *opinio juris*.

[147] The point is neatly put by Brigitte Stern: 'les deux "éléments constitutifs" de la coutume ne sont pas deux entités juxtaposées, mais ne sont que deux aspects d'un même phénomène: une certaine action qui est subjectivement exécutée, ou perçue d'une certaine façon' ('La Coutume au coeur du droit international: quelques réflexions', *Mélanges Reuter* (1981), p. 482).

[148] On this, see the passage from the *Nicaragua* v. *United States* judgment quoted on pp. 4–5 above.

[149] It may be objected that the tribunal is not a State; but when the tribunal declares what the respondent State should have done in the circumstances, it may, for purposes of State practice, be deemed to have done it (cf. W.S. Gilbert: 'When Your Majesty says "Let a thing be done", it's as good as done—it *is* done': *The Mikado*, Act II). This is one explanation of the role of judicial decisions as a subsidiary source of international law.

[150] *North Sea Continental Shelf*, *ICJ Reports*, 1969, p. 44, para. 77.

[151] But, as Judge Gros realistically observes, 'it is not the habit of States to make each other free gifts'—note also his reference to the *Hammaken* case (*ICJ Reports*, 1970, p. 278, para. 61 and footnote 1).

There is of course a distinction in time between the act which gave rise to the injury and the act of agreeing to make, or making, reparation, but for this purpose the two may be conflated: to accept the legal responsibility for injury caused by an act is equivalent to refraining from committing that act, because it is recognized as illicit. The only circumstances in which the two acts might have to be considered separately would seem to be where questions of intertemporal law might arise.[152]

In the period under consideration, the *Barcelona Traction* case and the *Nicaragua* v. *United States* case raised the question of customary law in relation to international responsibility; the first has been examined above (section 1(2)), and the second will be examined in its place, below.

(2) *The* opinio juris sive necessitatis

(a) *Nature of the* opinio juris

Despite the emphasis laid by the Court in the *North Sea* cases on the need for a 'subjective element' in the creation of a rule of customary law, it has been argued, for example by Dr Peter Haggenmacher,[153] that enquiry into the existence of that element was, in those specific cases, unnecessary, since the practice relied on was in any event insufficient to support the existence of the custom alleged. The Court stated specifically that:

> Not only must the acts concerned amount to a settled practice, but they must also be such, or be carried out in such a way, as to be evidence of a belief that this practice is rendered obligatory by the existence of a rule of law requiring it. The need for such a belief, i.e., the existence of a subjective element, is implicit in the very notion of the *opinio juris sive necessitatis*. The States concerned must therefore feel that they are conforming to what amounts to a legal obligation.[154]

The logical paradox to which this classic definition of the *opinio juris* gives rise is well known: once a custom is established, States complying with it can do so in the belief that the 'practice is rendered obligatory by the existence of a rule of law requiring it'; but how can such a belief accompany the earliest acts constitutive of the practice, unless an unfounded belief is sufficient?[155] A charming parallel is offered by Brigitte Stern: 'Mais il suffit

---

[152] Given the slow pace of international claims negotiation, this is not so unlikely: for the resulting judicial problems, see this *Year Book*, 60 (1989), p. 134.

[153] Peter Haggenmacher, 'La Doctrine des deux éléments du droit coutumier dans la pratique de la Cour internationale', *Revue générale de droit international public*, 1986, p. 5.

[154] *ICJ Reports*, 1969, p. 44, para. 77.

[155] See, for example, Akehurst, this *Year Book*, 47 (1974–5), p. 32. Münch has suggested that the problem arises from an ill-advised analogy from codified municipal law:

'Les codes, lorsqu'ils admettent localement ou subsidiairement un régime coutumier, pouvaient très bien renvoyer au critère de la durée accompagnée de l'*opinio juris*: ils n'avaient pas à s'occuper de la formation de nouvelles règles. Mais dans une matière non écrite et dans un ordre non écrit, la question se pose différemment': 'Le Rôle du droit spontané', *Pensamiento juridico y sociedad internacional (Mélanges Truyol Serra)* (Madrid, 1986), vol. 2, pp. 833, 834.

parfois de croire à l'amour pour qu'il existe'.[156] However, the suggested solution put forward by the present writer,[157] among others, is that at the initial stage of the development of the custom, it is sufficient that the States concerned regard the practice as what the Court, in a different context, referred to as 'potentially norm-creating',[158] as conforming to a rule which either already exists or is a useful and desirable rule which should exist.[159] This 'sociological' approach has been criticized[160] as a distortion of the concept, which, it is said, is essentially that of *opinio obligationis*; but it is questionable whether the history of the concept in practice suffers such fine distinctions. If it could be shown that States had held an *opinio necessitatis juris* in the 'sociological' sense, but had not and could not have an *opinio juris* in the strict sense of the Court's definition in the *North Sea* cases, and that the consequence had been the non-appearance of a custom, it would undoubtedly be necessary to abandon this interpretation as itself unsupported by practice.[161]

The alternative, that proposed by Haggenmacher in the study referred to, is to abandon the *opinio juris* entirely as a required element in the formation of custom, and base it solely upon the accumulation of practice of an appropriate kind.[162] Certainly the traditional justification of the need for a subjective element, restated by the Court in the *North Sea* cases, is of doubtful validity:

The frequency, or even habitual character of the acts is not in itself enough. There are many international acts, e.g., in the field of ceremonial and protocol, which are performed almost invariably, but which are motivated only by considerations of courtesy, convenience or tradition, and not by any sense of legal duty.[163]

It may however be doubted whether there is in fact any real risk of confu-

---

[156] 'La Coutume au coeur de droit international: quelques réflexions', *Mélanges offerts à Paul Reuter* (1981), p. 487. Miss Stern's solution is however, in effect, not so much sensualist as consensualist.

[157] *International Customary Law and Codification*, pp. 53–4.

[158] *ICJ Reports*, 1969, p. 42, para. 72.

[159] Cf. Sorensen, 'Principes de droit international public', *Recueil des cours*, 101 (1960–III), p. 50; Charpentier, 'Tendances de l'élaboration du droit international public coutumier', *L'Elaboration du droit international public* (Société française pour le droit international, 1974), p. 115. The approach of Judge Lachs in the *North Sea Continental Shelf* cases appears to be similar: *ICJ Reports*, 1969, p. 231.

[160] Haggenmacher, loc. cit. above (n. 153), p. 110, n. 334.

[161] Another cogent criticism is that of Akehurst:
'Practice accompanied by a sense of social or moral obligation does not always create a rule of customary law. The immorality of aggressive war was recognized centuries before its illegality. Most, if not all, developed countries give aid to poorer countries and would probably admit that they have a moral obligation to do so, but how many of them recognize a legal obligation to give aid?': 'Custom as a Source of International Law', this *Year Book*, 47 (1974–5), p. 35.
The distinction is however precisely between recognition of a moral obligation and recognition that that obligation ought to be or become a legal one.

[162] Loc. cit. above (n. 153), pp. 124–5; essentially his view is that relevant practice is a single phenomenon, the separation of the two elements being an unnecessary juristic refinement. A variant of this approach is to preserve the requirement of *opinio juris*, but to make its existence a matter of rebuttable presumption, as suggested by Lauterpacht: *The Development of International Law by the International Court* (1958), p. 380.

[163] *ICJ Reports*, 1969, p. 44, para. 77.

sion between established, but non-binding, protocolary practices, and rules of customary international law.[164]

There is, however, at least one other subjective aspect to be borne in mind in considering whether a State's acts in a particular field are contributory to the growth of custom. It may be that it is not strictly necessary that the State should have acted in the conviction that it was complying with a rule of customary law; but is essential that it should *not* have been acting in compliance, or in the belief that it was complying, with an obligation of a different character,—specifically, a treaty obligation. In the *North Sea* cases the Court, when analysing the examples of practice of the use of the equidistance method for the delimitation of the continental shelf, rejected a considerable number of examples offered:

> To begin with, over half the States concerned, whether acting unilaterally or conjointly, were or shortly became parties to the Geneva Convention, and were therefore presumably, so far as they were concerned, acting actually or potentially in the application of the Convention. From their action no inference could legitimately be drawn as to the existence of a rule of customary international law in favour of the equidistance principle.[165]

Leaving aside for the moment the question of States which at the relevant time were not yet parties to the 1958 Geneva Convention, the logic is unassailable: if the act of the State, in order to contribute to the formation of customary law, must have been accompanied by the intention of conforming to an existing or nascent rule of customary law, an act performed in compliance with a treaty obligation is without significance for this purpose. It does not constitute evidence to the contrary, since a State may in fact recognize the existence of a customary-law rule requiring the same conduct as that which is imposed upon it by the treaty; but this would have to be proved, and even so the act would not be accompanied by the requisite intention.

This raises something of a paradox in the context of the influence of multilateral treaties on the development of custom. It is of the essence of a rule of general customary law that it is applicable to, and binding upon, States which have not contributed to its formation. If a sufficient number of States adopt a consistent practice, accompanied by this slippery concept of *opinio juris*, the customary rule so created will bind other States (subject to exceptions of the kind exemplified by Norway in the *Fisheries* case).[166] But if the same group of States conclude a multilateral treaty requiring the practice in question to be followed, no customary rule will come into existence,

---

[164] Cf. Haggenmacher, loc. cit. above (n. 153), pp. 7–8; Akehurst, 'Custom as a Source of International Law', this *Year Book*, 47 (1974–5), pp. 32–4.

[165] *ICJ Reports*, 1969, p. 43, para. 76. It appears that Judge Lachs differed from the majority on this point, since he refers, in his study of State practice in his dissenting opinion, to 'States, both parties and not parties to the Convention' (ibid., pp. 228–9).

[166] The 'persistent objector' or 'single recalcitrant State': see section 5 below.

and other States will be able to rely on the principle *pactum tertiis nec nocet nec prodest*.

The reference in the *North Sea* judgment to the acts of delimitation by States which *subsequently* became parties to the 1958 Geneva Convention is intriguing. Clearly at the moment when such States entered into the relevant agreements, or adopted the relevant legislation, they were not acting in execution of a duty imposed by the Convention. Their subsequent accession to the Convention may point to the conclusion that at the time of the delimitation they already thought the Convention regime a good one, suitable for application even without, or prior to, acceptance of the Convention. Can it be said that this negatives the possibility of the existence of *opinio juris* in the classic sense?

It might be argued that the Court's dictum constitutes precisely the contradiction of the 'sociological' conception of the *opinio juris* referred to above. The Court, it may be said, refused to accept as practice contributory to the development of a custom acts which were accompanied by a conviction that the rule applied would be a desirable one, a conviction that took subsequent practical shape in accession to the Geneva Convention. Is this then not a rejection of 'sociological' *opinio juris* in favour of the rigid *opinio obligationis*?

It is suggested that it is not—for two reasons. First, the acceptance of the 1958 Geneva Convention implies conviction that the Convention regime as a whole is a satisfactory one for the State accepting it, in the context of the multilateral treaty-relationship; it does not necessarily imply approval of a particular aspect of the treaty in isolation—Article 6 and the equidistance/special circumstances rule—as a desideratum. It may of course be motivated by such approval, but since this cannot be demonstrated, the acceptance of the whole Convention is not *opinio juris*. As the Court observed, in a slightly different context in the *Nicaragua* v. *United States* case,

> Rules which are identical in treaty law and in customary international law are also distinguishable by reference to the methods of interpretation and application. A State may accept a rule contained in a treaty not simply because it favours the application of the rule itself, but also because the treaty establishes what the State regards as desirable institutions or mechanisms to ensure implementation of the rule.[167]

Secondly, the *opinio juris* under discussion is the conviction that the rule applied pursuant to that conviction is desirable as a rule of customary law, with a consequent vocation to universality,[168] not simply as a rule to be enshrined in a multilateral treaty.

This distinction, or something very close to it, is also referred to in the judgment of the Chamber in the *Gulf of Maine* case. The Chamber pre-

---

[167] *ICJ Reports*, 1986, p. 95, para. 178.

[168] In the case of a regional custom, universality must be taken as universality within the region. Different considerations apply to the special case of bilateral custom: see the discussion of the *Right of Passage* case, below pp. 102 ff.

faced its inquiry into the 'principles and rules of international law applicable in the matter', as required by the Special Agreement, with a distinction drawn between such principles and rules, on the one hand, and 'what could be better described as the various equitable criteria and practical methods'.[169] In the view of the Chamber, customary international law 'can of its nature only provide a few basic legal principles, which lay down guidelines to be followed with a view to an essential objective',[170] and not the appropriate 'equitable criteria' and 'practical methods' for achieving that objective. The Chamber however continues:

> The same may not, however, be true of international treaty law. There is, for instance, nothing to prevent the parties to a convention—whether bilateral or multilateral—from extending the rules contained in that convention to aspects which it is less likely that customary international law might govern.[171]

This is essentially the reason why the Chamber rejected not only the equidistance method, but virtually any specific method of delimitation in the maritime sphere, as an element of customary international law.

Whether or not this rejection is regarded as a correct finding, the distinction drawn is, it is suggested, logically sound, and relevant to the present discussion of the 'sociological' interpretation of *opinio juris*. For the Chamber, the inclusion of the equidistance method in the 1958 Geneva Convention did not, even in conjunction with other practice, lead to the conclusion that equidistance had become, or could become, a method required by customary international law, because while it could be, and clearly was, regarded by States as an appropriate element for inclusion in a treaty governing the matter, this did not *per se* signify approval of it as an actual or potential customary-law rule—approval which would rank as *opinio juris* in the sociological sense.

(b) *Application of* opinio juris *by the Court*

Whatever the theoretical weaknesses of the classical theory of *opinio juris* as one of the two elements of custom, the Court itself has continued, in decisions since the *North Sea Continental Shelf* cases, to remain faithful to it. In the case of the *Continental Shelf (Libyan Arab Jamahiriya/Malta)*, it stated that

> It is of course axiomatic that the material of customary international law is to be looked for primarily in the actual practice and *opinio juris* of States . . . ,[172]

a dictum which was quoted with approval the following year in the case concerning *Military and Paramilitary Activities in and against Nicaragua*

[169] *ICJ Reports*, 1984, p. 290, para. 80.
[170] Ibid., p. 290, para. 81; cf. also ibid., p. 300, para. 114.
[171] Ibid., p. 290, para. 82.
[172] *ICJ Reports*, 1985, p. 29, para. 27. It is not clear what other source the Court had in mind when including the word 'primarily' in the sentence.

(Nicaragua v. *United States of America).*[173] The *Libya/Malta* case does not however throw light on the Court's conception of what precisely *opinio juris* signifies, or how it has to be proved. The parties offered competing interpretations of State practice constituted or exemplified by over 70 maritime delimitation agreements. The Court commented that, for its part, it 'has no doubt about the importance of State practice in this matter'.[174] It continued however:

> Yet that practice, however interpreted, falls short of proving the existence of a rule prescribing the use of equidistance, or indeed of any method, as obligatory.[175]

Whether this conclusion is based upon considerations similar to those stated in the *Gulf of Maine* case, or other considerations relating to *opinio juris*, or upon, for example, lack of sufficient consistency in the practice relied on, is not explained.

Judge Sette-Camara, in his separate opinion, also reached a negative conclusion based on absence of practice, but in relation to the distance provisions of Article 76, paragraphs 1 and 5, of the Montego Bay Convention. In his view, anything other than the 'old rule' of natural prolongation 'lacks evidence of *opinio juris sive necessitatis* and of *usus*'.[176]

In the case concerning *Military and Paramilitary Activities in and against Nicaragua (Nicaragua* v. *United States of America)*, the Court was dealing with an extreme example of the sort of *dédoublement fonctionnel* between treaty and custom which it had to consider in the *North Sea Continental Shelf* cases. Virtually every State whose actions and attitudes might be scrutinized for evidence of *opinio juris* was a party to a multilateral treaty—the United Nations Charter—the provisions of which covered essentially the same ground as the customary law rules whose existence and content was in question, even though

> On a number of points, the areas governed by the two sources of law do not exactly overlap, and the substantive rules in which they are framed are not identical in content.[177]

Thus apart from the additional problem that the rules in question were prohibitory, which complicates proof of *opinio juris*, the situation was, in the terms of the *North Sea* decision, that

> the States concerned, whether acting unilaterally or conjointly, were . . . parties to the [Charter], and were therefore presumably, so far as they were concerned, acting . . . in the application of the [Charter]. From their action no inference could legitimately be drawn as to the existence of a rule of customary international law in favour of the [alleged] principle.[178]

[173] *ICJ Reports*, 1986, p. 97, para. 183.
[174] *ICJ Reports*, 1985, p. 38, para. 44.
[175] Ibid.
[176] Ibid., p. 69.
[177] *ICJ Reports*, 1986, p. 94, para. 175.
[178] *ICJ Reports*, 1969, p. 43, para. 76, slightly adapted.

The Court in 1986 did not refer specifically to this difficulty, or tackle it squarely.[179] It selected for scrutiny, however, a particular field of State action in which the difficulty adverted to did not arise. For the purposes of ascertaining whether there existed in customary international law 'an *opinio juris* as to the binding character' of refraining from the threat or use of force, the Court stated:

> This *opinio juris* may, though with all due caution, be deduced from, *inter alia*, the attitude of the Parties and the attitude of States towards certain General Assembly resolutions, and particularly resolution 2625 (XXV) entitled 'Declaration on Principles of International Law concerning Friendly Relations and Co-operation among States in accordance with the Charter of the United Nations'. The effect of consent to the text of such resolutions cannot be understood as merely that of a 'reiteration or elucidation' of the treaty commitment undertaken in the Charter. On the contrary, it may be understood as an acceptance of the validity of the rule or set of rules declared by the resolution by themselves.[180]

The passage is full of interest, and will be examined again in connection with the question of State practice. For the present, the significant aspect is the choice of the action to serve as evidence of *opinio juris*. For a State to refrain from the threat or use of force could be 'explained away' as a mere compliance with the Charter. The Charter requires States to refrain from the use of force; but it does not in terms require States to vote in favour of resolutions or declarations which endorse or recognize the principle of non-use of force.[181] Therefore if States do vote in favour of such texts, this amounts to a recognition of a rule outside the Charter, a rule of customary law.

What then of the statement in the *North Sea* cases that 'implicit in the very notion of the *opinio juris sive necessitatis*' is the need for a 'subjective element', the belief on the part of States that the practice in question 'is rendered obligatory by the existence of a rule of law requiring it'?[182] As the present writer has observed elsewhere,

> On any traditional interpretation, the only rule which could be created by the combination of *opinio juris* and voting in the General Assembly, the act of voting constituting practice, would be a rule imposing, in certain circumstances, a duty to cast an affirmative vote in the General Assembly, which would be a rule without much practical content.[183]

The argument in the *Nicaragua* v. *United States* case proceeds from the existence of a defined rule, laid down in the Charter, which can neverthe-

---

[179] The passage just quoted concerning differences between customary law and Charter law was addressed to the problem of the effect of the United States multilateral treaty reservation.

[180] *ICJ Reports*, 1986, pp. 99–100, para. 188.

[181] Actually to vote *against* such a resolution might come close to a breach of the Charter rule; but an absention would surely be lawful. On General Assembly resolutions as giving rise to *opinio juris*, see the separate opinion of Judge Dillard in the *Western Sahara* case, *ICJ Reports*, 1975, p. 121.

[182] *ICJ Reports*, 1969, p. 44, para. 77.

[183] *International Customary Law and Codification* (1972), p. 67.

less, at least in theory, exist simultaneously as a rule of customary law,[184] together with the existence of a State practice showing an *opinio* in favour of the rule, and not itself required by the Charter, to deduce therefrom a quasi-identical customary rule. It involves treating the *opinio* expressed in the vote as equivalent, not to a view that member States are bound by a customary rule to vote for a resolution endorsing non-use of force, but to a view that, because member States are bound, outside and independently of the Charter, to refrain from the use of force, it would be inconsistent with, or a non-recognition of, this rule not to vote in favour of such a resolution. It is a bold construction.[185] Unfortunately, the exceptional nature of the circumstances in which the Court found itself obliged to make it, which are unlikely to recur,[186] means that it is not one which can be expected to be confirmed or developed by later cases.

When it turned to the principle of non-intervention in the affairs of other States, the Court in the *Nicaragua* case adopted a similar approach, even though this principle is not specifically laid upon member States as an obligation by the Charter:

Of course, statements whereby States avow their recognition of the principles of international law set forth in the United Nations Charter cannot strictly be interpreted as applying to the principle of non-intervention by States in the internal and external affairs of other States, since this principle is not, as such, spelt out in the Charter. But it was never intended that the Charter should embody written confirmation of every essential principle of international law in force.[187]

Thus it is conceded that there is here no treaty-law obligation deriving from the Charter; at a stroke the problem of the possible double foundation of the obligation, which makes it difficult to find practice unambiguously signifying *opinio juris*, disappears. One might therefore expect a simple reliance on a practice of non-intervention; and indeed in the next sentence the Court states that

The existence in the *opinio juris* of States of the principle of non-intervention is backed by established and substantial practice.[188]

No such practice is specifically described; and the next step in the argument seems to be a retrograde one:

It has moreover been presented as a corollary of the principle of the sovereign

---

[184] See the first article in this series, this *Year Book*, 60 (1989), pp. 147 ff.

[185] For an alternative assessment, that 'The Court thus completely misunderstands customary law', see d'Amato, 'Trashing Customary International Law' in 'Appraisals of the ICJ's Decision: *Nicaragua v. United States (Merits)*', *American Journal of International Law*, 81 (1987), p. 102.

[186] This ill-starred 'multilateral treaty reservation' is no longer with us since the United States withdrawal of its Optional Clause declaration, and not, we may hope, likely to be revived.

[187] *ICJ Reports*, 1986, p. 106, para. 102.

[188] Ibid.

equality of States. A particular instance of this is General Assembly resolution 2625 (XXV), the Declaration on the Principles of International Law concerning Friendly Relations and Co-operation among States.[189]

To re-attach the principle, as a corollary, to a Charter principle, seems likely to re-introduce the problem of unambiguous practice; and in the following paragraphs the Court again relies on 'numerous declarations adopted by international organizations and conferences', including the General Assembly.

(c) *Whose* opinio juris?

(i) *The relevance of the views of the parties*. The existence of a dispute before the Court on the application of a rule of customary law normally implies that the parties will be at odds over the content, or even the existence, of the rule relied on by one of them. It might be supposed that if the parties were agreed as to the existence and content of a customary rule, then—assuming that there was nevertheless a dispute between them requiring settlement by the Court—it would not be necessary for the Court to go behind that agreement and ascertain whether such a rule truly existed. In the *Fisheries Jurisdiction* cases the Court noted that both parties had accepted and applied the concept of a twelve-mile fishery zone, so that 'this matter is no longer in dispute between the Parties'.[190] It did not enquire further into the existence of a 'general practice accepted as law' in support of the concept; but this was because it had no need to do so, since it was not asked to make any finding on the matter: the dispute before the Court concerned areas more than twelve miles off the coast.

The Chamber formed to deal with the *Gulf of Maine* case, however, when considering the significance for customary international law of the United Nations Conference on the Law of the Sea, referred to 'certain provisions of the [UNCLOS] Convention, concerning the continental shelf and the exclusive economic zone' as having been 'adopted without any objections'. It continued

The United States, in particular, in 1983, that is to say after the Special Agreement had come into force, proclaimed an economic zone on the basis of Part V of the 1982 Convention. This proclamation was accompanied by a statement by the President to the effect that in that respect the Convention generally confirmed existing rules of international law. Canada, which has not at present made a similar proclamation, has for its part also recognized the legal significance of the nature and purpose of the new 200-mile régime. This concordance of views is worthy of note . . .[191]

---

[189] Ibid.

[190] *ICJ Reports*, 1974, p. 24, para. 54; p. 192, para. 46.

[191] *ICJ Reports*, 1984, p. 294, para. 94. Cf. also the 'fortunate' circumstance of the parties' agreement on the fundamental norm: ibid., p. 299, para. 111 (p. 57, below).

Furthermore, in the case concerning *Military and Paramilitary Activities in and against Nicaragua (Nicaragua v. United States of America)*, the Court observed as follows:

> The Court notes that there is in fact evidence, to be examined below, of a considerable degree of agreement between the Parties as to the content of the customary international law relating to the non-use of force and non-intervention. This concurrence of their views does not however dispense the Court from having itself to ascertain what rules of customary international law are applicable. The mere fact that States declare their recognition of certain rules is not sufficient for the Court to consider these as being part of customary international law, and as applicable as such to those States. Bound as it is by Article 38 of its Statute to apply, *inter alia*, international custom 'as evidence of a general practice accepted as law', the Court may not disregard the essential role played by general practice. Where two States agree to incorporate a particular rule in a treaty, their agreement suffices to make that rule a legal one, binding upon them; but in the field of customary international law, the shared view of the Parties as to the content of what they regard as the rule is not enough. The Court must satisfy itself that the existence of the rule in the *opinio juris* of States is confirmed by practice.[192]

It should first be noted that the Court is not here dealing with any question of *consent* of States to a particular rule of customary law. The reference to, and rejection of, the treaty-law analogy rather confuses the argument, since to conclude a treaty laying down a rule of conduct is to consent to the application of that rule to oneself. The Court is however careful to speak in terms of 'recognition' and of the 'shared view of the Parties as to what they regard as the rule'.

It is of course vital to the existence of customary law that it be not dependent on consent, in the sense that a general rule of customary international law binds States which have not participated in its formation, and even if they are not agreeable to its application (reserving always the situation of the 'persistent objector'). It might be suggested that if the two States before the Court have a shared *opinio juris* as to the existence and content of a particular rule, then that rule must exist at least as a rule of special or bilateral customary law. This would however only be correct if the rule in question were one appropriate to apply solely in the restricted context of relations between the States, and were regarded as such by them. A belief that a rule exists as a rule of general international law cannot, however, be treated as *opinio juris* directed to a rule of special or bilateral custom.[193] Thus the existence or otherwise of the consent of the parties to the case to a particular rule will, if it is a rule of general law, be irrelevant. With regard to the *opinio juris*, the situation is somewhat different. Obviously, it cannot be *necessary* that the two parties before the Court have a 'shared view' as to the content of the relevant customary rules, since it will usually be absence

[192] *ICJ Reports*, 1986, pp. 97–8, para. 184.
[193] If the matter in dispute is one which concerns solely the reciprocal rights and obligations of the two States concerned, as in the *Right of Passage* case, or the *Temple of Preah Vihear* case, the line between consent and *opinio juris* is blurred to the point of invisibility. See also section 4 below.

of such a shared view which has caused the dispute to arise. The Court in the *Nicaragua* case was ruling that it is also not *sufficient* that there be such a shared view.

This approach cannot be faulted on the theoretical level. To show the existence of *opinio juris* in the thinking of only two States of the world would not normally be regarded as a very convincing demonstration of the existence of a rule of general international law; and the moment one excludes consent as a factor from the equation, the fact that these two States are the very parties before the Court does not affect the issue.[194] In the *Fisheries Jurisdiction* cases, the Court noted, in connection with the customary law rule providing for preferential fishing rights of the coastal State in certain circumstances, the existence of agreements to which the applicant States were parties recognizing such preferential rights. It was not however on this basis that the Court found that there was such a rule of customary law, but on the basis of 'State practice on the subject of fisheries' as evident in, *inter alia*, the work of the 1958 and 1960 Conferences on the Law of the Sea.[195] Similarly, in the case concerning the *Continental Shelf (Libyan Arab Jamahiriya/Malta)*, the Court first found that 'the institution of the exclusive economic zone . . . is shown by the practice of States to have become a part of customary law', before going on to observe that 'in any case, Libya itself seemed to recognize this fact' by a proposal during negotiations.[196]

At the same time, again because we are not talking of consent but of conviction of the existence of the rule, the Court's approach in the *Nicaragua* case may be regarded as slightly unrealistic:[197] it is not very likely that, in a situation of dispute, the State in whose interest it is to deny the rule would concede it unless there is in fact a solid background of *opinio juris* in its favour among States of the world.

(ii) Opinio juris *of States not before the Court*. Except in cases where the custom relied on is bilateral,[198] any assertion of the existence of a rule of customary international law must involve the Court in an examination of the conduct of States other than those parties to the case, in order to determine whether such conduct is indicative of *opinio juris* supporting the alleged rule. Theoretically at least, therefore, the Court may find itself having to include as an element in its reasoning, even if only an unavowed one,

[194] Cf. the observations in the previous article in this series (this *Year Book*, 60 (1989), pp. 39–43) on the juridical significance, if any, of previous statements by a party as to the state of the law on the question at issue.
[195] *ICJ Reports*, 1974, p. 26, para. 58.
[196] *ICJ Reports*, 1985, p. 33, para. 34.
[197] Akehurst ('Custom as a Source of International Law', this *Year Book*, 47 (1974–5), pp. 4–5) draws attention to some arbitral decisions in which the tribunal did not look behind the previous statements and shared view of the parties as to the content of a given rule: e.g., *Mexican Union Railways Claim, Reports of International Arbitral Awards*, vol. 5, p. 115. In Akehurst's view, such statements were treated as constitutive of State practice, which, in the present writer's view, is to read altogether too much into these decisions.
[198] See below, pp. 102 ff.

an assessment of such conduct as in accordance with or not in accordance with international law. In some cases, to rule that the conduct of other States relied on by an applicant State to show *opinio juris* does not support that claim will not involve a finding or implication that such conduct is contrary to an existing rule; it may be not unlawful, but not significant as *opinio juris*. This would be so if it were either 'not contrary to international law' or 'action . . . in a field which international law does not purport to regulate at all'.[199] This may not always be so, however; and it is obviously a delicate matter for a court to express or imply a view as to the legality of action of States not before it.[200]

The Court adverted to this problem in its judgment in the *Nicaragua* v. *United States* case, when discussing the question of the existence and content of a rule of customary law prohibiting intervention by one State in the affairs of another. It quoted the well-known passage from the *North Sea Continental Shelf* decision, concerning the need for 'evidence of a belief that [the] practice is rendered obligatory by the existence of a rule of law requiring it',[201] as implicit in the notion of *opinio juris*. It then continued:

The Court has no jurisdiction to rule upon the conformity with international law of any conduct of States not parties to the present dispute, or of conduct of the Parties unconnected with the dispute; nor has it authority to ascribe to States legal views which they do not themselves advance. The significance for the Court of cases of State conduct prima facie inconsistent with the principle of non-intervention lies in the nature of the ground offered as justification. Reliance by a State on a novel right or an unprecedented exception to the principle might, if shared in principle by other States, tend towards a modification of customary international law. In fact however the Court finds that States have not justified their conduct by reference to a new right of intervention or a new exception to the principle of its prohibition.[202]

There is of course something of an elision in the argument at this point. According to the traditional rule expressed in the quotation from the *North Sea* judgment, what is to be looked for is evidence that States acted as they did because they felt obliged to do so by a customary rule. This is quite different from ascertaining whether States felt that they were justified, or at least not forbidden, by an existing rule.

The definition of *opinio juris* in the *North Sea* cases requires however to be glossed in certain respects. First, as observed by MacGibbon,[203] *opinio juris* is primarily of importance from the standpoint of customary rules

---

[199] Cf. the discussion in the first article in this series, this *Year Book*, 60 (1989), pp. 84 ff., particularly p. 86 and p. 90.

[200] Contrast the attitude of the Court in the *Corfu Channel* case, where it would apparently have been prepared to make a finding, had the evidence supported it, that the mines had been laid by the Yugoslav Government, not a party to the case, with the celebrated ruling in the *Monetary Gold* case, declining to reach a finding on the responsibility of Albania because Albania was not before the Court.

[201] *ICJ Reports*, 1969, p. 44, para. 77, quoted in *ICJ Reports*, 1986, p. 109, para. 207.

[202] *ICJ Reports*, 1986, p. 109, para. 207.

[203] 'Customary International Law and Acquiescence', this *Year Book*, 33 (1957), p. 115.

expressed as obligations rather than expressed as rights: a claim to act in a particular way will hardly be a matter of duty, while there may well be a duty to admit the claim, or not to protest against it, if it is recognized as being justified by international law. Secondly, as the present writer has observed elsewhere, 'a State which asserts a claim will be guided by what it believes to be the law in fixing the *extent* of its claim'.[204]

In the particular instance under consideration in the *Nicaragua* v. *United States* case, the question was what was the significance of practice which was prima facie in contravention of a generally recognized rule of customary law, that of non-intervention. That practice might be significant of negative *opinio juris*, in the sense that it showed that the State acting did not regard itself as obliged by a customary rule requiring it to refrain from intervention; and that *opinio* might be totally negative, in the sense of a denial of the rule, or only *sub modo*, in the sense of a view that the general prohibition did not extend to action in the particular circumstances.

It is in this situation that comment on the legality of action of States not before the Court becomes unavoidable if the question is to be answered whether there exists such a rule of customary law as is asserted. An alternative approach is of course not to answer that question, if the decision can be made to rest on another ground. This course was adopted in the *Fisheries Jurisdiction* cases: to uphold the thesis advanced by the United Kingdom, that the Icelandic claim to a 50-mile exclusive fishery zone was 'without foundation in international law' might have meant declaring that the actions of other States in promulgating similar claims did not indicate an *opinio juris* supporting their legality. This would necessarily imply that at least the enforcement of such claims against other States might have been in violation of international law.

Only Judge Gros was prepared to press the principle *fiat justitia, ruat coelum* to this point:

> It has also been said that a claim extending beyond 12 miles is not *ipso jure* unlawful, because there have been many claims of this kind; . . .
>
> There is no escaping the fact that if the States which oppose the extension cannot do so on the basis of a rule of international law, their opposition is ineffective, and this must be said; but if they can base their opposition on such a rule, it is equally necessary not to hesitate to say that.[205]

(3) *State practice*

(a) *The nature of the practice required to establish a rule of customary law*

In 1972 the present writer advanced the following view as to the nature of State practice required to contribute to the formation of a rule of customary international law:

---

[204] *International Customary Law and Codification* (1972), p. 49. Cf. McNair in the *Fisheries* case, relying on State practice as to identification of the base-line of territorial waters: 'Governments are not prone to understate their claims' (*ICJ Reports*, 1951, p. 162).

[205] *ICJ Reports*, 1974, p. 135; cf. also the view of Judge Onyeama, ibid., p. 171, para. 17.

State practice as the material element in the formation of custom is, it is worth emphasising, *material*: it is composed of acts by States with regard to a particular person, ship, defined area of territory, each of which amounts to the assertion or repudiation of a claim relating to a particular apple of discord. Claims may be made in the widest of general terms; but the occasion of an act of State practice contributing to the formation of custom must always be some specific dispute or potential dispute.

The mere assertion *in abstracto* of the existence of a legal right or legal rule is not an act of State practice; but it may be adduced as evidence of the acceptance by the State against which it is sought to set up a claim, of the customary rule which is alleged to exist, assuming that that State asserts that it is not bound by the alleged rule. More important, such assertions can be relied on as *supplementary* evidence both of State practice and of the existence of the *opinio juris*; but only as supplementary evidence, and not as one element to be included in the summing up of State practice for the purpose of assessing its generality.

Practice or usage consists of an accumulation of acts which are material or concrete in the sense that they are intended to have an immediate effect on the legal relationships of the State concerned; and acts which are relevant only as assertions in the abstract, such as the recognition by a representative of a State at a diplomatic conference that an alleged rule exists are not constitutive of practice and thus of custom, but only confirmatory of it.[206]

---

[206] *International Customary Law and Codification*, p. 58, (original emphasis). The views here referred to had already been criticized in 1975 by Akehurst: 'Custom as a Source of International Law', this *Year Book*, 47 (1974–5), at p. 4, on the basis of, *inter alia*, the *Fisheries Jurisdiction* judgments. In the interstices of these footnotes, perhaps I may be permitted to comment on these and other criticisms. First, Ferrari Bravo argues in favour of taking account, as acts of State practice, of the views expressed by States at (in particular) codification conferences because for many of them the problem may never arise as a practical issue: such conferences 'sont souvent les seuls endroits où, d'une manière ou de l'autre, la voix de ces pays qui, autrement, n'auraient vraisemblablement pas l'occasion de participer à la formation des règles coutumières se manifeste' ('Méthodes de recherche de la coutume internationale dans la pratique des Etats', *Recueil des cours*, 192 (1985–III), p. 254). It is significant that Ferrari Bravo argues from this that States should be careful what they say at such conferences; it is precisely because States with no direct interest in a matter may not be restrained from putting forward inappropriate views that it is my contention that it is not correct to regard the expression of such views as an example of practice. More searching is the criticism made by Akehurst, that

'the distinction between assertions made in the context of some concrete situation and assertions made *in abstracto* is also unrealistic, because it emphasizes appearances at the expense of reality. For instance, at a conference on the law of the sea the Arab States and Israel may appear to be making abstract assertions about the right of passage through straits, but it is probable that what they really have in mind is the right of passage through the Straits of Tiran. Conversely, a State may adopt a particular attitude in the context of a particular dispute, not because it has a real interest in the facts of the case, but because it wishes to secure acceptance of a general principle (e.g. Argentina's protests over the kidnapping of Eichmann). Thus assertions about a particular dispute are dressed up as assertions *in abstracto*, and vice versa; it may not even be possible for an outside observer to tell whether this has happened. In short, there is no clear dividing line between the two classes of assertions; they merge into one another.' ('Custom as a Source of International Law', this *Year Book*, 47 (1974–5), p. 4.)

There is much force in this criticism; but the difficulty of distinguishing between abstract statements and statements directed to a concrete issue is to my mind a further reason for not including statements at conferences or in the General Assembly in the category of State practice. As to the contrary case, it would seem that Argentina's actual protest to Israel must constitute an act of State practice, whatever its motivation, and all the more so if it was designed to ensure acceptance of a general principle; thus a complaint of Israel's action by Argentina in (say) the General Assembly has a claim to be taken into account if such statements are to rank as State practice at all.

Of the decisions of the Court the subject of the present series of articles, only the *Right of Passage* and *North Sea Continental Shelf* judgments had been given at the time of the text above was written. It may thus serve as a working hypothesis to be tested against the subsequent decisions of the Court involving questions of customary law, to see to what extent they confirm or conflict with it.

The bulk of the decisions in the period considered in which it was necessary to consider the current state of customary international law consists of cases of maritime delimitation. A preliminary point to be examined, in view of the particular nature of the law in this field, and the way in which it has developed, is what sort of rules or principles of law the Court was required to ascertain and declare: rules extending to the actual methods by which delimitation of sea or sea-bed areas should be delimited, or simply rules as to the result to be achieved, coupled perhaps with non-binding guidelines on how to achieve it?

The Chamber in the *Gulf of Maine* case took up a very clear position on this, as set out in the following passages from its judgment:

One preliminary remark is necessary before we come to the essence of the matter, since it seems above all essential to stress the distinction to be drawn between what are principles and rules of international law governing the matter and what could be better described as the various equitable criteria and practical methods that may be used to ensure *in concreto* that a particular situation is dealt with in accordance with the principles and rules in question.

In a matter of this kind, international law—and in this respect the Chamber has logically to refer primarily to customary international law—can of its nature only provide a few basic legal principles, which lay down guidelines to be followed with a view to an essential objective. It cannot also be expected to specify the equitable criteria to be applied or the practical, often technical, methods to be used for attaining that objective—which remain simply criteria and methods even where they are also, in a different sense, called 'principles'.[207]

Emphasizing the specific, 'monotypic', character of each delimitation, the Chamber concluded that

This precludes the possibility of those conditions arising which are necessary for the formation of principles and rules of customary law giving specific provisions for subjects like those just mentioned.[208]

At a later stage in its judgment, the Chamber rejected the arguments of both parties as to the relevant rules and principles, asserting that 'The error lies precisely in searching general international law for, as it were, a set of rules which are not there'.[209] In the view of the Chamber,

A body of detailed rules is not to be looked for in customary international law which in fact comprises a limited set of norms for ensuring the co-existence and

---

[207] *ICJ Reports*, 1984, p. 290, paras. 80 and 81.
[208] Ibid., p. 290, para. 81.
[209] Ibid., p. 298, para. 110.

vital co-operation of the members of the international community, together with a set of customary rules whose presence in the *opinio juris* of States can be tested by induction based on the analysis of a sufficiently extensive and convincing practice, and not by deduction from preconceived ideas. It is therefore unrewarding, especially in a new and still unconsolidated field like that involving the quite recent extension of the claims of States to areas which were until yesterday zones of the high seas, to look to general international law to provide a ready-made set of rules that can be used for solving any delimitation problems that arise. A more useful course is to seek a better formulation of the fundamental norm, on which the Parties were fortunate enough to be agreed, and whose existence in the legal convictions not only of the Parties to the present dispute, but of all States, is apparent from an examination of the realities of international legal relations.[210]

The adoption of this view of the matter must entail as a practical conclusion that in this field the examination of the practice of States, in the quest for whatever customary rules may exist, be undertaken in a very different spirit from that which might previously or otherwise be employed, and which was in fact employed in the *North Sea Continental Shelf* cases. There is no point in comparing all known continental-shelf delimitations to see if they support the view that, for example, the equidistance method is a 'general practice accepted as law' if it has been asserted *a priori* that international law does not condescend to contain rules for the detail of delimitation practice.[211]

Yet the problem of the establishment of a legal rule or principle by reference to State practice and *opinio juris* is not avoided by the approach adopted by the *Gulf of Maine* Chamber. The fundamental norm referred to in the passage quoted above is apparently also a matter of customary law; it exists in 'the legal convictions . . . of all States', and it is to be discerned 'from an examination of the realities of international legal relations'. The Chamber does not however give any specific indication of the State practice from which it derives the norm.

When, however, one examines the fundamental norm as stated by the Chamber, it becomes more apparent why this is so.

What general international law prescribes in every maritime delimitation between neighbouring States could therefore be defined as follows:

(1) No maritime delimitation between States with opposite or adjacent coasts may be effected unilaterally by one of those States. Such delimitation must be sought and effected by means of an agreement, following negotiations conducted in good faith and with the genuine intention of achieving a positive result. Where, however, such agreement cannot be achieved, delimitation should be effected by recourse to a third party possessing the necessary competence.

(2) In either case, delimitation is to be effected by the application of equitable criteria and by the use of practical methods capable of ensuring, with regard to the

---

[210] Ibid., p. 299, para. 111.
[211] The full Court in 1985 differed from the Chamber on this point: it did examine the practice for precisely this purpose. See below, pp. 68–9.

geographic configuration of the area and other relevant circumstances, an equitable result.[212]

The first paragraph of this definition is largely derived, as the Chamber in fact indicates, from the judgment in the *North Sea Continental Shelf* cases. It derives less from positive international practice than from the nature of things: unilateral delimitation in an area where other States are interested is bound to be ineffective, if only because, in the absence of a more specific legal criterion, there is no means of reconciling two conflicting unilateral delimitations, or allowing one to prevail over the other. As for the second paragraph, if a delimitation is achieved by agreement, the result must presumably be equitable, since (again in the absence of specific criteria which are part of the applicable law—exactly what the *Gulf of Maine* Chamber excluded) it is impossible for a third party to say that what each party accepted as equitable is not in fact so. The result is that the 'fundamental norm' can in this respect be based upon State practice, in the sense that any and every agreed delimitation supports it, but at the same time it is a norm with no real content, in the sense of guidance or directives for achieving valid delimitation in the future. Whatever the States concerned agree to is by definition in conformity with the fundamental norm . . . but what if they are unable to agree?

Against this background, it is understandable that it has even been doubted whether maritime delimitation law is customary law at all. Prosper Weil attributes the development of international law in this field solely to judicial and arbitral decisions, which have in his view left aside the practice expressed in delimitation agreements, and themselves undertaken the definition of the appropriate law:

La conquête de la délimitation maritime par le droit n'est en fin de compte l'oeuvre ni de la convention ni de la coutume, mais celle de la jurisprudence qui, loin d'apparaître comme une source subsidiaire du droit international, remplit ici la mission d'une source primaire et directe de droit, même si elle a choisi modestement d'en porter le crédit au compte du droit coutumier.[213]

The approach of the *Gulf of Maine* Chamber certainly appears to bear out Weil's contentions; but to what extent is it typical of the Court's handling of the problem? A chronological survey of the delimitation cases will help us to answer this question also.

(i) *The North Sea cases.* The Court in the *North Sea* cases had to examine the question whether a customary rule of international law, requiring continental shelf delimitation by the equidistance method, had come into existence either prior to the adoption of the 1958 Geneva Convention on the Continental Shelf, or subsequently, to some extent as a result of that Convention. It noted that the claim of Denmark and the Netherlands that

---

[212] *ICJ Reports*, 1984, pp. 299–300, para. 112.
[213] *Perspectives du droit de la délimitation maritime*, p. 12.

such a rule bound the Federal Republic, so far as asserted on a positive law basis, was

based on the work done in this field by international legal bodies, on State practice and on the influence attributed to the Geneva Convention itself, —the claim being that these various factors have cumulatively evidenced or been creative of the *opinio juris sive necessitatis*, requisite for the formation of new rules of customary international law.[214]

When examining the claim that the equidistance rule had become established through positive law processes,[215] the Court noted that the parties making this claim

had not in fact contended that the delimitation article (Article 6) of the Convention 'embodied already received rules of customary law in the sense that the Convention was merely declaratory of existing rules'. Their contention was, rather, that although prior to the Conference, continental shelf law was only in the formative stage, and State practice lacked uniformity, yet 'the process of the definition and consolidation of the emerging customary law took place through the work of the International Law Commission, the reaction of governments to that work and the proceedings of the Geneva Convention'; and this emerging customary law became 'crystallized in the adoption of the Continental Shelf Convention by the Conference'.[216]

The Court's response to this contention was guarded:

Whatever validity this contention may have in respect of at least certain parts of the Convention, the Court cannot accept it as regards the delimitation provision (Article 6), . . . the principle of equidistance, as it now figures in Article 6 of the Convention, was proposed by the Commission with considerable hesitation, somewhat on an experimental basis, at most *de lege ferenda*, and not at all *de lege lata* or as an emerging rule of customary international law. This is clearly not the sort of foundation on which Article 6 of the Convention could be said to have reflected or crystallized such a rule.[217]

The Court appears to have been prepared to admit, perhaps with some reluctance, that the 'definition and consolidation of the emerging customary law' could be effected in the way suggested; this is not however to say that, in the absence of State practice in the more traditional sense, a rule of customary law could have been created solely through those processes. It is noteworthy that 'the work of the International Law Commission' is an element relied upon along with governmental reaction; but the work of the ILC, where members participate in a personal capacity, cannot be equated

---

[214] *ICJ Reports*, 1969, p. 28, para. 37.

[215] As distinct from its emergence as a matter of 'juristic inevitability': see above, pp. 32–3.

[216] Ibid., p. 38, para. 61.

[217] Ibid., p. 38, para. 62. It may be noted that the Court did not consider specifically and independently whether pre-1958 State practice might have added up to a custom, irrespective of the attitude of the ILC or of governments at the 1958 Conference. The reason was presumably not simply that the parties had not asserted this—since the Court was to be expected to follow the maxim *iura novit curia*—but that the parties did not assert it because the evidence of State practice was patently insufficient.

with State practice, or evidence an *opinio juris*. What it can and does of course do is put into shape and give expression and definition to a more or less amorphous State practice.

The Court's approach to the question of the possible establishment of a customary rule after the adoption of the 1958 Convention was strongly influenced by the existence of the Convention—that was indeed the way in which the matter was presented by the parties. In parenthesis, it may however be remarked that in theory a succession of acts of delimitation on an equidistance basis, by a sufficient number of States not parties to the Convention, would presumably have been capable of generating an independent rule of customary law; but the realities of the situation do justify the Court's approaching the question from the angle it did.

Having first laid down the requirement that, for a treaty provision to generate a customary rule,

the provision concerned should, at all events potentially, be of a fundamentally norm-creating character such as could be regarded as forming the basis of a general rule of law,[218]

the Court then referred to 'the other elements usually regarded as necessary before a conventional rule can be considered to have become a general rule of international law'. These are, presumably, State practice and *opinio juris*. For the purpose of such 'other elements', the court held that

it might be that, even without the passage of any considerable period of time, a very widespread and representative participation in the convention might suffice of itself, provided it included that of States whose interests were specially affected.[219]

The participation in the Geneva Convention at that time was, in the view of the Court, insufficient; turning to the 'time element', it noted that the relevant time periods were short, and continued:

Although the passage of only a short period of time is not necessarily, or of itself, a bar to the formation of a new rule of customary international law on the basis of what was originally a purely conventional rule, an indispensable requirement would be that within the period in question, short though it might be, State practice, including that of States whose interests are specially affected, should have been both extensive and virtually uniform in the sense of the provision invoked; —and should moreover have occurred in such a way as to show a general recognition that a rule of law or legal obligation is involved.[220]

The practice referred to here is presumably not, or at all events not limited to, participation in the relevant treaty, since that participation had already been examined and found wanting.

---

[218] Ibid., pp. 41–2, para. 72.
[219] Ibid., p. 42, para. 73.
[220] Ibid., p. 43, para. 74.

The next paragraph of the judgment in fact begins:

The Court must now consider whether State practice *in the matter of continental shelf delimitation* has, subsequent to the Geneva Convention, been of such a kind as to satisfy this requirement,[221]

and it is clear from the rest of the paragraph and subsequent paragraphs that the practice referred to is the actual international delimitations effected by agreement between States. There is no reference in this part of the judgment to attitudes of States expressed at international conferences or in other international fora. Admittedly, once the 1958 Conference had concluded, there was no particular context in which such expressions of attitude might be looked for.

When the Court, having declared that the equidistance rule was not a rule of customary law, turns to a statement of what in its view the applicable rules were, there is no further reference to State practice or to the *opinio juris*. To the extent that the 'principles and rules of international law applicable' stated in the operative part of the judgment are to be regarded as customary in nature, they must presumably be taken to be entailed in the concept of the continental shelf and of the rights over it established by customary law on the basis of practice beginning from the 1945 Truman Proclamation.

(ii) *The Barcelona Traction case.* The judgment in this case has already been discussed in Section 1(2) above, where it was noted that although the decision was made in a field governed (as between the parties) by customary law, the Court expressed itself in terms of 'general law' and did not specifically base the principal conclusions of its decision on custom established by practice and *opinio juris*. In one respect, however, practice was invoked in the judgment and extensively examined by an individual Member of the Court.

It was argued that, even if in general there is no recognized right of diplomatic protection of shareholders in respect of injury done to a company, such a right is exercisable when the national State of the company is for any reason disabled from exercising protection. It was therefore necessary to consider whether Canada, under whose laws Barcelona Traction had been incorporated, was the 'national State' of the company, and if so whether it was able to exercise diplomatic protection on its behalf. The Court's examination of the first of these questions was firmly based on the practice of States.

In allocating corporate entities to States for purposes of diplomatic protection, international law is based, but only to a limited extent, on an analogy with the rules governing the nationality of individuals. The traditional rule attributes the right of diplomatic protection of a corporate entity to the State under the laws of which it is incorporated and in whose territory it has its registered office. These two criteria have been confirmed by long practice and by numerous international instruments.

[221] Ibid., p. 43, para. 75, emphasis added.

This notwithstanding, further or different links are at times said to be required in order that a right of diplomatic protection should exist. Indeed, it has been the practice of some States to give a company incorporated under their law diplomatic protection solely when it has its seat (*siège social*) or management or centre of control in their territory, or when a majority or a substantial proportion of the shares has been owned by nationals of the State concerned. Only then, it has been held, does there exist between the corporation and the State in question a genuine connection of the kind familiar from other branches of international law. However, in the particular field of the diplomatic protection of corporate entities, no absolute test of the 'genuine connection' has found general acceptance. Such tests as have been applied are of a relative nature, and sometimes links with one State have had to be weighted against those with another.[222]

It had also been suggested that if Canada had sought to exercise protection of the company, it might have been argued by Spain that the Canadian nationality of the company was only formal or apparent, its interests being wholly in Spain, and its management in effect directed from London and Brussels; and that on that basis its nationality was not opposable to Spain, for lack of a 'genuine link' between the company and Canada, of the kind insisted on in the *Nottebohm* case. Although the decision in that case has given rise to much controversy, the rule of the 'genuine link' or 'effective connection' was certainly treated by the Court as one of customary law.[222a]

In the *Barcelona Traction* case, the Court dealt with this point very shortly:

> In this connection reference has been made to the *Nottebohm* case. In fact the Parties made frequent reference to it in the course of the proceedings. However, given both the legal and factual aspects of protection in the present case the Court is of the opinion that there can be no analogy with the issues raised or the decision given in that case.[222b]

Judge Jessup, in a separate opinion, dealt extensively both with the question of customary law as to the nationality of corporations for the purposes of diplomatic protection, and the application to corporations of the 'link' concept.[222c] Judge Sir Gerald Fitzmaurice also dealt with the *Nottebohm* rule, though only to indicate why he thought the Court should have gone more thoroughly into the question, and he did raise the question whether the *Nottebohm* case was rightly decided;[222d] he did not therefore examine or analyse State practice.

Both these Judges had much to say on a point not dealt with in the major-

---

[222] *ICJ Reports*, 1970, p. 42, para. 70.

[222a] Although its treatment of State practice was, it is generally agreed, very unsatisfactory. Brownlie regards the decision rather as 'a natural reflection of a fundamental concept which has been inherent, in the materials concerning nationality on the international plane' (*Principles of Public International Law* (4th edn., 1990), p. 407; see also 'The Relations of Nationality in Public International Law', this *Year Book*, 39 (1963), p. 349).

[222b] *ICJ Reports*, 1970, p. 42, para. 70, *in fine*.

[222c] Ibid., pp. 183–4, 196–9, and ibid., pp. 186–91.

[222d] Ibid., pp. 80–2, and see note 27 on p. 81.

ity judgment: the doctrine of continuous nationality, i.e., the rule that for diplomatic protection to be exercised, the individual claimant must have had the nationality of the protecting State both when the injury was done, and when the international claim is presented.[222e] Judge Fitzmaurice placed himself on the plane of legal theory and the opinion of writers rather than on that of State practice.[222f] Judge Jessup, however, referred to diplomatic practice and to the work of mixed claims commissions.[222g]

(iii) *The Fisheries Jurisdiction cases.* In these two cases in 1974 the Court was faced with the problem of finding the applicable rules of customary law in a field which was in rapid development, where varying claims were advanced and pressed, and gave rise to protests and objections, and where the records of international conferences contained a multiplicity of assertions of what the law was or should be.

On the subject of the breadth of the territorial sea and the extent of fishery rights, the Court referred to the 1958 and 1960 Conferences on the Law of the Sea, and continued:

The 1960 Conference failed by one vote to adopt a text governing the two questions of the breadth of the territorial sea and the extent of fishery rights. However, after that Conference the law evolved through the practice of States on the basis of the debates and near-agreements at the Conference. Two concepts have crystallized as customary law in recent years arising out of the general consensus revealed at that Conference.[223]

On the question of preferential fishery rights of the coastal State, the Court's analysis was as follows:

State practice on the subject of fisheries reveals an increasing and widespread acceptance of the concept of preferential rights for coastal States, particularly in favour of countries or territories in a situation of special dependence on coastal fisheries. Both the 1958 Resolution and the 1960 joint amendment concerning preferential rights were approved by a large majority of the Conferences, thus showing overwhelming support for the idea that in certain special situations it was fair to recognize that the coastal State had preferential fishing rights. After these Conferences, the preferential rights of the coastal State were recognized in various bilateral and multilateral international agreements.[224]

The Court then proceeded to enumerate the international agreements which it found significant in this respect.

These passages, particularly the second, seem to show that the attitude of States at an international conference can show an 'acceptance of a concept', or 'support for an idea' as to the appropriate rule, but that it is actual prac-

---

[222e] See, for example, *Panevezys-Saldutiskis Railway*, *PCIJ*, Series A/B, No. 76, p. 16.
[222f] *ICJ Reports*, 1970, pp. 99–102.
[222g] Ibid., p. 203.
[223] *ICJ Reports*, 1974, p. 23, para. 52.
[224] Ibid., p. 26, para. 58.

tice—in this latter context, fishery agreements—which causes the rule to become one of international law.[225]

The value of State proposals at international conferences was specifically discussed in the joint opinion of five judges[226] in that case, in a passage which merits quotation in full:

> In this respect, attention must be drawn to declarations made, or proposals filed by a number of States in relation to or in preparation for the Third Conference on the Law of the Sea. It is true that, as the Court's Judgment indicates, the proposals and preparatory documents made in the aforesaid context are *de lege ferenda*. However, it is not possible in our view to brush aside entirely these pronouncements of States and consider them devoid of all legal significance. If the law relating to fisheries constituted a subject on which there were clear indications of what precisely is the rule of international law in existence, it may then have been possible to disregard altogether the legal significance of certain proposals, declarations or statements which advocate changes or improvements in a system of law which is considered to be unjust or inadequate. But this is not the situation. There is at the moment great uncertainty as to the existing customary law on account of the conflicting and discordant practice of States. Once the uncertainty of such a practice is admitted, the impact of the aforesaid official pronouncements, declarations and proposals must undoubtedly have an unsettling effect on the crystallization of a still evolving customary law on the subject. Furthermore, the law on fishery limits has always been and must by its very essence be a compromise between the claims and counter-claims of coastal and distant-water fishing States. On a subject where practice is contradictory and lacks precision, is it possible and reasonable to discard entirely as irrelevant the evidence of what States are prepared to claim and to acquiesce in, as gathered from the positions taken by them in view of or in preparation for a conference for the codification and progressive development of the law on the subject?[227]

Thus for the five judges, statements and proposals at international conferences are valuable in the quest for rules of customary international law as 'evidence of what States are prepared to claim and to acquiesce in', in other words as items of State practice. (As frequently happens, evidence of practice and evidence of *opinio juris* related to that practice are to some extent merged, but there are special problems, discussed in section 3(2)(d) below, in discerning *opinio juris* in attitudes taken at international conferences.)

The judgments in the *Fisheries Jurisdiction* cases do not contain any consideration or analysis of the practice of States in the more traditional sense: claims and agreements as to maritime rights outside the context of international conferences. When comparing these cases with the cases concerning the delimitation of the continental shelf, it has of course to be borne in mind that shelf delimitation is, in most geographical circumstances, a prac-

---

[225] Thus it seems an over-simplification when Akehurst states that the Court cited the 1958 resolution and the 1960 amendment 'as State practice which had helped to create a rule of customary law': 'Custom as a Source of International Law', this *Year Book*, 47 (1974–5), p. 5.

[226] Forster, Bengzon, Jiménez de Aréchaga, Nagendra Singh, Ruda.

[227] *ICJ Reports*, 1974, p. 48, para. 12.

tical necessity, and that in the *North Sea* cases the Court had emphasized the legal requirement of agreement to that end. The definition of claims over maritime spaces in the direction of the open sea may however be less pressing a matter, at least as regards the definition of the outward limit, so that the possibility is greater of persistence of a situation of uncertainty or indefinition. Hence, the practice outside the context of conferences is likely to be more sparse.

(iv) *The Western Sahara case*. The first question asked of the Court by the General Assembly in the *Western Sahara* case was the following: 'Was Western Sahara . . . at the time of colonization by Spain a territory belonging to no one (*terra nullius*)?' After determining that the law was to be determined for the period beginning in 1884, that being the 'time of colonization by Spain', the Court turned to the meaning of the expression '*terra nullius*', concluding that:

a determination that Western Sahara was a '*terra nullius*' at the time of colonization by Spain would be possible only if it were established that at that time the territory belonged to no-one in the sense that it was then open to acquisition through the legal process of 'occupation'.[228]

In order to determine in what circumstances a territory was or was not regarded as open to acquisition, the Court turned to contemporary State practice.

Whatever differences of opinion there may have been among jurists, the State practice of the relevant period indicates that territories inhabited by tribes or peoples having a social and political organization were not regarded as *terra nullius*. It shows that in the case of such territories the acquisition of sovereignty was not generally considered as effected unilaterally through 'occupation' of *terra nullius* by original title but through agreements concluded with local rulers.[229]

The Court did not think it necessary to go into any detail of the practice which it took into account for this purpose. The material before it however included an excellent survey of the question, comprised in the written statement of Mauritania.[230] The practice there cited includes instructions given by governments to explorers or representatives; treaties concluded with native chiefs; and international diplomatic claims and negotiations.

(v) *The Tunisia/Libya case*. In its judgment in the case of the *Continental Shelf (Tunisia/Libya)*, the Court referred to its dicta in the *Fisheries Jurisdiction* cases as to the work of UNCLOS.[231] This was in the context of the provision in the Special Agreement, discussed elsewhere, that the Court should refer to the 'new accepted trends' in the law of the sea. It is striking to what extent this reference to UNCLOS marked, or took the

---

[228] *ICJ Reports*, 1975, p. 39, para. 79.
[229] Ibid., p. 39, para. 80.
[230] *Pleadings*, vol. 3, pp. 28–51. The authorship may with some confidence be attributed to Professor Jean Salmon.
[231] *ICJ Reports*, 1982, p. 37, para. 23.

place of, the underlying State practice constituted by actual claims or delimitations. The Court observed that

> Since the Court gave judgment in the *North Sea Continental Shelf* cases, a period has elapsed during which there has been much State practice in this field of international law, and it has been under very close review, particularly in the context of the Third United Nations Conference on the Law of the Sea.[232]

There is however no further reference in the judgment to the practice in question, and in particular no enquiry whether that practice was in fact consistent with developments at UNCLOS. To some extent this approach is justified by the parties' direction to take account of the 'new accepted trends' in UNCLOS; though if it could have been shown that State practice outside the context of the Conference added up to recognition of a rule of customary law contradicting, or contradicted by, the provisions of the UNCLOS draft Convention, it would undoubtedly have been the Court's duty to apply the customary rule and disregard the 'trend'.

It is in fact striking to what extent the argument of the judgment in the *Tunisia/Libya* case proceeds by logical construction on bases of principle, or even on an *a priori* basis, without reference to what States had actually done by way of maritime delimitation. One example of this is the discussion of the parties' contentions as to the role (if any) of economic factors in the delimitation process, already discussed in Chapter I, section 2(4). After setting out what the parties had contended on the point, the Court rejects any reference to such factors, because

> They are virtually extraneous factors since they are variables which unpredictable national fortune or calamity, as the case may be, might at any time cause to tilt the scale one way or the other.[233]

A more direct answer would have been simply that there is no trace in State practice of account being taken of the comparative economic wealth of the States concerned; the reason given by the Court is one possible reason why this is so, and thus situate at a higher level of abstraction. In the field of customary law, it is however surely essential to consider first what States actually do before considering why they do it.[234]

There are virtually only two references to delimitation practice in the *Tunisia/Libya* judgment: the first is a passage directed to showing that equidistance had not been universally employed in delimitation agreements, [235] a point on which there was no real controversy. The second appears in the Court's treatment of the effect on the delimitation line of the Kerkennah Islands, where it recalls

---

[232] Ibid., p. 47, para. 45.

[233] Ibid., p. 77, para. 107. It is something of a mystery why the Court dealt with the question, since it was raised as a rhetorical flourish rather than a serious argument, and not pressed at the hearings. See *Pleadings*, vol. 1, p. 72, para. 3.51; vol. 2, p. 154, para. 17; vol. 5, p. 21.

[234] Commenting on the *North Sea* judgment, the Court referred to 'the actual practice of States which is expressive, or creative, of customary rules': *ICJ Reports*, 1982, p. 46, para. 43.

[235] Ibid., p. 79, para. 109.

that a number of examples are to be found in State practice of delimitations in which only partial effect has been given to islands situated close to the coast; the method adopted has varied in response to the varying geographical and other circumstances of the particular case. One possible technique for this purpose, in the context of a geometrical method of delimitation, is that of the 'half-effect' or 'half-angle'.[236]

It is however evident that the Court is not here referring to use of the 'half-effect' in State practice to demonstrate the existence of a rule of customary law requiring the use of that technique in certain definable circumstances. Having reached a conclusion that to give full effect to the Kerkennahs would produce an inequitable result, and thus conflict with customary law, it delves into the armoury of methods offered by State practice to find a means of avoiding that result that has in previous cases found favour with States.

(vi) *The Gulf of Maine case*. This case has already been discussed above: the attitude of the Chamber as to the nature of the rules it was called on to apply was such as to dispense it from examination of the abundant examples of delimitation agreements supplied by the parties as evidence of State practice. As to the possibility of reliance on the UNCLOS texts for this purpose, the Chamber's approach will be referred to in section 3(2)(*d*) below.

(vii) *The Nicaragua v. United States case (Jurisdiction)*. In the phase of the case concerning *Military and Paramilitary Activities in and against Nicaragua (Nicaragua v. United States of America)* devoted to questions of jurisdiction and admissibility, a question of the effect of State practice underlay, but was not referred to in, the argument of one passage of the judgment; it was referred to in the dissenting opinions.

The United States had asserted that the Nicaraguan acceptance of jurisdiction under the Optional Clause, which contained no provision for its termination, was liable to immediate termination without previous notice, and that accordingly, by reciprocity, the United States could similarly terminate its own declaration. The Court did not resolve the basic question; it observed that 'the right of termination of declarations with indefinite duration is far from established', and went on to base itself on 'the requirements of good faith' to deduce that declarations 'should be treated, by analogy, according to the law of treaties, which requires a reasonable time for withdrawal'.[237]

Among the judges who disagreed, and thought that there was such a right of immediate termination, was Sir Robert Jennings: the interesting aspect of his opinion, for present purposes, is that he considered that such a right had come into existence since the date (1929) of Nicaragua's declaration:

---

[236] Ibid., p. 89, para. 129. The recourse to this method is criticized by Judge Gros, ibid., p. 150, para. 14, and Judge Oda, ibid., p. 269, para. 179.

[237] *ICJ Reports*, 1984, p. 420, para. 63.

I believe that there is ample evidence that States belonging to the Optional-Clause system have now generally the expectation that they can lawfully withdraw or alter their declarations of acceptance at will, provided only that this is done before seisin. Certainly there is no lack of precedents where this has been done without effective protest, and, in recent cases, without any protest whatsoever.[238]

. . .

In face of the unmistakable trend of recent developments, I feel bound to conclude that States now—though the position was probably different during the earlier, more promising period of the Optional Clause jurisdiction—have the right, before seisin of the Court, to withdraw or alter their declarations of acceptance, with immediate effect, and, moreover, even in anticipation of a particular case or class of cases.[239]

A similar view was taken by Judges Oda and Schwebel, but they are less specific as to the question of development over time.

Judge Jennings' reference to the absence of protest will be noted: it is solely here, on the part of other States, that an *opinio juris* can be traced—a conviction that immediate denunciation of a declaration is authorized by international law, and must therefore be accepted.

(viii) *The Libya/Malta case*. Much more specific reference to State practice is to be found in the Court's judgment in the case of the *Continental Shelf (Libya/Malta)* in 1985. At an early stage in that judgment the Court observes that

It is of course axiomatic that the material of customary international law is to be looked for primarily in the actual practice and *opinio juris* of States . . . [240]

and the qualification which immediately follows refers, not to the possible relevance of statements and proposals at international conferences, but to the recognized role of multilateral treaties in relation to the formation of custom:

. . . even though multilateral conventions may have an important role to play in recording and defining rules deriving from custom, or indeed in developing them.[241]

The circumstances were of course more favourable: UNCLOS had concluded its work, so that the possible contribution of the 'new accepted trends' was now to be looked for in the Convention as adopted at Montego Bay.

Later in the judgment, the Court considered State practice in the context of the status of the equidistance method, and noted that

the Parties have in fact discussed the significance of such practice, as expressed in published delimitation agreements, primarily in the context of the status of equidistance in present international law. Over 70 such agreements have been iden-

---

[238] Ibid., p. 550.
[239] Ibid., p. 553.
[240] *ICJ Reports*, 1985, p. 29, para. 27.
[241] Ibid., pp. 29–30, para. 27.

tified and produced to the Court and have been subjected to various interpretations.[242]

After noting the parties' divergent interpretations, the Court continued:

> The Court for its part has no doubt about the importance of State practice in this matter. Yet that practice, however interpreted, falls short of proving the existence of a rule prescribing the use of equidistance, or indeed of any method, as obligatory.[243]

At a later stage in its judgment, however, the Court reverted to the practice of States as exemplified in maritime delimitation agreements. For the purpose of the delimitation required in the case before it, the Court had found it appropriate to begin by defining the position of a median line between the coasts of the two parties. It hastened to add, however, that it

> could hardly ignore the fact that the equidistance method has never been regarded, even in a delimitation between opposite coasts, as one to be applied without modification whatever the circumstances.[244]

In support of this, it cited the 1958 Geneva Convention, and the UNCLOS draft which had referred to equidistance, and continued:

> Moreover in the practice of States as reflected in the delimitation agreements concluded and published, analysis of the delimitation line chosen, in relation to the coasts of the parties, or the appropriate basepoints, reveals in numerous cases a greater or lesser departure from the line which would have been produced by a strict application of the equidistance method.[245]

There is something unsatisfactory in the logical correlation of these two arguments from the same body of State practice. If the practice is insufficient to show the existence of a rule requiring the use of equidistance, or indeed of 'any method', for delimitation, it follows that States are free to employ the equidistance method or not to employ it, according as they consider it appropriate or inappropriate for the purpose of achieving the 'equitable result'. If so, it must equally be open to them to employ modified equidistance. In short the conclusion demonstrated in the later passage in the judgment is already contained in the earlier; and what is more, the conclusion would follow even if the State practice examined were wholly consistent with the use of unmodified equidistance. The departures from strict equidistance found in the practice are relevant rather to the conclusion that equidistance, modified or unmodified, is not an obligatory rule at all, than to the question whether a hypothetical equidistance rule is one of pure or modified equidistance.

At all events, the Court was unwilling to be as radical as the Chamber in the *Gulf of Maine* case, and deny the possibility of finding in State practice any rule prescribing particular methods; but the practical outcome was the

[242] Ibid., p. 38, para. 44.
[243] Ibid.
[244] Ibid., p. 48, para. 65.
[245] Ibid.

same. Equidistance had the best claim to have received the accolade of conversion into a customary rule by consistent practice; if even that method was insufficiently consecrated by consistency, no other could rank even as *proxime accessit*.

The separate opinion filed jointly by Judges Ruda, Bedjaoui and Jiménez de Aréchaga dealt with a point not examined in the judgment: a claim by Malta 'based on the radial projection of its coasts in all directions'. The authors of the opinion examined in detail

a considerable State practice which demonstrates that States, in their bilateral agreements, end their agreed lines of delimitation exactly at the point in which the opposition ceases to exist between the directly facing coasts of the parties, and a different opposition commences vis-à-vis the coasts of a third State.[246]

The agreements examined are numerous, and geographically widely-spread. Thus, *pace* the *Gulf of Maine* Chamber, delimitation agreements can and apparently do rank as State practice contributing to the development of custom.

(ix) *The Nicaragua v. United States case*. In its judgment on the merits in the case concerning *Military and Paramilitary Activities in and against Nicaragua*, the Court reiterated once more the need for it to 'direct its attention to the practice and *opinio juris* of States',[247] and quoted its own dictum in the *Libya/Malta* case emphasizing this, but qualifying it by reference to the 'important role' to be played by multilateral conventions 'in recording and defining rules deriving from custom, or indeed in developing them'.[248] The references to actual practice in the fields of customary law relevant to the decision are however sparse, and it is significant that the Court observed, with reference to the role of multilateral conventions, that

In this respect the Court must not lose sight of the Charter of the United Nations and that of the Organization of American States, notwithstanding the operation of the multilateral treaty reservation.[249]

The phraseology employed is striking; so far from the Court 'losing sight of' these two instruments, they appear to have bulked so large as to block the view of any distinct customary practice.

The Court's angle of approach to the existence of relevant practice is also unusual; in the next following paragraph of the judgment it explains:

The Court notes that there is in fact evidence, to be examined below, of a considerable degree of agreement between the Parties as to the content of the customary international law relating to the non-use of force and non-intervention. This concurrence of their views does not however dispense the Court from having itself to ascertain what rules of customary international law are applicable. The mere fact

---

[246] Ibid., p. 78, para. 7. See also the reliance of Judge Valticos on State practice in support of the median line: ibid., p. 107.
[247] *ICJ Reports*, 1986, p. 97, para. 183.
[248] *ICJ Reports*, 1985, pp. 29–30, para. 27, quoted above, p. 68.
[249] *ICJ Reports*, 1986, p. 97, para. 183.

that States declare their recognition of certain rules is not sufficient for the Court to consider these as being part of customary international law, and as applicable as such to those States. Bound as it is by Article 38 of its Statute to apply, *inter alia*, international custom 'as evidence of a general practice accepted as law', the Court may not disregard the essential role played by general practice. Where two States agree to incorporate a particular rule in a treaty, their agreement suffices to make that rule a legal one, binding upon them; but in the field of customary international law, the shared view of the Parties as to the content of what they regard as the rule is not enough. The Court must satisfy itself that the existence of the rule in the *opinio juris* of States is confirmed by practice.[250]

Thus, instead of examining what States actually do in a particular area of international relations, and deducing from their actions that certain forms of behaviour are regarded as required, or as forbidden, by custom, the court starts from the postulated existence of a rule, and examines State practice to see whether States in fact live up to it.

The circumstances of the case were, however, unusual, to say the least. So far from denying the existence of a customary rule outlawing the use of force in international relations, the United States had argued for the existence of a customary rule identical in virtually all respects with the requirements of the United Nations Charter in that respect, in order to argue that the 'multilateral treaty reservation' in its acceptance of jurisdiction debarred the Court from dealing with the Nicaraguan claim based on customary law. Once the Court had rejected this argument, the United States contentions as to the existence of customary law rules could be turned against it; but the Court wisely declined to base its decision solely on the United States admission of the existence of a customary rule banning the use of force.

The practice to which the Court referred was however not practice related to the actions and reactions of States *inter se* as regards instances of the threatened or actual use of force, but rather the attitude of States to resolutions proposed in the General Assembly relating to the question. Furthermore, these attitudes were not in fact presented by the Court in its judgment as instances of practice, but rather of *opinio juris*.

The Court thus finds that both Parties take the view that the principles as to the use of force incorporated in the United Nations Charter correspond, in essentials, to those found in customary international law. The Parties thus both take the view that the fundamental principle in this area is expressed in the terms employed in Article 2, paragraph 4, of the United Nations Charter. They therefore accept a treaty-law obligation to refrain in their international relations from the threat or use of force against the territorial integrity or political independence of any State, or in any other manner inconsistent with the purposes of the United Nations. The Court has however to be satisfied that there exists in customary international law an *opinio juris* as to the binding character of such abstention.[251]

Pausing there, one may note the curious reference in the third sentence

[250] Ibid., pp. 97–98, para. 184.
[251] Ibid., p. 99, para. 188; cf. sub-section (*c*)(i) above.

of the paragraph to a 'treaty-law obligation'; in the context of the Court's acceptance of the 'multilateral treaty reservation' as a limitation on the extent of its competence, and in the sequence of its argument, this reference is so unexpected as to make one wonder whether it might be a *lapsus calami*, 'customary-law obligation' being meant.[252]

The judgment continues:

> This *opinio juris* may, though with all due caution, be deduced from, *inter alia*, the attitude of the Parties and the attitude of States towards certain General Assembly resolutions, and particularly resolution 2625 (XXV) entitled 'Declaration on Principles of International Law concerning Friendly Relations and Co-operation among States in accordance with the Charter of the United Nations'. The effect of consent to the text of such resolutions cannot be understood as merely that of a 'reiteration or elucidation' of the treaty commitment undertaken in the Charter. On the contrary, it may be understood as an acceptance of the validity of the rule or set of rules declared by the resolution by themselves. The principle of non-use of force, for example, may thus be regarded as a principle of customary international law, not as such conditioned by provisions relating to collective security, or to the facilities or armed contingents to be provided under Article 43 of the Charter. It would therefore seem apparent that the attitude referred to expresses an *opinio juris* respecting such rule (or set of rules), to be thenceforth treated separately from the provisions, especially those of an institutional kind, to which it is subject on the treaty-law plane of the Charter.[253]

In short, the Court begins by accepting the existence of an *opinio juris*, at least as regards the parties, and announces the need to discover practice in support; but when it looks at what States, including the parties, have done, it treats such action as evidence of *opinio juris* and not as practice. Either the element of practice has dropped out of the equation somehow; or else action which 'expresses an *opinio juris*' is to be treated as *ipso facto* constituting an element of practice. Neither conclusion is very satisfactory.

When dealing with the question of the rules of customary law concerning non-intervention in the affairs of States, the Court similarly finds first that

> Expressions of an *opinio juris* regarding the existence of the principle of non-intervention in customary international law are numerous and not difficult to find,[254]

before going on to assert that

> The existence in the *opinio juris* of States of the principle of non-intervention is backed by established and substantial practice;[255]

but at this point no details whatever of such practice are given. The Court then deals with assertions of the principle in the context of General

---

[252] To prevent more weight being attached to this suggestion than it deserves, may I emphasize that it is not based on any 'inside knowledge' of the drafting of the judgment. See the introduction to the first of these articles, this *Year Book*, 60 (1989), p. 7.

[253] *ICJ Reports*, 1986, pp. 99–100, para. 188.

[254] Ibid., p. 106, para. 202.

[255] Ibid.

Assembly resolutions, before reverting to the question whether the practice is 'sufficiently in conformity' with the principle accepted in such resolutions 'for this to be a rule of customary international law'.[256]

The practice actually examined is somewhat specialized:

. . . before reaching a conclusion on the nature of prohibited intervention, the Court must be satisfied that State practice justifies it. There have been in recent years a number of instances of foreign intervention for the benefit of forces opposed to the government of another State. The Court is not here concerned with the process of decolonization; this question is not in issue in the present case. It has to consider whether there might be indications of a practice illustrative of belief in a kind of general right for States to intervene, directly or indirectly, with or without armed force, in support of an internal opposition in another State, whose cause appeared particularly worthy by reason of the political and moral values with which it was identified. For such a general right to come into existence would involve a fundamental modification of the customary law principle of non-intervention.[257]

Although the Court does not say so, the particular practice here examined corresponds most closely to what the United States was accused of having done in Nicaragua, so that the concentration of the Court's attention on this particular practice was fully justified.

(x) *The Frontier Dispute Case*. The task of the Chamber in the *Frontier Dispute* between Mali and Burkina Faso was to determine the course of a frontier which had come into existence as an administrative boundary between two French overseas territories. It therefore had little opportunity or need to examine questions of customary international law. However, the basic postulate of the case was that the international frontier between the two independent States was identical with the colonial boundary; and since there had been no treaty to that effect between the two States or legislative provision at the time of independence, this was a matter of general law. Specifically, in the view of the Chamber, the matter was governed by the principle of *uti possidetis juris*.

The Preamble to the Special Agreement by which the Chamber was seised stated that the parties desired to achieve a settlement of the frontier dispute 'based in particular on respect for the principle of the intangibility of frontiers inherited from colonization',[258] and this might have been regarded as sufficient to justify the application of that principle without further enquiry.[259] The Chamber however explained that it wished to emphasize the general scope of the *uti possidetis* principle, and devoted seven paragraphs to examination of it.

In effect, the Chamber took it as established that *uti possidetis* was an element of the international law applicable to the frontiers of the former

---

[256] Ibid., p. 108, para. 205.
[257] Ibid., p. 108, para. 206.
[258] Ibid., p. 557.
[259] But cf. the observations of the Court in the *Nicaragua* v. *USA* case, ibid., p. 97, para. 184, quoted at p. 51 above.

Spanish colonies in Latin America; the question of interest was that of its application to other ex-colonial territories, specifically in Africa. It set the principle in the context of the 1964 Addis Ababa resolution of the OAU which 'deliberately defined and stressed the principle of *uti possidetis juris* contained only in an implicit sense in the Charter of the Organization'.[260]

The Chamber considered that 'there is no need, for the purpose of the present case, to show that this is a firmly established principle of international law'; its approach was in fact to set *uti possidetis* above customary law, as 'a general principle, which is logically connected with the phenomenon of the obtaining of independence, whenever it occurs',[261] but one which nevertheless found expression in State practice:

It was for this reason that, as soon as the phenomenon of decolonization characteristic of the situation in Spanish America in the 19th century subsequently appeared in Africa in the 20th century, the principle of *uti possidetis*, in the sense described above, fell to be applied. The fact that the new African States have respected the administrative boundaries and frontiers established by the colonial powers must be seen not as a mere practice contributing to the gradual emergence of a principle of customary international law, limited in its impact to the African continent as it had previously been to Spanish America, but as the application in Africa of a rule of general scope.[262]

The suggestion that *uti possidetis* might have the status of a 'general principle of law' is not very convincing;[263] a more convincing view of it would

---

[260] Ibid., pp. 565–6, para. 22. It has been said that any analogy between the OAU resolution and *uti possidetis* in Latin America 'is both false and misleading' (McEwen, *International Boundaries of East Africa* (1971), p. 27). One of the main differences adverted to in this respect is the vagueness of definition of Spanish administrative boundaries in America, as a result of which

'The fact that not all the Spanish administrative divisions were effectively occupied was clearly recognized by the new republics themselves, and *uti possidetis* was used by them not merely as a title to what they already possessed in fact but as a legal claim to the unoccupied remainder of what, in effect, was regarded by them as a sphere of influence' (McEwen, op. cit., p. 28: see also Brownlie, *Principles of Public International Law* (4th edn., 1990), pp. 134–5).

This contrasts, it is said, with the requirement in Africa of effective occupation. The Chamber did not overlook the point, but considered that this was only one aspect of the principle, and that 'The essence of the principle lies in its primary aim of securing respect for the territorial boundaries at the moment when independence is achieved' (*ICJ Reports*, 1986, p. 566, para. 23).

[261] *ICJ Reports*, 1986, p. 565, para. 20.

[262] Ibid., p. 565, para. 21.

[263] So far as the suggested 'general principle' might be one derived from consistent parallels in municipal law, as contemplated by Article 38, paragraph 1(*c*), of the Statute, it is by no means apparent in what aspect of municipal law one might seek a source of analogy to the enfranchisement of neighbouring colonial territories. Nor is it self-evident that two adjoining administrative units in a colonial territory should necessarily become two independent States with the same boundaries; the history of the territories formerly composing the German Protectorate of Kamerun (see *Northern Cameroons, ICJ Reports*, 1963, pp. 21–4) suggests otherwise, and instances are not far to seek in which post-independence boundaries in Africa might have been better drawn on, for example, a tribal basis than following the colonial boundaries: in this sense, cf. the Chamber's judgment, *ICJ Reports*, 1986, p. 633, para. 149. *Uti possidetis* is more evidently appropriate when, as in Spanish America, independence is asserted from below, as it were, by the individual regional entities, than when achieved by the consent of the former colonial power or powers. This consideration may be taken to accentuate the regional character of the custom, or to limit its essential application to independence arising from conflict.

be that it developed as a rule of regional customary law,[264] albeit one of such eminent rationality and usefulness as to verge on a logical corollary of decolonization, as the Chamber suggested. In view of this aspect of it, very little in the way of practice or *opinio juris* was needed to extend its application to the African continent, and it may today be regarded as a rule of general international customary law.

From this point of view, elements of practice are mentioned by the Chamber, though seen from its own standpoint of a general principle:

The elements of *uti possidetis* were latent in the many declarations made by African leaders in the dawn of independence. These declarations confirmed the maintenance of the territorial status quo at the time of independence, and stated the principle of respect both for the frontiers deriving from international agreements, and for those resulting from mere internal administrative divisions. The Charter of the Organization of African Unity did not ignore the principle of *uti possidetis*, but made only indirect reference to it in Article 3, according to which member States solemnly affirm the principle of respect for the sovereignty and territorial integrity of every State. However, at their first summit conference after the creation of the Organization of African Unity, the African Heads of State, in their Resolution mentioned above (AGH/Res. 16(I)), adopted in Cairo in July 1964, deliberately defined and stressed the principle of *uti possidetis juris* contained only in an implicit sense in the Charter of their organization.[265]

(b) *Practice of or within an international organization*

Generally, the practice of States relevant for the determination of a rule of customary law is their conduct in their relations with each other as independent sovereign entities. Special considerations may apply to the possibility of generation of custom by their actions as members of an international organization. A distinction is necessary for this purpose between actions in relation to questions of the operation of the organization, and actions which, it may be suggested, are significant for the establishment of general customary law, governing their relations outside the organization.

(i) *Action in relation to the operation of the organization*. In the *Namibia* case, the resolution of the Security Council requesting an advisory opinion of the Court had been adopted by a vote on which three members of the Council, including two permanent members, had abstained (Poland, USSR, United Kingdom).[266] It was contended by South Africa that the decision therefore did not comply with the requirement in Article 27, paragraph 3, of the Charter that decisions require 'an affirmative vote of nine

---

[264] Cf. the declaration of Judge Moreno Quintana in the case of the *Arbitral Award of the King of Spain*, referring to it as a legal question 'of particular concern' to Spanish-American States: *ICJ Reports*, 1960, p. 217.

[265] *ICJ Reports*, 1986, pp. 565–6, para. 22.

[266] *Namibia, Pleadings*, vol. 1, p. 201, para. 350. The Secretary-General, when transmitting the resolution to the Court, did not mention the vote: ibid., pp. 3–4.

members including the concurring votes of the permanent members', and was therefore invalid.[267] It was well established that, in practice, resolutions had at least since 1949[268] generally been treated as adopted even if one or more permanent members had abstained. The Court's ruling on the point was as follows:

> However, the proceedings of the Security Council extending over a long period supply abundant evidence that presidential rulings and the positions taken by members of the Council, in particular its permanent members, have consistently and uniformly interpreted the practice of voluntary abstention by a permanent member as not constituting a bar to the adoption of resolutions. By abstaining, a member does not signify its objection to the approval of what is being proposed; in order to prevent the adoption of a resolution requiring unanimity of the permanent members, a permanent member has only to cast a negative vote. This procedure followed by the Security Council, which has continued unchanged after the amendment in 1965 of Article 27 of the Charter, has been generally accepted by members of the United Nations and evidences a general practice of that Organization.[269]

The second sentence of this paragraph seems to represent a break in the reasoning: it appears to be addressed to the point, raised by South Africa, whether an abstention can be said to be equivalent to 'concurrence', especially when the State concerned explains its abstention on the grounds that it is unable to support the proposed resolution. The essential ground of the Court's decision is however that there is a 'general practice of the Organization' endorsing the adoption of resolutions over the abstentions of one or more permanent members.[270]

How does the concept of a 'practice of the Organization' fit into the framework of a 'general practice accepted as law' under Article 38 of the Statute? The Court's reference to the practice as being 'of' the Organization is presumably intended to refer, not to a practice followed by the Organization as an entity in its relations with other subjects of international law, but rather a practice followed, approved or respected throughout the Organization. Seen in this light, the practice is not so much a set of acts of abstention by the permanent members, with the intention of neither blocking the proposed resolution, nor going on record as endorsing it, as rather a recognition by the other members of the Security Council at the relevant moment, and indeed by all member States by tacit acceptance, of the validity of such resolutions.

The practice is evidently treaty-related: it has no meaning except

---

[267] *Pleadings*, vol. 2, pp. 403–17; in fact South Africa challenged the validity of all the non-procedural resolutions relevant in the case on the grounds of non-compliance with Article 27, paragraph 3.

[268] See Stavropoulos, 'The Practice of Voluntary Abstentions by Permanent Members of the Security Council under Article 27, paragraph 3, of the Charter of the United Nations', *American Journal of International Law*, 61 (1967), at p. 746.

[269] *ICJ Reports*, 1971, p. 22, para. 22.

[270] The contention that the practice was a matter of customary law was made by Stavropoulos on behalf of the Secretary-General: *Pleadings*, vol. 2, p. 39.

between those entities for whom Article 27 of the Charter is a binding instrument. It is therefore material to ask whether it was truly a custom-generating practice which the Court had in mind or whether it was not rather an example of 'subsequent practice in the application of a treaty which establishes the agreement of the Parties regarding its interpretation'.[271] The difficulty with any such approach, which South Africa did not fail to point out to the Court, is that

> Whatever value the practice of an organization might have as an aid to the interpretation of its constitution, it cannot override the clear meaning of the text, particularly where, as in the present case, the meaning accords with the actual intentions of its authors.[272]

South Africa was able to point to indications in the *travaux préparatoires*[273] which showed practically irrefutably that the contemporary intention behind the text had been that, for purposes of the paragraph in question, an abstention should be equivalent to a negative vote.

The Court's ruling has therefore to be interpreted as a finding of a practice effective to give rise to a rule of customary law, though the second sentence, suggesting that the rule was not wholly inconsistent with the letter of the text, perhaps points to an inclination toward the idea of interpretation practice also.[274] One way of looking at the matter is to regard the Charter as having been in effect amended by the subsequent practice of the parties to it. Fitzmaurice himself in his series of articles referred specifically to the abstention question as an example of 'a common principle on the part of parties to a treaty' which 'may constitute a means whereby the strict effect of the treaty can be modified',[275] or of 'an amendment to the treaty by a tacit unwritten consensus'.[276] This is also a view espoused by Tunkin.[277]

The question whether the rule is one of general or of specific customary law is, for once, virtually meaningless: in view of the near-universal participation in the Charter, it could be called a rule of general law, but if it is only meaningful for members of the United Nations, it could for that reason be

---

[271] Vienna Convention on the Law of Treaties, Article 31(3)(*b*). Practice of this kind was resorted to by the Court in the *Certain Expenses* case to establish the meaning of terms in the Charter: *ICJ Reports*, 1962, pp. 160–1, para. 165.

[272] *Pleadings*, vol. 1, p. 412, para. 26.

[273] Ibid., pp. 405 ff. These had been played down by Stavropoulos in his 1967 article, loc. cit. above (n. 268), but not entirely convincingly.

[274] The argument addressed to the Court on the point, by the Secretary-General and the United States of America, also tended to blur the distinction between customary practice and interpretation of treaty by practice.

Judge Dillard in fact appears to have based his support of the opinion on the latter ground: *ICJ Reports*, 1971, p. 153.

[275] This *Year Book*, 28 (1951), p. 22; *Collected Edition*, I, p. 63, n. 1.

[276] This *Year Book*, 30 (1953), p. 63; *Collected Edition*, I, p. 185, n. 1.

[277] *Droit international public* (1965), pp. 94–5, quoted in Stavropoulos, loc. cit. above (n. 268), pp. 746–7.

called special.[278] To ascertain whether this is so, the question which has to be asked is whether, for a non-member of the United Nations, there is any difference in the legal impact of a Security Council resolution adopted in accordance with the letter of Article 27 of the Charter, and a resolution adopted over the abstention of a permanent member. It is difficult to see how much difference could be justified. In the particular case of Namibia, the Court defined as follows the position of non-members:

As to non-member States, although not bound by Articles 24 and 25 of the Charter, they have been called upon in paragraphs 2 and 5 of resolution 276 (1970) to give assistance in the action which has been taken by the United Nations with regard to Namibia. In the view of the Court, the termination of the Mandate and the declaration of the illegality of South Africa's presence in Namibia are opposable to all States in the sense of barring *erga omnes* the legality of a situation which is maintained in violation of international law: in particular, no State which enters into relations with South Africa concerning Namibia may expect the United Nations or its Members to recognize the validity or effects of such relationship, or of the consequences thereof. The Mandate having been terminated by decision of the international organization in which the supervisory authority over its administration was vested, and South Africa's continued presence in Namibia having been declared illegal, it is for non-member States to act in accordance with those decisions.[279]

The argument is complicated by the fact that the 'supervisory authority' referred to is not the Security Council but the General Assembly; but the essential message is that the Mandate, the League supervision, and the situation of the United Nations as an organization in relation to the Mandate all form part of a single whole which outsiders must take as they find it. Thus if a Security Council decision is taken in a manner which is, as regards the membership of the Organization, regular and valid by virtue of a customary rule binding on the membership, it is not for an outsider to question the validity of that decision in assessing the legal effects upon itself of the whole situation. In these circumstances, the question whether the customary law is or is not binding in itself upon non-member States is a wholly artificial question.

Only two years before the *Namibia* advisory opinion, the Court had reiterated the requirement of *opinio juris* for the creation of a rule of custom-

---

[278] Similarly, the problem discussed in the first of this series of articles (this *Year Book*, 60 (1989), pp. 147 ff.), of the simultaneous existence of treaty and custom covering the same ground, does not here arise. Only the parties to the Charter are bound, as a matter of treaty law, by Article 27; but they must be taken all to have accepted the customary rule which interprets that Article or regulates its effect. What does raise intriguing questions is the position of a State which only became a member of the United Nations after the establishment of the custom; does it, by acceding to the Charter, subject itself to the custom? Does the acceptance of 'the obligations contained in the present Charter' contemplated by Article 4, paragraph 1, extend to the acceptance of a custom which adheres, barnacle-like, to the hull of the Charter? An alternative would be to see the custom as already general, and binding thus on non-members, *in posse* as it were, so that on their acceding to the Charter their potential subjection to the custom becomes actual.

[279] *ICJ Reports*, 1971, p. 56, para. 126.

ary international law.[280] It is noteworthy that the *Namibia* advisory opinion refers only to practice, and does not comment on the question of *opinio juris*. The problem of the subjective element in the creation of rules by practice in the United Nations context had earlier been adverted to by Judge Winiarski in his dissenting opinion in the *Certain Expenses* case. He did not think, as the Court did, that in that case 'practice can furnish a canon of construction' of the Charter, and therefore went on to consider whether it might 'have contributed to the establishment of a legal rule particular to the Organization' *praeter legem* or even *contra legem*. In this respect he observed:

> It is sometimes difficult to attribute any precise legal significance to the conduct of the contracting parties, because it is not always possible to know with certainty whether they have acted in a certain manner because they consider that the law so requires or allows, or for reasons of expediency.[281]

Reasons of expediency would suffice for an *interpretative* practice; but would they suffice to constitute *opinio juris*?

In the *Namibia* case what was required, it appears, is that it could be shown that at some stage the regularity of Security Council decisions adopted over one or more abstentions by permanent members had become accepted to such a degree that member States considered that they were bound to accept such resolutions as valid, and could no longer question such validity. No evidence to this precise effect was available:[282] but once the practice became set as a practice, it would obviously acquire a self-confirming force, and it would become less and less likely to occur to a State which disliked a particular resolution to challenge it on the ground of non-compliance with Article 27, paragraph 3. The mental attitude thus created is as close to 'a belief that this practice is rendered obligatory' as one is likely to get.

In the *North Sea Continental Shelf* cases, the Court had also referred to the relevance of the participation in a practice of 'States whose interests were specifically affected'.[283] The representatives of the United States suggested in the *Namibia* case that this qualification was applicable to the permanent members of the Security Council, so that their acceptance of the validity of resolutions despite abstentions carried particular weight.[284]

Could South Africa have claimed to stand aloof from the practice, as a

---

[280] 'Not only must the acts concerned amount to a settled practice, but they must also be such, or be carried out in such a way, as to be evidence of a belief that this practice is rendered obligatory by the existence of a rule of law requiring it' (*North Sea Continental Shelf, ICJ Reports*, 1969, p. 44, para. 77).

[281] *ICJ Reports*, 1962, p. 232.

[282] Note however that according to Stavropoulos the practice had been unquestioned from 1949 to 1966, when Portugal and South Africa expressed reservations: loc. cit. above (n. 268) at pp. 737 and 746. South Africa, contending that there was no common intention to modify the Charter, observed that 'the practice appears to have been accepted in many quarters as being in consonance with the Charter': *Pleadings*, vol. 1, p. 413, which, if correct, is very nearly an indication of the necessary *opinio juris*.

[283] *ICJ Reports*, 1969, p. 42, para. 73.

[284] Mr Stevenson, *Pleadings*, vol. 2, p. 498.

'persistent objector' on the model of Norway in the *Fisheries* case? It did argue that while in principle all Security Council resolutions adopted otherwise than in accordance with the letter of Article 27, paragraph 3, were initially invalid, for the most part they had been validated by 'acquiescence, lapse of time, estoppel or similar provisions';[285] this was however not so as regards Security Council resolutions relevant to the question of South West Africa, in none of which South Africa had acquiesced. This however is clearly insufficient: once the matter is placed in the domain of customary law, the only conduct which could reserve for a State the position of a 'persistent objector' would be refusal to accept the validity of any resolution, on whatever subject, which depended upon the custom-based deviation from the strict terms of Article 27, paragraph 3.

(ii) *General Assembly resolutions and general customary law.* No support can be found in the jurisprudence of the Court for the theory that resolutions of the United Nations General Assembly constitute a new and autonomous source of international law.[286] On the other hand, commentators have been able to point to decisions of the Court in the period considered which suggest that General Assembly resolutions or declarations may crystallize or generate international customary law.[287]

There is first the reference in the advisory opinion in the *Namibia* case to Resolution 1514 (XV), the Declaration on the Granting of Independence to Colonial Countries and Peoples. The Court surveyed the events subsequent to the adoption of the Mandate instrument, and observed that

the subsequent development of international law in regard to non-self-governing territories, as enshrined in the Charter of the United Nations, made the principle of self-determination applicable to all of them . . . A further important stage in this development was the Declaration of the Granting of Independence to Colonial Countries and Peoples (General Assembly resolution 1514 (XV) of 14 December 1960), which embraces all peoples and territories which 'have not yet attained independence'.[288]

The Court then explained its approach to interpretation of the Mandate, applying what has been referred to in the first of these articles as 'intertemporal *renvoi*':[289]

Mindful as it is of the primary necessity of interpreting an instrument in accordance with the intentions of the parties at the time of its conclusion, the Court is bound to take into account the fact that the concepts embodied in Article 22 of the Covenant—'the strenuous conditions of the modern world' and 'the well-being and

---

[285] *Pleadings*, vol. 1, p. 417.

[286] See for example Skubiszewski, 'Enactment of Law of International Organizations', this *Year Book*, 41, (1965–6), p. 198, 'A New Source of the Law of Nations: Resolutions of International Organizations', *Mélanges Guggenheim* (1968), p. 508, and the comments of the present writer, *International Customary Law and Codification*, pp. 43–5.

[287] One of the best treatments of the subject is that of Jiménez de Aréchaga, 'International Law in the Past Third of a Century', *Recueil des cours*, 159 (1978–I), pp. 30–4.

[288] *ICJ Reports*, 1971, p. 31, para. 52.

[289] This *Year Book*, 60 (1989), p. 135.

development' of the peoples concerned—were not static, but were by definition evolutionary, as also, therefore, was the concept of the 'sacred trust'. The parties to the Covenant must consequently be deemed to have accepted them as such. That is why, viewing the institutions of 1919, the Court must take into consideration the changes which have occurred in the supervening half-century, and its interpretation cannot remain unaffected by the subsequent development of law, through the Charter of the United Nations and by way of customary law.[290]

Though the point is not spelled out explicitly, it is reasonable to link the mention of Resolution 1514 (XV) to the subsequent reference to 'development of law, through the Charter of the United Nations and by way of customary law'. The exact manner in which that resolution contributed to customary law however remains ill-defined.

Resolution 1514 (XV) was again in question in the *Western Sahara* advisory opinion; and it has been argued that 'it results from the Court's pronouncement in this respect that the resolution became a rule of positive customary law through the subsequent action of States, particularly within the United Nations'.[291] The advisory opinion is, however, again very reticent as to the precise status of the resolution and its relationship to customary law, and does not, in the present writer's view, take the matter much further.

The *Nicaragua* v. *United States* case has already been examined above from the standpoint of *opinio juris* and State practice; the references there to the significance of voting for General Assembly resolutions need to be read in the context of the very particular problem examined, viz., the possible customary-law status of a rule embodied or implied in the United Nations Charter.[292]

Until the Court is called upon, by the circumstances of a case before it, for a specific ruling, widely differing views as to the impact on customary law of General Assembly resolutions may thus continue to be held without inconsistency with the Court's authority.[293]

---

[290] *ICJ Reports*, 1971, p. 31, para. 53.
[291] Jiménez de Aréchaga, loc. cit. above (n. 287), p. 33.
[292] See above, pp. 47–8 and 67–8.
[293] The present writer maintains the views he expressed in *International Customary Law and Codification* in 1972:

'There would appear to be no objection of theory to the assertion that a General Assembly resolution may be evidence of the *opinio juris* with regard to a practice of which there is, apart from the resolution itself, adequate evidence of usage. It is in this way, and probably only in this way, that weight can be attached to the resolution itself, rather than to the multiple consents involved in its adoption by States; if a resolution stating or declaring the state of the law on a given subject is adopted by a sufficient majority to be regarded as generally representative, and provided the majority does not exclude the States most directly concerned, then it will probably be impossible to challenge the authority of the rules so stated on the ground that the *opinio juris* is lacking or unproved.' (p. 66).

'Of far greater practical importance, . . . if proved, is the contention that the adoption of a resolution declaring or stating the law can itself constitute the necessary practice. If this argument is accepted, the question of resolutions as evidence of *opinio juris* becomes practically academic, since States which solemnly declare certain rules to be law, in the knowledge that by doing so they make

(c) *Divergent practice*

If a dispute brought before the Court raises questions of customary international law, one of the difficulties will frequently be that the practice in the field in question is sufficiently varied to permit of differing interpretations. It is rare for the Court to be called upon to pronounce on a customary rule which is clearly established by widespread and consistent practice.[294] As the Court said of the rules concerning the use of force in the *Nicaragua* v. *United States* case, 'It is not to be expected that in the practice of States the application of the rules in question should have been perfect', in the sense that States should have acted 'with complete consistency'.[295] The Court continued:

> The Court does not consider that, for a rule to be established as customary, the corresponding practice must be in absolutely rigorous conformity with the rule. In order to deduce the existence of customary rules, the Court deems it sufficient that the conduct of States should, *in general*, be consistent with such rules . . . [296]

Divergent practice may, on examination, prove to be capable of explanation and analysis in a number of different ways. It may be so divergent as to compel the conclusion that there exists no rule of customary law in the matter. New practice may have overturned or reversed a previous rule, or effected a modification or qualification of it. If practice apparently inconsistent with a general rule shows enough internal consistency, it may reveal the existence of a local or special custom differing from the general rule; or of an exception to the general rule where special circumstances exist (e.g., the preferential fishing rights of a coastal State exceptionally dependent on fishing resources). Divergent practice may be asserted to be justified by an exception or qualification of the general rule; if such exception or qualification does not in fact exist, the practice is unjustified in itself, but does not weaken the force of the general rule (subsection (ii) below). Finally one or more States may claim, justifiably or not, the status of 'persistent objector', to whom the general rule is not opposable (section 5 below).

them law so far as the requirement of practice is concerned, must be taken to know and intend those rules to be binding.' (p. 67.)

'A State which asserts the existence of a right to which it claims to be entitled is simultaneously contributing a formal act to the corpus of practice on the subject, and asserting its view that the matter is one of law, not of convenience, courtesy or unsettled practice, and that its claim is co-terminous with its right and thus providing evidence of the *opinio juris*. Nevertheless, it is suggested that it is essential to make the distinction, and to decline to admit into the body of the law, not only alleged rules which rest only on practice with no evidence of the belief of States in their obligatory nature, but also rules which, although widely regarded as binding in law, have never in fact been applied in practice. This is not to say that such rules cannot exist, that all rules of law must have their roots in the soil of actual usage, but only that it is of the essence of a *customary* rule to be firmly earthbound, built upon a foundation of actual experience in the relations of States.' (p. 68).

[294] In the case of the *Diplomatic and Consular Staff in Tehran* this could have been the case if the Court had had jurisdiction to pronounce on the applicable customary law (cf. *ICJ Reports*, 1980, p. 41, para. 90), instead of being limited to ruling on breaches of the Vienna Conventions.

[295] *ICJ Reports*, 1986, p. 98, para. 186.

[296] Ibid. (emphasis added).

(i) *Does divergent practice negative or merely qualify an alleged rule?* Reference has already been made[297] to the Court's treatment of the alleged 'equidistance/special circumstances rule' of maritime delimitation in the case concerning the *Continental Shelf (Libyan Arab Jamahiriya/Malta)*. The Court declined to see in the accumulation of delimitation agreements produced by the Parties evidence of the existence of such a customary rule applicable to all delimitations. It also however deduced from (*inter alia*) the departures from strict equidistance which were apparent on the face of these agreements that 'the equidistance method has never been regarded . . . as one to be applied without modification whatever the circumstances'.

This exemplifies the problem of distinguishing between practice which constitutes evidence against the existence of a particular rule, and practice which shows the degree of flexibility of the rule, or the existence of exceptions to it. When dealing, in the *Fisheries* case, with the practice of a single State (practice, however extending over a long period of time), the Court considered that

too much importance need not be attached to the few uncertainties or contradictions, real or apparent, which the United Kingdom Government claims to have discovered in Norwegian practice. They may be easily understood in the light of the variety of the facts and conditions prevailing in the long period which has elapsed since 1812, and are not such as to modify the conclusions reached by the Court.[298]

The problem is multiplied when it is the practice of all States of the world which may be offered for consideration.

A new customary rule need not, and in most cases does not, grow up in a field previously unregulated by international law; nor, if there is an existing rule, need it overturn that rule—as being what Virally has neatly termed the *'lex delenda'*[299]—and substitute itself for it. It is much more common for a new rule to graft itself on to existing law, tempering, limiting or extending the effect of existing rules.

The process at work is seen clearly in the *Fisheries Jurisdiction* cases. Iceland had claimed to extend its fisheries jurisdiction unilaterally over areas which had previously formed part of the high seas. The Court began its survey of the historical development of the law by referring to the rule, codified in the 1958 Geneva Convention on the High Seas, that the high seas are 'all parts of the sea that are not included in the territorial sea or the internal waters of a State', and the rule that freedom of the high seas includes freedom of fishing.[300] It then examined subsequent developments, in particular at the 1960 Conference on the Law of the Sea, and found that

---

[297] Above, p. 69.
[298] *ICJ Reports*, 1951, p. 138.
[299] Virally, 'A propos de la *lex ferenda*', *Mélanges offerts à Paul Reuter* (1981), p. 531.
[300] *ICJ Reports*, 1974, p. 22, para. 50.

Two concepts have crystallized as customary law in recent years arising out of the general consensus at that Conference. The first is the concept of the fishery zone, the area in which a State may claim exclusive fishery jurisdiction independently of its territorial sea; the extension of that fishery zone up to a 12-mile limit from the baselines appears now to be generally accepted. The second is the concept of preferential rights of fishing in adjacent waters in favour of the coastal State in a situation of special dependence on its coastal fisheries.[301]

The rule of freedom of fishing in the high seas thus continues to exist, but the definition of the high seas has come to be modified, first by an additional exclusion, that of a fishery zone, extending certainly twelve miles and possibly more to seaward, and secondly by a concept of 'preferential rights of fishing in adjacent waters'.

The appearance in customary law of the exclusive economic zone may also be regarded as a modification of existing law by a new rule: the Court observed in the case concerning the *Continental Shelf (Libyan Arab Jamahiriya/Malta)* that

the institution of the exclusive economic zone, with its rule on entitlement by reason of distance, is shown by the practice of States to have become a part of customary law.[302]

Once again the area of the high seas underwent a marked curtailment; but the concept or institution of the high seas remained intact.

The same judgment suggests the existence of a certain presumption, when applying a recently-emerged rule of law, against treating the older law as 'lex delenda'—or possibly a certain reluctance on the part of the Court to admit openly a *revirement de jurisprudence*. There had been much argument before the Court—and elsewhere—as to the relationship between the concept, consecrated by the *North Sea Continental Shelf* decision, of the continental shelf as the natural prolongation of the land territory and the criterion of distance from the coast as a basis of delimitation. From the development of the exclusive economic zone as part of customary law, and its relationship with the continental shelf, as the Court found,

It follows that, for juridical and practical reasons, the distance criterion must now apply to the continental shelf as well as to the exclusive economic zone; . . .

The Court however hastened to add that

This is not to suggest that the idea of natural prolongation is now superseded by that of distance. What it does mean is that where the continental margin does not extend as far as 200 miles from the shore, natural prolongation, which in spite of its physical origins has throughout its history become more and more a complex and juridical concept, is in part defined by distance from the shore, irrespective of the physical nature of the intervening sea-bed and subsoil. The concepts of natural

---

[301] Ibid., p. 23, para. 52.
[302] *ICJ Reports*, 1985, p. 33, para. 34.

prolongation and distance are therefore not opposed but complementary; and both remain essential elements in the juridical concept of the continental shelf.[303]

The re-assurance offered by the first sentence of this passage is perhaps somewhat hollow; as pointed out, in particular, by Weil, the 1985 judgment effected a radical change in the basis of the legal title to the continental shelf; and while the term 'natural prolongation' was not abandoned, it acquired a new legal meaning.[304]

(ii) *Recognition of the rule of law but assertion of an exception*. In the particular instance of its consideration in the *Nicaragua* v. *United States* case of the law governing the use of force, the Court, after making the observation quoted above as to consistency of practice 'in general', went on to observe that, in order to deduce the existence of customary rules, it was necessary that

instances of State conduct inconsistent with a given rule should generally have been treated as breaches of that rule, not as indications of the recognition of a new rule. If a State acts in a way prima facie incompatible with a recognized rule, but defends its conduct by appealing to exceptions or justifications contained within the rule itself, then whether or not the State's conduct is in fact justifiable on that basis, the significance of that attitude is to confirm rather than to weaken the rule.[305]

There are here two ideas, both of which are essential to the idea of practice as creative of custom. First, if a State does not comply with a generally adopted practice, its conduct will not interfere with the development, or continued existence, of a general customary rule (or indeed be capable of giving rise to a different rule), if that conduct has been met with protests or other actions showing that it is regarded as aberrant in relation to a custom. The second idea is related to the non-conformist State's own declared attitude, if this may be understood as saying 'Yes, I know the rule is thus and thus, but my position is exceptional, so that I am entitled to depart from it'. If the alleged exception relied on is asserted as being so wide as to exempt the State wholly and permanently from the rule, the situation becomes that of the 'persistent objector', to be examined below. What the Court seems to have in mind is rather the position of a State which endorses the rule prohibiting the use of force in international relations, but claims on a particular occasion to have been justified in using force on the ground of an exception to the rule, either a recognized exception or one asserted *ad hoc*.

Clearly, in the latter case, the alleged exception must stand or fall on its merits, on the basis of the reaction of other interested States, and in the light of any subsequent confirmatory practice. What the Court was concerned to emphasize was the fact that conduct of this kind does not weaken

[303] Ibid.
[304] See Prosper Weil, *Perspectives du droit de la délimitation maritime* (1988), pp. 44 ff.
[305] *ICJ Reports*, 1986, p. 98, para. 186.

the general rule to which the exception is claimed. Full compliance may be better than lip service, but even lip service is at least a recognition that there is a rule.

3. *The Influence of Treaties on Custom*

(1) *Individual treaties as elements of State practice*

It is of course well established that by the conclusion of a bilateral or plurilateral treaty a State may be effecting an act of practice capable of contributing to the formation of a rule of international customary law in the domain to which the treaty relates.

In the period under review, it has repeatedly been contended by parties before the Court that maritime delimitation agreements concluded between States have had such an effect in the law of the sea. For various reasons, these claims have not been upheld; but the Court has at no time rejected the possibility that an accumulation of such agreements might afford convincing evidence of a 'general practice accepted as law'. There is of course a well-known paradox or difficulty in regarding treaties as acts of State practice, to which attention has already been drawn above:[306] the inclusion of a particular provision in successive treaties may be seen either as a recognition of an existing rule, or as a recognition that there is no such rule, so that it is necessary to include a treaty stipulation to cover the point.

It was not this difficulty which impeded the Court in the *North Sea Continental Shelf* cases from deriving a rule of customary law in favour of equidistance from the corpus of delimitation agreements. The problem was not whether the *existence* of an agreement implied a *need* for an agreement because customary law would not serve on its own: on the contrary, this was, as the Court found, a field in which the customary law of the sea required delimitation by agreement. The problem was the proof that the delimitation was accompanied by the necessary *opinio juris*. After explaining, in a classic passage already quoted,[307] the need for not only a settled practice but also 'evidence of a belief that this practice is rendered obligatory by the existence of a rule of law requiring it', the Court found that

the position is simply that in certain cases—not a great number—the States concerned agreed to draw or did draw the boundaries concerned according to the principle of equidistance. There is no evidence that they so acted because they felt legally compelled to draw them in this way by reason of a rule of customary law obliging them to do so—especially considering that they might have been motivated by other obvious factors.[308]

The idiosyncratic treatment of the matter by the Chamber formed to deal with the *Gulf of Maine* case has already been adverted to above.[309]

---

[306] p. 40, above.
[307] p. 40, above.
[308] *ICJ Reports*, 1969, pp. 44–5, para. 78.
[309] pp. 56–7, above.

In the case concerning the *Interpretation of the Agreement of 25 March 1951 between the WHO and Egypt*, the Court examined 'a considerable number' of host agreements between international organizations and the Governments of the States where such organizations had their seat, or an office, and deduced that these 'confirm the recognition by international organizations and host States of the existence of mutual obligations incumbent upon them'.[310] For reasons explained above, the case was however not a straightforward matter of customary law based on acts of State practice, including treaties.[311]

(2) *The contribution of multilateral conventions to customary law*

There are, as a number of writers have remarked,[312] three ways in which the existence of a multilateral treaty may be relevant to the establishment of a rule of customary international law. Two of these are simple enough in conception, though it may in practice not always be easy to ascertain whether the processes effecting them have or have not occurred. First, a treaty may be codifying, in the sense of stating conveniently in specific form a rule of customary law which already existed before the treaty—the treaty may simply 'reflect' customary law. Secondly, the treaty may be, wholly or to a great extent, innovatory, so that the rules which it lays down go beyond, or contradict, existing rules of customary law; but a practice may develop subsequently, among States not parties to the treaty, which gives rise to a new or varied rule of customary international law following the path mapped out by the treaty stipulation.

The third possibility (which from a chronological point of view is the second) is that at the time of the conclusion of the treaty it cannot be said that there exists an established rule of customary law conforming to the provisions of the treaty, but State practice and legal thinking has reached a stage at which little more would be needed for an existing 'general practice' to be 'accepted as law', in the terminology of Article 38 of the Statute. The conclusion of the treaty might then be regarded as having the effect of 'crystallizing' an 'emerging rule of customary law'.

It may be remarked that it is not essential to any of the three processes in view that the multilateral convention in question should have come into force as a treaty, and many of the instances to be examined concern treaties which were not yet in force.

Each of these three processes has been scrutinized by the Court during the period under consideration. They will be dealt with here in the order in which they may chronogically appear in relation to a given rule.

---

[310] *ICJ Reports*, 1980, p. 94, para. 45. The advisory opinion does not indicate which agreements these were, or how they were brought to the Court's notice; the *Pleadings* volume in the case give no enlightenment. Judge Oda, however, with characteristic industry, analyses 8 or 9 such agreements in his separate opinion: *ICJ Reports*, 1980, pp. 149–52.

[311] p. 39, above.

[312] See, for instance, Jiménez de Aréchaga, 'International Law in the Past Third of a Century', *Recueil des cours*, 159 (1978–I), pp. 14–15.

(a) *Treaties codifying or reflecting custom*

The Court has fairly frequently made reference to a multilateral convention in support of a finding as to the existence of a rule of customary law, but it has not on any such occasion found it necessary to enter into any detailed consideration of the claim of such convention to be considered declaratory of customary law. It has not therefore contributed to the debate on the well-known problem of distinguishing between 'codification' and 'progressive development' in law-making treaties.[313] Only in the merits phase of the *Fisheries Jurisdiction* cases did the Court, following Sir Gerald Fitzmaurice in his separate opinion in the jurisdiction phase of the same cases, refer to the fact that the 1958 Geneva Convention on the High Seas had stated in its Preamble that it was adopted as being 'generally declaratory of established principles of international law'.[314]

What is noticeable in the Court's language when referring in this context to multilateral treaties is a (wholly laudable) care to avoid attributing declaratory effect to such a treaty beyond what is strictly necessary for the decision in the current case.

In the *Namibia* case, the Court referred to the Vienna Convention on the Law of Treaties in the context of the right of termination of a treaty on account of breach, but it did so in such a way as to show that the rule was one clearly established in customary law, and the Vienna Convention constituted no more than a convenient expression of a recognized exception to the rule, without impact on the emergence or development either of the rule itself or of the exception. It stated, in a cautious formulation to be employed, with variants, in later cases, that

> The rules laid down by the Vienna Convention on the Law of Treaties concerning termination of a treaty relationship on account of breach (adopted without dissenting vote) may in many respects be considered as a codification of existing customary law on the subject.[315]

The qualification 'in many respects' has the effect of not excluding from the codifying category aspects of the text other than the one directly relevant to the Court's decision, while not making any finding wider than necessary. The reference to the absence of a dissenting vote as signifying or confirming the codifying nature of the provision is a matter to be discussed below (sub-section (*d*)).

More specifically, the Court discussed

> the general principle of law that a right of termination on account of breach must be presumed to exist in respect of all treaties, except as regards provisions relating

---

[313] For a recent study on this, see Do Nascimento e Silva, 'Treaties as Evidence of Customary International Law', *International Law at the Time of its Codification* (1987), vol. 1, pp. 392 ff.

[314] *ICJ Reports*, 1973, pp. 25, 70; *ICJ Reports*, 1974, p. 22, para. 50; p. 191, para. 42.

[315] *ICJ Reports*, 1971, p. 47, para. 94.

to the protection of the human person contained in treaties of a humanitarian character (as indicated in Art. 60, para. 5, of the Vienna Convention).[316]

Similarly in the *Fisheries Jurisdiction* cases, the Court observed in its judgments on jurisdiction that

There can be little doubt, as is implied in the Charter of the United Nations and recognized in Article 52 of the Vienna Convention on the Law of Treaties, that under contemporary international law an agreement concluded under the threat or use of force is void.[317]

The judgments in the same cases also contain a re-appearance of the cautious formulation noted in the *Namibia* case:

International law admits that a fundamental change in the circumstances which determined the parties to accept a treaty, if it has resulted in a radical transformation of the extent of the obligations imposed by it, may, under certain conditions, afford the party affected a ground for invoking the termination or suspension of the treaty. This principle, and the conditions and exceptions to which it is subject, have been embodied in Article 62 of the Vienna Convention on the Law of Treaties, which may in many respects be considered as a codification of existing customary law on the subject of the termination of a treaty relationship on account of change of circumstances.[318]

In the *Appeal relating to the Jurisdiction of the ICAO Council*, the language used by the Court appears at first sight to go further in admitting the codification status of the Vienna Convention; the relevant passage, which will not be quoted here, is paragraph 38 of the judgment.[319] However, the Court was seised only of a procedural question; it was considering whether or not Pakistan's claim before the ICAO Council disclosed the existence of a 'disagreement . . . relating to the interpretation or application' of certain treaties. For this purpose, the Court explained the implications of the claims of India before the Council, which relied on principles of treaty law regarded by India as codified in the Vienna Convention; the Court did not have to adopt any position as to whether India's arguments in this respect were sound.[320]

In the case concerning *United States Diplomatic and Consular Staff in Tehran*, the jurisdiction of the Court was founded primarily on the Optional Protocols to the Vienna Conventions on Diplomatic Relations and Consular Relations, and secondarily on a Treaty of Amity; it was therefore empowered to give judgment only on claims of breach of the two Conventions and that Treaty, not on claims for breach of rules of customary law. Nevertheless, the Court formally decided that Iran had violated obligations

---

[316] Ibid., p. 47, para. 96.
[317] *ICJ Reports*, 1973, p. 14, para. 24; p. 59, para. 24.
[318] Ibid., p. 18, para. 36; p. 63, para. 36.
[319] *ICJ Reports*, 1972, p. 67.
[320] Jiménez de Aréchaga ('International Law in the Past Third of a Century', *Recueil des cours*, 159 (1978–I), p. 129) therefore goes too far in treating this as a finding by the Court on Article 60 of the Convention.

to the United States 'under international conventions in force between the two countries, as well as under long-established rules of general international law'.[321] When enumerating the obligations of which a breach had occurred, the Court stated that in its view those obligations

are not merely contractual obligations established by the Vienna Conventions of 1961 and 1963, but also obligations under general international law.[322]

The Court did not explain whether or not the relevant rules of general international law antedated the Conventions, but the treatment in the judgment of the rules of diplomatic law suggests an implied finding that all relevant provisions of it were of respectable antiquity and merely codified by the Vienna Conventions. This interpretation is confirmed by reference to the Court's earlier order indicating provisional measures in the case, which emphasizes the historical background, and refers specifically to the 'imperative obligations inherent' in diplomatic and consular relations as being 'now codified in the Vienna Conventions of 1961 and 1963'.[323]

The Vienna Convention on the Law of Treaties is referred to also in the advisory opinion given in 1980 on the *Interpretation of the Agreement of 25 March 1951 between the WHO and Egypt*, but the way in which the Court conceived the relationship between customary law and the provisions of the Convention is less easily grasped and defined than in previous cases. Mention has already been made in the present Chapter (section 1(3)) of the fact that the advisory opinion in this case does not employ the term 'customary law' but refers rather to 'general international law'. On the basis of such law, the Court found that, on the termination of a host agreement between a State and an international organization, there was a mutual obligation to co-operate in good faith; and certain provisions in existing host agreements provided 'certain general indications' of what that obligation might involve in such a situation.[324] The Court continued:

A further general indication as to what those obligations may entail is to be found in the second paragraph of Article 56 of the Vienna Convention on the Law of Treaties and the corresponding provision in the International Law Commission's draft articles on treaties between States and international organizations or between international organizations. Those provisions, as has been mentioned earlier, specifically provide that, when a right of denunciation is implied in a treaty by reason of its nature, the exercise of that right is conditional upon notice, and that of not less than twelve months. Clearly, these provisions also are based on an obligation to

---

[321] *ICJ Reports*, 1980, p. 44. See the previous article in this series, this *Year Book*, 60 (1989), pp. 152–3.

[322] *ICJ Reports*, 1980, p. 31, para. 62.

[323] *ICJ Reports*, 1979, p. 20, para. 41; cf. ibid., pp. 19–20, paras. 39–40. For an authoritative statement of the rationale of the codification effected by the Convention, see Fitzmaurice, 'The Future of Public International Law and the International Legal System in the Circumstances of Today' (Institut de droit international, Special Report, 1973), p. 29, para. 32.

[324] *ICJ Reports*, 1980, p. 94, para. 46.

act in good faith and have reasonable regard to the interests of the other party to the treaty.[325]

The Court went on to consider 'what periods of time may be involved in the duties to consult and negotiate' between the organization and the host State, and stated:

Some indications as to the possible periods involved, as the Court has said, can be seen in provisions of host agreements, including Section 37 of the Agreement of 25 March 1951, as well as in Article 56 of the Vienna Convention on the Law of Treaties and in the corresponding article of the International Law Commission's draft articles on treaties between States and international organizations or between international organizations.[326]

Clearly the Court was not going so far as to suggest that the Vienna Convention had codified the law as to the obligations of the parties on the termination of a treaty containing no provisions for termination: the use of the term 'indication' is quite inconsistent with such an interpretation. The coupling of the Vienna Convention with existing host agreements however shows that the Court was regarding Article 56 of the Convention as in some sense an embodiment or distillation of State practice in the matter. The subject-matter of the obligations which the Court was seeking to define was, however, one in which it was hardly to be expected that any strict or rigid rules could come into existence. Questions of the modalities of consultation and negotiation, and the appropriate time-periods, lay behind the primary norm of an obligation to co-operate in good faith, rather as, for the *Gulf of Maine* Chamber, questions of methods of maritime delimitation lay behind a fundamental norm of negotiation in good faith with a view to an agreement achieving an equitable result.[327] In both cases, therefore, practice is not capable of creating an obligation of customary law of any degree of specificity; and accordingly, the question whether a multilateral convention on the point is or is not codifying does not arise.

In the case concerning the *Continental Shelf (Tunisia/Libyan Arab Jamahiriya)*, the Court noted, when discussing the significance of the land frontier between the two States, that 'the rule of continuity *ipso jure* of boundary and territorial treaties was . . . embodied in the 1978 Vienna Convention on Succession of States in respect of Treaties',[328] thus clearly attributing a codifying effect to the relevant provision of that Convention. In the same case the Court also referred to 'an attempt by a unilateral act to establish international maritime boundary lines regardless of the legal position of other States' as being contrary to 'recognized principles of international law, as *laid down, inter alia,* in the Geneva Conventions of 1958 on the Law of the Sea'.[329] Reference is made particularly to the Convention

---

[325] Ibid., pp. 94–5, para. 47.
[326] Ibid., p. 96, para. 49.
[327] *Gulf of Maine*, judgment, *ICJ Reports*, 1984, pp. 299–300, para. 112.
[328] *ICJ Reports*, 1982, p. 66, para. 84.
[329] Ibid., p. 66, para. 87.

on the Territorial Sea and the Contiguous Zone and the Convention on the Continental Shelf 'which provide that maritime boundaries should be determined by agreement'. In view of the 'crystallizing' rather than codificatory effect attributed to the Continental Shelf Convention by the Court in 1969, the reference in 1982 may be taken to be non-committal on the possibility that those Conventions had a codificatory character *stricto sensu*.[330]

The United Nations Convention on the Law of the Sea raises acutely the problem of determining the extent to which such a Convention is declaratory or codificatory of existing law and that to which it is innovatory. In the case concerning the *Continental Shelf (Libyan Arab Jamahiriya/Malta)*, there is a reference, in the final paragraphs of the judgment, in which the Court stated that it would 'summarize the conclusions reached', to Articles 76 and 83 of the UNCLOS Convention. It is there stated that the customary law development 'concerning the relationship between the concept of the continental shelf as the natural prolongation of the land territory of the coastal State and the factor of distance between the coasts' is 'reflected in' those articles.[331]

The treatment of this question in the body of the judgment is too complex to go into here: it will be considered in a later article in this series, under the rubric of the law of the sea. All that need be said here is that it would not be correct to read the reference to this development being 'reflected in' the UNCLOS Convention as signifying that the Convention was *pro tanto* codifying.

A more direct—and uncontroversial—statement of a codifying effect of the UNCLOS Convention appears in the judgment in the *Nicaragua* v. *United States* case:

it is true that in order to enjoy access to ports, foreign vessels possess a customary right of innocent passage in territorial waters for the purposes of entering or leaving internal waters; Article 18, paragraph 1(*b*), of the United Nations Convention on the Law of the Sea of 10 December 1982, does no more than codify customary international law on this point.[332]

A similar direct reference to 'codifying conventions' is to be found in the judgment of the Chamber in the *Frontier Dispute* case: the conventions given this description are the Vienna Convention on the Law of Treaties and the Vienna Convention on Succession of States in respect of Treaties.[333]

In the case concerning *Border and Transborder Armed Actions (Nicaragua* v. *Honduras)*, the Court stated that reservations to a treaty

may, in accordance with the rules of general international law on the point as codi-

---

[330] Cf. also the reference to the status of low-tide elevations under the Continental Shelf Convention: ibid., p. 89, para. 128.

[331] *ICJ Reports*, 1985, p. 55, para. 77.

[332] *ICJ Reports*, 1986, p. 111, para. 214.

[333] Ibid., p. 536, para. 17.

fied by the 1969 Vienna Convention on the Law of Treaties, be made only at the time of signature or ratification of the Pact or at the time of adhesion to that instrument.[334]

(b) The 'crystallization' of a customary-law rule

The term 'crystallization' as a means of defining an element in the process of formation of a rule of customary international law appears, apparently for the first time, in the Court's judgment in the *North Sea Continental Shelf* cases; the credit for it must however apparently be ascribed to Sir Humphrey Waldock as counsel for the Netherlands in that case.[335] In particular, when replying to a question by Judge Fitzmaurice as to the significance of the 1958 Convention on the Continental Shelf, Sir Humphrey stated that the position of the Governments of Denmark and the Netherlands was

that the doctrine of the coastal State's exclusive rights over the adjacent continental shelf was in process of formation between 1945 and 1958; that the State practice prior to 1958 showed fundamental variations in the nature and scope of the rights claimed; that, in consequence, in State practice the emerging doctrine was wholly lacking in any definition of these crucial elements as it was also of the legal régime applicable to the coastal State with respect to the continental shelf; that the process of the definition and consolidation of the emerging customary law took place through the work of the International Law Commission, the reaction of governments to that work and the proceedings of the Geneva Conference; that the emerging customary law, now become more defined, both as to the rights of the coastal State and the applicable régime, crystallized in the adoption of the Continental Shelf Convention by the Conference; and that the numerous signatures and ratifications of the Convention and the other State practice based on the principles set out in the Convention had the effect of consolidating those principles as customary law.[336]

This passage was summarized by the Court itself in its judgment as representing the views of the two governments.[337]

The essence of crystallization as a process is that it is a fairly abrupt passage from an amorphous state to one of regularity, definition and compara-

---

[334] *ICJ Reports*, 1988, p. 85, para. 35.

[335] See *Pleadings*, vol. 2, pp. 109, 242. The expression 'crystallization of unwritten rules of law' is however found as long ago as 1939 in the dissenting opinion of Judge van Eysinga in the *Panevezys-Saldutiskis Railway* case (*PCIJ*, Series A/B, No. 76, p. 35). See also the Report of M Borchard on 'La Protection diplomatique des nationaux à l'étranger', *Annuaire de l'Institut*, 1931–I, p. 282. The term also made its appearance in international law in the context of the 'critical date' in relation to international disputes: according to Fitzmaurice, the first use of the notion of the 'crystallization' of a dispute was in the United Kingdom oral argument in the *Minquiers* case: this *Year Book*, 32 (1954–5), p. 23; *Collected Edition*, I, p. 263.

[336] *Pleadings*, vol. 2, p. 242.

[337] *ICJ Reports*, 1969, p. 38, para. 61.

tive permanence of form.[338] In the analysis of the development of the law presented by Sir Humphrey, the moment of crystallization appears to be that at which the legal rule becomes defined, in the sense that, in the context of varying or fluid practice, it becomes clear what is the rule and what is the exception, and the moment at which, in consequence, the rule becomes binding, or passes from being a rule *in posse* to a rule *in esse*.

The Court rejected the contention of Denmark and the Netherlands, but for reasons which did not conflict with the idea that such a crystallization process might be a possible one, and indeed itself employed the expression in its rejection.[339] Furthermore, it accepted that the process had in fact occurred in relation to other provisions of the Continental Shelf Convention: it referred to Articles 1 and 3 as being those 'which, it is clear, were regarded as reflecting, or as crystallizing, received or at least emergent rules of customary international law'.[340] Its conclusion was that 'the Geneva Convention did not embody or crystallize any pre-existing or emergent rule of customary law'[341] requiring delimitation on the basis of an equidistance/special circumstances rule.

A key feature of the 'crystallization' process in the formation of a rule of customary international law is the existence of a text, giving form and shape to what may previously and otherwise have been an amorphous body of practice. There is no reason why this text should necessarily be a convention or draft convention; any text which was widely known in the community of States, and emanated from a source worthy of respect—a resolution of the Institut de droit international, or a 'Restatement'—would, at least in theory, serve as well. In the circumstances of today, however, it is unlikely that anything other than a convention or draft convention, or a proposal in precise terms made at a codifying conference, would have the focusing effect.

In the *Fisheries Jurisdiction* cases, the Court referred to the 1960 Conference on the Law of the Sea, and quoted (*inter alia*) the joint United States-Canadian proposal concerning a six-mile territorial sea and an additional six-mile fishing zone, with provision for preferential rights of the coastal State in the adjacent areas of the high seas. It found that

after that Conference the law evolved through the practice of States on the basis of the debates and near-agreements at the Conference. Two concepts have crystallized as customary law in recent years arising out of the general consensus revealed at that Conference. The first is the concept of the fishery zone, the area in which a State may claim exclusive fishery jurisdiction independently of its territorial

---

[338] ' . . . in the crystalline state matter is ordered in a certain geometrical way, while in the liquid and gaseous state it lacks this order' (*Encyclopedia Britannica* (1971), vol. 6, p. 852, *sub nom*. 'Crystallography'). Analogies should not be pressed too far: circumstances favourable to crystallization are a cooling-off after a period of high temperature, or (sometimes) a thorough shake-up!

[339] 'This is clearly not the sort of foundation on which Article 6 of the Convention could be said to have reflected or crystallized such a rule': *ICJ Reports*, 1969, p. 38, para. 62.

[340] Ibid., p. 39, para. 63.

[341] Ibid., p. 41, para. 69. See also the following paragraph on the same page.

sea; . . . The second is the concept of preferential rights of fishing in adjacent waters in favour of the coastal State in a situation of special dependence on its coastal fisheries, . . . [342]

In the jurisprudence of the Court, at least, crystallizing effect has been attributed, apart from concluded conventions, to one particular draft convention—the draft United Nations Convention on the Law of the Sea.

In the case of the *Continental Shelf (Tunisia/Libya)*, the Court referred to the Third United Nations Conference on the Law of the Sea, which was then in progress, and observed of the draft convention there elaborated that

> it could not ignore any provision of the draft convention if it came to the conclusion that the content of such provision is binding upon all members of the international community because it embodies or crystallizes a pre-existing or emergent rule of customary law.[343]

This reference was made in the context of the Court's examination of a provision in the Special Agreement whereby the Court in its decision was to take into account 'the new accepted trends in the Third Conference on the Law of the Sea'. If this provision meant anything, it must have meant that the Court was not restricted to applying such international legal rules as had already 'crystallized', since, as the Court pointed out in the passage quoted above, it would in any event have had to apply such 'crystallized' rules. The Court however found it necessary to interpret the Special Agreement restrictively:

> It would no doubt have been possible for the Parties to have identified in the Special Agreement certain specific developments in the law of the sea of this kind, and to have declared that in their bilateral relations in the particular case such rules should be binding as *lex specialis*. The Parties have however not been so specific, and in the light of their replies to a question put by a Member of the Court on the point, it does not appear that it was their intention to go so far as to impose additional or supplementary rules on themselves in this way in the context of this case. According to Tunisia, the 'trends', so far as they do not constitute general international law, are to be taken into account as 'factors in the interpretation of the existing rules'.[344]

The Court also added, *ex abundanti cautela*, a sentence to show that recourse to the 'trends' in the specific case was had only by virtue of the Special Agreement, and conferred no customary or crystalline status on such trends:

> In any event, however, any consideration and conclusion of the Court in connection with the application of the 'trends' is confined exclusively to the legal relations of the Parties in the present case.[345]

---

[342] *ICJ Reports*, 1974, p. 23, para. 52. This paragraph in fact anticipates the discussion of the 1960 Conference, at p. 25, para. 57.

[343] *ICJ Reports*, 1982, p. 38, para. 24.

[344] Ibid.

[345] Ibid.

In the event, the Court did not find it necessary to refer further to its power to take note of the 'new accepted trends'. Judge Jiménez de Aréchaga however endorsed Tunisia's view of the meaning of the Special Agreement, which he stated to be that

even if a new accepted trend does not yet qualify as a rule of customary law, it still may have a bearing on the decision of the Court, not as part of applicable law, but as an element in the interpretation of existing rules or as an indication of the direction in which such rules should be interpreted.[346]

The practical significance of recourse of this kind to the 'trends' was, for Judge Jiménez de Aréchaga, as follows

Therefore, it is legitimate to take into consideration that the whole process of the Conference is indicative of a new accepted trend, which is to minimize and 'tone down' the role assigned to equidistance in Article 6 of the 1958 Convention.[347]

Judge Jiménez thus rejected the contention that equidistance was a 'privileged method' of delimitation, that there was a presumption in favour of its use. In this however he did not differ from the judgment of the Court.[348]

The status of the 'new accepted trends' remains therefore obscure, even in the approach of Judge Jiménez de Aréchaga. It does not appear that the consent of the parties to the trends being taken into account caused him to come to a decision different from that which he would have reached on the basis solely of positive law. He merely felt able to look at the trends and find that they pointed in the same direction as his conclusion on the basis of law; presumably the maximum impact which they could have had would have been, if they had proved to point in the opposite direction, to cause him to review his conclusions on the basis of positive law, in order to be sure of their soundness on that basis. But even if the Special Agreement had not referred to the matter, it can hardly be thought that the judges would have closed their eyes to the proceedings of the Conference; they would on the contrary at all events have seen them as straws in the wind. Positive law must be interpreted and applied in its context; the UNCLOS debates were part of the context; they could assist in interpretation of the law but not contradict it, nor even weaken it.

The interest of the handling, by the Court and by Judge Jiménez de Aréchaga, of the question of the 'new accepted trends' is that it confirms the appropriateness of the 'crystallization' metaphor. Crystals grow in size, but the transition in a saturated solution from liquid to the presence of crystals is a qualitative change, having a 'before' and an 'after'. Similarly a potential rule can exist as an idea for some time, changing and developing, but if it becomes a rule of positive law then, at least in theory, one can point to a time when it was not such a rule and a time when it was. It is not a matter of gradations of legalness, but of the crossing of a line.

---

[346] Ibid., p. 108, para. 33.
[347] Ibid., p. 109, para. 35.
[348] Ibid., p. 79, para. 110.

(c) *Growth of a customary rule subsequently to a convention*

As already noted, the crystallization metaphor has been employed in the Court's decisions in relation to the impact on customary law of a text, primarily one produced by the conclusion, or the negotiation, of a multilateral treaty. Despite the use of the term in the *Fisheries Jurisdiction* cases for, apparently, a passage into customary law subsequent to the 1960 Law of the Sea Conference, it appears that the emphasis is most appropriate when text and consensus are synchronized. In the *North Sea Continental Shelf* cases, the Court held that certain provisions of the 1958 Geneva Convention had reflected, embodied or crystallized international customary law; but when it came to examine whether the rule alleged by Denmark and the Netherlands had come into existence subsequently to the conclusion of the Convention, it employed other terminology. The argument submitted to it was stated to be that

even if . . . no such rule was *crystallized* in Article 6 of the Convention, nevertheless such a rule has *come into being* since the Convention.[349]

This contention, in the view of the Court, involved treating Article 6 of the Convention

as a norm-creating provision which has constituted the formation of, or has generated a rule which, while only conventional or contractual in its origin, has since passed into the general *corpus* of international law, and is now accepted as such by the *opinio juris*, so as to have become binding even for countries which have never, and do not, become parties to the Convention. There is no doubt that this process is a perfectly possible one and does from time to time occur; it constitutes indeed one of the recognized methods by which new rules of customary international law may be formed.[350]

After adding the caution that 'this result is not lightly to be regarded as having been attained', the Court lays down as a first requirement

that the provisions concerned should, at all events potentially, be of a fundamentally norm-creating character such as could be regarded as forming the basis of a general rule of law.[351]

The Court then turns to the time element:

With respect to the other elements usually regarded as necessary before a conventional rule can be considered to have become a general rule of international law, it might be that, even without the passage of any considerable period of time, a very widespread and representative participation in the convention might suffice of itself, provided it included that of States whose interests were specially affected . . .[352]

. . . Although the passage of only a short period of time is not necessarily, or of

---

[349] *ICJ Reports*, 1969, p. 41, para. 70.
[350] Ibid., p. 41, para. 71.
[351] Ibid., pp. 41–2, para. 72.
[352] Ibid., p. 42, para. 73.

itself, a bar to the formation of a new rule of customary international law on the basis of what was originally a purely conventional rule, an indispensable requirement would be that within the period in question, short though it might be, State practice, including that of States whose interests are specially affected, should have been both extensive and virtually uniform in the sense of the provision invoked;—and should moreover have occurred in such a way as to show a general recognition that a rule of law or legal obligation is involved.[353]

The present writer has expressed the view elsewhere, on the basis of the first of these two passages, that

with all necessary reservations, the view of the Court was that in appropriate cases 'widespread and representative' participation in a Convention may suffice both as evidence of *opinio juris* and as sufficient State practice.[354]

This view has been criticized, in particular by Akehurst, who considers that it is clear from the second passage that '*opinio juris* is not something which can be inferred from practice, however extensive; it is an additional requirement'.[355] It seems to us however that, in the face of widespread participation in a potentially norm-creating convention, to call for independent evidence of *opinio juris* is to make it impossible ever to conclude that such participation can 'suffice of itself'. It should be borne in mind that if a State holds an *opinio* that a particular rule, stated in a recent convention, is *already* a rule of customary law, its conclusion from this is less likely to be that it should ratify the convention, than that it matters little whether it ratifies or not, since it considers that the rule exists and is binding in any event.[356]

(d) *The significance of conventions: voting, participation and the 'package deal'*

Having surveyed the possible ways in which international conventions may be treated as relevant to the establishment of a rule of customary law, we should pause to consider the rationale of taking account of conventions, as State practice, evidence of *opinio juris*, or otherwise.

In the case of conventions treated by the Court as codifying instruments, the authority of the customary rule applied is established, in principle independently of the convention, which merely affords a convenient statement of the rule. Whether the convention is in force, for the States parties to the case or at all, and the extent of State participation in the treaty is, in this respect, irrelevant. However, it is natural, in face of a disposition of a multilateral convention which is in point, and which may correspond to a

---

[353] Ibid., p. 43, para. 74.

[354] *International Customary Law and Codification*, p. 86.

[355] 'Custom as a Source of International Law', this *Year Book*, 47 (1974–5), p. 50.

[356] For a more radical interpretation of these dicta, see d'Amato, 'Manifest Intent and the Generation by Treaty of Customary Rules', *American Journal of International Law*, 64 (1970), p. 895, and the criticism by Jiménez de Aréchaga, 'International Law in the Past Third of a Century', *Recueil des cours*, 159 (1978–I), pp. 22–3.

customary rule, to reverse the intellectual process, and consider, not (i) what is the customary rule; and (ii) does this provision correspond to it, but rather (i) does this conveniently defined rule sum up and express previous established practice sufficient to produce a customary rule, and even (ii) what do the circumstances of the adoption of this convention suggest that it was intended to do?[357] This last question is entirely appropriate where the process being enquired into is a possible crystallization of a customary rule by the convention; and since it may not be possible—or necessary—in some cases to distinguish clearly, or at the least not *a priori*, between the codifying or crystallizing effect of a convention, it cannot be objected to even when the convention, as it turns out, was codificatory of established pre-existing law.

Thus, as we have seen, the Court in the *Namibia* case mentioned the fact that a particular provision of the Vienna Convention on the Law of Treaties was 'adopted without a dissenting vote' as relevant to the finding that it 'may in many respects be considered as a codification of existing customary law on the subject'.[358]

In the context of a suggestion that a particular convention, draft convention, or similar instrument had a crystallizing effect, the extent to which States voted for it or participated in it is treated as relevant. In the *Fisheries Jurisdiction* cases, the Court, when discussing 'State practice on the subject of fisheries', referred to developments at the 1958 and 1960 Conferences on the Law of the Sea, and observed that

Both the 1958 Resolution and the 1960 joint amendment concerning preferential rights were approved by a large majority of the Conferences, thus showing overwhelming support for the idea that in certain special situations it was fair to recognize that the coastal State had preferential fishing rights.[359]

The amount of support for a proposal is, however, far from being the sole relevant criterion. In the *North Sea Continental Shelf* cases, the Court made no reference whatever to the extent of support shown at the 1958 Conference for the criterion of equidistance for continental shelf delimitation, because that criterion, which was put forward by the International Law Commission,

was proposed by the Commission with considerable hesitation, somewhat on an experimental basis, at most *de lege ferenda*, and not at all *de lege lata* or as an emerging rule of customary international law. This is clearly not the sort of foundation on which Article 6 of the Convention could be said to have reflected or crystallized such a rule.[360]

[357] This is the approach strongly condemned by d'Amato in the context of the *Nicaragua* v. *United States of America* case: 'Trashing International Customary Law', 'Appraisals of the ICJ's Decision: Nicaragua v. United States of America (Merits)', *American Journal of International Law*, 81(1987), p. 102.

[358] *ICJ Reports*, 1971, p. 47, para. 94; see p. 88, above.

[359] *ICJ Reports*, 1974, p. 26, para. 58; p. 195, para. 50.

[360] *ICJ Reports*, 1969, p. 38, para. 62.

A striking linkage between support for the adoption of a draft convention and a customary-law impact is found in the Court's judgment in the case concerning the *Continental Shelf (Libyan Arab Jamahiriya/Malta)*, in connection with the 1982 United Nations Convention on the Law of the Sea.

It is of course axiomatic that the material of customary international law is to be looked for primarily in the actual practice and *opinio juris* of States, even though multilateral conventions may have an important role to play in recording and defining rules deriving from custom, or indeed in developing them . . . it cannot be denied that the 1982 Convention is of major importance, having been adopted by an overwhelming majority of States; hence it is clearly the duty of the Court, even independently of the references made to the Convention by the Parties, to consider in what degree any of its relevant provisions are binding upon the Parties as a rule of customary international law.[361]

The introductory sentence permits of two interpretations of the reference to the adoption of the Convention by 'overwhelming majority': that this is indicative of *opinio juris*, or that the attitudes so expressed by States constitute State practice. For reasons already explained, the present writer prefers the former reading, and would emphasize the need for actual State practice to be shown in addition.[362]

There is in this respect a further difficulty, which the Court does not refer to, but should be referred to here. Sir Robert Jennings, writing before the Conference had completed its work, drew attention to the deliberate use of consensus rather than voting, and to the negotiation of texts on the basis of a 'package deal' between States with differing or opposing interests. Referring to the Negotiating Text as it then stood (ICNT Rev. 2), he observed:

it would seem to follow that it also offers impressive evidence of that '*opinio juris*' which is the most important element of established customary law. Yet at the same time, insofar as those draft provisions are only elements of a package deal, which package may or may not be realized, it would seem that they are not necessarily evidence of *opinio juris* at all but of elements of a bargain. The I.C.N.T. is, after all, as has been insisted throughout the conference, only a negotiating text; and a negotiating text cannot as such logically be evidence of what is already established.[363]

After the adoption of the UNCLOS Convention, the problem was further studied in 1985 by Caminos and Molitor in an important article in the *American Journal*, where they observe that the same difficulty arises if it is

---

[361] *ICJ Reports*, 1985, pp. 29–30, para. 27.
[362] It is an over-simplification, though an attractive one, to say that
'international law has only one source—the common will of States. A new rule is created by its general acceptance by all the States concerned. The States themselves are the masters of the method by which they agree to express their common will': Sohn, 'Unratified Treaties as a Source of Customary International Law', *Realism in Law-Making (Mélanges Riphagen)* (1986), p. 245.
Consensus or unanimous voting does not always signify the existence of a 'common will'.
[363] 'Law-making and the Package Deal', *Mélanges offerts à Paul Reuter* (1981), p. 349.

sought to treat provisions of the Convention as having a crystallizing effect.[364]

The Court does not so far seem to have shown awareness of this problem. The Chamber formed to deal with the *Gulf of Maine* case, however, referred to the 'consensus reached on large portions of' the UNCLOS Convention and recalled that 'certain provisions of the Convention, concerning the continental shelf and the exclusive economic zone, . . . were adopted without any objections'; its conclusion was that

> In the Chamber's opinion, these provisions, even if in some respects they bear the mark of the compromise surrounding their adoption, may nevertheless be regarded as consonant at present with general international law on the question.[365]

Judge Oda also, in his dissenting opinion in the *Tunisia/Libya* case, did refer to the problem:

> It should be crystal clear that Article 76 of the draft convention is essentially a product of compromise—not consensus—between the conflicting positions of various groups which have different, and sometimes opposite, interests in the use of sea-bed areas. Well may the draft convention be expected eventually to become binding upon many nations, once it has become widely accepted and received a sufficient number of ratifications. Until that time, there is no doubt that Article 76 is not a provision of any worldwide multilateral convention, and can hardly be considered as enshrining established rules of international law.[366]

Further on he referred specifically to the 'package deal' concept:

> the Court should not have taken the relevant provisions of the 1981 draft convention on the Law of the Sea at their face value, on the sole ground that they had been formulated as a result of the consensus formula, special procedures and 'package deal' of UNCLOS III, even through the Special Agreement had requested it to take account of the 'tendances récentes admises' or 'new accepted trends' at that Conference. The Court should have examined more thoroughly the progress of the discussions underlying those provisions and considered the trends in the law of the sea for the past few decades in a much wider perspective.[367]

In 1985, commenting on Article 82 of the Convention, he observed that 'The suggested provision which emerged as a political compromise at the later stage of UNCLOS III can hardly be regarded as reflecting customary international law'.[368]

Another aspect of the same problem is the question whether States can

---

[364] Caminos and Molitor, 'Progressive Development of International Law and the Package Deal', *American Journal of International Law*, 79 (1985), pp. 871 ff.

[365] *ICJ Reports*, 1984, p. 294, para. 94. As Sinclair points out, 'More should not however be read into this *dictum* of the Chamber than its content warrants. It is a very broad-brush statement and probably should not be construed as giving to all the detailed provisions of Parts V and VI of the Convention the status of general, or customary international law': 'The Impact of the Unratified Codification Convention', *Realism in Law-Making* (*Mélanges Riphagen*) (1986), p. 218.

[366] *ICJ Reports*, 1982, p. 220, para. 104.

[367] Ibid., p. 247, para. 146.

[368] *ICJ Reports*, 1985, p. 155, para. 58.

'pick and choose' between the various provisions of a codifying convention, treating as customary law what suits them, and rejecting what does not: this problem is addressed by Judge Mbaye in his separate opinion in the *Malta/Libya* case.[369]

4. *General, Special and Bilateral Customary Law*

(1) *Bilateral custom: the* Right of Passage *case*

Traditional theory divides international customary law into the categories of general custom, applicable in principle to all States of the international community, and special or regional custom, applicable only within a group of States linked together by geographical proximity or other shared connection. The *Right of Passage* case in 1960 added to this simple taxonomy the concept of bilateral custom—rules of law applicable only between a particular pair of States.[370]

Before examining the *Right of Passage* case itself, we may note one particular aspect of a bilateral custom. The reliance by one State against another on a rule said to be of customary international law may in general take one of two forms, depending on whether or not the respondent State is or is not alleged to have participated in the practice giving rise to or evidencing the custom. The applicant State may say: numerous States have acted and do act in these circumstances in this particular way; now that you find yourself in the same circumstances, you too must act in this way, because the practice is indicative of a rule of customary law binding upon you. Or the applicant may say: you have acted thus and thus in analogous circumstances in the past, and have so shown your recognition of a customary rule of law; therefore you must act consistently with that rule in the present instance. Either situation may involve assertions of a rule of general or of special customary law; but the assertion of a bilateral custom can, by definition, only correspond to the second hypothetical situation.

In terms of the Statute definition of customary law, the distinction relates to the expression 'a general practice accepted as law'; does the word 'accepted' refer to the State against which the custom is asserted, or to the generality of States making up either the international community as a whole or the group of States within which it is claimed there exists a special custom? As regards a general customary rule, the latter interpretation is generally accepted—and indeed if it were not so it would not be possible to apply a general custom to a State which had taken no part in the practice

---

[369] Ibid., pp. 98–9.
[370] It must however be acknowledged that Fitzmaurice had already foreseen this possibility in his comments on the *US Nationals in Morocco* case, under the heading of 'Custom, Usage':

'Special rights, i.e., such as would not exist under ordinary rules, may, however, be acquired by one State, not against the world in general . . . , but against another particular State, e.g. in its territory or waters or with reference to its vessels or nationals' (this *Year Book*, 30 (1953), p. 69; *Collected Edition*, I, p. 199).

which went to its making. Where however a bilateral custom is asserted, the only practice which can be relied on to define the custom is that in which the respondent State has taken part; and the *opinio* of the general body of States, or even of the States of the region, is without impact.[371]

It is therefore hardly surprising that the possibility of a bilateral custom should have been doubted; but the Court in the *Right of Passage* case specifically based its decision on that ground:

> It is difficult to see why the number of States between which a local custom may be established on the basis of long practice must necessarily be larger than two. The Court sees no reason why long continued practice between two States accepted by them as regulating their relations should not form the basis of mutual rights and obligations between the two States.[372]

The proof of the practice in a case of alleged bilateral custom should present no more difficulty than in the case of any other custom—in fact rather less difficulty than in many cases of general custom where variations in practice might make the limits of the common element difficult to define, or even cast doubt on the existence of a generally shared practice. The subjective element however has, for the reason explained above, to be approached in a quite different way. The Court had very little to say on this:

> This practice having continued over a period extending beyond a century and a quarter unaffected by the change of regime in respect of the intervening territory which occurred when India became independent, the Court is, in view of all the circumstances of the case, satisfied that that practice was accepted as law by the Parties and has given rise to a right and a correlative obligation.[373]

In effect, the Court appears to have considered that the existence for so long of such a consistent practice was itself sufficient evidence of the existence of an appropriate subjective element. This interpretation of the Court's approach is supported by a somewhat curious paragraph which concludes its brief treatment of Portugal's reliance on general customary law and the general principles of law.

---

[371] Note that in the *Right of Passage* case Portugal also relied on general custom, but the Court found it unnecessary to examine 'whether general international custom . . . may lead to the same result' (*ICJ Reports*, 1960, p. 43).

[372] Ibid., p. 39. Haggenmacher ('La Doctrine des deux éléments du droit coutumier dans la pratique de la Cour internationale', *Revue générale de droit international public*, 1986, p. 57), relies on the (non-authoritative) French text of the preceding sentence:

'En tant que cette prétention du Portugal à un droit de passage est formulée par ce pays sur la base de la coutume locale, il est allégué au nom de l'Inde qu'aucune coutume locale ne saurait se constituer entre deux Etats seulement'

and contends that the words 'coutume locale' in the first half of the sentence refer only to a '*pratique* coutumière locale', and in the second half to a '*norme* coutumière locale'. This interpretation does not appear tenable, first because the authoritative English text uses 'local custom', prefaced by no definite article, in both halves of the sentence; and because Portugal did rely on an alleged customary norm, not a mere practice, so that to interpret the sentence in this way would signify that the Court was mis-stating a party's contention.

[373] *ICJ Reports*, 1960, p. 40.

The Court is here dealing with a concrete case having special features. Histori-cally the case goes back to a period when, and relates to a region in which, the rela-tions between neighbouring States were not regulated by precisely formulated rules but were governed largely by practice. Where therefore the Court finds a practice clearly established between two States which was accepted by the Parties as governing the relations between them, the Court must attribute decisive effect to that practice for the purpose of determining their specific rights and obligations. Such a particular practice must prevail over any general rules.[374]

To say that 'a practice clearly established between two States' was 'accepted by the Parties as governing the relations between them' leaves a lot of ques-tions unanswered. Presumably what is meant is at least that the extent of the right of passage was established by practice: each side recognized that transit of goods would cause no objections, but passage of soldiers or armed police required express permission. But could the practice be stopped or altered, and if so how? In the case of a general custom, the two questions are linked: if a practice between two States conforms to a more widely established norm, then it is an expression of customary rights and obli-gations, which cannot be extinguished or modified except by agreement between those concerned. But in a bilateral customary relationship this dimension is lacking.

The significance of the time element is also not without obscurities. In the *North Sea* cases, the Court, dealing with the possibility of the develop-ment of a rule of customary law on the basis of a conventional rule, observed that

Although the passage of only a short period of time is not necessarily, or of itself, a bar to the formation of a new rule of customary international law . . . an indis-pensable requirement would be that within the period in question, short though it might be, State practice . . . should have been both extensive and virtually uniform . . . and should moreover have occurred in such a way as to show a general recognition that a rule of law or legal obligation is involved.[375]

(2) *Relationship between general custom and special custom*

It would seem axiomatic that, as between States bound by a rule of special or regional customary law, that rule prevails over any incompatible rule of general customary law[376]—subject of course to any considerations of *jus cogens*. In practice, any actual conflict between such rules is somewhat unlikely: the function of special custom is less likely to be to derogate from general rules of customary law than to establish between a particular group of States certain reciprocal rights and obligations which simply do not exist in general law, as was the situation in the *Asylum* case.

In the *Right of Passage* judgment in 1960, the Court, after finding the

---

[374] Ibid., p. 44.
[375] *ICJ Reports*, 1969, p. 43, para. 74.
[376] In this sense Akehurst, this *Year Book*, 47 (1974–5), p. 29.

existence of a special custom between Portugal and India providing for passage to and from the enclaved villages, continued:

> Portugal also invokes general international custom, as well as the general principles of law recognized by civilized nations, in support of its claim of a right of passage as formulated by it. Having arrived at the conclusion that the course of dealings between the British and Indian authorities on the one hand and the Portuguese on the other established a practice, well understood between the Parties, by virtue of which Portugal had acquired a right of passage in respect of private persons, civil officials and goods in general, the Court does not consider it necessary to examine whether general international custom or the general principles of law recognized by civilized nations may lead to the same result.[377]

The finding of the Court based on special custom had not however amounted to acceptance of the whole of Portugal's claim: it had rejected the assertion of a right of passage of troops and armed police. The possibility therefore remained that such a right, even though not part of the special custom, was one recognized by general international law. The Court did not neglect this aspect of the matter, but completed its argument as follows:

> As regards armed forces, armed police and arms and ammunition, the findings of the Court that the practice established between the Parties required for passage in respect of these categories the permission of the British or Indian authorities, renders it unnecessary for the Court to determine whether or not, in the absence of the practice that actually prevailed, general international custom or the general principles of law recognized by civilized nations could have been relied upon by Portugal in support of its claim to a right of passage in respect of these categories.[378]

In the first stage of its argument, the Court considered that since a special custom of passage was established in favour of Portugal, judgment could, to that extent, be given in favour of Portugal, so that further consideration of what general customary law might provide was superfluous. This is a perfectly recognized and respectable judicial technique, numerous examples of which will be considered later in these articles.

In the second stage, the Court was in effect finding not merely that the special custom did not include a right of passage for troops and armed police, but that that custom included, as it were, a non-right of passage for those categories; or better expressed, a right of India to insist on its permission to be obtained for such passage.

The first stage of the argument raises the interesting theoretical question whether a special custom, to exist at all, may not have to diverge to a significant extent from the general law. Setting aside the special aspect of the case relating to the passage of troops and armed police, if there existed a rule of general customary law permitting passage in such circumstances as those of Damao and the enclaved villages, how could any special custom come into existence or be discernible? If the practice of unimpeded passage grows up

---

[377] *ICJ Reports*, 1960, p. 43.
[378] Ibid., pp. 43–4.

wherever in the world there is an enclosed territory, any individual special customs, in existence or *in statu nascendi*, are presumably merged, like droplets of mercury coming together, into the general custom. In strict theory, therefore, to find that there exists a special custom to a particular effect implies a finding that there is no general custom to that effect, or at least not to identical effect.

So far as the second argument is concerned, the logic is unimpeachable; the only hesitation one may have is at the level of assessment of the facts. If Portugal could have established that wherever else in the world the question arose, troops and armed police enjoyed the fullest freedom of transit, the record of permissions granted by India might have had to be regarded in a different light. India's conduct would then be an exercise of normal sovereignty in a field in which an established general custom recognized a limitation of sovereignty. Failing establishment of the status of 'persistent objector',[379] India might have been obliged to bow to the pressure of general practice. These are however theoretical considerations not entailing any criticism of the finding actually made by the Court.

5. *Customary Law and the 'Persistent Objector'*

Fitzmaurice did not in his series of articles deal with the rule, for which a dictum of the Court in the 1951 *Fisheries* case[380] affords the main jurisprudential authority, that a State which has consistently opposed the application to itself of a new rule of customary law, from a time before that rule crystallized as such, is not bound by the rule. He did however discuss it in his lectures at The Hague Academy in 1957, under the heading of 'The problem of the single recalcitrant State',[381] where he accepted the possibility within narrow limits:

namely—open dissent, expressly manifested at the time of the promotion of the rule, and consistently maintained subsequently.[382]

At the same time he questioned 'whether in those circumstances the alleged rule [i.e. that dissented from by the persistent objector] would really be a rule at all'.[383] The principle that the status of exemption, as a persistent objector, from an otherwise well-recognized general rule of customary law is at least theoretically possible, is however now well-established. The justification for it cannot be better expressed than it has been, in this *Year Book*, by Akehurst:

If a State were unable to opt out of a developing rule of customary law by dissenting from it *ab initio*, the creation of new rules of customary law would be sur-

---

[379] See below, section 5.

[380] *ICJ Reports*, 1951, p. 131: 'In any event, the . . . rule would appear to be inapplicable as against Norway, in as much as she has always opposed any attempt to apply it to the Norwegian coast'.

[381] *Recueil des cours*, 92 (1957-II), p. 99.

[382] Loc. cit. above (n. 7), p. 100.

[383] Ibid.

rounded by all kinds of logical and practical difficulties. If the dissent of a single State could prevent the creation of a new rule, new rules would hardly ever be created. If a dissenting State could be bound against its will, customary law would in effect be created by a system of majority voting; but it would be impossible to reach agreement about the size of the majority required, and whether (and, if so, how) the 'votes' of different States should be weighted . . . Recognition of a right of dissent removes these difficulties.[384]

In its discussion in the *North Sea Continental Shelf* cases of the formation of customary international law, the Court did not specifically advert to the question of the persistent objector.[385] Two of the dissenting judges however found themselves obliged to deal with the point in their dissenting opinions, in view of their conclusion, in which they differed from the majority, that the equidistance rule for continental shelf delimitation was binding on the Federal Republic of Germany as a rule of general customary law.

Judge Lachs referred first to this possibility as a reason for not allowing divergences of practice to lead to the conclusion that no general rule existed:

Nor can a general rule which is not of the nature of *jus cogens* prevent some States from adopting an attitude apart. They may have opposed the rule from its inception . . .[386]

It is worth remarking however that if the rule is not one of *jus cogens*, a State does not have to show an established status as persistent objector to be able to depart from the rule *by agreement with other States*—which is precisely the situation here contemplated (delimitations agreed on bases other than equidistance).

Later in his opinion Judge Lachs concluded that the equidistance rule had 'attained the identifiable status of a general law', but continued:

This may be contested in a particular case by a State denying its opposability to itself. Then, of course, the matter becomes one of evidence.[387]

On the facts, Judge Lachs rejected any assimilation of the position of the Federal Republic to that of Norway in the *Fisheries* case.[388]

Similarly Judge Sørensen, after quoting the *Fisheries* dictum, observed that:

Similarly, it might be argued in the present case that the Convention on the Continental Shelf would be inapplicable as against the Federal Republic, if she had

[384] 'Custom as a Source of International Law', this *Year Book*, 47 (1974–5), p. 26.

[385] Unger (*Völkergewohnheitsrecht—objektives Recht oder Geflecht bilateraler Beziehungen: seine Bedeutung für einen 'persistent objector'* (Tuduv, 1978), p. 94) quotes Müller, *Vertrauensschutz im Völkerrecht*, as advancing the view that the 'persistent objector' doctrine was applied in paragraph 33 of the *North Sea Continental Shelf* judgment. Unger considers, in my view correctly, that that paragraph deals with a different point, whether the Federal Republic was estopped by conduct from denying the application of the equidistance rule.

[386] *ICJ Reports*, 1969, p. 229.

[387] Ibid., p. 232.

[388] Ibid., p. 238.

consistently refused to recognize it as an expression of generally accepted rules of international law and had objected to its applicability as against her. But far from adopting such an attitude, the Federal Republic has gone quite a long way towards recognizing the Convention.[389]

In the *Fisheries Jurisdiction* cases, the finding of the Court that the extension of Iceland's fishing zone was 'not opposable' to the two applicants, the United Kingdom and the Federal Republic of Germany, has certain affinities with the principle of the status of the 'persistent objector'. The Court however made no express reference to that principle.[390]

6. Jus cogens *and Customary International Law*

In the judgment on the merits in the case of *Military and Paramilitary Activities in and against Nicaragua (Nicaragua v. United States of America)* the Court quoted, in support of its view that the prohibition of the use of force in Article 2(4) of the Charter was a rule of customary international law, certain statements that that prohibition was one of *jus cogens*.[391]

The first observation to be made on this is that the Court, without comment and apparently without adverting to the question, took up a definite position on a question the subject of doctrinal controversy, namely whether rules of *jus cogens* can come into existence only through customary law processes, or may also have their source in a treaty instrument, e.g., a multilateral convention. If it were accepted that a treaty could give rise to rules of *jus cogens*, it could not be argued that because a given rule is one of *jus cogens*, it is therefore a rule of customary law.[392] Accordingly, the Court must be taken to have been ruling implicitly that only customary law can produce obligations of *jus cogens*.

There have however been two distinct schools of thought among legal

---

[389] Ibid., p. 247.

[390] Akehurst, in the article already referred to (this *Year Book*, 47 (1974–5), p. 25, n. 5), quotes Judge de Castro as upholding in his separate opinion the 1951 *Fisheries* dictum. In fact however, in respect of the alleged customary rule authorizing the claim of a coastal State to a 12-mile fishery zone, Judge de Castro said:

'According to the most authoritative writers, and following the doctrine of the Court itself (*ICJ Reports*, 1950, p. 65; *ICJ Reports*, 1951, p. 131; *ICJ Reports*, 1969, p. 42, para. 73) the express will of a State during such a period [as the formative period] prevents the coming into existence of a custom' (*ICJ Reports*, 1974, p. 92).

Thus Judge de Castro was referring to a different passage on page 131 of the *Fisheries* judgment where the Court concluded that 'the ten-mile rule has not acquired the authority of a general rule of international law'. The Judge also placed Norway in the category referred to in the *North Sea* judgment as that of 'States whose interests were specially affected' by the development of a new customary rule.

[391] *ICJ Reports*, 1986, p. 100, para. 190.

[392] It could be suggested that the Court's argument may have been proceeding on the basis of a suppressed premise, namely that there was no relevant treaty in sight, from which it might have been suggested that the rule derived. In view of the express reference to the Charter this is however a dubious interpretation.

writers.[393] According to one view, the function of multilateral treaties in relation to *jus cogens* is purely declaratory; according to the other view, a norm of *jus cogens*, binding on all States, can arise from a widely supported conventional provision, even in the absence of unanimous acceptance, and Article 53 of the Vienna Convention on the Law of Treaties is referred to in this connection.[394]

In addition, however, to prove that a rule is one of customary law by demonstrating that it is one of *jus cogens* appears to be putting the cart before the horse. If a rule which is one of *jus cogens* must be one of general, non-treaty, law, rules of *jus cogens* are a sub-category of customary law rules. Thus to argue that a rule is one of *jus cogens* and therefore must be one of customary law resembles first establishing that a furry object with whiskers, four legs and a tail is a cat, in order to go on to deduce from this that the object is an animal.

However the circumstances in which the argument was used were exceptional. The existence of a rule prohibiting the use of force was universally admitted: the question was whether its sole basis was conventional, in Article 2, paragraph 4, of the Charter, or whether it also existed as a rule of customary international law, behind or alongside the Charter rule. The intellectual process of the Court's reasoning was not spelled out in the judgment, but appears to have been as follows. If the rule expressed in Article 2, paragraph 4, is one of *jus cogens*, then any agreement derogating from it is void, even if the Charter were abolished by mutual agreement between the parties to it. Therefore if the nature of the rule is such that it would survive the Charter, it can only be a rule of customary law.

Seen in this light, the agreement is logically sound, though it does not necessarily follow that the underlying rule of customary law is binding on United Nations members *as a customary rule* so long as they continue to be bound by the Charter. Less convincing is the Court's process of demonstration that the rule is one of *jus cogens*: it relies for this purpose on assertions to that effect by the parties to the case in their pleadings, and on a commentary of the International Law Commission. The Court however had in an earlier paragraph of its judgment held that 'in the field of customary international law, the shared views of the Parties as to the content of what they regard as the rule is not enough'.[395]

A rigorous view would be that for it to be demonstrated that a particular rule of customary international law is one of *jus cogens*, a twofold process is

[393] For an excellent survey of this question, with exhaustive references, see Fois, 'La funzione degli accordi di codificazione nella formazione dello *jus cogens*', *International Law at the Time of its Codification* (1987), vol. 1, p. 287.
[394] Cf. also remarks of Yasseen, Chairman of the Drafting Committee, in A/CONF 29–II, p. 514. Article 53 of the Convention seems to have contributed to the confusion between rules of law which are universally binding, but remain *jus dispositivum*, and rules of *jus cogens*; see, for example, Ziccardi, 'Il contributo della Convenzione di Vienna sul Diritto dei Trattati alla determinazione del diritto applicabile dalla Corte internazionale di giustizia', *Communicazioni e studi* (1975), p. 1043, particularly p. 1055.
[395] *ICJ Reports*, 1986, p. 98, para. 184.

required. For the rule itself to be one of customary law, practice and *opinio juris* must be shown—probably not a difficult exercise in the case of most rules of a significant degree of gravity and stability to be candidates for the status of *jus cogens*. The definition of the rule as one of *jus cogens* is however the effect of a separate, distinct, rule of international law, apparently either fundamental or of customary origin, which also requires to be proved by the demonstration of relevant practice and *opinio juris*. This may perhaps be too exigent a test for the establishment of a rule of *jus cogens*, but something more is surely required than a dictum of the International Law Commission.

In the specific context of the *Nicaragua* v. *United States* case, a further difficulty presents itself. The United States there argued that the customary law on the subject of non-recourse to force was so identified with the provisions of the Charter that the Court could not rule on the customary law obligations of the United States without interpreting the Charter, which it was debarred from doing by the 'multilateral treaty reservation' in the United States declaration of acceptance of the Optional Clause. The Court's response to this argument is that in this field 'The areas governed by the two sources of law thus do not overlap exactly, and the rules do not have the same content'.[396] One is therefore entitled to ask how it can be that a rule of treaty law can diverge from a rule of customary law which is one of *jus cogens*, i.e., one the essence of which is that no derogation from it by treaty is possible? The answer must presumably be that the divergences do not go to the essence of the rule, the elements of it from which it is not permissible to derogate by treaty, but only to the details of its application. Nevertheless the fact that the objection can be raised shows both the artificiality of the process in which the Court found itself engaged in the *Nicaragua* v. *United States* case and the caution with which it is necessary to approach claims that a particular rule is one of *jus cogens*.

CHAPTER IV:

GENERAL PRINCIPLES OF LAW RECOGNIZED BY CIVILIZED NATIONS[397]

1. *Introduction*

No decision of the Court, or indeed of the Permanent Court, has yet been based explicitly upon a principle or rule of law drawn from the

[396] Ibid., p. 94, para. 176.
[397] See Fitzmaurice, this *Year Book*, 27 (1950), pp. 10–11, 18–19, *Collected Edition*, I, pp. 10–11, 18–19.

'general principles of law recognized by civilized nations' referred to in Article 38, paragraph 1 (c), of the Statute.[398] It is comparatively rare for a State to base a claim before the Court on such principles, so that it is correspondingly infrequent for the Court to have occasion to refer to them for the purposes of its decision. Even where referred to by a party to proceedings, the general principles tend to be employed as something of a makeweight or last resort, a supplementary argument in case the contentions based on customary law or treaties fail to convince; with the result that the Court hardly if ever needs to refer to them. On the other hand, individual Members of the Court invoke general principles more frequently: Judge Ammoun was particularly attached to them, though he had strong objections to the use in the Statute of the term 'civilized nations'.[399]

It must be assumed that, save in such exceptional circumstances as those of the *Military and Paramilitary Activities* case, where the Court was debarred by the jurisdictional basis from applying multilateral treaties, all the sources of law referred to in the Statute may be drawn upon for the decision, even though the parties to the case may have based their claims only on particular grounds. There is of course a need to steer carefully between the hazard of judging, or appearing to judge, *ultra petita*, and that of neglecting a provision of law not invoked by the parties, and thus failing to decide 'in accordance with international law'. Yet it would not appear right for any one of the recognized sources to be excluded *a priori*.

It is therefore somewhat puzzling to find the Chamber formed to deal with the *Gulf of Maine* case, when indicating how it proposed to 'ascertain the principles and rules which in general govern the subject of maritime delimitation', stating that it would refer to

conventions (Art. 38, para. 1 (*a*)) and international custom (para. 1 (*b*)), to the

---

[398] A member of the Court has however gone on record, in an extra-judicial capacity, to the following effect:

'The silence observed in this matter by the International Court of Justice or other international tribunals must [not] be misinterpreted as any neglect of the importance of examining the common ground of national systems. However, as far as my experience goes, basic principles common to national legal systems are normally not disputed. The *jus gentium* applied by the Roman *praetor peregrinus* is still a reality. The main question is, however, how a generally accepted principle can provide an appropriate solution in the actual case under consideration. Studies of national legislations which have been submitted to the Court in the past are very helpful in clarifying the concepts and solutions found in national law, but usually they cannot offer the precise criteria for the application and interpretation of international law in the given case. The presentation of the various solutions of national legislations paraphrasing the basic principle involved, would often not be in conformity with the style of a judgment, the reasoning of which must proceed in a continuous chain of thought and argument to the operative part. I admit, however, that it would be welcomed not only by the parties but also by the international legal world if the reasoning of judgments and advisory opinions were to explain that the Court had examined, by comparative methods, the assertion—sometimes baldly stated—that a general principle of law, having a specified meaning and significance, forms part of binding general international law':

Mosler, 'To what extent does the variety of legal systems of the world influence the application of the general principles of law within the meaning of Article 38(1)(c) of the Statute of the International Court of Justice?', *International Law and the Grotian Heritage* (1985), p. 180.

[399] See below, section 6.

definition of which the judicial decisions (para. 1 (*d*)) either of the Court or of arbitration tribunals have already made a substantial contribution.[400]

The omission of Article 38, paragraph 1 (*c*), is pointed, and can only have been deliberate. As we shall see, an attempt to rely on general principles in the field of maritime delimitation had been made unsuccessfully in the *North Sea Continental Shelf* cases; but this would not justify the assumption 15 years later that such principles could necessarily still have nothing to say on the matter.

The approach adopted by the *Gulf of Maine* Chamber would have a curious result in a case in which the Montego Bay Convention was applicable as between the parties. Articles 74 and 83 of the Convention provided for delimitation 'by agreement on the basis of international law, as referred to in Article 38 of the Statute of the International Court of Justice, in order to achieve an equitable solution'. The reference to Article 38 must be taken to be a reference to the whole of that Article,[401] so that the general principles, having been rejected as a source for immediate application, would still come in on the back of an international convention as referred to in paragraph 1 (*a*) of Article 38, paragraph 1.

An aspect of the concept of general principles of law which has perhaps not been sufficiently remarked on is the following. When the Court takes into consideration an alleged rule or principle of law, it is doing so, as it were, retrospectively, in order to measure against it the conduct or the claims of a State. It must however be possible equally to refer to the same rule or principle prospectively: a State which is considering a particular course of action must be able to ascertain whether that course would or would not infringe a rule of law. The general principles contemplated by Article 38, paragraph 1 (*c*), of the Statute are to be derived from, or evidenced by, the consistent provisions of the various municipal legal systems. The legal adviser of a foreign ministry is however unlikely to be a specialist in comparative law; and while, at least in the developed countries, such specialists can be found in the universities, a foreign minister may be reluctant to delay implementing his chosen policy pending the completion of an exhaustive study of comparative legislation and jurisprudence. Paragraph 1 (*c*) of Article 38 was in fact included with an eye to retrospective consultation of general principles; the intention was to enable the Court to fill the gaps in the body of law deriving from convention and custom.[402] It is however fundamental—indeed it is itself one of the general principles recognized by civilized nations—that no one may be condemned for breach of a law which he neither knew of nor could know of.

The conclusion must be that it is insufficient to point to unanimity of

---

[400] *ICJ Reports*, 1984, pp. 290–1, para. 83.

[401] Or rather, the whole of paragraph 1, since a solution *ex aequo et bono* under paragraph 2 is by definition not a decision 'on the basis of international law'.

[402] *Proceedings of the Advisory Committee of Jurists*, p. 336.

municipal legal systems on a particular point unless the rule which it is sought to derive from them possesses such a degree of reasonableness and appropriateness for application on the international plane for a State which acts in a contrary manner at least to have been conscious of a possibility that a rule of law might point in the opposite direction. Put another way, the point is that the Court will be slow to recognize the existence of a general principle of law, even if there is good evidence of unanimity of municipal legal systems, unless it is such that it would be likely to guide or inspire State action.

Some consideration of this kind may have underlain the only decision during the period under review in which the Court ruled directly on a claim or assertion that a given rule could be derived from the general principles of law. In its judgment in 1966 in the *South West Africa* cases the Court was examining what it referred to as the 'necessity' argument:

> The gist of the argument is that since the Council had no means of imposing its views on the mandatory, and since no advisory opinion it might obtain from the Court would be binding on the latter, the mandate could have been flouted at will. Hence, so the contention goes, it was essential, as an ultimate safeguard or security for the performance of the sacred trust, that each member of the League could be deemed to have a legal right or interest in that matter and, in the last resort, be able to take direct action relative to it.[403]

The Court rejected this argument on grounds not here material: but it also ruled that it could not be upheld on the basis of the general principles of law.

> Looked at in another way moreover, the argument amounts to a plea that the Court should allow the equivalent of an '*actio popularis*', or right resident in any member of a community to take legal action in vindication of a public interest. But although a right of this kind may be known to certain municipal systems of law, it is not known to international law as it stands at present: nor is the Court able to regard it as imported by the 'general principles of law' referred to in Article 38, paragraph 1 (*c*), of its Statute.[404]

It is not easy to interpret this laconic ruling. It could be taken as an indication that a right cannot be regarded as reflecting a general principle of law if it is only 'known to certain municipal systems of law', but not to all. The tone of the passage rather suggests, however, that the Court would not have accepted the *actio popularis* as part of international law even if it had been universally recognized in municipal systems. A number of better reasons can be thought of for why the argument based on Article 38, paragraph 1

---

[403] *ICJ Reports*, 1966, p. 46, para. 85.

[404] Ibid., p. 47, para. 88. For the views of Fitzmaurice as to the alternative institutions of international law serving the same end, see 'The Future of Public International Law and the International Legal System in the Circumstances of Today' (Institut de droit international, Special Report, 1973), pp. 131–2.

(c), fails to convince;[405] and it is more likely that the Court, possibly influenced by a combination of these reasons, and not satisfied of the 'transferable' character of the alleged rule, thought the argument so devoid of merit as not to require any detailed answer.

The Court did not, as a result of the limited ground upon which it based its decision, have to deal with the contention of the applicants as to the existence in international law, on the basis of general principles of law, of a norm of non-discrimination and non-segregation (see section 3, below).

2. *Nature and Derivation of General Principles of Law*

It is fairly well established that the general principles contemplated by Article 38, paragraph 1 (c), of the Statute are at least primarily those which reveal themselves in the consistent solutions to a particular problem adopted in the various systems of municipal law—what Mr Elihu Root called, during the discussions of the 1920 Committee of Jurists, those which were 'accepted by all nations *in foro domestico*'.[406] It is necessary, though not always easy, to distinguish these principles from, on the one hand, what Sorensen has called 'les principes fondamentaux de la structure du droit international',[407] which were the subject of a previous section of these articles,[408] and from, on the other hand, mere arguments from analogy by reference to institutions or rules found in one or more systems of municipal law.[409] These distinctions were the subject of much argument between the parties in the *Right of Passage* case.

A more difficult and controversial question is whether these latter principles are also included in the category defined by Article 38, paragraph 1 (c), of the Statute.[410] Fitzmaurice expressed the view that they were so included; he emphasized that States parties to the Statute have 'duly consented to the application of those principles by the Court', even though he

---

[405] In so far as the matter is one of procedure, there is controversy as to whether there exist general principles of law in the field of procedure: see pp. 126–7 and n. 464, below. The radically different nature of judicial jurisdiction in the international and municipal spheres militates against a transfer or analogy from the one to the other. There must be doubt whether a general principle of this kind, assuming it to exist, can prevail over a specific provision in the Mandate.

[406] *Procès-verbaux* of the Committee, p. 335.

[407] *Les Sources du droit international*, p. 116. The interpretation of Article 38(1)(c) as restricted to principles derivable from municipal law recognition does not of course signify the exclusion of other general principles from the corpus of law applicable by the Court. Mosler, following Anzilotti, observes that the more basic principles need no transformation into international law, whereas the principles commonly accepted in municipal systems do need to be so transformed, hence the inclusion of Article 38(1)(c) in the Statute: 'Bedeutungswandel in der Anwendung "der van den zivilisierten Staaten anerkannten allgemeinen Rechtgrundsätze" ', *Pensamiento juridico y sociedad internacional* (*Mélanges Truyol Serra*) (Madrid, 1986), vol. 2, p. 823.

[408] This *Year Book*, 60 (1989), pp. 7–76.

[409] Also discussed in the previous article: this *Year Book*, 60 (1989), pp. 127–8.

[410] Or, to put the problem in terms expressed by Bin Cheng, whether the principles of Article 38(1)(c) are principles of natural law: *General Principles of Law as applied by International Courts and Tribunals* (1953), p. 3.

also regards them as 'constituting a separate source of international law independent of the specific consent of States'.[411] The question has attracted a vast literature[412] which it would be inappropriate to examine here. For our purposes, it is sufficient to note first that the Court itself has not, either in the period under examination or previously, given any specific indication of a view on the nature of the 'general principles', and secondly that the Court has applied general principles of a broad kind not derived from analysis of municipal legal systems without making any reference to Article 38, paragraph 1 (c).

A number of examples of such principles was discussed in the first article in this series.[413] In addition, an aspect of the case of the *Temple of Preah Vihear* may be cited. The view has been expressed by Verdross[414] that the Court was in that case applying a general principle of law, within the meaning of Article 38, paragraph 1 (c), in the following passage:

> It is an established rule of law that the plea of error cannot be allowed as an element vitiating consent if the party advancing it contributed by its own conduct to the error, or could have avoided it, or if the circumstances were such as to put that party on notice of a possible error.[415]

Verdross considers that it would be very difficult, if not impossible, to show that this principle is backed by international custom; and therefore considers that the Court had recourse to a general principle of law. Yet, even bearing in mind the Court's reticence in referring to municipal law,[416] it is striking that there is here no suggestion that the principle is one derived from the common experience of domestic legal systems. In marked contrast Judge Alfaro in the same case asserted that 'the principle of the binding effect of a State's own acts with regard to rights in dispute' was a general principle of law since it was 'known to the world since the days of the Romans'.[417]

---

[411] 'The Future of Public International Law and of the International Legal System in the Circumstances of Today' (Institut de droit international, Special Report, 1973), p. 130. An interesting suggestion made by Judge Mosler is that Article 38, paragraph 1(c), restricts the Court, and possibly other judicial bodies, to the category of principles there referred to, but that 'Es ist denkbar, dass es Grundsätze gibt, die in der Völkerrechtsordnung allgemein gelten, ohne dass sie zu denjeningen gehören, die Internationale Gerichte anwenden' ('Bedeutungswandel in der Anwendung "der von den zivilisierten Staaten anerkannten allegemeinen Rechtsgründsätze" ', *Pensamiento juridico y sociedad internacional* (*Mélanges Truyol Serra*) (1986), vol. 2, pp. 816–17). This however would seem to conflict with the Court's duty to 'decide in accordance with international law'.

[412] A useful list will be found at the beginning of a valuable recent survey of the problem: Lammers, 'General Principles of Law Recognized by Civilized Nations', *Essays on the Development of the International Legal Order* (*Mélanges Panhuys*) (1980), p. 53.

[413] This *Year Book*, 60 (1989), pp. 7–76.

[414] 'Les Principes généraux du droit dans le système de sources de droit international public', *Mélanges Guggenheim* (1968), pp. 529–30.

[415] *ICJ Reports*, 1962, p. 26.

[416] Cf. Mosler, quoted in n. 398, above.

[417] *ICJ Reports*, 1962, pp. 42–3.

The present article will therefore be based on the working hypothesis that Article 38, paragraph 1(c), refers only to general principles derived from national legal systems, not to the broader and more fundamental principles already discussed in the first of these articles.

Although the categories of, for example, customary law and general principles are clearly distinguishable in theory, there may well be some overlapping in content, so that a particular rule of law might be attributed convincingly to either of these categories. A rule which can boast an unimpeachable pedigree in custom and practice of States may at the same time correspond closely to a rule found in the majority, if not all, of municipal systems. This phenomenon, a tribute to the practical utility and intellectual satisfactoriness of the rule, is in fact the essential justification of such general principles as a source. If one were to reverse the hierarchy of sources in Article 38, paragraph 1, of the Statute, and analyse positive law in terms of general principles distilled from municipal law, only falling back on custom where municipal law support was lacking, it might prove surprising how infrequently such fall-back was unavoidable. Thus Judge Ammoun was able to contend that so well established a principle as the obligation to make reparation for injury caused by fault, besides being 'one of the traditional bases of law', was 'one, if not indeed the most important, of the principles common to nations in the sense of Article 38, paragraph 1(c), of the Court's Statute'.[418] He was also prepared to consider (but rejected) the possibility that the rule of diplomatic protection was derived from such a general principle.[419] In the *Certain Expenses* case, Sir Percy Spender discussed the principle of interpretation of an agreement by subsequent conduct of the parties as a matter of universal municipal law, and continued: 'That conduct on the part of both parties to a treaty should be considered on the same footing is incontestable'.[420] In the jurisdictional phase of the *Nicaragua* v. *United States* case, Judge Mosler specifically referred to acquisitive prescription as having the status of a general principle of law within the meaning of Article 38, paragraph 1(c), of the Statute.[421]

Reference should also be made to Judge Dillard's view in the *Namibia* case that in treaty law, where a long-term engagement is subjected to unexpected interruption,

emphasis in attempting a reasonable interpretation and construction of its meaning and the obligations it imposes shifts from a textual analysis to one which stresses the object and purpose of the engagement in light of the total context in which the engagement was located.

---

[418] Separate opinion in *Application for Review of Judgment No. 158 of the United Nations Administrative Tribunal, ICJ Reports*, 1973, p. 247. Similarly for the principle that costs follow the event: ibid., p. 250.

[419] Separate opinion in *Barcelona Traction, ICJ Reports*, 1970, pp. 300–1.

[420] Separate opinion in *Certain Expenses of the United Nations, ICJ Reports*, 1962, p. 190.

[421] *ICJ Reports*, 1984, p. 464.

Judge Dillard continues

This generalization can be amply supported by recourse to 'the general principles of law recognized by civilized nations' as revealed in the application of doctrines of impossibility and frustration to long-term engagements.[422]

3. *The Process of Analogy or 'Transfer' of Municipal Principle: the* South West Africa *cases*

A question going to the fundamental nature of the general principles contemplated by Article 38 arose in the *South West Africa* cases; it did not come to be treated in the judgment, but was discussed by Judge Tanaka. The applicants in those cases contended that there existed in international law a norm of non-discrimination, which the respondents had breached; and they derived it from, *inter alia*, the general principles of law recognized by civilized nations. It was suggested that one could

regard the presence of laws and regulations against social discrimination and segregation, in the municipal systems of virtually every State, as establishing, by comparative law analysis, an essential precondition for the assertion of the norm of non-discrimination and non-separation as a 'general principle of law' within the meaning of Article 38 (1)(c).[423]

Judge *ad hoc* van Wyk dealt with this contention robustly: apart from denying the existence of a generally accepted norm of non-discrimination in municipal systems, he pointed out that Article 38, paragraph 1(c),

does not authorize the application of the laws of civilized nations, it limits the Court to 'the general principles of law' of these nations. It certainly does not mean that by legislating on particular domestic matters a majority of civilized nations could compel a minority to introduce similar legislation.[424]

The argument of South Africa on the point was however rather more complex, and—it is suggested—more convincing. It contended that 'this suggested application of a principle by civilized nations is not a correct analogy and application as contemplated by Article 38 (1)(c)'.[425] In the view of South Africa, the general principles of law

are taken from the realm of municipal law, they are elevated by analogy from that law into international law relationships and applied there; and they are applied not because they in themselves define a right or an obligation or bring about the origination of a right or an obligation on the part of a State, a subject of the international law. They relate to the definition of legal relationships in domestic law . . . and from those relationships they are then taken by way of analogy [and] applied in the sphere of relationships as they obtain in international law . . . [426]

---

[422] *ICJ Reports*, 1971, p. 157.
[423] *Pleadings*, vol. 9, p. 353 (Gross).
[424] *ICJ Reports*, 1966, p. 170, para. 56.
[425] *Pleadings*, vol. 10, p. 47 (de Villiers).
[426] *Pleadings*, vol. 10, p. 44 (de Villiers).

The point is perhaps a subtle one, but important. One does not have to be an uncompromising dualist to accept that the function of international law is to regulate relations between the subjects of international law— States, international organizations, etc.,—and the function of a given system of municipal law is to govern relations between the natural and corporate persons who are subject to it. When having recourse to municipal law, in search of a principle which may be sufficiently general to warrant its being treated as 'accepted' by nations, the principle must be defined in a pure form: the individual subjects of law between whom it operates must be replaced, as in an algebraic equation, by x and y. Then, in the context of international law, x and y may be given the values 'State A' and 'State B', or 'State' and 'international organization', for example, and the congruity of the principle assessed.[427] The argument of the applicants in the *South West Africa* cases represented a short-circuiting of this analysis: it involved transferring the alleged principle to the international plane with the subjects of municipal law still in place, as it were. Such an argument might serve to support an asserted rule of customary law—if there were sufficient consistent practice and evidence of *opinio juris*—but is not appropriate to recourse to general principles of law.

The approach expounded by South Africa indeed appears to represent the classic view of the mechanism of recourse to general principles of law; and it was accepted even by Judge Tanaka, who nevertheless considered that the norm of non-discrimination, as a matter of international law, could be based upon Article 38, paragraph 1(*c*).

If we limit the application of Article 38, paragraph 1(*c*), to a strict analogical extension of certain principles of municipal law, we must recognize that the contention of the Respondent is well-founded.[428]

If Judge Tanaka was nevertheless able to uphold the contentions of the applicants as to the norm of non-discrimination, it was because he adopted a wider concept of 'general principles', containing a much more marked element of natural law.

This aspect of the *South West Africa* cases emphasizes the important role of analogy in the application of Article 38, paragraph 1(*c*). It is essential to consider the suggested principle against the whole pattern of relationships in the municipal system, and then to test the principle by superimposing it on the analogous pattern on the international plane. Possibly the only case in which provisions of municipal law could be relied on as embodying 'general principles' as they stand, and not by way of analogy, would be if such provisions had been incorporated in a multilateral treaty. It has been

---

[427] Cf. the argument of South African counsel that the alleged norm would mean, on the international plane, that an international organization 'is not entitled to differentiate as between various nations on the basis of their belonging to one race or the other, but that all nations are to be treated equally': *Pleadings*, vol. 10, pp. 47–8 (de Villiers).

[428] *ICJ Reports*, 1966, pp. 296–7.

suggested[429] that the Court's reliance, in the *Nicaragua* v. *United States* case, on common Article 3 of the Geneva Conventions could be justified as an appeal to 'general principles' under Article 38, paragraph 1(c), in view of the fact that some of the provisions of Article 3 'are rooted in national legal systems'. This is, however, to stretch the concepts of Article 38, paragraph 1(c), to their limits.

The distinction between the use of municipal law analogies and the identification of a 'general principle recognized by the civilized nations' may perhaps be practically a question of degree. For the purposes of analogy no widespread consistency of municipal systems is required: it suffices to suggest that the current problem in international law is analogous to one which arises in the municipal sphere, and that the municipal solution is one which recommends itself for disposing of the international law problem. Thus Judge Dillard in the *Appeal relating to the Jurisdiction of the ICAO Council* relied on jurisprudence of United States courts in support of his views on the question of recourse to a compromissory clause in a treaty alleged to have been terminated.[430] Although he referred in passing in this connection to Article 38, paragraph 1(c), of the Statute, his argument is simply one of analogy to a particular legal system, not an appeal to general principles of law shared by municipal law systems. On the other hand, when Judge Schwebel, citing Anzilotti, relies in his dissenting opinion in the *Nicaragua* v. *United States* case on the rule *inadimplenti non est adimplendum* as a general principle of law,[431] this is clearly the kind of case contemplated by Article 38, paragraph 1(c), even though no specific municipal laws are cited. A general principle, however, is demonstrated to be such by the ubiquity or near-ubiquity of its presence in municipal systems. It is not, it appears, required to be universally present;[432] in the view of Judge Tanaka, 'the recognition of a principle by civilized nations . . . does not mean recognition by *all* civilized nations'.[433] Nevertheless, the existence in one or more municipal systems of a solution to the problem which is attributable to a quite different principle undermines the credibility of the principle asserted as a *general* principle.

---

[429] Meron, 'The Geneva Conventions as Customary Law', *American Journal of International Law*, 81 (1987), p. 357.

[430] *ICJ Reports*, 1972, pp. 109–14.

[431] *ICJ Reports*, 1986, p. 381, para. 240.

[432] It has been suggested that a principle present in all the municipal systems of a particular group of States could be applied, by analogy to regional customary law, in a dispute between two States members of that group. Akehurst has pointed out that

'Much of the difficulty of proving general principles of law could be avoided if international tribunals confined themselves to applying general principles of law which were common to the disputing parties, without enquiring whether these principles existed in the law of other States': 'Equity and General Principles of Law', *International and Comparative Law Quarterly*, 25 (1976), p. 824.

For the ICJ, however, the reference in Article 38(1)(c) to 'civilized nations' can only be interpreted as general in scope.

[433] *ICJ Reports*, 1966, p. 299.

4. *General Principles in the Hierarchy of Sources: the* Right of Passage *case*

In the *Right of Passage* case, Portugal presented what is perhaps one of the clearest examples in the case law of the Court of a reliance on general principles of law, claiming that

the municipal laws of the civilized nations are unanimous in recognizing that the holder of enclaved land has a right, for purposes of access to it, to pass through adjoining land; whereas it is rare to find a principle more clearly emerging from the universal practice of States *in foro domestico* and more perfectly meeting the requirements of Article 38, paragraph 1(*c*), of the Statute of the Court.[434]

In support of this claim, Portugal presented a comparative study of 64 different legal systems,[435] of which 61, in the view of the author of the study, provided for rights of access to enclaved land. Portugal however based its claim primarily on general and special custom, and the Court, having upheld the substance of the claim on the basis of special custom, found it unnecessary to go further: having arrived at that conclusion, 'the Court does not consider it necessary to examine whether general international custom or the general principles of law recognized by civilized nations may lead to the same result'.[436]

The Court did not however overlook the possibility that examination of the general principles might lead to a *different* result. The claim of Portugal to passage of troops, armed police and ammunition had not been upheld, inasmuch as the Court had found that passage in these respects was subject to prior permission by India; it was arguable that the right of access to enclaved territory deriving from the general principles of law was not so limited. The Court observed however that its finding on this point

renders it unnecessary to determine whether or not, in the absence of the practice that actually prevailed, general international custom or the general principles of law recognized by civilized nations could have been relied on by Portugal in support of its claims to a right of passage in respect of these categories.[437]

Emphasizing the importance of practice in the particular historical and geographical context, the Court continued:

Where therefore the Court finds a practice clearly established between two States which was accepted by the Parties as governing the relations between them, the Court must attribute decisive effect to that practice for the purpose of determining their specific rights and obligations. Such a particular practice must prevail over any general rules.[438]

As has been observed above,[439] the finding of the Court as to the passage of troops and armed police was not a finding of the absence of a customary

[434] Portuguese final submissions, *ICJ Reports*, 1960, pp. 11–12.
[435] *Pleadings*, vol. 1, pp. 714 ff.; vol. 2, pp. 858 ff.
[436] *ICJ Reports*, 1960, p. 43.
[437] Ibid.
[438] Ibid., p. 44.
[439] Above, p. 105.

right, but of the existence of a custom requiring permission; and on that basis any contrary rule that might have been derived from the recognized general principles would clearly have been excluded. This aspect of the case however also points up a particular difficulty in transferring rules from the national to the international level.

The intellectual process involved in Portugal's claim corresponded to that argued by South Africa in the *South West Africa* cases, discussed above, which, it is suggested, is the true mechanism of Article 38, paragraph 1(c): the transfer to the international plane of a principle governing relationships between subjects of law on the domestic plane, and fitting it to the relationships of the subjects of international law. However, as India pointed out in argument, the relationship of the owner of an enclaved piece of land with his neighbours is not the same as the relationship between sovereign States: sovereignty is not mere ownership of territory. Even if municipal laws agreed in recognizing a right of way to an enclave over adjoining land which was usable for all purposes,[440] none of the purposes for which the owner of the 'dominant tenement' might use it would have the same impact on the rights of the owner of the 'servient tenement' as would the passage of armed troops on the sovereignty of India over its territory.

Judge Wellington Koo, the only member of the Court to deal with the point, saw no difficulty. In his separate opinion, he found Portugal's claim fully justified, including the claim for the passage of troops and armed police, on the basis of a local custom; he went on however to state 'additional grounds' for upholding the full extent of Portugal's claim. In his view, the problem was one of reconciling the sovereignty of India over its territory with Portugal's sovereignty over the enclaves, to which the passage of troops and armed police was indispensable.

The existence of two conflicting rights, however, is not an uncommon phenomenon in international law. In the complexities of intercourse between nations such a situation is often unavoidable. It is, however, not an intractable problem; its solution only calls for mutual adaptation and adjustment. By reference to, and application of, the general principles of law as stipulated in Article 38, paragraph 1(c), of the Statute, as well as to customary international law, similar situations have found solutions in the past.

In municipal law, as disclosed by a comparative study by Professor Max Rheinstein, the right of access to enclaved property is always sanctioned. Admittedly, there are important distinctions between a right of passage of an international enclave and that of an enclaved land owned by a private individual. But in whatever mould municipal law may be cast, in whatever technical framework it may be installed, in harmony with national tradition or out of preference for a particular legal fiction, the underlying principle of recognition of such a right, in its essence, is the same. It is the principle of justice founded on reason.[441]

---

[440] Which was, apparently, not so: see the limitations on the 'noodweg' in the Roman-Dutch law of South Africa, *Right of Passage, Pleadings*, vol. 1, p. 716.

[441] *ICJ Reports*, 1960, p. 66.

5. *Eclipse of General Principle by Conflicting Principle of International Law: the* North Sea Continental Shelf *cases*

The contention of the Federal Republic of Germany in the *North Sea Continental Shelf* cases, that delimitation of the continental shelf should be such as to allot to each riparian State its 'just and equitable share', a contention initially of somewhat uncertain provenance,[442] became, from the Reply onward, based on an appeal to the general principles referred to in Article 38, paragraph 1(*c*), of the Statute.[443] The German pleadings were not supported on this point by any study of comparative law, on the lines of that produced by Portugal in the *Right of Passage* case, a deficiency which its opponents did not fail to point out. It might in fact have been difficult to supply such a study: while the underlying idea of *justitia distributiva* undoubtedly plays a part in many if not all legal systems, it is not apparent what specific area of municipal law could have been regarded as analogous to the right of riparian States to or over the continental shelf.

The Court's rejection of the Federal Republic's thesis was however not grounded on any refusal to recognize the existence in municipal law of such a concept of a 'just and equitable share'. The essential reason for its decision was that the Court regarded the concept as inconsistent with what the Court found to be the nature of continental shelf rights as established by customary law.

More important is the fact that the doctrine of the just and equitable share appears to be wholly at variance with what the Court entertains no doubt is the most fundamental of all the rules of law relating to the continental shelf, enshrined in Article 2 of the 1958 Geneva Convention, though quite independent of it,— namely that the rights of the coastal State in respect of the area of continental shelf that constitutes a natural prolongation of its land territory into and under the sea exist *ipso facto* and *ab initio*, by virtue of its sovereignty over the land, and as an extension of it in an exercise of sovereign rights for the purpose of exploring the sea bed and exploiting its natural resources.

. . .

It follows that even in such a situation as that of the North Sea, the notion of apportioning an as yet undelimited area, considered as a whole (which underlies the doctrine of the just and equitable share), is quite foreign to, and inconsistent with, the basic concept of continental shelf entitlement, according to which the process of delimitation is essentially one of drawing a boundary line between areas which already appertain to one or other of the States affected. The delimitation itself must indeed be equitably effected, but it cannot have as its object the awarding of an equitable share, or indeed of a share, as such, at all,—for the fundamental concept involved does not admit of there being anything undivided to share out.[444]

The process at work may be seen as the ousting of a possible general prin-

---

[442] Though the German Memorial does refer to it as 'a generally recognized principle inherent in all legal systems, including the legal system of the international community': *Pleadings*, vol. 1, p. 30.

[443] *Pleadings*, vol. 1, pp. 392–3.

[444] *ICJ Reports*, 1969, p. 22, paras. 19–20.

ciple by a rule of customary law, on the basis either of *lex specialis derogat generali*, or of the hierarchy of sources established by Article 38 of the Statute.[445] It may also, and perhaps better, be seen as rejection of an appeal to an alleged principle recognized in municipal law, of a very high degree of generality, which may well have a role to play in international law, on the ground that it is, in the particular field considered, inconsistent with the whole nature of the legal concept at stake.

For Judge Ammoun, in fact, the decision of the Court was not merely not a rejection of general principles of the kind referred to in Article 38, paragraph 1(c); it was based upon such a principle, though not exactly that invoked by the Federal Republic. Judge Ammoun put the question

Is there a general principle of law recognized by the nations from which would follow a rule to the effect that the continental shelf could be delimited equitably between the Parties?[446]

His reply was that there was such a principle: the principle of equity; and he buttressed his view with references to the common law, Muslim law, Chinese law, Soviet law, Hindu law and the law of other African and Asian countries.[447] It is an impressive performance.

6. The Significance of the Expression 'Civilized Nations': Philosophy of Judge Ammoun

In his separate opinion in the *North Sea Continental Shelf* cases, Judge Ammoun took strong exception to the continued presence in the Statute of the post-war Court of the reference to recognition of general principles 'by civilized nations'. In his view, the use of the term 'is incompatible with the relevant provisions of the United Nations Charter',[448] in particular the reference there to the 'sovereign equality' of the member States.[449] His objection is related to the former Europe-centred nature of all discussion or statement of the rules of international law, from which, in his view, the terms of Article 38, paragraph 1(c), were inherited.

Thus it is that certain nations, to whose legal systems allusion was made above, which did not form part of the limited concert of States which did the law-making, up to the first decades of the 20th century, for the whole of the international community, today participate in the determination or elaboration of the general principles of law, contrary to what is improperly stated by Article 38, paragraph 1(c), of the Court's Statute.[450]

[445] In the *Right of Passage* case Judge Moreno Quintana stated that Article 38, paragraph 1, 'establishes a legal order of precedence in the application of sources of international law', but added the mysterious gloss that 'the validity of a general principle may take the place of international custom, and the existence of international custom the place of a treaty' (*ICJ Reports*, 1960, p. 90).
[446] *ICJ Reports*, 1969, p. 135, para. 34.
[447] Ibid., pp. 139–40, para. 38.
[448] Ibid., p. 132.
[449] Ibid., p. 133.
[450] Ibid., pp. 133–4. See also the same judge's separate opinion in the *Barcelona Traction* case, *ICJ Reports*, 1970, p. 309.

This sensitivity on behalf of non-European, and particularly developing, nations is understandable, but may, it seems, rest on a misunderstanding. Judge Ammoun's practical proposal is to read the text of the paragraph as though the word 'civilized' were omitted; but it is suggested that this is unnecessary. In the first place, the only intention of the inclusion of the word was surely to limit consideration of municipal systems to those which are sufficiently developed to reveal the extent to which they share common underlying principles,[451] rather as in the *Abu Dhabi* arbitration[452] it was necessary to exclude the local law simply because that law had nothing to say on the subject. Secondly, the reference to 'civilized nations' is surely a classic case for application of what has been referred to, in the first of these articles, as 'intertemporal *renvoi*'.[453] The category of 'civilized nations' was not defined once and for all in 1920; it remains open, and subject (at least in theory) to fluctuation. There is therefore no difficulty in accepting Judge Ammoun's thesis that States which did not exist in 1920, or States which existed but were regarded as insignificant in relation to the development of international law, can and should be taken into account for purposes of application of Article 38, paragraph 1(c). Nor could it be complained that they are not so taken into account: the comparative survey presented by Portugal in the *Right of Passage* case includes, for example, Ghana, Burma, Pakistan, India, China, Turkey and the Philippines.[454]

7. Renvoi *to Municipal Law distinguished from Application of General Principles: the* Barcelona Traction *case*

The reference to municipal law in the *Barcelona Traction* case has already been discussed in the first of these articles.[455] It may however be asked whether the Court was not there also basing itself on the general principles of law contemplated by Article 38, paragraph 1(c), of the Statute, without expressly saying so, when, for example, it said that

> It is to rules generally accepted by municipal legal systems which recognize the limited company whose capital is represented by shares, and not to the municipal law of a particular State, that international law refers.[456]

---

[451] While the word 'civilized' clearly derives from Baron Descamps' proposed reference to the 'legal conscience of the civilized nations', its incorporation in Mr Root's revised draft gives it quite a different coloration: cf. de Lapradelle in *Procès-verbaux*, p. 335, and Verdross:

'En recourant à cette formule, le Comité n'a pas, cependant, voulu établir une distinction entre les diverses nations; il a simplement exprimé l'idée que ces principes doivent avoir une base objective dans la conscience juridique concordante des peuples': 'Les Principes généraux du droit dans le système des sources de droit international public', *Mélanges Guggenheim* (1968), p. 523.

[452] *Petroleum Development (Trucial Coast) Ltd.* v. *Sheikh of Abu Dhabi* (1951), 18 ILR 144. On this, see the illuminating comments of Friedmann, 'The Uses of "General Principles" in the Development of International Law', *American Journal of International Law*, 57 (1963), pp. 283–4.

[453] This *Year Book*, 60 (1989), pp. 135 ff.

[454] *Right of Passage, Pleadings*, vol. 1, pp. 714 ff.

[455] This *Year Book*, 60 (1989), pp. 117–25.

[456] *ICJ Reports*, 1970, p. 37, para. 50.

It is suggested that this is not so: that the judgment cannot be explained on the basis of an appeal to Article 38, paragraph 1(c).

The essence of a recognized general principle contemplated by that text is that it is a principle taken over by and incorporated into international law, so as to regulate the conduct of States or other subjects of international law, because it can be regarded, on the basis of the universal or near universal testimony of municipal legal systems, as part and parcel of universal justice. The logic of the *Barcelona Traction* judgment is however different from this: it begins by defining the question to be asked as follows:

has a right of Belgium been violated on account of its nationals having suffered infringement of their rights as shareholders in a company not of Belgian nationality?[457]

Thus the violation of a right of Belgium is dependent on the infringement of the rights 'as shareholders' of its nationals. Rights 'as shareholders' can however only exist as rights of municipal law; as the Court observes, it has to take account of 'the relevant institutions of municipal law' because 'there are no corresponding institutions of international law to which the Court could resort'.[458] Similarly the Court distinguished the position of the company from that of the shareholders:

International law may not, in some fields, provide specific rules in particular cases. In the concrete situation, the company against which allegedly unlawful acts were directed is expressly vested with a right, whereas no such right is specifically provided for the shareholder in respect of those acts. Thus the position of the company rests on a positive rule of both municipal and international law. As to the shareholder, while he has certain rights expressly provided for him by municipal law as referred to in paragraph 42 above, appeal can, in the circumstances of the present case, only be made to the silence of international law. Such silence scarcely admits of interpretation in favour of the shareholder.[459]

Could the Court have based its decision in the case on a general principle of law derived from municipal experience? It seems doubtful whether this could have been done. The central point of difficulty in the case was the relationship between the rights of Belgium to exercise diplomatic protection and the rights (or interests) of the Belgian shareholders alleged to have been infringed. Certainly the Court's thinking seems to have been influenced by the idea that it is generally accepted in municipal systems that when wrong is done to a corporate body, e.g., a company, only that body can seek legal redress, not its members individually. But a *transference* of such a rule to the international plane would produce something much more like the rule in the *Reparation for Injuries* case, that an international organization, rather than its individual members, can seek redress for injury done to the servant of the organization in that capacity. The difficulty is essen-

---

[457] Ibid., pp. 32–3, para. 35.
[458] Ibid., p. 37, para. 50.
[459] Ibid., p. 38, para. 52.

tially the same as that which arose in the *South West Africa* cases in respect of the alleged norm of non-discrimination: to try to import a rule of municipal law into international law without fitting it to the pattern of relationships of the subjects of international law is to distort the mechanism of application of general principles.

8. *General Principles in Procedural Law: the Maltese Intervention in* Continental Shelf (Tunisia/Libyan Arab Jamahiriya)

In support of its application for permission to intervene in the case concerning the *Continental Shelf (Tunisia/Libyan Arab Jamahiriya)*, Malta presented to the Court, in the course of the oral proceedings in respect of that intervention, a consultation by Professor Walter Habschied on 'Les conditions de l'intervention volontaire dans un procès civil', in which the author carried out 'une étude comparative sur la notion, les formes et les conditions de *l'intervention volontaire* dans le procès civil'.[460] The purpose of this study, which covered systematically the various municipal procedures belonging to the principal legal systems of the world, was

fournir des éléments pouvant contribuer à éclairer le contexte général dans lequel le Statut de la Cour internationale de justice, et en particulier les articles 62 et 63, a été élaboré et à faciliter l'interprétation de ces dispositions.[460]

Viewed in this light, the purpose would appear to be not so much to appeal to the general principles of law contemplated by Article 38, paragraph 1(*c*), of the Statute as to interpret the term 'intervene' in the Statute in the light of the systems of municipal law with which the draftsmen in 1920 might be supposed to have been familiar.[461] At the hearings, however, counsel for Malta went considerably further than this; he derived six propositions from the comparative-law study, all designed to show that Malta's application ought to succeed.[462]

Counsel for Libya, while referring to French law in support of his contentions, refused to see any usefulness in the comparative-law study offered by Malta, stating roundly that

En réalité, je ne crois pas qu'en matière de procès il y ait réellement de véritables principes généraux communs aux différents droits internes qui auraient exercé en tant que tels, une influence marquée sur le développement du procès international.[463]

In this the speaker, Professor Malintoppi, was in fact aligning himself with his compatriot, Sereni, who had already attacked Bin Cheng for including

---

[460] *Pleadings*, vol. 3, p. 459.

[461] It is curious therefore that the consultation does not attempt, in accordance with the intertemporal law principle, to analyse the various systems as they stood in 1920, but rather takes them as they stood in 1981.

[462] *Pleadings*, vol. 3, pp. 341–4.

[463] Ibid., p. 393.

procedural principles among the general principles of law contemplated by Article 38 of the Statute.[464]

Neither the Court nor any of the judges who appended opinions to the judgment referred in any way to the possible relevance of municipal-law analogies or the applicability of Article 38, paragraph 1(c), of the Statute. At most, one might see the Court's rejection of 'the direct yet limited form of participation in the subject-matter of the proceedings' sought by Malta,[465] and of the notion that an interest in the applicable principles might be sufficient to justify an intervention,[466] as indicating that the comparative-law analysis, and the arguments based on it, failed to carry weight. Whether this was because, in matters of intervention, the procedural background at the international level offers too little analogy with that of municipal systems, or because of a more far-reaching doubt as to the existence of general principles in the procedural sphere, must remain a matter for speculation.

CHAPTER V:

SUBSIDIARY SOURCES: JUDICIAL DECISIONS

The 'subsidiary means for the determination of rules of law' contemplated by Article 38, paragraph 1(d), of the Statute of the Court, namely 'judicial decisions and the teachings of the most highly qualified publicists of the various nations', did not afford matter for comment by Fitzmaurice in the decisions of the Court during the period reviewed by his articles. During the period now under review, while it is still the case that no decision has been wholly or partly based upon such sources—indeed, on account of their subsidiary nature this is hardly to be expected—the influence of at least some arbitral decisions has become more overt. As to doctrine, the Court has maintained its policy of not quoting or referring to individual writers in its decisions, though Judges in separate and dissenting opinions have continued to make explicit their debt to 'the teachings of the most highly qualified publicists'.

The fact that Article 38 of the Statute prefaces its reference to 'judicial decisions' with the words 'subject to the provisions of Article 59' signifies that the decisions contemplated must include previous decisions of the Court itself (and of the Permanent Court of International Justice).[467] Also relevant may be decisions of municipal courts, and of international arbitral tribunals (including mixed claims commissions, etc.).

---

[464] See Bin Cheng, *General Principles of Law as applied by International Courts and Tribunals* (Stevens, 1953), Part IV, *passim*; Sereni, 'Principi generali di diritto e processo internazionale', *Quaderni della Rivista di diritto internazionale* (1955).

[465] *ICJ Reports*, 1981, p. 19, para. 34; cf. Habschied consultation, *Pleadings*, vol. 3, p. 478.

[466] On this cf. the recent decision of the Chamber in the *Land, Island and Maritime Frontier Dispute (El Salvador/Honduras), ICJ Reports*, 1990, p. 124, para. 76.

[467] In this sense, Judge van Wyk in *South West Africa, ICJ Reports*, 1962, p. 576.

1. *Decisions of Municipal Courts*

Although a number of references may be found in Judges' separate and dissenting opinions during the period under review to decisions of municipal courts, on examination they prove not to be applications of Article 38, paragraph 1(*d*). That text contemplates that a decision of a national court may be a subsidiary means 'for the determination of rules of law', i.e., rules of international law; the finding of a municipal court on a problem of public international law arising before it may be good evidence of the existence of a rule, particularly a rule created by practice as one of customary law. This is intellectually distinguishable from, on the one hand, the decision of a municipal court as an act of State practice contributing to the creation of a rule of customary law; and, on the other hand, from such a decision as an element of evidence of the existence of a 'general principle of law recognized by civilized nations', or as a valuable analogy which may assist in defining an otherwise amorphous rule based on another formal source.

Reference to municipal case law in the context of the 'general principles of law' and as sources of analogy has already been discussed in these articles.[468] An example of reliance on a municipal court decision as an element of State practice, in a field in which customary international law was in a state of flux or development, can be found in Judge Ammoun's reference, in the *North Sea* cases, to the decision of a Peruvian court on the legal bases of Peru's claim to areas formerly part of the high seas.[469]

While at one time the decisions of municipal courts, for example, prize courts,[470] formed a valuable source of material 'for the determination of rules of law', developments in international relations, including the greater prominence of other law-making, or at least law-defining, agencies, have deprived this subsidiary source of its importance. There appears to be no true case of recourse to Article 38, paragraph 1(*d*), of the Statute in relation to municipal decisions during the period under review.

2. *Arbitral Decisions*

Specific references in the decisions of the Court to the jurisprudence of arbitral tribunals have in the past been extremely rare.[471] During the period under review, however, in addition to a re-appearance[472] of the *Alabama*

---

[468] This *Year Book*, 60 (1989), pp. 7–76 and 127–8; above, pp. 114 ff.

[469] *ICJ Reports*, 1969, p. 107, n. 4.

[470] See for example O'Connell, *International Law*, vol. 1, p. 34.

[471] The only example known to the present writer is the passing citation of the *Alabama* decision in *Nottebohm, ICJ Reports*, 1953, p. 119. There would seem to be no harm in revealing the existence, at the time the writer entered the service of the Court (1968), of an unwritten rule of drafting that the Court only referred specifically to its own jurisprudence, never to arbitral awards. This rule appears now to have been abandoned.

[472] See previous note and *ICJ Reports*, 1988, p. 34.

decision in the text of a judgment, one particular arbitral award has been quite frequently referred to: the 1977 decision of the Anglo-French Arbitration Tribunal on the *Delimitation of the Continental Shelf*.[473]

Reference to that decision need not, however, in view of its nature, constitute an appeal to a judicial decision as a 'subsidiary means for the determination of rules of law'. In the domain of delimitation of maritime areas, a particular delimitation constitutes—*pace* the *Gulf of Maine* Chamber[474]— an act of State practice; and the fact that a particular delimitation is effected, not by direct agreement but by third-party settlement on the basis of agreement to refer the problem to such settlement, need not, and, it is suggested, should not, deprive it of that character. The basic principle that maritime delimitation is to be effected by agreement signifies that a tribunal seised of such a dispute must be deemed to be declaring the solution which the parties themselves ought to have, or would have, agreed upon.[475] Accordingly, an arbitral award defining a maritime boundary may have the status of an act of State practice contributing to the development of customary law.

The initial references in the Court's decision to the Anglo-French arbitration in fact partake more of the nature of a reference to State practice than that of recourse to a judicial precedent: in the *Tunisia/Libya* case, the Court, discussing the significance attached by the parties to geomorphological features, observed that 'so substantial a feature as the Hurd Deep was not attributed such a significance in the Franco-British Arbitration of 1977 concerning the Delimitation of the Continental Shelf'.[476] Similarly, later in the same judgment the Court includes the 1977 decision, along with a Franco-Spanish Convention, as examples of a practice of combination of equidistance with other factors.[477]

It is in the *Gulf of Maine* judgment that Article 38, paragraph 1(*d*), of the Statute is seen in operation in relation to the *Anglo-French* decision.[478] When analysing the development of customary international law in respect of maritime delimitation, the Chamber follows its discussion of the *North Sea Continental Shelf* cases with the following:

> Subsequently, the Court of Arbitration's Decision of 30 June 1977 on the delimitation of the continental shelf between France and the United Kingdom confirms on this point the Court's conclusions in the *North Sea Continental Shelf* cases and enunciates as follows the general rule of customary international law on the matter:

---

[473] Cmnd. 7438.

[474] See pp. 56 ff., above.

[475] In this sense the *Gulf of Maine* judgment, *ICJ Reports*, 1984, p. 292, para. 89, referring to 'un accord direct, ou éventuellement . . . une voie de substitution'. *Contra*, Prosper Weil, *Perspectives du droit de la délimitation maritime*, pp. 117 ff.

[476] *ICJ Reports*, 1982, p. 57, para. 66.

[477] Ibid., p. 79, para. 109.

[478] The State practice element also appears in the form, once again, of reference to the Hurd Deep: *ICJ Reports*, 1984, p. 274, para. 46.

'failing agreement, the boundary between States abutting on the same continental shelf is to be determined on equitable principles' (Decision, para. 70).[479]

A still more explicit recourse to the 1977 decision as a 'means for the determination of rules of law' is found in a passage dealing with the alleged 'equidistance-special circumstances rule': a passage is quoted from the decision as clearly showing

the different levels at which the various rules concerned are situated: the provisions of Article 6 of the 1958 Convention at the level of special international law, and, at the level of general international law, the norm prescribing application of equitable principles, or rather equitable criteria, without any indication as to the choice to be made among these latter or between the practical methods to implement them. The Chamber considers that such is the current state of customary international law.[480]

The significance of, in particular, the last sentence needs no underlining.

A further reliance on the 1977 decision as part of 'international jurisprudence', to be referred to in the same breath as decisions of the Court itself, will be found in paragraph 187 of the *Gulf of Maine* judgment;[481] it need not be quoted here.

The development which appears to have occurred, at least in the degree of explicitness with which an arbitral decision may be referred to, is evident if the *Gulf of Maine* decision is compared with that in the *Barcelona Traction* case fourteen years earlier. The Court specifically noted in that case that in respect of certain specific issues dealt with in its judgment the parties had 'relied on international instruments and judgments of international tribunals',[482] and that 'The Parties have also relied on the general arbitral jurisprudence which has accumulated in the last half-century'.[483] Yet the Court did not mention any specific example of the arbitral jurisprudence to which it referred: it was left to judges in their separate or dissenting opinions to refer to some twenty individual decisions. The Court explained its attitude to the general arbitral jurisprudence as follows:

However, in most cases the decisions cited rested upon the terms of instruments establishing the jurisdiction of the tribunal or claims commission and determining what rights might enjoy protection; they cannot therefore give rise to generalization going beyond the special circumstances of each case. Other decisions, allowing or disallowing claims by way of exception, are not, in view of the particular facts concerned, directly relevant to the present case.[484]

Yet in the next succeeding paragraphs the Court went on to discuss the special situation of possible action by shareholders where a company has ceased to exist, without however referring, as did two individual Judges[485]

---

[479] Ibid., p. 293, para. 92.
[480] Ibid., p. 303, para. 123.
[481] Ibid., p. 324.
[482] *ICJ Reports*, 1970, p. 40, para. 62.
[483] Ibid., p. 40, para. 63.
[484] Ibid.
[485] Sir Gerald Fitzmaurice, ibid., p. 72, note; Judge Ammoun, ibid., pp. 319, 325.

in their opinions, to the precedent, cited by the parties, of the *El Triunfo* case.[486]

From the nature of the subject of the dispute, the *Barcelona Traction* case involved the parties in considerable reference to arbitral decisions, and this is, as already observed, reflected in the separate and dissenting opinions appended to the judgment. In other cases during the period under review, arbitral jurisprudence was less directly relevant; but a few instances of its citation in Judges' opinions may be recorded here.[487]

3. *Decisions of the Court Itself*

Where a single case before the Court involves a series of decisions, for example a decision on a preliminary objection or on a jurisdictional issue followed by a decision on the merits, it is evident that the prior decision is *res judicata* and questions settled by it[488] cannot be re-opened. At the other extreme, the Court may, and frequently does, quote dicta from previous decisions if they afford a convenient statement of the law even if the previous decision was in a case involving not merely different parties, but totally different claims and arguments. The Court may in the latter case, but not in the former, be said to be mining the deposits of its own judicial wisdom as 'subsidiary means for the determination of rules of law' as contemplated by Article 38, paragraph 1(*d*), of the Statute. There may however be cases where previous decisions must apparently have some influence, but which fall somewhere between the two categories.

An example of this was the question, which arose in the *South West Africa* cases in 1962, of the significance or weight to be given to the 1950 advisory opinion on the *International Status of South West Africa*. Judge van Wyk, in his dissenting opinion in 1962, took a strict view on the point:

Article 59, referred to in Article 38(*d*), provides that a decision of this Court has no binding force except between the parties and in respect of that particular case. It follows that 'judicial decisions' mentioned in Article 38(*d*) include the decisions of this Court. There are no parties to Opinions of this Court and in terms of Article 59 such opinions have no binding force. It follows that Opinions of this Court,

---

[486] *Reports of International Arbitral Awards*, vol. 15, p. 464.

[487] *Finnish Vessels*: *ICJ Reports*, 1959, p. 87; *Dalmas*: *ICJ Reports*, 1959, p. 254; 1962, p. 46; 1969, p. 115; *Clipperton Island*: *ICJ Reports*, 1959, p. 255; *Island of Timor*: ibid., p. 256; *Grisbadarna*: *ICJ Reports*, 1959, p. 255; 1960, p. 83; 1984, p. 309; *Orinoco Steamship Co.*: *ICJ Reports*, 1960, p. 226; *Indemnities to Russian Individuals*: *ICJ Reports*, 1960, p. 96: 1962, p. 47; 1969, p. 134; *Yukon Lumber Claim*: *ICJ Reports*, 1962, p. 46; *Venezuelan Preferential Claims*: ibid.; *The Lisman* and *The Mechanic*: ibid., p. 49; *Life Insurance Claims*: ibid., p. 51; *North Atlantic Coast Fisheries*: *ICJ Reports*, 1969, p. 113; *Norwegian Shipowners' Claim*: ibid., pp. 134, 135; *W.J. Armstrong and Co* v. *Vickers Ltd*: ibid., p. 142; *Frederick and Co*: ibid.; *Lake Lanoux*: *ICJ Reports*, 1982, p. 145; *Petroleum Development (Trucial Coast)* v. *Sheikh of Abu Dhabi*: ibid., p. 173; *Forests of Central Rhodope*: *ICJ Reports*, 1988, p. 62.

[488] It may of course not be totally free from doubt or controversy exactly what questions *were* settled by the earlier decision. Some at least of the criticism addressed to the 1966 judgment in the *South West Africa* case appears to derive from a lack of appreciation of this point.

even if they relate to the same legal issues now being considered, cannot be more than a subsidiary means for the determination of the rules of international law.[489]

Nor is this view necessarily inconsistent with the Court's treatment, in the 1962 judgment, of the 1950 advisory opinion.

A further example is the decision on the preliminary objections of Thailand in the *Temple of Preah Vihear* case.[490] As the Court there stated:

> The first preliminary objection as advanced by Thailand is evidently based wholly on the alleged effect on Thailand's 1950 Declaration of the conclusion reached by the Court in its decision in the *Israel* v. *Bulgaria* case as to the correct sphere of application of Article 36, paragraph 5, of the Statute.
>
> . . .
>
> The Court's decision in the *Israel* v. *Bulgaria* case was of course concerned with the particular question of Bulgaria's position in relation to the Court and was in any event, by reason of Article 59 of the Statute, only binding, *qua* decision, as between the parties to that case. It cannot therefore, as such, have had the effect of invalidating Thailand's 1950 Declaration.[491]

The Court did classify the previous judgment as 'a statement of what the Court regarded as the correct legal position', and went on to explain why the question raised by the preliminary objection was not *in pari materia*.

The problem was more immediate for those Members of the Court who had dissented from the majority view in the *Israel* v. *Bulgaria* case. One of these, Judge Tanaka, made a declaration, in which he was joined by Sir Gerald Fitzmaurice, who had not sat in the earlier case, in which the two Judges explained that, while voting for the judgment, they had 'an additional and, for us, a more important reason for rejecting the first preliminary objection':

> Since . . . the objection necessarily presupposes the correctness of the conclusion reached in the *Israel* v. *Bulgaria* case, the view that this conclusion was in fact incorrect would, for anyone holding that view, furnish a further reason for rejecting the objection, and a much more immediate one than any of those contained in the present Judgment.
>
> This is precisely our position since, to our regret, we are unable to agree with the conclusion which the Court reached in the *Israel* v. *Bulgaria* case as to the effect of Article 36, paragraph 5, of the Statute. We need not give our reasons for this, for they are substantially the same as those set out in the Joint Dissenting Opinion of Judges Sir Hersch Lauterpacht and Sir Percy Spender, and of Judge Wellington Koo. Furthermore, it is not our purpose to call in question or attempt to reopen the decision in that case.[492]

There seems no reason to conclude that the process here at work is the use of a previous decision as a 'subsidiary means for the determination of rules of law'. Clearly it is irrelevant for this purpose that the point at issue is

---

[489] *ICJ Reports*, 1962, p. 576.
[490] *ICJ Reports*, 1961, p. 17.
[491] Ibid., p. 27.
[492] Ibid., pp. 36, 37.

one of jurisdiction,[493] not one of substance of the dispute brought before the Court, nor that it is one of interpretation of the Statute, so long as it is one to which 'rules of law', derivable from the recognized sources, are applicable. From the nature of things, a question of interpretation of the Court's Statute is more likely than many other legal questions to have been the subject of a previous decision: the subjects of litigation may be almost infinitely varied, but the Statute will apply in every case, and may have to be interpreted in many.[494]

More difficult is the question whether in such circumstances the previous decision may operate to determine the rules of law in a binding way; the question whether this may only be so for Judges, like Judge Tanaka, who took part in the previous decision, not for new Judges, like Judge Fitzmaurice; the question whether, without being technically binding, the previous decision may enjoy some kind of presumption of authority, rebuttable in some circumstances;[495] and similar questions. These are however matters going to the nature of the judicial function, more appropriate for treatment in a later article in the present series.

The only further question to be commented on is the significance in this respect of the expression 'subsidiary means' in Article 38, paragraph 1(d). Are judicial decisions a formal source of law, in the sense that a judicial decision on a point unresolved by practice or international convention suffices of itself to give rise to a rule of law; or are they only a material source, in the sense that a judicial decision may conveniently state, formulate or even 'crystallize'[496] a rule of law, but that rule must be assignable to the category of customary law or 'general principles of law'?[497] In connection with the decisions of the Court itself, this question appears to be capable of resolution as a matter of simple logic: if, by having recourse to a previous decision of its own, the Court determines the existence of a rule of law whose sole source is that decision, it must follow that the previous decision applied a rule with no underpinning whatever in a recognized source of law: *quod est absurdum*.

---

[493] We are of course not here dealing with the position of a Judge who has unsuccessfully voted against a finding of jurisdiction in a previous phase of the *same* case, where the relevant principle is that of *res judicata*. Cf. the declarations of Judges Dillard and Waldock appended to the Court's orders of 20 December 1974 in the *Nuclear Tests* cases, *ICJ Reports*, 1974, pp. 532, 537.

[494] Cf. also the problems of reconciling the decisions of 1981 and 1984 on intervention in the *Tunisia/Libya* and *Libya/Malta* cases, a Gordian knot cut through by the 1990 judgment of the Chamber in the *Land, Island and Maritime Frontier Dispute (El Salvador/Honduras)* case.

[495] Cf. the implication in the passage of the *South West Africa* decision quoted above that the Court in 1962 might depart from its view of 1950 if good reason were shown to do so.

[496] See Chapter II, section 3, above.

[497] If it has a treaty basis, it is unlikely that any judicial decision will be needed to indicate the rule's *existence*, though it may be a valuable guide to its *interpretation*.

COLLECTIVE RESPONSES TO THE UNILATERAL DECLARATIONS OF INDEPENDENCE OF SOUTHERN RHODESIA AND PALESTINE: AN APPLICATION OF THE LEGITIMIZING FUNCTION OF THE UNITED NATIONS*

By VERA GOWLLAND-DEBBAS‡

I. INTRODUCTION

The proclamation in 1988 of the independent State of Palestine has underlined once again a major function which the United Nations has assumed by default, namely that of collective legitimization, and its corollary, collective illegitimization. A comparison with the attempted creation of another controversial State this century—that of Rhodesia—sheds light on this significant development of the United Nations.

It will be recalled that on 11 November 1965 a European minority under the leadership of Ian Smith unilaterally declared the independence of the British colony of Southern Rhodesia. The purported new State of Rhodesia had serious claims to fulfil the traditional criteria of statehood. It possessed a defined territory, permanent population and a government clearly manifesting its effectiveness both in terms of authority over the population, and in terms of independence from external control.

Twenty-three years later, on 15 November 1988, the Palestine National Council, at its 19th Extraordinary Session in Algiers, adopted the decision to declare 'in the Name of God and on behalf of the Palestinian Arab people, the establishment of the State of Palestine in the land of Palestine with its capital at Jerusalem'. Whilst there clearly was an identifiable population, there was no *elected* government, and an apparent lack of effective authority over defined territory.

In terms therefore of the traditional criteria for recognition of statehood, the contrasts between these two cases may seem to be evident. Yet in the former, the 'State of Rhodesia' was effectively denied recognition and entry into the international community by the United Nations until its accession to independence in 1980 as the State of Zimbabwe on the basis of majority rule. In the latter case, the proclamation of an independent State of Pales-

* © Dr Vera Gowlland-Debbas, 1991.

‡ Ph.D; Graduate Institute of International Studies, Geneva. A shorter article on the same theme, entitled 'Legal Significance of the Legitimizing Function of the United Nations: the Cases of Southern Rhodesia and Palestine', has appeared in *Le Droit international au service de la paix, de la justice et du développement. Mélanges Michel Virally* (Paris, Editions A. Pedone, 1991).

tine was officially acknowledged by the General Assembly of the United Nations in December 1988, and granted recognition by close to 100 States.[1]

This apparent paradox may be explained by reference to an underlying common denominator: in effect in both these cases the traditional criteria of statehood, in particular the principle of effectiveness, were overridden by the legitimizing principle of self-determination of peoples, the United Nations acting as the 'dispenser of approval or disapproval' of these unilateral claims to independent status in accordance with their conformity or non-conformity with this principle.

The political and moral impact of this United Nations function of legitimization has been underlined by a number of commentators.[2] In briefly reviewing the collective responses to these two unilateral proclamations of independent statehood, the present article seeks to demonstrate, however, that in both cases the United Nations went well beyond a political or moral function. For in its unanimous condemnation of the UDI, and its legitimization of the proclamation of a Palestinian State, it is contended that the United Nations majority resorted to a series of pronouncements having a quasi-legal function: the collective defence of the right to self-determination, a norm now considered as of fundamental concern to the international community, and which has proved to be the cornerstone of subsequent claims to full sovereignty in both the legal and the material sense.

II. The Unilateral Declarations of Independent Statehood under International Law

(a) The Background

The origins of the two unilateral declarations are by now sufficiently well known to be recalled only briefly.

The constitutional relationship between the territory of Southern Rhodesia and the United Kingdom differed from that of other more classic colonies as a result of its particular circumstances. Instigated by Cecil Rhodes, the British had in 1888 first acquired a sphere of influence in the territory

---

[1] Keesing's Record of World Events, 34 (1988), p. 36321.

[2] Claude, 'Collective Legitimization as a Political Function of the United Nations', International Organization, 20 (1966), 367–79; Virally, L'Organisation mondiale (Paris, Armand Colin, 1972), pp. 430–1 and 454–6; id., 'Le Role des organisations internationales dans l'atténuation et le règlement des crises internationales', Politique étrangère, 14 (1976), pp. 529–62 (reprinted in Virally, Le Droit international en devenir. Essais écrits au fil des ans (Paris, IUEHI-Genève/Presses universitaires de France, 1990), pp. 357–79). With a passing reference to Rhodesia and the PLO, he states: 'La composition multilatérale de l'organisation internationale, la finalité d'"intérêt général" . . . confère aux actes de ses organes une autorité morale spécifique. Par là-même, elle est en mesure de conférer ou de refuser le label de la légitimitée aux situations créées par les Etats ou d'autres acteurs internationaux, ou à leurs aspirations . . . . Les conséquences pratiques de l'exercice de cette fonction n'ont pas besoin d'être longuement commentées': ibid., pp. 540–1.

and had then secured exclusive mineral rights from the local chief, following this up by occupation in 1890 and conquest in 1894. The origins of the Southern Rhodesian crisis that was to erupt in November 1965 can be traced to the initial British policy of entrusting local administration to a chartered company, and then to the gradual delegation of powers to the European settlers, leading to the grant to this minority of a considerable measure of internal self-government (Constitutions of 1923 and 1961).[3] Whilst there was no formal system of *apartheid* in existence and legislation was not overtly based on racist lines, deliberate white Rhodesian governmental policies ensured that African participation in the political process and the rate of African political advancement were kept to a minimum. As a result, whilst Southern Rhodesia's two northern neighbours acceded to independence in 1964 as Zambia and Malawi, the United Kingdom, under pressure from the international community not to abandon this large unenfranchised black majority, denied the territory independence so long as the white minority refused to give certain guarantees for their political advancement.[4]

It was the resentment of white Rhodesians over this, following the failure of negotiations with the United Kingdom to obtain independence by constitutional means, that led to a unilateral declaration of independence on 11 November 1965 by which the 'Government of Rhodesia' purported to enact a constitution for an independent sovereign State. Significantly, the 'Independence Proclamation', whilst echoing the 1776 American Declaration of Independence, omitted the assertion that 'all Men are created equal', and made no reference to 'the Consent of the Governed'.[5]

Palestine, it will be recalled, as one of the territories detached from the Turkish Empire, had been placed in 1922 under the League of Nations mandate system with Great Britain designated as the Mandatory Power. Article 22 of the Covenant of the League provided that the Mandates should be governed by the principle 'that the well-being and development of such peoples form a sacred trust of civilization', and with respect to Class A Mandates, which included Palestine, provided for the provisional recognition of 'their existence as independent nations . . . subject to the rendering of administrative advice and assistance by a Mandatory'. After the Second World War, however, Great Britain, finding itself, in the face of the inherent contradictions of the Mandate and the growing tension in the territory, unable to establish political institutions leading towards self-government, placed the matter in April 1947 in the hands of the General Assembly of the United Nations. The result was the adoption of resolution 181 (II)

---

[3] For the constitutional relationship see Palley, *The Constitutional History and Law of Southern Rhodesia 1888–1965, with Special Reference to Imperial Control* (Oxford, Clarendon Press, 1966).

[4] For further analysis of the question of Southern Rhodesia see Gowlland-Debbas, *Collective Responses to Illegal Acts in International Law: United Nations Action in the Question of Southern Rhodesia* (Dordrecht, Martinus Nijhoff, 1990).

[5] Rhodesia Proclamation No. 53 of 1965. Text in Windrich, *The Rhodesian Problem. A Documentary Record 1923–1973* (London/Boston, Routledge/Kegan Paul, 1975), pp. 210–11. See Palley, op. cit. above (n. 3), p. 750.

on 29 November 1947 recommending a 'Plan of Partition with Economic Union' which provided for the establishment of independent Arab and Jewish States and of a special international regime for the City of Jerusalem. This was never implemented. The consequences are only too well known. Following the 1948–9 Arab-Israeli conflict, the newly proclaimed State of Israel appropriated territories not assigned to it under the Partition Plan, and Egypt and Jordan ended up administering the Gaza Strip and the West Bank respectively,[6] both of which territories were occupied by Israel following further hostilities in 1967.

There were several milestones leading to the declaration of an independent Palestinian State: the formation of the Palestine Liberation Organization by the National Congress of Palestine in 1964; the recognition of the PLO as the sole and legitimate representative of the Palestinian people by the 8th Arab Summit in Rabat in October 1974; the Palestinian uprising, the *intifidah*, begun in the occupied territories in December 1987; and King Hussein's decision on 31 July 1988 to give up legal and administrative links with the West Bank.[7]

In contrast to the Rhodesian 'Independence Proclamation', the 'Declaration of Independence' of Palestine was made, *inter alia*:[8]

> By virtue of the natural, historical and legal right of the Palestinian Arab people to its homeland, Palestine . . .
> . . . on the basis of the international legitimacy embodied in the resolutions of the United Nations since 1947, and
> Through the exercise by the Palestinian Arab people of its right to self-determination, political independence and sovereignty over its territory . . .

The Declaration also affirmed the establishment in the State of Palestine of, *inter alia*, a democratic parliamentary system and full equality of rights, and affirmed respect for the principles of the UN Charter.

(b) *The Unilateral Declarations of Independence and the Criteria of Statehood*

Under international law, such unilateral declarations of independence can only be considered as a claim to personality and a request for recog-

---

[6] On the origins of the Palestine problem and the legal issues raised see Boyle, 'Creating the State of Palestine, *Palestine Yearbook of International Law*, 4 (1987/88), pp. 15–43; Cattan, *Palestine and International Law. The Legal Aspects of the Arab-Israeli Conflict* (London, Longman, 1973); Kassim, 'Legal Systems and Development in Palestine', *Palestine Yearbook of International Law*, 1 (1984), pp. 19–35; W.T. and S.V. Mallinson, *The Palestine Problem in International Law and World Order* (Harlow, Longman, 1986); Pellet, 'La Destruction de Troie n'aura pas lieu', *Palestine Yearbook of International Law*, 4 (1987/88), pp. 44–84.

[7] Text in *International Legal Materials*, 27 (1988), pp. 1637–54. Regarding the prior status of the West Bank, see Kassim, loc.cit. above (n. 6), pp. 27–8; Pellet, loc.cit. above (n. 6), p. 60.

[8] For the English text of the Declaration of Independence and accompanying political communiqué, see *International Legal Materials*, 27 (1988), pp. 1660–71, and UN Doc. A/43/827 and S/20278, Ann. III (1988). See also Flory, 'Naissance d'un Etat Palestinien', *Revue générale de droit international public*, 93 (1989), pp. 385–407.

nition. Actually to attain that end, fulfilment of the international legal criteria for independent statehood has traditionally been required (as a preliminary step or a determining factor in the achievement of international personality, depending on whether one argues from the constitutive or declaratory viewpoints of the effects of recognition).[9] In particular, the need for effective governmental control has been underlined.[10] Debate relating to the fulfilment of these criteria by Rhodesia and Palestine has been waged on both sides. This debate can be summarized as follows.

1. Southern Rhodesia and the criteria of statehood

In 1965 the purported new State of Rhodesia had serious claims to fulfil these criteria. The first two conditions regarding territorial boundaries and permanent population did not come into question. With respect to the criteria of effectiveness and independence, it appeared that the domestic effectiveness of the Smith regime, a regime given judicial blessing by the Rhodesian courts,[11] was assured. It wielded effective control over the organs of government, successfully set up new governmental institutions under new constitutional arrangements, issued passports and introduced a decimal currency and UDI stamps. There was no serious challenge at the time from within, the threat of guerrilla warfare having initially been contained. Southern Rhodesia's independence from the United Kingdom was also clearly demonstrated in the face of that State's futile attempts to assert its sovereignty, whilst refusing at the same time to use force against 'kith and kin'. Finally, Southern Rhodesia's dependence on South Africa's support was said not to affect its legal independence. These arguments concerning statehood were bolstered by the fact that the regime maintained itself in power for over fourteen years, despite considerable external pressures.

On the other hand, serious doubts were expressed at the time, which in retrospect proved to be only too well-founded, concerning the 'reasonable prospects of permanency' of a regime which denied political participation to the majority in the territory on a racially discriminatory basis, and the stability of a State the independence of which had been opposed by the entire international community.[12]

---

[9] Article 1 of the Montevideo Convention on the Rights and Duties of States of 1933, *League of Nations Treaty Series*, vol. 19, p. 165, which states: 'The State as a person of international law should possess the following qualifications: (a) a permanent population; (b) a defined territory; (c) government; and (d) capacity to enter into relations with the other States'. See also the American Law Institute, *Restatement (Third) of the Foreign Relations Law of the United States* (St. Paul, Minnesota, 1987), vol. 1, para. 201.

[10] e.g. Brownlie, *Principles of Public International Law* (Oxford, Clarendon Press, 4th edn., 1990), p. 73; Crawford, *The Creation of States in International Law* (Oxford, Clarendon Press, 1979), pp. 36 ff.; Thierry, Combacau, Sur and Vallée, *Droit international public* (Paris, Editions Montchrestien, 1984), pp. 198–211.

[11] *Archion Ndhlovu and others* v. *The Queen*, Appellate Division, High Court of Rhodesia, 13 September 1968, [1968] (4) SALR 515.

[12] For arguments and references, see Gowlland-Debbas, op.cit. above (n. 4), pp. 205–15.

2. *Palestine and the criteria of statehood*

The greater part of this debate has arisen from the request of Palestine for a change from its observer status to full membership of certain of the specialized agencies (so far, the WHO and UNESCO), since the constituent instruments of these organizations make admission to full membership contingent on 'statehood'.[13] This discussion has not at the time of writing been conclusive, compromise resolutions being adopted in both organizations which effectively shelved the admission for an indeterminate period.[14]

However, certain conclusions regarding statehood may be drawn from this stage of the debate. Not surprisingly, the representative from Israel considered that 'the declaration from Algiers proclaims a so-called independent Palestinian State, with no territory, no borders and with Jerusalem, my home town and the capital of Israel, as its declared capital. That declaration has no meaning in reality.'[15] Other States such as Canada, Australia, the United States, Spain (speaking in the name of the European Community) and Norway also declared that, in their view, the proclaimed Palestinian State did not conform with the criteria of international law for the recognition of statehood.[16]

The French Foreign Minister in a more nuanced statement declared:

Si cette 'reconnaissance par la France d'un Etat palestinien ne soulève aucune diffi-

[13] Letters dated 1 and 27 April 1989 from Mr Yasser Arafat in his capacity as President of the State of Palestine and Chairman of the Executive Committee of the PLO, to the Directors-General of WHO and UNESCO (WHO Doc. A42/INF.Doc./3 and UNESCO Doc.25 C/106, Annex 1). The application for admission to the WHO, for example, refers to 'the desire of the State of Palestine to become a full member of the WHO in accordance with Article 6 of the Constitution' (which provides that 'States . . . may apply to become Members and shall be admitted as Members when their application has been approved by a simple majority vote of the Health Assembly'), and undertakes 'to fulfil all duties and responsibilities arising from the full membership of the State of Palestine in WHO'.

[14] At the 42nd Session of the World Health Assembly an Arab draft resolution requesting admission of the State of Palestine (WHO Doc. A42/Conf. Paper No. 2) gave way to a compromise resolution WHA42.1 (see WHO Doc.A/42/VR.10) adopted on 13 May 1989 by secret ballot, with 83 votes to 47, and 20 abstentions, which authorized the Director-General, *inter alia*, to make a complete study of the various implications of the application for admission of Palestine to the work of the WHO. The findings of the Director-General's study having been considered inconclusive (WHO Doc.A/43/25), the matter was again postponed at the 43rd Session for an indeterminate period (Res WHA43.1).

The application for admission to UNESCO was also deferred, the 25th General Conference of UNESCO approving without a vote a resolution proposed by the Executive Board (see UNESCO Docs.131 EX/Decision 9.3, 132 EX/Decision 9.4, Doc.25 C/106, Doc.25 C/VR/2 prov.), deciding to associate Palestine more closely with the work of the organization and to include this question on the agenda of its next session (UNESCO Doc.25 C/Res. 62).

The application of Palestine for membership of the World Tourism Organization (WTO) by letter of 27 June 1989 was also deferred after a vote by secret ballot (WTO General Assembly Resolution A.Res.233 (VIII)).

[15] UN Doc.A/43/PV.79, p. 32, and letter from the Permanent Representative of Israel to the Director-General of the WHO, 21 April 1989, reproduced in WHO Doc.A42/INF.Doc./3.

[16] Letters from the Permanent Missions or representatives in Geneva of Canada, Australia, the United States, Spain and Norway to the Director-General of the WHO (WHO Doc. A42/INF.Doc./3, May 1989), and statement by USA at 43rd World Health Assembly (A43/VR/8, pp. 3–4). These views were reiterated by the United States and Japan in the General Assembly (UN Doc.A/43/PV.82, USA, p. 47; Japan, p. 8).

culté de principe', il est toutefois 'contraire à sa jurisprudence de reconnaître un Etat qui ne dispose pas d'un territoire défini'.[17]

The Federal Department of Foreign Affairs of Switzerland, with respect to a communication of 21 June 1989 from the Permanent Observer of Palestine to the UN concerning the participation of Palestine in the four 1949 Geneva Conventions and 1977 Additional Protocols, informed the contracting parties that

due to the uncertainty within the international community as to the existence or the non-existence of a State of Palestine and as long as the issue has not been settled in an appropriate framework, the Swiss Government, in its capacity as depositary of the Geneva Conventions and their additional Protocols, is not in a position to decide whether this communication can be considered as an instrument of accession in the sense of the relevant provisions of the Conventions and their additional Protocols. . . . [18]

As for writings on the subject, in a recent article concerning the admission of Palestine to the specialized agencies, one author was led to conclude: 'It is very doubtful that "Palestine" currently qualifies as a State under international law'.[19]

The case for fulfilment of the criteria of statehood is, however, convincing. In so far as the requirement of population is concerned, it is hard to dispute the existence of a Palestinian people with its own separate cultural identity. This existence has been recognized in a number of international instruments,[20] numerous General Assembly resolutions[21] and State unilateral and collective declarations.[22] It has also been argued that the *intifidah*

---

[17] *Le Monde*, 18 November 1988. See also statement by the President of the French Republic, underlining 'le principe de l'effectivité, qui implique l'existence d'un pouvoir responsable et indépendant s'exerçant sur un territoire et une population. Ce n'est pas encore le cas . . . ': ibid., 24 November 1988.

[18] Note of Information dated 13 September 1989.

[19] Kirgis, 'Admission of "Palestine" as a Member of a Specialized Agency and Withholding the Payment of Assessments in Response', *American Journal of International Law*, 84 (1990), pp. 218–30, at pp. 219 and 230, although he concludes that this does not necessarily determine its eligibility for admission to the specialized agencies or to the United Nations, since these also take into account other factors than that of statehood under customary international law, such as ability to carry out the ongoing obligations of membership (ibid., pp. 220–1).

[20] An explanatory memorandum dated 12 May 1989 from six Afro-Asian States (UNESCO Doc. 131 EX/43, pp. 1–2) refers to Article 16 of the Treaty of Sèvres (1920), the Treaty of Lausanne (1923) and the Mandate over Palestine entrusted to the United Kingdom on the basis of Article 22 of the League Covenant.

[21] GA Res. 181 of 29 November 1947 on the partition of Palestine and relevant resolutions adopted since 1967 recognizing the right to self-determination of the Palestinian peoples (below).

[22] The Declaration of Venice (12 June 1980) of the Heads of State, Heads of Government and Ministers of Foreign Affairs in the name of the European Community, in which it is explicitly mentioned that 'the Palestinian people, which is conscious of existing as such . . . ' should exercise in full its right to self-determination (cited in UNESCO Doc. 131 EX/43, p. 2). See also declaration of the President of the French Republic: 'D'ores et déjà émerge la nation palestinienne, identifiée comme telle aux yeux des autres nations du monde': *Le Monde*, 24 November 1988.

'has shown that even 20 years of occupation cannot destroy the aspirations of a people'.[23]

As for defined territory, it has been pointed out that the declaration of independence and political communiqué of 15 November 1988, combined with recognition of the right of Israel to exist, have now served to remove past ambiguities. These decisions accept the convening of an International Conference on the basis of Security Council Resolution 242 (1967) which, together with General Assembly Resolution 181(II), would delimit the frontiers of the State of Palestine within the confines of the Palestinian territory occupied since 1967.[24] It may be added that though the Proclamation purports to establish Jerusalem as the capital of an independent Palestinian State (contrary to the *corpus separatum* established by Resolution 181), this has clearly been limited to Arab Jerusalem.[25] It can also be contended that a new State may exist despite undefined boundaries[26]—witness the creation of Israel in 1948, admitted to the United Nations on 11 May 1949 despite not only undefined frontiers but also claims relating to its territory as a whole.[27] Furthermore, it may be argued that as a result of the withdrawal of Jordanian administration, there is an absence of other valid claims to this territory since (in accordance with the well-established principle of international law concerning non-acquisition of territory through the use of force) Israel cannot be said to have acquired sovereignty over the territories which it presently occupies.[28]

As for the requirement of effectiveness, it has been argued that the State is endowed with legitimate and representative political powers, namely, an

[23] UN Doc. A/43.PV.80, Austria, p. 21; Flory, loc. cit. above (n. 8), p. 397; Pellet, loc. cit. above (n. 6), pp. 60–1.

[24] Arguments in UNESCO Doc.131 EX/43, pp. 2–4. See GA Res.43/176 calling for an International Peace Conference on the Middle East, particularly Art. 3(*a*) and statement by the United Kingdom in UN Doc. A/43/PV.782, p. 83. The Palestine National Council's declaration of independence says that the 'state of Palestine . . . rejects the threat or use of force, violence and intimidation against its territorial integrity and political independence or those of any other state'. See also statement by the United States: 'The PLO has explicitly announced its acceptance of Security Council Resolutions 242 (1967) and 338 (1973), recognition of Israel's right to exist and renunciation of terrorism', on the basis of which the US declared that it was prepared to engage in a substantive dialogue with the PLO (A/43/PV.82, p. 43).

[25] Cf. Arafat's statement in the General Assembly (UN Doc.A/43/PV.78, p. 27).

[26] See, e.g., *North Sea Continental Shelf* cases, in which the Court stated that 'there is no rule that the land frontiers of a State must be fully delimited or defined . . . ' (*ICJ Reports*, 1969, at p. 32); Brownlie, op. cit. above (n. 10), p. 73.

[27] Verhoeven, *La Reconnaissance internationale dans la pratique contemporaine. Les Relations publiques internationales* (Paris, Editions A. Pedone, 1975, p. 28), states with regard to the creation of Israel: 'Les critères juridiques semblent en effet n'avoir guère joué de rôle dans les reconnaissances américaine et soviétique qui donnèrent une impulsion décisive à l'Etat nouveau', quoted in UNESCO Doc. 131 EX/43, p. 9; see also Crawford op. cit. above (n. 10), pp. 37–8; Dugard, *Recognition and the United Nations* (Cambridge, Grotius Publications Limited, 1987), pp. 60–1; Salmon, 'La Proclamation de l'état palestinien', *Annuaire français de droit international*, 34 (1988), pp. 37–62 at pp. 46–7.

[28] As a number of UN General Assembly resolutions have continued to affirm: see below. See also Pellet, loc. cit. above (n. 6). However, in the Israeli view, these territories had no legitimate sovereignty from the end of the Mandate to the Israeli occupation in 1967. See Tabiri, 'Humanitarian Law: Deportation of Palestinians from the West Bank and Gaza', *Harvard International Law Journal*, 29 (1988), pp. 552–8, at pp. 554–5.

Executive Committee entrusted by the Palestinian National Council (the supreme body of the PLO) with governmental functions, exercising responsibility outside the Palestinian territory in full independence and, inside the territory, carrying out certain (clandestine) functions (social, educational, cultural, etc., by the intermediary of clandestine popular committees) since it is temporarily deprived of exercising territorial authority.[29] It must be pointed out, however, that despite allusions to precedents such as the Czechoslovak and Polish National Committees (1917–18) and the French Committee of National Liberation (1943),[30] the status of the Palestinian government remains difficult to define, since the Executive Committee is only entrusted with governmental functions pending the constitution of a provisional Palestinian government and there is a deliberate intention to avoid the term 'government-in-exile'.[31]

However, whilst in these two cases of Rhodesia and Palestine States continue to give lip service to the traditional criteria of statehood, it is remarkable that in both cases these should have been considered irrelevant by the United Nations majority, as reflected in the collective response by the organization to the two declarations of independence. The reason may be sought in the United Nations function of legitimization.

III. The United Nations Function of Legitimization

The concept of legitimacy plays an important role in international society. Moreover, whereas the function of legitimization was once exclusively assumed by individual States through the medium of State recognition, the institutionalization of State relations has provided a means for the international community as a whole to pronounce on the legitimacy of new situations.[32]

It has been pointed out quite rightly that legitimacy is not to be identified necessarily with legality. It has been stated: 'Même si la distinction n'est pas absolue, il convient cependant de tenir pour *légitime* ce qui est conforme à une valeur alors qu'est légal ce qui est conforme au droit'.[33] Indeed, legitimacy affirmed within a moral or political framework on the basis of notions of justice or community interests may serve to counter the existing legal order. In turn, however, where this process is successful, what was previously only legitimate may well become identified with a new legality. The function of legitimization has thus been closely associated to the doc-

---

[29] UNESCO Doc. 131 EX/43, pp. 4–7.

[30] Ibid., pp. 6–7. See Verhoeven, op. cit. above (n. 27), pp. 132–40, for an analysis of the status of these various entities.

[31] Flory, loc. cit. above (n. 8), p. 399. See, e.g., statement by Arafat, in UN Doc. A/43/PV.78, p. 26. See, however, Salmon, loc. cit. above (n. 27), at p. 53.

[32] See Virally, *L'Organisation mondiale* (n. 2, above), pp. 430–2; R.-J. Dupuy, *La Communauté internationale entre le mythe et l'historie* (Paris, Economica/UNESCO, 1985); Franck, 'Legitimacy in the International System', *American Journal of International Law*, 82 (1988), pp. 705–59.

[33] Verhoeven, op. cit. above (n. 27), p. 587 (original emphasis).

trine of collective non-recognition traced back to the 1932 Stimson doctrine but revived in modern form. This doctrine is envisaged as a collective response to an act or situation contrary to international law and consisting in the withholding of legitimation, the function of legitimization being used here in a negative fashion to prevent the consolidation of illegal but otherwise effective changes which would have had, under traditional international law, a law-creating function.[34]

This evolution has been well illustrated in contemporary international society where, under the impetus of the so-called new States, the political process set in motion by the UN majority on the basis of a proclaimed new legitimacy has resulted—largely though not exclusively by means of the passage of General Assembly declaratory resolutions—in the establishment of new rules of conduct for States.

In this sense, therefore, the function of legitimization—and its corollary, that of illegitimization—assumed by the political organs of the United Nations may no longer be exclusively analysed within a political context of upholding what is moral, or just, but applied within the framework of a new *legal* order, considered to be more in conformity with contemporary notions of justice and community interests, and which has seen the erosion of the monolithic structure of traditional international law by a hierarchization (or relativization)[35] of norms resulting from novel concepts: those of *'jus cogens'* (endorsed by the 1969 Vienna Convention on the Law of Treaties), of 'obligations *erga omnes'* (enunciated by the International Court in the *Barcelona Traction* case) and of 'international crimes' (introduced into the Draft Articles on State Responsibility of the International Law Commission).[36] The process of legitimization—and illegitimization—

---

[34] See generally Cassese, *International Law in a Divided World* (Oxford, Clarendon Press, 1986), p. 27; Dupuy, op. cit. above (n. 32), p. 106; Dugard, op. cit. above (n. 27), pp. 24–5. The Stimson Doctrine enunciated by the US Government on 7 January 1932 (text in *American Journal of International Law*, 26 (1932), p. 342), following on the Japanese invasion of Manchuria which was to lead to the proclamation of the puppet State of Manchukuo in March 1932, has been reaffirmed in the *Third Restatement*, vol. 1, para. 202, as follows: 'A State has an obligation not to recognize or treat as a state an entity that has attained the qualifications for statehood as a result of a threat or use of armed force in violation of the United Nations Charter' (Kirgis, loc. cit. above (n. 19) p. 228).

[35] See Weil, 'Towards Relative Normativity in International Law?', *American Journal of International Law*, 77 (1983), pp. 413–42.

[36] See Articles 53 and 64 of the 1969 Vienna Convention on the Law of Treaties; *Barcelona Traction, Light and Power Co. Ltd.*, *Second Phase*, *ICJ Reports*, 1970, p. 32 (' . . . an essential distinction should be drawn between the obligations of a State towards the international community as a whole, and those arising vis-à-vis another State in the field of diplomatic protection. By their very nature the former are the concern of all States. In view of the importance of the rights involved, all States can be held to have a legal interest in their protection; they are obligations *erga omnes*'); Article 19 of Part I of the International Law Commission's Draft Articles on State Responsibility, para. 2 ('An internationally wrongful act which results from the breach by a State of an international obligation so essential for the protection of fundamental interests of the international community that its breach is recognized as a crime by that community as a whole, constitutes an international crime': *Yearbook of the ILC*, 1980, vol. 2, part 2). See, generally, P.-M. Dupuy, 'Action publique et crime international de l'Etat: à propos de l'article 19 du projet de la Commission du Droit international sur la responsabilité des Etats', *Annuaire*

by the United Nations has therefore also become a legal process, as a tool in the collective defence of those norms of the new legal order which are considered fundamental to the international community.

Whilst not explicitly stated in the Charter, this UN function has evolved through practice on the basis of (a) declaratory resolutions affirming the existence of certain fundamental rules, e.g. the prohibition of the use of force in international relations and the right to self-determination, and (b) resolutions determining or characterizing certain situations or acts—in particular those relating to territorial changes effected through the use of force, and to the birth of new entities—as valid or invalid, as the case may be, a change being considered legitimate only if carried out in conformity with such rules. Unarguably, therefore, the function of legitimization has become part of a legal process, despite its evident political impetus, in the sense that a whole number of legal consequences (underlined by the International Court of Justice) flow from these declaratory resolutions and from determinations which have 'operative design',[37] thus impinging on and modifying the prior legal situation.

Nowhere is this so evident as in the role played by the United Nations in the promotion of the fundamental right to self-determination. Under the vehicle of Resolution 1514(XV) on the Declaration of Independence to Colonial Countries and Peoples, and subsequent General Assembly resolutions,[38] the principle, formulated as the right of a majority of a people not yet constituted into a State to determine its external and internal political status, was gradually given shape and expanded to include colonialism in all its forms and manifestations.[39] It was to find its way into treaty law and judicial pronouncements, and is now considered to form part of the body of rights fundamental to the international community, breaches of which are deemed to warrant a different and more serious legal response.[40]

français de droit international, 25 (1979), pp. 539–53; Gaja, 'Jus Cogens Beyond the Vienna Convention', Recueil des cours, 172 (1981–III), pp. 271–316, and Gowlland-Debbas, op. cit. above (n. 4), pp. 241 ff.

[37] Legal Consequences for States of the Continued Presence of South Africa in Namibia (South West Africa) notwithstanding Security Council Resolution 276 (1970), ICJ Reports, 1971, p. 50 ('It would not be correct to assume that because the General Assembly is in principle vested with recommendatory powers, it is debarred from adopting, in specific cases within the framework of its competence, resolutions which make determinations or have operative design'). See the by now classic work of Castañeda, Legal Effects of United Nations Resolutions (London, Columbia University Press, 1969).

[38] The most famous of which is certainly the Declaration on Principles of International Law concerning Friendly Relations and Co-operation among States in accordance with the Charter of the United Nations (Res. 2625(XXV)).

[39] These 'forms and manifestations' of alien domination include racist regimes in colonies of settlement, and foreign occupation (see, e.g., GA Res.2105(XX), 2621(XXV); Abi-Saab, 'Wars of National Liberation and the Laws of War', Annales d'Etudes internationales/Annals of International Studies, 3 (1972), pp. 93–117, at pp. 93, n. 1, and 102).

[40] The right to self-determination is included in common Article 1 of the 1966 International Human Rights Covenants and Article 1(4) of the 1977 Protocol I Additional to the Geneva Conventions of 12 August 1949 relating to the protection of victims of international armed conflicts, and has been consecrated by the Court in the Namibia opinion. It is considered to have become a rule of jus cogens. Moreover, Article 19(3) of Part I of the Draft Articles on State Responsibility states that on the basis of the rules of international law in force, an international crime may result, inter alia, from '(b) a serious

Placed within the context of the right to self-determination, the questions of Southern Rhodesia and Palestine were to constitute important precedents in this process.

IV. The Collective Responses to the Unilateral Declarations of Independence

Action with respect to Southern Rhodesia had been initiated in 1961 at the international level as a result of the concern of the UN majority over the progressive evolution towards independence of a territory placed under a local administration of settlers and based on racial discrimination and a denial of political and other rights to the African majority.[41] In seeking the means to oppose and eradicate this system before it could slide into the formal *apartheid* system of its Southern neighbour, and to substitute for it the only goal acceptable, that of self-determination for its people, the UN majority sought to ground international jurisdiction on the international status of Southern Rhodesia. In 1962 this status was determined by the General Assembly, over the protests of the United Kingdom but in the light of international standards and criteria, to be that of a non-self-governing territory under Chapter XI of the Charter (General Assembly Resolution 1747(XVI)), and hence a self-determination unit to which could be applied the body of law on decolonization which had progressively been shaped.[42] In this context, it is easy to understand why the UN opposed efforts by the European minority in 1965 to perpetuate colonialism in another form by unilaterally declaring the independence of a State based on minority rule and racial discrimination.

It is contended that the United Nations went well beyond a verbal condemnation in determining, on the basis of a series of quasi-judicial pronouncements (Security Council Resolutions 216, 217 (1965)),[43] that this unilateral declaration of independence made by a racist minority, as well as the situation arising from it, was not only unconstitutional but also *illegal and invalid under international law* as it ran counter to the rights of the majority.

The United Nations then called for collective sanctions in the form of a dual response: (1) The refusal to validate the purported changes in the status of the territory, by the initiation of a policy of collective non-recognition (one of the most significant revivals of the pre-war Stimson doctrine) (Security Council Resolutions 216, 217 (1965), 277 (1970));[43a]

---

breach of an international obligation of essential importance for safeguarding the right of self-determination of peoples such as that prohibiting the establishment or maintenance by force of colonial domination' (*Yearbook of the ILC*, 1980, vol. 2, part 2, pp. 30–4).

[41] In 1965 there were 210,000 Europeans out of 4.5 million Africans.

[42] Gowlland-Debbas, op. cit. above (n. 4), chapter 2.

[43] See also 277 (1970); 288 (1970); 328 (1973).

[43a] See also 288 (1970), 328 (1973), 423 (1978), 445, 448 (1979); GA Res. 2012 and 2022(XX).

and (2) the imposition, for the first time in UN history, of a panoply of economic, financial and diplomatic sanctions under Article 41 of the Charter on the basis of a determination that the illegality of the situation resulting from the unilateral declaration of independence constituted a threat to international peace and security under Chapter VII of the Charter (Security Council Resolutions 232(1966), 253 (1968)).[43b] As a corollary, UN resolutions affirmed the legitimacy of the National Liberation Movements of Southern Rhodesia, entailing their right to representation in the international arena, recognition of the legitimacy of their struggle by all means at their disposal and their right to assistance by third parties.[44]

Thus whilst seemingly prepared to concede to Rhodesia a certain degree of effectiveness, the United Nations nevertheless denied independence to that entity irrespective of the traditional indicia of statehood. It is evident that the United Nations was here distinguishing between ordinary recognition problems predicated on the existence of statehood, and where questions of legality do not arise, and this type of collective non-recognition of a situation based on a determination that an act contrary to international law has occurred. This becomes apparent from an analysis of the function, content and legal effects of this policy, duplicated in the call for non-recognition of South Africa's continued presence in Namibia[45] and the proclaimed independence of the South African bantustans.[46] For behind the apparent object of an independent State of Rhodesia, what States were called on not to recognize was in fact the illegal and invalid situation created by the UDI. Hence efforts to argue from the existence or non-existence of the criteria of statehood in this situation obscured the true function of non-recognition—the refusal to validate the act of UDI and its consequences, considered contrary to international law and hence null and void.[47]

Whilst, after the adoption of Resolution 181 (II), and the subsequent establishment of a State of Israel, the Palestine question was not immediately associated with the decolonization process, the Palestinians initially being looked upon as refugees and treated within the context of an individual right of return,[48] the General Assembly after 1969 shifted its perspective to acknowledge their status as a people belonging to a self-determination unit. At the same time the United Nations sought to illegitimize all Israeli actions contrary to this right.

Thus in a number of resolutions the Assembly affirmed the following: (1) the legitimate inalienable right of the Palestinian people to self-

---

[43b] See also 277 (1970), 333 (1973), 388 (1976) and 409 (1977).

[44] For an analysis of these resolutions see Gowlland-Debbas, op. cit. above (n. 4), chapters 3–6.

[45] SC Res.276 (1970) and 283 (1970).

[46] GA Res. 31/6A, SC Res. 402 (1976) and 407 (1977): UN Doc. S/13549 and S/14794.

[47] Gowlland-Debbas, op. cit. above (n. 4), pp. 274ff.

[48] See GA Res. 194(III), 513(VI), 2452 (XXIII), 2535 (XXIV) and 2963 (XXVII); Mallinson, op. cit. above (n. 6), pp. 178–87. See also *The Right of Return of the Palestinian People* (United Nations, New York, 1978).

determination, including the right to establish its own independent State; (2) the legitimacy of its representatives—the PLO—granted observer status in the General Assembly and a right to participate on an equal footing with member States in Security Council debates on the Middle East, as well as in all conferences on the Middle East held under the auspices of the UN; and (3) the illegality under international law and UN resolutions of Israel's occupation of Arab territories since 1967, including Jerusalem, considered contrary to the *jus ad bellum* (the principle of the inadmissibility of the acquisition of territory by force) as well as the *jus in bello* (the 1949 Geneva Conventions), and the consequent invalidity of all legislative and administrative measures and actions taken by Israel purporting to alter their character and status, in particular, the so-called 'Basic Law' on Jerusalem, the establishment of settlements, the destruction of homes and property and the policy of deportations. However, the right of all States in the region to exist within secure and internationally recognized boundaries was also affirmed.[49]

The Assembly's response to the decision of the Palestine National Council of 15 November 1988 in the form of General Assembly Resolution 43/177 acknowledging the proclamation of an independent State of Palestine must therefore be taken in the same vein as, but acting in an opposite direction to, the Assembly's response to the Southern Rhodesian unilateral declaration of independence. This proclamation is considered in the preamble to be in line with Resolution 181(II) *'and in exercise of the inalienable rights of the Palestinian people . . . '*. The resolution *'affirms* the need to enable the Palestinian people to exercise their sovereignty over their territory occupied since 1967' and decides that, effective as of 15 December 1988, the designation 'Palestine' should be used in place of the designation 'Palestine Liberation Organization' in the United Nations system.[50]

[49] See, e.g., on the right to self-determination of the Palestinian people and the legitimacy of its representatives, GA Res. 2535B (XXIV); 2672C (XXV); 3210 (XXIX); 3236 (XXIX); 3237 (XXIX); 3375(XXX); 3376(XXX); ES 7/2; 35/207; S/10470; S/21306; on Jerusalem and occupied territories, SC Res.242 (1967), 338 (1973), 446 (1979), 452 (1979), 456 (1980), 476 (1980), 478 (1980); GA Res. 2253 (XXII); and more recently, SC Res.605, 607 and 608 (1988), GA Res. 43/21. See also Declaration on Palestine, in *Report of the International Conference on the Question of Palestine. Geneva, 29 August–7 September 1983* (United Nations, New York, 1983); W.T. and S.V. Mallinson, *An International Law Analysis of the Major United Nations Resolutions concerning the Palestine Question* (United Nations, New York, 1979); Tabiri, loc. cit. above (n. 28), pp. 552–8; Travers, 'The Legal Effect of United Nations Action in Support of the Palestine Liberation Organization and the National Liberation Movements of Africa', *Harvard International Law Journal*, 17 (1976), pp. 561–80.

[50] The resolution, one of three adopted on Palestine on 15 December 1988, was carried by 104–2 (Israel and the United States) with 36 abstentions. The General Assembly took no vote at its 44th Session in 1989 on a draft resolution the operative paragraph of which would have decided 'that the designation Palestine shall be construed, within the United Nations, as the State of Palestine, without prejudice to the acquired rights of the Palestine Liberation Organization in accordance with the relevant United Nations resolutions and practice' (UN Doc. A/44/L.50). The decision to defer consideration of the draft resolution occurred as a result of an appeal by the President of the General Assembly (press release GA/7937 of 5 December 1989) following a United States threat to withold its assessed contribution to the budget of the UN, which the President of the General Assembly insisted was 'an obligation under the Charter'. See Kirgis, loc. cit. above (n. 19), p. 220, for the view that there are no legal grounds in this case justifying US withholding of its contributions.

Not surprisingly, controversy arose over the legal significance of this 'acknowledgement'.[51] The United States declared that by this resolution the General Assembly had expressly withheld the attribution of statehood from 'Palestine' since it was specified that the change of the designation of the PLO to 'Palestine' was 'without prejudice to the observer status and functions of the PLO within the United Nations system'.[52] Japan, Australia and the United Kingdom, amongst others, expressed reservations on the fact that the draft resolution presupposed the establishment of the State of Palestine.[53]

However, it is clear that the function of this resolution was to recognize and affirm the intrinsic legality of a situation—the declaration of independence—considered to be in conformity with General Assembly Resolution 181 and other resolutions recognizing the right to self-determination of the Palestinian people, including the right to a State of its own, and the consequent intrinsic illegality, despite its effectiveness, of the Israeli occupation which was preventing the State of Palestine from exercising authority over this territory. The Assembly was not concerned with cognition, in the sense of affirmation of the existence of the criteria of statehood, but with a process of legitimization. In a sense, by implicitly acknowledging that the conditions for the establishment of a Palestinian State had now been met, several years after the adoption of Resolution 181, the Assembly may be said to have been asserting its competence, assumed on a number of occasions, and upheld by the Court as a discretionary right,[54] to determine the forms and procedures by which the right to self-determination was to be realized. It may be seen, therefore, as the crowning of the decolonization process in Palestine.

The debate surrounding the adoption of this resolution supports this view. Arafat reiterated in the General Assembly that the independent State of Palestine had been declared by virtue, *inter alia*, of 'our belief in international legitimacy'.[55] Several member States spoke in similar vein. Egypt, amongst others, stated: 'We are thus called upon to adopt resolutions consistent with the norms of international legitimacy and the purposes and principles enshrined in the UN Charter.'[56] It was argued that 'some of the legal pretexts used to justify non-recognition of the State of Palestine are clearly no longer part of the spirit of our age'.[57] Even those States which had not yet recognized the State of Palestine stated that they nevertheless

---

[51] The wording of the French text is 'prend acte de', which Flory considers to correspond 'à une sorte de reconnaissance par l'Organisation': loc. cit. above (n. 8), p. 402; but see Salmon, loc. cit. above (n. 27), p. 39.

[52] A/43/PV.82, United States, pp. 46–7.

[53] See A/43/PV.82, Australia, p. 81, Japan, p. 82, United Kingdom, p. 83, Canada, p. 86, France, p. 87. Kirgis states: 'The United Nations did not thereby recognize a Palestinian state, nor did it call the PLO a provisional government' (loc. cit. above (n. 19), p. 220).

[54] *Western Sahara* case, *ICJ Reports*, 1975, p. 36.

[55] A/43/PV.78, pp. 23, 27, 32–3.

[56] See A/43/PV.78, p. 48. See also Saudi-Arabia, p. 72; Iraq, p. 87; A/43/PV.80, Sudan, p. 6.

[57] A/43/PV.78, Iraq, p. 87.

welcomed the proclamation as the exercise of the right to self-determination, including the establishment of a State of its own, by the Palestinian people through its legitimate representatives, differing only in the view that recognition of statehood could take place only within the context of a comprehensive Middle East settlement.[58]

There have been similar claims to establish a State on the basis of legitimacy. Indeed the declaration of independence of a Palestinian State reflects the wording of the Declaration on the Establishment of the State of Israel made also 'by virtue of our Natural and Historic Right and on the Strength of the Resolution (181)'.[59]

Another significant precedent was admission of Namibia to membership of, *inter alia*, the International Labour Organization despite the clear absence of the traditional criteria of statehood, on the basis that the ILO was not prepared to allow the legitimate rights of the Namibian people to be frustrated by the illegal occupation of South Africa, in the absence of which Namibia would have qualified for independent statehood. The resolution reads:[60]

Noting that Namibia is the only remaining case of a former mandate of the League of Nations where the former mandatory Power is still in occupation,

Considering that an application for membership in terms of article 1 is prevented only by the illegal occupation of Namibia by South Africa, the illegal nature of this occupation having been confirmed by the International Court of Justice in its Advisory Opinion of 21 June 1971,

Affirming that the International Labour Organisation is not prepared to allow the legitimate rights of the Namibian people to be frustrated by the illegal actions of South Africa,

Making it clear that in now granting the application for membership it does not overlook the wording of article 1 and believes that in the near future the illegal occupation of Namibia by South Africa will be terminated,

Decides to admit Namibia to membership in the Organisation, it being agreed that, until the present illegal occupation of Namibia is terminated, the United Nations Council for Namibia, established by the United Nations as the legal administering authority for Namibia empowered, *inter alia*, to represent it in international organisations, will be regarded as the Government of Namibia for the purpose of the application of the Constitution of the Organisation.

---

[58] A/43/PV.79, Sweden, p. 74; A/43/PV.80, Chile, pp. 18–20, Austria, pp. 21–2, New Zealand, p. 132, Canada, pp. 172–6; A/43/PV.82, Australia, p. 81, Japan, p. 82, France, pp. 87–8.

[59] Quoted in Dugard, op. cit. above (n. 27), pp. 60–61.

[60] ILO, 64th Session (Geneva, June 1978), *Provisional Record*, No. 24, pp. 19–20. It will be recalled that the Mandate for South West Africa was revoked in 1966 by the General Assembly on the ground that South Africa had failed to fulfil its obligations under it (GA Res. 2145 (XXI)). A UN Council for Namibia was subsequently established to administer the territory. Following SC Res.276(1970), the International Court, in its 1971 *Namibia opinion* (*ICJ Reports*, 1971, p. 16), affirmed the illegality of South Africa's presence in Namibia and held that member States were under an obligation to recognize that illegality, which was opposable even in respect of non-member States. In 1976 the General Assembly, by Res.31/149, requested the specialized agencies to consider granting full membership to Namibia, which a number of specialized agencies proceeded to do.

As has been pointed out,[61] the ILO was, by the adoption of this resolution, exercising its function of legitimization. Whilst General Assembly Resolution 43/177 was not related to admission of the State of Palestine, it nevertheless appeared to be implying much the same thing.

V. Legal Consequences of Legitimization

Security Council Resolution 277 (1970) calling for collective non-recognition of an independent State of Rhodesia was clearly a mandatory resolution adopted by the Council on the basis of powers conferred under Chapter VII.[62] General Assembly Resolution 43/177 on Palestine, on the other hand, can place no corresponding obligation on member States to acknowledge the proclamation or *a fortiori* to recognize the State of Palestine, in the absence of admissions procedures,[63] though naturally it has determinative effect on the status of the entity for internal purposes (the change of appellation in particular).

However, the characterization by the Organization of the situation could not remain without legal effect.[64] In the case of Southern Rhodesia, there existed, beyond the conventional obligation, a general international law duty on the part of States not to recognize a situation determined to be contrary to a fundamental norm—that of self-determination—and hence invalid.[65] It could therefore be argued along the same lines that acknowledgment by the Assembly of the proclamation of an independent State of Palestine, a proclamation determined in this case to be *in conformity* with that right, could not similarly remain without legal effects.

This means, at the very minimum, that recognition by States of this entity cannot be held to be illegal in the sense of premature recognition. This is not to say that in recognition of statehood, the traditional criteria

---

[61] Osieke, 'Admission to Membership in International Organizations: The Case of Namibia', this *Year Book*, 51 (1980), pp. 189–229, at pp. 214–15. Referring to this resolution Osieke concludes: 'Here then lies the justification, the *raison d'être*, for the admission of Namibia as a Member of the ILO. By regarding the rights of the Namibian people as subsisting irrespective of the illegal occupation of their territory by South Africa, and by refusing to recognize the illegal acts committed by South Africa or to allow that country to benefit from such acts, the Conference appears to have resorted to the principle *ex injuria jus non oritur* according to which 'an illegality cannot as a rule, become a source of legal right to the wrongdoer' (ibid., p. 217).

[62] Gowlland-Debbas, op. cit. above (n. 4), pp. 288–95.

[63] Even where admission to the United Nations is involved, there has been controversy as to the effects of such admission on recognition of the entity as a State. The majority of authors agree that in the case of ordinary recognition problems, i.e. where a question of legality does not arise, it is not a function of the United Nations to grant or to withhold recognition, since admission to the United Nations is only predicated on the existence of statehood for purposes of the Charter, and other considerations, such as ability to fulfil the obligations of membership, may be relevant. Dugard has, however, convincingly argued that admission to the United Nations constitutes or confirms the existence of a State (op. cit. above (n. 27), p. 79). (It is generally agreed, however, that membership of an international organization does not impose an obligation of recognition on member States of that organization.)

[64] See *Namibia* opinion, *ICJ Reports*, 1971, pp. 47–51, 54.

[65] Gowlland-Debbas, op. cit. above (n. 4), pp. 281 ff.

have been totally replaced, but that where this concerns certain postulated legal rules considered essential for the international community, different considerations operate depending on whether a situation of legality or illegality is involved and whether the object is the upholding of the maxim *ex injuria jus non oritur* over its rival principle *ex factis jus oritur* or the law-creating influence of facts.[66]

As a legal mechanism, this process of legitimization, which attempts to override considerations of effectiveness, may be criticized for creating an unbridgeable gap between the facts and the law. However, just as the lack of legal title may serve to weaken a situation of fact, assumption of legal title may serve to strengthen it. It is undeniable that the ostracism and diplomatic isolation of the European minority regime in Rhodesia and denial to it of international personality had a constitutive effect to the extent that it undermined its effectiveness: it is enough to think of the corollary of UN policy, had Rhodesia been accepted into the United Nations under a white minority regime in 1965.[67] The application of a similar process of legitimization to Namibia, where the maintenance of the fiction of a United Nations territory contributed to undermining the effectiveness of South Africa's hold over the territory, has had a similarly successful outcome.

Whilst, therefore, in the case of Palestine the UN may be accused of perpetuating a legal fiction, it may be argued that acknowledgment of the legitimacy of the proclamation of an independent Palestinian State, coupled with individual State recognition, may likewise serve to create the very effectiveness that is said to be lacking and contribute towards consolidation of its status. Cassese states that traditionally international law has provided that only those claims and situations which are effective can produce legal effects, in other words claim international legitimacy.[68] Today, however, there is evidence that only those claims and situations which are legitimate can produce legal effects and hence be effective.

United Nations collective responses in terms of the denial of legal effects to acts or situations in breach of certain norms deemed fundamental, by a determination that such acts or situations are both illegal and invalid, and by the application, in consequence, of a policy of collective non-recognition, have had an extensive and consistent basis.[69] The contrary

---

[66] Lauterpacht, *Recognition in International Law* (London, Cambridge University Press, 1947), pp. 426–7. Dugard points out that criteria such as effective government and independence are no longer strictly insisted on in matters of admission to the United Nations where they run counter to developments in international law regarding the right of self-determination (op. cit. above (n. 27), p. 72).

[67] Gowlland-Debbas, op. cit. above (n. 4), pp. 661–3. See also Abi-Saab, Foreword to Gowlland-Debbas, ibid., pp. 18–20.

[68] Op. cit. above (n. 34), pp. 26–7.

[69] In addition to the cases of Southern Rhodesia, the occupation of Arab territories by Israel, Namibia, and the independence of the South African bantustans, already referred to above, one can cite the cases of the declaration of a Turkish Cypriot Republic (SC Res. 541 (1983) and 550 (1984)); and the condemnation by the General Assembly in GA Res.35/169B of all partial agreements and separate treaties violating the recognized rights of the Palestinian people (alluding to the Treaty of Peace between Egypt and Israel of 1980).

process of legitimization of the proclamation of an independent Palestinian State is in line with and strengthens this practice. This practice has been considered as important evidence in the process of identifying and shaping fundamental norms, recognized as essentially dynamic concepts, the content of which evolves in accordance with the changing requirements of the international community.[70]

This tendency to entrust to political organs the task of validating or invalidating claims and situations by means of legal judgments has been contested, but it may be said that it is in keeping with the contemporary tendency to reject, at the international level, municipal law concepts of separation of powers, as the *Nicaragua* case underlined.[71] It is in keeping with the concept formulated by the International Law Commission, in relation to the defence of fundamental norms, of the need for collective action within an *institutionalized* framework.[72] Finally, it is in keeping with a noticeable tendency of the contemporary international community to promote a more dynamic and hence interventionist international law, concerned no longer merely with jurisdictional issues but with the evolution, if not transformation, of the international system.[73]

---

[70] See references in Gowlland-Debbas, op. cit. above (n. 4), pp. 255–8.

[71] See *ICJ Reports*, 1984, para. 92, where the Court refers to Nicaragua's statement regarding the US arguments as to the delineation of powers between the Security Council and the Court.

[72] *Yearbook of the ILC*, 1976, vol. 1, pp. 60 and 78–9.

[73] Virally states, with reference to the problem of legitimization: 'dans certains cas, loin d'éliminer les causes de conflit, l'ONU peut perpétuer certaines situations génératrices de tensions et de crises, en refusant de sanctionner le fait accompli. Cette attitude n'est pas contradictoire, si on admet que l'objectif à atteindre n'est pas d'entériner n'importe quel règlement qui mette un terme à une crise . . . mais bien de parvenir à un règlement durable, qui puisse être accepté sincèrement par toutes les parties concernées, parce qu'il tient compte de leurs intérêts légitimes': *L'Organisation mondiale* (n. 2, above), p. 432.

DIPLOMATIC PROTECTION OF PRIVATE BUSINESS COMPANIES: DETERMINING CORPORATE PERSONALITY FOR INTERNATIONAL LAW PURPOSES*

By CHRISTOPHER STAKER‡

I. INTRODUCTION

GIVEN that '[t]hroughout its history, the development of international law has been influenced by the requirements of international life',[1] it has had inevitably to take account of the emergence over the last century of the limited liability company as the major vehicle for international trade and investment. It was already recognized last century that business companies, as juridical persons, could be protected diplomatically in a similar way to natural persons.[2] Numerous matters brought before the International Court of Justice and its predecessor have involved the diplomatic protection of companies,[3] and this subject is now a standard part of general works on international law.[4]

Over the decades, municipal company laws have evolved and increased dramatically in complexity in response to rapidly changing commercial realities. In customary international law, however, the topical issues are much

---

* © Christopher Staker, 1991.

‡ BA, LLB (Hons.), Attorney-General's Department, Canberra. The views expressed in this article are the personal views of the author and not necessarily those of the Commonwealth of Australia or any of its Departments, authorities or other officers. This article was written while the author was on leave as a Sir Robert Menzies Memorial Scholar in Law at the University of Oxford. He gratefully acknowledges the valuable advice provided by Professor Ian Brownlie, his supervisor.

[1] *Reparation for Injuries* case, *ICJ Reports*, 1949, p. 174 at p. 178.

[2] See, e.g., *Compañia Anglo Chilena de Salitre, etc.* case (1896), Tribunal Anglo-Chileno, 1894–6, vol. 1, p. 128, referred to in Al-Shawi, *The Role of the Corporate Entity in International Law* (Ann Arbor, 1957), at p. 33; Moore, *International Law Digest*, vol. 6, pp. 641–4; McNair, *International Law Opinions* (Cambridge, 1956), vol. 2, p. 36.

[3] PCIJ: *German Interests in Polish Upper Silesia* case, Series A, Nos. 6 (1925) and 7 (1926); *Chorzów Factory* case, Series A, Nos. 9 (1927), 12 (1927), 13 (1927) and 17 (1928); *Peter Pázmány University* case, Series A/B, No. 61 (1933) (involving a corporation other than a business corporation); *Losinger & Co.* case, Series A/B, No. 67 (1936); *Panevezys-Saldutiskis Railway* case, Series A/B, Nos. 75 (1938) and 76 (1939); *Electricity Company of Sofia and Bulgaria* case, Series A/B, No. 77 (1939); *Société Commerciale de Belgique* case, Series A/B, No. 78 (1939). ICJ: *Anglo-Iranian Oil Company* case, *ICJ Reports*, 1951, p. 89, and 1952, p. 93; *Interhandel* case, *ICJ Reports*, 1957, p. 105, and 1959, p. 6; *Barcelona Traction* case, *ICJ Reports*, 1964, p. 6, and 1970, p. 3; *Elettronica Sicula SpA (ELSI)* case, *ICJ Reports*, 1989, p. 15. Many of these cases involved the application of treaty provisions, but some were decided under general principles of customary international law.

[4] e.g. Brownlie, *Principles of Public International Law* (4th edn., Oxford, 1990), at pp. 421–4, 489–94; Verdross, *Völkerrecht* (5th edn. by Verosta and Zemanek, Vienna, 1964), at pp. 314–15; Rousseau, *Droit international public* (Paris, 1983), vol. 5, at pp. 128–51.

the same as those of a century ago. That the literature on the diplomatic
. protection of companies is so vast is due to the controversy surrounding this
area of the law, rather than its complexity. There are in fact only two issues
that are commonly discussed. The first is the question of how to determine
which State is entitled to protect a given company. The second is the issue
of whether the separate legal personalities of the company and the shareholders in *municipal law* preclude a State from protecting its nationals who
are shareholders in a company in respect of damage inflicted on the company, where that State would not be entitled to protect the company itself.
The International Court of Justice in the *Barcelona Traction* case,[5] relying
on this fundamental distinction between the legal personalities of a company and its shareholders in systems of municipal law generally, answered
the latter question by saying that:

. . . where it is a question of an unlawful act committed against a company representing foreign capital, the general rule of international law authorizes the national
State of the company alone to make a claim.[6]

As to the first question, the Court noted that:

The traditional rule attributes the right of diplomatic protection of a corporate
entity to the State under the laws of which it is incorporated and in whose territory
it has its registered office.[7]

Notwithstanding the possibility of each of these international law rules
being subject to exceptions or qualifications,[8] their simplicity contrasts
starkly with the increasing complexity of municipal systems of company
law.[9] Writers have pointed out that international lawyers (unlike political
and economic scientists) have given insufficient attention to the evolution
of multinational and transnational companies,[10] leaving international law in
a highly unsatisfactory state.[11] This was freely admitted in the separate
opinions of some of the judges in the *Barcelona Traction* case,[12] and was
explained in the judgment on the basis that a body of rules could only have
developed with the consent of all concerned, while 'the law on the subject
has been formed in a period characterized by an intense conflict of systems
and interests . . . The difficulties encountered have been reflected in the

---

[5] *ICJ Reports*, 1970, p. 3.

[6] At p. 46. See also, e.g., Jones, 'Claims on Behalf of Nationals who are Shareholders in Foreign
Companies', this *Year Book*, 26 (1949), p. 225 at p. 232.

[7] At p. 42.

[8] As to which, see below.

[9] Not all members of the *Barcelona Traction* Court accepted the correctness of these rules, as is
apparent from the discussion below. However, judges and writers have all tended to address the same
issues referred to above and to address them with equally simple rules.

[10] Kopelmanas, 'L'Application du droit national aux sociétés multinationales,' *Recueil des cours*, 150
(1976–II), p. 295 at p. 301.

[11] Oliver, 'Historical Development of International Law: Contemporary Problems of Treaty Law',
ibid. 88 (1955–II), p. 417 at p. 459.

[12] *per* President Bustamante y Rivero (at p. 57): ' . . . the whole subject is bedevilled, on the international plane, with the existence of gaps in the law'; *per* Judge Fitzmaurice (at p. 76): 'international
law is in this respect an under-developed system as compared with private law'.

evolution of the law on the subject'.[13] Given these inadequacies, further studies in this area do not require justification.

As one such contribution, this article examines a question which logically arises before either of the issues referred to above needs to be dealt with. This is the question of the circumstances in which the existence of a private company created under the municipal law of a State will be recognized as existing for the purposes of the international law rules on diplomatic protection. If the juridical personality of a given company in municipal law is not transposed on to the international plane, an injury inflicted on the company in the municipal sphere would presumably be treated in the international sphere as having been inflicted on the members of the company, whose national State(s) could bring claims on their behalf in respect of the injury. In the *Barcelona Traction* case, for instance, Belgium was claiming against Spain on behalf of Belgian nationals who allegedly owned some 88 per cent of the shares in the Barcelona Traction company, which was incorporated in Canada. These shareholders had allegedly lost almost the total value of their investment when the company's assets were despoiled by, or with the connivance of, the government authorities in Spain. Belgium was held not to be entitled to claim on behalf of the shareholders in respect of an injury inflicted on the company, and was held unable to protect the company itself, the national State of which was Canada.[14] However, if the situation had not been one in which the juridical personality of the Canadian company existed for international law purposes, Belgium's *jus standi* would have been indisputable, and discussion of the nationality of the company and the possibility of 'piercing the corporate veil' would have been unnecessary.

All of the judges agreed that for the purposes of that claim, the company had personality separate from that of its shareholders. Except for Judge Morelli,[15] none of the judges indicated expressly on what basis this was to be determined. Astonishingly, this issue appears also to have escaped the attention of writers.[16] This absence of discussion makes any analysis of the issues difficult. However, there are three main possibilities. First, international law could refer to the municipal law of the State of incorporation of a company to determine that it has legal personality separate from that of its members. In this case, corporate personality under municipal law could either be recognized *ipso facto* for international law purposes, or be recognized subject to qualifications imposed by international law. Alternatively, in any claim in which the legal personality of a company is in issue, international law could refer to the municipal law of the defendant State. A third possibility is that international law determines the existence of the indepen-

---

[13] Ibid., p. 47. The Court suggested that these inadequacies could only be overcome by recourse to treaty stipulations or special agreements. Also President Bustamante y Rivero at p. 57.

[14] Judgment, pp. 45–6.

[15] As to which, see below, Part IV.

[16] This author is aware of no detailed discussion of the question, although some writers are aware of the problem: see, e.g., Brownlie, op. cit. above (n. 4), at pp. 484, 487.

dent personality of a company on the basis of relevant facts, rather than the municipal law of any State. Parts II to V of this essay discuss each of these possibilities in turn. The discussion will give particular emphasis to the comments made by judges in the *Barcelona Traction* case, which is the one case decided by the World Court to consider extensively the area of the diplomatic protection of companies in customary international law. Some general conclusions are drawn in Part VI.

II. UNQUALIFIED REFERENCE TO THE LAW OF THE INCORPORATING STATE

If, as the *Barcelona Traction* Court indicated, international law has no substantive rules of company law and is referring in this area to principles of municipal law,[17] it would seem logical to make recognition of the existence of a company dependent on the company having had juridical personality conferred upon it under the municipal law of some State. This appears all the more necessary if one accepts the 'traditional rule' which ascribes to companies the nationality of the State of incorporation.[18] It would be possible for international law to treat the fact of a company having a separate legal personality from its members under the municipal law of its State of incorporation as conclusive for international law purposes. However, such a regime would seem to run counter to the views traditionally espoused by both developing and industrialized States. Developing nations have long argued that it should not be possible for a State having no connection with a business enterprise to assume a right to protect it, merely by conferring corporate personality on the enterprise under its municipal law, or for investors from small States to bring their business activities under the protection of a large and powerful industrial State simply by incorporating a company under the laws of that State and conducting their business through that corporation.[19] Industrialized States would argue that while companies today are frequently incorporated under the laws of States other than the national State of any of the incorporators,[20] the motivation of the incorporators is normally to obtain tax or other municipal law advantages. It will in fact usually be the case that the State of incorporation of a company will have no interest in protecting it internationally in the absence of some substantial

[17] Judgment, p. 37.

[18] Above, n. 7 and accompanying text.

[19] This essay is concerned only with the position in customary international law. It is in fact common today for States to conclude bilateral treaties which determine the companies one party is entitled to protect against the other and which may effectively preclude this possibility. Such treaties vary significantly in approach. An example is the treaty between the United States and Italy discussed in the *ELSI* case (loc. cit. above, n. 3). Article XXIV (5) of that treaty provided that each party could deny the privileges accorded under that treaty to corporations created under the laws of the other party in which nationals of third countries had a controlling interest.

[20] And subsidiary companies are incorporated under the laws of States other than the State of incorporation of the parent company.

local connection.[21] Thus, the result of automatically recognizing such companies for international law purposes may in practice be to deprive the company and its shareholders of any possibility of protection in respect of the interests held through the company: the national State of the company would not be willing to protect it, while the fact of the existence of the company would preclude the national State or States of the shareholders from protecting them. This is precisely the situation in which the Barcelona Traction company and its shareholders found themselves.[22]

There is, moreover, a substantial body of opinion that a State is not entitled to protect a locally incorporated company in the absence of a genuine link between the company and that State.[23] This would mean that not only may States be *disinclined* to protect locally incorporated companies in the absence of a genuine link, but they would be *legally incapable* of so doing. In the *Barcelona Traction* case, Judges Petrén and Onyeama[24] were clearly willing to accept this. They agreed with the Court that the company's separate legal personality prevented Belgium from protecting the shareholders in respect of damage inflicted on the company. However, they regarded Canada's right to protect the company itself to be an open question, rather than a necessary incident of the company's incorporation under Canadian law. This result appears to conflict with the current trend of international law, which is towards greater protection of the rights of individuals. The Court in that case said that 'considerations of equity cannot require more than the possibility for some protector State to intervene',[25] and Judge Lachs considered Canada's right to protect the company to be an essential premiss of the Court's reasoning.[26]

This problem of the 'statelessness' of companies could be addressed by a rule which permitted a State other than the State of incorporation of a company to be the company's national State, either in addition to or instead of the State of incorporation. Judges Petrén and Onyeama cannot have envisaged this possibility, since it would have required them to consider whether, if Canada had been unable to protect the company, the national State of the company might not have been Belgium, with which the company was closely linked, at least on Belgium's submissions, by virtue of the

[21] On the well-known practice of the United States and the United Kingdom, see Brownlie, op. cit. above (n. 4), at p. 485.

[22] Judge Ammoun, who in the *Barcelona Traction* case spoke at length of the need for international law to take account of 'the material and intangible interests of the weaker and deprived peoples' (at p. 290), may well have had this in mind when he expressed the view (pp. 295–6) that a State always has a right to protect a company incorporated under its laws, irrespective of whether or not there is a genuine link between the company and the State.

[23] Brownlie, op. cit. above (n. 4), p. 486 and references cited therein. Also Judge Jessup at pp. 186–9 and references cited therein. While this view was rejected in the judgment in the *Barcelona Traction* case, the Court did point out (at p. 42) numerous links it considered that company had with Canada, thereby demonstrating an uneasiness with the notion of a State being entitled to protect a company solely on the basis of incorporation under its municipal law.

[24] In a joint declaration appended to the judgment, at p. 52.

[25] At p. 48.

[26] At p. 53.

preponderant Belgian interests in it.[27] A similar position appears to have been adopted by Judge Padilla Nervo.[28] The main support in that case for the opposite view was provided by Judge Jessup, who said:[29] 'With all due respect to the Court, I must point out the irrational results of applying a rule which would provide that only the State in which a company is incorporated may extend diplomatic protection'. Judge Fitzmaurice,[30] while considering the test of incorporation to be 'the better view', considers Judge Jessup's opinion to be 'a highly tenable proposition', at least where the State of incorporation is disqualified from acting for want of a genuine link.

This proposition gives rise to the question of how to determine the standing of a State other than the State of incorporation of a company to protect it, given that States do not by municipal legislation confer nationality on companies in the same way as they do on individuals.[31] It would be necessary to establish such standing on the basis of sufficient factual connections, though the relevance of particular connections and their relative weight would be a question of international law.[32] While this suggestion would greatly diminish the instances of stateless companies, statelessness presumably still could occur where under each of these connecting factors the company had diffuse links with numerous States. Moreover, a State inflicting an injury on a foreign-incorporated company will, under these criteria, be likely to have sufficient links with the company to be a 'national' State, and therefore presumably not be internationally responsible for the injury.[33]

This approach also runs counter to the general principle, well established in the case of nationality of natural persons, that international law does not allocate individuals to States; rather, it is for each State to claim persons as its nationals. While a State by incorporating a company under its municipal

[27] Although this was technically unnecessary, as Belgium was only claiming on behalf of the shareholders said to be Belgian, one would have expected the point to be considered.

[28] At p. 254: 'For juridical persons as for natural persons, "nationality" expresses a link of legally belonging to a specific State. The requirement for juridical persons as for natural persons, is that the existence of the link of legally belonging to a specific country must, if it is to serve as a plea at the international level, be accompanied by that of a "real" link with the same country.' The link of 'legally belonging to a specific country' is, in the case of juridical persons, presumably intended to mean the fact of incorporation under that country's laws, so that a country other than that of incorporation could not be a national State, while this State is still only able to protect the company if there are other factual links. See also Judge Tanaka at pp. 122–3 and 128–9.

[29] At p. 200.

[30] At p. 83.

[31] Although under municipal systems of private international law, companies will be considered to have a nationality for certain purposes. De Visscher, 'La Protection diplomatique des personnes morales', *Recueil des cours*, 102 (1961–I), p. 395 at pp. 438–9, 462, suggests that this should serve as the test of nationality for public international law purposes. However, this would mean that the only State capable of protecting a company would be the State of incorporation or, in some cases, the State where the *siège social* is located.

[32] Cf. Judge Fitzmaurice: the test might be 'that of where the real weight of real interest lies' (at p. 83 n. 29); Judge Jessup: international law 'cannot be oblivious' to links such as the place of management, the place of operation and payment of taxes and the nationality of those who exercise control, in addition to the law of incorporation (at p. 200).

[33] Judge Jessup did not consider whether the Barcelona Traction company might have had Spanish nationality.

law may thereby raise a presumption that it intends to consider the company a national (in the same way that a State, by conferring on an individual its 'citizenship' for municipal law purposes, is thereby presumed to be conferring nationality in international law), this view would lead to companies being deemed the 'nationals' of certain States in the absence of any action on the part of those States. While analogies between companies and the nationality of natural persons cannot be taken to extremes, and while Judge Jessup only refers to factual connections giving States a *permissive right* of protection without any duty to afford the company national treatment, the view does seem a radical departure from established principles.[34]

III. Qualified Reference to the Law of the Incorporating State

So far, our examination has been confined to the difficulties which will arise if international law determines the existence of a company for its purposes by reference to the municipal law of the incorporating State and makes that recognition automatic. There is no reason, though, why international law should not make recognition of this legal personality in municipal law subject to qualifications. It could do this for instance by requiring a genuine link between the company and incorporating State, not as a requirement for recognizing the nationality of the company, but as a requirement for recognizing the very existence of the company. Because a company incorporated in the absence of such a link would simply not be recognized in international law, issues of nationality and of the possibility of 'piercing the corporate veil' would not arise. There would be no company to protect; the national State of the persons behind the company would be free to protect these.

This approach would be consistent with that pertaining in other situations in which the operation of international law depends on the content of municipal law, such as the nationality of natural persons and the delimitation of the territorial sea. Here it is well established that while international law refers to municipal law, the effect of municipal law on the international plane remains a question of international law. In relation to maritime boundaries, the International Court of Justice said in the *Fisheries* case: 'Although it is true that the act of delimitation is necessarily a unilateral act, because only the coastal State is competent to undertake it, the validity of the delimitation with regard to other States depends upon international law'.[35]

---

[34] While the *Cayuga Indians* arbitration (1926), *Reports of International Arbitral Awards*, vol. 6, p. 173, did establish the possibility of natural persons being deemed to have a nationality on the basis of a factual connection, this proposition was clearly of limited application. The award rested on the assumption that the individuals in question were persons 'in a state of pupillage' to whom the national government stood '*in loco parentis*'. It would be untenable to suggest that natural persons generally could be attributed nationality on the basis of their place of residence or business activities, etc.

[35] *ICJ Reports*, 1951, p. 116 at p. 132.

In relation to the nationality of natural persons, it said in the *Nottebohm* case:[36]

> It is . . . for every sovereign State, to settle by its own legislation the rules relating to the acquisition of its nationality . . . It is not necessary to determine whether international law imposes any limitations on its freedom of decision in this domain . . . [But it] is international law which determines whether a State is entitled to exercise protection and seise the Court.[37]

As with nationality laws, municipal company laws are enacted with municipal legal effects in mind, and there is no reason to question the limits of a State's jurisdiction to create juridical persons for its own municipal purposes.[38] Whether this municipal legal personality will be transposed onto the international plane is a question of international law, and there is no reason why international law should *ipso facto* give it unqualified effect.[39] Judge Jessup notes[40] that in international law 'there was growing recognition of the rule that if a State wishes to have its "unilateral acts" recognized and given effect by other States, those acts must conform to the principles and rules of international law'. Strangely, this comment is made in the context of the nationality of corporations, without any mention of its relevance to the issue of the very existence of corporations for international law purposes.

Because this point has never been the subject of detailed discussion, it is difficult to say, assuming recognition of the existence of a company is conditional upon its having some minimum connection with the incorporating State, what manner of connection is required. A convenient solution would be to require a connection similar to that required to make the company's nationality of that State effective. In that case, either the company would be recognized and the incorporating State would be competent to protect it, or the company would not be recognized and the persons behind it could be protected by their national State.[41] This is the effect of Judge Fitzmaurice's suggestion[42] that shareholder claims should be permitted in cases where the company's State of incorporation is unable to protect it for want of sufficient connection. Judge Jessup reaches a slightly different conclusion, however. He assumes that shareholder claims are always permitted, whether or not some other State is concurrently entitled to protect the com-

---

[36] *ICJ Reports*, 1955, p. 4 at pp. 20–1.

[37] Similarly, while it is for each State to determine for itself with which States it is at war, the question of belligerent status for international law purposes is one of international law: *Interhandel* case, *ICJ Reports*, 1959, p. 6 at p. 25.

[38] The judgment in the *Barcelona Traction* case noted (at p. 33) that the creation of companies by States is 'in a domain essentially within their domestic jurisdiction', just as nationality laws are 'in principle within this reserved domain': *Nationality Decrees in Tunis and Morocco* case (1923), *PCIJ*, Series B, No. 4, at p. 24.

[39] A point made vehemently by Judges Gros and Riphagen: see below, n. 73.

[40] At p. 188.

[41] The solution assumed by Brownlie, op. cit. above (n. 4), at p. 487.

[42] At pp. 79–80.

pany itself.[43] Moreover, although he expressly says that Canada was incapable of protecting the Barcelona Traction company,[44] this appears not to have affected its existence in international law. If Belgium had succeeded in proving to his satisfaction an 88 per cent Belgian interest in the company, presumably Belgium might on his criteria have been capable of protecting the company itself as one of its 'national' States.[45]

Comments by Judge Tanaka could be taken as the strongest support for the view that the creation of a company in municipal law does not automatically entail its recognition in international law,[46] if he too did not, quite surprisingly, reach exactly the opposite conclusion. He assumes the existence and Belgian nationality of Sidro (a parent company of Barcelona Traction) by virtue of its incorporation under Belgian law and the location of its *siège social* in Belgium, considering irrelevant all other factors.[47] Like Judge Jessup, however, he considers that concurrent shareholder claims will always be possible.[48]

Of course, even if the recognition of the existence of a company in international law required a genuine link between the company and the State of incorporation, this would not obviate discussion about the possibility of concurrent shareholder claims, particularly in situations where damage is inflicted by the State of incorporation on a company owned by non-nationals, but also where the State of incorporation is, for whatever reason, disinclined to protect the company in which nationals of other States have substantial interests. The precise nature of the link required would also still need to be determined for the purposes of the rule.[49]

The existence of a genuine link rule would also give rise to the question of the point in time at which the genuine link must exist. Is a genuine link with the State of incorporation required only at the time of incorporation, or only at the time that its existence is in issue (so that it will be recognized if there is a genuine link at the time of injury and of the bringing of the claim, even if there was none at the time of actual incorporation), or is a genuine connection required continuously from the time of incorporation to the time of bringing the claim?

If the correct answer were the first, many companies would exist for the purposes of international law despite having lost the original connection with their State of incorporation (by virtue of changes in share ownership,

---

[43] At pp. 195–200.

[44] At pp. 188–91.

[45] See above, n. 32 and accompanying text. But cf. at p. 183.

[46] e.g. at p. 121: 'Law relating to corporations is concerned with matters of private law . . . and belongs to the plane of municipal law . . . [I]t belongs to an entirely different plane of law the prevailing principle of which is quite extraneous to that of diplomatic protection.'

[47] At p. 140.

[48] At pp. 128–9. He considers that a claim could be brought on behalf of the holder of even a single share. Cf. Judge Jessup at p. 206.

[49] In the *Barcelona Traction* case, in discussing the issue of nationality, the Court considered in its judgment that there were genuine links between the company and Canada, while Judges Jessup and Gros found none.

places of operation, etc.). Because of this, the State of incorporation may not be inclined to protect it, while the existence of the company would prevent claims by the national States of the shareholders, leading again to either *de facto* statelessness or the need to permit protection by States other than the State of incorporation.

If the correct answer were the second, the result would be to render the existence of a company in international law quite unstable. As its shares are traded and its board of management changes over time, it may periodically cease to exist and resume existence on the international plane as links with the State of incorporation are lost and reestablished. However, its existence in the municipal law of the State of incorporation, and presumably in that of every State in which it engages in activities, would be unaffected.

If the correct answer were the third, the existence in international law of many public corporations whose shares are widely traded in a number of countries is likely to be ephemeral, particularly if they are holding companies for subsidiaries incorporated elsewhere, since at some stage of their history it is likely that their connection with the State of incorporation may be severed, if only for a short period, by changes in ownership. It would also be necessary for the State of incorporation, when bringing the claim, to demonstrate the continuous existence of this connection, which in practice could prove extremely difficult.[50] Similar difficulties would be faced by a State seeking to assert the existence of the company to resist a claim by the national State of the shareholders.

Before seeking to draw conclusions on these issues, it will first be necessary to examine the possibility that the question of the existence of a company for international law purposes does not depend at all on the municipal law of the State of incorporation.

IV. REFERENCE TO THE LAW OF THE DEFENDANT STATE

The one judge in the *Barcelona Traction* case to address directly the question of the circumstances in which corporations created by municipal law will be recognized by international law was Judge Morelli, and, interestingly, he did not consider the law of the incorporating State to be the relevant factor, but rather the law of the defendant State in any case in which a claim is brought on behalf of a company. This stems from his view on the general principle of respect for acquired rights. On this he says:

. . . the international rule . . . has regard solely to interests which, within that [municipal] legal order, have already received some degree of protection through

---

[50] As is evidenced by Belgium's failure to satisfy several of the judges in the *Barcelona Traction* case of the Belgian nature of the Sidro-Sofina group. If nationals of the State of incorporation owned 51 per cent of the company's shares, the ability of the claimant State to establish such a connection would mean the difference between being able to claim for damages equivalent to 100 per cent or 51 per cent of the damage sustained by the company.

the attribution of rights or other advantageous personal legal situations (faculties, legal powers or expectations): an attitude on the part of the State legal order which in itself is not obligatory in international law.

It is on the hypothesis that this state of affairs has arisen in the municipal legal order that the international rule lays upon the State the obligation to observe a certain line of conduct with regard to the interests in question: with regard, one might thenceforward say, to the rights whereby the interests in question stand protected in the municipal legal order . . . [51]

This view (which this writer has previously termed the 'Morelli principle'[52]) was supported in that case by Judge Padilla Nervo.[53] Judge Morelli goes on to say that:

From the considerations I have set forth it needs must follow that, in terms of general international law at least, a State is free even to deny companies—or certain companies—legal personality . . . It is only in the event that certain rights and, consequently, legal personality are conferred on a company within the municipal order that the State is bound by certain international obligations with regard to the judicial protection of those rights and respect for the same.

Where the municipal legal order denies a company legal personality, this signifies that the municipal order in question considers the corporate property as the subject-matter of rights pertaining to the members. In that event it is in relation to these rights, freely conferred on the members by the municipal order, that there is incumbent upon the State an international obligation of protection and respect.

If, on the other hand, the municipal legal order allows the company legal personality, it can but treat the members' rights accordingly. Consistently with the attribution of the corporate property to the company, considered as a juristic person, the members will in this case enjoy no more than limited rights, the subject-matter of which will not be the corporate property.[54]

In other words, as every State is only obliged to respect those rights of an alien which it has itself recognized the alien as having, every State is free to determine for itself whether to recognize a foreign corporation as a juridical person capable of enjoying rights and, if so, what these rights are. Protection can only be exercised in respect of a violation of those rights. Thus, it is not a matter of determining generally whether a particular company is recognized as existing in international law. Rather, in every particular case in which a State seeks to bring a claim in respect of the violation of the rights of one of its nationals, it will be necessary to determine in whom, if anyone, the defendant State recognized those rights as vesting. If it has recognized them as vesting in a company, only the national State of the

---

[51] At p. 233.

[52] Staker, 'Public International Law and the *Lex Situs* Rule in Property Conflicts and Foreign Expropriations', this *Year Book*, 58 (1987), p. 151 at p. 156.

[53] At p. 250: 'It is indispensable [to a valid State claim on behalf of a national] that the protected person be himself the possessor of a right which would entitle him to formulate a claim for damages in the internal judicial order'.

[54] At p. 235.

company will be entitled to bring a claim. The corporate personality of a company in international law is then, on this view, a relative status, depending on whether the defendant State has recognized it, and, presumably, to what extent it has recognized it.

This view is not without doctrinal support,[55] although Judge Morelli is very much in the minority.[56] It is appealing in that it provides for a single, simple test for determining whether a company is to be treated as existing on the international plane that avoids the complications of other tests and which is consistent with the principle of State sovereignty. However, it is submitted, with respect, that Judge Morelli's views do not reflect the present position in international law.

First, the present writer has previously argued that the Morelli principle of acquired rights is not a correct statement of the law with respect to tangible property or debts (although it applies in the case of intangible property such as intellectual and industrial property).[57] It was argued that in the case of tangible real or personal property, every State is not entirely free to determine for itself in whom rights under its municipal law shall vest. In the case of tangible property brought into the territory of a State, the State is obliged by international law to recognize any title to it acquired under the law of a previous situs. Where under that law title belongs to a person not a national of the State of the new situs, the failure of this State to recognize the title will amount to a failure to respect the acquired rights of an alien, and will effectively be a confiscation of that property. If this is so, the Morelli principle of acquired rights cannot be relied upon as a basis for the Morelli view of corporate personality.

Secondly, it is fundamentally difficult to assert that a State is completely free to decide, as property is brought into its territory, in whom that property vests, irrespective of the municipal laws of any other State. Logically, if this is the case, not only would it be possible (to use the example of the *Barcelona Traction* case) for Spain to deny recognition to a company validly incorporated under the laws of Canada by nationals of Belgium (and recognize the Belgian shareholders as being the actual owners), but it could, for instance, 'recognize' property brought into its territory by a group of Belgian nationals as belonging to a Canadian company, even though under Canadian law no such company exists. If this were the case, every State could avoid possible diplomatic claims in respect of assets brought to its territory by foreigners by 'recognizing' them as the property

---

[55] Caflisch, *La Protection des sociétés commerciales et des intérêts indirects en droit international public* (The Hague, 1969), at p. 19: ' . . . c'est à la législation de l'Etat défendeur que l'on se réfère pour mesurer l'étendue de la personnalité juridique attribuée à la société'.

[56] Comments by President Bustamante y Rivero may be taken to support the view: '[Diplomatic protection of a company presupposes that a] legal bond has first been established between the holding company which forms the subject of diplomatic protection and the State whose acts are the subject of complaint' (at p. 56). Judge Padilla Nervo, while agreeing with the Morelli principle of acquired rights (above, n. 53), does not apply it to the issue of the existence of companies, relying instead on the 'situation of the shareholder as defined by the various legal systems' (at p. 256).

[57] Loc. cit. above (n. 52).

of companies of third States having no interest in protecting them. By 'recognizing' a non-existent Canadian company, Spain would in effect itself be creating the company and conferring Canadian nationality on it.[58] This runs counter to the well-established rule that one State cannot confer the nationality of another. Yet Judge Morelli expressly says that even if the Barcelona Traction company were dissolved under Canadian law, Spain could still 'recognize' the existence of the company and thereby resist any claim brought by Belgium on behalf of the Belgian shareholders. He adds that Canada would still be entitled to protect the company in international law although it did not exist as a matter of Canadian law![59]

As a matter of principle, it is surely not tenable to argue that Spain's discretion could go beyond a decision whether or not to recognize a company which has been established under Canadian law. Even so, while considerations of State sovereignty may support the view that in the international legal relations between Canada and Spain, the unilateral acts of Canada should not bind Spain without the latter's consent, those same considerations would seem to undermine the suggestion that Spain may unilaterally determine the validity of the acts of a third party for the purposes of Spain's international legal relations with Belgium. Surely Belgium had as much right as Spain to determine for itself whether it would recognize the existence of the Barcelona Traction company for the purposes of its international legal relations with Spain. Admittedly, in the *Barcelona Traction* case itself, Belgium had in fact in its pleadings admitted the existence of the Barcelona Traction company. However, it surely would not have done so if it had not considered itself bound to. None of the Judges suggested that Belgium had any discretion in the matter.

The Morelli principle of corporate personality gives rise to the further question of what actions of the defendant State can be taken to imply recognition of a foreign corporation. Judge Morelli simply said that both parties had agreed the company enjoyed legal personality in the legal order of Spain.[60] This was also evident in that case from the nature of the injury complained of: a bankruptcy judgment pronounced by a Spanish court against the company which necessarily implied the existence of the company in Spanish law. However, the issue could arise for instance in a case of an injury that consisted only of the physical seizure by a State of property in transit through its territory allegedly belonging to a foreign corporation that transacted no business in that State and had no other assets there. Presumably it would be sufficient for the claimant State to show that under the defendant State's municipal law, the existence of the company would have been recognized if this had ever been put in issue before its courts at a time

---

[58] Judge Morelli does not give a test for determining the nationality of companies, but appears to assume that once a company has been recognized, it may be protected against the recognizing State by the State of incorporation.

[59] At p. 240.

[60] At p. 236.

prior to the infliction of the injury.[61] This means that those States which grant automatic recognition to all foreign business companies (which are the majority)[62] can be taken to have recognized for international law purposes every company in the world in the abstract, leaving the discretion suggested by Judge Morelli little practical operation.

V. Existence of a Company as an Issue of Fact

So far we have examined the possibilities of the existence of a company for international law purposes being dependent on the municipal law of either the State of incorporation or the defendant State in any claim brought on behalf of a company, and have questioned the relevance of the municipal law of the claimant State in cases where the company is incorporated in a State not party to the claim. There is, however, a further possibility that the question whether a company exists for international law purposes does not depend on the municipal law of any State at all. It could be possible that international law confers on a State a right to protect a business undertaking (even if the individuals who own the undertaking are not all nationals of that State) where there are sufficient factual links between the State and the undertaking as a whole, regardless of whether the undertaking has separate legal personality in the municipal law of any State.

The Court's observation in the *Barcelona Traction* case that international law has no substantive rules of company law and that it therefore has to refer to the relevant rules of municipal law suggests that to be protected, a company must have been incorporated in some system of municipal law. However, the Court noted[63] that 'It is to rules generally accepted by municipal legal systems which recognize the limited company whose capital is represented by shares, and not to the municipal law of a particular State, that international law refers. In referring to such rules, the Court cannot modify, still less deform them.' The Court decided the case on the basis of the 'concept and structure of the company'[64] generally, without referring to specific provisions of either Canadian or Spanish law.[65] Judge Ammoun simply asked: 'Ought not international law . . . to align itself on this point with the generality of systems of municipal law, from which . . . there derive the concept of juristic personality and the limits assigned thereto?'[66] More recently, Judge Oda in the *ELSI* case considered whether a

---

[61] The issue is likely to come before the defendant State's courts *after* infliction of the injury if local remedies are exhausted, but the international legal position could not be affected by the subsequent conduct of the defendant State.

[62] Rabel, *The Conflict of Laws: A Comparative Study* (2nd edn. by Drobnig, Ann Arbor, 1960), vol. 2, pp. 133 ff.

[63] At p. 37.

[64] At p. 34.

[65] Also Judges Fitzmaurice at pp. 67, 70, Jessup at pp. 167–8, Padilla Nervo at p. 256.

[66] At p. 322, although he avoids being specific, referring to ' . . . the generality of municipal legal systems . . . in particular, the legal systems of Canada, of Belgium and of Spain'(p. 323).

treaty between the United States and Italy was intended to add to 'those rights of shareholders guaranteed to them under Italian law as well as under the general principles of law concerning companies'.[67]

These comments suggest that even if Canadian or Spanish law did confer on shareholders direct rights in respect of an injury to the company, this might be disregarded by international law as a 'modification' or 'deformation' of the rules generally accepted by municipal legal systems.[68] Taken to their logical conclusion, these comments would also mean that international law may recognize as a juridical person for the purposes of diplomatic protection an entity that does not have juridical personality under the municipal law of any State on the basis of a general principle of law that a collectivity which in reality exists as an entity distinct from its constitutive members should be recognized as having a separate personality in law.[69] Thus, despite the Court's insistence that international law has no rules of its own in the area of company law, it would on this view indeed have a body of rules independent of any municipal system, based on general principles accepted by all systems.[70]

It is beyond the scope of this essay to deal at length with the arguments in support of this view, and unnecessary, given the conclusions which follow.[71] It is, however, a tenable argument that as the specific rules for regulating the rights and obligations *inter se* of company, members and officers on the municipal plane do not have, and are not intended to have, any relevance to the rights *inter se* of States on the international plane, they should not be relied on at all in international law.[72] Some of the comments by Judges Gros and Riphagen could be cited in support of the argument.[73]

---

[67] *ICJ Reports*, 1989, p. 15 at pp. 87–8. See also *Starrett Housing Corp.* v. *Iran, Iran–US Claims Tribunal Reports*, 7 (1984–III), p. 119 at p. 120, *per* Kashani (dissenting op.): 'Under the legal systems of Iran and the United States, as well as under international law . . .'.

[68] Judge Jessup (at pp. 167–8) considers the possibility of a rule based on general principles *allowing* shareholder claims in international law, irrespective of the provisions of municipal law. Cf. Judge Gros, at p. 273, who assumes that under the Court's view, shareholder claims would be admissible in international law if provided for in the municipal law of either Canada or Spain.

[69] An approach which would prefer the 'reality' theory of corporate personality over the 'fiction theory'. It is not possible to deal here with the details of these theories: see Caflisch, op. cit. above (n. 55), at pp. 5–10; de Visscher, loc. cit. above (n. 31), at pp. 399–408. The two theories were referred to by some of the judges in the *Barcelona Traction* case: see, e.g., Judge Tanaka at p. 120. There are in fact municipal law authorities in support of the existence of a general principle that in the absence of legislation for incorporating companies, the formation of juristic persons should be legally recognized: see the 1913 decision of the Chinese Supreme Court reproduced in Cheng (tr.), *The Chinese Supreme Court Decisions* (Peking, 1923), p. 9.

[70] Judge Ammoun explains this apparent contradiction by treating 'the law of the commercial legal order' (p. 327) — i.e. the generality of municipal legal systems (p. 322) — as a separate body of law, a '*lex fori*', to which international law refers (see pp. 325–8).

[71] Below, nn. 82–4 and accompanying text.

[72] And here the arguments raised above in Part III are equally pertinent.

[73] *per* Judge Gros: ' . . . the *renvoi* to municipal law leads eventually, in the present case, to the establishment of a superiority of municipal over international law which is a veritable negation of the latter' (at p. 272); 'The Court does not have to apply the rules of municipal law, as a municipal court of last instance would, to the relationships between the company and the shareholder; it takes account of them as being facts for the purpose of its appraisal of the legal situation laid before it by Parties and in order to see whether that situation as a whole is in conformity with the rules of international law or not'

VI. Conclusions

Given the wide disagreement between the members of the *Barcelona Traction* Court on the various aspects of the diplomatic protection of companies, it is difficult to find any clear guidance in that case as to the rules which determine whether the existence of a company will be recognized for the purposes of international law. The disagreements between the judges were due in part to the differing outlooks of those from industrialized and those from developing countries. Moreover, some of the judges were apparently attempting to develop, rather than merely apply, the existing rules.[74]

There is no reason even to assume that there is one set of rules for all purposes of international law. There may be different rules depending on whether the existence of a company is sought to be established for the purposes of the international law rules on diplomatic protection or for some other purpose of international law.[75] Even within the domain of diplomatic protection, the rules may depend on the type of juridical person involved. The *Barcelona Traction* judgment noted[76] that there was no need in that case 'to investigate the many different forms of legal entity provided for by the municipal laws of States' because the Court was 'concerned only with . . . a limited liability company whose capital is represented by shares'. Judge Riphagen even suggested that there may be different rules for different types of limited liability companies,[77] while other judges discussed the possibility of distinct rules applying to holding companies.[78] Judge Riphagen also suggested that the applicable rules may depend on the type of injury inflicted,[79] while there has long been support for the view that the rules on the existence of a corporate personality may be affected by the relationship between the company and the defendant State, so that the existence of the company can be disregarded where the defendant State is the State of incorporation.[80] There is even the possibility that there are 'regional' rules of customary international law, so that the rule may vary depending on whether the parties to which it is applied are two industria-

---

(ibid.); 'In this case, proof has not been supplied in a manner satisfying for a court that Barcelona Traction, in continuous fashion, predominantly — or even substantially — represented an investment on the part of the Belgian economy' (at p. 282). *per* Judge Riphagen: 'It is . . . not possible to regard the company's legal personality under municipal law as an exclusive touchstone' (at p. 343); 'The essential point is thus the existence or non-existence of a link between the undertaking and the Belgian State sufficient for it to be considered on the international plane that the international commerce of the latter State is affected by those measures' (at pp. 345–6).

[74] e.g. Judges Tanaka (at p. 131) and Padilla Nervo (at pp. 247–8). Judge Fitzmaurice agreed with the sentiments of Judge Jessup's judgment, but considered it to be applying rules that were *de lege ferenda* only. Cf. Judge Jessup (pp. 165–6, 170), who purported to apply the rules as they existed in 1948, the time of the alleged injury.

[75] e.g. the determination of belligerent status in wartime: see the reference to the *Interhandel* case, above, n. 37.

[76] At p. 34.

[77] At pp. 342 ff.

[78] President Bustamante y Rivero (at pp. 54–7); Judge Gros (at pp. 268, 280).

[79] At pp. 348 ff.

[80] Referred to in the judgment (at p. 48) and most of the separate opinions.

lized States, or an industrialized State and a developing State.[81] It is in the face of these variables and uncertainties that it will now be attempted to reach some kind of conclusions in the case of the diplomatic protection of companies limited by shares.

First, it is the case that diplomatic claims on behalf of companies will inevitably concern issues of acquired rights under municipal law. Even where a State claim on behalf of a company is based on an alleged denial of justice *stricto sensu* (such as a denial of proper access to the courts, irrespective of whether the municipal law of the defendant State confers a right of access), the company concerned will have been denied justice while attempting to assert or defend an acquired right. (The Barcelona Traction company, for instance, had allegedly been deprived of the assets of its operating subsidiaries in Spain as a result of a denial of justice.) Since a company cannot acquire rights in municipal law without being recognized in municipal law, it is submitted that international law does not permit the diplomatic protection of a company which has not been incorporated under some system of municipal law. While it is true that international law may protect interests of individuals not amounting to rights in municipal law,[82] it seems superfluous for international law to create for its own purposes legal entities capable of having interests. The mere fact that an entity exists as a social and economic reality should not of itself in the absence of incorporation in municipal law mean that diplomatic protection is exercisable on behalf of the entity as a whole. In such cases all rights and interests belong to the individual members and are protectable as such. This view is supported in the case of business companies by comments in the judgment of the PCIJ in the *Panevezys-Saldutiskis Railway* case,[83] and is consistent with the authorities on other types of juridical person created by municipal law.[84]

Judge Gros suggests that independently of issues of diplomatic protection, a State may bring a claim against another on the basis that illegal actions of the defendant State towards a business entity (whether incorporated or not, and if so, regardless of the State of incorporation) adversely

---

[81] See Judge Jessup, at p. 164. The suggestion is rejected by Judge Gros at p. 277.

[82] See Judge Jessup at pp. 167–8.

[83] (1939) *PCIJ*, Series A/B, No. 76, p. 17. Thus, claims cannot be brought on behalf of partnerships which have no separate legal personality in the system of law under which they were created. Claims must be brought on behalf of individual partners. See Brownlie, op. cit. above (n. 4), at pp. 483–4; Judge Tanaka at pp. 117, 119; Judge Ammoun at p. 298. This is also consistent with the Court's comment that the creation of companies is within the domestic jurisdiction of States (above, n. 38). It may however be sufficient that the company has been created by treaty rather than municipal law: in the *Panevezys-Saldutiskis Railway* case it was argued that the effect of the Treaty of Tartu between the Soviet Union and Estonia 'was to preserve the existence of the Russian company and convert it automatically into an Estonian company'. In that case, Estonia sought to assert the existence of this company against a third party, Lithuania.

[84] In the *Peter Pázmány University* case, loc. cit. above (n. 3), the existence of a university as a body corporate was determined in accordance with Hungarian law. In 1834, the King's Advocate advised Lord Palmerston that the question whether certain religious houses in Portugal were corporations for the purposes of diplomatic protection, separate from the members who were British subjects, depended on the law of Portugal: McNair, op. cit. above (n. 2), at pp. 32–3.

affected the economy of the claimant State.[85] Whether any such action exists in international law need not be discussed here. There is, however, no *a priori* rule that a State violates international law by conducting itself in a manner prejudicial to the economy of another State,[86] and other judges on the *Barcelona Traction* Court did not support a rule applying in the case of illegal conduct towards companies that are nationals of third States.[87]

However, while the incorporation of a company in municipal law may be necessary for its recognition on the international plane, this may not necessarily be sufficient. In this area, as in the case of nationality, international law could adopt a functional approach. Thus, where a company has been incorporated under some system of municipal law, but as a matter of social and economic reality it has no existence independent from its members, it would seem reasonable for international law not to permit claims on behalf of the company, but to require instead that claims be brought in respect of the shareholders interested in the company (or, to use different terminology, the corporate personality of such a company should not be recognized for the purposes of diplomatic protection). In the case of an enterprise conducted by a 'one-person' company incorporated in State A, in which the 'one person' is a national of State B, State A has no greater, and State B no lesser, interest in protecting the company than in a case in which the enterprise was conducted in the person's own name. As there is no reason for international law to apply automatically the consequences of municipal law, it is submitted that the better view is that any injury inflicted on such an enterprise should be the subject of a potential claim by State B only. This should apply whether the 'one person' is a natural person or another company, so that if the Barcelona Traction company had been a wholly owned subsidiary of Sofina, and Belgium's right to espouse a claim on behalf of the latter had been established, Belgium should have been able to claim in respect of the alleged injury to Barcelona Traction.[88] Similarly, where a company has been incorporated for the sole purpose of holding and managing property jointly owned by its members (e.g. an item of real estate or an investment portfolio), such that the company cannot be said to represent more than the joint property interests of its members, State claims on behalf of the company should not be admissible, but the property interest of each of the members should be capable of protection by their national State(s). The same reasoning could also apply where in reality a corporation is a joint venture of two or more companies or persons, in which, despite the corporate form, the separate interests and activities of the co-venturers remain readily identifiable.[89]

---

[85] At esp. pp. 278–9.

[86] Judgment, at p. 46.

[87] See especially the judgment at pp. 45–6.

[88] In fact, Belgium was in that case seeking in effect to apply such a rule, since the assets seized by the Spanish authorities in fact belonged to various wholly-owned subsidiaries of Barcelona Traction, incorporated in Canada and Spain.

[89] This would answer the problem raised by Judge Jessup at pp. 200–1.

Conversely, where a company incorporated and enjoying certain rights under municipal law in fact constitutes an entity separate from its constituent members, it is more convenient for the claimant State, the defendant State, the company itself and its members for one claim to be brought in international law in respect of the rights as a whole of the company itself, and the municipal law concept of the incorporated company as a separate legal entity is one which commends itself to adoption on the international plane. For the existence of a company to be recognized for the purposes of diplomatic protection, there do not appear to be any requirements other than incorporation under some municipal legal system and an existence in reality independent of the members. In particular, there appears to be no requirement of a genuine link between the company and the State under the laws of which it is incorporated. All of the judges in the *Barcelona Traction* case accepted the existence for international law purposes of the Barcelona Traction company, even those who found that there was no genuine link between the company and Canada.[90] If a company exists as a matter of social reality, the fact that it has assumed a charter of convenience appears irrelevant, especially as it will presumably be recognized under the private international law rules of every State with which it does have a genuine connection (it being difficult to imagine the charter being otherwise chosen). It may be arguable that if neither party to a State claim has recognized a company in its law, each should be estopped from asserting its existence against the other in international law.

It is submitted that, contrary to the principle advanced by Judge Morelli, the recognition of a company for international law purposes does not depend on recognition in the municipal law of the defendant State. Moreover, the defendant State does not necessarily have an international law duty to recognize all companies which would be recognized for international law purposes. If a company is incorporated in State A and acquires tangible movable property under the law of that State which is subsequently taken to the territory of State B, the latter State will be under an international law duty to recognize the company's title to that property.[91] It is submitted that State B will have sufficiently discharged this duty if under its system of municipal law the existence of the company is not recognized,[92] but the members of the company are considered the joint owners of the corporate property. However, if State B confiscated the property, a

---

[90] Even the links found by the Court (continuity of registration in Canada, location of registered office, accounts and share register in Canada, holding of board meetings there during a period and registration with the Canadian tax authorities) were largely the necessary consequences of incorporation in Canada rather than an independent connection with it.

[91] Under the *lex situs* rule which is part of international law. See above, n. 52.

[92] It is hoped to deal at a later date with the question of the extent to which States have a duty in international law to recognize in their municipal law companies incorporated under the law of another State. Rabel, op. cit. above (n. 62), gives examples of countries imposing conditions on the recognition of foreign stock companies.

State claim could be brought on behalf of the company by its 'national' State.

The question of when a company can be taken to exist for international law purposes is an essential one. However, if the above conclusions are correct, the problem remains that a company may be recognized as existing in international law for the purposes of diplomatic protection while having no genuine connection with its State of incorporation. In addressing this question, no new answers have therefore been found to the problems of the nationality of companies in international law and the possibility of concurrent diplomatic claims on behalf of shareholders. These latter issues remain unsettled and will need to be the subject of further study in future.

PERSONALITY AND PRIVACY UNDER THE EUROPEAN CONVENTION ON HUMAN RIGHTS*

By L. G. LOUCAIDES‡

I. PROTECTION OF THE INDIVIDUAL AS A PERSON

Freedom of the person is a paramount and fundamental human right in every liberal State. For this freedom to be meaningful and to serve man in a modern humane society, it must embrace the whole spectrum of his psychosomatic and intellectual entity and activity. If freedom of the person is exclusively defined by reference to the abstract relationship of the individual to the State or individual to society, without taking account of the particular personal qualities of the individual, it will be of limited practical value. For man to be able to function freely, in the full sense of the term, he must have the possibility of self-definition and self-determination: the right to be himself.

Thus, the achievement of effective protection of freedom of the person requires legal recognition and safeguarding of the individuality of man, i.e. of the qualities, abilities and characteristics that distinguish and individualize a particular person; all those attributes that give to every human being his special and original signification in society; in other words, his personality.[1]

In the domain of the domestic legal order the constitutions of some European countries expressly recognize a specific right 'to free development of one's personality'. Thus Article 2 of the Basic Law of the Federal Republic of Germany provides as follows:

Every one shall have the right to the free development of his personality in so far as he does not violate the rights of others or offend against constitutional order or the moral code.

A similar provision is contained in Article 5 of the Greek Constitution of 1975. But even in the domain of international law the necessity of protect-

* © L.G. Loucaides, 1991.

‡ Deputy Attorney-General of Cyprus; Member of the European Commission of Human Rights.

[1] The concept of personality is not to be confused with that of the individual as a biological entity. For a useful compendium of articles on this subject, see Kluchkohn and Murray (eds.), *Personality in Nature, Society and Culture* (2nd edn., 1953). Friedrich emphasizes that the 'core objective' of a constitution should be 'that of safeguarding each member of the political community' as 'a person' and adds: 'Each man is supposed to possess a sphere of genuine autonomy. The constitution is meant to protect the *self*; for the self is believed to be the (primary and ultimate) value': *Constitutional Government and Democracy* (4th edn., 1968), p. 8. For the 'autonomy' of the individual, see generally Burdeau, *Traité de science politique*, vol. 6 (1971), pp. 189 ff., and vol. 7 (1973), pp. 602 ff.

ing the personality of the individual as a whole has gradually been recognized. Already, in the field of international efforts for the protection of human rights, man is not regarded as an abstract concept of the positive law of States, but as a real psychosomatic being according to the true relations and conditions of social life.[2] This 'personalized' approach is also expressed by the specific reference to the 'personality' of man in the Universal Declaration of Human Rights adopted by the General Assembly of the United Nations in 1948.[3] In Article 22 of this Declaration it is provided:

Everyone, as a member of society, has the right to social security and is entitled to realization, through national effort and international co-operation and in accordance with the organization and resources of each State, of the economic, social and cultural rights indispensable for his dignity and the free development of his personality.

Article 29 of the same Declaration provides:

Everyone has duties to the community in which alone the free and full development of his personality is possible.

In the same year the concept of personality was again referred to in the American Declaration of the Rights and Duties of Man:

It is the duty of the individual so to conduct himself in relation to others that each and every one may fully form and develop his personality.[4]

II. The European Convention on Human Rights

In the European Convention on Human Rights, which came into force in 1953, there is no express reference to the concept of the personality of individuals. However, the system of protection provided thereby was intended to cover significant aspects of the human personality. In its preamble reference is made to the Universal Declaration of Human Rights as a source for its inspiration. Moreover the Convention was drafted in the aftermath of the Second World War and was the product of the abhorrent experiences of Nazism.[5] It is therefore natural to assume that the enhancement of the protection of the individual as a person must have been one of the primary aims of the Convention.

[2] Cf. Burdeau, op. cit. (previous note), vol. 7, pp. 589 ff.

[3] A more recent reference to the concept of personality in UN instruments can be found in the Convention against Discrimination in Education of 1960, Article 5: 'Education shall be directed to the full development of the human personality . . . '; and in the International Covenant on Economic, Social and Cultural Rights of 1966, Article 13: 'The States Parties . . . agree that education shall be directed to the full development of the human personality . . . '.

[4] Article XXIX; see also the Preamble to the American Convention on Human Rights of 1969 where it is expressly recognized that the 'essential rights of man are not derived from one's being a national of a certain state, but are based upon attributes of the human personality, and that they therefore justify international protection in the form of a convention reinforcing or complementing the protection provided by the domestic law of the American states.'

[5] Cf. Doswald-Beck, 'The Meaning of the "Right to Respect for Private Life" under the European Convention on Human Rights', *Human Rights Law Journal*, 4 (1983), p. 283 at pp. 286, 287.

The personalized inclination of the system is indicated by the particular human rights which are expressly recognized and protected and which constitute aspects of the personality of the individual in a democratic and pluralistic society (the right to respect for private and family life, home and correspondence, freedom of thought, of expression and of association, the right to education, the right to marry, etc.).

The principle of protecting the individual as a person has also influenced those responsible for the interpretation of the Convention. In fact, the interpretation of the Convention by the organs of the Convention, and in particular by the Commission and the Court of Human Rights, has played a decisive role in the substantial recognition and protection of the personality of the individual in its widest expression. This has been achieved through a constant widening of the relevant provisions and their adjustment to progressive social ideas and changing perceptions. The result is the extension of protection to a large and continually developing spectrum of specific situations.

The most interesting and substantial contribution in this field involves the interpretation and application of the right to 'respect for private life', which is defined in Article 8 of the Convention as follows:

1. Everyone has the right to respect for his private and family life, his home and his correspondence.
2. There shall be no interference by a public authority with the exercise of this right except such as is in accordance with the law and is necessary in a democratic society in the interests of national security, public safety or the economic well-being of the country, for the prevention of disorder or crime, for the protection of health or morals, or for the protection of the rights and freedoms of others.

(a) 'Private Life' and 'Personality'

Professor Velu, in a treatise of 1970,[6] expressed the view that the right to respect for private life was, in effect, a miscellany of rights covering a wide field of individual activities, and added:

In particular, this right protects the individual against:
(1) Attacks on his physical or mental integrity or his moral or intellectual freedom.
(2) Attacks on his honour and reputation and similar torts.
(3) The use of his name, identity or likeness.
(4) Being spied upon, watched or harassed.
(5) The disclosure of information protected by the duty of professional secrecy.[7]

In the meantime, the case law of the Council of Europe on the scope of

---

[6] 'The European Convention on Human Rights and the Right to Respect for Private Life, the Home and Communications', in Robertson (ed.), *Privacy and Human Rights* (1973), p. 12 at p. 92. See also Opsahl, 'The Convention and the Right to Respect for Family Life', ibid., p. 182; Jacobs, *The European Convention on Human Rights* (1975), p. 126.

[7] This analysis seems to have been the prevailing view in the colloquy held in 1970 by the Council of Europe and the Belgian universities to study the content of Article 8 of the European Convention: see Robertson, op. cit. (previous note), pp. 425, 428.

the right in question has developed in an impressive and progressive manner and has abandoned certain of its earlier and more conservative jurisprudence. While extending the meaning of the right to respect for private life, the Commission and the Court of Human Rights of the Council of Europe have not, as yet, attempted to give an exhaustive definition of this right.[8] This fact, together with the established approach that the Convention is a 'living instrument' whose interpretation may develop over the years,[9] promises that new rights derived from the notion of 'private life' will continually be recognized whenever required by the conditions of social life.[10]

The first authoritative analysis of the right of 'privacy' was made in the report of the Commission of Human Rights in Application No. 6825/74.[11] The case concerned a complaint by an owner of a dog in Iceland that legislation which prohibited the keeping of dogs, with the exception of dogs necessary in connection with farming, violated his right to respect for his private life. In dismissing the application the Commission observed:

> For numerous anglo-saxon and French authors the right to respect for 'private life' is the right to privacy, the right to live, as far as one wishes, protected from publicity . . .
>
> In the opinion of the Commission, however, the right to respect for private life does not end there. It comprises also, to a certain degree, the right to establish and to develop relationships with other human beings, especially in the emotional field for the development and fulfilment of one's own personality.
>
> The Commission cannot, however, accept that the protection afforded by Article 8 of the Convention extends to relationships of the individual with his entire immediate surroundings, insofar as they do not involve human relationships and notwithstanding the desire of the individual to keep such relationship within the private sphere.
>
> No doubt the dog has had close ties with man since time immemorial. However, given the above considerations, this element alone is not sufficient to bring the keeping of a dog into the sphere of private life of the owner. It can further be mentioned that the keeping of dogs is by the very nature of that animal necessarily associated with certain interferences with the life of others and even with the public life.[12]

This decision is bold enough in accepting the idea that private life extends to certain relationships of man which are necessary for 'the development of his personality'—even though in applying this approach to the particular

---

[8] No guidance as to the meaning of this right can be derived from the *travaux préparatoires* of the Convention, as there is no discussion at all of such right therein.

[9] e.g. *Tyrer* v. *UK, European Human Rights Reports* (hereinafter *EHRR*), vol. 2, p. 1; Series A, No. 26, para. 31.

[10] Cf. Vlachos, *Sociology of the Rights of Man* (1979), p. 163. According to McDougal, Lasswell and Chen, *Human Rights and World Public Order* (1980), p. 844, 'even in the absence of a concise international definition of privacy, existing transnational prescriptions concerning privacy or private life are undergoing an expansion in general community expectation that will permit their application to many important emerging threats to civic order'.

[11] *Decisions and Reports of the European Commission of Human Rights* (hereinafter *Decisions and Reports*), vol. 5, p. 86.

[12] At p. 87.

facts of the case the decision appears to be quite conservative. Through this decision the concept of 'the personality' of the individual is accepted for the first time as the basis for the determination of the scope of private life.

Equally important for the elaboration of the right in question is the report of the Commission in the case of *Bruggeman and Scheuten* v. *Germany*,[13] which concerned a complaint of violation, again, of the right to respect for private life, based, this time, on the prohibition of abortion. The majority of the Commission dismissed the application on the ground that pregnancy 'cannot be said to pertain uniquely to the sphere of private life. Whenever a woman is pregnant her private life becomes closely connected with the developing foetus'[14] (without deciding whether the unborn child is to be considered as a 'life' or 'entity' for the purposes of the Convention). Professor Fawcett disagreed with the approach adopted by the majority, and his dissenting opinion in support of a wider scope of private life appears to be convincing.[15] 'Private life', he stated, 'must cover pregnancy, its commencement and its termination: indeed, it would be hard to envisage more essentially private elements in life'.[16]

The Commission in this case again referred to the concept of the personality of the individual and stated:

> The right to respect for private life is of such a scope as to secure to the individual a sphere within which he can freely pursue the development and fulfilment of his personality. To this effect, he must also have the possibility of establishing relationships of various kinds, including sexual, with other persons. In principle, therefore, whenever the State sets up rules for the behaviour of the individual within this sphere, it interferes with the respect for private life and such interference must be justified in the light of para. (2) of Art. 8.

> However, there are limits to the personal sphere. While a large proportion of the law existing in a given State has some immediate or remote effect on the individual's possibility of developing his personality by doing what he wants to do, not all of these can be considered to constitute an interference with private life in the sense of Art. 8 of the Convention. In fact, as the earlier jurisprudence of the Commission has already shown, the claim to respect for private life is automatically reduced to the extent that the individual himself brings his private life into contact with public life or into close connection with other protected interests.[17]

In the case of *Paton* v. *UK*,[18] which concerned a complaint by a potential father relating to an abortion obtained by his wife without his permission, the Commission accepted that this constituted an interference with the applicant's right to respect for his private and family life, but found that

---

[13] Application No. 6959/75, *Decisions and Reports*, vol. 10, p. 100.

[14] At para. 59.

[15] See also Duffy, 'The Protection of Privacy, Family Life and Other Rights under Article 8 of the European Convention on Human Rights', *Yearbook of European Law*, 2 (1982), pp. 191, 194, 224. In the US case *Roe* v. *Wade*, 410 US 113 (1973), the Supreme Court invalidated a law banning abortion on the ground that it violated the right of 'privacy': see below, p. 191.

[16] At para. 1.

[17] At paras. 55–6.

[18] Application No. 8416/78, *Decisions and Reports*, vol. 19, p. 244.

such interference was justified under paragraph 2 of Article 8 as being necessary for the protection of another person, i.e. to avert the risk of injury to the physical or mental health of his wife.

Another interesting case regarding the concept of private life is *Arrondelle* v. *UK*,[19] where the Commission found admissible a complaint of interference with the applicant's right of privacy as a result of the noise caused by aircraft using an airport close to the applicant's property which subjected her to intolerable stress, the applicant being deprived at the same time of the means to change residence.

Of particular significance is the decision of the European Court of Human Rights in the case of *Airey* v. *Ireland*.[20] The Court in this case found that the applicant was justified in complaining that the State did not provide her with sufficient protection of her private life, as required by Article 8 of the Convention, inasmuch as she was not furnished with sufficient means to obtain a judicial separation from her husband. In particular the applicant complained that she had been unable to bring proceedings for judicial separation because the procedure was too technical for her to act as a litigant in person, whilst the absence of legal aid and the high legal costs prevented her, as a poor woman, from obtaining legal assistance.

The decision is significant in two ways. On the one hand it has recognized that the State, over and above its obligations to abstain from actions that amount to interference with the right to respect for the private life of an individual (unless justified under paragraph 2 of Article 8), has positive obligations to protect this right.[21] On the other hand, the concept of private life has been extended so as to include the right to obtain a legal separation from a spouse.[22] The Court found a breach of Article 8 and stated in its judgment:

> The Court does not consider that Ireland can be said to have 'interfered' with Mrs Airey's private or family life: the substance of her complaint is not that the State has acted but that it has failed to act . . . . In Ireland, many aspects of private or family life are regulated by law. As regards marriage, husband and wife are in principle under a duty to cohabit but are entitled, in certain cases, to petition for a decree of judicial separation; this amounts to recognition of the fact that the protection of their private or family life may sometimes necessitate their being relieved from the duty to live together.

[19] Application No. 7889/77, *Decisions and Reports*, vol. 19, p. 186.

[20] *EHRR*, vol. 2, p. 305; Series A, No. 32.

[21] In its decision of 26 March 1985 in *X and Y* v. *Netherlands*, *EHRR*, vol. 8, p. 235; Series A, No. 91, the European Court of Human Rights has reconfirmed this position as follows: 'The Court recalls that although the object of Article 8 is essentially that of protecting the individual against arbitrary interference by public authorities, it does not merely compel the State to abstain from such interference; in addition to this primarily negative undertaking, there may be positive obligations inherent in an effective respect for private or family life . . . These obligations may involve the adoption of measures designed to secure respect for private life even in the sphere of the relations of individuals themselves' (para. 23).

[22] In a more recent case (*Johnston and others* v. *Ireland*, 18 December 1986, *EHRR*, vol. 9, p. 203; Series A, No. 112) the Court distinguished the right to separate from the right to divorce and found that the latter was not safeguarded by Article 8; consequently the Court rejected the applicants' claim

Effective respect for private or family life obliges Ireland to make this means of protection effectively accessible . . . to anyone who may wish to have recourse thereto. However, it was not effectively accessible to the applicant . . . She has therefore been the victim of a violation of Article 8.[23]

The case law of the Council of Europe has not, as yet, defined what particular positive obligations are imposed on a State for the effective protection of respect for private life. It is clear that the case law on this subject will continue to evolve in the future, depending on the facts of the relevant cases.[24] It should be noted, however, that in a recent case[25] the Court pointed out that 'the notion of "respect" is not clear-cut, especially as far as the positive obligations are concerned: having regard to the diversity of the practices followed and the situations obtaining in the Contracting States the notion's requirements will vary considerably from case to case'. The Court added that 'this is an area in which the Contracting Parties enjoy a wide margin of appreciation in determining the steps to be taken to ensure compliance with the Convention with due regard to the needs and resources of the community and of individuals'.[26]

The recognition of positive obligations on the part of the State has paved the way for the application of the Convention in cases where there is interference with the rights of an individual by other *individuals*. If the Convention's obligations were only negative, it would be difficult to establish State responsibility for interference by private individuals with the rights safeguarded thereby. However, from the moment that it is accepted that States are also obliged to take positive measures, in order to ensure effective implementation of Convention rights, it is reasonable to assume that a State is also responsible whenever it seriously fails to take the appropriate measures to ensure that private individuals cannot violate the rights protected under the Convention.[27]

Another interesting point arising from *Airey* is that in case of failure to fulfil the positive obligation of effective protection of the right of private life, there can be no question of justifying the violation on the basis of the provisions of paragraph 2 of Article 8 of the Convention, for such provisions apply only to 'interferences' and not to 'omissions'. In any event, the fixing of the scope of a positive obligation for the purposes of that article presupposes that the limitations provided therein have already been taken

against Ireland that there was an obligation on its part to introduce measures permitting the applicants' divorce and remarriage. The Court took into consideration the fact that Article 12, which deals specifically with the 'right to marry', does not guarantee a right to divorce.

[23] At paras. 32–3.

[24] The view has been propounded that it is very probable that some welfare benefits come within the scope of Article 8 of the Convention and that a minimum welfare provision may possibly now constitute a positive obligation inherent in the effective respect for private life by the States: Duffy, loc. cit. above (n. 15), p. 199.

[25] *Abdulaziz, Cabales and Balkandali*, 28 May 1985, EHRR, vol. 7, p. 471; Series A, No. 94, para. 67.

[26] See also *Johnston and others*, loc. cit. above (n. 22).

[27] Ibid.

into account. In other words, recognition of a particular positive obligation on the part of the State to protect the right of private life under Article 8 of the Convention in a concrete situation presupposes that the obligation in question has been considered to be not inconsistent with the interests for the protection of which restrictions are permitted by virtue of paragraph 2 of Article 8. As the Court observed in the *Rees* case,[28]

In determining whether or not a positive obligation exists, regard must be had to the fair balance that has to be struck between the general interest of the community and the interests of the individual, the search for which balance is inherent in the whole of the Convention.[29] In striking this balance the aims mentioned in the second paragraph of Article 8 may be of a certain relevance, although this provision refers in terms only to 'interferences' with the right protected by the first paragraph—in other words is concerned with the negative obligations flowing therefrom.[30]

The jurisprudence of the Convention organs relating to the right to respect for private life appears to be of particular interest for the purposes of the subject under examination as regards the following four categories of situations: prisoners; sexuality; police investigations and secret surveillance; retention of personal information.

1. *Prisoners*

With respect to prisoners, reference should be made to the *Prisoners' Correspondence* case,[31] which relates directly to the right of correspondence but has at the same time consequences in respect of the scope of the right to respect for private life. The case concerned a variety of complaints by prisoners about restrictions on their right to correspondence. The Commission indicated generally when restrictions of prisoners' rights can be considered 'necessary in a democratic society'. It observed:

In the context of present-day conditions of imprisonment, the requirements of a democratic society involve the striking of a balance between the legitimate interests of public order and security and that of the rehabilitation of prisoners (e.g. encouragement of and assistance to a prisoner 'to lead a good and useful life', to maintain his 'self-respect and a sense of personal responsibility' and 'to establish and maintain such relations with persons and agencies outside prison as may . . . best promote the interests of his family and his own social rehabilitation').[32]

The Commission, in the same report, recognized that 'there is a basic human need to express thoughts and feelings, including complaints about real or imagined hardships. This need is particularly acute in prison, as

---

[28] 17 October 1986, *EHRR*, vol. 9, p. 56; Series A, No. 106.
[29] See, *mutatis mutandis*, amongst others, the *James and others* judgment of 21 February 1986 (*EHRR*, vol. 8, p. 123; Series A, No. 98, para. 50) and the *Sporrong and Lönnroth* judgment of 23 September 1982 (*EHRR*, vol. 5, p. 35; Series A, No. 52, para. 69).
[30] See, *mutatis mutandis*, the *Marckx* judgment of 13 June 1979 (*EHRR*, vol. 2, p. 330; Series A, No. 31, para. 31).
[31] Application No. 5947/72 and others, *EHRR*, vol. 3, p. 475.
[32] At para. 290.

prisoners have little choice of social contacts, hence the importance of having access to the outside world.'[33] The Commission also observed that Article 8 required 'that prisoners should be allowed to maintain effective family connections, sharing their experience and grievances with their close relatives. Such considerations require the strictest limitation of the ordinary and reasonable requirements of imprisonment.'[34] Finally, the Commission found that there was a violation as a result of the rule against communicating with persons who were not relatives or persons known to the prisoner concerned prior to the imprisonment.[35] The Commission also found a breach in the prohibition of letters containing grossly improper language, and in this respect observed that 'it is an essential feature of freedom of expression in a democratic society that the individual may freely correspond in whatever terms he or she desires, even though such terms may be vulgar, controversial, shocking or offensive. This freedom may be particularly important for persons such as prisoners subject to the daily frustrations of a closed community life.'[36]

The correlation of the right to correspondence with the requirements of private life and the personality of the individual in the above case is obvious. The reasoning of this jurisprudence could easily be applied, *mutatis mutandis*, so as to cover other rights interwoven with the personality of individuals in detention. The Commission had already, in a decision of 1982,[37] found that the right of private life of prisoners includes maintaining as far as practicable their contact with the outside world, 'in order to facilitate their re-integration in society on release, and this is effected, for example, by providing visiting facilities for the prisoners' friends' (under restrictions necessary for the security and effective administration of prisons).[38]

The Commission had the opportunity to consider the issue of whether prisoners are entitled to conjugal visits during their imprisonment. The Commission replied in the negative, even in the case where the husband and wife are detained in the same prison.[39] In its decision on this point the Commission took into account the general practice in States parties to the Convention, according to which sexual relations in prison are not allowed, a practice considered by the Commission to be justified for the prevention of disorder in prison. However, the understanding which the Commission showed for the fact that in certain European countries conjugal visits to prisons are allowed, as well as the general tenor of the decision, show a certain dissatisfaction with the existing situation; and this makes it possible that in the future the case law on this issue will eventually change.

---

[33] At para. 322.
[34] At para. 324.
[35] At para. 335.
[36] At para. 406.
[37] Application No. 9054/80, *Decisions and Reports*, vol. 30, p. 113.
[38] At p. 115.
[39] e.g. Application No. 8166/78, *Decisions and Reports*, vol. 13, p. 241.

In *McFeeley* v. *UK*[40] the Commission confirmed its previous decision in case 6825/74[41]—in which the Commission referred for the first time to the concept of personality and in particular to 'the right to establish and to develop relationships with other human beings, especially in the emotional field for the development and the fulfilment of one's own personality'—and concluded that 'this element in the concept of privacy extends to the sphere of imprisonment'.[42] As a result, the Commission found that the prohibition of association of the applicants with other prisoners constituted an interference with their right to privacy. However, in view of the facts of the particular case, this interference was considered justified on the basis of the provisions of paragraph 2 of Article 8 of the Convention as 'necessary in a democratic society . . . for the prevention of disorder'.

In the same case the Commission found that the requirement that the applicants wear prison uniforms again constituted an interference with their right to respect for their private lives. However, this interference was considered to be 'necessary in a democratic society in the interest of public safety and for the prevention of crime', on the ground that the uniform facilitated the identification of a prisoner with a view to preventing his escape or securing recapture in the event of an escape.

In another case[43] the Commission found that the refusal to permit a prisoner to attend his mother's funeral constituted interference with his right to private life, but was justified on grounds of 'public safety'.

The element of security, on the basis of the facts of each particular case, had, as expected, a decisive effect on the limitation of the right of private life of prisoners. Nevertheless, the jurisprudence is significant especially in so far as it determines in effect the scope and the application of the right of private life on the basis of the requirements of the personality of the individual, thus extending the protection of this right even within the confines of prisons.

2. *Sexuality*

In *Dudgeon* v. *UK*[44] the Commission had the opportunity to elaborate on the right to respect for private life in relation to the sexual activity of individuals. The applicant was a homosexual and complained of prohibitive provisions of the criminal law of Northern Ireland as regards homosexual activities even between consenting adults in private. Both the Commission and the Court in their decisions found that these provisions constituted interference with the right of private life of the applicant 'which included his sexual life', even though no criminal proceedings were brought against him on the basis of such provisions. The mere existence of the relevant

---

[40] *Decisions and Reports*, vol. 20, p. 44.
[41] See p. 178 and n. 11, above.
[42] At para. 82.
[43] Application No. 5229/71.
[44] *EHRR*, vol. 3, p. 40 (report of the Commission); ibid., vol. 4, p. 149; Series A, No. 45 (judgment of the Court).

legislation was considered to constitute 'a continuous and direct interference' with the right in question. The Court in its decision acknowledged 'the legitimate necessity in a democratic society for some degree of control over homosexual conduct notably in order to provide safeguards against the exploitation and corruption of those who are especially vulnerable by reason, for example, of their youth'.[45] However, this did not apply, in the opinion of the Court, in this case, which concerned an absolute prohibition.

The Commission had already found in the case of *X* v. *UK*[46] that the prohibition of homosexual relations between consenting adults aged 18 to 21 years was justified on the basis of the provisions of paragraph 2 of Article 8 of the Convention. In the same case the Commission rejected allegations of discrimination against male homosexuals, as compared with lesbians, to whom the relevant prohibition did not apply. With regard to lesbianism the Commission observed that the social danger posed by it was less than in the case of male homosexuals.

The Commission repeated this position in a more recent decision in respect of Application No. 9721/82[47] in which a 17-year-old applicant complained that the criminal prohibition of homosexuality between young persons under 21 'actually damages their personalities'.

In 1977 and 1978 the Commission declared admissible two applications by trans-sexuals who had undergone sex-change operations and complained that their changes of sex were not officially recognized, and that as a result they were subject to embarrassment. The Commission in its report in one of these two cases[48] unanimously found that there was a violation of Article 8 of the Convention on the ground that the refusal to allow rectification of the official documents, as claimed by the applicant, would have obliged him sometimes to explain the difference between his appearance and his civil status.[49] The Commission took into account the fact that in the country to

---

[45] At para. 62.

[46] Application No. 7215/75, *EHRR*, vol. 3, p. 63; *Decisions and Reports*, vol. 11, p. 36.

[47] *EHRR*, vol. 7, p. 145.

[48] *Van Oosterwijck* v. *Belgium*, Application No. 7654/76, *EHRR*, vol. 3, p. 581. The case was later brought before the Court, which declined to deal with the merits because of its finding that the applicant had failed to exhaust domestic remedies: see judgment of 6 November 1980, *EHRR*, vol. 3, p. 557; Series A, No. 40.

[49] In the more recent *Rees* case (judgment of 17 October 1986, loc. cit. above (n. 28)) the Court found that the mere refusal to alter the register of births or to issue a birth certificate whose content and nature differed from those of the birth register, so as to correspond with the applicant's changed sex, was not a violation of Article 8 of the Convention. The Court took into account the fact that, except for the birth certificate, all official documents referred to the applicant by his new name together with the prefix 'Mr'. The Court found that the refusal in question was, in the circumstances, within the margin of appreciation left to the State and was justifiable because of the administrative problems and the consequent duties on the rest of the population resulting from the alteration sought by the applicant. The Court based its decision on the necessity to strike a 'fair balance between the general interest of the community and the interests of the individual' (para. 37). However, the Court stressed, 'The Convention has always to be interpreted and applied in the light of current circumstances. The need for appropriate legal measures should therefore be kept under review having regard particularly to scientific and societal developments' (para. 47).

which the complaint related, i.e. Belgium, sex-change operations were allowed.[50]

The case is of particular importance for the topic of this study in view of the application of the right to respect for private life by express reference to the concept of personality as follows:

> The State has . . . not interfered with the applicant's behaviour and the relationships into which he has freely entered and which express and compose his personality. But it has refused to recognise an essential element of his personality: his sexual identity resulting from his changed physical form, his physical make-up and his social role.[51]

The Commission, in a more recent decision,[52] has expressly stated that the concept of private life covers the physical and moral integrity of an individual, which includes his sexual integrity. Applying its previous jurisprudence,[53] according to which the State, over and above its obligation to abstain from interfering in the private life of the individual, has positive obligations effectively to protect such right, the Commission found that the absence in the Netherlands of criminal legal provision for the prosecution of those who have sexual intercourse with mentally handicapped persons (as in the case under consideration) constituted a violation of the right to respect for private life as safeguarded by Article 8 of the Convention. The Commission in its decision stated:

> In the sphere of private life . . . it is generally accepted in the Contracting States that some degree of regulation is required in order to protect all members of society and in particular those who for reasons of lack of maturity, mental disability or state of dependence are especially vulnerable and incapable of protecting themselves. . . . There not being any . . . criminal legal provision applicable to the present case, it follows that the system of criminal legal protection afforded to particularly vulnerable members of the Dutch society is incomplete.[54]

Finally, the Commission considered that the existence of civil legal remedies did not fill the gap because of the cumbersome and time-consuming nature of the procedure, as compared with criminal proceedings which, according to the Commission, are a far more effective means of protecting the sexual integrity of persons who are in an especially vulnerable position. For this reason it was found that only protection of this nature can fulfil the exigencies of the right to respect for private life.[55]

---

[50] For this reason the case cannot be considered as an authority for the existence of an obligation on the part of every State to recognize sex-changes resulting from operations.

[51] At para. 52.

[52] Application No. 8978/80, *EHRR*, vol. 6, p. 311 (5 July 1983).

[53] *Airey* case, loc. cit. above (n. 20).

[54] At paras. 80, 85.

[55] The decision of the Commission in this case was affirmed by the Court: judgment of 26 March 1985, *EHRR*, vol. 8, p. 235; Series A, No. 91.

3. *Police investigations and secret surveillance*

In 1979 the Commission admitted for the first time complaints under Article 8 of the Convention relating to police methods of investigation. The case concerned persons who had been detained in England for 45 hours after their arrival from Ireland.[56] The Commission found that the searching, questioning, fingerprinting and photographing of the applicants during their detention amounted to interferences in their private life, but that, in that particular case, these were justified 'for the prevention of crime' under paragraph 2 of Article 8 of the Convention. As regards retention by the police of the applicants' fingerprints and photographs after their release, the Commission, after mentioning that the Convention must be interpreted and applied in the light of present-day conditions, found that these interferences in the private life of the applicants were justified in order to combat terrorist activity prevailing in modern life. The Commission took into account that the applicants' records were held separately from ordinary criminal records and were exclusively reserved for use in the campaign against terrorism. The Commission's reasoning shows how much it was influenced by the particular facts of the case in combination with the need to allow States to combat terrorism effectively. Accordingly, there is still room for the view that the general practice of keeping records of all persons questioned by the police, whether or not eventually charged or even suspected of an offence, constitutes unjustified violation of their right to privacy in the wide sense of the term, consistently with the case law referred to in this study.[57] In its decision, the Commission left this matter open, distinguishing the case under consideration on the ground that it referred exclusively to 'the retention of the information which the applicants themselves provided during their examination, together with fingerprints and photographs'.[58]

In the same case, the Commission found that refusal to allow the applicants to contact their wives during their detention amounted to a breach of Article 8. In its decision the Commission mentioned that unless there were specific reasons relating to a danger that accomplices would be alerted, such restrictions would be unjustified.

In *Klass* v. *Germany*[59] the Court found that secret surveillance of telephone calls interfered with the right to respect for private life and that, in any exceptional case where such a measure is necessary in the interest of public security, it must be specifically reasoned and relevant legislation must provide adequate and effective criteria and other safeguards against its abuse. The Court also indicated that in principle it is desirable that such measures be under judicial control.

---

[56] Applications Nos. 8022, 8025 and 8027/77, *EHRR*, vol. 5, p. 71; *Decisions and Reports*, vol. 25, p. 15.
[57] See Duffy, loc. cit. above (n. 15), at p. 232.
[58] At para. 226.
[59] *EHRR*, vol. 2, p. 214; Series A, No. 28.

Another decision on the same subject is *Malone* v. *UK*,[60] which concerned the tapping of the applicant's telephone for the purpose of collecting evidence in a criminal case against him. The English courts dismissed a civil action by the applicant on the ground that no right safeguarded by English law had been infringed.[61] However, both the Commission and the Court found a violation of the applicant's right of privacy which could not be justified on the basis of paragraph 2 of Article 8 of the Convention, because the particular legal provision in England, which allowed telephone-tapping, did not define the extent and the manner of exercise of the relevant governmental power with sufficient precision to give the public adequate protection against abuse. In the circumstances, it was found that the interference was not 'according to law' as required by the relevant provisions of paragraph 2 of Article 8, given that this term presupposes, according to the Court, adequate legal regulation easily accessible to the public and defining specific conditions for the application of the relevant restrictions.

In the same case the Court agreed with the Commission that the existence of laws and practices permitting and establishing a system for effecting secret surveillance amounted in itself to an interference with the applicant's rights under Article 8 of the Convention, apart from any measures actually taken against him. The Commission in a more recent case[62] decided that the principle just mentioned could not be interpreted so broadly as to encompass every person who fears that the security services may have compiled information about him. It was, however, found to be sufficient, in the area of secret measures, if it could be established that practices permitting secret surveillance existed and that there was a reasonable likelihood that the security services had compiled and retained information concerning private life.[63] Furthermore, it was decided by the Court in the *Malone* case that there could be interference with the right of a person to respect for his private life through measures of secret surveillance even though such person was not directly subjected to surveillance ('indirect interception', i.e. the recording of information about a person which appeared in the telephone or mail intercepts of others).

4. *Retention of personal information*

According to recent case law of the Commission and the Court, retention of confidential information about a person's life may of itself amount to

[60] *EHRR*, vol. 5, p. 385 (report of the Commission); ibid., vol. 7, p. 14; Series A, No. 82 (judgment of the Court of 2 August 1984); followed and applied by the Court in the *Kruslin* case (judgment of 24 April 1990) and in the *Huvig* case (judgment of 24 April 1990).

[61] [1979] 2 All ER 620. Sir Robert Megarry V-C, in dismissing the action, applied, *inter alia*, the principle that 'everything is permitted except that which is expressly forbidden'. It is submitted that this public law principle was misunderstood, for it can only be invoked to justify acts of individuals and not acts of the State at the expense of the freedom of the individual.

[62] Application No. 12175/86 (report of 9 May 1989).

[63] Application No. 12015/86 (report of 6 July 1988).

unjustified interference with the right of privacy, irrespective of the purpose of such retention, depending on the facts of each particular case.[64]

In the *Leander* case[65] the Court found that the storing and the release of confidential information relating to the applicant, which were coupled with refusal to allow him an opportunity to refute it, amounted to an interference with his right to respect for private life. However, such interference was found to be justified as necessary in the interests of national security in the light of the particular facts of the case. In the more recent *Gaskin* case[66] the applicant's complaint was of the refusal to allow him access to a confidential file containing information compiled and maintained by a local authority and relating to the applicant's identity, i.e. recording his early childhood and formative years during the period that the applicant was in care. The Court decided that there was a breach of the provisions of Article 8 of the Convention because of the lack of a procedure providing that an independent authority should finally decide whether access was to be granted in cases where a contributor to the records either was not available or refused consent to such access. The Court found that the absence of such a procedure made the system incompatible with the principle of proportionality.

(b) *Widening of the Meaning of 'Private Life'*

So, in their case law, the organs of the Convention have gone beyond the established traditional meaning of private life,[67] and with a clearly personalized approach have extended this meaning so as to cover a wide range of elements and manifestations of the individual's personality, supporting in this way the view that private life should be considered as coextensive with the needs of the personality—thus affording protection to individual rights which are derived from such needs but are not expressly safeguarded by the Convention. This view gains further support from the wording of several decisions of these organs, which from the first years of application of the Convention have felt the need to protect the right of privacy on the basis of the requirements of personality. In fact, as long ago as 1969 the Commission in one of its reports stated expressly that it had examined the complaint of the applicant on the basis of the assumption that Article 8 of the Convention guarantees 'the right to the free development of the

---

[64] Mention should be made in this respect of the Convention for the Protection of Individuals with regard to Automatic Processing of Personal Data, 1988 (Council of Europe No. 108), which was inspired by Article 8 of the European Convention on Human Rights and which provides protection of the right of privacy with regard to automatic processing of personal data.

[65] 26 March 1987, *EHRR*, vol. 9, p. 433; Series A, No. 116.

[66] 7 July 1989, Series A, No. 160.

[67] As admitted by the Commission itself: Application No. 6825/74, *Decisions and Reports*, vol. 5, p. 87.

personality'.[68] In any case, with the later development of its case law, the Council of Europe has reached the point of admitting in substance that protection of private life means protection of the personality. A typical example is a decision of the Commission in 1981[69] in a case where it was argued that there was interference with the applicant's private life as a result of the refusal of the German authorities to allow him to have his ashes scattered in his garden on his death. The Commission stated in its decision:

> Whilst those arrangements are made for a time after life has come to an end, this does not mean that no issue concerning such arrangements may arise under Article 8, since persons may feel *the need to express their personality* by the way they arrange how they are buried. The Commission, therefore, accepts that the refusal of the German authorities to allow the applicant to have his ashes scattered in his garden on his death is so closely related to *private life* that it comes within the sphere of Article 8 of the Convention.[70]

The reference to the concept of personality or (to use the expression of the Commission) 'the need to express one's personality' as a basis and a yardstick for the determination of the meaning of private life, for the purposes of Article 8 of the Convention,[71] explains the extension and application of this term to aspects of an individual's personality that can hardly be considered as falling within the ambit of the term 'private life' in its traditional sense.[72]

(c) *Broadening of Human Rights through the Method of Interpretation—'Privacy' and 'Personality' in the USA*

The method of broadening fundamental rights by judicial interpretation, guided by the totality of the provisions and aims of a convention or constitution which safeguards them, and at the same time taking account of current human and social values, is a well-established practice. It is illustrated by the American case law according to which the right of private life, though not expressly mentioned in the American Constitution, was considered to be constitutionally protected by derivation from other constitutional provisions. A typical example is the decision in *Griswold* v.

---

[68] ' . . . moreover, even if it were to be admitted that Article 8 of the Convention guaranteed in the same way as for example Article 2, paragraph 1 of the Basic Law of the Federal Republic of Germany, the right to the free development of the personality, it must be conceded that such free development was not seriously interfered with in the case . . . ': Application No. 2929/66. In a more recent case (Application No. 8042/77, *Decisions and Reports*, vol. 12, p. 202), where the Commission was asked to interpret private life so as to cover the general right to protection of personality, in order that the applicant be entitled to use her maiden name during a pre-election campaign instead of her husband's name, the Commission found that it need not decide the issue because in any case the applicant was able to use her maiden name after her husband's, and thus could be reasonably identified. See also in this respect Doswald-Beck, loc. cit. above (n. 5), at p. 299.

[69] Application No. 8741/79, *Decisions and Reports*, vol. 24, p. 137.

[70] At para. 2 (emphasis added).

[71] Cf. Doswald-Beck, loc. cit. above (n. 5), at p. 308.

[72] Cf. Henkin, quoted at p. 192, below, for a similar judicial attitude as regards the concept of private life in the United States.

Connecticut[73] where the Supreme Court of the United States annulled an anti-contraceptive statute as an infringement of the right of marital privacy. Mr Justice Douglas, writing the opinion of the Court, asserted that the 'specific guarantees in the Bill of Rights have penumbras, formed by emanations from those guarantees that help give them life and substance. Various guarantees create zones of privacy . . . .'[74] Thus, while privacy is nowhere mentioned in the American Constitution, it was recognized as 'one of the values served and protected by the First Amendment through its protection of associational rights',[75] and by the complex of other Amendments. Mr Justice Goldberg, concurring, stated:

> The right of privacy is a fundamental personal right, emanating from the totality of the Constitutional scheme under which we live . . . The Makers of our Constitution recognized the significance of man's spiritual nature, of his feelings and of his intellect. They knew that only a part of the pain, pleasure and satisfaction of life are to be found in material things. They sought to protect Americans in their beliefs, their thoughts, their emotions and their sensations. They conferred as against the Government, the right to be let alone—the most comprehensive of rights and the right most valued by civilized men.[76]

Justices Harlan and White based their conclusions regarding annulment of the statute in question on the fact that it 'violates basic values implicit in the concept of ordered liberty'.[77]

The creative role of the US Supreme Court in *Griswold* was reaffirmed and further extended in 1973 in *Roe* v. *Wade*.[78] In *Roe* the Court invalidated a Texas law banning abortion except on 'medical advice for the purpose of saving the life of the mother' on the ground that it violated the right of privacy as 'founded in the Fourteenth Amendment's concept of personal liberty and restrictions upon state action'.[79]

In a more recent case, *Carey* v. *Population Services International*,[80] the line of cases on privacy was significantly extended so as to make the 'decision whether or not to beget or bear a child' a 'constitutionally protected right of privacy'.[81] This constitutional protection of individual autonomy in matters of childbearing led the Court to invalidate a State statute that banned the distribution of contraceptives to adults except by licensed pharmacists and that forbade any person to sell or distribute contraceptives to a minor under sixteen.

What is of additional interest regarding the American case law recogniz-

---

[73] 381 US 479 (1965).
[74] At p. 484.
[75] *Constitution of the United States of America, Analysis and Interpretation* (Senate Document 92–82, 1973), p. 1258.
[76] At p. 494.
[77] At p. 500.
[78] 410 US 113 (1973).
[79] At p. 153.
[80] 431 US 678 (1977).
[81] At p. 685.

ing the right of privacy is the fact that it relates to aspects of the personality beyond those covered by the strict meaning of 'privacy'.[82] Referring to this case law, Henkin writes:

> What the court has been talking about is not at all what most people mean by privacy. None of the . . . cases . . . which the justices have swept together into the basket labelled 'right of privacy' deals with any of the matters that are the subject of the now massive literature on privacy . . . The court has been vindicating not a right to freedom from official intrusion, but to freedom from official regulation, i.e. a right to autonomy. . . . We will know which rights are and which are not within the zone only case by case, with lines drawn and redrawn in response to individual and societal initiatives and the imaginativeness of lawyers.[83]

Referring to the same topic, Kalven stresses that ' . . . the topic is really freedom, and . . . calling it privacy tends to obscure matters'.[84] Further, McDougal, Lasswell and Chen point out:

> It will be observed that all these cognate terms and verbalisms about privacy reflect a struggle to secure a policy that transcends particular factual contexts and guarantees optimum freedom of choice to human beings. . . . While in the United States the protection of civic order finds increasingly vigorous expression through the expanding right to privacy, comparable protection has been achieved in other legal systems under a 'general right of the personality'.[85]

(d) Delimitation of the Protected Scope of Personality

The manifestations of personality which are to be legally protected cannot be exhaustively determined *in vacuo* and in the abstract. The personality of the individual functions in an environment involving a continuous process of 'give and take' between the individuality of man and the requirements of society as a whole. Manifestations of the personality are inevitably affected by the passage of time and their recognition for purposes of legal protection depends upon social conditions. Indeed, a new right attached to the personality only appears when conditions of social life so require.

This relativity is illustrated by the case law of the European Commission and European Court of Human Rights in respect of private life. Many aspects of the individuality of man, as, for example, in the field of sexuality, that were originally considered to fall outside the ambit of the relevant right, were later recognized and protected.

Under the influence of prevailing moral and social values and conditions, developing jurisprudence determines the scope of the concept of private

---

[82] See McDougal, Lasswell and Chen, op. cit. above (n. 10), at pp. 850–4.
[83] ' "Selective Incorporation" in the Fourteenth Amendment', *Yale Law Journal*, 73 (1963–4), p. 74.
[84] ' "Privacy and Freedom"—A Review', *Record of the New York City Bar Association*, 23 (1968), p. 185 at p. 187.
[85] Op. cit. above (n. 10), at pp. 850, 854.

life.[86] In some cases the case law gives a wider meaning to the term in order to cover a new situation, and in other cases the term is limited and its application excluded. Many decisions of the European Commission and European Court of Human Rights dismiss complaints for interferences with private life on the ground that the alleged interference was outside the 'private' sphere of the individual which—according to the interpreters of the Convention—requires recognition and protection. In this context it is useful to bear in mind the decision of the Commission in the *Bruggeman* case[87] where it stated:

. . . there are limits to the personal sphere. While a large proportion of the law existing in a given State has some immediate or remote effect on the individual's possibility of developing his personality by doing what he wants to do, not all of these can be considered to constitute an interference with private life in the sense of Article 8 of the Convention.[88]

Similarly the European Court, adopting the same position in *Golder* v. *UK*,[89] stated that there are 'bounds delimiting the very content of any right'.[90]

Thus, applications were dismissed for complaints directed against the following alleged interferences: the obligation of drivers and passengers of motor vehicles to wear safety belts;[91] the obligation of motor-cyclists to wear helmets;[92] the obligation, in order to profit from unemployment benefits, to accept a certain job;[93] the prohibition of pigeon-feeding in public streets;[94] conviction for aiding and abetting the suicide of others;[95] deportation of one of the partners of a homosexual couple,[96] etc.[97] This case law may very well be the result of applying the principle that 'such invasions as are "socially adequate" i.e. recognized as reasonable and inevitable within the community concerned, do not give rise to any liability'.[98]

Any determination of the content of the right itself depends on the facts of the case, especially the degree of severity of the consequences of the particular situation to which the complaint refers. According to one view,

The activity wished to be pursued must be something of a serious nature, the

---

[86] See also pp. 177–90, above. For the interpretation of the European Convention according to changing conditions, see Waldock, 'The Evolution of Human Rights Concepts and the Application of the European Convention on Human Rights', *Mélanges offerts à Paul Reuter* (1981), p. 535.

[87] Loc. cit. above (n. 13).

[88] At para. 56.

[89] *EHRR*, vol. 1, p. 524; Series A, No. 18.

[90] At para. 38.

[91] Application No. 8707/79, *Decisions and Reports*, vol. 18, p. 255.

[92] Application No. 6454/74.

[93] Application No. 7602/76, *Decisions and Reports*, vol. 7, p. 161.

[94] Application No. 9101/80.

[95] Application No. 10083/82, *EHRR*, vol. 6, p. 140.

[96] Application No. 9369/81, *EHRR*, vol. 5, p. 581 (so long as the link with the deporting State is not a material element in the relationship).

[97] *Digest of Strasbourg Case-Law*, vol. 3, pp. 41 ff.

[98] Stromholm, *Right of Privacy and Rights of the Personality: A Comparative Survey* (1967), at pp. 56–7.

forbidding or regulation of which clearly has an adverse effect on the applicant's development of his personality or recognition thereof.[99]

Seriousness of the consequences of a certain situation was recognized as an element in determining the limits of the right to respect for private life by a decision of the Commission[100] which dismissed a complaint against rules requiring the wearing of school uniform on school premises and during school hours. The Commission considered that this case could not be equated with the obligation of prisoners to wear a uniform, because prison uniforms bear a certain stigma and the obligation to wear them is continuous, whether the prisoner is working or at leisure. In the Commission's view the obligation to wear a school uniform was not, in the circumstances, 'so serious as to constitute an interference with the right to respect for private life'.

The right in question can also be limited by such well-recognized defences as, for example, consent. Furthermore, as was earlier indicated, the right to respect for private life may be limited when 'the individual himself brings his private life into contact with public life or into close connection with other protected interests'.[101] Like any other individual right, the right under consideration stops at the point where the corresponding right of another person begins.[102] Of course, a major problem is delimitation in practice of the right of personality of an individual by reference to the corresponding rights of others, as each of two legally equivalent rights relates to the subjectivities of the persons involved and extends to an undefined scope. This difficult problem can only be left to the courts, to weigh the conflicting claims and define their limits on the basis of the concrete situation and the values at stake.

Beyond these inherent limits on the right, its scope is also limited by express restrictions in the interests of society as a whole. Such restrictions are stipulated in the provisions setting out the right. These restrictions must be interpreted strictly and in a way not permitting recognition by implication of any limitations beyond those which are expressly allowed.[103] As explained above, a basic prerequisite for the validity of the imposition of the express restrictions in question is their regulation by a law which is accessible to the public and which determines their extent with sufficient precision to enable individuals to foresee to a degree reasonable in the circumstances the consequences of their actions, thereby enabling them to regulate their conduct accordingly.[104] Thus a restriction based on a vague

---

[99] Doswald-Beck, loc. cit. above (n. 5), at p. 309.

[100] Application No. 11674/85 (report of 3 March 1986).

[101] Application No. 6959/75, loc. cit. above (nn. 13, 17).

[102] Cf. Article 4 of the French Declaration of the Rights of Man and the Citizen of 1789: 'Freedom consists of the power to do anything that does not harm another'.

[103] *Golder* case, loc. cit. above (n. 89).

[104] *Malone* case, loc. cit. above (n. 60); see also the decision in *Sunday Times* v. *UK, EHRR*, vol. 2, p. 245; Series A, No. 30. Cf. Loucaides, 'Nullum crimen sine lege certa', *Cyprus Law Review*, 3 (1983), pp. 474 ff. For these restrictions in general see also Duffy, loc. cit. above (n. 15), pp. 204 ff.

law or on a law which does not provide effective safeguards against abuse must be regarded as legally ineffective.

General terms such as 'public safety' cannot be invoked for the imposition of restrictions on individual rights in an absolute and uncontrolled manner. As stated by the European Court in *Klass* v. *Germany*,[105] which concerned a measure of secret surveillance 'in the interest of public safety', the contracting States do not

> . . . enjoy an unlimited discretion to subject persons within their jurisdiction to secret surveillance. The Court, being aware of the danger such a law poses of undermining or even destroying democracy on the ground of defending it, affirms that Contracting States may not, in the name of the struggle against espionage and terrorism, adopt whatever measures they deem appropriate.
>
> The Court must be satisfied that whatever system of surveillance is adopted, there exist adequate and effective safeguards against abuse.[106]

Indeed, States cannot invoke general restrictive provisions in order to serve democracy or social interest in an arbitrary or abstract manner at the expense of the personality of the individual. 'Social' interest is not an open field where governmental activity can operate freely and without restriction.[107]

Inherent in the concepts of democracy and social interest is the achievement of the freedom of the individual by securing to each individual the necessary conditions for its exercise. Freedom should be more complete within ordered society than outside.[108] It is submitted that the individual, by subjecting himself to the rules of a liberal society, should not be regarded as sacrificing his freedom. On the contrary, his freedom must be effectively secured by the State authorities.

Again, 'public safety', 'public health', 'public order', etc., should be construed and applied as intended to serve and implement the subjective rights attached to personality, and consequently general restrictions based on these concepts should be seen as nothing other than supplementary safeguards of individual freedoms of the citizens as a body.[109] Only for the sake of making these freedoms more effective can such restrictions be imposed by the State. It is submitted that the State cannot impose restrictions detaching them from their true context which is governed by the concept of personality.[110] On that basis, any actual imposition of restrictions can only be justified to the extent that it in fact secures the personality of individuals in an organized society by protecting its members from concrete and real dangers applicable at that time and place, and does not on any particular

---

[105] Loc. cit. above (n. 59).

[106] At paras. 49–50.

[107] Vlachos, op. cit. above (n. 10), at p. 192.

[108] Bastid, *Sieyès et sa pensée* (1939), p. 345; Sieyès, *L'Exploitation raisonnée des droits de l'homme et du citoyen*.

[109] Burdeau, op. cit. above (n. 1), vol. 6, p. 197.

[110] Cf. Vlachos, op. cit. above (n. 10), at p. 190.

occasion take the form of measures which are disproportionate and exceed what is necessary.

As is rightly observed by Burdeau, 'The role of the State is to widen all the more the possibilities offered to the freedom that is inherent in the individual. Man is free; he does not need to be liberated. What power can secure to him is the possibility to enjoy his freedom.'[111]

III. CONCLUSION

Modern legal trends seem to acknowledge the necessity of extending legal recognition to the whole spectrum of the personality of the individual as a prerequisite for the meaningful and effective protection of the freedom of the person. Basic aspects of the personality of the individual are expressly safeguarded in international instruments on human rights and in contemporary constitutions. Far-reaching supplementary protection is afforded by the constitutions of some European countries through direct recognition of a specific right to 'free development of one's personality'. It is submitted that comparable protection has also been achieved through the expanding right of privacy under the European Convention on Human Rights as interpreted and applied by the organs of the Convention. This case law has expounded and upheld the protection of privacy to such a degree that, for all practical purposes, the right of privacy has become a functional equivalent of a right of personality, potentially embracing all those constituent parts of the personality of the individual that are not expressly safeguarded by the European Convention. Thus the right of privacy, despite the not inconsiderable controversy involved in its delimitation,[112] has been employed and proved useful to the strategy of effectively protecting freedom of the person.[113] These developments pave the way for a similar approach in the legal systems of the European countries which are parties to the Convention and of those countries whose constitutional catalogue of human rights includes a right of privacy.

In the light of the case law of the organs of the European Convention on Human Rights[114] it appears that protection of the privacy of the individual implies not only abstention from interference with the right but also positive action on the part of the State for its effective implementation. This is an extremely promising area for legal development in the future, in the form of elaboration and recognition of the required specific measures and of the conditions to be fulfilled by States, in order to secure to individuals the

---

[111] Op. cit. above (n. 1), vol. 6, p. 198.

[112] See Wacks, *The Protection of Privacy* (1980), pp. 10–12, 21–2.

[113] Referring to the modern legal trends on the concept of privacy, McDougal, Lasswell and Chen (op. cit. above (n. 10), p. 844) observe: ' "Privacy" is quickly becoming the potent catch symbol for a constellation of demands which, functionally, are demands for civic order—for the utmost practicable freedom of choice in the shaping and sharing of aggregate values'.

[114] *Airey* case, loc. cit. above (n. 20).

necessary opportunities and means to enable them to exercise effectively the freedom to express and develop their personalities.

The right of personality implies the widest possible freedom of choice and, hence, the minimum of coerced choices for individuals. State intervention restrictive of such freedom should be subject to adequate safeguards—under judicial control—and be limited to what is necessary for the common interest, conceived as an interest in protecting and securing the effective development of the personality of every individual in an organized society on an equal basis and in accordance with the hierarchy of values as determined by the prevailing social conditions.[115]

[115] As observed by McDougal, Lasswell and Chen (op. cit. above (n. 10), p. 800): 'The aggregate common interest need not be conceived as in antithesis to the individual interest. The aggregate interest may, however, be more than the sum total of particular individual interests, since an appropriate accommodation or integration can raise the level of value production ultimately available for all.' As aptly indicated by Judge Lauterpacht, 'All social laws are, in the last resort, laws for the protection of individuals; all laws for the protection of individuals are, in a true sense, social laws': *Guardianship of Infants Convention of 1902* case, *ICJ Reports*, 1958, p. 55 at p. 85.

THE INTERNATIONAL LEGAL REGIME
REGULATING NUCLEAR DETERRENCE
AND WARFARE*

By WILLIAM R. HEARN‡

* © William R. Hearn, 1991.
  ‡ Lawyer, Cassels, Brock & Blackwell, Toronto; BA, LL B (Toronto), LL M (Cantab.); member of
the Ontario Bar. This article is based on a paper submitted in April 1989 in partial fulfilment of the
requirements for the LL M Degree at Cambridge University.

I. INTRODUCTION

THIS article examines whether, and if so to what extent, international law regulates the threat to use, or actual use of, nuclear weapons. It seeks to demonstrate the relevance of law to such weapons and to articulate an overview of the present international legal regime regulating nuclear deterrence and warfare. What follows is a discussion first of the general nature and sources of international law and then of specific aspects of the laws of armed conflict. This article does not, however, address legal issues of arms control arising from the testing, development, manufacture, possession or proliferation of nuclear weapons; rather, the focus here is on the related though conceptually distinct legal regime respecting when and how States may threaten, or engage in, nuclear war.

It might be thought entirely out of step with improved East-West relations (especially given recent developments in Eastern Europe and in the Soviet Union) to dwell on chilling matters such as nuclear deterrence and warfare (let alone, for other reasons discussed in the next section, their 'legal' aspects). Some will undoubtedly argue that such a focus is misguided. The purpose, however, is not to detract from the importance of nuclear arms control, but to draw attention to the serious legal problems concerning nuclear deterrence and warfare; problems that should be resolved but that unfortunately are often overlooked (or worse, assumed away) by governments and writers alike. This article therefore focuses on a flawed, and for decades inert, legal regime (rooted in what might be called 'cold war values') in the hope that States might now, after over forty years in the wilderness, negotiate meaningful improvements in its content.

The recent spate of writings[1] applying the laws of armed conflict to nuclear weapons is evidence that it is at least a fashionable jurisprudential

---

[1] In addition to the many articles written in the 1980s referred to in this article, see the collection of essays in Pogany (ed.), *Nuclear Weapons and International Law* (1987), the proceedings of the Canadian Conference on Nuclear Weapons and the Law in Cohen and Gouin (eds.), *Lawyers and the Nuclear Debate* (1988), and the text by Singh and McWhinney, *Nuclear Weapons and Contemporary International Law* (1989).

endeavour. One commentator attributes this expanding body of literature to 'the cavalier nuclear warfighting rhetoric propounded by the Reagan Administration in the aftermath of the 1980 election'.[2] Whatever the impetus, the question of the legality of nuclear weapons has received considerable attention from international lawyers in the past decade, putting to rest the curious claim of some commentators[3] that the international legal community has been largely silent on the subject. Indeed, at least in terms of scholarship, the alleged 'legal silence' is a fallacy. A cursory reading of any published bibliography on the subject evidences a sustained (and, arguably, distinguished) tradition of legal writing.[4]

Generally, writers on the subject of international law and nuclear weapons fall into one of three camps. Writers in the self-proclaimed 'political realists' camp scotch the inquiry at the outset, arguing that international law is irrelevant to matters of high international politics such as nuclear deterrence and warfare. For them, meaningful legal analysis ends with the threshold jurisprudential question of the role of international law. By contrast, writers in the other two camps share the view that international law is at least relevant to nuclear weapons, but disagree widely on the effect of its application. One camp argues that under the existing laws of armed conflict nuclear weapons are illegal as such, while the other maintains that the legality of nuclear weapons depends on the specific context of their threatened or actual use. Generally, 'contextualist' writers look to whether there is a 'disproportionate and unnecessary destruction of values in light of the military advantage to be secured'.[5] As might be expected, there is a wide range of views within the 'contextualist' camp.[6]

After dealing first with the jurisprudential challenge of the 'political realists', this article will scrutinize the 'illegal as such' and 'contextualist' arguments in an effort to articulate, by way of overview, the present international legal regime regulating nuclear deterrence and warfare. Admittedly the categories of nuclear deterrence and warfare are closely related, but so dividing the discussion orders the analysis of the laws of armed conflict that follows roughly in terms of the traditional distinction between the laws respecting the resort to force (*jus ad bellum*) and those

---

[2] Boyle, 'The Relevance of International Law to the "Paradox" of Nuclear Deterrence', *Northwestern University Law Review*, 80 (1986), p. 1407.

[3] Falk, Meyrowitz and Sanderson, 'Nuclear Weapons and International Law', *Indian Journal of International Law*, 20 (1980), p. 541 at p. 542; and Arbess, 'The International Law of Armed Conflict in Light of Contemporary Deterrence Strategies', *McGill Law Journal*, 30 (1984), p. 89 at p. 91.

[4] A stronger argument, however, can be made respecting the silence of the laws of war themselves: for example, see Roberts, 'The Relevance of the Laws of War in the Nuclear Age', in Dewar *et al.* (eds.), *Nuclear Weapons, the Peace Movement and the Law* (1986), p. 25 at p. 31. A sense of the extent of the literature on the subject may be gleaned from Roehrenbeck, 'The Use of Nuclear Weapons under International Law', in Miller and Feinrider (eds.), *Nuclear Weapons and Law* (1984), p. 215.

[5] Arbess, loc. cit. above (n. 3), quoting McDougal and Feliciano at p. 105.

[6] Contrast, for example, the different contextualist analyses and conclusions in Kalshoven, 'Arms, Armaments and International Law', *Recueil des cours*, 191 (1985-II), p. 191 esp. pp. 266 ff., and Weston, 'Nuclear Weapons versus International Law: A Contextual Reassessment', *McGill Law Journal*, 28 (1983), p. 542.

governing the conduct of hostilities (*jus in bello*). While today the *jus ad bellum* and *jus in bello* are often applied concurrently and indeed may even overlap in some situations, for clarity of thought they should remain conceptually distinct from one another (treated as parallel and not fused regimes).[7]

In essence, this article will elaborate the following propositions. First, the traditional laws of armed conflict are not obsolete in the nuclear age and therefore apply to determine when and how States may lawfully threaten to use, or actually use, nuclear weapons. Secondly, what is called in this article the 'functional-positivist' approach to international law[8] properly and best articulates the present international legal regime regulating nuclear deterrence and warfare. And thirdly, as to this regime, no binding rule or principle of international law directly or by analogy outlaws nuclear weapons as such; rather, the legality of any particular nuclear weapon (as with most conventional ones) depends on the circumstances of its threatened or actual use. This article will also highlight what this writer views as the main problem with the present legal regime—namely, that it is based largely on vague, general principles susceptible to excessively subjective and evasive interpretations. The intention here is not to legitimate cold war attitudes (though admittedly much of this article's analysis might be relied on to do so), but rather to stress the need for States now to negotiate, in the climate of improved East-West relations, better laws on the subject.

II. Preliminary Matters of International Legal Theory

(a) *Relevance of the Laws of Armed Conflict to Nuclear Weapons*

As already mentioned, writers in the so-called 'political realists' camp, most notably Morgenthau[9] and Hoffman,[10] deny the relevance of international law to that sector of international relations dealing with matters of 'vital national interest' or 'high international politics' (a sector into which

---

[7] Greenwood, 'The relationship between *ius ad bellum* and *ius in bello*', *Review of International Studies*, 9 (1983), p. 221. As Greenwood notes, ' . . . each is capable of operating on its own since neither is logically dependent on the other . . . [and] the two systems of rules operate in somewhat different ways and the consequences which flow from the violations are not always the same' (at p. 231).

[8] See below at pp. 205–8.

[9] Before challenging the relevance of international law entirely, Morgenthau argued that the gap existing between law and politics in the realm of international relations might be bridged by replacing the positivist approach to international law with a functionalist analysis: see his article 'Positivism, Functionalism and International Law', *American Journal of International Law*, 34 (1940), p. 260. However, apparently disillusioned by the experience of World War II, Morgenthau abandoned the task of developing a 'functionalist jurisprudence' of international law and helped to establish the 'political realists' school of political science: see his book *Politics Among Nations* (1948).

[10] Hoffman, 'International Law and the Control of Force', in Deutsch and Hoffman (eds.), *The Relevance of International Law* (1971).

threats to use, or uses of, nuclear weapons clearly fall).[11] This view was forcefully put in 1963 by the United States Secretary of State, Dean Acheson, when he addressed the American Society of International Law on the Cuban missile crisis. In an oft-quoted passage, he said:

> I must conclude that the propriety of the Cuban quarantine is not a legal issue. The power, position and prestige of the United States had been challenged by another state; and law simply does not deal with such questions of ultimate power—power that comes close to the sources of sovereignty . . . The survival of states is not a matter of law.[12]

Regrettably, this argument underestimates the descriptive worth and prescriptive validity of international law. Moreover, given the account of the crisis by Abram Chayes,[13] then Legal Advisor to the Department of State, Acheson's assertion can be dismissed as hyperbole. Without claiming that legal considerations dictated decision, Chayes documents how law did critically mould the approach the United States ultimately adopted to resolve the crisis.[14] Furthermore, Acheson's argument relies unduly on an Austinian notion of law (that is, as a sovereign command backed by an organized and effective sanction for non-compliance) and so mistakenly deems international law merely a matter of 'positive morality', depending only on the moral conscience and practical discretion of States.[15] As is well known, the political realists' error is that they assume international law must function in a manner similar to municipal law in order for it to possess 'legal quality'.[16] In so doing, they overlook crucial distinctions between national societies and international society and preclude the possibility that international law is 'law' in a different sense from municipal law.

Admittedly international law lacks the coherent, recognized and comprehensive framework of sanctions present in municipal law. However, some conformity with international law is fostered by the enlightened self-interest of States—that is, through their concern with reciprocal treatment by other States, as well as with eliciting where possible and politically prudent favourable domestic and world public opinion (or at least avoiding world opprobrium). This conformity helps States to ensure a minimum standard of order in their international relations. Therefore, even if international law is not readily enforceable, the fact that it provides a framework within which States overtly conduct their international relations, and which

---

[11] A less extreme variation of this argument is the contention of some writers that nuclear weapons have made the laws of armed conflict obsolete: see, for example, Stowell, 'The Law of War and the Atomic Bomb', *American Journal of International Law*, 39 (1945), p. 784, and Thomas, 'Atomic Bombs in International Society', ibid., p. 736; cf. Fried, 'International Law Prohibits the First Use of Nuclear Weapons', *Revue belge de droit international*, 16 (1981), p. 33 at pp. 50–2.

[12] *Proceedings of the American Society of International Law*, 1963, p. 13 at p. 14.

[13] Chayes, *International Crises and the Role of Law—The Cuban Missile Crisis* (1974).

[14] For example, see summary, ibid. at pp. 4–5.

[15] Campbell, 'Can Law Control Force', in Dewar, op. cit. above (n. 4), p. 72 at pp. 76–7.

[16] Boyle, *World Politics and International Law* (1985), p. 20; see also Janis, 'Do "Laws" Regulate Nuclear Weapons?' in Pogany, op. cit. above (n. 1), p. 53.

is modestly adhered to, is sufficient justification for its retention. Moreover, breaches of international law do not, of themselves, demonstrate its inefficacy, for as the International Court of Justice stated in *Military and Paramilitary Activities in and against Nicaragua (Merits)*:

> If a State acts in a way *prima facie* incompatible with a recognized rule, but defends its conduct by appealing to exceptions or justifications contained within the rule itself, then whether or not the State's conduct is in fact justifiable on that basis, the significance of that attitude is to confirm rather than to weaken the rule.[17]

Hence the weakness of international law in the realm of high international politics reflects more the primitive state of international society (or perhaps, better put, emerging 'world' society) than a fundamental flaw in law as a source of world public order. Thus those who deem irrelevant that which may be in embryo, to use a hackneyed expression, 'throw the baby out with the bath water'.

Even accepting the relevance of international law to high international politics, one must be mindful of the scepticism pervading Lauterpacht's observation in 1952 that 'if international law is, in some ways, at the vanishing point of law, the law of war is, perhaps even more conspicuously, at the vanishing point of international law'.[18] Indeed, one might be tempted to add to this sobering comment that the laws respecting the means of warfare (especially those regulating nuclear weapons) are at the vanishing point of the laws of war! But to do so, it is submitted, would be to overlook the true character of the laws of armed conflict which, as Lauterpacht summarizes, 'is almost entirely humanitarian in the literal sense of the word, namely to prevent or mitigate suffering and, in some cases to rescue life from the savagery of battle and passion'.[19] To be sceptical then is not to say that the laws of armed conflict are irrelevant in the nuclear age.[20] Rather, it is a prudent warning, perhaps especially directed at international lawyers, to limit one's expectations of, and views on the efficacy of, this particular area of law which, at best, only partially restrains the behaviour of States.[21] As Kalshoven notes, 'the law of armed conflict is a reflection of, and finds its limits in, the perceived interests and political will of States, not the idealistic notions of kind souls'.[22]

---

[17] *ICJ Reports*, 1986, at p. 432, para. 186.

[18] Lauterpacht, 'The Problem of the Revision of the Laws of War', this *Year Book*, 29 (1952), p. 360 at pp. 381–2.

[19] Ibid., at pp. 363–4. It is noted that some commentators take a different view—for example, McDougal and Feliciano argue that 'The common interest which sustains the law of war is the interest of all participants in economy in the use of force—in the minimization of the unnecessary destruction of values': quoted in Arbess, loc. cit. above (n. 3), at p. 102 n. 47.

[20] Roberts, loc. cit. above (n. 4), at p. 43.

[21] Cassese, *International Law in a Divided World* (1986), p. 255.

[22] Kalshoven, loc. cit. above (n. 6), at p. 288. Put another way, 'international lawyers examining the legality of nuclear weapons should distinguish clearly between what the law is and should be and not narcotize themselves into transferring preference into prescription': Reisman, 'Deterrence and International Law', in Miller and Feinrider (eds.), *Nuclear Weapons and Law* (1984), at p. 129.

In short, to admit the relevance of the laws of armed conflict to nuclear weapons is to do no more than make the rather simple observation that law and politics cannot be divorced and are engaged in a crucial symbiotic relationship. As Shaw notes, 'it does neither discipline a service to minimize the significance of the other'.[23] Moreover, given the serious risks to 'global survivability' of adopting wholeheartedly the political realist approach to controlling nuclear force (namely, with greater opposing force), the rationale for concepts of law having a significant role in the management of force is even more compelling. Surely the preferred route is to develop better a non-violent approach to the control of force, and law is an integral aspect of this approach.[24]

(b) Merits of the 'Functional-Positivist' Approach to International Law

As is well demonstrated by Allott,[25] one's conception of the nature and sources of international law determines, in large part, one's articulation of its substantive content. This is perhaps a trite point, but one that bears elaboration—especially in the context of presenting international law at its fringe, which arguably is the case with the international law regulating threats to use, or uses of, nuclear weapons.

The conception of the nature of international law underlying the analysis in this article is largely positivist, as classically expressed by Oppenheim.[26] Accordingly, the so-called 'sense of legal right or obligation' is seen primarily as stemming from the consent of States as international society's principal actors. Some critics will undoubtedly (and, in this writer's view, mistakenly) reject such a paradigm as it might appear rooted in the nineteenth century.[27] On this rather traditional approach Allott chides, 'it treat[s] international law as a rabbit to be produced from the hat of any international lawyer who [can] win the acquiescence of his admiring audience'.[28] Still, even recognizing some of the theoretical problems with this approach (for example, the fiction of 'consent' respecting new States in international society and the competing law-creating processes fostered by the growth of international institutions in the twentieth century and the

[23] Shaw, International Law (2nd edn., 1986), p. 56.
[24] Campbell, loc. cit. above (n. 15), at p. 73.
[25] Allott, 'State Responsibility and the Unmaking of International Law', Harvard International Law Journal, 29 (1988), p. 1 at pp. 24–6.
[26] Oppenheim, 'The Science of International Law: Its Task and Method', American Journal of International Law, 2 (1908), p. 313.
[27] Indeed, in adopting the alternative 'policy-science approach', Weston claims to 'avoid the many pitfalls of the traditional theories', 'demythologize the business of law-making' and base his analysis on 'jurisprudential realism': see Weston, loc. cit. above (n. 6), at p. 552. As will be discussed below, these claims are open to doubt.
[28] Allott, 'Language, Method and the Nature of International Law', this Year Book, 45 (1971), p. 79 at p. 121.

increased global role of individuals and private organizations), this writer argues that it is better to refine (not reject) the tenets of positivism and, therefore, admits that the consent of States, while primary, is not the sole basis of international law.

The preferred approach, it is submitted, is what might be called 'functional-positivism'[29]—as already noted, an approach broached but never fully developed by Morgenthau.[30] The approach is 'positivist' because it embraces traditional, State-centric and observable institutions of positive law for making, recognizing and applying binding rules. It is 'functionalist' because it recognizes that these institutions serve specific value objectives—at the most basic level raised in this article, the avoidance of mutual destruction and assurance of global survivability.[31] The essential point is that 'functional-positivism' regards international law as a contrivance, not discovery, of humanity—principally through the consent of States.[32] The weakness of the rival natural law approach is that it tempts States to distort moral reasoning by appealing to selective and self-serving notions of innate and universal law. Consequently, it is said to be 'dangerously anarchical and distracts our attention from the essential task of contriving positive laws of justiciable form and content'.[33] By contrast, the functional-positivist approach stresses shared (albeit few and often vague) international values and posits piecemeal integration to secure these values, assisted largely by State-created, not divined, law. Hence, in the context of nuclear weapons, it has been said that this approach regards international law as 'an authoritative contrivance for securing the overriding objective of human survival'.[34]

By adopting functional-positivism, this article rejects not only natural law theory but also, in part, the self-styled 'human value oriented jurisprudence' of international law developed by McDougal and his associates at Yale Law School.[35] This article is not the place for a comprehensive summary of this theory of jurisprudence; suffice it to say that, in the lexicon of the 'policy-science school', law-making is a process of co-ordinate communication which creates in a target audience a complex set of expectations

[29] Campbell, loc. cit. above (n. 15), at p. 80.

[30] See above, n. 9.

[31] Campbell, loc. cit. above (n. 15), at p. 80.

[32] Ibid., at p. 81.

[33] Ibid., at p. 85.

[34] Ibid., at p. 87.

[35] See, for example, McDougal and Feliciano, 'International Coercion and World Public Order— The General Principles of the Laws of War', Yale Law Journal, 67 (1958), p. 771; McDougal and Lasswell, 'The Identification and Appraisal of Diverse Systems of Public Order', American Journal of International Law, 53 (1959), p. 1; and McDougal and Reisman, 'The Prescribing Function in World Constitutive Process: How International Law is Made', Yale Studies in World Public Order, 6 (1980), p. 249. This approach to international law was applied to the question of the legality of nuclear weapons in Weston, loc. cit. above (n. 6). See, however, the critique of this application in Reisman, 'Nuclear Weapons in International Law', New York Law School Journal of International and Comparative Law, 4 (1983), p. 339.

respecting policy content, authority and control.[36] Notwithstanding the contextualist analysis this approach endorses, it is rejected by this writer mainly because it ignores the fact that States generally accept international law as it is (that is, in traditional terms) and obey its dictates.[37]

This approach is also rejected because it espouses a view of international law-making that is, arguably, 'an atavistic return to the promotion of Grotian natural law concepts dressed up in the jargon of mid-twentieth century social science'.[38] References to *global* policy', *world* public order' and *universal* human dignity' aside, McDougal's jurisprudence is inextricably and (despite labels to the contrary) transparently grounded in the *Western* liberal tradition of natural rights, as expressed archetypally by Locke, and thus reduces to a kind of 'international utilitarianism'.[39] Such excessively value-laden jurisprudence, based on Lockean liberal values (such as the central importance of the sanctity of private property), cannot realistically serve as the basis for the formation of a system of world public order encompassing States and peoples espousing widely varying and often antithetically opposed sets of values.[40] While consistent with a world view that might be attributed to the United States, McDougal's jurisprudence ignores the possibility (indeed, reality) of other systems of world public order such as, for example, might emanate from the social philosophies of Rousseau, Bentham and Marx. It hardly bears noting that the systems ascribed to these social philosophers adopt a rather different theory of government and its relationship to the individual, starting with the premiss that there is no such thing as natural rights, but only those within the context of a civil society. The point here is not to wade through this philosophic bog, but to emphasize the incongruity of McDougal's perception of international law-making that is at once parochial in value content and universal in ambition.

The quest for improving the quality of public order in international society, in the light of its heterogeneity, is better served by the more modest, less messianic goals of functional-positivism. Despite what critics might say, such an approach is not an inherently static reliance on rules and endorses no less a process of law-making than the policy-science approach. Moreover, functional-positivism is not open to the criticism of dubbing one set of values 'a public order of human dignity' in a thinly veiled argument for a 'melting-pot' of international society. Rather, it accepts that

---

[36] Paraphrased from McDougal and Reisman, loc. cit. (previous note), at p. 250.

[37] Shaw, op. cit. above (n. 23), at p. 55.

[38] Boyle, op. cit. above (n. 16), at p. 63. Cf. Higgins, 'The Identity of International Law', in Cheng (ed.), *International Law: Teaching and Practice* (1982), p. 27 at p. 41, where, in an article neither embracing nor criticizing McDougal's theory of international jurisprudence, she writes: 'The particular language of the policy-science school may be inelegant, but it is useful in communication of certain concepts and ideas, and is by no means difficult if a small, serious effort is made to understand its methodology.'

[39] Allott, loc. cit. above (n. 28), at p. 126.

[40] Boyle, op. cit. above (n. 16), at p. 67.

international law accommodates an international society of diverse constituent States.[41]

Consistently with the functional-positivist approach to the nature of international law, this article takes Article 38(1) of the Statute of the International Court of Justice[42] as its starting point for the sources (or, as some writers prefer to say, 'evidence') of international law. The analysis, however, goes beyond the categories enumerated in Article 38(1) (which, in any event, does not purport to be a list of the 'sources' of international law, but only what the International Court of Justice will apply in deciding cases).[43] It is well established that the orthodox categories, especially treaties and custom between States, need revision.[44] But this does not necessarily mean that the categories must be abandoned altogether.[45] The better view, it is submitted, is to revise this traditional view of the sources of international law to accommodate the law-making capacity of various international institutions and non-State actors. Consequently, in addition to traditional sources, this article will draw on other potential sources of international law, such as United Nations General Assembly resolutions, national legislation and court decisions as well as acts of private organizations (like the International Committee of the Red Cross (the ICRC)), to name a few.

Having dealt with the jurisprudential preliminaries of the relevance of the laws of armed conflict to nuclear weapons and of the merits of the functional-positivist conception of the nature and sources of international law—or, perhaps in the terms of Allott's cynical simile, having shown the reader an empty black hat and said 'Nothing up my sleeve!'—this article proceeds to the less abstract task of articulating the present international legal regime regulating nuclear deterrence and warfare.

III. Nuclear Deterrence—Threats to Use Nuclear Weapons

(a) *Jus ad bellum*

The legal regime regulating the use of nuclear weapons as a deterrent

---

[41] See the critique of the policy-science approach in Dorsey, 'The McDougal-Lasswell Proposal to Build a World Public Order', *American Journal of International Law*, 82 (1988), p. 41, and reply in McDougal, 'The Dorsey Comment: A Modest Retrogression', ibid., p. 51.

[42] See Brownlie (ed.), *Basic Documents in International Law* (3rd edn., 1983), p. 387 at p. 397.

[43] Brownlie, *Principles of Public International Law* (3rd edn., 1979), at p. 3.

[44] See, for example, Jennings, 'The Identification of International Law', in Cheng, op. cit. above (n. 38), p. 3 at p. 9. For a more detailed systematic critique, see McDougal and Reisman, loc. cit. above (n. 35), at pp. 259–68.

[45] Contrary to the straw man descriptions and critique of positivism by some writers—for example, Weston, loc. cit. above (n. 6), at p. 548—the functional-positivist model can 'conjoin law and social reality'. True, it treats international law mainly as a body of rules governing relations between States, but it also explains the process by which these rules are changed by a wide variety of global actors (though principally States).

derives mainly from the relationship between the prohibition of the threat or use of force in Article 2(4) of the UN Charter and the exceptional right of self-defence in Article 51.[46] Also important in this regard are the customary doctrines of anticipatory self-defence (for threats of first-use) and of self-defence and belligerent reprisals (for threats of second-use). Thus it can be said that nuclear deterrence raises considerations mainly of the *jus ad bellum*. Of course, such considerations are also raised by nuclear warfare; however, as they loom largest in the realm of nuclear deterrence (and to avoid repetition), they will be discussed in this section. Likewise, while considerations of the *jus in bello* are relevant to nuclear deterrence, they are concerned mainly with nuclear warfare and so the discussion of them will be confined to that section of this article.

Many writers treat the legal regime regulating nuclear deterrence as an afterthought or, at best, a logical extrapolation of the legal regime for nuclear warfare. They argue that if a given use of nuclear weapons is illegal, then logically any threat of such use must be illegal as well.[47] The result is usually a detailed analysis of the law on nuclear warfare (primarily the *jus in bello* giving short shrift to the *jus ad bellum*) followed by a cursory 'so too' for the law on nuclear deterrence.

By contrast, this article deals first with the legality of nuclear deterrence in terms of the *jus ad bellum* because the logical extrapolation asserted by some writers is at times more apparent than real. As Sadurska notes, 'effective threats will not have the same destructive consequences as the use of force' and 'may be an economical guarantee against open violence'.[48] On these grounds, Sadurska concludes that 'there is no reason to assume that the threat will always be unlawful if in the same circumstances the resort to force would be illicit'.[49] Indeed, the notion that the 'end justifies the means' is the core logic of deterrence for, it is submitted, even if deterrence is aggressive in means, its objective is defensive and it is probably the only form of defence to a nuclear attack.[50]

---

[46] Article 2(4) of the Charter states:
'All members shall refrain in their international relations from the threat or use of force against the territorial integrity or political independence of any state, or in any other manner inconsistent with the purposes of the United Nations.'
Article 51 of the Charter provides:
'Nothing in the present Charter shall impair the inherent right of self-defence if an armed attack occurs against a member of the United Nations, until the Security Council has taken measures necessary to maintain international peace and security.'

[47] See, for example, Arbess, loc. cit. above (n. 3), at p. 121; Grief, 'The Legality of Nuclear Weapons', in Pogany, op. cit. above (n. 1), p. 22 at p. 39; and Weston, loc. cit. above (n. 6), at p. 587.

[48] Sadurska, 'Threats of Force', *American Journal of International Law*, 82 (1988), p. 239 at p. 250.

[49] Ibid.

[50] The same point is made about the legality of the 'MAD *threat* of countervalue war' in O'Brien, *The Conduct of Just and Limited War* (1981), at p. 138. See also McGrath, 'Nuclear Weapons: The Crisis of Conscience' *Military Law Review*, 107 (1985), p. 191 at p. 208, where it is argued that while 'countervalue weapons are too terrible to fit within the framework of international law', they may 'make sense within the concept of mutual deterrence'.

(b) *Threats of First-Use in Anticipatory Self-Defence*

Some writers contend that any threat of the first-use of nuclear weapons is illegal.[51] They argue for a narrow reading of the right of self-defence, treating the articulation of it in Article 51 of the Charter as exhaustive, and so precluding the legality of any preventive action.[52] It is sometimes alleged that this proposition is supported by State practice—namely, that there has been no actual first-use of nuclear weapons since 1945, despite episodes of tension wrought by the cold war. Also, it has been said that this view is fortified by the unilateral verbal commitments to policies of 'no first-use' made by China and the Soviet Union on separate occasions in the UN General Assembly.[53] However, both of these proofs may easily be refuted. The former is specious simply for lack of *opinio juris* because, as O'Brien notes, non-use is more probably the result of the operation of the nuclear deterrent than any State's conviction or statement of belief that first-use is legally impermissible.[54] Moreover, even if it can be said that a State can bind itself by way of a unilateral declaration (as might be inferred from the reaction of the ICJ to the French declaration in the *Nuclear Tests* cases),[55] such a declaration does not, of itself, create an obligation on other States to comply with its terms. The latter 'proof' is weak because one can argue that even if the Chinese and Soviet declarations are credible, they are at best exceptional and permit the inference that these States do not view threats of first-use as illegal *per se*. Indeed, as Cassese notes, were threats of first-use prohibited in any event, it would not be necessary for States to assume a unilateral obligation on the matter.[56]

Contrary State practice also challenges the contention that all threats of the first-use of nuclear weapons are illegal. Western nuclear powers (i.e., the United States, United Kingdom and France) are not only reluctant to make 'no first-use' statements, but they have embraced the threat of first-use as the cornerstone of NATO deterrence policy in Europe.[57] These introductory points aside, the core of the inquiry into the legal regime of nuclear deterrence regulating threats of first-use is the scope of the right of anticipatory self-defence.

It is widely agreed by writers that the customary right of anticipatory self-defence was implicitly recognized in the exchange of notes between the United States and Great Britain following the *Caroline* incident of 1837

---

[51] Boyle, loc. cit. above (n. 2), at p. 1439; Singh, op. cit. above (n. 1), at p. 87.

[52] Singh argues that there is no right of self-defence where there is a 'mere threat, even though that threat may be with nuclear weapons': ibid. at p. 87. He maintains that nuclear weapons may only be legally used (or threatened) 'to repel a nuclear attack': ibid. at pp. 102–3.

[53] Boyle, loc. cit. above (n. 2), at p. 1443. See, e.g., the statement made on 11 June 1982 by the Chinese delegate to the Special General Assembly of the UN (text reproduced in *China and the World* (Bejhing, 1983), at p. 16), and the statement made by Gromyko in 1982 in UN Doc. A/S-12/PV.12 at p. 22.

[54] O'Brien, op. cit. above (n. 50), at p. 141.

[55] *ICJ Reports*, 1974, at pp. 253, 247.

[56] Cassese, op. cit. above (n. 21), at p. 270.

[57] Roberts, loc. cit. above (n. 4), at p. 33.

where the United States Secretary of State, Webster, declared that a State is entitled to take forcible measures in self-defence where it can demonstrate a 'necessity . . . instant, overwhelming, leaving no choice of means and no moment for deliberation'.[58] In addition to this imminence requirement, Webster stressed the requirement of proportionality—in his words, 'the act justified by the necessity of self-defence must be limited by that necessity and kept clearly within it'.[59]

Whether the right of preventive action set out in the *Caroline* formula survives in the era of the Charter has given rise to a protracted controversy. Brownlie, for example, argues that Article 51 of the Charter is exhaustive and so formative of the right of self-defence.[60] Bowett, on the other hand, maintains that the Charter has left the customary right of self-defence (in particular, preventive action) unimpaired.[61] The crux of the matter is the extent to which an 'armed attack' is a necessary precondition to the modern right of self-defence or, put another way, whether this right still accommodates preventive action with respect to an imminent armed attack.

Unfortunately, the Charter's *travaux préparatoires* are inconclusive, for quotations from State delegates at the San Francisco Conference can be produced to support either Brownlie's or Bowett's view.[62] For example, during a committee discussion of the text of Article 2(4), the United States delegate observed:

. . . the intention of the authors of the original text was to state in the broadest terms an absolute all-inclusive prohibition; the phrase 'or in any other manner' was designed to ensure that there should be no loopholes.[63]

On the other hand, Committee 1 of Commission I stated that 'the use of arms in legitimate self-defence remains admitted and unimpaired'.[64]

However, State practice subsequent to the Charter is somewhat less equivocal. To be sure, States have been reluctant to invoke the doctrine of anticipatory self-defence, some dubious exceptions being the claims of Pakistan invading Kashmir in 1948, Israel invading Egypt in 1956 and the Soviet Union invading Czechoslovakia in 1968 and Afghanistan in 1979. Still, even though the doctrine is open to abuse, States have not united in declaring that the Charter precludes resort to force in anticipatory self-defence.

This proposition is evidenced in the views of States during the debate in the UN Security Council following Israel's attack on Iraq's nuclear reactor, 'Osirak', in June 1981, where Israel alleged that she was acting in anticipat-

---

[58] *British Foreign and State Papers*, vol. 30, at p. 193.

[59] Ibid.

[60] Brownlie, *International Law and the Use of Force by States* (1963), at p. 273.

[61] Bowett, *Self-Defence in International Law* (1958), at pp. 184–5.

[62] For a fuller discussion of this point, see Pogany, 'Nuclear Weapons and Self-Defence in International Law', in Pogany, op. cit. above (n. 1), p. 63 at pp. 71–2.

[63] *Documents of the United Nations Conference on International Organization* (1945), vol. 6, at p. 335.

[64] Ibid. at p. 459.

ory self-defence. Even though the Security Council unanimously adopted a resolution condemning the Israeli operation, it did not reject the right of anticipatory self-defence as such.[65] In fact, during the debate, the delegates representing the United States, United Kingdom, Sierra Leone, Niger and, of course, Israel made statements implicitly recognizing a right of pre-ventive action.[66]

The post-Charter right of anticipatory self-defence, consistent with the *Caroline* formula, was also affirmed by the Nuremberg and Tokyo Inter-national Military Tribunals constituted after the Second World War to try German and Japanese war criminals, respectively. The Nuremberg Tri-bunal, for example, stated that ' . . . preventive action in foreign territory is justified only in case of an instant and overwhelming necessity for self-defence, leaving no choice of means, and no moment for deliberation'.[67] Likewise, the Tokyo Tribunal held that a State 'threatened with impending attack' may legitimately resort to force in self-defence.[68] While these tri-bunals were concerned with offences committed before the Charter, their findings were generally perceived by States as applicable after the War: for example, UN General Assembly Resolution 95(I) of 11 December 1946, unanimously adopted, affirmed 'the principles of international law recog-nized by the Charter of the Nuremberg Tribunal and the judgment of the Tribunal'.[69]

Still, it might be argued that the correctness of these judicial pronouncements is now questionable in light of the *Nicaragua* case where, concerning itself with the customary right of self-defence (as dis-tinct from its conventional articulation under Article 51 of the Charter), the ICJ held that, 'in the case of individual self-defence, the exercise of this right is subject to the State concerned having been the victim of an *armed attack*',[70] especially since the ICJ defined this precondition so as to appear to preclude anticipatory self-defence.[71] However, strictly speaking, the integrity of the judgments at Nuremburg and Tokyo remains intact because in the *Nicaragua* case the ICJ expressly disclaimed any intention

---

[65] Security Council Resolution 487, 19 June 1981, reprinted in 'Documents on Israel's Attack on Iraq's Nuclear Reactor', *International Legal Materials*, 20 (1981), p. 963 at p. 973.

[66] For example, the United Kingdom's delegate stated that the Israeli operation violated inter-national law in so far as 'there was no instant or overwhelming necessity for self-defence': S/PV 2282nd meeting, 15 June 1981 at p. 42; *International Legal Materials*, 20 (1981), at p. 977. Quoting a passage from Bowett, op. cit. above (n. 61), the Israeli delegate contended that 'No State can be expected to await an initial attack which, in the present state of armaments, may well destroy the State's capacity for further resistance and so jeopardize its very existence': ibid. at p. 973.

[67] Passage reproduced in Schwarzenberger, *International Law as Applied by Courts and Tribunals*, vol. 2 (1968), at pp. 28–9. It should be noted that even though Germany's argument of self-defence was rejected on the facts, the legal ruling in the case cannot be distinguished on this ground.

[68] Ibid. at p. 71.

[69] *UN Yearbook*, 1946–7, at p. 254.

[70] *ICJ Reports*, 1986, at p. 437, para. 195 (emphasis added).

[71] For example, in considering the nature of acts which can be treated as constituting armed attacks, the ICJ included acts by armed bands on a significant scale but excluded 'assistance to rebels in the form of the provision of weapons or logistical or other support': ibid. at pp. 102–3, para. 195.

to comment on the legality of preventive measures—for, in that case, an armed attack had in fact occurred. In its words:

> In view of the circumstances in which the dispute has arisen, reliance is placed by the Parties only on the right of self-defence in the case of an armed attack which has already occurred, *and the issue of the lawfulness of a response to the imminent threat of armed attack has not been raised. Accordingly, the Court expresses no view on that issue.*[72]

Even so, in the *Nicaragua* case the judgment's ambivalence on the question of anticipatory self-defence remains, and in an effort to clarify the matter Judge Schwebel, in dissent, emphasizes:

> The Court rightly observes that the issue of the lawfulness of a response to an imminent threat of armed attack has not been raised in this case, and the Court accordingly expresses no view on that issue. Nevertheless, its Judgment may be open to the interpretation of inferring that a State may react in self-defence, and that supportive States may react in collective self-defence, only if an armed attack occurs . . . I wish, *ex abundanti cautela*, to make clear that, for my part . . . I do not agree that the terms or intent of Article 51 eliminate the right of self-defence under customary international law, or confine its entire scope to the express terms of Article 51.[73]

Some writers go even further than accepting the customary right of anticipatory self-defence within the *Caroline* formula, contending that the formula is more rhetorical than substantive—particularly the requirement that threats be met instantly, for it is sometimes better to do so only after protracted calculation.[74] Indeed, this appears to be one of the lessons of the Cuban missile crisis. O'Brien, for example, suggests that the so-called 'principle of effectiveness' should guide interpretations of the right's scope.[75] Moreover, on Sadurska's reasoning,[76] even if the use may be disproportionate to the military objective sought, the threat of use may not and so may be legally permissible—to the extent that, accepting the logic of nuclear deterrence, such a threat is the only way to prevent nuclear war.

In sum, while not uncontroverted, there is some evidence of State practice, judicial decisions and writings to support the continued existence of the customary right of anticipatory self-defence, notwithstanding the prohibition of the threat or use of force in Article 2(4) of the Charter.[77] It follows, therefore, that the threat of the first-use of nuclear weapons is not

---

[72] Ibid., para. 194 (emphasis added).
[73] Ibid., at pp. 347–8, paras. 172–3.
[74] O'Brien, op. cit. above (n. 50), at p. 133.
[75] Ibid., at p. 132; see also Rauschning, 'Nuclear Warfare and Weapons', in Bernhardt (ed.), *Encyclopedia of Public International Law*, vol. 4 (1982), p. 44 at p. 49.
[76] See above, p. 209.
[77] cf. Dinstein, *War, Aggression and Self-Defence* (1988), where a distinction is made between 'anticipatory self-defence' (which he regards as excluded by the Charter) and 'interceptive self-defence' (which he argues remains legal). In Dinstein's view, legitimate interceptive self-defence contemplates an act against an attack that has been initiated, even though the final blow has not yet been delivered: at p. 180.

illegal as such and may be lawful if proportionate to, and issued in the face of, an imminent threat. For example, the mere threat of a low-yield counterforce strike (without more) would appear lawful to deter the imminent attack of a mobilized armoured column. Moreover, given the logic of this legal regime, it can be argued that even if a first countervalue strike would be dispropor- tionate to the military objective sought (e.g., to destroy the communication centre for a conventional attack) or otherwise unlawful under the *jus in bello*, the *threat* of such a strike would not necessarily be unlawful under the *jus ad bellum*, to the extent that it was the only available deterrent. Hence, inter- national law does not prohibit all threats of the first-use of nuclear weapons; rather, the legality of each threat depends on its context.

(c) *Threats of Second-Use in Self-Defence and Belligerent Reprisal*

Clearly, the strongest legal justification for the threat of the second-use of nuclear weapons is the right of self-defence under Article 51 of the Charter, for carrying out such a threat posits that an armed attack (indeed, a nuclear one) has already occurred. Prior to such an attack, the legality of threats of second-use may be justified by the customary right of anticipatory self- defence, discussed in the previous section.

An alternative and more controversial legal justification for threats of second-use is the customary law doctrine of belligerent reprisals. This sec- tion focuses on the scope of this customary doctrine and the extent to which it (like the customary right of self-defence) can be said to have survived in the era of the Charter. Admittedly, on its face, the Charter regime of Articles 2(4) and 51 (as well as Article 2(3)) appear conventionally to prohi- bit resort to any forcible reprisals.[78] Moreover, this prohibition is reiterated in the 1970 UN General Assembly Declaration on Principles of Inter- national Law concerning Friendly Relations and Co-operation among States which provides that 'States have a duty to refrain from acts of reprisal involving the use of force'.[79]

For several reasons, however, it can be argued that the customary right of belligerent reprisals (the requirements of which will be discussed below), like the customary right of anticipatory self-defence, today stands unim- paired by the Charter regime. First, given the failure of the Security Coun- cil to fulfil the policing role intended for it by the drafters of the Charter, any prohibition on belligerent reprisals that might have been intended by, or reasonably inferred from, the prohibition in Article 2(4) must be reinter-

---

[78] See, for example, Bowett, 'Reprisals Involving Recourse to Armed Force', *American Journal of International Law*, 66 (1972), p. 1 at p. 1; Brownlie, op. cit. above (n. 60), at p. 282; Grief, loc. cit. above (n. 47), at p. 46 n. 76; Kennedy, 'A Critique of United States Nuclear Deterrence Theory', *Brooklyn Journal of International Law*, 9 (1983), p. 35 at p. 59; and Zoller, ibid. at pp. 38–9.

[79] GA Res. 2625 (XXV), *General Assembly Official Records*, 25th Session, Supplement No. 28, at p. 121; UN Doc. A/8028 (1970).

preted so as not to leave the victim State without recourse to effective and legal action. Further, notwithstanding the 1970 Declaration of Principles and such Charter-era statements as the Security Council's 1964 resolution on the Harib Fort incident condemning 'reprisals as incompatible with the purposes and principles of the United Nations',[80] the prohibition of belligerent reprisals today suffers from what has been called a 'credibility gap'[81]—that is, even if illegal in theory, in practice a victim State can escape international censure for using force in reprisal against the use of force by another State provided the victim State satisfies requirements similar to those for belligerent reprisals at customary law. Hence, even if the original intent of the Charter regime was to prohibit all reprisals involving the use of force, and however earnestly some States continue to pledge their support to this political ideal at the UN, the contrary practice of States tolerating recourse to belligerent reprisals suggests a revival, if it was ever dead, of this customary law doctrine. It might, of course, be argued that there is no clear *opinio juris* on the part of States supporting this doctrine. However, this is not determinative of the issue because the lack of such statements of belief by States is more probably due to political expedience (in that because belligerent reprisals, by their very nature, follow an armed attack, the requirements of the less controversial right of acting in self-defence are met, so giving the victim State a better accepted legal justification) than to a widespread conviction among States that belligerent reprisals are legally impermissible.

Indeed, belligerent reprisals are contemplated in the United States Rules of Land Warfare where they are defined as:

. . . acts of retaliation in the form of conduct which would otherwise be unlawful, resorted to by one belligerent against enemy personnel or property for acts of warfare committed by the other belligerent in violation of the law of war, for the purpose of enforcing future compliance with recognized rules of civilized warfare.[82]

The scope of such reprisals at customary law is discussed in the award made by the tribunal of the *Naulilaa Incident* arbitration.[83] As this decision has been subsequently interpreted by most writers, a legitimate belligerent reprisal must:

1. be in response to a prior violation of the laws of armed conflict;
2. follow exhaustion of all reasonable means of peaceful settlement;

---

[80] SC Res. 188, UN Doc. S/5649 (1964).

[81] Bowett, loc. cit. above (n. 78), at p. 1, and Greenwood, 'International Law and the United States' Air Operation against Libya', *West Virginia Law Review*, 89 (1987), p. 933 at p. 950.

[82] United States of America War Office, Department of the Army, Field Manual No. 27–10: *The Law of Land Warfare* (1956), para. 497(a) at p. 177.

[83] *Germany–Portugal* arbitration (1928), *Reports of International Arbitral Awards*, vol. 2, p. 1012. On the facts of the case, the German response to the original act was disproportionate and the reprisal was therefore unlawful.

3. be a reasonably proportionate response to the prior delict;[84] and
4. be undertaken as a sanction for the laws of armed conflict and not merely for revenge—that is, taken not simply for punishment, but in an effort to put an end to a continuing wrong, deter repetition or secure reparation.[85]

Moreover, it follows from these conditions that counter-reprisals are not legally permitted against legitimate belligerent reprisals.[86]

The legal requirements for belligerent reprisals are therefore similar to those for self-defence. As Bowett notes, both stem from the same generic remedy of self-help but each has a different purpose—protection is the main aim of self-defence whereas punishment and deterrence are the goals of reprisals.[87] Another purpose often attributed to belligerent reprisals is 'signalling'—that is, indicating to the adversary that a given step up the ladder of violence is a measured sanction and not meant to inaugurate unrestricted warfare.[88]

The inherent vagueness of the proportionality requirement for belligerent reprisals has led to a range of opinions among writers as to whether reprisals with nuclear weapons must be 'in kind' (that is, in response to an illegal nuclear strike) to be legitimate.[89] Brownlie, for example, sees no scope for the doctrine of belligerent reprisals, especially in the context of nuclear weapons, arguing:

it is hardly legitimate to extend a doctrine related to the minutiae of the conventional theatre of war to an exchange of power which, in the case of the strategic and deterrent uses of nuclear weapons, is equivalent to the total war effort and is the essence of the war aims.[90]

Castrén maintains that reprisals with nuclear weapons are only legitimate if in kind.[91] Lauterpacht, by contrast, takes the view that nuclear reprisals that are 'not in kind' (say, in response to an egregiously brutal conventional attack) are legitimate where the enemy 'violates rules of the law of war on a scale so vast as to put himself outside the orbit of considerations of

---

[84] cf. McDougal and Feliciano, who maintain that the real test should be whether the reprisal is proportionate to the legitimate end to be achieved—i.e., preventing repetition of the unlawful act or ensuring that a continuing violation is terminated: see *Law and Minimum World Public Order* (1961), at p. 682.

[85] These conditions are variously described by Bowett, loc. cit. above (n. 78), at p. 3; Greenwood, 'Reprisals and Reciprocity in the New Law of Armed Conflict' (unpublished draft, 1988), at p. 3; and Grief, loc. cit. above (n. 47), at p. 31.

[86] Kalshoven, *Belligerent Reprisals* (1971), at p. 351.

[87] Bowett, loc. cit. above (n. 78), at p. 3; cf. Hampson, 'Belligerent Reprisals and the 1977 Protocols to the Geneva Conventions of 1949', *International and Comparative Law Quarterly*, 37 (1988), p. 818 at p. 821.

[88] Kalshoven, op. cit. above (n. 86), at p. 377.

[89] Grief, loc. cit. above (n. 47), at pp. 30–1.

[90] Brownlie, 'Some Legal Aspects of the Use of Nuclear Weapons', *International and Comparative Law Quarterly*, 14 (1965), p. 437 at p. 445.

[91] Castrén, 'The Illegality of Nuclear Weapons', *Toledo Law Review*, 1971, p. 89 at p. 98.

humanity and passion'.[92] Taking a less extreme view, Singh and Schwarzenberger admit that legitimate reprisals need not be identical, but stress the acute difficulty of assessing the proportionality of reprisals that are 'not in kind'.[93] Along the same lines, Kalshoven asks 'proportional to what?, to the explosive force of the weapons used by the enemy, to the suffering caused, or to the military effect achieved?'.[94]

In this writer's view, the confusion over applying the proportionality test is partly resolved by recognizing that the proportionality of a belligerent reprisal, however subjectively assessed by the victim State, is ultimately, for the purpose of international law, determined objectively by the community of States at large. Thus, all factors may be relevant as third party States assess retrospectively whether the act in reprisal was reasonably proportionate to the wrongful act to which it was a response (or, taking a wider view, whether it was proportionate to the mischief it sought to prevent). The consequence of this view, it is submitted, is not to limit legitimate belligerent reprisals with nuclear weapons only to those in kind, but to make rare (that is, only in the exceptional circumstances suggested by Lauterpacht) the legitimacy of belligerent reprisals with nuclear weapons that are not in kind.

While not free of doubt, there is some evidence for the proposition that the customary right of belligerent reprisals has survived to the present day. In the first place, the many prohibitions of reprisals against protected persons or property in the Geneva Conventions of 1949[95] and in Additional Protocol I of 1977[96] permit the inference that the customary doctrine of belligerent reprisals was not obliterated by an absolute prohibition under Article 2(4) of the Charter. Indeed, it can reasonably be argued that the

[92] Lauterpacht (ed.), *Oppenheim's International Law*, vol. 2 (7th edn., 1952), at p. 351. He cites the example of Germany during the Second World War since, by indulging in 'a systematic plan of putting to death millions of civilians in occupied territory', it exhibited conduct which might justify the use of nuclear weapons as a punishment. It is interesting to note that the UN Secretariat, 'Survey of Existing Rules of International Law concerning the Prohibition or Restriction of the Use of Specific Weapons', UN Doc. A/9215 of 7 November 1973, vol. 1, para. 99 at p. 154, states: 'A manual of the Federal Republic of Germany provides that the use of nuclear weapons in a manner which would otherwise be prohibited by international law is permitted by way of reprisal against a particularly grave violation of international law by an enemy.'
[93] Singh, op. cit. above (n. 1), at p. 168; Schwarzenberger, *The Legality of Nuclear Weapons* (1958), at p. 41.
[94] Kalshoven, op. cit. above (n. 86), at p. 558.
[95] For example, Convention I, Article 46, outlaws reprisals against the wounded, sick, personnel, buildings and equipment protected by the Convention; Convention II, Article 47, outlaws reprisals against the wounded, sick and shipwrecked persons, personnel, vessels and equipment protected by the Convention; Convention III, Article 13, outlaws reprisals against prisoners of war; and Convention IV, Article 37, outlaws reprisals against protected persons and their property. This summary is taken from Shaw, 'Nuclear Weapons and International Law' in Pogany, op. cit. above (n. 1), p. 1 at p. 17.
[96] For example, reprisals are outlawed against: the wounded, sick and shipwrecked and certain protected medical and other personnel, buildings and vehicles in Article 20; the civilian population in Article 51(6); civilian objects in Article 52(1); cultural objects and places of worship in Article 53(c); objects indispensable to the civilian population's survival in Article 53(4); the natural environment in Article 55(2); and works and installations containing dangerous forces in Article 56(4). These provisions are summarized and discussed in Greenwood, loc. cit. above (n. 85), at pp. 14 ff.

Charter provisions relate only to reprisals involving resort to force in the first instance. Also, there is some modern-day practice of States, most notably that of Israel (and, arguably that of the United States), where limited action has been taken and admitted as a belligerent reprisal.[97] Further, regarding such reprisals, the UN Security Council has sometimes exercised its political judgment so as not to condemn the act in belligerent reprisal where it has been deemed a 'reasonable' response.[98]

Admittedly, few other examples of State practice positively support the customary right of belligerent reprisals. As already noted, however, this may not reflect their illegality as such, but may be due to expedience because, in the first place, there can be no doubt that politically 'reprisals in war have a bad name';[99] as Cassese laments, 'reprisals are a primitive instrument through which violence escalates into barbarity'.[100] Moreover, as also noted, given that forcible reprisals usually

---

[97] On the practice of Israel, see, for example, the incidents at Qibya on 15 October 1953, Nahhalin on 28 March 1954 and Gaza on 28 February 1955, summarized in Bowett, loc. cit. above (n. 78), at p. 33. Israeli counterterror practice since Bowett's 1972 article is discussed in O'Brien, 'Reprisals, Deterrence and Self-Defence in Counterterror Operations', *Virginia Journal of International Law*, 30 (1990), p. 421 at pp. 426–62.

On the practice of the United States, see the discussion in O'Brien (loc. cit. above, at pp. 467–9) of US operations in the Persian Gulf—namely, American attacks on Iranian targets on 19 October 1987 (where the United States destroyed an Iranian oil platform as 'a measured and appropriate response' to Iran firing missiles at a US–flagged tanker) and on 18 April 1988 (where the United States attacked Iranian oil platforms and clashed with Iranian aircraft and boats (sinking an Iranian frigate and four gunboats) after Iranian mining of the Persian Gulf resulted in damage to a US ship).

Also, though on weaker grounds, it might be argued that the United States bombing raid of April, 1986 on Libyan leader Qadhafi's headquarters in Tripoli, despite American assertions of acting in self-defence, was more in the nature of a forcible reprisal. While Secretary of State Shultz spoke of Libya's sanctuary and support to terrorist groups such as that led by Abu Nidal as amounting to 'ongoing armed aggression' and 'a threat to US security' (see 'Documents Showing the Evolution of Sanctions Against Libya', *International Legal Materials*, 25 (1986), p. 173 at p. 206), other official American statements suggested that the United States military action was a belligerent reprisal against the string of terrorist attacks culminating in the attacks of 27 December 1985 on the airports at Rome and Vienna. For example, see Deputy Secretary of State Whitehead's comment that the United States will take measures 'to change Qadhafi's pattern of action': ibid at p. 218; see also Whitehead, 'Counterterrorism Policy', in *Department of State Bulletin*, 86 (1986), at p. 79, where, again, mixed with a claim of acting in self-defence, it is asserted that the United States military action was aimed partly at 'demonstrating that Qadhafi's continued pursuit of his policies would not be without direct cost to Libya'. For more detailed discussions of the 1986 United States' raid on Libya, see Brandenburg, 'The Legality of Assassination as an Aspect of Foreign Policy', *Virginia Journal of International Law*, 27 (1987), p. 655 at pp. 690–3, Greenwood, loc. cit. above (n. 81) and O'Brien's 1990 article noted above at pp. 463–7. The dual and so confusing character of the American bombing raid is reflected in Dinstein's characterization of the air strikes as 'acts of defensive armed reprisals', *War, Aggression and Self-Defence* (1988), at p. 212. This approach to characterizing reprisals is endorsed by O'Brien in his 1990 article noted above at p. 476. Of course, legalities aside, the United States argument rests on what now appears to have been dubious assumptions of fact—i.e., the earlier terrorist attacks were apparently sponsored by Syria, not Libya.

[98] See, for example, the Nahhalin incident of 28 March 1954; see the discussion in Bowett, loc. cit. above (n. 78), at pp. 20 and 29 ff. See also Hampson, loc. cit. above (n. 87), at p. 836, and Levenfield, 'Israel's Counter-Fedayeen Tactics in Lebanon: Self-Defence and Reprisal under Modern International Law', *Columbia Journal of Transnational Law*, 21 (1982), p. 1 at pp. 10–12. On the other hand, see the Security Council's condemnation of the British use of force as an illegal reprisal in the Harib Fort incident in 1964: SC Res. 188, UN Doc S/5649 (1964).

[99] Greenwood, loc. cit. above (n. 85), at p. 1.

[100] Cassese, op. cit. above (n. 21), at p. 274.

follow an armed attack, the requirements of self-defence are met and this presents the victim State with a better accepted legal justification for threats or use of force.[101]

Still, the scope of legitimate belligerent reprisals should be severely curtailed to guard against self-serving abuses solely for retribution but under the guise of punishment and deterrence that, as between intransigent belligerents, might escalate the violence of war to horrific proportions.[102] While it is tempting to treat the forcible responses of States to terrorist attacks as State practice supporting a widening view of belligerent reprisals, this temptation should be resisted. Since the exceptional use of force in self-defence is politically more palatable than its use in belligerent reprisal, such forcible acts might be better viewed as part of an emerging wider view of self-defence. Bowett's 'accumulation of events theory' accommodates this wider view, positing that if pinprick attacks (that is, attacks which if treated in isolation constitute relatively minor uses of force) emanating from the same State form a reasonably coherent and proximate pattern, they can be treated as a continuing attack upon the victim State. The consequence of Bowett's approach is two-fold: first, the victim State need not show that another attack is imminent before using force in self-defence so long as further attacks are likely; and secondly, the proportionality of the victim State's response is judged not against a single act or imminent threat but against the actual and anticipated attacks as a whole.[103] It would appear that this approach incorporates deterrence as integral to effective self-defence, especially in counterterror operations against a continuing threat. Although there is some evidence of State support for this theory,[104] it is still too early to say that it has come to represent international law.

While rife with problems of application, the significance of the enduring customary right of belligerent reprisals is that it can be used to justify the threat or use of nuclear weapons in reprisal even where such weapons would otherwise be illegal pursuant to the *jus in bello*.[105] Moreover, the right elaborates a legal regime of regulation largely dependent on the context of the threat or use.[106] In terms of nuclear deterrence, therefore,

---

[101] The synopsis of selected incidents in Bowett, loc. cit. above (n. 78), at pp. 33–6, supports this view.

[102] For an account of the modern-day trend substantially reducing the scope (in terms of objects and purposes) for taking lawful belligerent reprisals, see Greenwood, 'The Twilight of the Law of Belligerent Reprisals', *Netherlands Yearbook of International Law*, 20 (1989), p. 35.

[103] Greenwood, loc. cit. above (n. 81), at pp. 953–6.

[104] In addition to the State practice noted in n. 97, above, see, for example, the British plea of self-defence in the Harib Fort incident of 1964, rejected by the Security Council as an illegal reprisal, discussed by Greenwood, ibid., at p. 945. As to the aptness of the Caroline formula, O'Brien contends: 'Given the duration and magnitude of Israel's war with the PLO, 1964 to present, the interpretation of necessity is very different from that in a singular incident along the US–Canadian border in 1837': loc. cit. above (n. 97), at p. 471.

[105] Singh, op. cit. above (n. 1), at p. 168, and Schwarzenberger, op. cit. above (n. 93), at pp. 40–1.

[106] Weston, loc. cit. above (n. 6), at p. 558.

international law does not prohibit threats of second-use as such but determines their legality in the context of their issue.

(d) *Threats Through Extended Deterrence*

Extended deterrence is shorthand for the use of nuclear threats to deter attacks on allies and other third States.[107] While some writers treat the legality of extended deterrence as a special question,[108] it appears to make more sense to treat the subject as raising considerations of *jus ad bellum* similar to those already discussed—namely, the scope of the customary right of anticipatory self-defence, self-defence under Article 51 of the Charter and the customary doctrine of belligerent reprisals. Obviously, however, what differs with extended deterrence is that threats of force are issued against the aggressor State not individually but collectively by a protecting State on behalf of a victim State.

The decision of the ICJ in the *Nicaragua* case suggests that legitimate collective self-defence requires, in addition to the precondition of an 'armed attack', that the victim State formally request assistance from the protecting State (not itself under any direct armed attack).[109] While presumably this requirement is intended to safeguard the interests of victim States from over-zealous 'protecting' States abusing collective security arrangements, it does not, in this writer's view, materially alter the legal regime from that for individual self-defence. Moreover, in principle at least, the importance of this requirement of a 'formal agreement' is in some doubt given the strength of Judge Jennings' dissenting opinion, where he contends that it is unduly formalistic for the Court to require as a condition of lawful collective self-defence that a formal request for assistance from the victim State to the protecting State be made. In his view, while legitimate collective self-defence does not mean 'vicarious defence by champions', it may suffice that the State rendering assistance is, in addition to other requirements, in at least some measure, defending itself.[110] Similarly, Dinstein argues that there must be clear evidence that the security of the protecting State is endangered for, in his words, 'collective self-defence is above all the defence of self'; and he suggests that the ICJ's insistence in the *Nicaragua* case on a prior request for help by the victim State would be correct only where the protecting State's military action took place within the victim State's territory.[111]

Admittedly, unlike the customary right of collective self-defence, the

---

[107] As distinct from 'pure' deterrence, which is aimed at deterring attacks on one's own State.

[108] See, for example, Arbess, loc. cit. above (n. 3), at p. 128, where he argues that while 'pure' deterrence may be legally justified as it is a threat to dissuade nuclear attack, 'extended' deterrence is illegal as it is a threat to initiate nuclear war. This writer submits that there is nothing inherent in the notion of extended deterrence that makes it more 'aggressive' than pure deterrence. Indeed, the ultimate aim of each is to dissuade activity that might lead to a nuclear attack.

[109] *ICJ Reports*, 1986, at pp. 119–22, especially para. 232; see also paras. 195, 199.

[110] Ibid. at p. 545.

[111] Dinstein, op. cit. above (n. 77), at pp. 247–50, the quotation at p. 248. Bowett agrees with Dinstein's analysis in his review of the book: this *Year Book*, 59 (1988), p. 263 at p. 265.

scope for a customary right of collective belligerent reprisals charts new legal territory. It appears, however, that there is no reason in principle why such a right should not exist—subject, of course, to satisfaction of the requirements for legitimate individual belligerent reprisals discussed above plus, arguably, the requirement of a formal request for assistance from the victim State in certain circumstances. Hence, like threats of first- or second-use in pure deterrence, threats in extended deterrence are not absolutely prohibited but are regulated mainly by the vague principle of proportionality.

IV. NUCLEAR WARFARE—ACTUAL USE OF NUCLEAR WEAPONS

(a) *Jus in bello*

Shifting the analysis from when to how States may legally use nuclear weapons, it should be noted at the outset that several propositions about the *jus in bello* are widely accepted: that it applies regardless of the legality of an armed conflict under the *jus ad bellum*;[112] that it is broadly delineated by balancing the three underlying principles of military necessity, humanity and chivalry[113] (though this last principle may have lost some significance as warfare has become increasingly impersonal[114]); and that it is primarily concerned with establishing a minimum standard to alleviate the human suffering caused by warfare.[115] States have so far adopted a dual approach to the regulation of the means of warfare, namely, general principles and specific bans.[116] Unfortunately, it appears that this regime suffers from the weakness that the general principles are 'so loose as to be almost unworkable, save in extreme situations' and the specific bans are 'too few and easily circumvented by changes in weapons technology'.[117]

(b) *No Specific and Absolute Prohibition of Use*

1. *Treaties*

No treaty expressly declaring the use of nuclear weapons illegal as such has ever been concluded. True, there are various international agreements dealing with certain limitations on the deployment and proliferation of nuclear weapons. These include, for example, the peace treaties following

---

[112] Rauschning, loc. cit. above (n. 75), at p. 45.

[113] Roberts and Guelff (eds.), *Documents on the Laws of War* (1982), at p. 5. It is noted that this book is now in its second edition (1989); however, the page references for documents cited in this article are to the first edition.

[114] Weston, loc. cit. above (n. 6), at p. 554 n. 39.

[115] Cassese, op. cit. above (n. 21), at p. 269.

[116] Ibid.

[117] Cassese, 'Means of Warfare: The Traditional and the New Law', in Cassese (ed.), *The New Humanitarian Law of Armed Conflict* (1979), p. 161 at p. 170.

the Second World War prohibiting the deployment of nuclear weapons by Bulgaria, Finland, Hungary, Italy and Romania,[118] the treaties on nuclear-free areas,[119] and the many treaties on arms control[120] and non-proliferation.[121] Moreover, there are continuing negotiations on nuclear arms limitation directly[122] as well as attempts to link the discussion of nuclear weapons to other arms limitation talks.[123] However, if anything, these treaties and continuing negotiations respecting bans on certain uses of nuclear weapons and their possession by certain States permit the inference that certain other unspecified uses are not contrary to international law.[124] These international agreements and negotiations appear to operate on the basis of denying the illegality of nuclear weapons as such or, at least, without prejudice to this general question.

2. Custom

Customary international law is derived both from what States do and from what they say with an avowed sense of legal right or obligation—that is, in terms of *opinio juris*, the key factor is the State's statement of belief that it is acting in accordance with the law. This statement need not be genuine so long as other States concur or acquiesce in its assertion.[125] In assessing the customary law on nuclear weapons, special attention must be given to the practice with *opinio juris* of those States actually possessing such weapons.[126] It cannot be argued convincingly, however, that the non-

[118] Signed with the Allies on 10 February 1947. To the same effect, see also the Austrian State Treaty of 15 May 1955 and the North Atlantic Treaty (regarding accession of the Federal Republic of Germany on 23 October 1954).

[119] See, for example, the Antarctica Treaty, 1959; the Treaty on Principles Governing the Activities of States in the Exploration and Use of Outer Space, including the Moon and other Celestial Bodies, 1967; and the Treaty on the Prohibition of the Emplacement of Nuclear Weapons and other Weapons of Mass Destruction on the Seabed and Ocean Floor and in the Subsoil thereof, 1971. See also two treaties respecting inhabited areas, not yet in force, the Treaty for the Prohibition of Nuclear Weapons in Latin America, 1967, and the South Pacific Nuclear-Free Zone Treaty, 1985. For a discussion of these treaties, see Freestone and Davidson, 'Nuclear Free Areas', in Pogany, op. cit. above (n. 1), at p. 176.

[120] See the various treaties between the United States and the Soviet Union—for example: on testing, the Partial Nuclear Test Ban Treaty, 1963, and Treaties Prohibiting Certain Underground Nuclear Tests of 1974 and 1976; on limitation, the Treaty on Limitations of Anti-Ballistic Missile Systems, 1972, and the Intermediate-Range Nuclear Forces Treaty, 1987.

[121] See the Treaty on the Non-Proliferation of Nuclear Weapons, 1968.

[122] For example, the current round of Strategic Arms Reduction Talks in Geneva between the United States and the Soviet Union.

[123] See, for example, the effort by Arab and non-aligned States to link nuclear to chemical disarmament at the 1989 Paris Conference on Chemical Weapons: *The Times*, 12 January 1989, at p. 6. This effort was, however, rejected by Western and nuclear States and, at best, only vaguely catered for in the final declaration of the conference.

[124] This point is made by many writers including Bilder, 'Nuclear Weapons and International Law', in Miller and Feinrider, op. cit. above (n. 22), p. 3 at p. 6; Mallison, 'The Laws of War and the Juridical Control of Weapons of Mass Destruction in General and Limited Wars', *George Washington Law Review*, 36 (1968), p. 308 at p. 333; Rauschning, loc. cit. above (n. 75), at p. 11.

[125] This view is taken from Akehurst, 'Custom as a Source of International Law', this *Year Book*, 47 (1974–5), p. 1 at p. 10; cf. D'Amato, 'Reply to Akehurst', *American Journal of International Law*, 80 (1986), p. 148, who prefers to limit relevant 'law-making' State practice to what States actually do.

[126] This 'specially affected interest' doctrine is noted in the *North Sea Continental Shelf* cases, *ICJ Reports*, 1969, p. 3 at p. 42, para. 73.

use of nuclear weapons since 9 August 1945 is conclusive evidence of a customary prohibition for, as already noted, this is more likely to be due to considerations of deterrence than to convictions of illegality.

In this regard, the statements of belief of legal right and obligation asserted in the available military manuals of States possessing nuclear weapons reject the idea of an absolute prohibition and clearly contemplate certain legal uses of nuclear weapons. For example, Article 613 of the United States *Rules of Naval Warfare* (1955) declares that:

> There is at present no rule of international law expressly prohibiting States from the use of nuclear weapons in warfare. In the absence of any express prohibition, the use of such weapons against enemy combatants and other objectives is permitted.[127]

Likewise, the United Kingdom's *Manual of Military Law* states that:

> There is no rule of international law dealing specifically with the use of nuclear weapons. Their use, therefore, is governed by the general principles laid down in this chapter* . . .
> In the absence of any rule of international law dealing expressly with it, the use which may be made of a particular weapon will be governed by the ordinary rules and the question of the legality of its use in any particular case will, therefore, involve merely the application of the recognized principles of international law.**[128]

This view (that there is no specific and absolute prohibition of the use of nuclear weapons) is also confirmed in the military manuals of several non-nuclear States.[129] Hence, in light of these unambiguous assertions—particularly by States with nuclear weapons and so specially affected—it is hard to demonstrate that nuclear weapons are illegal *per se* and that the mere possession of such weapons is, of itself, unlawful.[130]

Still, military manuals are not the end of the matter and one must consider what States have said and done in other contexts, in particular, at the

---

[127] Quoted by Shaw, loc. cit. above (n. 95), at p. 2. This view is reiterated in the manuals of the other United States services—for example: in the Army, Field Manual No. 27–10, op. cit. above (n. 82), at para. 35, and in the Air Force, Air Force Pamphlet 110–31, *International Law—The Conduct of Armed Conflict and Air Operations* (1976), para. 6–5, where it is stated that 'The use of explosive "atomic weapons" whether by air, sea or land forces, cannot as such be regarded as violative of international law in the absence of any customary rule of international law or international convention restricting their employment'. See also, to the same effect, para. 10.2.1 of United States, Department of the Navy, Naval Warfare Publication 9, *The Commander's Handbook on the Law of Naval Operations* (1987).

[128] The War Office, *The Law of War on Land, being Part III of the Manual of Military Law* (1958), *para. 113 and ** para. 107 n. 1(b).

[129] See, for example, the field manuals of Austria, Federal Republic of Germany, the Netherlands and Switzerland, referred to in the UN Secretariat's 'Survey of Existing Rules of International Law Concerning the Prohibition or Restriction of Use of Specific Weapons', loc. cit. above (n. 92), vol. 1, para. 99 at pp. 153–4. See also paras. 511, 618 and 708 of the Canadian Forces, *Law of Armed Conflict Manual*, presently in draft form, which when issued in final form will be an official publication of the Canadian Forces.

[130] Bright, 'Nuclear Weapons as a Lawful Means of Warfare', *Military Law Review*, 30 (1965), p. 1 at p. 28.

UN. Some writers contend that certain UN General Assembly resolutions, purporting to declare the use of nuclear weapons illegal *per se*, are cogent evidence of customary international law.[131] The one most frequently relied on for this contention is Resolution 1653 (XVI) of 24 November 1961 entitled 'Declaration on the Prohibition of the Use of Nuclear and Thermo-Nuclear Weapons' which states, *inter alia*, that the use of nuclear weapons is 'a direct violation of the United Nations Charter', 'contrary to the rule of international law and to the laws of humanity' and 'a crime against mankind and civilization'.[132] Also often cited in this regard is Resolution 2936 (XXVII) of 29 November 1972 which speaks of 'the permanent prohibition of the use of nuclear weapons'.[133]

There are several problems, however, with the view that these UN General Assembly resolutions evidence existing (as opposed to emerging) customary law. First, under Article 10 of the Charter, General Assembly resolutions are strictly speaking only recommendatory and not of binding force; thus, to evidence customary international law, at least a high degree of support must be expressed by States at the time of adoption and subsequently in State practice.[134] The voting patterns, while reflecting widespread concern, hardly establish the requisite legal consensus among States. Resolution 1653 (XVI) was adopted by 55 votes to 20, with 26 abstentions. Those opposing the resolution included more than half the nuclear States (that is, those States specially affected—namely, the United States, United Kingdom and France). A similar pattern of voting has been in evidence with regard to other such resolutions.[135] Secondly, although strong, the language in the resolutions is far from convincing from a legal point of view. As Kalshoven notes, Resolution 1653 (XVI) lumps together all conceivable uses, fails to clarify such difficult and controversial questions as reciprocity or reprisals and, most importantly, after purporting to prohibit all uses, meekly requests the Secretary-General:

to consult the Governments of member States to ascertain their views on the possibility of convening a special conference for signing a convention on the prohibition of the use of nuclear and thermo-nuclear weapons for war purposes and to report on the results of such consultation to the General Assembly.[136]

This call upon States to establish a conventional prohibition appears to vitiate the claim for a customary prohibition evidenced by the resolution itself. And thirdly, a telling weakness with the customary law argument

---

[131] Falk *et al.*, loc. cit. above (n. 3), at p. 578; Grief, loc. cit. above (n. 47), at p. 38.

[132] Text reprinted in Singh, op. cit. above (n. 1), at p. 407.

[133] Other similar, more recent resolutions include Resolution 36/100 of 9 December 1981 entitled 'Declaration on the Prevention of Nuclear Catastrophe', and Resolution 39/63H of 12 December 1984 entitled 'Convention on the Prohibition of the Use of Nuclear Weapons'.

[134] See, for example, the opinion of arbitrator Dupuy in *Texaco v. Libyan Arab Republic* (1978), 53 ILR 389 at 486–7, especially para. 83.

[135] Despite the passing of numerous similar resolutions, the voting patterns at the UN have not changed significantly over the past three decades: Roberts, loc. cit. above (n. 4), at p. 40.

[136] Kalshoven, loc. cit. above (n. 6), at p. 277.

respecting these various UN General Assembly resolutions is the lack of follow-up mechanisms to generate continuous and effective pressure for compliance.[137]

In short, given the intrinsic limitations on the power of the UN General Assembly as well as the defects in the content and voting patterns of the relevant resolutions, it cannot be said that they evidence an existing customary law prohibition on the use of nuclear weapons. At best, they express political concern and possibly evidence an emerging customary norm. Moreover, it must be emphasized that the Western nuclear powers have consistently voted against resolutions banning the use of weapons and therefore could regard themselves as 'persistent objectors' should such an emerging customary norm ever crystallize. Grief contends that the claim of 'persistent objector' is not open to nuclear States because the 'ideas' underlying the various UN General Assembly resolutions prohibiting the use of nuclear weapons 'are based upon principles of international law which pre-date any objection which they may have made'.[138] This contention, however, is dubious on two grounds. First, the 'ideas' pre-dating the resolutions, as this article shows, do not absolutely prohibit but only regulate the use of nuclear weapons. And secondly, there is no reason in principle why the persistent objector rule should not apply. As noted by Charney, this rule 'may be seen to be closely linked to the doctrine that in order to determine whether a rule of [customary] international law exists, one must examine the views and practices of the States whose interests are particularly affected'.[139]

3. General principles

Looking for a 'specific' prohibition in 'general' principles is by definition a futile exercise and to belabour the point would smack of pedantry of the highest order. The point here is simply to note that in working through the categories set out in Article 38(1) of the ICJ Statute there is no basis for an absolute prohibition on the use of nuclear weapons emanating from the 'general principles of law recognized by civilized nations'.[140] By this phrase is meant those rules and principles that are so common to the various national legal systems of the world that they compose, independently of custom or treaty, general international law. It is widely considered that

[137] This requirement for assessing the possible impact of such resolutions on customary law is attributed to Abi-Saab and endorsed in Cassese, op. cit. above (n. 21), at pp. 194–5. See also Sloan, 'General Assembly Resolutions Revisited (Forty Years Later)', this *Year Book*, 58 (1987), p. 39 at p. 134.

[138] Grief, loc. cit. above (n. 47), at p. 39.

[139] See Charney, 'The Persistent Objector Rule and the Development of Customary International Law', this *Year Book*, 56 (1985), p. 1 at p. 23. It should be noted, however, that Charney sees only limited scope for the doctrine of the persistent objector: see, for example, his conclusion at p. 24.

[140] As expressed in Article 38(1)(c) of the Statute of the ICJ, in Brownlie, op. cit. above (n. 43), at p. 397.

equity is a principle within this category. In terms of the law on nuclear deterrence and warfare, the relevant general principles—namely, humanity, military necessity and chivalry—are helpful to formulate more specific rules on the laws of armed conflict[141] or even to draw reasoned analogies from existing rules, but by themselves they do not (indeed, as noted by their very designation as 'general principles', cannot) constitute a specific prohibition.[142]

4. Subsidiary sources: judicial decisions and writers

Although only 'subsidiary' under Article 38(1)(d) of the Statute of the ICJ, national court decisions are still an important means of developing standards within States from which the laws of armed conflict are, to a large extent, derived. Still, no decision as yet has directly addressed the question of the legality of the use of nuclear weapons as such.

The closest instance of a court doing so is the District Court of Tokyo decision in the *Shimoda* case[143] where it was held that the dropping of the atomic bombs on Japan was in violation of international law—specifically, that these bombings had in the circumstances violated the principles of military necessity and humanity as existing at the time of their occurrence. While the merits of the decision have been criticized,[144] it remains important as a legal precedent (if only as the one case in which a court has ruled on the legality of a particular use of nuclear weapons). It must be stressed, however, that the court's decision is narrowly drawn, focusing on the legality of the particular bombings and not of nuclear weapons generally.[145] From this writer's research, it appears that most other attempts to have national courts consider issues relating to the legality of nuclear weapons have failed and not one has succeeded in getting a judicial pronouncement that nuclear weapons are illegal as such.[146]

An even less fertile source of law on the subject is the jurisprudence of the ICJ (if only because of the merely persuasive value of its judgments, as under Article 59 of the Statute of the ICJ its decisions have no binding force except between parties in a case). The ICJ has never pronounced on the question of the legality of nuclear weapons. Moreover it is submitted, for reasons of judicial propriety, the ICJ is unlikely to do so in the

---

[141] Bright, loc. cit. above (n. 130), at p. 32.

[142] Schwarzenberger, op. cit. above (n. 93), at pp. 48–9.

[143] See the decision of 7 December 1963 translated in *Japanese Annual of International Law*, 8 (1964); digested in *American Journal of International Law*, 58 (1964), p. 1016.

[144] Roberts, loc. cit. above (n. 4), at p. 36.

[145] Falk, 'The Shimoda Case: A Legal Appraisal of the Atomic Attacks Upon Hiroshima and Nagasaki', *American Journal of International Law*, 59 (1965), p. 759 at p. 769.

[146] See, for example, the reluctance of national courts to make judgments about the legality of the security policies pursued by their governments in *Greenham Women against Cruise Missiles* v. *Reagan*, 591 F Supp. 1332 (1984), 755 F 2d 34 (1985) (a United States decision), and in *Operation Dismantle Inc. et al.* v. *The Queen et al.*, [1985] SCR 441 (a Canadian decision).

future[147] (notwithstanding the power of the General Assembly or Security Council to request an advisory opinion from the Court on 'any legal question' under Article 96(1) of the Charter).[148]

In sharp contrast to the judicial silence on the legality of nuclear weapons has been the cacophony of writers who have addressed the issue and reached a variety of conclusions. There is probably agreement on the existence of a strong presumption against the use of nuclear weapons, but on the question of an absolute prohibition there is widespread disagreement.[149] Moreover, many opinions—particularly those stated in the 1950s and 1960s—are outdated as developments in nuclear weapons and their means of delivery have changed the facts upon which these opinions were based.[150]

5. Private organizations and individuals

The importance of the views of private organizations and individuals as sources of international law is determined mainly by the extent to which they effectively lobby governments and so mobilize States to support certain norms of international conduct. There are several examples in the past decade of private organizations attempting to mobilize State support for a prohibition of the use of nuclear weapons—to name but a few, the Lawyers' Committee on Nuclear Policy based in New York and its 1983 'Statement on the Illegality of Nuclear Weapons', [151] Lawyers for Nuclear Disarmament, based in London, and its 1985 London Nuclear Warfare Tribunal and Interim Declaration,[152] and the Nuclear Weapons Legal Action Project, based in Ottawa, and its recent attempts to have the Canadian Government's support of NATO's policy advocating the first-use of nuclear weapons considered judicially by way of a reference to the Supreme Court of Canada.[153]

Without doubt, the most widely recognized private organization in this regard is the ICRC, which has acquired over time a respected and quasi-official role in the implementation as well as clarification and development of the humanitarian laws of armed conflict.[154] The work of the ICRC

[147] See Khosla, 'Nuclear Weapons, Global Values and International Law', in Miller and Feinrider, op. cit. above (n. 22), at p. 13, citing the pragmatic character of the decision taken by the ICJ in the *Nuclear Tests* cases (*Australia and New Zealand* v. *France*), *ICJ Reports*, 1974 at pp. 253 and 457, respectively. The conservative approach of the court in the *Northern Cameroons* case *ICJ Reports*, 1963, p. 15, is also instructive.

[148] Schwarzenberger, op. cit. above (n. 93), at p. 57.

[149] Roberts, loc. cit. above (n. 4), at pp. 38–9; see also Fujita, 'The Pre-Atomic Law of War and Its Applicability to Nuclear Warfare', *Kansai University Review of Law and Politics*, 6 (1985), p. 7 at pp. 32–43.

[150] Rauschning, loc. cit. above (n. 75), at p. 47.

[151] Reprinted in Weston (ed.), *Toward Nuclear Disarmament and Global Security* (1984), at p. 146.

[152] Discussed in Grief, loc. cit. above (n. 47), at p. 41.

[153] Discussed by Cotler, in Cohen and Gouin, op. cit. above (n. 1), p. 146 at pp. 149–50.

[154] As discussed in Weston, loc. cit. above (n. 6), at p. 569, the ICRC played a major role in the drafting and negotiation of the four Geneva Conventions of 1949 and the two Additional Protocols of 1977.

supports the view that there is no existing specific and absolute prohibition of the use of nuclear weapons. In its efforts to facilitate diplomatic conferences respecting the laws of armed conflict, it has drafted rules for submission to governments, going no further than to acknowledge that 'the general principles of the Law of War apply to nuclear and similar weapons'.[155]

(c) *No Absolute Prohibition of Use by Analogy*

Much ink has been spilt over whether legal prohibitions of certain kinds of weapons apply by analogy to nuclear weapons.[156] The main analogies drawn are between the primary blast and heat effects of nuclear weapons and incendiary weapons on the one hand and the secondary radiation effects of nuclear weapons and poison, poison gas, chemical or bacteriological weapons on the other.

As to the analogy between the primary nuclear blast and heat effects and incendiary weapons: even if the analogy is apt, it cannot be said that there is an absolute prohibition. The 1868 St Petersburg Declaration on inflammable bullets of a weight below 400 grammes[157] evidences more a concern with regulation and with the balance of military necessity and humanity in light of the 'no unnecessary suffering' principle than a concern with a prohibition of incendiaries as such. So, too, the provisions on incendiary weapons in Protocol III of the 1981 UN Convention on Specific Conventional Weapons do not set out an absolute prohibition, but rather regulate use to protect civilians and civilian objects.[158] This view (that there is no blanket prohibition on the use of incendiaries) is reflected in the United States *Army Field Manual* which provides that:

> The use of weapons which employ fire, such as tracer ammunition, flame-throwers, napalm and other incendiary agents, against targets requiring their use is not violative of international law. They should not, however, be employed in such a way as to cause unnecessary suffering to individuals.[159]

As to the analogies commonly drawn respecting the radiation effects of nuclear weapons: the focus of most writers has been on the poison/poison gas analogy, for it is doubtful that the analogy is sound with either chemical

---

[155] From Resolution XXVII adopted at the XXth International Red Cross Conference held in Vienna in October 1965; quoted and discussed in Kalshoven, loc. cit. above (n. 6), at p. 278.

[156] For arguments in favour of such analogies see, for example, Arbess, loc. cit. above (n. 3), at p. 97; Brownlie, loc. cit. above (n. 90), at p. 442; Castrén, loc. cit. above (n. 91), at p. 95; Falk *et al.*, loc. cit. above (n. 3), at p. 563; Schwarzenberger, op. cit. above (n. 93), at p. 35; Singh, op. cit. above (n. 1), at pp. 190–1; Weston, loc. cit. above (n. 6), at p. 559; cf. Bright, loc. cit. above (n. 130), at p. 17; Kalshoven, loc. cit. above (n. 6), at p. 283; Mallison, loc. cit. above (n. 124), at p. 325 and Rauschning, loc. cit. above (n. 75), at pp. 47–8.

[157] See Roberts and Guelff, op. cit. above (n. 113), at p. 30.

[158] Ibid. at p. 480.

[159] Op. cit. above (n. 82), para. 36 at p. 18.

weapons (because of State practice[160]) or bacteriological ones (likewise, because of State practice as well as for technical reasons[161]). Briefly put, the 'poison/poison gas analogy' argument rests on three conventional prohibitions which, it is widely accepted, have become part of customary law:[162] first, the Hague Declaration of 1899 outlawing 'the use of projectiles the sole object of which is the diffusion of asphyxiating and deleterious gases';[163] second, Article 23(a) of the Regulations annexed to Hague Convention IV of 1907 declaring it forbidden 'to employ poison or poisoned weapons';[164] and third, the Geneva Gas Protocol of 1925 prohibiting 'the use in war of asphyxiating, poisonous or other gases and of all analogous liquids, materials or devices'.[165]

Putting aside for the moment the vexed question of defining 'poison' in this context, the poison/poison gas analogy meets several initial objections. First, as regards the Hague Declaration of 1899, even if radiation were an 'asphyxiating or deleterious gas', this effect is not the 'sole object' of nuclear weapons. With the possible exception of enhanced radiation weapons like the neutron bomb,[166] radiation is not the main effect; rather, heat and blast effects are primary and therefore this provision is insufficient to support, by analogy, a blanket prohibition of the use of nuclear weapons.[167] Secondly, as regards the Geneva Gas Protocol of 1925, a similar point is made by Kalshoven:

> The drafting history of the Geneva Gas Protocol and the practice of states leaves no doubt that the purpose was to restrict weapons the primary effect of which is to asphyxiate or poison the adversary.[168]

And thirdly, also respecting the Geneva Gas Protocol of 1925, it is said that even if radiation is analogous to poison gas (which is doubtful given that some radiation consists of gamma rays and neutron particles), State practice makes it clear that the range of gases covered by the Protocol is not

---

[160] The 1989 Paris Conference on Chemical Weapons is a case in point: see above, n. 123. The point that States treat chemical weapons and nuclear weapons as separate and distinct categories is also made by Shaw, op. cit. above (n. 95), at p. 14.

[161] For technical reasons, bacteriological warfare is distinct: as Singh writes, 'There are no bacteria or living organisms in a nuclear explosion that cause somatic or genetic effects on mankind and hence nuclear warfare cannot be regarded as coming within the technical meaning of biological warfare. The fact that by reducing the power of resistance to disease in human beings, atomic explosion exposes the population to "susceptibility to secondary bacterial infection" is an indirect effect . . .': quoted in Fujita, loc. cit. above (n. 149), at p. 34. That States treat the two types of warfare as separate is evidenced by the Convention on the Prohibition of the Development, Production and Stockpiling of Bacteriological (Biological) and Toxin Weapons and on their Destruction of 1972 in International Red Cross Handbook (12th edn., 1983), at p. 370.

[162] Schwarzenberger, op. cit. above (n. 93), at p. 31; cf. Mallison, loc. cit. above (n. 124), at p. 327, who disputes this point with respect to the Geneva Gas Protocol, 1925.

[163] Roberts and Guelff, op. cit. above (n. 113), at p. 36.

[164] Ibid. at p. 52.

[165] Ibid. at p. 139.

[166] Paust, 'Controlling Prohibited Weapons and the Illegal Use of Permitted Weapons', McGill Law Journal, 28 (1983), p. 608 at p. 611; and Rauschning, loc. cit. above (n. 75), at p. 44.

[167] Schwarzenberger, op. cit. above (n. 93), at pp. 37–8.

[168] Kalshoven, loc. cit. above (n. 6), at pp. 283–4.

comprehensive and does not contemplate nuclear radiation. For example, on ratification of the Protocol in 1975, the United States Government stated that 'control agents and chemical herbicides' were not included;[169] more importantly, despite the notoriety among writers of the 'poison gas analogy' argument, the United States reservation of 1975 made no reference to nuclear weapons. In these circumstances, it is very difficult to argue that the United States unwittingly gave up the legality of its nuclear weapons. The United States would not have failed to have entered a reservation regarding nuclear weapons (as it did with Additional Protocol I of 1977), if the analogy with poison gas under the Geneva Gas Protocol of 1925 was regarded by States as a blanket prohibition of the use of nuclear weapons. Another point often made in relation to the weakness of the prohibition under the Geneva Gas Protocol of 1925 is that a large number of States have only become parties to it on the basis of a reciprocal 'no first-use' reservation, the effect of which is that if an enemy State ignores the Protocol, it (as the victim State) will be legally entitled to do so as well.[170]

Some writers contend that the argument by analogy with the 'poison' prohibition in Article 23 (a) of the Hague Regulations of 1907 is, however, iron-clad.[171] Yet, on scrutiny, even here there are chinks in the armour, so to speak. The main difficulty is with defining the term 'poison' under Article 23 (a), and so the ambit of the prohibition. Unfortunately, the Hague Regulations do not define 'poison'. In an effort to resolve the issue, most writers turn to modern dictionary definitions of 'poison'; but in the process reach different conclusions on the aptness of the analogy with nuclear weapons.[172] It is apparent, therefore, that the plain meaning approach of interpretation is inconclusive and the matter must be clarified in terms of the context of negotiations respecting the prohibition and how subsequent State practice can be said to have defined the term 'poison' in a special way.

In light of the practice of States concerning the prohibitions under the Hague Declaration of 1899 and the Geneva Gas Protocol of 1925, it is reasonable to infer that the prohibition under Article 23(a) refers only to weapons whose *primary* effect is poisonous. Therefore, as radiation (par-

---

[169] Ibid. at p. 269. Note that in 1970 the United Kingdom made a similar statement regarding 'CS and other such gases': Shaw, loc. cit. above (n. 95), at p. 14.

[170] See, for example, the reservations made by Australia, Canada, India, Iraq, United States, United Kingdom and Soviet Union in Roberts and Guelff, op. cit. above (n. 113), at pp. 144–5.

[171] For example, Singh writes, 'Even though the Geneva Gas Protocol is comprehensive, the single word 'poison' used in Article 23 has a still wider interpretation in the sense that anything which is poisonous is covered by it': op. cit. above (n. 1), at p. 127.

[172] Bright, reaching the conclusion that the analogy is not appropriate, uses the definition of 'poison' in the *Merriam Webster New International Dictionary*: 'any agent which introduced (especially in small amounts) into an organism, may chemically produce an injurious or deadly effect': loc. cit. above (n. 130), at p. 17; Schwarzenberger, reaching the opposite conclusion, uses the definition in the *Shorter Oxford Dictionary*: 'a substance that when introduced into or absorbed by a living organism destroys life or injures health': op. cit. above (n. 93), at p. 27. Agreeing with Bright, Rauschning defines poison as 'a substance that causes chemical reactions resulting in death or severe disability when, even in small quantities, it is ingested or inhaled or touches the skin': loc. cit. above (n. 75), at p. 47.

ticularly fall-out) is only a side effect of nuclear weapons (save the neutron bomb), it is not caught by the analogy, for poisoning is the main (if not the sole) effect of poison and poison gas.[173] This view is borne out by paragraph 35 of the United States *Army Field Manual* 27–10 which states that 'explosive' atomic weapons as such are not violative of international law in the absence of a rule restricting their employment. Moreover, it appears that the unpublished annotation to paragraph 35 explains that:

> The qualifying word 'explosive' is inserted . . . to save taking a position on the use of an atomic weapon, the effect of which is confined to radiation. Such an arm might conceivably run afoul of the prohibition of paragraph (a), Article 23, H.R.[174]

It has also been argued that the prohibition of poison under Article 23(*a*) only applies if poisoning is superfluous to the object of the weapon or perfidiously introduced;[175] thus, as the poisonous effect of radiation, if it is such, is essential to the working of nuclear weapons, the prohibition does not apply. A similar, though more cynical, purposive interpretation is suggested by Mallison, who contends that the prohibition is really about ineffective or obsolete weapons and, as nuclear weapons are neither, it does not apply.[176]

Even if the arguments for a special meaning of 'poison' under Article 23(*a*) are rejected, it must again be stressed that the application of the so-called ordinary meaning of the word to nuclear weapons is not problem-free. For instance, it is contended by some writers that radiation emitted immediately upon blast (mainly gamma rays and neutrons) is more analogous to thermal radiation (or heat), which does not involve introducing or absorbing a damaging substance into the body.[177] Moreover, while conceding that fall-out in the form of radioactive aerosols may be introduced into the body in a way analogous to poison, its injurious effect in all circumstances might be questioned.[178] Furthermore, even ignoring these medical arguments and admitting that initial and residual radiation are capable of damaging biological tissue and causing a variety of illnesses (including death), it remains the case that not all exposures have such consequences. Rather, the amount of radiation emitted from a nuclear explosion depends very much on the type of weapon as well as on whether the blast occurred on the surface or in the air (in addition to local environmental and meteoro-

---

[173] Akehurst, *A Modern Introduction to International Law* (5th edn., 1984), at p. 232; cf. Grief, loc. cit. above (n. 47), at p. 30.

[174] For the full text of this paragraph in the Manual, see above, n. 127. For the unpublished annotation, see Fujita, 'First Use of Nuclear Weapons: Nuclear Strategy vs International Law', *Kansai University Review of Law and Politics*, 3 (1982), p. 57 at p. 75.

[175] Argument canvassed by Schwarzenberger, op. cit. above (n. 93), at pp. 28–9; cf. Castrén, loc. cit. above (n. 91), p. 94.

[176] Mallison, loc. cit. above (n. 124), at p. 331.

[177] Bright, loc. cit. above (n. 130), at p. 18; Rauschning, loc. cit. above (n. 75), at p. 47.

[178] Ibid.

logical factors).[179] Thus, as Rauschning notes, 'it cannot be concluded . . . that all nuclear weapons and all means of their employment constitute poisoning in the sense of the prohibition of poison'.[180]

Admittedly, the arguments on the poison/poison gas analogy are chilling and finely balanced. What tips the scale in this writer's view is the cogent evidence that nuclear States and their non-nuclear allies do not find the analogy close enough to be persuasive and therefore do not consider themselves legally bound by any such prohibition. Thus, even if the prohibition were to apply by analogy, it would do so in a manner which is far from clear-cut and its effectiveness would be minimal. Hence, as with specific prohibitions, the arguments in favour of prohibitions by analogy of the use of nuclear weapons are not compelling.

(d) *Regulation of Use*

1. *Established principles of humanitarian law*

The so-called established principles of humanitarian law, while expressed in a variety of specific conventions, are widely regarded by States and writers as part of customary international law and applicable to wars on land, sea and air. Yet, while these principles attempt to balance the precepts of military necessity and humanity, they are vague and subjective, leaving interpretation of them mainly to the discretion of the belligerents.[181]

(i) *Means not unlimited/proportionality.* Article 22 of the Hague Regulations of 1907 provides that 'the right of belligerents to adopt means of injuring the enemy is not unlimited'.[182] This principle is reaffirmed in Article 35 (1) of Additional Protocol I of 1977.[183] Unfortunately, neither the Hague Regulations nor Additional Protocol I gives any indication of the precise way in which belligerent rights are 'limited'. However, as Cassese notes, it is reasonable to interpret the provision as excluding the inference that weapons which are not banned are *ipso facto* allowed.[184] Moreover, the content of the provision is partly illuminated by the allied principle of proportionality—that the damage caused by use of a given weapon must not be blatantly disproportionate to the military objective achieved.[185]

Viewed thus, the provision appears to deem unlawful all-out nuclear war—that is, massive and indiscriminate countervalue and counterforce

---

[179] Bright, loc. cit. above (n. 130), at p. 6; Rauschning, loc. cit. above (n. 75), at p. 48; and Shaw, loc. cit. above (n. 95), at p. 14.

[180] Rauschning, loc. cit. above (n. 75), at p. 48; see also Bright, loc. cit. above (n. 130), at p. 19; cf. Singh, op. cit. above (n. 1), at pp. 190–1, where he contends that 'There is also clear "use of poison" involved in every kind, size and shape of nuclear weapons in so far as "poison radiation" is its invariable concomitant.'

[181] Shaw, loc. cit. above (n. 95), at p. 3.

[182] Roberts and Guelff, op. cit. above (n. 113), at p. 52.

[183] Ibid. at p. 409.

[184] Cassese, loc. cit. above (n. 117), at p. 162.

[185] Kalshoven, loc. cit. above (n. 6), at p. 286.

strikes;[186] the only possible legal justification for a general nuclear war would be defence against a general nuclear attack.[187] The provision does not, however, rule out all uses of nuclear weapons given the arguable possibility for States effectively to wage limited nuclear war.

Many writers argue that the risk of escalation is so high that the proportionality principle is breached with even a small low-yield counterforce strike in a remote area.[188] However, even if the probability of escalation is great, it is not inevitable[189] and, arguably, no greater with the use of nuclear weapons than it is with the use of conventional weapons.[190] Indeed, escalation is likely in any armed conflict between the superpowers. It therefore takes the escalation argument too far to insist on an absolute qualitative distinction between nuclear and conventional weapons for, regrettably, both run the risk of escalating conflict. Moreover, notwithstanding the potential of some nuclear weapons to cause serious damage, the horrific effect of large-scale conventional warfare is often understated. Hence, as Greenwood concludes:

> The use of battlefield nuclear weapons against military targets by a State faced with a massive conventional attack which it was unable to repel by conventional means would not appear wholly disproportionate when the alternative was the destruction or subjugation of the State concerned.[191]

In short, under the principle 'means not unlimited', the illegality of any weapon, nuclear or conventional, will depend on the circumstances of its use.

(ii) *No unnecessary suffering.* Article 23(e) of the Hague Regulations of 1907 prohibits the use of 'arms, projectiles or material calculated to cause unnecessary suffering'.[192] This principle is reaffirmed in Article 35(2) of Additional Protocol I of 1977.[193]

Unfortunately, the provision is vague.[194] However, State practice and writers suggest that it has two aspects. First, the suffering must be unnecessary. It is not sufficient that the suffering be 'massive, protracted

---

[186] Ibid.

[187] O'Brien, op. cit. above (n. 50), at p. 135.

[188] For example, Weston writes, 'once unleashed, the probability that tactical nuclear warfare could be kept at theater or battlefield level would be small': loc. cit. above (n. 6), at p. 583.

[189] Kalshoven, loc. cit. above (n. 6), at p. 287.

[190] Röling, 'International Law, Nuclear Weapons, Arms Control and Disarmament', in Miller and Feinrider, op. cit. above (n. 22), p. 181 at p. 183.

[191] Greenwood, 'Self-Defence and the Conduct of Armed Conflict' (unpublished, 1988), at p. 7. In support of this view, see Kalshoven, loc. cit. above (n. 6), at p. 287; Mallison, loc. cit. above (n. 124), at p. 330; McGrath, loc. cit. above (n. 50), at p. 213; O'Brien, op. cit. above (n. 50), at p. 134; and Shaw, loc. cit. above (n. 95), at p. 9; cf. Brownlie, loc. cit. above (n. 90), at pp. 446 and 450; Falk *et al.*, loc. cit. above (n. 3), at p. 560; Grief, loc. cit. above (n. 47), at p. 22; and Weston, loc. cit. above (n. 6), at p. 561.

[192] Roberts and Guelff, op. cit. above (n. 113), at p. 52.

[193] Ibid. at p. 409.

[194] Cassese contends it 'is barren of practical effects save in extreme cases': loc. cit. above (n. 117), at pp. 162–3; Bright argues, 'such a non-specific provision cannot effectively deter any particular means of warfare': loc. cit. above (n. 130), at p. 16.

and exquisite';[195] rather, it must be superfluous or disproportionate to the military objective of the weapon's use.[196] On this test, the more effective a weapon is at securing a significant military advantage, the less likely it is that the suffering caused by its use will be deemed unnecessary.[197] Of course, if a less severe, reasonably alternative weapon exists to achieve the same military objective, the test obliges the use of this alternative weapon.[198] That a balance is struck favouring military necessity over humanity is evidenced in the preamble to the St Petersburg Declaration of 1868 banning explosive projectiles under 400 grammes weight, which provides:

That the only legitimate object which States should endeavour to accomplish during war is to weaken the military forces of the enemy; That for this purpose it is sufficient to disable the greatest possible number of men . . . [199]

Similarly, the United States Department of the Air Force has noted that the critical factor in the prohibition of unnecessary suffering is 'whether the suffering is needless or disproportionate to the military advantages secured by the weapon, not the degree of suffering itself'.[200] Elaborating this prohibition, the practice of States supports the view that it is illegal as such to use projectiles filled with glass or other materials inherently difficult to detect medically; so, too, dum dum bullets are illegal as they unnecessarily enlarge wounds caused by their use.[201]

The second aspect of the 'no unnecessary suffering' principle is calculation or subjective intent—that is, the nature of the weapon itself or the use to which it has been put must be such as to have been calculated to cause the unnecessary suffering.[202] The main application of this principle is with respect to the radiation effects of nuclear weapons. For example, Grief contends that:

No legitimate military advantage could justify the use of weapons which would produce such inhumane effects not only at the time of an attack and immediately afterwards, but even for generations.[203]

---

[195] Kalshoven, loc. cit. above (n. 6), at p. 284.

[196] See, for example, Rauschning, loc. cit. above (n. 75), at p. 48, and Weston, loc. cit. above (n. 6), at p. 555.

[197] Greenwood, loc. cit. above (n. 188), at p. 6.

[198] O'Brien, op. cit. above (n. 50), at p. 134.

[199] Roberts and Guelff, op. cit. above (n. 113), at pp. 30–31.

[200] Air Force Pamphlet 110–31, loc. cit. above (n. 127), ch..6, para. 6–3(b)2.

[201] For example, in discussing Article 23(e) the British *Manual of Military Law*, loc. cit. above (n. 128), at para. 110, states: 'Under this heading may be included such weapons as lances with a barbed head, irregularly shaped bullets, projectiles filled with glass and the like.'

[202] Cf. Grief who contends that 'Although the 1907 provision appears to demand a subjective test, the authoritative French text confirms that, irrespective of a belligerent's intention, weapons are prohibited if they are apt to cause unnecessary suffering': loc. cit. above (n. 47), at p. 22. Even if this textual argument for an 'objective' test of intention is accepted, the questions of whether the suffering is 'unnecessary' and whether the use of a particular nuclear weapon is 'apt to cause' unnecessary suffering remain.

[203] Grief, loc. cit. above (n. 47), at p. 25.

However, in view of the two aspects of the principle discussed above and given the effectiveness of nuclear weapons, it cannot be said that there is an absolute prohibition of their use. For example, counterforce uses are not covered by the prohibition to the extent that nuclear weapons are effective at killing and so repelling the enemy's military personnel.[204] Moreover, most but not all countervalue strikes are prohibited; again, the decisive factor is the balance between considerations of military necessity and humanity. As Rauschning notes, even the fact that nuclear weapons may not cause immediate death or as a side-effect may cause genetic damage, terrible as this may be, does not outlaw the use of such weapons if they are effectively employed to gain a sufficiently important military advantage.[205] What is a 'sufficiently important military advantage' in this context is, of course, a matter of serious debate. But given the inherent vagueness and excessive subjectivity of the test, it is wishful thinking to rely on it to ground an absolute prohibition.

(iii) *Discrimination between combatants and non-combatants.* The prohibition of weapons or tactics that cause indiscriminate harm as between combatants and non-combatants is another argument against the legality of nuclear weapons.[206] It is expressed in Articles 25 and 27 of the Hague Regulations of 1907[207] and Articles 22 and 24 of the draft Hague Rules of Aerial Warfare of 1923.[208] This prohibition was not adhered to during the aerial bombings of the Second World War, but nevertheless was subsequently confirmed by States as customary international law. For example, on 18 December 1968 the UN General Assembly unanimously adopted Resolution 2444 (XXIII) stating that 'a distinction must be made at all times between persons taking part in the hostilities and members of the civilian population to the effect that the latter be spared as much as possible'.[209] Also in 1972 the United States Department of Defence said that it regarded this principle as 'declaratory of existing customary international law',[210] a view reiterated in United States Air Force Pamphlet 110–31 of 1976.[211] Moreover, this principle was restated and even expanded upon in Articles 48 and 51 (especially paragraphs (4) and (5)) of Additional Protocol I of 1977.[212]

However, as with the other established principles of humanitarian law discussed in this article, this prohibition is vague and somewhat subjective, requiring a balance of the considerations of military necessity and humanity. Unfortunately, on the prohibition's own terms and in the light

[204] Rauschning, loc. cit. above (n. 75), at p. 48.
[205] Ibid.
[206] Ibid.
[207] Roberts and Guelff, op. cit. above (n. 113), at p. 53.
[208] Ibid. at pp. 126–7; though these rules were never adopted in legal form.
[209] Quoted from Cassese, loc. cit. above (n. 117), at p. 163.
[210] In *American Journal of International Law*, 67 (1973), p. 122, quoted from Cassese, loc. cit. above (n. 117), at pp. 163–4.
[211] Loc. cit. above (n. 127), at para. 3–4(a).
[212] Roberts and Guelff, op. cit. above (n. 113), at pp. 414–16.

of State practice, the more vital the target militarily, the more international law condones incidental civilian damage.[213] Moreover, as Schwarzenberger notes, the distinction between combatants and non-combatants is somewhat blurred and certainly not limited to 'soldiers in the field'; rather, a legitimate target is anyone connected with the war effort (which may include those working in centres of communication, large industrial and administrative establishments and any other area likely to become important for the conduct of hostilities).[214] The residue of non-combatants, who may not be regarded as a legitimate target, is therefore only those unconnected with the war effort and removed from important target areas.[215]

Given these factors, the prohibition obviously applies to forbid pure countervalue strikes (say on a residential area),[216] as well as the use of inaccurate missiles (in the extreme case, 'blind weapons' such as the V1 and V2 rockets used by Germany during World War II) where civilian damage is inevitable. On the other hand, restricted counterforce uses of nuclear weapons do not appear to be covered by the prohibition[217]—for example, the use of a low-yield nuclear weapon in an air burst to attack a military objective such as a war munitions plant or the use of a moderate yield nuclear weapon in a ground burst to destroy a defined military target such as a hardened missile silo.[218] Of course, this view assumes that the risk of escalation in a limited nuclear war is not inevitable or, at least, no more likely than in a conventional war.

The more difficult question is how the prohibition applies to attacks on military objectives which cause incidental damage to civilians.[219] Here, again, the balance between the general considerations of military necessity and humanity is decisive. This balance appears to prohibit even the counterforce use of a high-yield nuclear weapon in a ground burst (given the widespread damage to non-combatants likely to follow); however, it must be stressed that the more vital the military target in question, the more collateral non-combatant damage the present legal regime condones.[220] In this respect, State practice respecting 'target area bombing' during the Second World War is instructive—such attacks were regarded as lawful (and to this extent not indiscriminate) where it was otherwise impractical to achieve the vital military objective sought.[221]

[213] Weston, loc. cit. above (n. 6), at p. 556. Note the *Shimoda* case, where the Japanese court, in holding that the atomic bombings of Hiroshima and Nagasaki by the United States were illegal, stressed the fact that the two cities were not valid military objectives: *Japanese Annual of International Law*, 8 (1964), at p. 212.

[214] Schwarzenberger, op. cit. above (n. 93), at pp. 21–2.

[215] Ibid. at p. 48.

[216] McGrath, loc. cit. above (n. 50), at p. 213; O'Brien, op. cit. above (n. 50), at p. 137.

[217] O'Brien, op. cit. above (n. 50), at p. 139.

[218] Rauschning, loc. cit. above (n. 75), at p. 49.

[219] The salience of this question is underlined by Falk's claim that there are over sixty military objectives targeted by the United States within the city limits of Moscow: see Falk, 'Toward a Legal Regime for Nuclear Weapons', *McGill Law Journal*, 28 (1983), p. 519 at p. 528.

[220] Rauschning, loc. cit. above (n. 75), at p. 49.

[221] Whiteman, *Digest of International Law*, vol. 10 (1968), at p. 481.

In short, States are clearly prohibited from attacking civilian targets as such, but as nuclear weapons are not inevitably indiscriminate,[222] the principle of discrimination between combatants and non-combatants does not establish an absolute prohibition of their use.

(iv) *Belligerent duties and protections under the Geneva Conventions of 1949.* Some writers[223] contend that the use of nuclear weapons would inevitably result in the violation of certain duties and protections under the Geneva Conventions of 1949.[224] Briefly put, their argument is that the use of high-yield nuclear weapons would make it impossible for belligerents to perform duties under the Geneva Conventions and would also cause damage to legally protected persons and property. Many provisions are cited: on belligerent duties, for example, those relating to the collection of the wounded or dead, individual burial, evacuation of prisoners and the ban on exposing them to unnecessary danger[225] as well as those relating to child welfare;[226] and on protections of persons and property, for example, those relating to wounded and sick members of the armed forces,[227] hospital ships and medical transport,[228] property of prisoners-of-war,[229] and hospital and safety zones.[230]

No attempt will be made to address the detail of these various provisions for the argument respecting the Geneva Conventions is open to three fundamental objections. First, and least importantly, as Schwarzenberger notes, the category of 'protected persons' under Geneva Convention IV in all but one of its four parts is somewhat limited. In his words, 'protected persons are only those citizens who, in case of conflict or occupation, find themselves in the hands of a party to the conflict or occupying power of which they are *not* nationals'.[231] Secondly, as Kalshoven demonstrates, the drafting history of the Geneva Conventions shows that State delegates, mindful of the use of nuclear weapons from the recent experience of the Second World War, expressly rejected the notion of a specific and absolute ban on their use.[232] Thirdly, and most importantly, the argument is based on a bad example. No doubt some uses of nuclear weapons would violate

---

[222] Grief, loc. cit. above (n. 47), at p. 29.

[223] See, for example, Falk *et al.*, loc. cit. above (n. 3), at pp. 569–70; Fried, loc. cit. above (n. 11), at p. 40; Grief, loc. cit. above (n. 47), at pp. 33–4; and Singh, op. cit. above (n. 1), at pp. 151–61.

[224] Geneva Convention I for the Amelioration of the Condition of the Wounded and Sick in Armed Forces in the Field; Geneva Convention II for the Amelioration of the Condition of Wounded, Sick and Shipwrecked Members of the Armed Forces at Sea; Geneva Convention III Relative to the Treatment of Prisoners of War; and Geneva Convention IV Relative to the Protection of Civilian Persons in Time of War: in Roberts and Guelff, op. cit. above (n. 113), at pp. 169; 193; 215; and 271, respectively.

[225] Convention I, Articles 15–17; Convention II, Articles 18–20; and Convention III, Articles 10, 22 and 23, ibid. at pp. 177; 200; and 224, respectively.

[226] Convention IV, Article 24, ibid. at p. 281.

[227] Convention I, Article 12, ibid. at pp.12–13.

[228] Convention II, Articles 38–39, ibid at pp. 206–7.

[229] Convention III, Article 18, ibid. at p. 224.

[230] Convention IV, Article 14, ibid. at pp. 277–8.

[231] Schwarzenberger, op. cit. above (n. 93), at p. 47 (emphasis added).

[232] Kalshoven, loc. cit. above (n. 6), at pp. 272–3 and 285.

these provisions, and Singh is correct to say that 'thermo-nuclear megaton weapons' suffer from the 'intrinsic difficulty of restricting their devastating effects to legally permissible objects of destruction'.[233] Yet, as already noted in the discussion of other principles of humanitarian law, other more limited uses of nuclear weapons are possible. Moreover, as escalation is not inevitable (or, at least, no more likely than with conventional weapons), it cannot be said that the Geneva Conventions of 1949 establish an absolute prohibition of the use of nuclear weapons.

(v) *Crimes under the Genocide Convention of 1948 and the Nuremberg Principles.* Some writers[234] contend that any use of nuclear weapons involves commission of the crime at customary international law of genocide as described in the UN Genocide Convention of 1948. True, any massive nuclear exchange between the superpowers would entail grave consequences for the belligerents as well as for humanity, but this is not what the Genocide Convention is about.[235]

Article II of the Convention defines genocide as acts[236] 'committed with intent to destroy, in whole or in part, a national, ethnical, racial or religious group, as such'.[237] Thus, the key to the crime is not the suffering or destruction as such, but its intention—i.e., that the act is committed with intent to destroy a particular group as a group.[238] Grief argues that the requisite intention is present if the act is done with the knowledge of its likely consequences, and he contends that as escalation is likely in any nuclear exchange, any use of nuclear weapons is genocide.[239] However, as with similar arguments on other general principles of humanitarian law, this argument takes too extreme a view of the risk of escalation in a limited nuclear war. Even assuming that an objective intention test is all that the Convention requires and admitting that nuclear weapons could be used to commit genocide, it is not the inevitable consequence of their use.[240] Of course, the Convention will apply to a belligerent deliberately employing nuclear weapons to obliterate all or part of a group of the enemy's civilian

---

[233] Singh, op. cit. above (n. 1), at p. 156.

[234] See, for example, Brownlie, loc. cit. above (n. 90), at p. 443; Falk *et al.*, loc. cit. above (n. 3), at pp. 568–9; and Grief, loc. cit. above (n. 47), at p. 36.

[235] Kalshoven, loc. cit. above (n. 6), at p. 284.

[236] The acts listed under Article II are:

'(a) Killing members of the group;

(b) Causing serious bodily or mental harm to members of the group;

(c) Deliberately inflicting on the group conditions of life calculated to bring about its physical destruction in whole or in part;

(d) Imposing measures intended to prevent births within the group;

(e) Forcibly transferring children of the group to another group':

Roberts and Guelff, op. cit. above (n. 113), at pp. 158–9.

[237] Ibid. at p. 158.

[238] Shaw, loc. cit. above (n. 95), at p. 15.

[239] Grief, loc. cit. above (n. 47), at p. 36. He also argues that the number of victims could be evidence of intention.

[240] Shaw, loc. cit. above (n. 95), at p. 15.

population as such.[241] But it is fanciful to call a low-yield counterforce strike to destroy an advancing line of troops an 'act of genocide'.

A second problem with the argument that the Genocide Convention establishes an absolute prohibition of the use of nuclear weapons is noted by Kalshoven. In his words, 'It follows moreover from the *travaux préparatoires* of the Convention that the notion of genocide was expressly defined in such a manner as to prevent a mixing up with the law of war'.[242] In the light of these considerations, the Genocide Convention does not establish an absolute prohibition of the use of nuclear weapons; rather, the commission of the crime of genocide depends on the particular context in which these weapons are used.

Akin to the Genocide Convention argument, some writers contend that the use of nuclear weapons would entail the commission of international crimes as defined in Article 6 of the Nuremberg Charter—namely, 'crimes against the peace' under 6(*a*), 'war crimes' under 6(*b*) and 'crimes against humanity' under 6(*c*).[243] The Nuremberg Charter was considered by the Nuremberg Military Tribunal as expressing international law existing at the time of its creation,[244] and this view was subsequently approved by the unanimous adoption of UN General Assembly Resolution 95(I) on 11 December 1946.[245]

There are, however, obvious problems with this argument. As already noted, the use of nuclear weapons does not necessarily involve a war of aggression or the violation of an international obligation, and, therefore, it cannot be prohibited outright as a crime against the peace under 6(*a*). So too, not all uses of nuclear weapons are violations of the laws of war, and therefore a crime under 6(*b*). And likewise, not all uses lead to 'murder, extermination, enslavement, deportation and other inhumane acts committed against the civilian population', and so a crime against humanity under 6(*c*). Moreover, respecting the 'crimes against humanity' argument, Schwarzenberger states:

> In view of the process of shrinkage to which, by tacit consent of the Powers, the sector of the civilian population appears to be subject, the prohibition implied in this rule, establishing an additional type of extraordinary criminal jurisdiction under municipal law, would be relevant at most in exceptional cases.[246]

[241] Boyle cites the example of 'counter-ethnic targeting', a strategy allegedly discussed by United States government officials during the Carter administration which contemplated the destruction of major population centres inhabited primarily by the Great Russian people solely because of their constituent ethnicity: loc. cit. above (n. 2), at pp. 1437–8.

[242] Kalshoven, loc. cit. above (n. 6), at p. 285.

[243] Roberts and Guelff, op. cit. above (n. 113), at p. 155.

[244] This can reasonably be inferred from the final argument of counsel in defence of Goering, reproduced in *Nazi Conspiracy and Aggression, Supplement B.*, Office of the United States Chief of Counsel for Prosecution of Axis Criminality (United States Government Printing Office, Washington, 1947), at p. 48.

[245] *UN Yearbook*, 1946–7, at p. 254, discussed in Schwarzenberger, op. cit. above (n. 67), at pp. 526–8.

[246] Schwarzenberger, op. cit. above (n. 93), at p. 45.

As an example of such an exceptional case, Schwarzenberger notes:

> . . . it would apply if nuclear weapons of a size which precluded the protection of the civilian population, in the most limited sense of the term, were employed or nuclear weapons were intentionally used against the civilian population for purposes of terrorization.[247]

Thus, while the Nuremberg Principles (like the Genocide Convention) apply to prohibit certain unlikely uses of nuclear weapons, they do not establish a blanket prohibition.

(vi) *The Martens Clause*. First enunciated in the preamble to Hague Convention II of 1899, the so-called 'Martens Clause' has become part of customary international law and for ease of reference has been repeated in many subsequent conventions.[248] As set out in Article 1(2) of Additional Protocol I of 1977, it provides:

> In cases not covered by this Protocol or by other international agreements, civilians and combatants remain under the protection and authority of the principles of international law derived from established custom, from the principles of humanity and from the dictates of public conscience.[249]

The values generated by the Martens Clause are legally significant in two instances: when existing principles of the laws of armed conflict are interpreted and when new principles are considered.[250]

Contrary to the view of some writers,[251] the present writer believes that the triad of 'established custom', 'principles of humanity' and 'dictates of public conscience' does not measurably enhance existing principles so that the use of nuclear weapons is absolutely prohibited. At best, it only scotches the argument that the existing principles have no application to constraining the use of nuclear weapons.[252] As Schwarzenberger notes:

> Considerations of humanity, requirements of civilization or other formative factors are no substitute for prohibitive rules of international law and, by themselves, do not constitute evidence of rules prohibiting the use of nuclear weapons.[253]

Hence, in relation to nuclear weapons, the Martens Clause does no more than reaffirm the existing international legal regime's attempt to strike a relative balance between considerations of military necessity and humanity—unfortunately, a balance, it seems, with a bias that inevitably

---

[247] Ibid.

[248] See, for example, the preamble to Hague Convention IV of 1907; Article 63 of Geneva Convention I of 1949; Article 62 of Geneva Convention II of 1949; Article 142 of Geneva Convention III of 1949; Article 158 of Geneva Convention IV of 1949; Article 1(2) of Additional Protocol I of 1977; and the preamble to the UN Convention on Prohibitions and Restrictions on the Use of Certain Conventional Weapons of 1981, in Roberts and Guelff, op. cit. above (n. 113), at pp. 45; 192; 213; 270; 325; 390; and 469, respectively.

[249] Ibid. at p. 390.

[250] Röling, loc. cit. above (n. 190), at p. 189.

[251] Falk *et al.*, loc. cit. above (n. 3), at p. 558, and Fried, loc. cit. above (n. 11), at p. 47.

[252] Schwarzenberger, op. cit. above (n. 93), at p. 45.

[253] Ibid. at p. 47.

shifts further from the latter with each advance in the lethality of a weapon system.[254]

2. *Applicable rules under Additional Protocol I of 1977*

Additional Protocol I of 1977[255] contains many provisions which, at first sight, appear directly relevant to the international legal regime regulating nuclear warfare, especially those in Part III concerning 'Methods and Means of War, Combatant and Prisoner-of-War Status'[256] and Part IV concerning the 'Civilian Population'.[257] Yet any consideration of these provisions must begin with the question of the Protocol's status respecting nuclear weapons.

This threshold question arises in the light of the declarations on signing in 1977 made by both the United Kingdom and the United States—namely, in the words of the United Kingdom's statement that 'the new rules introduced by the Protocol are not intended to have an effect on and do not regulate or prohibit the use of nuclear weapons'.[258] It is submitted that even though the United States declaration is worded slightly differently, its effect is the same as the United Kingdom's declaration.[259] All other nuclear States, save China, took positions similar to the United States and United Kingdom at the conference.[260] Given the crucial importance of this issue, as perceived by the nuclear States and consistently evidenced in their pronouncements throughout the conference, it can reasonably be contended that the statements of the United Kingdom and United States on signing are at least 'interpretative declarations'—that is, statements that do not derogate from the treaty but that indicate a preferred perception of it for the purpose of resolving future disputes over its interpretation.[261] Alternatively, even if it can be said that despite the objections of nuclear States Protocol I established new rules on nuclear weapons, the

---

[254] Shaw, loc. cit. above (n. 95), at p. 3.

[255] Roberts and Guelff, op. cit. above (n. 113), at p. 389.

[256] Ibid. at p. 409.

[257] Ibid. at p. 414.

[258] Ibid. at p. 482.

[259] The United Kingdom's declaration speaks of 'new rules introduced' (whereas the United States declaration refers to 'rules established') by the Protocol. The United States declaration does not exclude the operation of all rules under Protocol I, just those 'established' conventionally by it. The declaration thus does not (indeed cannot) remove nuclear weapons from the purview of those provisions of Protocol I that codify customary international law.

[260] France did not sign the Protocol but at the end of the conference stated *inter alia* that 'the rules of the Protocol do not apply to the use of nuclear weapons': see Fujita, 'Status of Nuclear Weapons in International Humanitarian Law', *Kansai University Review of Law and Politics*, 7 (1986), p. 1 at pp. 18–19. The Soviet Union, while not making any mention of the relationship between the Protocol and the use of nuclear weapons on signing (see ibid. at p. 19), agreed during the conference that the Protocol was not to address the issue of the use of weapons of mass destruction as such (relying on the Soviet delegate's speech to the conference on 21 March 1975, see Bring and Reimann, 'Redressing a Wrong Question: The 1977 Protocols Additional to the 1949 Geneva Conventions and the Issue of Nuclear Weapons', *Netherlands International Law Review*, 33(1986), p. 99 at p. 103).

[261] The distinction between a 'mere interpretative declaration' and a 'true reservation' is discussed in McRae, 'The Legal Effect of Interpretative Declarations', this *Year Book*, 49 (1978), p. 155. See also Bowett, 'Reservations to Non-Restricted Multilateral Treaties', ibid. 48 (1976–7), p. 67.

declarations of the United States and United Kingdom must then be viewed as 'true reservations' that modify the legal effect of the Protocol, as contemplated by Article 2(1)(d) of the Vienna Convention on the Law of Treaties.[262]

If viewed as reservations in derogation of the Protocol, the question becomes one of whether these reservations are permissible. As Protocol I has no express provision on permissibility of reservations, the compatibility test set out in Article 19(c) of the Vienna Convention[263] applies—namely, to be permissible, the reservation must not be 'incompatible with the object and purpose of the treaty'. Some writers contend that as reservations the statements are impermissible because they are incompatible with the Protocol's purpose, construed by such writers in the widest sense to be 'the protection of victims of international conflict'.[264] However, this argument is ill-founded for, as Kalshoven and others have documented,[265] the diplomatic conference that produced the Protocol operated throughout on the tacit understanding that the new rules which it established would not apply to nuclear weapons. This perspective was evident at the outset of the conference in the introductory comments on the draft Protocol which the ICRC presented for discussion, which stated:[266]

> Problems relating to atomic, bacteriological and chemical warfare are subjects of international agreements or negotiations by governments and in submitting these draft Additional Protocols the ICRC does not intend to broach these problems.[267]

Hence, in light of this tacit agreement between States—namely, that the Protocol was to have the limited object of improving the protection of victims in international conflict without providing new rules for nuclear weapons—the United States and United Kingdom's reservations (if indeed they can be characterized as such) are permissible.[268]

---

[262] See Brownlie, op. cit. above (n. 42), at p. 351.

[263] Ibid. at p. 357. It is submitted that for Protocol I the compatibility test is more appropriate than the unanimity test and that Article 19(c) of the Vienna Convention is established customary international law in light of the *Genocide Reservations* case, *ICJ Reports*, 1951, at p. 15, UN General Assembly Resolution 598 (VI) of 12 January 1952, UN General Assembly Resolution 1452 (XIV) of 7 December 1959 and the 1962 International Law Commission Report and Draft Articles for the Vienna Convention on the Law of Treaties.

[264] Arbess, loc. cit. above (n. 3), at p. 101; Fujita, loc. cit. above (n. 174), at p. 77; Grief, loc. cit. above (n. 47), at p. 32; and Weston, loc. cit. above (n. 6), at p. 567.

[265] Kalshoven, loc. cit. above (n. 6), at pp. 282–3; see also Fujita, loc. cit. above (n. 260), at pp. 13–20, and Bring and Reimann, loc. cit. above (n. 260), at p. 103, and the extended n. 83 in Roach, 'Certain Conventional Weapons Convention: Arms Control or Humanitarian Law?', *Military Law Review*, 105 (1984), p. 3.

[266] Bring and Reimann, loc. cit. above (n. 260), at p. 101.

[267] See, for example, Fujita, loc. cit. above (n. 260), at p. 12.

[268] Akin to the argument that the United States and the United Kingdom's reservations are impermissible, some writers (e.g., Grief, loc. cit. above (n. 47), at p. 25) contend that, as signatories, the United States and the United Kingdom have not refrained from acts which would defeat the object and purpose of the Protocol (as required under Article 18(a) of the Vienna Convention on the Law of Treaties: Brownlie, loc. cit. above (n. 42), at p. 357). Again, the better view, it is submitted, is that the

Since the United States and United Kingdom have not yet ratified the Protocol (and under Article 23(2) of the Vienna Convention[269] will have to confirm their reservations on signing when they do), the entire reservation argument is somewhat speculative. Yet, in light of the foregoing, it is hardly conceivable that if the Protocol is ever ratified, the United States and United Kingdom will not confirm their reservations (unless, of course, they are to be treated as interpretative declarations). As permissible reservations, they will then be opposable[270] to any State that fails to object in accordance with the terms of Article 20 of the Vienna Convention.[271] The point here is not, as Arbess derides, that 'few [States] have specifically expressed agreement [with the reservations]'.[272] Rather, opposability of the reservations will turn on whether, following ratification by the United States and the United Kingdom (with confirmations of the reservations), other States fail to object within a period of twelve months or by the date of their consent, whichever is later.[273] In any event, whether or not other States object to the reservations (or, as they are entitled to do, to the entry into force as between them and the reserving States of the entire treaty), given the ambiguous operation of Article 21 of the Vienna Convention, the new rules established by Protocol I will still not be applicable to nuclear weapons.[274]

In the light of Protocol I's limited applicability, whether the statements are treated as interpretative declarations or as permissible reservations, some of the main provisions which simply reaffirm existing customary law and so have a clear bearing on nuclear weapons include:

1. Article 35(1)[275]—that the right to choose the 'methods or means' of

---

Protocol has the more limited object of the new rules not being applicable to nuclear weapons, and therefore the United States and the United Kingdom have not breached this provision of the Vienna Convention.

[269] Brownlie, loc. cit. above (n. 42), at p. 359.

[270] This distinction between permissible and opposable reservations is drawn in Bowett, loc. cit. above (n. 261), at p. 88, to elaborate the legal effects of reservations under Article 21 of the Vienna Convention: Brownlie, loc. cit. above (n. 42), at pp. 358–9.

[271] Ibid. at pp. 357–8. It should be noted that India opposed the United States and United Kingdom's declarations on signing but received no other State's support: Fujita, loc. cit. above (n. 260), at p. 25.

[272] Arbess, loc. cit. above (n. 3), at p. 100.

[273] This is the combined effect of Article 23(2) of the Vienna Convention, which provides that in the case of a confirmation of a reservation on ratification, 'the reservation shall be considered as having been made on the date of its confirmation', and Article 20(5): Brownlie, loc. cit. above (n. 42), at pp. 358–9.

[274] If a State does not object to the reservation, then the Protocol is modified as between the accepting and reserving States 'to the extent of the reservation': Article 21(1)(a) of the Vienna Convention (i.e., the new rules do not apply to nuclear weapons). Likewise, if a State objects to the reservation, then the provisions in the Protocol to which the reservation relates do not apply as between the objecting and reserving States 'to the extent of the reservation': Article 21(3) of the Vienna Convention (i.e., again, the new rules do not apply to nuclear weapons). So too, if a State objects to the reservation and the treaty coming into force between itself and the reserving State, then the Protocol does not come into effect as between these two States (and, obviously, any new rules in it do not apply to nuclear weapons or indeed to any weapons): Article 21(3) of the Vienna Convention.

[275] Roberts and Guelff, op. cit. above (n. 113), at p. 409.

warfare is not unlimited (though even here it is argued that the inclusion of the word 'methods' is an extension of the law);

2. Article 35(2)[276]—that it is prohibited to employ means or 'methods' of warfare of a nature to cause unnecessary suffering (though, again, here it is argued that the word 'methods' extends the provision at customary law); and

3. Article 48[277]—that a distinction must be made between military objectives and civilian objects and between combatants and the civilian population.

Some of the provisions regarded as new or significant extensions of existing customary law (and so not applicable to nuclear weapons) include:[278]

1. Article 51(5)[279]—the wide definition of attacks considered indiscriminate;

2. Article 51(6)[280]—the specific and absolute prohibition of reprisals against civilians;

3. Article 56[281]—the special protection of works and installations containing dangerous forces;

4. Article 57[282]—the sophisticated rules elaborating the principle of proportionality and precautionary measures to protect civilians from the effects of military attacks; and

5. Articles 35(3) and 55[283]—the protection of, and prohibition of reprisals against, the natural environment.

In sum, the rules of customary law codified in Protocol I apply to nuclear weapons (as they do to all weapons), but the new rules in Protocol I, having their source in the treaty itself, do not. As already discussed, the applicable customary rules regulate the use of nuclear weapons, but do not ban their use entirely.

(e) *Environmental Protection*

Some writers[284] contend that the use of nuclear weapons, even on a small scale, would violate certain provisions of international law respecting protection of the environment, namely:

1. Article 1(1) of the UN Convention on Environmental Modification Techniques of 1977[285] prohibiting 'military or any other hostile use of

---

[276] Ibid.

[277] Ibid. at p. 414.

[278] Kalshoven, loc. cit. above (n. 6), at p. 283.

[279] Roberts and Guelff, op. cit. above (n. 113), at p. 416.

[280] Ibid.

[281] Ibid. at p. 418.

[282] Ibid. at pp. 419–20.

[283] Ibid. at pp. 409 and 418. For further discussion of these sections, see below, pp. 245–6.

[284] Arbess, loc. cit. above (n. 3), at p. 97; Grief, loc. cit. above (n. 47), at p. 34; Röling, loc. cit. above (n. 190), at p. 188; and Weston, loc. cit. above (n. 6), at p. 567.

[285] Roberts and Guelff, op. cit. above (n. 113), at p. 379.

environmental modification techniques having widespread, long-lasting or severe effects'; and

2. Article 35(3) of Additional Protocol I of 1977[286] prohibiting 'methods or means of warfare which are intended or may be expected to cause widespread, long-term and severe damage to the natural environment' as supplemented by Article 55(1)[287] (in the context of protecting civilian objects) and Article 55(2)[288] prohibiting reprisals against the natural environment.

It is argued that these provisions are 'declaratory of emerging customary law',[289] especially in view of such other instruments as the 1970 Stockholm Declaration of the UN Conference on the Human Environment[290] (in particular, Principles 21 and 22) and the confirming reference to the prohibition in the preamble to the 1981 UN Convention on Specific Conventional Weapons.[291] Indeed, Röling even speaks of an incipient crime of 'ecocide'.[292]

Upon scrutiny, however, the provisions fall short of establishing an absolute prohibition on the use of nuclear weapons. In the first place, even if the provisions evidence an emerging principle of customary law, it cannot be said to have crystallized as yet. Therefore, the source of the legal obligation remains the text and applicability of the treaties themselves; and it is far from clear to what extent these treaties regulate the use of nuclear weapons. For instance, the UN Convention of 1977 concerns attacks launched directly on the environment or use of the environment itself as a weapon[293] and adopts a test for damage establishing the prohibition that is vague and open to subjective interpretation—despite attempts by States to elaborate it in committee.[294] Therefore, given that environmental damage from a low-yield counterforce use is an uncertain and incidental effect (in any event, not the primary object of use) and that escalation of a limited nuclear war is not inevitable, not all uses of nuclear weapons are necessarily 'environmental modification techniques' proscribed by the Convention.

The prohibition in Articles 35 and 55 of Additional Protocol I of 1977 differs from that in Article 1(1) of the UN Convention of 1977 in several

---

[286] Ibid. at p. 409.

[287] Ibid. at p. 418.

[288] Ibid.

[289] Weston, loc. cit. above (n. 6), at p. 567. Grief refers to the provisions as expressing an 'emerging principle of customary law': loc. cit. above (n. 47), at p. 34.

[290] UN Doc. A/CONF. 48/14; also in *International Legal Materials*, 11 (1972), at p. 1416.

[291] Roberts and Guelff, op. cit. above (n. 113), at p. 469.

[292] Röling, loc. cit. above (n. 190), at p. 188.

[293] Roberts and Guelff, op. cit. above (n. 113), at p. 378.

[294] The first 1976 'Understanding' of the Conference of the Committee on Disarmament interpreted the terms of the test 'widespread', 'long-lasting' and 'severe' as follows:

'(a) "widespread": encompassing an area on the scale of several hundred square kilometres;

(b) "long-lasting": lasting for a period of months, or approximately a season;

(c) "severe": involving serious or significant disruption or harm to human life, natural and economic resources or other assets':

Roberts and Guelff, op. cit. above (n. 113), at p. 377.

respects. First, the concern in Protocol I is more clearly with weapons that cause damage to the environment.[295] Secondly, it adopts a slightly different and narrower test of damage for the prohibition—referring to 'long-lasting' not 'long-term' and using 'and' not 'or' (which suggests the prohibition is limited to damage satisfying all three factors, not just one). And thirdly, it appears to adopt an 'objective' test of intention to cause damage with the phrase 'may be expected' which is wider than the test under the UN Convention of 1977. However, Protocol I also employs a criterion based upon certain types of damage which is vague and open to subjective interpretation, despite similar attempts by States to clarify the matter.[296] Still, even resolving these definitional problems, the main defect of the argument for a prohibition under Protocol I is that, given the statements on signing of the United States and United Kingdom (whether characterized as interpretative declarations or permissible reservations) discussed above, the provisions (as new law) do not apply to nuclear weapons.

Again, therefore, the provisions respecting environmental protection establish, at best, a regime of regulation, not outright prohibition, of the use of nuclear weapons. Clearly, this regime prohibits the use of large dirty bombs but, arguably, not the use of a neutron bomb to counter an advancing tank column (where the radiation effects, though primary, are not long-term, given the low half-life of the fall-out).

(f) Protections for Non-Participating States

Some writers[297] contend that any use of nuclear weapons would violate the neutrality rights of States not participating in the conflict, given the possibility of fall-out being transmitted (mainly by wind) from the area of conflict to the territory of such States. The basic rule usually cited is that set out in Article 1 of Hague Convention V of 1907—namely, that 'the territory of neutral powers is inviolable'[298]—which is widely regarded as a prin-

---

[295] Ibid. at p. 378.

[296] The following clarifying statement was submitted to Committee III of the Conference negotiating the Protocol:
'It was generally agreed that battlefield damage incidental to conventional warfare would not normally be proscribed by this provision. What is proscribed in effect is such damage as would be likely to prejudice over a long-term the continued survival of the civilian population or would risk long-term major health problems for it': CDDH/111/286 at p. 9, discussed in Kalshoven, 'Reaffirmation and Development of International Humanitarian Law Applicable in Armed Conflicts: The Diplomatic Conference, Geneva, 1974–1977', Netherlands Yearbook of International Law, 9 (1978), p. 107 at p. 130.

[297] See, for example, Arbess, loc. cit. above (n. 3), at p. 98; Brownlie, loc. cit. above (n. 90), at p. 444; Falk et al., loc. cit. above (n. 3), at p. 567; Fried, loc. cit. above (n. 11), at p. 42; Grief, loc. cit. above (n. 47), at p. 34; Singh, op. cit. above (n. 1), at p. 186; and Weston, loc. cit. above (n. 6), at p. 559.

[298] Roberts and Guelff, op. cit. above (n. 113), at p. 63. Note that this general rule is elaborated in Article I of Hague Convention III of 1907 as regards neutrality in sea warfare and in Article 39 of the draft Hague Rules of Aerial Warfare of 1923, ibid. at pp. 110 and 131 respectively. Note also that Grief contends that Article 2(4) of the Charter is violated on the grounds that any fall-out would be a 'use of force against the territorial integrity' of a State: loc. cit. above (n. 47), at p. 35.

ciple of customary law binding upon all States.[299] The example often given is the possible violation of the rights of the permanently neutralized countries of Switzerland and Austria should nuclear weapons causing significant fall-out be used in Europe.[300]

Even assuming the continuing validity of the basic rights of neutral States,[301] though recognizing that some of the corresponding duties have been modified particularly in light of the collective security system under the UN Charter,[302] two problems remain with the argument that the rights of non-participating States establish an absolute prohibition on the use of nuclear weapons. First, fall-out affecting a neutral State is not the inevitable consequence of every use of a nuclear weapon. Moreover, not only is it uncertain, but any fall-out is likely to be incidental and may be deemed proportionate to the military objective secured.[303] And secondly, the rights of neutral States have historically been regarded more as a basis for intervention, or of liability for reparations, than as a basis for prohibiting certain activity.[304] Thus, while the protections for non-participating States place obligations on States contemplating the use of nuclear weapons, they do not prescribe an outright ban.

V. Conclusion

The traditional laws of armed conflict are not obsolete in the nuclear age and so apply to determine when and how States may lawfully threaten, or engage in, nuclear war. Unfortunately, much of the comfort this conclusion engenders dissipates upon scrutiny of the substance of these laws.

[299] Brownlie, loc. cit. above (n. 90), at p. 444. As set out in Roberts and Guelff, op. cit. above (n. 113), at pp. 68–9, all nuclear States are parties to Hague Convention V of 1907, save the United Kingdom.

[300] Fried, loc. cit. above (n. 11), at p. 42; Grief, loc. cit. above (n. 47), at p. 34.

[301] It is submitted that this is a reasonable assumption. As Weston notes:
'For all the vicissitudes that the law of neutrality has suffered over the years, from the bodyblows of maritime warfare during World War I, to the coming into being of the United Nations collective security system, to the more-or-less routine overflight of planes, rockets and satellites for intelligence retrieval and space exploration purposes, two key claims continue to be honored to substantial degree: the claim that belligerents have no warrant to carry their hostilities into the territory of a non-participating State and the accompanying claim that non-participating States have the right to exclude the entry of belligerent forces into their territory': loc. cit. above (n. 6), at p. 559.

[302] Despite notions of 'non-belligerence' and 'qualified neutrality', releasing neutrals from certain traditional duties, the basic right of neutrality 'is indicated by the many references to neutral States, neutral territory, etc. which are to be found in international agreements concluded since the establishment of the United Nations: for example, the four 1949 Geneva Conventions refer to neutral powers, countries and territory; and 1977 Geneva Protocol I refers to "neutral and other States not Parties to the conflict" ' (in Article 2(c): Roberts and Guelff, op. cit. above (n. 113), at p. 390; quoted from ibid. at p. 62); see also Bindschedler, 'Neutrality, Concept and General Rules', in Bernhardt (ed.), Encyclopedia of Public International Law, vol. 4 (1982), p. 9 at p. 13.

[303] The importance of military necessity in the context of assessing violations of a neutral's rights is discussed obiter in the American Electric and Manufacturing Company case (United States–Venezuela Mixed Claims Commission), Reports of International Arbitral Awards, vol. 9, p. 145 at p. 146.

[304] See Singh, op. cit. above (n. 1), at p. 187.

Taking what might be called a 'functional-positivist' approach to the nature and sources of international law, this article has endeavoured to articulate an overview of the present international legal regime regulating nuclear deterrence and warfare. The concern, therefore, has been with what the law is, not what it ought to be (for moral, political, economic or other reasons). As discussed at some length, it would appear that no binding rule or principle of international law directly or by analogy outlaws nuclear weapons as such; rather, the legality of any particular nuclear weapon depends on the circumstances of its threatened or actual use.

Of course, it might be said that the present regime has the merit of inviting States to consider all the legal factors of any given nuclear weapon's threat or use (as opposed to compelling them to ignore international law altogether because it is either irrelevant or prohibitive in any event). However, the present regime remains unsatisfactory for at least two reasons. First, as noted, it is based largely on vague, general principles susceptible to excessively subjective and evasive interpretations. And secondly, even making charitable assumptions about the ability of States to wage limited nuclear war (as admittedly has been done throughout this article), it must be recognized that such 'luxury of analysis'—that is, muddling through decisions based on vague and subjective general legal principles—is unlikely to exist in times of nuclear crisis.

Consequently, prudence dictates (the political will of States, especially of nuclear States, permitting) that the substance of the laws of armed conflict regulating nuclear weapons be improved. This may best be done, it is submitted, by embellishing the present general principles with specific rules applied according to objective criteria.[305] It may well prove that, as Baxter has argued, it is not possible to frame any workable rules on the employment of nuclear weapons falling short of an outright prohibition.[306] But States must strive to achieve greater specificity and objectivity in this area of the law; for only thus can be secured the true value, in times of a nuclear crisis, of the laws of armed conflict as a practical guide of legality for governments and as a reasonable assurance of survival for humanity. With the marked improvement in East-West relations of late, opportunities have now arisen that demand to be seized.

---

[305] As Cassese notes, 'The best way of supplementing and strengthening the existing general principles is linking them with the enactment of specific bans': loc. cit. above (n. 117), at p. 179.

[306] See Boyle, loc. cit. above (n. 2), p. 1472 at n. 73.

SOME LEGAL ASPECTS OF TRADE IN THE NATURAL RESOURCES OF NAMIBIA*

By CALEB M. PILGRIM‡

I. INTRODUCTION[1]

The German Imperial Mining Decree of 1905 granted to any person, except natives and coloureds, a general right to prospect anywhere in South West Africa.[2] South Africa perpetuated this policy of discrimination when, as a result of Germany's defeat in the First World War, South West Africa became a 'C' mandate under the terms of the League of Nations mandate.

South Africa and various multinational corporations exploited Namibia from the inception of the mandate. Although the mandate was terminated in 1966,[3] this exploitation continued through the production, processing, trading and use of Namibia's resources by South Africa and various multinational corporations.[4] The majority of UN member States and the council for Namibia were of the opinion that this exploitation was undertaken without the consent of the Namibian people or the Council for Namibia,[5] and

---

* © Dr Caleb M. Pilgrim, 1991.

‡ Ph. D (Cantab.), JD (Yale). The author's interest in this subject originated with a suggestion by Mr E. Lauterpacht in a lecture at Cambridge University in 1979–80 that the question of the legal title to the natural resources of Namibia should be vindicated before the courts. Research for this paper was initiated at Yale Law School during the academic year 1988–9.

[1] There have been an increasing number of studies on Namibia since Allard K. Lowenstein's *Brutal Mandate* (1962). See, for example, Slonim, *South West Africa and the United Nations: An International Mandate in Dispute* (1973); Sagay, *Legal Aspects of the Namibian Dispute* (1975); SWAPO Department of Information and Publicity, *To be Born a Nation: The Liberation Struggle for Namibia* (1981); Green, Kiljunen and Kiljunen, *Namibia: The Last Colony* (1981); Dore, *The International Mandate System and Namibia* (1985); Soggott, *Namibia: The Violent Heritage* (1986); Commonwealth Secretariat, *The Mineral Industry of Namibia: Perspectives for Independence* (a study by Roger Murray); United Nations Institute for Namibia, *Namibia: Perspectives for National Reconstruction and Development* (1986), and *Namibia: The Legal Framework and Development Strategy Options for the Mining Industry* (1987); also, Cooper (ed.), *Allies in Apartheid: Western Capitalism in Occupied Namibia* (1988).

[2] See Wellington, *South West Africa and the Human Issues* (1967); also Calvert, *South West Africa during the German Occupation, 1884–1914* (1969), at pp. 25–7, and *Namibia: The Legal Framework and Development Strategy Options* (previous note), at pp. 64–9.

[3] GA Res. 2145 (XXI).

[4] For the argument that the South African colonial regime delinked the mineral sector from the rest of the economy and that that sector was developed purely as an 'enclave' sector of the economy, see *Namibia: The Legal Framework and Development Strategy Options* (above, n. 1), at pp. 1, 15–19.

[5] The Council for Namibia was established pursuant to United Nations General Assembly Resolution 2145 (XXI), 27 October 1966, and Resolution 2248 (S-V), 19 May 1967: *Compendium of Major Resolutions, Decisions and Other Documents Relating to Namibia*, UN Doc. A/AC. 131/1984/CRP.17 (29 March 1984) (hereinafter *Compendium*), at p. 34. The powers and functions of the Council include the right 'to administer South West Africa (Namibia) until independence' in order to safeguard the interests of Namibia and its people in anticipation of the independence of Namibia. The Council is,

damaged Namibia and its people.[6] The UN Council for Namibia therefore adopted Decree No. 1 and other measures in an attempt to remedy this mischief and safeguard the interests of the Namibian people.[7] The Decree merits quotation in full. It provided that:

The United Nations Council for Namibia,

Recognizing that, in terms of General Assembly resolution 2145 (XXI) of 27 October 1966 the Territory of Namibia (formerly South West Africa) is the direct responsibility of the United Nations,

Accepting that this responsibility includes the obligation to support the right of the people of Namibia to achieve self-government and independence in accordance with General Assembly resolution 1514 (XV) of 14 December 1960,

Reaffirming that the Government of South Africa is in illegal possession of the Territory of Namibia,

Furthering the decision of the General Assembly in resolution 1803 (XVII) of 14 December 1962 which declared the right of the peoples and nations to permanent sovereignty over their natural wealth and resources,

Noting that the Government of the Republic of South Africa has usurped and interfered with these rights,

Desirous of securing for the people of Namibia adequate protection of the natural wealth and resources of the Territory which is rightfully theirs,

Recalling the advisory opinion of the International Court of Justice of 21 June 1971,[8]

Acting in terms of the powers conferred on it by General Assembly resolution

---

from the standpoint of the United Nations, vested with power 'to promulgate such laws, decrees and administrative regulations as are necessary' for that administration. For a brief history of UN handling of the Namibian question, see *Namibia: Perspectives for National Reconstruction and Development* (above, n. 1), at pp. 46–50.

[6] Although mining accounts for more than one-third of Namibia's GDP and about 85 per cent of its exports, blacks—95 per cent of the population—do not realize much of that revenue. Average per capita income for blacks is 1/18th that of whites. The ratio of white to black per capita expenditure in 1984 was 8 to 1. 5,000 white-owned farms take up 77 per cent of all viable farming land. Blacks form a labour pool; contracted migrants help to keep wages low and profits high in South Africa: Mittelman, 'Cutting the Weak Link in the Apartheid Chain: Namibia', *Africa Today*, vol. 35, no. 2 (1988), at p. 521; Curtin Knight, 'Namibia's Transition to Independence', *Current History*, May 1989, at p. 227. Similarly, an anthropologist with direct work experience in Namibia cites a Government report released in 1984 showing the condition of the Namibian Bushmen: annual per capita income is $21; 90 per cent of children between ages 5 and 19 are not in school; at least 40 to 50 per cent of children die before age 10; the total 'Bushman' population declined at least 5 per cent in the decade of the 1970s. The anthropologist concludes that so long as land rights are unprotected and communal land is controlled solely by the State, the majority of Namibians will remain vulnerable squatters on their own land; thousands will join the fate of the 'Bushmen': letter from John Marshall, *New York Times*, 17 November 1988. The writ of summons in the *URENCO* case alleges 'great and irreparable damage': United Nations, *Namibia Bulletin*, vol. 9, no. 7, para. 2 at p. 2. See also UN General Assembly Resolution 2145 (XXI), adopted 145th plenary meeting, 27 October 1966: *Compendium* at p. 32; and United Nations, *Plunder of Namibian Uranium: Major Findings of the Hearings on Namibian Uranium held by the United Nations Council for Namibia in July 1980*, DPI/715–40520–June 1984–10M.

[7] Adopted by the Council for Namibia at its 209th meeting on 27 September 1974 and approved by the General Assembly of the United Nations at its 29th Session on 13 December 1974: *Compendium*, p. 118.

[8] *Legal Consequences for States of the Continued Presence of South Africa in Namibia (South West Africa) notwithstanding Security Council Resolution 276 (1970)*, advisory opinion, *ICJ Reports*, 1971, p. 16.

2248 (S-V) of 19 May 1967 and all other relevant resolutions and decisions regarding Namibia,

Decrees that

1. No person or entity, whether a body corporate or unincorporated, may search for, prospect for, explore for, take, extract, mine, process, refine, use, sell, export, or distribute any natural resource, whether animal or mineral, situated or found to be situated within the territorial limit of Namibia without the consent and permission of the United Nations Council for Namibia or any person authorized to act on its behalf for the purpose of giving such permission or consent;

2. Any permission, concession or licence for all or any of the purposes specified in paragraph 1 above whensoever granted by any person or entity, including any body purporting to act under the authority of the Government of the Republic of South Africa or the 'Administration of South West Africa' or their predecessors, is null, void and of no force or effect;

3. No animal resource, mineral or other natural resource produced in or emanating from the Territory of Namibia may be taken from the said Territory by any means whatsoever outside the territorial limits of Namibia by any person or body, whether corporate or unincorporated, without the consent and permission of the United Nations Council for Namibia or of any person authorized to act on behalf of the said Council;

4. Any animal, mineral or other natural resource produced in or emanating from the Territory of Namibia which shall be taken from the said Territory without the consent and written authority of the United Nations Council for Namibia or of any person authorized to act on behalf of the said Council may be seized and shall be forfeited to the benefit of the said Council and held in trust by them for the benefit of the people of Namibia;

5. Any vehicle, ship or container found to be carrying animal, mineral or other natural resources produced in or emanating from the Territory of Namibia shall also be subject to seizure and forfeiture by or on behalf of the United Nations Council for Namibia or of any person authorized to act on behalf of the said Council and shall be forfeited to the benefit of the said Council and held in trust by them for the benefit of the people of Namibia;

6. Any person, entity or corporation which contravenes the present decree in respect of Namibia may be held liable in damages by the future Government of an independent Namibia;

7. For the purposes of the preceding paragraphs 1, 2, 3, 4 and 5 and in order to give effect to this decree, the United Nations Council for Namibia hereby authorizes the United Nations Commissioner for Namibia, in accordance with resolution 2248 (S-V), to take the necessary steps after consultations with the President.

The Decree prohibited trade in Namibia's natural resources and provided that the government of an independent Namibia might sue companies violating the Decree.

In order to conserve Namibia's resources, the Council for Namibia brought suit in 1987 against the Dutch Government and companies trading in Namibian uranium.[9] Notwithstanding recent agreements, these proceed-

---

[9] United Nations, 'The URENCO Case', *Namibia Bulletin*, Special Issue, vol. 11, no. 7 (July 1988), and see below.

ings are still pending[10] since this litigation is considered independent of the recent agreements.[11] Moreover, under the terms of the Decree, the government of an independent Namibia still has standing to maintain an action for compensation for illegal trade in its resources.[12]

II. THE PROBLEM STATED

At first sight, it might be thought that the question of trade in Namibia's resources presents a typical decolonization problem of the type encountered in mineral rich territories, e.g. in Zambia and Angola on accession to independence.[13] But Namibia's status hitherto as an international territory under the *de jure* administration of the United Nations, and until recently under the *de facto* control of South Africa, distinguishes it from other cases.[14]

The Namibian question is partly a matter of the relationship of municipal law to public international law. The main object of this article is to

[10] On the *URENCO* case, see below, pp. 266–73.

[11] For the recent agreements, see below, pp. 273–7.

[12] 'Sanctions busting' by Shell and BP in Rhodesia after UDI could be analogous here, in that notwithstanding the evidence amassed by Tom Bingham QC in the *Bingham Report*, 1979, and threats of legal action by President Kaunda of Zambia, no concrete legal action was ever taken to recover compensation for damage caused as a result of violations of UN sanctions and UK sanctions legislation by the oil companies.

Whether a sovereign Namibian Government would wish to pursue this matter of compensation for violations of Decree No. 1 is so far unclear; but Art. III.B(7) of SWAPO's Constitution adopted by the Central Committee 28 July–1 August 1976 at Lusaka, Zambia, declares as one of SWAPO's basic aims and objectives 'To ensure that the people's government exercises effective control over the means of production and distribution and pursues a policy which facilitates the way to social ownership of all the resources of the country'. Art. IX.K.(5) provides that SWAPO's Secretary for Legal Affairs 'shall study all treaties' purportedly entered into on behalf of Namibia by previous colonial administrations and the illegal South African regime and make recommendations thereon to the National Executive Committee: SWAPO Department for Publicity and Public Information, *SWAPO: Constitution of the South West Africa People's Organization* (1976), pp. 4, 21.

[13] Carlsson, *Address to the University of Bremen*, at p. 1, states that 'Namibia . . . should be seen as a major issue of decolonization' which should not be linked with the problem of *apartheid*.

[14] In terms of UK constitutional law, an agreement to transfer power from the metropolis to the colony normally resulted in issuance of an Order in Council with a provision designating the new independent government as successor in title to the rights and contractual obligations of the colonial government (for example Zambia, 1964). See 'Note on the Question of Treaty Succession on the Attainment of Independence by Territories Formerly Dependent Internationally on the United Kingdom', in Wilson, *International Law and Contemporary Commonwealth Issues* (1971), at p. 205. Cf. note 18, below. Arguably, the law of trusts could have provided an equally useful framework for analysing the particular problem of Namibia. In so far as the law of trusts provides for reversion of property to the original settlor, the UNGA, upon revocation of the mandate from South Africa, could have restored the mandate to the UK, the original settlor, rather than establishing the Council for Namibia as the governing body of Namibia. The question of Namibia would then have become a straightforward decolonization matter. The author is indebted to Mr S. Jituboh, Counsel for the Council for Namibia, for this insight.

At the time of the establishment of the Council, the UK was so actively opposed to the Unilateral Declaration of Independence (UDI) by the Smith regime in Rhodesia that it is doubtful whether they could have consistently opposed self-government and independence for a Namibia restored to UK trusteeship, notwithstanding the fact that the UK had once sought to integrate Namibia into South Africa.

delineate the differences between the legal situation existing before independence, the applicable law, the rights of the Namibian people over their
resources, and the adequacy of the legal regime which governed and still
governs the handling, management and disposal of these resources, and the
situation likely to evolve after independence.

The question of trade in Namibia's natural resources is important for
several reasons: not least because of the actors involved,[15] the type and
value of resources traded (strategic and other minerals including uranium,
gold, diamonds and other important commodities),[16] the deleterious effects
of that trade on the Namibian people, and possible recourse for the
Namibian people and any other people similarly situated. The question
remains important, not just in terms of the outcome of a single case, the
URENCO case, but also in terms of any future trading regime with an independent Namibia.

This article assesses certain legal aspects of trade in Namibia's natural
resources prior to independence. In so doing, it focuses on two problems:
first, the question of possible liability for trade in Namibia's natural
resources at the time when Namibia was under South Africa's occupation.
In this context, special attention is paid to the URENCO case. Secondly,
some limited consideration is given to the significance of recent agreements,
specifically, the Agreement between Angola, Cuba and South Africa on
Namibia's independence.[17] The Military Withdrawal Agreement between
Cuba and Angola necessarily falls outside the scope of this paper.[18]

III. Legal Requirements for Valid Title

Traditional public international law recognized seven methods of acquiring
territory: occupation, accretion, prescription, voluntary cession, assimila-

---

[15] For a comprehensive survey of TNCs based in Europe, North America and South Africa, and
active in Namibia, see *Reference Book on Major Transnational Corporations Operating In Namibia*
(1985), UN Sales No. E.85 II.A.5 (hereinafter the *Reference Book*). Schermers, 'The Namibia Decree
in National Courts', *International and Comparative Law Quarterly*, 26 (1977), p. 87, attributed some
value to the Decree as a deterrent: 'The Decree seems to have had some effect. Several companies have
withdrawn from Namibia.' The *Reference Book* suggests, however, that whereas 17 corporations had
ceased operations in Namibia, 43 others, 22 of which were based in the USA and Western Europe, continued to operate and invest in Namibia.

[16] 'Even before the commencement of large-scale uranium production in 1976, Namibia ranked
fourth among African countries (after South Africa, Zambia and Zaire) and seventeenth in the world in
the value of minerals (other than petroleum) produced. In addition to the identified reserves of dia-
mond, uranium, copper, arsenic, silver, cadmium, lead and zinc, significant reserves of other minerals
were also found. . . . There are not many countries in the world where the mineral wealth per capita is
as large as in Namibia. While the territory has a strong mineral resource base, this resource is being
depleted fast': *Namibia: The Legal Framework and Development Strategy Options for the Mining
Industry* (above, n. 1), at p. 2.

[17] S/20346, A/43/989.

[18] Agreement between the Government of the Republic of Cuba and the Government of the People's
Republic of Angola for the conclusion of the International Mission of the Cuban Military Contingent,
done at UN Headquarters on 22 December 1988. See S/20345.

tion, peace treaties and conquest. The entry into force of the UN Charter ended the legality of acquisition of title to territory through conquest.[19]

The question of title to territory must be distinguished from the question of title to resources. With the Agreement on Namibia's independence, the issue of title to territory might be considered settled.[20] However, the issue remains relevant as regards Walvis Bay.[21] International trade in the resources of Namibia prior to independence and any trade in resources within Walvis Bay necessarily raise questions as to title to these resources.

The main legislation followed by the South African authorities in Namibia has been the Mines, Works and Mineral Ordinance, No. 20 of 1968, and regulations published on 1 October 1968 in the *Official Gazette* of the South West Africa Administration, repealing the Mines, Works and Minerals Ordinance, No. 26 of 1954. The 1968 Ordinance was amended in 1969 by proclamation R89 (published in the South African *Government Gazette*) to incorporate changes resulting from the administrative incorporation of most of the major branches of the South West African administration into ministries of the Republic, under the South West Africa Affairs Act, No. 25 of 1969. These involved changes in the nomenclature reflecting the placing of mining affairs under the direct control of the South African Department of Mines ('Minister of Mines' for the 'Administrator of South West Africa', 'Department for Mines Division' etc.), together with a section defining the powers of supervision and control of the mining industry in Namibia by the Department of Mines.

Deeds Registry Proclamation No. 37 of 1939, which set out the functions of the Deeds Registry in Windhoek, was also amended in 1969 by the Mining Titles Registration Proclamation R90 to provide for establishment of a Mining Titles Office in Windhoek for the registration of all documents relating to the mining rights, granted or acquired, under the 1968 Ordi-

---

[19] Art. 2, para. 4, prohibited member States from using or threatening the use of force. To obtain territory through conquest would clearly violate obligations assumed under the Charter and could not result in good title.

[20] Professor Brownlie has argued that 'it is doubtful if the United Nations has a "capacity to convey title", in part because the Organization cannot assume the role of territorial sovereign: in spite of the principle of implied powers the Organization is not a state and the General Assembly only has a power of recommendation': *Principles of Public International Law* (3rd edn., 1979), at p. 174.

[21] On one hand, SWAPO considers the question already settled through SC Res. 435, which states that the bay is 'in fact an integral part of Namibia'. On the other hand, South African officials, e.g. Deputy Defence Minister Wynand Breytenbach, have made it clear that 'Walvis Bay will always be part of South Africa': 'Walvis Bay Time Bomb: In an Independent Namibia who will rule Walvis Bay?', *The Namibian*, 9 September 1988, pp. 10–11. The position of the UN is that Walvis Bay is an integral part of Namibia: see, e.g., SC Res. 385 (1976), para. 7 of which sought 'free elections under the supervision and control of the United Nations to be held for the whole of Namibia as one political entity', and SC Res. 432 (1978), which unanimously recognized Walvis Bay as an integral part of Namibia: *Compendium*, pp. 19, 24. Art. 4 (4) of Namibia's Constitution provides that 'The national territory of Namibia shall consist of the whole territory recognized by the international community through the organs of the United Nations as Namibia, including the enclave, harbour and port of Walvis Bay, as well as the offshore islands of Namibia, and its southern boundary shall extend to the middle of the Orange River'. See also below, pp. 262–3, 274.

nance. The Ordinance governs base minerals, precious metals and stones (including diamonds). Separate provisions for the prospecting and mining of source minerals—uranium and radioactive metals—are contained in the Atomic Energy Act, No. 90 of 1967.[22]

But most States considered South Africa's occupation of Namibia unlawful. With the exception of South Africa, no State has in recent memory officially questioned the illegality of South Africa's occupation of Namibia.[23] Rights acquired since the ICJ advisory opinion of 1971 declaring South Africa's occupation illegal were, from the standpoint of the UN majority, potentially null and void.[24] UN Decree No. 1 built on an international process condemning South Africa's occupation, attempted to nullify South African legislation controlling Namibia, and sought to provide a basis for compensation for the adverse effects of South Africa's occupation of Namibia.

The arguments as the non-binding nature of UN General Assembly resolutions are too well known to be worth repeating here. It is worth recalling that the ICJ 1971 advisory opinion, in upholding the General Assembly's termination of the mandate, found that the General Assembly 'is not debarred from adopting in specific cases within the framework of its competence resolutions which make determinations or have operative design'.

[22] Commonwealth Secretariat, *The Mineral Industry of Namibia*, pp. 67–8; for a brief but comprehensive survey of the domestic legal arrangements governing the Namibian mining industry, see *Namibia: The Legal Framework and Development Strategy Options for the Mining Industry* (above, n. 1), pp. 70–118.

[23] The ICJ in its advisory opinion of 21 June 1971 held that:
(1) the continued presence of South Africa in Namibia being illegal, South Africa is under obligation to withdraw its administration from Namibia immediately and thus put an end to its occupation of the Territory;
(2) States members of the United Nations are under obligations to recognize the illegality of South Africa's presence in Namibia and the invalidity of its acts on behalf of or concerning Namibia, and to refrain from any acts and in particular any dealings with the Government of South Africa implying recognition of the legality of, or lending support or assistance to, such presence and administration;
(3) it is incumbent upon States which are not members of the United Nations to give assistance within the scope of sub-paragraph (2) above, in the action which has been taken by the United Nations with regard to Namibia: *ICJ Reports*, 1971, p. 58.
The defendants, URENCO and UCN, argue that advisory opinions of the ICJ are not binding (Statement of Defence of URENCO Nederland and Ultra-Centrifuge Nederland NV, 'The URENCO Case', loc. cit. above (n. 11), at p. 13. Their position is in this respect identical to that of the South African Government *vis-à-vis* earlier ICJ advisory opinions. South Africa refused to abide by those opinions, stating that they were not binding because they were purely advisory: *General Assembly Official Records*, 8th Session (1953), 4th Committee, 357th meeting, p. 267. The importance of the ICJ advisory opinions which were handed down in 1950, 1955, and 1956 lay in the fact that they destroyed any vestige of legitimacy which South Africa might have claimed for its administration of the territory. The opinions also vindicated the role of the UN as the lawfully governing authority of Namibia: *ICJ Reports*, 1950, p. 137; ibid. 1955, p. 76; ibid. 1956, p. 27. Moreover, as one expert points out, 'When competent organs of the United Nations make a determination that a situation is illegal, the States which are addressees of the resolution or resolutions concerned are under an obligation to bring that situation to an end': Brownlie, op. cit. above (n. 20), at p. 515, citing the 1971 opinion. Arguably, the same holds true for corporations established under the laws of such States. Ideally both States and corporations should abide by the ICJ opinions.

[24] See below, text accompanying nn. 38–40.

Many subsequent UN resolutions confirming the illegality of South Africa's occupation of Namibia and its handling of Namibia's resources easily fit within the definition of 'resolutions which make determinations or have operative design'.

Moreover, as Professor Falk suggested almost twenty years ago:

> The time has come for the ICJ to confirm the role of *international consensus* as a source of international law within the meaning of Article 38 of the Statute of the Court, consensus being used to refer to an overwhelming majority, a convergence of international opinion; a predominance, to something more than a simple majority but something less than unanimity or universality. Only with this rudimentary legislative capacity will it become possible to use the resources of law to implement the will of the international community against those who defy it. And if the resources of law are not available, then what? Only force is left to implement that will. This competence to use force is possible in the context of a threat or breach of international peace or act of aggression without awaiting the consent of all states. Why should this false notion of universality be an impediment to legal order when something less than force is at stake?[25]

However, it should be borne in mind that attempts at implementing UN resolutions through the use of national courts have been largely unsuccessful, sometimes because of domestic legal constraints, sometimes because of a lack of political will resulting in failure to embody the policy objectives underlying UN resolutions, including Decree No. 1, in national legislation.

In a typical case, *Diggs* v. *Dent*,[26] the plaintiffs brought an action for declaratory and injunctive relief in respect of the defendants' dealings with the Government of South Africa concerning the importation of seal skins from Namibia. The plaintiffs argued that such trade violated the UN Charter, UN Security Council Resolutions 276[27] and 301[28] and the ICJ advisory opinion on the *Legal Consequences for States of the Continued Presence of South Africa in Namibia (South West Africa) notwithstanding Security Council Resolution 276 (1970).*[29] The District Court for the District of Columbia held that notwithstanding the plaintiffs' standing to sue, the limited nature of UN resolutions deprived the court of jurisdiction. According to the Court, the treaty provisions of the UN Charter were not self-executing and did not vest in any of the plaintiffs any individual legal rights which they could assert before the court. It was the court's view that:

> Even if the court had subject matter jurisdiction, it would be forced to conclude that the issues before it are ones within the foreign policy authority of the President and are non-justiciable. It is not for the court to say whether a treaty has been

---

[25] Falk, *The Status of Law in International Society* (1970), at p. 134. Cf. D'Amato's argument that South Africa's objections to all UN resolutions against it defeat a consensus claim: 'On Consensus', *Canadian Yearbook of International Law*, 8 (1971), pp. 117–21.

[26] *International Legal Materials*, 14 (1975), p. 797.

[27] Ibid. 10 (1971), p. 295.

[28] Ibid., p. 1296.

[29] *ICJ Reports*, 1971, p. 16.

broken or what remedy shall be given, *Whitney v. Robertson* 124 US 190, 194–195 (1888); *Z & F Assets Realizations Corp. v. Hull*, 114 F 2d, 464, 471 (DC Cir. 1940) aff'd 311 US 470 (1941). Nor should the Court direct the manner in which the Executive is to carry out his foreign relations responsibilities.[30]

IV. *De jure* Administration versus *de facto* Control

Arguably, the failure of the UN Council for Namibia to enforce the Decree could call into question the validity of the Decree. In its deliberations on Namibian uranium, the States General of the Netherlands may well have interpreted a lack of action on the part of the Council as proof that the Council could not make a case for the Decree's legality in the courts of the Netherlands. On the other hand, the UN Office of Legal Affairs has argued that the lack of *de facto* control over the territory does not affect the internationally recognized legal authority of the Council and its standing as 'the only authority that has any legal right to administer Namibia'.[31]

(a) *Decree No. 1 and other UN Resolutions applied to Namibia*

Decree No. 1 was based primarily on UN majority recognition of the legitimate claim of the peoples of Namibia to exercise their right to self-determination, and to control and dispose of their natural resources.[32] Yet

---

[30] *Diggs v. Dent*, loc. cit. above (n. 26), at pp. 804–05. Similarly, in *Diggs v. Shultz*, 470 F 2d 461 (1972), an action by the plaintiffs to enjoin importation of metallurgical chromite from Southern Rhodesia into the United States, the US Court of Appeals, citing *Frothingham v. Mellon*, 262 US 447, 489, 43 S Ct. 597, 601, held that 'To attempt to decide whether the President chose properly among the three alternatives confronting him "would be, not to decide a judicial controversy, but to assume a position of authority over the governmental acts of another and coequal department, an authority which we plainly do not possess".'

[31] *Report of the Mission to Western Europe to Seek Legal Advice on the Implementation of Decree No. 1 for the Protection of the Natural Resources of Namibia, 24 April to 12 May, 1984*, UN Doc. A/AC.131/133 (13 July 1984), para. 54 at p. 10; also *Report of the Delegation of the Council to the Symposium on International Efforts to Implement Decree No. 1 for the Protection of Natural Resources of Namibia, held at Geneva from 27 to 31 August 1984*, UN Doc. A/AC.131/149 (10 January 1985), para. 23 at p. 4.

[32] The rise of the principle of self-determination after the First World War, its subsequent application to the colonial empires, especially after adoption of the Declaration on the Granting of Independence to Colonial Countries and Peoples, UNGA Res. 1514 (XV), and post-1945 State practice, notwithstanding a few exceptions involving wars of national liberation, lead to the conclusion that self-determination is almost universally accepted as a legal principle and States generally conduct themselves in accordance with it. This does not in any way gainsay the problem of diverse and even conflicting interpretation to which the principle of self-determination is susceptible. See also Brownlie, op. cit. above (n. 20), at pp. 515 (self-determination as *jus cogens*), 593–6 (status of the principle in general), and 540–1 (the relationship between the principles of self-determination and permanent sovereignty over natural resources).

the Decree, despite near universal acceptance of the validity of the sentiments underlying it, was never implemented by the Netherlands and other Western States.[33] The position of the United Nations has been that the Decree is 'highly unique' within the international legal system, for although it is an international act in the form and method of its adoption, its substance takes the form and characteristics of national law.[34] It is a law adopted by an international legal authority and is designed to have a legal effect in a particular territory. Since the Council for Namibia was the internationally recognized legally administering authority for Namibia, the Decree was to be considered Namibian domestic law. 'The removal of any natural resource from Namibia in violation of the Decree therefore implied that those in possession of Namibian resources had no legal title to them.'[35]

The Council styled this resolution a Decree. In assessing its validity, it is necessary to determine, first, the specific powers of the Council and, secondly, the scope of these powers. What is the scope of these powers under the law of the Charter? Does the Charter empower the General Assembly through the Council to issue such a Decree? Are such Decrees binding under the law of the Charter?

The powers and functions assigned to the Council by General Assembly Resolution 2248 (S-V) included the power

(*a*) to administer Namibia until independence with the maximum participation of its inhabitants;

(*b*) to promulgate legislation required for the administration of the territory until a legislative assembly could be elected on the basis of universal adult suffrage;

(*c*) to take immediate measures in consultation with the inhabitants to

---

[33] The *Report of the Delegation of the Council to the Symposium on International Efforts to Implement Decree No. 1* noted that:

'The Decree remained unimplemented although 10 years had elapsed since its promulgation. It was generally accepted, however, that the Council's inability to implement effectively the Decree was due to those foreign economic interests which, in collaboration with South Africa, were engaged in the systematic plunder of Namibia's resources, in defiance of the resolutions of the United Nations, as well as the lack of political will of some countries to implement the Decree. . . . Among the suggestions made by the participants for the effective implementation of the Decree was the institution of legal proceedings against those transnational corporations and other foreign economic interests which were operating illegally in Namibia':

Report, loc.cit. above (n. 31), at p. 2.

Schermers, although critical of the Decree, concludes that 'There can be little doubt about the legality of the Namibia Decree'. And he goes on to argue that the Decree should be followed since 'Non-application of the decree would violate international public policy and therefore be contrary to the national public policy as well': 'The Namibia Decree in National Courts', *International and Comparative Law Quarterly*, 26 (1977), p. 97.

[34] Schermers, loc. cit. (previous note), at p. 89, concludes that UN Decrees on Namibia 'have the same effect within the legal orders of the member States as decrees of foreign States would have. The legal situation then is the same as it is when the Namibia Decree is considered as a decree of the only lawful authority in regard to Namibia.'

[35] United Nations Council for Namibia: *Report of the Delegation of the Council to the Symposium on International Efforts to Implement Decree No. 1*, loc. cit. above (n. 31), at p. 4.

establish a constitutional assembly with the object of drawing up a Constitution;

(d) to maintain law and order;

(e) to transfer all powers to the people of the territory following the declaration of independence.

Finally, the Assembly requested the Council to entrust executive and administrative tasks, as it deemed necessary, to a United Nations Commissioner for Namibia.[36]

It is by no means clear that the constituent document of the Council authorized resource management and control by the Council. It is possible that a narrow interpretation of the scope of the powers and functions of the Council would have confined the Council to administration and preparation for elections. It would possibly have excluded the resource question. The Council, in promulgating Decree No. 1, would in effect have acted ultra vires. On the other hand, had the Council, as trustee, ignored the pillage of Namibia's resources, the material well-being of the inhabitants, and their economic and social development, the Council would have been derelict in its supervisory duty.

The drafters of Decree No. 1 clearly intended it to be legally binding. The Council for Namibia was empowered to enact laws and regulations with respect to Namibia. Decree No. 1 thus provided that those trading in the resources of Namibia, without the consent of the Council or the consent of the Namibian people, could be held liable in damages by the government of an independent Namibia.

The UN Decree and other resolutions on Namibia were intended to effect a fundamental alteration in the domestic law applied by the South African authorities in Namibia. The Decree and the various resolutions are consistent with the principles of self-determination, independence, and sovereignty over natural resources which are well established in international law.

The Decree asserts, in paragraph 1, that any dealings in the resources situated within the territorial limits of Namibia require 'the consent and permission of the United Nations Council for Namibia or any person authorized to act on its behalf for the purpose of giving such permission or consent'.[37] It thus claims a power on the part of the Council to consent to the exploitation of Namibia's resources. This provision covers TNCs and their subsidiaries incorporated in Namibia.

The Decree further provides that any permission, concession or licence granted by any party purporting to act on the authority of the Government of the Republic of South Africa or the 'Administration of South West

---

[36] *Compendium*, p. 34. The Council originally comprised 11 member States, and was later expanded to 31. SWAPO's representative participated as an observer in the work of the Council.

[37] See text at p. 251, above.

Africa' is null, void and of no force or effect.[38] In short, under the Decree it is no defence if one claims to have acted under South Africa's authorization or the authorization of her predecessors. This may well be the case where TNCs acted subsequent to the ICJ opinion declaring South Africa's occupation of Namibia illegal.

But what is the position of contracts existing at the time of the Decree's enactment?[39] Was the Decree intended to have retroactive effect? Possibly it was, given that it refers to permission given by the 'predecessors' of the Government of the Republic of South Africa or the Administration of South West Africa. The drafters may have intended this clause to reach such 'unequal treaties' as may have resulted in earlier concessions to MNCs and the South African authorities. It is, however, anathema to those who cling to the notion of sanctity of contracts.[40] Nonetheless, the Decree by itself does not fully resolve this question, which is directly related to compensation in the event of future nationalizations or action under the Decree by a future independent Namibian Government.[41]

The Decree further provides that resources produced in or emanating from the territory of Namibia without the Council's consent 'may be seized and shall be forfeited to the benefit of the said Council and held in trust by

---

[38] Para. 2: see text at p. 251, above. Security Council Res. 301 (1971) declares that franchises, rights, titles or contracts relating to Namibia granted to individuals or companies by South Africa after the adoption of General Assembly Resolution 2145 (XXI) of 27 October 1966 were not subject to protection or espousal by their States against claims of a future lawful Government of Namibia. Such a resolution could operate as estoppel with regard to those member States which did not vote against the resolution.

SWAPO has also stated that an independent Namibian State will not be liable for the funds raised by the post-mandate-revocation South African occupation regime. The lenders who lent to the South African regime and who secured guarantees from the South African State 'must turn to the South African treasury for their payment'. Since 1980, Pretoria has raised at least R 750 million from foreign institutions on behalf of Namibia: *The Namibian*, 26 August 1988, at p. 17. Cf. Curtin Knight, loc. cit. above (n. 6), at p. 228. This particular policy of SWAPO would possibly have been inconsistent with membership of, and definitely encounter the hostility of, the IMF, the IBRD and various Western banks. More recent statements by SWAPO have evidenced some 'moderation'.

[39] For example, in 1970 the British Atomic Energy Authority signed a major contract with the South African subsidiary of Rio Tinto Zinc (RTZ) for the purchase of uranium from the Rossing mine. In 1973 a partnership and sales agreement was concluded between RTZ and the French company, Total Compagnie Minéaire et Nucléaire, a wholly owned subsidiary of the French Government-owned Compagnie Française des Pétroles (CFP). This gave Total a 10 per cent holding in Rossing Uranium in return for a long-term contract for a 'substantial quantity' of uranium concentrate during the 1980s: Barbara Rogers, *Namibia's Uranium: Implications for South Africa's Occupation Regime* (1975), at p. 3, cited in *Namibia: The Legal Framework and Development Strategy Options* (above, n. 1), n. 45 at p. 47.

[40] Moreover, there is a common law presumption against the retrospective operation of a statute 'so as to impair an existing right or obligation, otherwise than as regards matters of procedure, unless that effect cannot be avoided without doing violence to the language of the enactment': *per* Wright J in *Re Athlumney*, [1898] 2 QB 547, 552.

[41] The situation varies. The drafters of the Decree would give it indefinite retrospective application. The US Government would not protect US investors against claims by a future lawful Namibian Government where their investments were made after 1966; the Netherlands would only forego protection where its nationals invested after 1974 (below n. 66); the British, French and West German Governments do not recognize the legislative capacity of the Council and would therefore presumably espouse investments by their nationals before and after enactment of the Decree.

them for the benefit of the people of Namibia'.[42] This provision is permissive only, and suggests recognition of the practical limits to the Council's ability to enforce the Decree. Are the powers of seizure and forfeiture within the ambit of the Council's powers? Moreover, as we have seen, the idea of 'holding in trust' is suggestive of trust law. If so, has the Council, as fiduciary, acted diligently and met the applicable legal 'prudent man' standard? What, for instance, is the effect of the Council's apparent inactivity over a prolonged period?

In response, it can be said that any inactivity on the part of the Council has been more apparent than real. Since it became operational, the Council has pursued a number of activities involving the protection of Namibia's interests. It has publicized the Decree, arranged studies of the conditions in the territory, organized symposia, initiated suit, and constantly helped initiate UN resolutions on Namibia. It is nevertheless also true that, through no fault of its own, it was unable to administer the territory. However, this inability to administer the territory did not extinguish the Council's rights to administer the territory until independence.

The idea of forfeiture is not new in the law. It was not unknown to the English common law. Recent legislation in the United States also provides for the forfeiture of goods used or acquired by the defendant in drug related offences. So long as the Council for Namibia was the validly constituted administering authority of Namibia, the forfeiture provisions in themselves would present no immediate legal problem.

The Decree permits 'the future Government of an independent Namibia' to hold anyone who violates the Decree liable in damages.[43] Arguably, this could be interpreted to mean that the Decree lacked any provision for compensation or damages, except by way of litigation by the Government of an independent Namibia. However, under the doctrine of 'implied powers', the Council, as the internationally recognized, legal, administering authority for Namibia, could be held to be legally competent and to have standing to sue for compensation or damages on behalf of the Namibian people. The relevant provisions in the Decree need not in practice exclude recovery

---

[42] Para. 4: text at p. 251, above.

[43] Operative para. 6 of the Decree provides that 'Any person, entity or corporation which contravenes the present decree in respect of Namibia may be held liable in damages by the future Government of an independent Namibia'. This provision is permissive only and should be read to mean that the Government of an independent Namibia will take steps to have the matter adjudicated. But under whose courts? Under the Charter of Economic Rights and Duties of States this could be the courts of an independent Namibia. Art. 1 of the CERDS reaffirms the right of States to exercise sovereignty over their natural resources. Art. 2 declares that 'Each State is entitled to regulate foreign investment in accordance with its laws and regulations and in conformity with its national objectives and priorities'. Art. 2D further declares that each State has the right to nationalize or requisition foreign property for a public purpose, provided that just compensation in the light of all relevant circumstances shall be paid. Under CERDS, where controversies arise over compensation, they should be settled under the domestic laws of the nationalizing State and by its tribunals unless it is agreed otherwise.

TNCs and several Western States have opposed these provisions of CERDS and would naturally oppose any action by a new independent Namibian Government premised on them.

of compensation or damages except by a future government of an independent Namibia. The future government of an independent Namibia will
only be the recognized successor of the internationally recognized, legal
authority set up by the United Nations to administer Namibia, namely, the
Council for Namibia.[44] Presumably the new Namibian Government should
either join the *URENCO* case as plaintiff or at least file an amicus brief in
that case. Pursuit of the *URENCO* case would serve to maintain leverage in
negotiations with the MNCs and Western governments.

Perhaps a more pertinent criticism of the Decree concerns the failure of
the Council to declare an exclusive economic zone (EEZ) off Namibia. In
declaring an EEZ off Namibia, the Council would have established a legal
framework which could be used to control and tax offshore fishing in the
interests of the people of Namibia.[45] This would have rendered the Decree
more comprehensive and brought the legal regime into line with the growing tendency among LDCs to establish an EEZ with a view to protecting
their maritime rights, their fishing rights and various marine resources.[46]

Another major defect in Decree No. 1 is that it did not mention Walvis

---

[44] With regard to the *URENCO* case, a domestic law model solution could possibly be found in the
notion of fluid class recovery. A revolving fund could easily be set up and held in trust for the benefit of
the inhabitants of Namibia. Cf. *Morton Eisen* v. *Carlisle & Jacquelin, et al.*, 417 US 156 (1974), where
the District Court suggested that 'fluid class recovery would have allowed damages to be distributed to
future odd-lot traders rather than to specific class members actually injured'. The Court suggested that
a fund equivalent to the amount of the unclaimed damages might be established and the odd-lot differ-
ential reduced in an amount determined reasonable by the Court until such time as the fund was
depleted. Shareholders in American Metal Climax, Inc. and Newmont Mining Corporation which
operate the Tsumeb mines in Namibia have submitted resolutions to the annual meeting of shareholders
calling upon the companies to recognize and deal with the UN and put into escrow the profits from their
operations in Namibia against the day when they deal with the Government of an independent Namibia: United Nations, *Namibia Bulletin*, Special Issue, vol. 11, no. 6 (June 1988), at p. 5. It follows
that a shareholder in corporations including the above as well as Rio Tinto Zinc could possibly have
been used to bring suit before the US and UK courts.

[45] Namibia's fishing industry has enormous potential, but observers believe that it has been seriously
damaged by overfishing by South African cartels and fleets of international trawlers. According to Curtin Knight, loc. cit. above (n. 6), at p. 227, South African authorities have not restrined the companies
from depleting the pelagic fish stocks (pilchard and anchovy) and 'fleets of foreign trawlers have fished
with impunity in national waters because the government in Windhoek, regarded as illegal by the UN,
could not declare an internationally recognized Exclusive Economic Zone'.

[46] On 10 December 1982 the Council for Namibia, as the legal Administering Authority signed the
United Nations Convention on the Law of the Sea adopted by the Third United Nations Conference on
the Law of the Sea on 30 April 1982. Among other things, the Law of the Sea Convention established a
200-mile exclusive economic zone in which the coastal State would have control over all natural
resources. The Council's signature of the Convention may have been an attempt to remedy the original
omission in the Decree. However, the Council arguably still did not go far enough to protect a dependent Namibia, e.g. in the event of oil spills and environmental damage. Cf. *Namibia: Perspectives for
National Reconstruction and Development* (above, n. 1), pp. 213–15, 951–2. For our immediate purposes, accession to the UNCLOS Convention is more important as recognition of the Council's treaty-
making power and elements of its legal personality. UN practice supports this conclusion as evidenced
by the Council's accession to the Geneva Conventions of 12 August 1949, and signature of the Final Act
of the United Nations Conference on Succession of States in respect of State Property, Archives and
Debts: GA Res. 38/36C, *Compendium*, at p. 105. Whereas most of the Western States abstained on this
resolution, the Netherlands voted in favour of adoption.

Bay.[47] This omission is all the more striking since the General Assembly has reiterated over repeated South African objections that:

Walvis Bay is an integral part of Namibia and condemned South Africa in the strongest possible terms for its decision to annex Walvis bay, thus violating the principle of the territorial integrity of Namibia . . . [and] reiterated that this decision is illegal, null and void and an act of aggression against the Namibian people. The existence of South African military bases in Walvis Bay is a threat to the national security of Namibia. The illegal annexation of Walvis Bay, the main port and vital economic avenue of Namibia is a deliberate attempt to undermine the territorial integrity, economic independence and national security of Namibia.[48]

On the principle that whatever is not expressly mentioned is excluded, the Decree does not cover Walvis Bay and the resources situated therein. From this view, the resources situated within Walvis Bay could be lawfully exploited by South Africa or any TNC with South Africa's permission. Proponents of this view will claim that their argument is strengthened by the fact that none of the recent agreements mentions Walvis Bay. This point will assume increased importance at a future date in view of Walvis Bay's economic and strategic importance as a harbour[49] and its fisheries, and given that sedimentary deposits have also suggested the presence of oil off the Bay.[50]

(b) *Violations of the Decree and the Council's Decision to Litigate*

The purpose of the Decree was to permit the Council to use foreign domestic courts, in countries which recognize the Council's authority over

---

[47] South Africa's occupation of Walvis Bay would allow South Africa to dictate Namibia's external trade. It would also pose a military threat to the exercise of self-determination by the Namibian people and an independent Namibian Government. For background, see Moorsom, *Walvis Bay: Namibia's Port* (1984), at pp. 59, 63; also *Objective: Justice—Walvis Bay: An Integral Part of Namibia*, UN Office of Public Information, Special Supplement No. 2 (June 1978), UN Doc. DPI/617–85–40778–June 1985–10M; and see n. 21, above.

[48] Declaration on Namibia and Programme of Action in Support of Self-Determination and National Independence for Namibia, S-9/2, adopted by the General Assembly 3 May 1978: *Compendium*, at pp. 36–40.

[49] Walvis Bay was seized by Britain in 1878 to counter Bismarck's colonial ambitions. When Germany took over South West Africa, the Governor of the then British ruled Cape Colony annexed Walvis Bay. Its strategic significance can be gauged from the fact that in September 1977, one year after adoption of Res. 385, Pretoria claimed full control over the enclave. In 1985 South Africa conducted 'Operation Riksha' off Walvis Bay. In August 1988 South Africa also conducted 'Operation Magersfontein' off Walvis Bay. South Africa has maintained a strong military presence in Walvis Bay, and the South African air force uses the nearby airport. The Southern African Development Coordination Conference (SADCC), which aims to lessen the economic dependence of member States on South Africa, today relies on South African ports, the Mozambican ports of Maputo, Beira and Nacala, and Benguela and Luanda in Angola, which are at the mercy of the South African-backed MNR and UNITA. Control of Walvis Bay is therefore of the utmost importance in this context.

South Africa's 'historical claim' to Walvis Bay has always threatened to wreck the settlement negotiations. It has now apparently been easier to leave the issue in abeyance until after Namibia's independence.

[50] *Namibia: The Legal Framework and Development Strategy Options* (above, n. 1), at p. 12.

Namibia, to recover natural resources exported from South West Africa, there being precedents for such action in the case of unlawfully expropriated property belonging to aliens.[51]

There are three main reasons why the Decree was never implemented by the Western States and their corporations. First, those governments, corporations and individuals which did not comply with the Decree continued to realize substantial profits from an illicit trade under South African auspices. Secondly, their domestic law did not require them to comply with the Decree. Thirdly, the parties who continued to invest in Namibia probably believed that the Council for Namibia had no power to bring charges against those violating the Decree.

In January 1984, a Mission of the Council of Namibia visited France, Germany and the UK to consult with non-governmental organizations (NGOs) and solicit the opinions of jurists in these countries concerning effective implementation of Decree No. 1, notably on the possibility of bringing suit before domestic courts. The Mission concluded that Decree No. 1 only had executive force in the Netherlands, where such actions stood the best chance of success since the Government of the Netherlands had accorded full recognition to both the Decree and the competence of the Council to enact it.[52] The Mission had rather limited success, and the General Assembly by Resolution 39/72 subsequently asked the Federal Republic of Germany, Holland and the United Kingdom expressly to exclude uranium from the Treaty of Almelo which regulates URENCO activities.[53]

A subsequent UN symposium on international efforts to implement Decree No. 1, held in Geneva from 27 to 31 August 1984, again condemned the operation of Western-based corporations and concerns in Namibia, under the illegal South African administration in violation of the Decree, particularly the increased involvement of UK-based corporations, such as Rio Tinto Zinc Corporation and Consolidated Gold Fields Ltd.[54] After rejecting the tendency in some political circles to view the problem as part of a regional political problem, thereby 'ignoring the illegality under international law of South Africa's illegal occupation of Namibia', the symposium recommended, *inter alia*, that the Commissioner for Namibia 'take a decision to institute legal proceedings in the Netherlands to prepare

---

[51] See Dugard, *Annual Survey of South African Law*, 1974, at p. 55, citing *Anglo-Iranian Oil Co. v. Jaffrate (The Rose Mary)*, [1957] 1 WLR 246, and Lauterpacht, 'Implementation of Decisions of International Organizations through National Courts', in Schwebel (ed.), *The Effectiveness of International Decisions* (1971), pp. 57, 63–5.

[52] *Report of the Mission to Western Europe to Seek Legal Advice on the Implementation of the Decree No. 1 for the Protection of the Natural Resources of Namibia* (above, n. 31), para. 127.

[53] See Tavernier, *Annuaire français de droit international*, 30 (1984), p. 567 at pp. 587–8.

[54] UN Council for Namibia, *Conclusions and Recommendations of the Participants in the Regional Symposium on International Efforts to Implement Decree No. 1. for the Protection of the Natural Resources of Namibia, held at Geneva, from August 27—31, 1984*, UN Doc. A/AC.131/148 (19 September 1984). The *Report of the Delegation of the Council to the Symposium* (above, n. 31), at p. 4, also cites the Western States and Israel as the prime violators of the Decree.

appropriate briefs in order to commence legal proceedings in the courts of the Netherlands to implement the Decree at the earliest opportunity'. Similar legal action was urged in other countries known to be involved in mining or transporting, processing or receiving Namibian minerals, particular attention being given to Belgian companies, since Belgium was a member of the Council. Many of the other recommendations concerned the formalities of legal notice to possible future defendants or other parties (possibly) as intervenors in any foreseeable litigation.[55]

The UK and the USA are the developed countries most involved in trade with Namibia. In the UK, the Thatcher Government steadfastly opposed the imposition of sanctions against South Africa. Any action along the lines contemplated by the Council would moreover be unlikely to prevail in the UK courts. France appeared supportive of the Council's endeavours. Belgium was non-committal, claiming to be only a port of transit. In addition, it was felt that there was little chance of success before the European Court. The member States, when questioned on the subject, normally replied that uranium is the property of EURATOM under the EURATOM Treaty. The question of title is not addressed. The Council's position is that the parties are knowingly importing Namibian uranium which is then supplied to customers. This is tantamount to theft under the Decree and so the defendants must answer. When the question of uranium is raised in the European Parliament, there is no response—almost a conspiracy of silence, as though the question did not exist.

The US Anti-Apartheid Act of 1986 banned importation of Namibian uranium into the United States. The Council for Namibia possibly believed that no useful purpose would be served by bringing suit before the US or Canadian courts, not only because of domestic legal obstacles,[56] but also because of the recent policy initiatives by the US and Canada, and their role as members of the Western contact group. But as observed in a United Nations Report:

Despite the new sanctions bill by the United States Congress which provides for tightening South African mineral imports to the United States, the import of Namibian or South African uranium converted to hexafluoride is still allowed . . .

The Canadian connection with South African uranium resources is substantial . . . The Canadian–South African uranium collaboration has not been limited to the private sector. In 1972, Canada was part of a secret uranium cartel with the Governments and uranium producers of France, Australia and South Africa. Documentary evidence indicates that RTZ played a strong role in initiating the cartel for the purpose of protecting its investments in Rossing . . .

Even though Canada does not recognize the legality of the occupation regime of

---

[55] Ibid. The point is of continuing relevance as regards whether the new Namibian Government will join with the Council as plaintiff, or pursue the *URENCO* case, if the Council is disbanded by order of the General Assembly.

[56] On this subject, see Shockey, 'Enforcement in United States Courts of the United Nations Council for Namibia's Decree on Natural Resources', *Yale Studies in World Public Order*, 2 (1976), p. 285.

South Africa in Namibia, the Canadian Government, equally, does not recognize the authority of the United Nations Council for Namibia or its Decree No. 1.[57]

It is thus distinctly possible that the Council believed that just as there was little or no hope of success in the courts of the UK, the FRG or the EEC Court, so too with the Canadian and US courts. That the legal status of the Decree varies from legal order to legal order, and from country to country, presented a serious obstacle to mounting a relatively unified and consistent challenge to what the United Nations considers an illegal trade in Namibia's resources.

As a matter of legal strategy, the Council selected the court in the Netherlands because it was thought to offer the best chance of success. First, the Netherlands Government accepted public international law as part of the law of the Netherlands. Secondly, the Netherlands, in contrast to the Federal Republic of Germany and the United Kingdom, recognized the legislative power of the Council.

As indicated above, shareholders in corporations investing in Namibia could have been used to raise the matter in US and UK domestic courts.[58] With hindsight, two other avenues might also have been fruitfully pursued. First, the Council could have sought an advisory opinion from the ICJ as to the legal status of Decree No. 1 before it began suit in the *URENCO* case. A favourable ruling by the ICJ would have had a persuasive effect on any subsequent negotiations and on any litigation involving Namibia's resources. Whether the Decree's critics would have construed such a request as reflecting the Council's doubts as to the legality of the Decree is not unimportant from the standpoint of legal strategy. Secondly, at the international political level, the Council could have urged friendly States at the Commonwealth Heads of Government Conference, the Conference of Heads of State or Government of Non-Aligned Countries, and at the UN actively to consider enactment of Decree No. 1 or legislation based on the Decree into their national legislation.[59]

(c) *South Africa and the Trade in Namibia's Resources: the* URENCO *case*

Although the *URENCO* case concerns a single commodity—uranium— any decision in that case would set a precedent for litigation in connection

---

[57] United Nations, 'Developments with Regard to Implementation of Decree No. 1: The *URENCO* Case', *Namibia Bulletin*, Special Issue, vol. 11, no. 6 (June 1988), at p. 14.

[58] See above, n. 44.

[59] The Declaration on Namibia adopted at the Seventh Conference of Heads of State or Government of Non-Aligned Countries, New Delhi, March 1983, para. 42, called on 'all countries, transnational corporations and other organizations exploring and exploiting the resources, including marine resources in the territorial waters of Namibia . . . to comply with the relevant UN resolutions and the relevant paragraphs of the Algiers Declaration adopted in 1981 in consonance with Decree No. 1 . . . and terminate their activities on the territory of Namibia, including Walvis Bay, Penguin and other adjacent off shore islands forthwith': *Compendium*, at p. 198.

with other resources exploited in Namibia.[60] The Council's argument is that South Africa's exploitation of Namibia is unlawful since it violates norms enunciated in:

(i) the League of Nations documents 21/31/14D of 17 December 1920, which contained the conditions of the mandate issued by the League and accepted by the Union of South Africa, according to which the mandatory, *inter alia*, was to promote to the utmost the well-being of the people of Namibia and to refrain from establishing military bases in Namibia, which obligations, according to the ICJ advisory opinion of 11 July 1950,[61] continued to apply notwithstanding the dissolution of the League of Nations;

(ii) the UN Charter incorporating the principle of self-determination of peoples which subsequently developed into and was recognized as the right to self-determination as demonstrated and confirmed by, *inter alia*, the Declaration on the Granting of Independence to Colonial Countries and Peoples, contained in General Assembly Resolution No. 1514 (XV) of 14 December 1960, the International Covenant on Civil and Political Rights and the International Covenant on Economic, Social and Cultural Rights, both adopted by the General Assembly in 1966, and the advisory opinion of the International Court of Justice of 16 October 1975 concerning *Western Sahara*;[62]

(iii) the Declaration on Permanent Sovereignty over Natural Resources, contained in General Assembly Resolution No. 1803 (XVIII) of 14 December 1962, incorporating the right of people to permanent sovereignty over their natural resources;

(iv) General Assembly Resolution No. 2145 (XXI) whereby the mandate was terminated on account of its violation by the mandatory, as well as subsequent resolutions of the General Assembly, according to which the exercise of power and the exploitation of Namibia should cease immediately and all States, as well as enterprises under their control, should refrain from any dealings with respect to the exploitation of Namibia;

(v) Resolution No. 283 of 29 July 1970, as well as other resolutions of the United Nations Security Council, according to which the Republic of South Africa must terminate its exercise of power in and over Namibia and all States and enterprises controlled by them should refrain from any dealings with respect to commercial or industrial enterprises or concessions in Namibia, as well as from any support of enterprises not controlled by them which could contribute to the exercise of power by South Africa and Namibia's exploitation;

---

[60] For example, diamonds, lead and zinc.
[61] *ICJ Reports*, 1950, p. 128.
[62] *ICJ Reports*, 1975, p. 12.

(vi) the advisory opinion of the International Court of Justice of 21 June 1971[63] according to which the Republic of South Africa should withdraw from Namibia immediately and States members of the United Nations should refrain from any acts tending to support the exercise of power by South Africa; and

(vii) Decree No. 1 of 27 September 1974, enacted by the Council for Namibia in accordance with its purpose, power, and task.[64]

The *URENCO* plaintiffs have alleged that uranium ore is mined from the Rossing mine in Namibia and ultimately used for the production of electricity.[65] By carrying out orders placed on the basis of purchases of Namibian uranium-concentrate, the conversion, enrichment and fuel element fabrication plants have substantially contributed towards the exploitation of Namibian uranium, profited thereby and furthered Namibia's exploitation.

The defendants allegedly engaged in the business of enriching uranium, carrying out, *inter alia*, orders placed on the basis of Namibian uranium-concentrate.[66] The defendants, including the State,[67] have argued that although it is to be assumed that at least part of the uranium-hexafluoride supplied to Urenco Nederland is of Namibian origin, they, the defendants,

---

[63] *ICJ Reports*, 1971, p. 16.

[64] The manner in which Namibian uranium is exploited, without the consent or permission of the Namibian people or the Council for Namibia, and the processing and purification uranium undergoes prior to use in a nuclear reactor, are discussed in the writ of summons submitted by the Council for Namibia to the District Court in the Netherlands: 'The URENCO Case', loc. cit. above (n. 9), at pp. 7–8.

[65] 'South Africa has also used the uranium resources under its control to evolve and implement a strategy for its survival through the development of a nuclear weapons programme deriving from the delivery systems supplied by France, the Federal Republic of Germany and other western countries with a view to guaranteeing the continuation of white minority rule and the maintenance of the political and economic status quo in the region': United Nations, loc. cit. above (n. 57), at p. 9.

[66] Urenco Nederland, Urenco (UK) and Urenco Deutschland oGH, and their respective managing partners (Ultra-Centrifuge Nederland NV, British Nuclear Fuels plc and Uranit GmbH), are engaged in the business of enriching uranium, and belong to the Urenco Group, which was formed after the conclusion of the Treaty of Almelo between the Federal Republic of Germany, the Netherlands and the United Kingdom: *Treaty Gazette*, 1970, at p. 41.

[67] The Netherlands position is that it is practically impossible to determine the source of uranium, and the Netherlands is bound to process uranium sent to it under the Treaty of Almelo. The Council for Namibia has responded to this argument by invoking Arts. 25 and 103 of the UN Charter. Art. 25 provides that 'The Members of the United Nations agree to accept and carry out the decisions of the Security Council in accordance with the present Charter'. Art. 103 provides that 'In the event of a conflict between the obligations of the Members of the United Nations under the present Charter and their obligations under any other international agreement their obligations under the present Charter shall prevail'. See United Nations, loc. cit. above (n. 57), at p. 22, and United Nations Council for Namibia, *Implementation of Decree No. 1 for the Protection of the Natural Resources of Namibia: Study on the Possibility of Instituting Legal Proceedings in the Domestic Courts of States—Report of the United Nations Commissioner for Namibia*, UN Doc. A/AC.131/194 (23 October 1985), at p. 30.

The State, according to the plaintiffs, (a) is represented on the Joint Committee established by the Treaty of Almelo, (b) is the majority shareholder in UCN, and through the rights it has pursuant to the Treaty of Almelo, as well as through the special rights granted to it in the Articles of Association of UCN and the powers of UCN with respect to URENCO Nederland, is able to influence decisively URENCO Nederland and UCN in order to prevent URENCO Nederland from acts in contravention of the ban on the importation of uranium from Namibia.

are not to blame therefor because Urenco Nederland cannot ascertain when and to what extent this is the case.[68]

The Council attempts to rebut this by arguing that this assertion cannot exculpate the defendants, not only because Urenco Nederland can demand the assurance that no Namibian uranium-concentrate has been used in the production of the uranium-hexafluoride supplied to it, but also because by carrying out orders placed on the basis of purchases of Namibian uranium-concentrate, the enrichment plant has made an indispensable contribution towards exploitation of Namibian uranium, has profited thereby and has furthered Namibia's exploitation regardless of when and to what extent Namibian concentrate has been used in the production of the uranium-hexafluoride supplied to the plant. The suit thus seeks to compel the defendants to refrain from carrying out any order of enriched uranium placed wholly or partly on the basis of a purchase of Namibian uranium.

In response, the Dutch Government argues that the Council's claims cannot be accepted. First, the Dutch Government argues that in principle the organs of legal entities are not empowered to act as a party to civil proceedings. The United Nations as an international organization is not a party to the proceedings. The Council, an organ of that body, is the plaintiff. Moreover, the Council intends to act independently as a party to these proceedings, and not on behalf of the United Nations. The Council, it is therefore contended, lacks independent legal personality and cannot sue in the absence of specific enabling legal provision.[69] The mere fact that the organ concerned is a governmental organ with the freedom to determine its own policies is insufficient grounds for making an exception in this case.[70]

The Dutch Government maintains that according to Dutch international private law, the question whether an organization has legal personality in principle has to be judged according to the law of the country under which the organization concerned has been constituted (the so-called incorpor-

---

[68] It is not clear why this is not mere dissembling on the part of the defendant Dutch Government. Neither the Government of the Netherlands nor URENCO denies the fact that Namibian uranium is being enriched in the Netherlands. Uranium suppliers and their clients swap uranium from one source for uranium from other sources either to disguise the identity of the uranium being shipped or to change the identity completely. Namibian uranium converted to hexafluoride in France, Canada, the USA and the UK assumes the nationality of the country of its conversion. On the other hand, uranium produced in the USA, Canada or Australia retains its original identity throughout the nuclear fuel cycle as a safeguard against diversion by third countries. In the industry this is known as 'flagging' or 'origin accounting': United Nations, loc. cit. above (n. 57), at p. 9. Documents of specific origin could similarly be required for uranium imported into the Netherlands. The EEC Rules for the Establishment of Certificates of Origin 'are left to the discretion of national authorities': *Official Journal of the European Communities*, No. L 166/12 (7 April 77), Appendix, p. 111.

[69] The Netherlands, as did the United States and the United Kingdom, abstained on GA Res. 2248 (S-V) establishing the Council. Arguably, the decision of these States not to vote against the resolution obliges them not to work to frustrate the objectives of the Council.

[70] The State further refers to a case involving the courts 'which are independent by definition: Court of Appeal Amsterdam, January 22, 1987 . . . . In this decision a claim against an investigating judge was deemed unreceivable because *inter alia* a judge cannot appear in court in such capacity.' It is not clear that this decision is authority for anything other than the well-established principle of judicial immunity of judges.

ation system). The plaintiff in its writ of summons does not clarify why it is of the opinion that it has legal personality or personal *locus standi in judicio*. The mere assertion that the Council has been constituted and exists according to the law of the United Nations is insufficient for that purpose. The Dutch Government argues that neither the resolution by which the Council was constituted, nor its functions or objectives, justify the recognition of a legal personality for conducting legal proceedings such as the present ones.

It is tempting to dismiss this as sheer nonsense. Whatever the position under Dutch international private law, it would be a curious government which was not intended to and which did not have legal personality. Indeed, according to the Dutch Permanent Representative to the United Nations:

> . . . in those cases where the UN itself functions as the administering authority of a trust territory, it is the General Assembly which possesses the legal powers necessary for the exercise of the administration. Such administrative powers with regard to a specific territory are of an entirely different character than the general powers of the Assembly concerning questions dealt with by the UN. They are, therefore, by no means limited to the making of recommendations provided for in Article 10 of the Charter.
>
> In respect of Namibia, the General Assembly has delegated the exercise of those executive powers to the Council for Namibia. In its resolution 2248 (S-V) the General Assembly has entrusted to the Council the powers and functions to administer the territory and, among other things, to promulgate such laws, decrees and administrative regulations as are necessary for the administration of the territory. My government holds the opinion that the General Assembly was legally fully competent to do so.
>
> . . . In the Netherlands' view, the Council was legally entitled indeed to decree that the exploitation etc. of the natural resources in Namibia would henceforward require the consent and permission of the UN Council for Namibia . . . In the opinion of my government, the Council has the right and duty to represent Namibia in international forums . . . [71]

The Council, in pursuing alleged violations of the Decree before the Dutch courts, has acted in accordance with the legislative mandate entrusted to it by the General Assembly, rendering formal approval by the General Assembly unnecessary.

The legal personality of the Council, i.e. its rights, duties, powers and obligations, is conferred on it by the system under which it operates, the UN system. Its legal personality is evident in its remedial rights as well as its duties towards the ultimate beneficiaries in this case, the Namibian people. It is submitted that the Dutch Government's clear recognition of

---

[71] Statement by J.H. Burgers, Representative of the Netherlands to the United Nations, in the Fourth Committee of the General Assembly, 21 October 1975: Press Release issued by the Netherlands Mission to the UN, summarized in UN Doc. A/C.4/SR.2151, at pp. 15–16.

the Council's powers to administer the territory, of its powers 'to promulgate laws and administrative regulations', of its 'right and duty to represent Namibia in international forums', as well as its recognition of the fact that the Council was legally entitled to decree that the exploitation of Namibia's resources was unlawful, except with consent of the Council or the Namibian people, is incompatible with the claim now urged by the Dutch Government that the Council lacks legal personality in respect of defending Namibia's interests.

The second argument urged by the Dutch Government is that in the decisions of the Council and the General Assembly there is no mention of proceedings against a sovereign State or the State of the Netherlands, but of proceedings against 'corporations or individuals'. Paragraph 65 of resolution 40/97A of the General Assembly of 13 December 1985 *inter alia* approves a decision of the Council for Namibia of 2 May 1985: 'to initiate legal proceedings in the domestic courts of States against corporations or individuals involved in the exploitation . . . '. Paragraph 68 of resolution 41/93A of the General Assembly of 20 November 1986, *inter alia*, approves: 'the continued efforts of the UN Council for Namibia to initiate legal proceedings in the domestic courts of States against corporations or individuals involved in the exploitation . . . '. The Dutch Government maintains that the terms 'corporations or individuals' do not include sovereign States. But the term 'corporation' is not necessarily limited to private corporations. The term 'corporations' also includes 'public service corporations' and corporations 'affected with a public interest'.

The language in Decree No. 1 also logically encompasses State entities. For instance, by paragraph 1, 'No *person or entity, whether a body corporate or unincorporated*, may search for, prospect for, explore for, take, extract, mine, process, refine, use, sell, export, or distribute any natural resource . . . found to be situated within the territorial limits of Namibia'. Paragraph 3 forbids the removal of any resource from Namibia 'by any *person or body, whether corporate or unincorporated*', without the consent of the Council. Paragraph 6 states that 'Any *person, entity or corporation* which contravenes the Decree . . . may be held liable in damages . . . '. 'Persons' here are legal persons; 'entities' necessarily include the State and State entities. Nothing in the language of the Decree prevents suit against the Dutch Government or against any other government.

Nor is there anything, explicit or implicit, in other resolutions, supported by the Government of the Netherlands, that could prevent the plaintiff from bringing suit against the Dutch Government or any other government. For instance, Resolution 37/233C, paragraph 14 (*j*), decided that the Council should 'Take *all* measures to ensure compliance with the provisions of Decree No. 1 . . . including consideration of the institution of legal proceedings in the domestic courts of States and other appropriate bodies'. Resolution 38/36C, paragraph 15 (*j*), repeated this obligation verbatim. On both occasions the Dutch Government voted *in favour of* the particular resolutions. It could either have abstained or explained its vote as not contemplating suit against a sovereign State.[72]

Barring claims of sovereign immunity, it is difficult to see why the Council is not authorized to sue any government involved in the illegal exploitation of Namibia's uranium, if it is authorized to sue corporations or individuals involved in the same illegal activity, the illegal importation, trade and use of Namibia's uranium. If the State recognizes legal personality for the purposes of suing 'corporations or individuals', as does the Dutch Government in this case, surely it cannot deny legal personality for the purposes of suing the State? One either has legal personality, or one does not. If the Government's defence is one of sovereign immunity, this should be specified.

Recent international public policy has seen the imposition of selected sanctions against South Africa, and some discussion about lifting such sanctions in view of recent reforms in South Africa. The Comprehensive Anti-Apartheid Act of 1986[73] has as its major features a ban on US imports of South African steel, iron, uranium, coal, textiles and agricultural products, a prohibition of new corporate investment in South Africa and new loans to South African government agencies, a prohibition on US banks' acceptance of deposits from South African government agencies, and a revocation of landing rights in the United States for South African Airways.[74] The EEC banned, among other things, imports of iron, steel and gold coins from South Africa and prohibited new investment.[75] The Commonwealth Heads of Government, for their part, agreed to adopt certain measures and commend them to the rest of the international community for urgent adoption and implementation.[76] The major feature of the Commonwealth plan was a ban on the imports of iron, steel, uranium, coal and agricultural products from South Africa, a ban on new investment in, promotion of tourism to, and air links with South Africa, termination of all government assistance to, investment in, and trade with South Africa, and withdrawal of most consular facilities there and a ban on all new bank loans to South Africa. But the UK did not subscribe to these measures, agreeing

[72] There are any number of reasons for abstaining on UN resolutions. Lowenstein (*Brutal Mandate*, at p. 150) was on one occasion advised by the US representative on the 4th Committee that 'The US had to abstain' on a 4th Committee vote on South West Africa, 'to avoid jeopardizing visas for Americans who might wish to go to South Africa'. Mere abstention is not therefore converted into automatic opposition. The will of the international community, as reflected in a body of General Assembly resolutions is not defeated by mere abstention, especially where the State's pattern of voting in opposition or abstention is neither consistent nor clear.

[73] Pub. L. No. 99–440, 100 Stat. 1086 (1986).

[74] It has however been suggested that the decline of the US uranium industry , which was declared non-viable for three years in a row (1984, 1985 and 1986), led to importation of Namibian/South African uranium for domestic utilities from 1977: United Nations, loc. cit. above (n. 57), at p. 13. See also 'The URENCO Case', Statement of Defence of the State of the Netherlands submitted 3 May 1988, para. 11.3 at pp. 18–19.

[75] *New York Times*, 21 September 1986, at p. A1, col. 4. Note, however, that the Federal Republic of Germany blocked the ban on coal.

[76] Ibid., 6 August 1986, at p. A10, col. 2.

only to a voluntary ban on new investment in, and promotion of tourism to, South Africa and to the European community sanctions described above.

The significance of the *URENCO* case lies in the fact that the prospect of a finding of liability, let alone a finding itself, would have increased the risks of investing in Namibia under South African sponsorship. This heightened risk would have served to deter investors likely to be induced by high profits derived for a Namibia under South Africa's occupation.

The *URENCO* case has not been decided at the time of writing.[76a] An earlier decision, if a victory for the Council, would not necessarily have meant a defeat for the Netherlands and the various Western multinational corporations. It could have put future dealings with Namibia on a more stable and certain legal footing. On the other hand, a loss for the Council could have meant continued exploitation and depletion of Namibia's resources without legal redress; international outrage, and for a time frosty relations between African, Third World States and the Dutch Government; a new move in the ICJ by the General Assembly majority; and possibly some damage to the prestige of the UN in the aftermath of the Nobel Peace Prize awarded to it for its role in ending the Iran–Iraq War.

Namibia's accession to independence did not automatically render the *URENCO* case moot. The claims urged by the Council were still viable, whether urged by the Council itself or by the Namibian Government. The Council's mandate may or may not be extended by the UN General Assembly at some future session.[76a] However, from the Council's perspective, and that of the new government, logically, it would seem premature to abandon the case. Indeed, either party, depending on future circumstances, might be expected to pursue the case if only because this would enable the new government to retain some leverage in its negotiations with Western governments and multinationals.[77]

V. Recent Developments

(a) *The Agreement between Cuba, Angola and South Africa concerning Namibia's Independence (the Tripartite Agreement)*[78] *and Namibia's Independence*

As we have seen, Namibia's recent accession to independence is not necessarily the postscript for the UN Decree and the Council for Namibia. Like the Camp David Accords between Israel and Egypt which resulted only in a partial settlement to the Arab-Israeli dispute,[79] the Namibian Agreements presage at best an uneasy peace. That they have worked so far

---

[76a] But see n. 94, below.
[77] Cf. n. 12, above.
[78] UN Doc. 1/43/989, S/20346 (22 December 1988).
[79] The Camp David Accords essentially left unresolved the wider Arab-Israeli problem, the issue of reconciliation between the Arabs and Jews.

is more a tribute to human ingenuity than to agreements so loosely drafted as to be virtually useless.

The Tripartite Agreement deals mainly with the politico-military dimension of the Namibian question. There is no immediate link between the Decree and the recent agreements. The Tripartite Agreement, however, has some limited economic relevance. The Agreement's reaffirmation of 'the right of the peoples of the southwestern region of Africa to self-determination, independence and equality of rights, and of the States of Southwestern Africa to peace, development and social progress' necessarily implies recognition of Namibia's right to permanent sovereignty over its resources in accordance with UNGA Resolution 1803 as well as a right to development compatible with the UN Charter.[80]

Although the Agreement requires that 'The parties shall respect the territorial integrity and inviolability of the borders of Namibia', Walvis Bay is not expressly included in the Agreement. It is to be the subject of negotiation afterwards. Whether this concession should have been made is debatable. The assumption is that the elected or 'independent' Government of Namibia can successfully negotiate the return of Walvis Bay. This appears contrary to UN practice whereby States have usually become independent with full national and territorial integrity, e.g. Guyana and Belize. Also, the OAU Charter and OAU resolutions call for respect for borders set at the time of independence. Independent Namibia will therefore be a truncated Namibia,[81] and any trade in the resources of Walvis Bay sanctioned by the South African authorities while the Bay remains under their control is illegal from the standpoint of public international law.

(b) *Foreign Trade, Foreign Private Investment and the Namibian Constitution*

At one extreme, the transfer of mineral rights from the German colonial authorities to the South African Government in 1919 offers a precedent for the transfer of mineral rights from South Africa to the Council for Namibia and then to the Government of independent Namibia. The German administration had been ousted by force in 1915. The change of power was only subsequently legitimized by the League of Nations mandate. South African legislation unilaterally transferred title to minerals in the territory, often

---

[80] Several UN resolutions condemn South Africa's policies in Namibia, (e.g. SC Res. 264 (1969) (condemnation of the bantustans policy); SC Res. 366 (1974) (racially discriminatory and repressive laws and practices); SC Res. 385 (1976), 435 (1978) and 439 (1978) (unilateral measures by South Africa in relation to the electoral process, including the unilateral registration of voters and the transfer of power)): *Compendium*, at pp. 5, 18, 19–21, 24, 26.

[81] As such, the position of the South West African Administrator General has been that 'no voting or registration of voters would be conducted in Walvis Bay which South Africa considers part of its territory'. Namibians in Walvis Bay would have to cross the Swakop river for registration and voting either at centres in Swakopmund or elsewhere inland. South Africa would not allow anyone 'on its territory' to conduct political campaigns. 'The elections . . . registration of voters and voting will have to be done within the borders of Namibia': *The Namibian*, 24 March 1989, at p. 9.

without discussion with those affected. Existing rights and concessions of the colonial companies were in most instances cancelled without compensation, although many had been dormant and expropriation did not involve actual loss of plant or equipment. In such circumstances, strict adherence to the equitable principle that 'he who comes to equity, must come with clean hands' could conceivably mean little or no compensation for some corporations investing in Namibia in disregard of the ICJ 1971 advisory opinion and UN resolutions.

At the level of public international law, such protection as international law would ordinarily afford an investor, expropriated by the host government, would not automatically extend to those investing in Namibia after termination of the mandate or contracting with the South African Government in disregard of Security Council resolutions and the ICJ advisory opinion.[82] The cumulative effect of such UN resolutions and the 1971 ICJ advisory opinion places the Government of newly independent Namibia in a strong legal position with respect to MNC trade in Namibia's resources. Western industrialized countries from which the MNCs originate have not normally endorsed this view. However, the United States has accepted the principle with respect to those companies and individuals investing after termination of the mandate.[83] But nothing portends exceptionalism for newly independent Namibia.[84] An ex-colony, rich in natural resources, confronting potentially divisive racial and ethnic diversity, politically sovereign, but territorially truncated, Namibia could well remain dependent on the erstwhile colonial powers, South Africa and the West.[85]

[82] The situation however is still not entirely clear. For example, 'France regards the resolutions of the Security Council in this regard as recommendatory only, and thereby not binding on member states': Weil in Lauterpacht and Collier (eds.), *Individual Rights and the State in Foreign Affairs: An International Compendium* (1977), p. 289.

[83] See the Davis Statement, *Department of State Bulletin*, 73 (1975), p. 270. The US also voted in favour of SC Res. 301 (1971) of 20 October 1971 which declared franchises, rights, titles or contracts relating to Namibia after the adoption of GA Res. 2145 (XXI) not subject to protection or espousal by their States against claims of a future lawful Government of Namibia.

[84] In elections in November 1989, 97 per cent of the registered electorate voted for the 72-member assembly which drafted the new constitution. SWAPO won 57 per cent of the November vote, thus failing to win the two-thirds majority which could have meant 'exclusive' authorship of the Constitution by SWAPO. See *UN Chronicle*, December 1989, pp. 4–10; *The Economist*, 11 November 1989, pp. 49–50, and 18 November 1989, pp. 46–7; also *American Spectator*, January 1990, p. 48.

[85] Most commentators agree on this point. Kapstein, 'Self-Rule in Namibia Won't Break South Africa's Stranglehold', *Business Week*, 2 October 1989, p. 56, argues that South Africa will maintain its stranglehold over Namibia by controlling vital trade links and most of the mining operations that dominate the country. Similarly, Curtin Knight, loc. cit. above (n. 6), at p. 240, suggests that 'As an independent country, Namibia will remain dependent on South Africa for transport, trade and, probably, currency transactions. A positive model for the future of Namibia might be Botswana, which enjoys political independence and economic advantages as a member of the South African Rand zone. A less positive model is Lesotho, which has economic advantages because of its relations with South Africa but has no political independence.' Sparks, 'Namibia: Prospects for the Economy at Independence' (unpublished paper, December 1989), p. 4, cautions that if the transition period does not go 'smoothly' (from South Africa's perspective) there would be: a marked exodus of key personnel in the mining and transportation sectors, a withdrawal of South African financial support, a massive capital flight (there are no restrictions on moving Rand back to South Africa), transportation bottlenecks centring around Walvis Bay and the railroads, withdrawal of credit by South African private interests, and a general breakdown

So far, the new Constitution provides only the most tentative and general framework for resolving questions of past and future trade and investment in Namibia's resources. Most of the pertinent provisions are set out in Chapter 11, 'Principles of State Policy', and conform with principles of traditional public international law. Article 96(*d*) provides that the new State will endeavour to ensure that it 'fosters respect for international law and treaty obligations'. This merely reiterates the principle *pacta sunt servanda*.[86] Article 98 provides for a mixed economy. Typically, the economy shall be based on following forms of ownership:

(a) public;
(b) private;
(c) joint public-private;
(d) cooperative;
(e) co-ownership; and
(f) small-scale family.

The cautiousness of the drafters of the new Constitution is further reflected in Article 99 which provides that

Foreign investment shall be encouraged within Namibia subject to the provisions of an Investment Code to be adopted by Parliament.

It is again reflected in Article 100 which explicitly provides for sovereign ownership by the State only where

Land, water and natural resources below and above the surface of the land and in the continental shelf and within the territorial waters and the exclusive economic zone of Namibia . . . are not otherwise lawfully owned.

Moreover, these provisions (Articles 95–100) are not legally binding,[87] and it remains to be seen how much deference will be shown to them by Namibian and other courts. Future legislation by Parliament is expected to fill gaps in existing law and policy. However, it is unlikely that there will be a radical departure from the constitutional norms articulated above.

Two other provisions appear relevant here: Article 140 and Article 144. First, Article 140(1) provides that

Subject to the provisions of this Constitution, all laws which were in force immediately before the date of independence shall remain in force until repealed by Act of Parliament or until they are declared unconstitutional by a competent Court.

of the economy's modern sector. Sparks labels the period during which SWAPO rejected all co-operation with South Africa the 'fantasy land period'. The period since 1988 he labels the 'real world period' because it shows some attempt by SWAPO to reach a negotiated overall settlement: at pp. 66–71. See also Sikorski, 'Africa's Next Basket Case?', *National Review*, 15 September 1989, pp. 21–7.

[86] Cf. Art. 26 of the Vienna Convention on the Law of Treaties, which provides that 'Every treaty in force is binding upon the parties to it and must be performed by them in good faith'.

[87] Art. 101 provides that 'The principles of state policy . . . shall not of and by themselves be legally enforceable by any Court, but shall nevertheless guide the Government in making and applying laws to give effect to the fundamental objectives of the said principles. The Courts are entitled to have regard to the said principles in interpreting any laws based on them.'

This provision in effect makes much South African sponsored legislation the law of Namibia. Secondly, Article 144 provides that

Unless otherwise provided by this Constitution or Act of Parliament, the general rules of public international law and international agreements binding upon Namibia under this Constitution shall form part of the law of Namibia.

Again, this provision appears complementary of Article 96(d) and argues for continuity in terms of the policies of the new Namibian Government relative to the majority of existing treaties and agreements.[88]

VI. CONCLUSION

Any new Third-World government, such as Namibia's, seeks economic growth, expansion of employment, integration of the sectors of the national economy, more equitable re-distribution of income, the abolition of colonial structures and attributes of the economy and, ultimately, economic independence. The challenge for the new Government in independent Namibia is how to correct distortions which are the legacy of South African occupation without destroying the national economy. Although much of the wealth generated in Namibia is repatriated in the form of corporate profits, it is unlikely that the new Government will undertake any outright nationalization in the immediate future.[89] The Government will continue to depend for some time on foreign technology, aid and expertise if it is to develop the national economy.[90] However, this does not rule out increasing governmental participation, comparable to other LDC experience.[91] In this scenario, if there is to be nationalization of Namibia's main resources and foreign exchange earners, 'creeping nationalization' appears more likely

---

[88] Cf. n. 38, above. This article is not concerned with the subject of *apartheid*. However, Namibia's constitution, insofar as it deals with some international law issues, such as *apartheid* in Art. 23, already reflects relevant international law conventions. International law is therefore *ab initio* part of Namibia's law, its precise scope yet to be determined. Cf. also Art. 140.

[89] The new Government considers the articulation of a legal framework laying down the investment, mining and petroleum code as one of its most urgent tasks. Mr Ya Toivo has indicated that the government would take steps to create 'a favorable climate for mineral development by reviewing and revising the relevant investment conditions through appropriate legislation covering the whole range of the modern system of mineral and petroleum management': *The Namibian*, 26 January 1990.

[90] The Oslo Declaration issued by the International Conference on the Independence of Namibia held from 21 to 22 November 1989 thus appealed to all governments to provide generous political, financial, technical and material assistance in order to help Namibia solve the urgent socio-economic injustices resulting from years of colonial domination, and reduce its dependency on South Africa: *The Namibian*, 24 November 1989, p. 5. Bilateral discussions on aid are already taking place. Cf. *The Economist*, 4 November 1989, pp. 16–19, which said in an editorial that countries giving foreign aid to a newly independent Namibia would be wise to attach strings so as to encourage democracy.

[91] The pronouncements by SWAPO representatives have been most cautious. 'The mineral development policy must be effected consistently with and within the context of the national development policy. Our point of departure and guiding principle is that the Namibian mineral resources are the common property and patrimony of all the Namibian people and must therefore be developed to benefit the broad majority of our people': SWAPO's Shadow Minister of Mines, Andima Ya Toivo, addressing the Namibian Chamber of Mines, *The Namibian*, 26 January 1990, p. 1.

than immediate outright nationalization. The new Namibian Government could allow TNCs to continue to operate in Namibia,[92] but pay increased taxes and royalties and require improved and increased training and managerial opportunities for Namibian workers, as well as improvement in their wage levels, health, living and working conditions.[93] It need not be emphasized that any government of a sovereign Namibia will need to balance the exigencies of foreign trade and investment against its concerns about conserving finite natural resources and resolving environmental problems incidental to the mining industry.[94]

[92] Dr Otto Herrigel, SWAPO's Shadow Finance Minister, said it was preferable to finance economic development through internal resources and foreign investment rather than through foreign aid and loans: *The Namibian*, 9 February 1990, p. 2.

[93] See *Namibia: The Legal Framework and Development Strategy Options* (above, n. 1), at pp. 52–3. Observers have criticized the health, safety and working conditions of black Namibians. J. Apter described the conditions of miners' families working for the Zinc and Lead Company Ltd. as worse than conditions at Robben Island, South Africa's notorious prison: 'Worse than Robben Island', *Progressive*, July 1989, at pp. 15–16. In another vein, *The Lancet*, 'Namibia: Health Care in a War Zone', 12 November 1988, at p. 1131, asserted that the 'stationing of the South African army in Namibia . . . had a detrimental impact on the health of the people and the provision of health care in that country'. See also Namibian Constitution, Art. 95.

[94] On 4 December 1990, after this article had gone to press, the *URENCO* case was withdrawn at the request of the solicitors for the UN Council for Namibia. No reasons were formally given, but it appears that the Namibian Government had instructed the Council to discontinue the case. The Council itself was dissolved at the 44th Session of the General Assembly.

RESTRICTIONS ON RIGHTS OF ACTION AND THE EUROPEAN CONVENTION ON HUMAN RIGHTS: THE CASE OF *POWELL AND RAYNER**

By FRANÇOISE J. HAMPSON‡

I. INTRODUCTION

Section 76(1) of the Civil Aviation Act 1982[1] provides that

No action shall lie in respect of trespass or in respect of nuisance, by reason only of the flight of an aircraft over any property at a height above the ground which, having regard to wind, weather and all the circumstances of the case is reasonable . . .

The section appears to preclude the bringing of an action in nuisance in the situation defined, where it would normally be available. This is not the only form which a restriction on a right of action may take. The European Commission of Human Rights has used different terminology in the cases to describe the effect of such a provision. It has sometimes spoken of an immunity granted to a class of defendants[2] or in relation to certain proceedings.[3] On other occasions it has spoken of an absolute defence.[4] These appear to raise the same issues as a bar to action imposed on the would-be plaintiff or on a cause of action.[5] Again, the Commission has cited domestic case law in which the issue has been characterized as a lack of jurisdiction[6] arising out of a statutory provision. Is this to be interpreted in the same way as such restrictions on a cause of action as effectively extinguish it?[7]

The European Commission and Court of Human Rights have consist-

---

* © Françoise J. Hampson, 1991.

‡ Senior Lecturer in Law and Member of the Human Rights Centre, University of Essex. The author was the legal representative of the applicants in the case of *Powell and Rayner* from the oral hearing before the Commission to the conclusion of the case. The author would like to thank Professor Kevin Boyle for his very helpful comments on a draft of this paper.

[1] See further at Part VII, below.

[2] Crown immunity: *Dyer* v. *UK*, No.10475/83, *Decisions and Reports of the European Commission of Human Rights* (hereinafter *D & R*), vol. 39, p. 246 at p. 251; statutory immunity: ibid; immunity: *Rayner* v. *UK*, No. 9310/81, Decision on Admissibility, 16 July 1986, para. 7.

[3] Immunity in relation to parliamentary proceedings: *Agee* v. *UK*, No. 7729/76, *D & R*, vol. 7, p. 164 at p. 175.

[4] Ibid. and *X* v. *UK*, No. 7443/76, *D & R*, vol. 8, p. 216 at p. 217.

[5] See generally *Ashingdane* case, European Court of Human Rights, Series A (hereinafter Series A), No. 93, para. 57; *Rayner* v. *UK*, No. 9310/81, Decision on Admissibility, 16 July 1986, para. 7.

[6] *Ashingdane* case, Series A, No. 93, para. 18(a); *Dyer* v. *UK*, No.10475/83, *D & R*, vol. 39, p. 246 at p. 251.

[7] *Dyer* v. *UK*, ibid. at p. 251, citing *K* v. *UK*, No. 9803/82, not published; *Rayner* v. *UK*, No. 9310/81, Decision on Admissibility, 16 July 1986, para. 7.

ently emphasized the autonomy of Convention concepts[8] and the need to look behind the form to the substance of an issue.[9] It is submitted that these questions of terminology are, in this context, matters of form. The issue in each case is whether there existed in domestic law a cause of action which the applicant could have invoked on the facts had it not been for a legal provision, whether statutory or not, denying him what would otherwise have been a right of access to court.

Provisions restricting the vindication of recognized rights must be distinguished from the provision in a statute of a limited period during which a claim may be brought, at the end of which the cause of action is extinguished.[10] Section 76(1) of the Civil Aviation Act does not address the question of the *existence* of a cause of action; *a fortiori*, it does not terminate or extinguish it. It merely provides that any such cause of action as may exist cannot be vindicated by legal action.

This raises the issue of whether the restrictions on the right of action represent a denial of access to court, in breach of Article 6 of the European Convention on Human Rights. In the case of *Powell and Rayner*,[11] the European Commission of Human Rights regarded the argument that section 76 of the Civil Aviation Act violated Article 6 of the Convention as inadmissible, being manifestly ill-founded.[12] By virtue of this finding, the issue was not considered on its merits by either the Commission or the

---

[8] *König* case, Series A, No. 27, paras, 88–9; *Feldbrugge* case, Series A, No. 99, paras, 26–7; *Deumeland* case, Series A, No. 100, paras. 60–1.

[9] *Dyer* v. *UK*, No. 10475/83, *D & R*, vol. 39, p. 246 at p. 251; *König* case, Series A, No. 27, para. 89. See also *Ringeisen* case, Series A, No. 13; case of *Sporrong and Lönnroth*, Commission Report of 8 October 1980, para. 150; *Kaplan* v. *UK*, No. 7598/76, *D & R*, vol. 21, p. 5 at p. 24, and cases cited at n. 8, above.

[10] More commonly called the limitation or prescription period; e.g. *X* v. *Switzerland*, No. 8407/78, *D & R*, vol. 20, p. 179 at p. 180; *Welter* v. *Sweden*, No 11122/84, ibid. vol. 45, p. 246 at p. 249. Where an application is brought out of time, the application to the European Commission of Human Rights will fail for non-exhaustion of domestic remedies under Art. 26 of the European Convention on Human Rights (ECHR). For text of Convention, see Council of Europe, *European Convention on Human Rights, Collected Texts*. During the period in which the applicant can bring the claim, he is not the 'victim' of the limitation provision (Art. 25 ECHR). It is difficult to envisage a situation in which an application challenging the limitation period could be admissible, unless the period was unreasonably short.

[11] Admissibility decisions: *Powell* v. *UK*, No. 9310/81, 16 October 1985; *Rayner* v. *UK*, No. 9310/81, 16 July 1986; Commission Report: *Powell and Rayner* v. *UK*, No. 9310/81, 19 January 1989. The applications were joined, together with that of *Baggs* v. *UK*, No. 9310/81, *D & R*, vol. 44, p. 13, which was the subject of a friendly settlement. Court judgment: case of *Powell and Rayner*, Series A, No. 172, judgment of 21 February 1990.

[12] Art. 27(2) ECHR. The Commission has jurisdiction to determine whether an application is admissible. If so, it goes on to consider whether a violation of the Convention has occurred. Most of the grounds of inadmissibility have nothing to do with the merits of a case (e.g. a case must be submitted within six months of the final domestic decision). In the case of 'manifestly ill-founded' as a criterion of inadmissibility, however, some review of the merits is necessary. The Commission uses the criterion to exclude not only claims which are obviously groundless or without foundation but also those in which '. . . there is no *appearance* of a breach of the substantive Convention provision', even though such a finding ' . . . does not preclude the possible fundamentally arguable nature of the claim, particularly in those cases where an application has been declared to be manifestly ill-founded by a narrow

European Court of Human Rights.[13] The object of this article is to examine the decision of the Commission in the light of the case law relating to restrictions on rights of action.

II. ARTICLE 6 AND THE RIGHT OF ACCESS TO COURT

Article 6(1) of the European Convention on Human Rights provides that

In the determination of his civil rights and obligations or of any criminal charge against him, everyone is entitled to a fair and public hearing within a reasonable time by an independent and impartial tribunal established by law. . . .

This does not, on the face of it, guarantee a right of access to court for a determination of a civil right. It appears to guarantee merely that, if the dispute does come before a court, then the requirements of a fair determination of the issue must be satisfied. In the case of *Golder*,[14] however, the European Court of Human Rights held that the protection of Article 6 rights would be meaningless if States were free to prevent applicants from bringing their claims before a court. Article 6 was therefore held necessarily to imply a right of access to court.[15] It is clear, however, that many different types of impediment may restrict access to court. It is necessary to consider the attitude of the Commission and Court to different types of obstacles.

III. BARRIERS IN THE EXERCISE OF THE RIGHT OF ACCESS TO COURT

In the *Golder* case, the barrier was a positive impediment placed in the way of the applicant. In order to bring a claim in defamation, Mr Golder had to be able to contact a solicitor to initiate the proceedings. The applicant was, at the time, a prisoner. The Home Secretary rejected Mr Golder's petition requesting permission to consult a solicitor.[16]

This type of positive impediment must be distinguished from the administrative provisions of a legal system which regulate the manner in which

---

majority in the Commission': case of *Powell and Rayner*, Series A, No. 172; verbatim record of the public hearings held on 27 September 1989, p. 4.

Once a particular complaint has been declared manifestly ill-founded, the Commission does not consider that complaint further. The jurisdiction of the European Court of Human Rights is confined to admissible issues. Where an applicant raised several issues before the Commission only one of which was declared admissible, the Court's jurisdiction is restricted to that issue. It cannot consider issues declared manifestly ill-founded by the Commission: ibid. judgment of the Court, para. 29; see also Hampson, 'The Concept of an "Arguable Claim" under Article 13 of the European Convention on Human Rights', *International and Comparative Law Quarterly*, 39 (1990), p. 891–9.

[13] Case of *Powell and Rayner*, Series A, No. 172, para. 29.

[14] Series A, No. 18.

[15] Ibid., paras. 35–6; see also *Hilton v. UK*, No. 5613/72, *D & R*, vol. 4, p. 177, *Kiss v. UK*, No. 6224/73, ibid. vol. 7, p. 55; *Campbell v. UK*, No. 7819/77, ibid. vol. 14, p. 186; *Reed v. UK*, No. 7630/76, ibid. vol. 19, p. 113.

[16] Series A, No. 18, paras. 16 and 18.

access to court is achieved. So, for example, any requirement that, in complicated cases, an applicant should use a lawyer is not a denial of access to court, provided that applicants have access to lawyers.[17] In the *Golder* case, the applicant's access to a lawyer was frustrated by a positive obstacle placed in his way.

No such positive impediment was placed in the way of the applicant in the *Airey* case.[18] Mrs Airey complained of a denial of access to court to seek a decree of judicial separation from her husband. That particular action had to be heard in the High Court. Mrs Airey's denial of access to court arose from a lack of financial resources. No solicitor would take her case and brief counsel because Mrs Airey had insufficient means of her own and no civil legal aid was available in the Republic of Ireland. The European Court of Human Rights held that it was not enough that no positive barrier was placed in the way of the applicant. The Convention obligations may sometimes impose positive duties on States.[19] The Court went out of its way to stress that it was not requiring the Irish Government to introduce civil legal aid.[20] Other means existed to enable Mrs Airey to obtain the decree she sought, such as giving district courts jurisdiction to hear such cases. The proceedings would have been much cheaper and would not have required the services of a barrister. The Irish Government tried to argue that the applicant could have represented herself in the High Court proceedings. The Court discovered that, in a seven-year period, no successful application had been made for a decree of judicial separation by a person representing him/herself.[21] The Court held that, in view of the complexity of the proceedings, the theoretical possibility of bringing one's own case was not sufficient. Article 6 guaranteed a right of *effective* access to court and not an illusory one.[22]

The criterion of effectiveness was also used in the final stage of the reasoning in the *Ashingdane* case.[23] That was the first case in which the relationship between the right of access to court and restrictions on a right of action in national law was considered by both the Convention organs. If the *Airey* case[24] represents a further logical development of the principle enunciated in the *Golder* case,[25] the *Ashingdane* case[26] does not. In the first

[17] e.g. *X* v. *Federal Republic of Germany*, No. 11564/85, *D & R*, vol. 45, p. 291 at p. 292; it is a requirement under Art. 78(1) of the German Code of Civil Procedure that parties before the family courts in matrimonial matters be represented by a lawyer. See also *Granger* case, Series A, No. 174.
[18] Series A, No. 32.
[19] Ibid., para. 25.
[20] Ibid., para. 26; when ratifying the Convention, the Irish Government entered a reservation to Art. 6(3)(c) limiting its obligations in the realm of criminal legal aid. As the Court held, ' . . . *a fortiori* it cannot be said to have implicitly agreed to provide unlimited civil legal aid'. The breach found was of Art. 6 on its own. The Court did not rely on Art. 14 in conjunction with Art. 6.
[21] Ibid., para. 24.
[22] Ibid.
[23] Series A, No. 93.
[24] Series A, No. 32.
[25] Series A, No. 18.
[26] Series A, No. 93.

two cases what was at issue was an impediment in the right of access to court which was totally independent of the cause of action. Had Mr Golder been able to consult a solicitor and had Mrs Airey been able to afford a barrister, their complaints would have been handled in a fashion consistent with Article 6.

The problem with a restriction on a right of action is different. The applicant's difficulty concerns the law as applied by the domestic court. The objection is that the law restricts the cause of action by arbitrarily denying it in certain circumstances. The nature of this claim requires a distinction to be drawn between two issues. First, does a cause of action exist at all as claimed by the applicant and second, if so, is it arbitrarily restricted so as to deny the applicant a right of access to court? Consider a situation in which an English applicant wished to claim that he had been denied access to court to bring a claim alleging an invasion of his privacy.[27] The lack of any remedy in domestic law for such a claim, unless it can be brought within the bounds of another remedy such as that for tortious invasion of property, may well be in violation of the Convention, but the applicant cannot claim a denial of access to court since he has no such civil right in English law which could be the subject of a determination. Whilst the distinction between the two issues seems clear in theory, it has posed difficulties in practice. The significance of the distinction is made all the greater by the fact that the Commission has said that it is principally for the national legal system to define causes of action.[28] In other words, if there is no cause of action as defined by the national legal system, that is usually the end of the matter. If, however, there is a cause of action, the Commission and Court will examine whether any impediment or restriction is such as to constitute a denial of access to court. The existence of a cause of action in domestic law is therefore a prerequisite for the applicability of Article 6 to an alleged civil right. That is true in any case and not just in one in which a statutory bar is in issue.[29]

IV. The Existence of a Cause of Action as a Precondition for the Applicability of Article 6

Article 6(1) of the Convention

. . . does not impose requirements in respect of the nature and scope of the relevant national law governing the 'right' in question. Nor does the Commission consider that it is, in principle, competent to determine or review the substantive

[27] See, for example, *Malone* case, Series A, No. 82.

[28] Case of *Sporrong and Lönnroth*, Commission Report of 8 October 1980, para. 150; see also *Kaplan v. UK*, No.7598/76, *D & R*, vol. 21, p. 5 at p. 24, para. 134; case of *James and others*, Series A, No. 98, para. 81; case of *Lithgow and others*, Series A, No. 102, para. 192.

[29] Case of *Sporrong and Lönnroth*, Commission Report of 8 October 1980, para. 150; see also case of *James and others*, Series A, No. 98, para. 81; case of *Lithgow and others*, Series A, No. 102, para. 192.

content of the civil law which ought to obtain in the State Party any more than it could in respect of substantive criminal law.[30]

The extent of the supervision which can be exercised by the Convention organs was stated by the Commission in the case of *Sporrong and Lönnroth*, in which it said:

whether a right is at all at issue in a particular case depends primarily on the legal system of the State concerned. It is true that the concept of a 'right' is itself autonomous to some degree. Thus it is not decisive for the purposes of Article 6 para. 1 that a given privilege or interest which exists in a domestic legal system is not classified or described as a 'right' by that system. However, it is clear that the Convention organs could not create by way of interpretation of Article 6 para. 1 a substantive right which has no legal basis whatsoever in the State concerned.[31]

The example given above of an individual seeking to claim that the absence of a right of action for invasion of privacy in English law violates Article 6 illustrates why the Convention organs might be tempted, inadvertently, into creating such a substantive right. Article 8 of the Convention guarantees the right to respect for privacy and family life. If there was an interference in the exercise of that right which was not justified under paragraph 2 of the article, there would be a violation of Article 8.[32] That does not mean that there is a violation of Article 6. The arguments necessary to establish such a violation require, as a precondition, that there exists a cause of action. If no such cause of action exists, there may be a violation of Article 13.[33] That article requires that there be a remedy from a national authority where an applicant establishes a violation of a Convention right, in this case that contained in Article 8.

One must therefore ask whether there was prima facie any cause of action in the case of *Powell and Rayner*,[34] in which the applicants complained that section 76(1) of the Civil Aviation Act, quoted at the outset, deprived them of their right to sue in nuisance on account of the noise levels around Heathrow airport. English law recognizes a cause of action in nuisance. The common law cause of action includes noise as a possible source of nuisance.[35] The European Court of Human Rights has recognized that the

---

[30] *Rayner* v. *UK*, No. 9310/81, Admissibility Decision of 16 July 1986, para. 7.

[31] Case of *Sporrong and Lönnroth*, Commission Report of 8 October 1980, para. 150; see also case of *James and others*, Series A, No. 98, para. 81; case of *Lithgow and others*, Series A, No. 102, para. 192.

[32] e.g. *Malone* case, Series A, No. 82.

[33] In the case of *Powell and Rayner*, Series A, No. 172, the Commission Delegate pointed out at the oral hearing before the Court that 'It is significant that . . . the Government have not sought to argue in their memorial to the Court that even if the applicants had an arguable Convention claim they had effective remedies at their disposal': verbatim record of the public hearings, 27 September 1989, p. 5. This suggests that had the Commission found the Art. 8 complaint admissible, the Court would have followed the Commission in finding a violation of Art. 13. See further Hampson, loc. cit. above (n. 12).

[34] Above, n. 11.

[35] e.g. *Christie* v. *Davey*, [1893] 1 Ch. 316; *Hollywood Silver Fox Farm Ltd.* v. *Emmett*, [1936] 2 KB 468; *Andreae* v. *Selfridge & Co. Ltd.*, [1938] Ch. 1. In *Bosworth-Smith* v. *Gwynnes Ltd.*, 122 LT 15, the noise created by the testing of an aircraft engine, the B.R.2, was held to be nuisance; see generally, Buckley, *The Law of Nuisance* (1981), pp. 11–12 and 24–5.

common law is part of the body of law applicable in England.[36] The detailed argument about the relationship between the cause of action and the restriction to which it is subject will be examined in the next section. At this stage, it is sufficient to note that the applicants in the case of *Powell and Rayner*[37] were not asking the Convention organs to 'create . . . a substantive right which has no legal basis . . . '[38] in English law. Prima facie, they had a cause of action in nuisance. Furthermore, the existence of such a cause of action will not have come as a surprise to the Commission and Court. In the case of *Zimmermann and Steiner*,[39] which involved different issues under Article 6, they expressed no surprise that the applicants should have a remedy in Swiss law for nuisance caused by the operation of aircraft.

Given the existence, prima facie, of a cause of action in nuisance, it becomes important to examine the relationship between an alleged cause of action and a restriction imposed on it, with a view to establishing a criterion or test which can be used to determine whether a cause of action exists in a case involving such a restriction.

V. The Relationship Between a Cause of Action and a Restriction Imposed on its Scope

Where a statutory provision states that 'no action shall lie', it would appear evident that it is the provision itself which excludes the action and thus denies a would-be claimant the right of access to court. That may, however, be an over-simplification.

In the *Ashingdane* case,[40] for example, the applicant sought a declaration that the Department of Health and Social Security was under a statutory duty to provide him with hospital accommodation at an appropriate local hospital and that it was acting *ultra vires* in refusing to admit him to a particular hospital on account of a ban imposed by a trade union on the admission of a particular type of patient. In the domestic proceedings, the department successfully relied on section 141 of the Mental Health Act 1959, which provided in subsection 1 that

No person shall be liable . . . to any civil . . . proceedings to which he would have been liable apart from this section

and in subsection 2 that

No civil . . . proceedings shall be brought against any person in any court in respect of . . .

an act purported to be done in pursuance of the Act. On the face of it, the

---

[36] *The Sunday Times* case, Series A, No. 30, para. 47.
[37] Above, n. 11.
[38] Case of *Sporrong and Lönnroth*, Commission Report of 8 October 1980, para. 150.
[39] Series A, No. 66.
[40] Series A, No. 93.

applicant was prevented from suing by virtue of the immunity conferred by the section. The distinction between an immunity from suit and a bar to action would appear to be irrelevant for the purposes of Article 6 of the European Convention, given the Commission and Court's emphasis on substance and effect, rather than form. It is sufficient to note that, irrespective of the form of the provision, the section appeared to bar legal action. As the European Court of Human Rights pointed out, however, ' . . . the claims Mr Ashingdane wished to assert in the domestic proceedings were founded on section 3 . . . ' of the 1977 National Health Service Act, which imposed a duty on the Secretary of State for Social Services to provide hospital accommodation throughout England and Wales ' . . . to such extent as he considers necessary to meet all reasonable requirements'.[41] The breach of a statutory duty can only give rise to an action if the statute creates an interest in an individual which Parliament intended to be protected by an action in tort.[42] Where the duty is of so vague a nature or involves major political questions such as resource allocation, it is unlikely that the courts would allow an individual to bring an action for breach of statutory duty. In other words, it does not appear that Mr Ashingdane would have had a cause of action, even disregarding section 141 of the 1959 Act. The line of reasoning of the judges in the domestic proceedings is not crucial here. The Convention organs are trying to establish whether a cause of action existed in domestic law. It seems unlikely that Mr Ashingdane had such a cause of action. From this analysis, it would appear that the Convention organs should apply a 'but for' test. The question should be whether the applicant would have had a cause of action 'but for' the restriction.

The importance of such a test is that it distinguishes quite clearly between the *applicability* of Article 6 and the question of its *breach*. So, for example, issues involving the aim of the restriction and the number and class affected, an aspect of proportionality, relate to whether Article 6 has been breached. They are not relevant to the question whether or not it is applicable. That depends on whether a cause of action exists in domestic law, even if the applicant cannot invoke it owing to a restriction imposed on its scope.

The proposed test must be examined to see first whether it is compatible with the criteria adopted in the cases involving such restrictions. Then its application in the case of *Powell and Rayner*[43] will need to be considered.

---

[41] Ibid., para.59.

[42]. e.g. 'The Secretary of State's duty under s. 3 [of the National Health Service Act 1977], to provide services "to such extent as he considers necessary", gave him in terms a discretion as to the disposition of financial resources. The court could only interfere if the Secretary of State acted so as to frustrate the policy of the Act, or as no reasonable minister could have acted': *R* v. *Secretary of State for Social Services, ex parte Hincks*, (1979) 123 SJ 436, *per* Wien J; see generally *Clerk and Lindsell on Torts* (16th edn., 1989), pp. 768–71; *Street on Torts* (8th edn. by Brazier, 1988), pp. 368–71; *Salmond and Heuston on the Law of Torts* (19th edn. by Heuston and Buckley, 1987), pp. 273–5.

[43] Above, n. 11.

VI. CASE LAW OF THE CONVENTION ORGANS AND THE 'BUT FOR' TEST

The cases which have involved an interference in access to court brought about by the restricted scope of a cause of action rather than by the financial circumstances of the applicant, or a practical obstruction or the expiry of a limitation period, have concerned principally the doctrine of parliamentary privilege, the denial of an action in negligence to members of the British armed forces, restrictions on actions brought against health service employees in the United Kingdom and the immunity of British Telecommunications from proceedings in tort.

(a) *Parliamentary Privilege*

In the case of *Agee* v. *United Kingdom*, the Commission stated that

. . . Article 6(1) must be interpreted with due regard to parliamentary immunity as traditionally recognised in the States parties to the Convention . . . In the present case the applicant cannot complain in the United Kingdom courts of the statements made in Parliament in view of the doctrine of Parliamentary privilege, which forms part of United Kingdom law. This affords absolute protection to persons making such statements. Although a person's rights under domestic law to protection of his reputation generally constitute 'civil rights' within the meaning of Art. 6(1), the applicant does not have any right in United Kingdom law to protection of his reputation insofar as it may be affected by the statements complained of. Art. 6(1) does not therefore guarantee the right to take proceedings in respect of these statements, since the applicant has no 'civil right' to protection of his reputation against them.[44]

This statement, it is submitted, confuses several discrete issues. The fact that the defendant can rely on an absolute defence does not mean that the applicant has no cause of action. Those are separate issues. It means merely that a claim would have no prospect of success. In other words, the recognized right of action in defamation is illusory where the statements in question are protected by parliamentary privilege. It is, nevertheless, open to a court to determine whether or not the statements come within the scope of the protection afforded by parliamentary privilege.[45] It should therefore fall to the Commission to examine whether the effect of the defence can be justified. It would appear that, since the

. . . principle of immunity in respect of such statements is generally recognised as a consequence of an 'effective political democracy' within the meaning of the Preamble to the Convention,[46]

---

[44] *Agee* v. *UK*, No. 7729/76, *D & R*, vol. 7, p. 164 at p. 175.

[45] These issues have been raised in the UK before both the courts and the House of Commons: see Wade and Bradley, *Constitutional and Administrative Law* (10th edn., 1985), pp. 212–17 and 221–2.

[46] *Agee* v. *UK*, No. 7729/76, *D & R*, vol. 7, p. 164 at p. 175. The protection afforded to speech in parliament must be distinguished from the proceedings a parliament may itself institute to protect its dignity. When a parliament is acting as a court in determining whether a person is guilty of a breach of privilege or contempt of parliament, it must afford the individual the procedural guarantees of Art. 6

the Commission would have no difficulty in restricting the cause of action in defamation to vanishing point in cases involving freedom of speech in Parliament.

A further confusion stems from the first. The Commission refers to the applicant's right to protect his reputation as being a 'civil right', but goes on to say that the applicant has no 'civil right' to protect his reputation against statements made in Parliament. The Commission is again confusing the applicability of Article 6 (whether there is a 'civil right') and the issue of a breach of the article (whether a particular limitation on access to court is justified).

What makes this confusion so dangerous is the way in which the Commission reaches its conclusion. It appears to suggest that it includes the limitation in its determination as to the existence of a cause of action. On this basis, there would never be a cause of action, and hence no denial of effective access to court, where a statutory provision or rule of law restricted such action as would otherwise be available. So, for example, if a legislative provision were to deny to all women the right to bring actions in defamation, the Commission would argue that they had no cause of action in domestic law. Article 6 would therefore be inapplicable to the issue since there was no 'civil right' which fell to be determined. If such a complaint were also held to fall outside the scope of Article 6, then on the basis of the case law, Article 14, the non-discrimination provision, would not be applicable either.[47] The women would not have been discriminated against with regard to a Convention right since they would have no 'civil right'. This surprising conclusion is inconsistent with the oft-stated view that the concept of a 'civil right' is autonomous,[48] that contracting States only enjoy a *certain* margin of appreciation and that the final decision as to the observance of the Convention's requirements rests with the Commission and Court.[49] By incorporating the limitation into the determination of whether there exists a cause of action, the Commission is effectively transferring to the domestic legal system the definition of civil rights.

The 'but for' test would not have led to a different conclusion but it would have relied on different reasoning. In trying to establish whether there existed a domestic cause of action, the Commission would have asked itself whether, in English law, a person can bring an action based on allegedly defamatory remarks, ignoring at this stage the fact that the statements

---

ECHR. Since a parliament, or a chamber of it, is not independent of the government or the parties (it is judging an offence against its own dignity), doubts arise as to its impartiality; see *Demicoli* v. *Malta*, No. 13057/87, currently before the European Court of Human Rights.

[47] e.g. *Belgian Linguistic* case, Series A, No. 6; case of *Abdulaziz, Cabales and Balkandali*, Series A, No. 94, para. 71; Fawcett, *The Application of the European Convention on Human Rights* (2nd edn., 1987), pp. 294–7; Cohen-Jonathan, *La Convention européenne des droits de l'homme* (1989), pp. 538–41.

[48] *König* case, Series A, No. 27, paras, 88–9; *Feldbrugge* case, Series A, No. 99, paras. 26–7; *Deumeland* case, Series A, No. 100, paras. 60–1.

[49] *Ashingdane* case, Series A, No. 93, para. 57; *Handyside* case, Series A, No. 24, paras. 47–50; *The Sunday Times* case, Series A, No. 30, paras. 58–9.

were protected by parliamentary privilege. The answer is clearly in the affirmative. Article 6 would therefore be applicable. It would then be for the Commission and Court to determine whether the total lack of any prospect of success where the statements had been made in Parliament was a legitimate restriction or whether it constituted a denial of access to court.

(b) *Exclusion of Actions in Negligence under Section 10 of the Crown Proceedings Act 1947*

The same confusion is seen in a series of cases raising a common problem. Under section 10 of the Crown Proceedings Act 1947, members of the armed forces on duty were removed from the general regime of civil liability where the injury they had received was treated as attributable to service for the purposes of entitlement to a disability pension. This was done by conferring an immunity from an action in tort on members of the armed forces and the Crown.[50] In a case decided in 1976, the Commission stated that

. . . even assuming that the applicant's claim concerns his civil rights as understood by Art. 6 (1) of the Convention, there was nothing that prevented him from bringing proceedings in the courts. He refrained from going to court because the Crown and any other persons he could have proceeded against would probably have had an absolute defence against his claim. . . . However, the Commission does not consider that the mere existence of this defence meant that the applicant was denied access to the courts.[51]

Once it is assumed that a civil right was at issue, then clearly there was a serious impediment in the applicant's access to court. The determination by the court has nothing to do with the merits of the claim; the absolute defence determines the result of the case at the outset. Where there is an absolute defence, any right of access is theoretical or illusory. Invoking the autonomy of Convention concepts, the Commission and Court have, in other areas, gone behind matters of form to investigate the substance of an

---

[50] Section 10 of the Crown Proceedings Act 1947 provides:

'(1) Nothing done or omitted to be done by a member of the armed fores of the Crown while on duty as such shall subject either him or the Crown to liability in tort for causing the death of another person, or for causing personal injury to another person, in so far as the death or personal injury is due to anything suffered by that other person while he is a member of the armed forces of the Crown if—

(a) at the time when that thing is suffered by that other person, he is either on duty as a member of the armed forces of the Crown or is, though not on duty as such, on any land, premises, ship, aircraft or vehicle for the time being used for the purposes of the armed forces of the Crown; and

(b) [the Secretary of State] certifies that his suffering that thing has been or will be treated as attributable to service for the purposes of entitlement to an award under the Royal Warrant, Order in Council or Order of His Majesty relating to the disablement or death of members of the force of which he is a member.'

This provision was replaced by the Crown Proceedings (Armed Forces) Act 1987, which repealed section 10 of the Crown Proceedings Act 1947 but provided for its revival in certain circumstances.

[51] *X* v. *UK*, No.7443/76, *D & R*, vol. 8, p. 216 at p. 217.

issue.[52] The effect of an absolute defence on the applicant's vindication of his civil rights is the same as a restriction on the scope of a cause of action. Each results in his being denied effective access to court. The question for the Commission and Court should therefore be whether the absolute defence is justifiable.

In a case decided in 1982, the Commission characterized the issue as one of Crown immunity and found that once a certificate of entitlement was issued ' . . . the right to sue in tort was effectively extinguished and replaced by a pension entitlement'.[53] The fullest consideration of the problem is to be found in *Dyer* v. *United Kingdom*, decided in 1984.[54] The parties accepted that

> . . . in general, the right to compensation for negligence constitutes a 'civil right' and therefore the right to bring a civil action for negligence is guaranteed by Article 6 para. 1.[55]

On the basis of the analysis suggested, the question should then have become whether Article 6(1) was breached or whether the absolute defence was justified. The Commission, however, went on to confuse the issue by asking

> . . . whether there can be said to be a 'civil right' where such a right, i.e., a right to compensation for negligence, has been expressly removed by a statutory immunity . . . [56]

The danger inherent in that approach has already been explained. The Commission then reaffirmed its earlier view that

> . . . the substitution of a pension entitlement for a right to compensation in tort *removes* the 'civil right' to sue for purposes of this provision.[57] (emphasis added)

Having deprived itself of jurisdiction, the Commission then asserted that it was for the Convention organs to determine whether a matter was a 'civil right' within the meaning of Article 6! It repeated the statement in the cases of *Sporrong and Lönnroth*[58] and *Kaplan*[59] to the effect that the Convention organs cannot

---

[52] e.g. 'Whether or not a right is to be regarded as civil within the meaning of this expression in the Convention must be determined by reference to the substantive content and effects of the right—and not its legal classification—under the domestic law of the State concerned': *König* case, Series A, No. 27, para. 89. See also *Ringeisen* case, Series A, No. 13; case of *Sporrong and Lönnroth*, Commission Report of 8 October 1980, para. 150; *Kaplan* v. *UK*, No. 7598/76, *D & R*, vol. 21, p. 5 at p. 24 and cases cited at n. 48, above.

[53] *Dyer* v. *UK*, No. 10475/83, *D & R*, vol. 39, p. 246 at p. 251, citing *K* v. *UK*, No. 9803/82, not published.

[54] Ibid.

[55] Ibid.

[56] Ibid.

[57] Ibid. (emphasis added).

[58] Case of *Sporrong and Lönnroth*, Commission Report of 8 October 1980, para. 150.

[59] *Kaplan* v. *UK*, No. 7598/76, *D & R*, vol. 21, p. 5 at p. 24.

. . . create by way of interpretation a substantive right which has no legal basis whatsoever in the State concerned.[60]

There is no doubt that the right to compensation for negligence is a recognized right in English law. In accepting that that right was a 'civil right', the parties necessarily recognized that it was a right. There is therefore no doubt that the case satisfied the criterion in the cases of *Sporrong and Lönnroth* and *Kaplan*. The Commission's analysis is internally inconsistent. Further to confuse the issue, the Commission itself pointed to the danger in the conclusion it had reached in determining that the right was 'removed' or 'effectively extinguished':

. . . Were Article 6 para. 1 to be interpreted as enabling a State Party to remove the jurisdiction of the courts to determine certain classes of civil claim or to confer immunities from liability on certain groups in respect of their actions, without any possibility of control by the Convention organs, there would exist no protection against the danger of arbitrary power . . . [61]

The Commission then examined ' . . . whether Section 10 of the 1947 Act constitutes an *arbitrary limitation* of the applicant's substantive civil claims',[62] making it clear that it was concerned ' . . . not only in respect of procedural limitations such as the removal of the jurisdiction of the court, as in the *Ashingdane* case, but also in respect of a substantive immunity from liability . . . '.[63] In other words, the Commission, having decided that Article 6 was inapplicable, then proceeded to examine whether the absolute defence was in breach of the Article! The Commission accepted that the absolute defence in section 10 of the Crown Proceedings Act was justified because of the special nature and risks of military service, the provision of a pension entitlement without proof of negligence and the possibility of its adjustment to take account of inflation and changes in the degree of disablement and because the immunity only applied where the injury was received in the course of the serviceman's duty.

The application of the 'but for' test would have simplified the issue but would not have led to a different conclusion. The question would have been whether English law recognized a right to sue in negligence for compensation for injury, disregarding section 10 of the 1947 Act. The second question would have been whether any such right was 'civil', within the meaning of the Convention. Both questions would be answered in the affirmative. The issue would then have been whether the interference in the exercise of the right was justified. As will be seen in Part VIII below, section 10 of the Crown Proceedings Act represented a statutory bar that was both legitimate and proportionate.

---

[60] Case of *Sporrong and Lönnroth*, Commission Report of 8 October 1980, para. 150; see also case of *James and others*, Series A, No. 98, para. 81; case of *Lithgow and others*, Series A, No. 102, para. 192.

[61] *Dyer* v. *UK*, No. 10475/83, *D & R*, vol. 39, p. 246.

[62] Ibid. at p. 252 (emphasis added).

[63] Ibid.

(c) *Restriction of Actions brought against British Health Service Employees*

The *Ashingdane* case[64] is the leading case on restrictions on the scope of a cause of action in relation to Article 6 and is the first of those examined here to have been decided by the European Court of Human Rights. The provision called into question was section 141 of the Mental Health Act 1959 which provided, in subsection 1, that 'No person shall be liable . . . to any civil proceedings to which he would have been liable apart from this section in respect of any act purporting to be done in pursuance of the Act . . . unless the act was done in bad faith or without reasonable care'. Subsection 2 provided that the leave of the High Court was required to bring a case alleging bad faith and that the High Court had to be satisfied that there was a substantial ground for the contention.

Mr Ashingdane alleged a breach of statutory duty under section 3 of the National Health Service Act 1977 on the part of the Secretary of State. As the Court explained, section 141

> . . . did not qualify section 3 of the 1977 Act as such, but had the effect of qualifying claims grounded on section 3 in so far as they related to measures carried out in purported pursuance of the 1959 Act . . . [65]

Section 3 is couched in very general terms and leaves a wide discretion to the Minister. This makes it most unlikely that the duty in section 3 would be amenable to judicial control by the courts.[66] In other words, the applicant's problem arose not from the restriction in section 141 of the 1959 Act but from the fact that he had no cause of action in English law since he could not sue for breach of statutory duty under section 3 of the 1977 Act. Having no 'right' in domestic law, Article 6 was inapplicable. That should have been sufficient to dispose of the issue. The Court, however, not only considered the criteria which such restrictions must satisfy in order to be legitimate but in fact did that *before* considering the relationship between section 141 of 1959 Act and section 3 of the 1977 Act.[67] This gives a certain confusion to the judgment.

The Court initially stated that it did not have to determine whether or not the claim related to a 'civil right' in English law, since ' . . . even assuming Article 6 para. 1 to be applicable, the requirements of this provision were not violated'.[68] After restating earlier case law, in particular the principle of access to court as enunciated in the *Golder* case,[69] the Court maintained that the

---

[64] Series A, No. 93.

[65] Ibid., para. 59.

[66] See n. 42, above, and accompanying text.

[67] The criteria for determining the legitimacy of restrictions imposed on a cause of action were considered in the *Ashingdane* case, Series A, No. 93, para. 57; the existence of the cause of action was discussed in para. 59.

[68] Ibid., para. 54. The Court so held by six votes to one. Judge Pettiti was of the view that Article 6(1) was both applicable and violated. Judge Lagergren, concurring with the opinion of the majority of the Court, appears to suggest that Article 6(1) was applicable but not violated.

[69] Series A, No. 18.

. . . applicant did have access to the High Court and then to the Court of Appeal, only to be told that his actions were barred by operation of law . . . . To this extent, he thus had access to the remedies that existed within the domestic system.[70]

This illustrates the difficulty that arises when the Commission and Court do not deal with the first question first. In Convention terms, there was no cause of action in domestic law. Had there in fact existed a cause of action, then an absolute defence or an immunity from suit would have been a substantial impediment, rendering the access to court theoretical and illusory.[71] It could *not*, in that case, be said that the applicant has access to the remedies that existed within the domestic system. It would be a matter of examining whether the impediment was justified.

Having claimed that the applicant did have access to the national remedies, the Court stated that

. . . This of itself does not necessarily exhaust the requirements of Article 6 para. 1. It must still be established that the degree of access afforded under the national legislation was sufficient to secure the individual's 'right to a court', having regard to the rule of law in a domestic society. . . . the limitations applied must not restrict or reduce the access left to the individual in such a way or to such an extent that the very essence of the right is impaired. . . . Furthermore, a limitation will not be compatible with Article 6 para. 1 if it does not pursue a legitimate aim and if there is not a reasonable relationship of proportionality between the means employed and the aim sought to be achieved.[72]

This important elaboration of the criteria to be used to assess the legitimacy of a restriction of the scope of a cause of action will be examined below.

The Court went on to examine the circumstances in which section 141 of the Mental Health Act 1959 was applied to Mr Ashingdane, having recognized that the avoidance of harassment by litigation was a legitimate aim. It was in this context, which represents an examination of the question of proportionality, that the Court considered the relationship between section 141 of the 1959 Act and section 3 of the National Health Service Act 1977. This issue, however, relates to the preliminary question of the existence of a cause of action and not to the matter of the proportionality of the restriction imposed on its scope.

The Court pointed out that section 141 of the 1959 Act only partially precluded actions for breach of statutory duty, as it would have allowed an action alleging bad faith or negligence, subject to leave of the High Court being obtained. This relates to the *scope* of the bar and is one of the elements in assessing proportionality. It is not relevant to a determination of whether a cause of action would exist, were it not for the statutory provision. Of the three reasons given by the Court (the legitimate aim, the lack of a right to sue in domestic law and the limited scope of the statutory bar),

---

[70] *Ashingdane* case, Series A, No. 93, para. 56.
[71] *Airey* case, Series A, No. 32, para. 24; see also n. 52, above.
[72] *Ashingdane* case, Series A, No. 93, para. 57.

only the second reason relates to the existence of the cause of action in domestic law. The other two are relevant only to the question of the legitimacy of the restriction imposed on its scope.

Whilst the Court avoided some of the confusion apparent in the reasoning of the Commission in other cases, its own analysis was not without difficulties. The application of the 'but for' test would not have led to a different result. Leaving aside section 141 of the Mental Health Act 1959, the applicant would not have been able to establish a right to sue for breach of statutory duty under domestic law. Article 6 would therefore not have been applicable.

(d) *Immunity of British Telecommunications (Telecom) from Proceedings in Tort*

In a recently reported case,[73] the Commission had to consider the compatibility of section 23(1) of the Telecommunications Act 1981 with Article 6 of the Convention. That section provides that proceedings in tort will not lie in respect *inter alia* of omissions from ' . . . a directory for use in connection with a telecommunications service'. The applicant, a solicitor, complained of the loss of business he suffered owing to the omission of his firm from the local telephone directory and from the Yellow Pages trade directory. The Commission characterized section 23 ' . . . as a provision defining the extent of a civil right and not as a provision removing the jurisdiction of the civil courts'.[74] The Commission stated that it could not determine ' . . . the substantive content of the civil law which ought to obtain in a State Party . . .' but that ' . . . a real threat to the rule of law could emerge if a State were arbitrarily to remove the jurisdiction of civil courts to determine certain classes of civil action . . . '.[75] It seems odd to speak of the removal of the jurisdiction of the civil courts when the Commission had just stated that the provision was not to be characterized in that way. Nevertheless, the Commission went on to state that ' . . . the scope of the Commission's review is limited to examining whether the limitation of the civil claim in question is arbitrary . . . '.[76] This assumes that the Commission recognizes a domestic right of action 'but for' section 23 of the Telecommunications Act. Only on that basis is the criterion in the case of *Sporrong and Lönnroth* satisfied. The Commission does not spell out the stages in its reasoning but its analysis is less internally inconsistent than in earlier case law. Whether this is as a result of its characterization of the issue is not clear. It should be noted that this case was decided after that of *Powell and Rayner*. The Commission accepted the legitimacy and proportionality of the restriction on a claim in tort because

---

[73] *Wallance-Jones* v. *UK*, No. 10782/84, *D & R*, vol. 47, p. 157.
[74] Ibid., at p. 159.
[75] Ibid.
[76] Ibid.

. . . in the field of telecommunications, such a limitation of liability is considered to be an essential condition of producing telephone directories which contain millions of user entries . . . as well as offering a telephone service to the public at a reasonable cost.

The Commission also noted ' . . . the existence of a compensation scheme, albeit of a limited nature, in respect of such omissions . . . '.[77] In this case, the Commission appears to have applied something akin to a 'but for' test.

In the cases examined so far, the application of a 'but for' test would not have resulted in a different conclusion but would have avoided the confusions apparent in the reasoning of the Convention organs.

VII. The Application of the 'But For' Test in the Case of POWELL and RAYNER

The applicants in the case of *Powell and Rayner*[78] alleged that the noise levels they experienced on account of the operations in and around Heathrow airport violated their right to respect for privacy. They claimed that their normal remedy, a suit in nuisance, was barred by section 76(1) of the Civil Aviation Act 1982, as a result of which they were denied access to court in breach of Article 6, and that the absence of any other remedy in domestic law constituted a breach of Article 13. Their complaint under Article 6 was, in a sense, the kernel of the case. The applicants suggested that the deterrent effect of their being able to sue in nuisance would be such as to ensure that the airport's operations would be conducted so as not to violate Article 8.[79]

The impugned statutory provision, section 76(1) of the Civil Aviation Act 1982, provides that

No action shall lie in respect of trespass or in respect of nuisance, by reason only of the flight of an aircraft over any property at a height above the ground which, having regard to wind, weather and all the circumstances of the case is reasonable, or the ordinary incidents of such flight, so long as the provisions of any Air Navigation Order or of any Orders . . . have been duly complied with . . .[80]

As was seen in the *Ashingdane* Case,[81] it cannot be assumed that a cause of action exists merely because a statutory provision excludes it. That must be established independently of the provision. Section 76(1) does not *grant* a cause of action where the height of the aircraft is unreasonable. It *excludes* the bringing of an action where the height is reasonable. In other words, the applicants do not rely on a right of action created by and within the

[77] Ibid.
[78] Above, n. 11.
[79] Verbatim record of the public hearing held on 27 September 1989, p. 37.
[80] Where material loss or damage is caused to a person or property by an aircraft in flight or an object falling from an aircraft, strict liability is imposed under s. 76(2) of the Civil Aviation Act 1982.
[81] Series A, No. 93.

limits of a statute but on a right of action arising outside the statute and excluded by its provisions.

The obvious remedy for the applicants was a suit in nuisance against the adjacent landowner, which at the time was the British Airports Authority. Nuisance is essentially a common law cause of action. On the basis of the case law, an actionable nuisance can be founded not only on tangible emissions, such as smoke, but also on account of unreasonable noise levels.[82] In order to establish nuisance, the plaintiff must show that the noise levels were unreasonable in all the circumstances. In the instant case, the applicants would have had to show that the noise levels were unreasonable, even bearing in mind that the operation in question was an international airport. The likelihood of their success is not relevant to establishing whether they had a cause of action. It need only be noted in this context that one of the applicants, Michael Rayner, believed that he could establish the unreasonableness of the noise levels.[83]

At common law, the applicants would have had a cause of action based on noise. The *source* of the noise—aircraft—is not relevant to the existence of the cause of action but it may be relevant in assessing unreasonableness. *A fortiori*, the height of the aircraft and their compliance or failure to comply with any Air Navigation Order is also irrelevant. The only criterion is the noise level generated by the activity.

In its admissibility decisions, the Commission considered whether there existed a cause of action or 'civil right'. Its conclusion dictated the scope of the case as a whole in its own subsequent consideration of the merits and in the Court's consideration of admissible issues.[84] The Commission first reiterated the principles in the *Golder* case[85] and in the case of *Sporrong and Lönnroth*.[86] It went on to distinguish the present case from those involving compensation for members of the armed forces[87] and the *Ashingdane* case[88] on the ground that

> . . . the provision in section 76 CAA does not confer an immunity from liability in respect of actions of certain and distinct groups of persons (such as soldiers or mental health patients . . .) but excludes *generally* any action in respect of trespass or nuisance caused by the flight of an aircraft at a reasonable height regardless of the status of the possible claimant. The Commission considers that the purpose and effect of section 76 CAA is to exclude generally any possible compensation claims

---

[82] Above, n. 35.

[83] Case of *Powell and Rayner*, Series A, No. 172, memorial of the applicants to the Court, p. 17. In an analogous situation, one of the elements taken into account in determining the grant of legal aid in the UK is the prospects of success. That is not the criterion used by the Court, which bases its decision on ' . . . whether the interests of justice . . . [require] . . . a grant of legal aid . . . in the light of the case as a whole': *Granger* case, Series A, No. 174, para. 46.

[84] Case of *Powell and Rayner*, Series A, No. 172, judgment of the Court, para. 29; see n. 4, above.

[85] Series A, No. 18.

[86] Commission Report of 8 October 1980.

[87] *X* v. *UK*, No. 7443/76, *D & R*, vol. 8, p. 216; *K* v. *UK*, No. 9803/82, cited in *Dyer* v. *UK*, No. 10475/83, *D & R*, vol. 39 p. 246.

[88] Series A, No. 93.

for trespass and nuisance and not just to limit jurisdiction of civil courts with regard to certain classes of civil action.[89]

It is not clear whether the Commission regards the distinction between restrictions on causes of action and those on jurisdiction as significant. It is difficult to see why the difference in form should be important.[90] The question is whether an applicant is denied access to court. It is the *effect* of the limitation that matters. Again, the distinction between imposing a bar on the plaintiffs or an immunity on the defendant appears to be a matter of form. The Commission apparently attached great significance to the fact that section 76 of the Civil Aviation Act did not exclude a suit in nuisance in relation to a defined class of plaintiffs or a defined class of defendants but generally. This will be discussed further in relation to proportionality.

In this context, it is sufficient to note the logic of the Commission's position by applying it to one area where the Commission does seem to have recognized that there was a cause of action, the soldiers' compensation cases. Rather than excluding claims for compensation for injury on the part of servicemen, the Government should have been advised to exclude all such claims against the Crown generally. The Commission would then have concluded that ' . . . the applicant, *therefore*, cannot invoke under English law a substantive right to compensation . . . '.[91] This flies in the face of the Commission's avowed concern for the rule of law.[92] It opens the way for the exclusion of civil causes of action at the arbitrary whim of a government. Provided it excludes the cause of action generally, the Commission will rely on the proposition that it cannot create by interpretation ' . . . a substantive right which has no legal basis whatsoever in the State concerned'.[93]

The use of the word 'therefore' is an indication of the source of the flaw in the reasoning of the Commission. Having examined the scope and terms of the bar to action, the Commission concludes that there is no ' . . . substantive right to compensation for the alleged noise nuisance'.[94] In other words, there no substantive right *because* the section excludes it![95] On the basis of this reasoning, every such bar to action would necessarily have the effect of extinguishing causes of action. If there is no substantive right recognized in the domestic legal system, there can be no 'civil right' for the purposes of Article 6. The article is therefore not applicable and *a fortiori* cannot be breached. The Commission and Court, on this line of reasoning, can have

---

[89] *Rayner* v. *UK*, No. 9310/81, Decision on Admissibility, 16 July 1986, para. 7.

[90] Above, n. 52.

[91] *Rayner* v. *UK*, No. 9310/81, Decision on Admissibility, 16 July 1986, para. 7 (emphasis added).

[92] e.g. *Golder* case, Series A, No. 18, para. 34; *Airey* case, Series A, No. 32, para. 24; *Ashingdane* case, Series A, No. 93, para. 57.

[93] Case of *Sporrong and Lönnroth*, Commission Report of 8 October 1980, para. 150; see also case of *James and others*, Series A, No. 98, para. 81; case of *Lithgow and others*, Series A, No. 102, para. 192.

[94] *Rayner* v. *UK*, No. 9310/81, Decision on Admissibility, 16 July 1986, para. 7.

[95] Case of *Powell and Rayner*, Series A, No. 172, para. 36. The Government appears to endorse this line of reasoning: ibid., memorial of the Government, pp. 36–8.

no jurisdiction to review the legitimacy and proportionality of statutory bars. Yet, in the *Ashingdane* case,[96] the Court went out of its way to assert its jurisdiction to consider limitations put on the right of access to court and to indicate the criteria it would apply.

The error of the Commission in the case of *Powell and Rayner*[97] was to confuse yet again the question of the existence of a cause of action with that of the legitimacy and proportionality of a restriction imposed on its scope. The first issue can only be examined by leaving out of consideration the particular statutory provision and applying the 'but for' test. In contrast to the earlier cases, the application of the test in the case of *Powell and Rayner*[98] *would* lead to a different result from that of the Commission. Leaving aside section 76 of the Civil Aviation Act, the applicants would clearly have had a common law right of action for nuisance. The principle of *Sporrong and Lönnroth*[99] is therefore satisfied. The statutory provision results in a denial of effective access to court. It is therefore necessary to examine the aim and proportionality of the limitation.

The Commission did not stop at holding that the applicants could not invoke under English law a substantive right to compensation for the alleged noise nuisance. It went on to observe that

. . . The mere fact that consequently an action in respect of aircraft noise nuisance would be devoid of all prospects of success is not equivalent to depriving the applicant of the right of access to a court.[100]

The use of the phrase 'prospects of success' assumes the existence of a cause of action. The Commission, however, had just asserted that the applicants had no substantive right in English law to sue on account of noise nuisance. The non-existence of a cause of action would indeed mean that the applicants had no prospect of success but, in that case, it is not clear to what 'action' the Commission is referring. The prospects of success would at best be relevant, where a cause of action did exist, if a limitation sought to exclude actions where there was no prima facie case.

The Commission is building upon its original error in that it can only conclude that there is no cause of action, thus depriving the applicant of a right of access to court, if it includes the restriction contained in section 76(1) of the Civil Aviation Act in its appraisal.

The Commission, inconsistently with its previous finding, then went on to recognize that section 76(1) of the Civil Aviation Act is in fact a bar to action. It says that ' . . . it cannot be considered to be clearly established that under English law he could invoke before a court a substantive right were he not *barred* from doing so . . . ' (emphasis added) because ' . . . to

96 Series A, No. 93.
97 e.g. *Rayner* v. *UK*, No. 9310/81, Decision on Admissibility, 16 July 1986, para. 7.
98 Above, n. 11.
99 Commission Report of 8 October 1980, para. 150; see also case of *James and others*, Series A, No. 98, para. 81; case of *Lithgow and others*, Series A, No. 102, para. 192.
100 *Rayner* v. *UK*, No. 9310/81, Decision on Admissibility, 16 July 1986, para. 7.

sue in nuisance one would have to prove unreasonable user'.[101] Again, the Commission is confusing the existence of a cause of action and the prospects of success. If the need to prove unreasonable user means that there is no substantive right in English law, all suits in nuisance would fall outside the protection of Article 6.[102]

To summarize the argument up to this point, only in the *Ashingdane* case[103] has there been a coherent attempt to consider first the applicability of Article 6 and only then the question of its breach. The applicability of the article depends upon there being a domestic substantive right which the Convention organs characterize as civil. The criterion in the case of *Sporrong and Lönnroth*[104] is not itself a problem. Its application may, however, pose difficulties in cases involving restrictions on the scope of a cause of action, since one cannot presume from the mere existence of an apparent bar that in fact a cause of action exists. The question must be, could the applicant sue but for the restriction? That can only be answered by ignoring the bar itself. The number and/or class of those affected, the scope of the bar and its object are irrelevant. The only issue is whether the impugned provision prevents the applicant from doing what he would otherwise do. If that is answered in the affirmative, Article 6 is applicable on the basis of the principles in the *Golder* case,[105] the *Airey* case,[106] and the case of *Sporrong and Lönnroth*.[107] Only then is it necessary to look at the rationale behind the restriction. Had the approach being suggested here been adopted, it does not appear that the result would have been any different in the soldiers' compensation cases[108] and the *Ashingdane* case.[109] In the case of the former, section 10 of the Crown Proceedings Act clearly did act as a bar to action, but the aim of the provision and its proportionality would have satisfied the criteria examined in the next section. In the *Ashingdane* case, it does not appear that the applicant would have had a cause of action in English law, notwithstanding the provisions of section 141 of the Mental Health Act 1959. In the case of *Powell and Rayner*,[110] however, the applicants would have had a cause of action but for section 76 of the

---

[101] Ibid.

[102] 'The essence of nuisance is a condition or activity which *unduly* interferes with the use or enjoyment of land': *Clerk and Lindsell on Torts* (16th edn., 1989), para. 24–01, p. 1354 (emphasis added), and chapter 24 generally. 'A person, then, may be said to have committed the tort of private nuisance when he is held to be responsible for an act indirectly causing physical injury to land or substantially interfering with the use or enjoyment of land or of an interest in land, where, in the light of all the surrounding circumstances, this injury or interference is held to be *unreasonable*': *Street on Torts* (8th edn. by Brazier, 1988), pp. 314–15 (emphasis added), and chapter 19 generally. See, generally, Buckley, *The Law of Nuisance* (1981), chapter 1.

[103] Series A, No. 93.

[104] Commission Report of 8 October 1980, para. 150; see also case of *James and others*, Series A, No. 98, para. 81; case of *Lithgow and others*, Series A, No. 102, para. 192.

[105] Series A, No. 18.

[106] Series A, No. 32.

[107] Commission Report of 8 October 1980, para. 150.

[108] Above, n. 87.

[109] Series A, No. 93.

[110] Above n. 11.

Civil Aviation Act. It therefore remains to be considered what criteria a restriction on the scope of a cause of action must satisfy in order not to violate the right of effective access to court in Article 6 of the European Convention and to apply them to the case of *Powell and Rayner*.

VIII. Criteria to Assess the Compatibility of a Restriction on the Scope of a Cause of Action with the Right of Access to Court

The Court in the *Ashingdane* case, whilst not needing to address the issue in order to determine the case, established the criteria to assess the compatibility of such restrictions with the right of access to court. The restriction must pursue a legitimate aim, must be proportionate and must not have the effect of extinguishing the applicant's access to court.[111] These criteria are the ones found in the case law on the application of the limitations in the second paragraphs of Articles 8–11.[112] Those provisions themselves define the only legitimate aims of the restrictions and further require that the limitations be 'necessary in a democratic society'.[113] The Convention organs have themselves added the requirement that the aim be pursued in a proportionate way. The legitimacy of the aim is not a blanket authorization for whatever measure the State seeks to implement.[114]

(a) *Legitimate Aim*

It will be recalled that the right of access to court is not expressly stated in Article 6.[115] It is the product of judicial interpretation. Permissible limitations on that right are therefore not to be found in the text of the Convention but in the case law. A further difficulty, in the case of *Powell and Rayner*, arises from the admissibility decisions in the two cases. Having decided, wrongly it is submitted, that there was no cause of action in domestic law, the Commission had no need to and the Court could not analyse possible legitimate aims for the denial of access to court and the proportionality of section 76(1) of the Civil Aviation Act in relation to those aims.[116] It is therefore necessary to speculate as to aims which may be legitimate on the basis of the confused case law.

An 'effective political democracy' has been held to require an immunity from suit in relation to statements made in Parliament.[117] It is not clear

---

[111] *Ashingdane* case, Series A, No. 93, para. 57.

[112] e.g. *Handyside* case, Series A, No. 24; *The Sunday Times* case, Series A, No. 30.

[113] *Handyside* case, Series A, No. 24, paras. 48–9.

[114] e.g. in the *Sunday Times* case, Series A, No. 30, the Court held that the grant of an injunction to restrain the publication of an article pursued the legitimate aim of maintaining the authority of the judiciary but that it was neither necessary nor proportionate: para. 67.

[115] *Golder* case, Series A, No. 18; see above, n. 14 and accompanying text.

[116] Case of *Powell and Rayner*, Series A, No. 172, para. 29; see n. 12, above.

[117] *Agee v. UK.* No. 7729/76, *D & R*, vol. 7, p. 164 at p. 175.

whether the Convention organs would review the scope of the immunity. Other Convention concepts have been held to be autonomous,[118] so the Commission and Court might be willing to determine for themselves which communications should be covered, whether any geographical limit is appropriate and whether the principle applies to any utterance of a Member of Parliament or only to those made in the performance of his/her duties.[119]

A second aim accepted by the Commission as legitimate is the substitution of an alternative remedy for the one excluded. It appears to have been material in the soldiers' compensation cases that the immunity only applied where the injury had been certified as attributable to service for the purposes of pension entitlement.[120] The Commission also pointed out that, in many jurisdictions, compensation is handled by means of an insurance scheme rather than litigation and that this has the benefit of avoiding the costs and difficulties of proving negligence.

The avoidance of vexatious litigation is also regarded as a legitimate aim. In a Scottish case,[121] the Commission accepted that the naming of a person as a vexatious litigant under the Vexatious Actions (Scotland) Act 1898, as a result of which he had to seek leave to bring any action at all, was legitimate since he would be given leave if he had a prima facie case. The Commission probably had a similar problem in mind in the *Ashingdane* case, where it referred to the aim of avoiding medical personnel being harassed by litigation.[122] In the first case, the procedures of the court are being abused, even if a different defendant is involved on each occasion. In the second case, the problem is rather the burden on particular individuals who, on account of their professional responsibilities, run the risk of being sued frequently. The legislation in question was the Mental Health Act. The harm sought to be avoided in both cases is the bringing of frivolous claims. The Court, in the *Golder* case, also expressly envisaged limits being placed on the access to court of minors and those of unsound mind.[123]

In the case of *Powell and Rayner*,[124] none of the aims, the legitimacy of

---

[118] *König* case, Series A, No. 27, paras. 88–9; *Feldbrugge* case, Series A, No. 99, paras. 26–7; *Deumeland* case, Series A, No. 100, paras. 60–1.

[119] These issues have been raised in the UK before both the courts and the House of Commons; see Wade and Bradley, *Constitutional and Administrative Law* (10th edn., 1985), pp. 212–17 and 221–2.

[120] *Dyer* v. *UK*, No. 10475/83, *D & R*, vol. 39, p. 246 at p. 251. The Commission made no reference to the fact that no pension was actually guaranteed: *Adams* v. *War Office*, [1955] 3 All ER 245. If, however, the applicants in the cases before the Commission have all in fact received pensions, no difficulty arises. The same principle did not apply in *Wallace-Jones* v. *UK*, No. 10782/84, *D & R*, vol. 47, p. 157, in which the *aim* of the restriction on a cause of action was not the provision of alternative compensation. Such compensation as was offered bore no relationship to the loss suffered by the applicant and appears to have been made, at least in part, *ex gratia* (ibid. at p. 158).

[121] *H* v. *UK*, No. 11559/85, *D & R*, vol. 45, p. 281.

[122] Series A, No. 93, para. 58. In *Wallace-Jones* v. *UK*, No. 10782/84, *D & R*, vol. 47, p. 157 at p. 159, it is not clear whether the Commission had in mind the possibility of harassment by litigation when it accepted that a limitation of liability in the field of telecommunications ' . . . is considered to be an essential condition of producing telephone directories which contain millions of user entries . . . '.

[123] Series A, No. 18, para. 39.

[124] *Rayner* v. *UK*, No. 9310/81, Decision on Admissibility, 16 July 1986; *Powell and Rayner* v. *UK*, No. 9310/81, Report of the Commission, 19 January 1989.

which has already been established, was in issue. No alternative remedy was available to the applicants. Whilst various administrative measures had been taken to control the noise levels around Heathrow airport, such as noise certification of aircraft, restrictions on night movements and the creation of minimum noise routes, these did not give individual applicants the means to challenge the noise levels.[125] Compensation for loss of value of houses and land from airport noise is provided for by the Land Compensation Act 1973 but does not apply to public works constructed before 1969 or to the intensification of existing use. The Noise Abatement Act 1960 specifically exempts aircraft noise from its operations, as does the Control of Pollution Act 1974. The aim found to be legitimate in the soldiers' compensation cases was therefore inapplicable in the case of *Powell and Rayner*; no alternative compensation was available.

The avoidance of vexatious litigation was not raised by either the Government or the Commission. The need to prove unreasonable user in an action for nuisance is an effective deterrent to the bringing of frivolous claims. Furthermore, the Government has seen no need to guard against frivolous litigation with regard to noise where aircraft happen to be flying unreasonably low. Even if such an aircraft is making less noise than one flying at a reasonable height, a plaintiff will be able to sue in nuisance provided the noise crosses the threshold of the unreasonable. Section 76(1) of the Civil Aviation Act 1982 does not apply in such circumstances. The Government pointed to the fact that section 76(1) of the Civil Aviation Act was not a complete bar to action and suggested that, in effect, this enabled the applicant to sue wherever he could have sued at common law. This is only true with regard to the height of aircraft and not to the noise they generate. Further, on the Government's reasoning, the bar to action is completely unnecessary. These arguments relate to the proportionality of the statutory bar, rather than to its legitimacy. There is no evidence of a risk of vexatious litigation.

It is also suggested that section 76 of the Civil Aviation Act was directly comparable to Article 1 of the Rome Convention on Damage Caused by Foreign Aircraft to Third Parties on the Surface, 1952.[126] It is not clear

---

[125] Case of *Powell and Rayner*, Series A, No. 172, verbatim record of the public hearings, 27 September 1989, p. 5 and pp. 32–4. In a different context, that of determining whether information given in confidence should be released to an interested party, both the Commission and Court commented on the lack, in the United Kingdom, of an ' . . . independent procedure to enable . . . [the applicant's] . . . request to be tested . . . ': *Gaskin Case*, Series A, No. 160, paras. 47 and 49. This lack of scrutiny by an authority independent of the Government is not uncommon in the United Kingdom; see also a series of cases involving parental rights in relation to children in the care of a local authority, *O and H* v. *UK*, Series A, No. 120; *W, B and R* v. *UK*, Series A, No. 121. The Court held that the powers of the English courts were not of sufficient scope to enable parents to challenge certain decisions of a local authority. In the context of aircraft noise, it is submitted that a judge is in a better position than the Government itself to balance competing rights and interests and to assess whether the Government's administrative regulations meet the need for effective regulation of noise levels.

[126] *United Nations Treaty Series*, vol. 310, p. 181; *American Journal of International Law*, 52 (1958), p. 593; *Powell and Rayner* v. *UK*, No. 9310/81, Report of the Commission, 19 January 1989, para. 27.

whether this was thought to make section 76 necessary or merely permissible. A State cannot plead one international obligation in order to justify breaching another.[127] It is up to the State to implement its commitments in a fashion consistent with its other obligations. Further, equivalent provisions to section 76 of the Civil Aviation Act existed in legislation which predated the Rome Convention.[128] The relevance of invoking the Rome Convention may have been confined to showing that the position in English law was consistent with an international obligation which dealt expressly with the matter at issue and that a similar situation obtained in other States party to the treaty.[129] In what sense this constitutes a legitimate aim is not clear. Even if the public policy need to implement international obligations were a legitimate aim, to invoke it the Government would have to show that section 76 of the Civil Aviation Act was *required* by the Rome Convention.

The relevant part of Article 1 of the Rome Convention provides that

. . . there shall be no right to compensation . . . if the damage results from the mere fact of passage of the aircraft through the airspace in conformity with existing air traffic regulations.

This would justify excluding actions in trespass, except in the case of damage coming within section 76(2) of the Civil Aviation Act. The 'mere fact of passage' might also be interpreted so as to exclude a right to compensation where the nuisance was necessarily attendant upon the mere fact of passage. That would exclude an action based on noise levels reasonably necessary to the passage of aircraft. Nothing in Article 1 would appear to exclude a right to compensation where the noise levels attendant upon the fact of passage were *un*reasonable, even though in conformity with air traffic regulations. The Rome Convention therefore does not appear to justify a restriction on the cause of action of the scope of section 76(1) of the Civil Aviation Act.

If no other form of compensation is available, there is no evidence of a risk of vexatious litigation and the Rome Convention cannot be used to justify the denial of access to court, the remaining possibility is that the exclusion of a right of action is designed to reduce the operating costs of

---

[127] e.g. Arts. 26 and 30 of the Vienna Convention on the Law of Treaties 1969, *UK Treaty Series*, No. 58 (1980), Cmnd. 7964; *American Journal of International Law*, 63 (1969), p. 875. There are difficulties in applying the latter provision to a treaty such as the ECHR which is ' . . . essentially of an objective character being designed rather to protect the fundamental rights of individual human beings from infringement by any of the High Contracting Parties than to create subjective and reciprocal rights for the High Contracting Parties themselves': *France, Norway, Denmark, Sweden and Netherlands v. Turkey*, No. 9940–9944/82, *D & R*, vol. 35, p. 143 at p. 169. The general principle nevertheless remains valid.

[128] S. 9(1) Air Navigation Act 1920; s. 40(1) Civil Aviation Act 1949. It should be noted that the first of these provisions came a year after the decision in *Bosworth-Smith v. Gwynnes Ltd.*; see n. 35, above.

[129] See the question asked of both the applicants and the Government by the Court: (89) 242; no. 24, 342. The Court itself had previously dealt with a case involving the right to sue in nuisance on account of aircraft noise in Swiss law: case of *Zimmermann and Steiner*, Series A, No. 66.

Heathrow airport and the airlines. The seeking of an economic advantage may perhaps be a legitimate aim, by analogy with the recognition given to the 'economic well-being' of a country in the Convention.[130] The connection between the economic advantage derived from a major international airport and the denial of a right to bring an action for nuisance on account of unreasonable noise levels may not, however, be sufficiently close to make the latter necessary to the achievement of the former aim, even assuming it to be legitimate. It is therefore not clear what arguably legitimate aim the restriction is pursuing; the best contender appears to be the avoidance of cost in the promotion of the economic well-being of the country.

(b) *Proportionality*

In assessing proportionality, the function of the Convention organs is not confined

> . . . to ascertaining whether a respondent State exercised its discretion reasonably, carefully and in good faith. Even a Contracting State so acting remains subject to . . . [their] . . . control as regards the compatibility of its conduct with the engagements it has undertaken under the Convention.[131]

The Commission and Court allow States a 'margin of appreciation'[132] but subject to their supervision. The scope of the 'margin of appreciation' varies as between the different aims which legitimize an interference in the exercise of a right.[133] Those notions which are 'more objective' than the concept of morals leave less scope for a broad 'margin of appreciation'. The Court gave the rights protected by Article 6 of the Convention as an example of a 'more objective notion'.[134]

The Commission and Court therefore clearly have a supervisory role but the basis on which they evaluate proportionality still has to be established. There is some evidence that they equate the criterion of necessity with that of proportionality.[135] The Court has said that 'necessary' is not synonymous with indispensable but does not have the flexibility of such terms as admissible or reasonable; it refers, rather, to a 'pressing social need'.[136]

---

[130] Art. 8 ECHR; see case of *Abdulaziz, Cabales and Balkandali*, Series A, No. 94; case of *Powell and Rayner*, Series A, No. 172, applicants' memorial to the court, pp. 23–4, and judgment, para. 12. In *Wallace-Jones* v. *UK*, No. 10782/84, *D & R*, vol. 47, p. 157 at p. 159, the Commission accepted as legitimate and proportionate a restriction based on the need to offer a telephone service to the public at a *reasonable cost*.

[131] *The Sunday Times* case, Series A, No. 30, para. 59; *Handyside* case, Series A, No. 24, para. 49.

[132] *Handyside* case, Series A, No. 24, para. 48.

[133] Ibid.; *The Sunday Times* case, Series A, No. 30, para. 59.

[134] *The Sunday Times* case, Series A, No. 30, para. 59.

[135] Ibid., paras. 62 and 67; *Handyside* case, Series A, No. 24, para. 48.

[136] *Handyside* case, Series A, No. 24, para. 48.

The Court examines the necessity of the restriction placed on a right ' . . . in the light of the case as a whole . . . '.[137]

The Convention organs are not however trying to balance two competing principles. The starting point is a Convention *right*, ' . . . subject to a number of exceptions which must be narrowly interpreted . . . '.[138] The need to construe exceptions restrictively, the view that the rights protected by Article 6 are 'objective', leaving less of a 'margin of appreciation' for the domestic authorities, and the significance attached by the Commission and Court to the 'rule of law',[139] all suggest that a government must make out a very strong case for a restriction on a right of access to court to be regarded as legitimate, necessary and proportionate. In the *Golder* case, for example, the Court said,

> The principle whereby a civil claim must be capable of being submitted to a judge ranks as one of the universally 'recognized' fundamental principles of law; the same is true of the principle of international law which forbids the denial of justice. Article 6§1 must be read in light of these principles.
>
> Were Article 6§1 to be understood as concerning exclusively the conduct of an action which had already been initiated before a court, a Contracting State could, without acting in breach of that text, do away with its courts, or take away their jurisdiction to determine certain classes of civil actions and entrust it to organs dependent on the Government. Such assumptions, indissociable from a danger of arbitrary power, would have serious consequences which are repugnant to the afore-mentioned principles . . . [140]

It is against this background that the proportionality of the denial of effective access to court produced by section 76 of the Civil Aviation Act 1982 must be assessed.

The applicants in the case of *Powell and Rayner*[141] wished to be able to invoke their right to sue in nuisance at common law on account of allegedly unreasonable noise levels but were prevented from doing so by that provision. In the previous section, it was suggested that there is no evidence of a risk of vexatious litigation and that the restriction on action is broader in scope than might be justified under Article 1 of the Rome Convention. The proportionality of the bar therefore only needs to be assessed in the context of the possibly legitimate aim of encouraging economic well-being.

That aim is pursued at the expense of the applicants. Approximately one thousand five hundred people[142] live within the 60 NNI contour around

[137] *The Sunday Times* case, Series A, No. 30, para. 60; *Handyside* case, Series A, No. 24, para. 50.
[138] *The Sunday Times* case, Series A, No. 30, para. 65, citing the case of *Klass and others*, Series A, No. 28, para. 42.
[139] *Golder* case, Series A, No. 18, paras. 34–5; *Airey* case, Series A, No. 32, para, 24; *Ashingdane* case, Series A, No. 93, para. 57; *Dyer* v. *UK*, No. 10475/83, *D & R*, vol. 39, p. 246 at p. 252.
[140] *Golder* case, Series A, No. 18, para. 35.
[141] Above, n. 11.
[142] Ibid., Report of the Commission, para. 20.

Heathrow airport.[143] Thirty-eight million passengers a year use the airport.[144] If it were a question of balancing competing rights, even a relatively 'small' interest on the part of the airport users would clearly balance out a serious burden placed on the small number of adjacent residents. The starting point, however, is the right of the applicants. They have the right to enjoy their property free from nuisance. The scale of the burden placed on them is more important than the numbers affected. Further, the cost of preventing the nuisance would be spread between the airport users, resulting in only a slightly increased cost per capita.

The Government does take a variety of administrative measures designed to reduce the noise to which the applicants are subjected.[145] The measures, however, lack two essential elements, as a result of which they come within the words of warning of the Court in the *Golder* case.[146] There is no control independent of Government and no evidence that reasonableness is the criterion used to evaluate the effectiveness of the measures taken.

These elements suggest that a disproportionate burden may be placed on the applicants, but it is necessary to examine in greater detail the scope of the restriction itself. The Government and the Commission suggested that two features of the scope of section 76 of the Civil Aviation Act ensure that the provision is proportionate in its effect and does not destroy the 'very essence of the right'[147] to sue in nuisance. First, the bar does not exclude all actions in nuisance. Where an aircraft is flying unreasonably low or in breach of an Air Navigation Order, an individual may be able to sue on account of unreasonable noise. This enables a plaintiff to exercise his right by reference to the height of aircraft when his complaint relates to noise. It adds insult to injury to tell an applicant that he may be able to succeed in an action in nuisance where the aircraft is flying low and quite possibly making less noise than an aircraft flying at a reasonable height. It is easier to cope with exceptional exposure to a high level of noise, as the NNI formula recognizes, than regular exposure to that or a lower level of noise disturbance. The possibility of a suit in a nuisance where an aircraft is flying too low, in other words in exceptional circumstances, preserves the penumbra of the right, but section 76(1) destroys its very essence by preventing a successful action in nuisance in normal circumstances, where it is most needed.

Second, the Commission suggested that a distinction should be drawn

---

[143] Noise and Number Index; the ' . . . long-term average measure of noise exposure which is used in the United Kingdom to assess the disturbance from aircraft noise . . . . It takes account of two features of the noise, namely the average noisiness and the number of aircraft heard during an average summer day': ibid., Series A, No. 172, para. 10. 60 NNI is recognized by the Government as an area of high noise annoyance, on account of which no development whatsoever is permitted.

[144] Case of *Powell and Rayner*, Series A, No. 172, verbatim record of the public hearings, 27 September 1989, p. 37.

[145] Above, n. 125 and accompanying text.

[146] Above, n. 140 and accompanying text; see also n. 119, above.

[147] *Ashingdane* case, Series A, No. 93, para. 57.

between this case and the soldiers' compensation cases[148] and the *Ashingdane* case,[149] in that those cases conferred ' . . . an immunity from liability in respect of actions of certain and distinct groups of persons', whereas, in the present case, the bar to action

. . . excludes *generally* any action in respect of trespass or nuisance caused by the flight of an aircraft at a reasonable height regardless of the status of the possible claimant.[150]

There are two objections to the Commission's analysis, the one challenging the analysis itself and the second the underlying assumption on which it is based. Section 76 of the Civil Aviation Act may not in terms confer an immunity on a 'certain and distinct' group or deny a right of action to a defined group but that is its effect in fact. The only persons protected against an action in nuisance are airport operators and the airlines, since only they could be sued at common law on account of unreasonable noise levels caused by aircraft. They represent a numerically smaller group than members of the armed forces or National Health Service employees. The only persons prevented from taking action to vindicate their right are adjacent landowners. They also represent a smaller group than members of the armed forces or National Health Service patients. If constituting a class or group is relevant, the requirement is satisfied by the victims of section 76(1) of the Civil Aviation Act.

It is submitted, however, that the requirement that the would-be plaintiff or defendant belong to a defined class or group is not only unnecessary but the very *antithesis* of the criterion that should be applied. Where a bar to action excludes legal action by a particular group, it is more likely to represent the proportionate achievement of a legitimate aim. The aim in the soldiers' compensation cases, for example, was to provide a different form of compensation. The only persons eligible for the particular type of pension were members of the armed forces injured whilst on duty. It was therefore necessary, if the exclusion was to be proportionate, that it should only apply to those eligible under the alternative scheme. The more widespread the effect of a restriction superimposed on a cause of action, the more likely it is to be inconsistent with the rule of law. It excludes a whole area of activity from the supervision of the courts. The Commission and Court have shown an awareness of this danger in relation to a similar problem in a different area, that of prisoners' correspondence.[151] The British authorities used to assume that all letter-writing by prisoners was a privilege. As a result of the decisions of the Convention organs, they have been obliged to recognize that a prisoner has a prima facie right to correspond and that it is

---

[148] *X* v. *UK*, No. 7443/76, *D & R*, vol. 8, p. 216; *K* v. *UK*, No. 9803/82, cited in *Dyer* v. *UK*, No. 10475/83, *D & R*, vol. 39, p. 246.

[149] Series A, No. 93.

[150] *Rayner* v. *UK*, No. 9310/81, Admissibility Decision of 16 July 1986, para. 7.

[151] e.g. *Golder* case, Series A, No. 18; case of *Silver and others*, Series A, No. 61; case of *Campbell and Fell*, Series A, No. 80; *Weeks* case, Series A, No. 114; case of *Boyle and Rice*, Series A, No. 131.

up to the government to justify *specific* limitations. In the case of restrictions on causes of action, this would suggest that only specific restrictions should be held to be proportionate.

Section 76(1) of the Civil Aviation Act does not exclude all possibility of a suit in nuisance. Nevertheless, in only leaving open that possibility in exceptional circumstances, it destroys the 'very essence' of the applicants' right. Their right of access to court is 'theoretical' and 'illusory'.[152]

Two arguments remain, concerning the proportionality of the restriction in the context of the case as a whole. The first is that the change sought, allowing individuals to exercise their right to sue in nuisance, would cost too much. It would cost the Government nothing. The unsuccessful plaintiff would have to bear his own costs and those of the defendant. The cost of paying damages to a successful plaintiff could be spread between the thirty-eight million passengers a year who use Heathrow airport. Since they are the ones who benefit from the activity, it would seem not inappropriate that they should bear the cost. Would-be plaintiffs probably hope that the possibility of legal action would have a deterrent effect.

Second, the Government would probably claim that it is within its 'margin of appreciation' to choose how to strike a balance between competing interests. It has chosen to proceed by way of administrative regulation, rather than letting the courts achieve the balance. It is submitted that this argument forgets that the applicants' interest is a *right* and one which is a fundamental element in the rule of law.[153] The Government itself is not independent but is, rather, an interested party. It does not use the reasonableness of the noise levels as the criterion for such measures as it does take. The nature of the interest to be protected is so fundamental that to allow a State to proceed by way of administrative regulation would appear to allow it to exceed its 'margin of appreciation'.

Finally, the possible effect of the change sought must be considered. Determining what constitutes a reasonable noise level is not a new task for judges. Not only do they make such determinations in common law actions in nuisance, but they have also been given that responsibility under statute. Under section 59(5) of the Control of Pollution Act 1974, a court determines whether the 'best practicable means' have been used to prevent or counteract the effect of noise. 'Practicable' is defined in section 72(1) as meaning 'reasonably practicable having regard among other things to local conditions and circumstances, to the current state of technical knowledge

---

[152] *Airey* case, Series A, No. 32, para. 24.

[153] Above, n. 140 and accompanying text; see also n. 125, above. If it were left to a government to exclude access to court where, in its opinion, the applicant would not win, the government would be substituting its opinion for that of an independent judge. The danger to the rule of law in such a situation is obvious, particularly where the government or a body for whose actions it bears responsibility under the ECHR (e.g. the British Airports Authority) is the would-be defendant. In an analogous situation, one of the elements taken into account in determining the grant of legal aid in the UK is the prospects of success. That is not the criterion used by the Court, which bases its decision on ' . . . whether the interests of justice . . . [require] . . . a grant of legal aid . . . in the light of the case as a whole': *Granger* case, Series A, No. 174, para. 46.

and to the financial implications'.[154] The only guide as to how judges would apply such a formula in the case of a major international airport is to be found in the way in which they assess the reasonableness of noise levels in an action in nuisance.[155] Judges have shown a particular concern for noise levels at night.[156] Whilst they might impose additional restrictions on the day-time operations at Heathrow airport, they would be more likely to restrict night-time operations, either quantitatively by extending the hours during which the night-time limits apply or qualitatively by setting a lower maximum noise threshold, or both.[157]

IX. CONCLUSION

It is submitted that, in the case of *Powell and Rayner*,[158] the Commission misapplied the principle in the case of *Sporrong and Lönnroth*.[159] The Commission should have found that a cause of action exists in domestic law but that it is barred by operation of section 76(1) of the Civil Aviation Act 1982. Had it done so, the Commission and Court would have had to consider what aim the restriction is pursuing and whether or not it is legitimate. The date of the first measure of this sort, predating the Rome Convention by thirty-two years, casts doubt on the claim that section 76(1) is required by that Convention. The provision is also unnecessarily broad, if that is its purpose. There is no evidence of a risk of vexatious litigation. The most likely reason for the restriction is the avoidance of cost in the promotion of Heathrow as Europe's leading international airport. The Commission and Court might regard this as the promotion of the economic well-being of the country and hold it to be a legitimate aim. It is suggested, however, that the way in which the aim is pursued imposes a disproportionate burden on the applicants by destroying the very essence of their right to sue in nuisance. The costs of Heathrow airport should be borne by the airport users, rather than by adjacent landowners.

Were the applicants to be able to exercise their right at common law to

---

[154] In *Baker* v. *Burbank-Glendale-Passadena Airport Authority*, 39 Cal. 3d 862, a decision of the Californian Supreme Court, it was held that unreasonable levels of aircraft noise give rise to an actionable 'continuing' nuisance, unless the authorities have done *everything technologically possible* to abate the noise. (The US Supreme Court denied certiorari of the decision on 24 February 1986.) A less strict criterion, the one used in the Control of Pollution Act 1974, is all that is being suggested here.

[155] Above, n. 35; in *Bosworth-Smith* v. *Gwynnes Ltd.*, 122 LT 15, concerning the noise created by the testing of an aircraft engine, Peterson J said, at p. 20, 'I am not satisfied that everything that is possible has been done for the purpose of mitigating the nuisance'.

[156] e.g. *Andreae* v. *Selfridge & Co. Ltd.*, [1973] 2 All ER 255 at 261, *per* Sir Wilfred Greene MR; see, generally, Buckley op.cit. above (n. 35), pp. 11–12.

[157] It is not clear whether the Government's definition of night for the purposes of regulating levels of aircraft noise is 2300–0700 hours or whether the effect of qualifications on the definition is to reduce it to 2330–0600 hours: case of *Powell and Rayner*, Series A, No. 172, memorial of the applicants to the Court, p. 27; see Appendix B of the memorial for noise infringement record. The figures for night-time infringements suggest that the Government does not effectively enforce its own restrictions.

[158] Above, n. 11.

[159] Case of *Sporrong and Lönnroth*, Commission Report of 8 October 1980.

sue in nuisance, they would only be able to obtain redress against *un*reasonable noise levels. A court would take into account, in assessing reasonableness, the fact that Heathrow airport is a major international airport. The Government maintains that the administrative measures which it takes are sufficient. In that case, it has nothing to fear from allowing actions in nuisance. The insistence on the need to restrict the cause of action creates the suspicion that the Government fears successful litigation. It is submitted that section 76(1) deprives the applicants of the 'very essence' of their right of access to a court for an objective determination of the reasonableness of the noise levels to which they are subjected. This is inconsistent with a due regard for the rule of law. Section 76(1) of the Civil Aviation Act 1982 therefore gives rise to a denial of the applicants' right of effective access to court, in breach of Article 6 of the European Convention on Human Rights.

SPLITTING THE PROPER LAW IN PRIVATE INTERNATIONAL LAW*

By CAMPBELL MCLACHLAN‡

'It is quite correct . . . that a transaction may in certain respects . . . be governed by the law of one country although it is governed by the law of another country in other respects. . . . but this does not mean that there are two different systems of law which can simultaneously govern and determine the general obligation of the contract . . . On the contrary, the whole theory which lies at the root of private international law, however difficult that theory may be in application, is that the law of one country, and one country alone, can be the proper or governing law of the contract . . . ':
per Evatt J, *Wanganui-Rangitikei Electric Power Board* v. *Australian Mutual Provident Society*, (1933-4) 50 CLR 581, 604 (HCA).

I. THE PROVINCE OF THE PROPER LAW

The doctrine of the split proper law has long been part of the orthodoxy of English choice of law rules. It has recently received renewed attention, and apparent endorsement, in two important commercial decisions: *Vesta* v. *Butcher*[1] and *Libyan Arab Foreign Bank* v. *Bankers Trust Co.*[2] Parliament has recently enacted the Contracts (Applicable Law) Act 1990 which, as from 1 April 1991, gives the Rome Convention on the Law Applicable to Contractual Obligations 1980 the force of law in the United Kingdom. The Covention adopts the notion of a split proper law in its set of uniform rules. Yet it is the purpose of this article to argue that the doctrine is a fallacy. So far from being supported by actual judicial decision and principle, it runs counter to the primary function of the proper law, to locate obligations within a legal matrix, and, as the recent cases illustrate, serves only to confuse analysis of transnational contracts. These themes will be worked out through a discussion of the English cases, of approaches adopted in other legal systems, and of *Vesta* v. *Butcher* and *Bankers Trust*. But it is first necessary to say something about the function of the proper law.

The necessity for rules of private international law arises from the multiplicity of diverse legal systems, which may potentially have an impact upon a given legal status, relationship or obligation. The primary function of the

* © Dr Campbell McLachlan, 1991.
‡ LL B (Hons.); Ph.D; Diploma *cum laude* (Hague Academy of International Law); Solicitor (New Zealand).
[1] *Forsikringsaktieselskapet Vesta* v. *Butcher*, [1989] AC 852 (HL and CA), affirming [1986] 2 All ER 488 (Hobhouse J).
[2] [1988] 1 Lloyd's Rep. 259.

choice of law process is to resolve the very real conflicts of laws which as a matter of fact arise when legal situations span national boundaries. In carrying out this function, the 'proper law' has, at least from an English perspective, a vital part to play.

In one sense, the notion of the proper law does little more than state the issue.[3] It does not in itself determine which law is the proper law to govern a particular situation. Yet, by determining the question, the proper law approach shapes a system of choice of law rules which seeks to locate obligations within a single legal system, and thereby reduce the range of conflict. Such an approach may be contrasted with the American 'Governmental Interest Analysis' theories[4] which focus on identifying the competing claims of policies underlying particular rules to apply to a given issue.

A proper law approach is, then, about identifying the system of rules applicable to a given obligation or relationship as a whole. However, it begs the question in this sense as well. It does not in itself determine the extent of the issues arising out of a legal relationship to be subjected to one law. Yet the choice of law process plainly involves a categorization of issues. A simple sales contract may involve different laws to govern the capacity of the parties, formal requirements, the obligations of the parties and transfer of title to the goods.

This division of issues, and of choice of law rules applicable to those issues, flows from fundamental definitions and distinctions, which are made in substantive law. Addressing these distinctions in a transnational context involves the same elemental step of legal reasoning, namely, determining the nature of the problem. But it should not be assumed that such basic categories are immutable or that factual situations will always fit neatly into them.

The type of division with which this paper is concerned involves situations where the courts have allowed or required two legal systems to apply within one of the broad categories established by choice of law rules. The cases examined here are all concerned with the notion of splitting the proper law applicable to a contract, but this need not be the only relevant context. The phenomenon has been considered much more broadly in civil law systems and in the United States under the term 'dépeçage'. As Lagarde comments: 'Le terme évoque directement l'art du boucher'.[5] But what is seen in Europe as an evil (necessary or unnecessary) has been adopted across the Atlantic as basic to the 'American Revolution' in the conflict of laws, since it is employed to denote isolation of the particular

---

[3] See Mann, 'The Proper Law in the Conflict of Laws', *International and Comparative Law Quarterly*, 36 (1987), p. 437.

[4] See Cavers, *The Choice of Law Process* (1965); Weintraub, 'Developments in Choice of Law for Contracts', *Recueil des cours*, 187 (1984–IV), p. 243; Juenger, 'Conflict of Laws: A Critique of Interest Analysis', *American Journal of Comparative Law*, 32 (1984), p. 1.

[5] Lagarde, 'Le "dépeçage" dans le droit international privé des contrats', *Rivista di diritto internazionale privato e processuale*, 11 (1975), p. 649.

issue whose applicable law is to be decided (as opposed to the determination of the law to govern a relationship or obligation as a whole).

The narrower framework for the problem in English law should not obscure the possible range of divisions which may be involved. A split proper law may be effected as a result of the choice of the parties or by judicial decision. It may involve a division between aspects of the obligation, such as between formation and performance; or between the law governing the obligations of each party; or between separate terms of the contract; or between separate parts of the contractual arrangement (such as the two constituent bank accounts of the contract in the *Bankers Trust* case).

Despite this wide compass, the cases on split proper law do betray a common concern with the need to respect party autonomy (whether it be the autonomy to choose different laws to govern different parts of a contract, or simply the need to secure the validity and efficacy of the contract); and the need to respect the claims of legal systems with a close connection to the contract.

The ongoing tension in the cases is between the judges' desire to give effect to those objectives and the whole function of a proper law.[6] As Kahn-Freund has put it:[7]

No contractual obligation can exist in more than one system, simultaneously or consecutively, any more than it can exist in none . . . .The proper law of the contract determines not only its interpretation, effect, and discharge, but also its validity e.g. the questions whether it was ever made, whether it is void for illegality, or voidable, by reason of mistake, fraud, duress, etc.

An outstanding judicial expression of this is the decision of the House of Lords in *Amin Rasheed Shipping Corp.* v. *Kuwait Insurance Co.*[8] In that case, it had been suggested, in an argument which had received some favour in the lower courts, that the contract under consideration was effectively 'internationalized'. Lord Diplock rejected this notion:[9]

My lords, contracts are incapable of existing in a legal vacuum. They are mere pieces of paper devoid of all legal effect unless they were made by reference to some system of private law which defines the obligations assumed by the parties to the contract by their use of particular forms of words and prescribes the remedies enforceable in a court of justice for failure to perform any of those obligations; and this must be so however widespread geographically the use of a contract employing a particular form of words to express the obligations assumed by the parties may be.

An awareness of the very real conflicts of laws which could arise if a contract

---

[6] On this in relation to other aspects of choice of law in contract, see McLachlan, 'The New Hague Sales Convention and the Limits of the Choice of Law Process', *Law Quarterly Review*, 102 (1986), p. 591.

[7] Kahn-Freund, *General Problems of Private International Law* (1976), p. 256.

[8] [1984] AC 50.

[9] Ibid. 65.

is subjected to more than one legal system has also informed the courts' approach to post formation choice of law. In a number of recent cases the courts have been confronted with choice of law clauses which purport to 'float' in the sense that the choice of law is left to the option of one party, or only crystallizes on the happening of a given event. This type of clause was rejected by the Court of Appeal in *The Armar*. Megaw LJ commented:[10]

> As a matter of legal logic, I find insuperable difficulty in seeing by what system of law you are to decide what, if any, is the legal effect of an event which occurs when a contract is already in existence with no proper law, but instead with a 'floating' non-law.

As Hobhouse J pointed out in *Vesta* v. *Butcher*, there may not be an irreducible conflict between party autonomy and a proper law approach, since:[11]

> . . . the primary function of the proper law is to give effect to the parties' intention not merely to agree, but also to make a legal contract, i.e. to create a legal relationship. This presupposes a legal system since a legal contract cannot be made without a reference to a legal system which is to give it its legal effect.

A split proper law undermines the whole function of the proper law which is to provide a basic infrastructure of legal rules in order to determine the existence, nature and extent of the parties' legal obligations, and provides no alternative basis for resolving the competing claims of legal systems. There are sound commercial reasons for the unifying function of the proper law: parties must be able to know the nature and extent of their obligations, which can only be discovered by reference to a given legal system.

A better answer to the underlying concerns which have motivated the courts to approve a split proper law is to be found in construing the nature of the contractual obligations assumed by the parties, and in considering the important distinction between reference and incorporation.[12]

Aside from the underlying law governing the contract, the parties may incorporate into a contract governed by one legal system some provision of another system. Thus, to give Dicey's example, the parties to an English contract may agree that the liability of an agent to his principal shall be determined in accordance with the relevant articles of the French Civil Code. The effect is not to make French law the proper law of the contract, but rather to incorporate the articles as contractual terms into an English contract. This is merely a shorthand alternative to setting out the French articles verbatim. While there may be difficulties, as a matter of construction, in deciding whether the parties have intended to choose the proper

---

[10] *Armar Shipping Co. Ltd.* v. *Caisse Algérienne d'Assurance et de Réassurance*, [1981] 1 WLR 207, 215, discussed by Pierce, 'Post-formation Choice of Law in Contract', *Modern Law Review*, 50 (1987), p. 176.

[11] [1986] 2 All ER 488, 504.

[12] Dicey and Morris, *The Conflict of Laws* (11th edn., 1987), pp. 1178–80; Kelly, 'Reference, Choice, Restriction and Prohibition', *International and Comparative Law Quarterly*, 26 (1977), p. 857.

law governing the whole of the contract, or merely to incorporate some terms of a foreign law, the distinction in principle is clear. In the case of incorporation it will still be the proper law which forms the basic infrastructure for the parties' contractual relations. Issues of interpretation are thus approached from the standpoint of the proper law. The distinction is important because, as will be argued, many of the fact situations where there is an apparent split proper law are in reality examples of incorporation.

The fallacies of a split proper law approach are exemplified by such English cases as have divided the law governing obligations under a contract, and by the comparative experience of dépeçage. The resurrection of the doctrine in the context of reinsurance (*Vesta* v. *Butcher*) and Eurodollar automatic funds transfer arrangements (the Libyan Bank cases) has shown that, whatever its superficial attractions, the doctrine provides a bad guide to decision. These considerations cause one to question the origins of the doctrine, and it is to the authorities that we must first turn.

II. Origins of the Doctrine in English Law

One of the first statements approving the split proper law in English law is to be found in the first edition of *Dicey*:[13]

... it may be, that part of the contract shall be governed by the law of one country e.g., of England, where it is made, and part of the contract by the law of another country e.g., of Scotland, where it is to be performed. The law or laws by which it is intended that a contract shall be governed may be conveniently termed the 'proper law of a contract'.

Dicey further accepted that separate laws could govern each party's obligations to perform.[14] Thus, where A agreed to deliver goods to X in Liverpool and X agreed to pay for them in New York, A's performance of the delivery would be governed by English law and X's performance of the payment would be governed by the law of New York.

He cited in support of the former proposition the case of *Hamlyn* v. *Talisker Distillery*.[15] That case concerned a dispute under a contract between an English and a Scottish firm, signed in London but to be performed in Scotland, which contained a stipulation that any dispute was to be heard by arbitration by two members of the London Corn Exchange. The dispute came before the Scottish Courts, which held that the arbitration clause was invalid (the clause not naming the arbitrators as required by Scots law). The House of Lords on appeal from Scotland held that the

---

[13] Dicey, *The Conflict of Laws* (1896), p. 540; cf. 11th edn. (1987), p. 1163.
[14] Ibid., pp. 572–3; cf. 11th edn., p. 1194.
[15] [1894] AC 202 (HL).

clause was valid, being governed by English law. Lord Herschell LC held:[16]

> Where a contract is entered into between parties residing in different places, where different systems of law prevail, it is a question, as it appears to me, in each case, with reference to what law the parties contracted, and according to what law it was their intention that their rights either under the whole *or any part of the contract* should be determined.

Fourteen years earlier, in *Chamberlain* v. *Napier*,[17] Hall VC had considered a matrimonial property agreement executed in Scotland between an Englishman and a Scotswoman, which contained trusts of the English real property of the husband in English form and of personalty in Scotland belonging to the wife in Scots form. The Vice Chancellor held:[18]

> . . . I think there is no difficulty on principle or in law, in holding that, in a contract framed as this is, a certain portion of it is to be treated as construed as English, when in all other respects it must be dealt with as Scotch.

These dicta were considered by Swinfen Eady J in *British South Africa Company* v. *De Beers Consolidated Mines Ltd.*,[19] a case which concerned a loan agreement between the defendant, a South African company, and the plaintiff, an English company, secured by charge on the plaintiff's assets (which included land and mines in Rhodesia). It was subsequently agreed that the plaintiff should grant the defendant a mining licence in consideration of the loan. By the law of Southern Rhodesia such an agreement would have been valid, but by English law it was invalid, the mining licence constituting a clog on the equity of redemption. Swinfen Eady J reviewed the general principles applicable to choice of law in contract and held that '. . . different laws may apply to different parts of a contract if the parties so intend'.[20]

The next two cases to consider the doctrine were argued consecutively before the House of Lords, and the decisions were delivered on the same day, 20 October 1949: *Kahler* v. *Midland Bank*[21] and *Zivnostenska Banka National* v. *Frankman*.[22] In these cases the House was concerned with the ability of Czech nationals to obtain delivery up of shares and debenture bonds respectively held to the order of or with the branch of Czech banks in London. Lord MacDermott held, in an oft-cited passage in *Kahler*:[23]

> If then, as I would hold, the proper law of the contract is to a substantial extent that of Czechoslovakia, must it be said on that account, and notwithstanding the circumstances, that that law is also the proper law of the mode of performance in

---

[16] Ibid. 207 (emphasis added).
[17] (1880) 15 Ch. D 614.
[18] Ibid. 631.
[19] [1910] 1 Ch. 354.
[20] Ibid. 383.
[21] [1950] AC 24.
[22] [1950] AC 57.
[23] [1950] AC 24, 42.

London? Though there is no authority binding your Lordships to the view that there can be but one proper law in respect of any given contract, it is doubtless true to say that the Courts of this country will not split the contract in this sense readily or without good reason. In my opinion, however, there is good ground for so doing in the somewhat unusual and, as I think, compelling circumstances of the present case.

In *Re Helbert Wagg & Co. Ltd.*[24] the English courts were again concerned with the effect of the upheavals of the 1930s and of the Second World War on financial arrangements. A loan was made by an English company to a German company. The German Moratorium Law of 1933 converted foreign debts expressed in foreign currency into Reichsmarks, and the debt was paid on this basis. After the war, the English company lodged a claim to rank as creditor with the Administrator of German enemy property in England for the full amount of the debt in sterling. Upjohn J, considering terms in the agreement which provided for security for the loan by means of mortgages over German immovable property, acknowledged that 'those considerations are not conclusive upon the question, for the parties may well contemplate that different parts of their contract shall be governed by different law'.[25]

In *Re United Railways of the Havana and Regla Warehouses Ltd.*,[26] Jenkins LJ cited *Hamlyn* and *Kahler* as authority for the proposition that 'the fact that one aspect of a contract is to be governed by the law of one country does not necessarily mean that that law is to be the proper law of the contract as a whole',[27] although he accepted that the courts would not split the contract readily and without good reason.

Recently, in *Tamari v. Rothfos*,[28] the Court of Appeal considered a clause in a contract for the sale of coffee which submitted claims as to the quality of the coffee to English law, but was silent as to the law applicable to the balance of the contract. By accepting that the law as to the contract as a whole was still at large, Lord Denning MR appears to have accepted that quality claims could be governed by a different law from other matters.

At first blush, therefore, there would seem to be considerable judicial authority for the doctrine of split proper law. However, closer examination shows that none of the cases cited above in fact involved a split proper law. In every case, while accepting the possibility, the court proceeded to reach a decision on another basis: either by finding the contract to be subject to a single law, or by finding two separate contracts, or by holding that a single contract, governed by a single proper law, had incorporated into it some provisions subject to foreign law.

It is plain that either of these latter alternatives was acceptable to Hall

---

[24] [1956] Ch. 323.
[25] Ibid. 340.
[26] [1960] Ch. 52.
[27] Ibid. 92.
[28] *Wahbe Tamari and Sons Co. v. Bernhard Rothfos Beteiligungsgesellschaft mbH*, [1980] 2 Lloyd's Rep. 553.

VC in *Chamberlain* v. *Napier*. In construing those parts of the contract which created an English trust over English real property, Hall VC held:[29]

I quite agree with what was said in argument, that the provisions of the contract generally are of a Scotch character, but, notwithstanding that, there are portions of the contract which are separable from the remainder of it, and seem to me *to contain an English contract*, which was meant by the parties to it to be construed by and to operate under English law.

He then went on to hold that the trust relating to the husband's equity must be construed in accordance with English law, because, having regard to the language and the subject-matter, this was the clear intention of the parties.

In *Hamlyn* v. *Talisker*, it was accepted either that the whole contract was governed by English law,[30] or that the clause nominating arbitration in England was a separate contract governed by English law. As Lord Shand put it:[31]

. . . the agreement which it contained for the settlement of disputes which might arise out of the contract was to be interpreted and governed by the law of England . . .

It is now accepted that *Hamlyn* v. *Talisker* is one of the earliest authorities for the view that an arbitration clause in a contract constitutes a self-contained contract collateral or ancillary to the main contract of which it forms a part.[32]

In *De Beers* the whole contract was held to be governed by English law.[33] In *Kahler* the proper law of the entire contract was held to be Czechoslovakian law. Lord MacDermott's comments on split proper law were made in his dissenting judgment. The same position was taken by the House in *Frankman*'s case. In *Helbert Wagg*, Upjohn J applied German law to the entirety of the contract. Finally, when the *United Railways* case reached the House of Lords *sub nom. Tomkinson* v. *First Pennsylvania Banking and Trust*

---

[29] (1880) 15 Ch. D 614, 631 (emphasis added). But see *contra* Swinfen Eady J in *De Beers*, [1910] 1 Ch. 354, 383:
'It will be observed that Hall V.-C. dealt with the case upon the footing that there was one contract, and not, as was suggested, two contracts in one document.'

[30] But see the comments of Lord Reid in *Compagnie d'Armement Maritime* v. *Compagnie Tunisienne de Navigation*, [1971] AC 572, 596:
'[*Hamlyn* v. *Talisker*] if carefully read, is a decision on the validity of the arbitration clause and on the law governing that clause. Their Lordships were most careful in their language to limit their decision as to the applicability of English law to the arbitration clause, whose validity was in question, and not to exclude the application of Scottish law, as the lex loci solutionis, to the rest of the contract.'

[31] [1894] AC 202, 216.

[32] Collins, 'The Law Governing the Agreement and Procedure in International Arbitration in England', in Lew (ed.) *Contemporary Problems in International Arbitration* (1986), p. 126 at p. 127; Mustill and Boyd, *The Law and Practice of Commercial Arbitration In England* (1982), pp. 78–82; Redfern and Hunter, *Law and Practice of International Commercial Arbitration* (1986), pp. 132–4; Thomas, 'Proper Law of Arbitration Agreements', *Lloyd's Maritime and Commercial Law Quarterly*, 1984, p. 304. The leading authority is *Bremer Vulkan Schiffbau und Maschinenfabrik* v. *South India Shipping Corp.*, [1981] AC 909. The principle of the autonomy of the arbitration clause is explicitly recognized in, for example, the UNCITRAL model law, Article 16(1).

[33] [1910] 1 Ch. 354, 386.

Co.,[34] it was held that the entire contract was to be governed by Pennsylvanian law, although it was accepted that Cuban law governed the formalities in the creation of the contract. In *Tamari* v. *Rothfos*, it was held, taking the coffee quality clause together with other relevant connecting factors, that the contract as a whole was governed by English law.

In a further line of cases, the courts made a sustained sally into dividing by operation of law the legal systems governing the fundamental obligations of a contract. This line of authority was concerned with determining the money of account in a contract, where the sum owed was expressed simply in pounds, without further elucidation as to which monetary system was indicated: the much discussed Privy Council 'money' cases.[35]

The controversy originated in the dictum of Lord Wright in *Adelaide Electric Supply Co. Ltd.* v. *Prudential Assurance Co. Ltd.*:[36]

It is established that prima facie, whatever is the proper law of the contract regarded as a whole, the law of the place of performance should be applied in respect of any particular obligation which is performable within a particular country other than the country of the proper law of the contract.

Lord Wright cited as authority the presumption in *Dicey* that when a contract is made in one country and is to be performed either wholly or partly in another, the proper law of the contract, especially as to the *mode of performance*, may be presumed to be the law of the country where the performance is to take place.[37] He also referred to *Ralli Bros.* v. *Compañia Naviera Sota y Aznar*,[38] a case which deals with the effect of illegality by the place of performance.

The *Adelaide* case concerned a company incorporated in England to transact business in Australia. In 1921, by special resolution of the shareholders, the whole conduct and control of its business was transferred to Australia, except for certain formal matters required by statute to be observed in England. The resolution provided that all dividends should be paid to the shareholders in Adelaide. In 1932 the shareholders claimed to be paid the nominal amount of their dividends in English pounds without deduction for Australian exchange. The House of Lords held that they were only entitled to be paid the nominal amount in Australian pounds, in spite of a difference of some 25 per cent in the value of the two currencies. A majority (Lords Warrington, Tomlin and Russell) took the rather unrealistic view that there was no difference between the English and Australian pound, and that thus the company could discharge its indebtedness in whatever was the legal tender at the place of payment, that is, in Australian pounds. Lord Wright, on the other hand, went further and held that,

---

[34] [1961] AC 1007.

[35] See Mann, *The Legal Aspect of Money* (4th edn., 1982), pp. 234–41; Morris, 'The Eclipse of the lex loci solutionis—a Fallacy Exploded', *Vanderbilt Law Review*, 6 (1953), p. 505.

[36] [1934] AC 122, 151.

[37] 1st edn., p. 570; 11th edn., Rule 186 (2).

[38] [1920] 2 KB 287 (CA).

although (as the House unanimously found) the contract was governed by English law, the question of the money of account was a matter for the law of the place of performance. In so doing, he expressly overruled the Court of Appeal's decision in *Broken Hill Pty. Co. Ltd.* v. *Latham*,[39] in which it had been held that, where the contract was governed by Australian law, even though the debenture-holders had the option to require payment in London, the money of account was a matter for the proper law of the contract, and therefore the amount due to them was to be calculated in Australian pounds.

Lord Wright proceeded to compound his mischief in *Auckland City Corp.* v. *Alliance Assurance Co.*[40] The Privy Council there considered debenture bonds issued by the Auckland City Corporation, which were repayable at the holder's option either in Auckland or in London. The proper law of the contract was that of New Zealand. The Board held that a debenture-holder which exercised its London option was entitled to receive the nominal amount of the debenture in English pounds without any deduction for the New Zealand rate of exchange. Lord Wright applied his own (minority) reasoning in the *Adelaide* case, though the terms of the judgment suggest increasing uneasiness about the concept of hiving off such a central aspect of the contract to be governed by the law of the place of performance rather than the proper law of the contract.

There are signs that Lord Wright sought to distance himself further from his own dictum in the decision of the Privy Council in *Mount Albert Borough Council* v. *Australasian Assurance Society Ltd*. In that case, Lord Wright, discussing the *Adelaide* case, said:[41]

> The House of Lords was not concerned there with . . . questions of the substance of the obligation which, in general, is fixed by the proper law of the contract under which the obligation is created. The House of Lords was concerned only with performance of that obligation, in regard to the particular matter of the currency in which payment was to be made . . .

Lord Wright's distinction is unconvincing, since the effect of the decision in *Adelaide* was indeed to alter radically the substance of the obligation, and not merely the manner of payment. This was highlighted by Fullagar J in *Goldsbrough, Mort & Co. Ltd.* v. *Hall*,[42] a decision affirmed by a majority of the High Court of Australia. As Fullagar J pointed out, 'it does seem a little unkind to tell a creditor in Melbourne that it is not a matter of substance whether he is entitled to receive from his debtor £1,000 or £1,250 in Australian currency'.[43] Putting the matter in broader terms, he held:[44]

> If there are different moneys of account then the question cannot be one of mode

---

[39] [1933] Ch. 37.
[40] [1937] AC 587.
[41] [1938] AC 224, 241.
[42] [1948] VLR 145, affirmed in (1949) 78 CLR 1.
[43] [1948] VLR 145, 152.
[44] Ibid. 151.

of performance but must be one of the substance of the obligation, and the substance of the obligation is a matter of construction and therefore governed not by the lex loci solutionis, but by the proper law of the contract.

This approach was decisively adopted by the Privy Council in the case which not only cast considerable doubt on Lord Wright's dictum in *Adelaide* but which also constitutes the *locus classicus* for the modern formulation of the English choice of law rule in contracts. *Bonython* v. *Commonwealth of Australia*[45] was again concerned with debentures expressed in pounds sterling, which were repayable in either Brisbane, Sydney, Melbourne or London at the holder's option. The debenture-holders once again claimed to be paid the nominal amount of the debentures in English pounds without any deduction for Australian exchange. The Privy Council rejected their appeal. It held that the proper law of the contract was that of Queensland and that the debenture-holders were entitled to no more than the nominal amount of their debentures in Australian pounds. Lord Simmonds, delivering the judgment of the Board, held:[46]

> It has been urged that, if London is chosen as the place of payment, then English law as the lex loci solutionis governs the contract and determines the measure of the obligation. But this contention cannot be accepted. The mode of performance of the obligation may, and probably will, be determined by English law; the substance of the obligation must be determined by the proper law of the contract.

Following *Bonython* it is possible to draw a clear distinction between the money of account (the substance of the obligation) and the money of payment (the instrument of payment). The money of account, being a question of construction, is governed by the proper law of the contract and not by the law of the place of payment.[47]

For present purposes, the significance of this line of cases is that, as Dr Morris puts it, 'chaos results when the law of the place of performance is allowed to encroach on the sphere of the law governing the substance of the obligation'.[48] As one of the most sustained attempts to split the law governing different obligations within a contract, the *Adelaide* case and those following it decisively illustrate the fallacies and difficulties involved. Not merely does it prove impossible in practice to distinguish between the role to be accorded to each legal system, but the courts may very rapidly reach the position where the law which is regarded as the fundamental law of the contract has an insignificant role in determining the nature of the obligation. No doubt there are questions of performance which are properly referable to the place of performance,[49] but these are matters which

---

[45] [1951] AC 201.
[46] Ibid. 219.
[47] Mann, op. cit. above (n. 35), p. 241; Goode, *Payment Obligations in Commercial and Financial Transactions* (1983), pp. 144-5.
[48] Morris, loc. cit. above (n. 35), p. 532.
[49] Dicey and Morris, op. cit. above (n. 12), Rule 186(2).

concern the details of the mode, place and time of performance, as to which the local law at the place of performance is clearly relevant as a matter of fact. Thus, if the parties provide that payment is to be made during the usual business hours in Paris, it will be for French law to determine what the usual business hours are.[50] This is little more than a practical recognition of the situation which must necessarily pertain.

In sum, therefore, the English cases do not stand as authority for the proposition for which they are cited, and the money of account cases highlight the flaws of a split proper law approach. What of the experience in other conflict of law systems?

III. COMPARATIVE AND INTERNATIONAL PERSPECTIVES

The tension between the unifying notion of the proper law and a division of the law governing different sets of obligations stems from the very origins of private international law. Savigny, in his *Treatise on the Conflict of Laws*,[51] enunciated the modern notion of the proper law in advocating that every obligation had a seat, whose law governed the parties' rights and duties under that obligation.[52] However, as he pointed out, the notion of the seat of an obligation was not without its difficulties. One such difficulty was that reciprocity occurs in many obligations, each party having mutual rights and duties. This was to be solved, in his view, by separating the two separate debts so that each of the two halves of the contract was governed by a separate law. He prayed in aid of this proposition the Roman Law concept of the contract of sale as including two distinct stipulations.[53]

As one of Savigny's earliest translators into English noted: 'It cannot be denied that in many cases this separation of the two halves of a bilateral obligation may cause doubts and perplexities, especially in regard to the local law'.[54] However, the notion did have a profound effect on the developing European systems of the conflict of laws.[55] Its influence on Dicey has already been noted.[56] The doctrine was, it appears, to have a more direct effect on the shape of German law, where the technique of splitting the contract into a separate set of obligations for each party was adopted by the courts.[57] The German courts attempted to split up the sale of goods contract by hiving off the seller's duties to deliver the goods, to be liable for warranties and conditions, or default, and to replace defective merchandise, from the law governing the existence and effect of the various

---

[50] Ibid., p. 1237.
[51] (1849), translated by Guthrie (2nd edn., Edinburgh, 1880).
[52] Ibid., p. 194.
[53] Ibid., p. 195.
[54] Ibid.
[55] Lando, 'Contracts', *International Encyclopedia of Comparative Law* (1976), vol. 3, ch. 24, pp. 8–13; Rabel, *The Conflict of Laws: A Comparative Study* (1960), vol. 2, pp. 469–72.
[56] See text at n. 14, above.
[57] Lando, loc. cit. above (n. 55), pp. 11–12.

duties of the buyer at the place where he had to pay the price and accept goods, accept a substitute, examine the goods and give notice, as well as any remedies the buyer might have on the ground of defects and non delivery.[58] As Rabel has argued:[59]

. . . this principle is based on the mistaken conception that a bilateral contract can be reasonably partitioned into two unilateral obligations. . . . The very nature of a *synallagma* is ignored when a sale contract is torn up into halves belonging to different legislations.

In the United States, a different form of splitting was introduced by Beale[60] under the influence of an extreme interpretation of the principle of territoriality, that every act should be determined according to the law of where it occurred.[61] Under this interpretation, the existence and effect of a contract were to be governed by the law of the place of contracting, and the duty of performance and the right to damages for breach were to be determined by the law of the place of performance. This principle was adopted in the first *Restatement of the Conflict of Laws*.[62] It was adopted by the courts following a dictum of Hunt J in *Scudder* v. *Union National Bank*, that:[63]

Matters bearing upon the execution, the interpretation and the validity of the contract are determined by the law of the place where the contract is made. Matters connected with its performance are regulated by the law prevailing at the place of performance. . . . A careful examination of the well considered decision of our country and of England will sustain these positions.

As Lando notes, 'It has been difficult for the present writer to find more than a few of these "well considered decisions" in England and the United States'.[64] This form of splitting was found by the courts to be no less unworkable than Savigny's split laws of performance.[65] A moment's consideration shows that it is simply not possible to distinguish sensibly between two such central areas. As Rabel has put it:[66]

. . . there is no consistent dividing line possible between the extent of a contractual obligation and its performance. Both together form the purpose of the contract and are its very core. Whether an event making performance impossible or onerous frees the debtor from his entire duty, or only from paying damages, or not at all, is determined by the distribution of effort and risk implied in the contract.

This has now been recognized in Switzerland, where this form of splitting

---

[58] Rabel, op. cit. above (n. 55), pp. 469–70.
[59] Ibid, pp. 470–1.
[60] Beale, *A Treatise on The Conflict of Laws* (1935), vol. 2, p. 1077.
[61] Lando, loc. cit. above (n. 55), p. 8.
[62] (1934), sections 332 and 358.
[63] 91 US 406, 412 (1875).
[64] Lando, loc. cit. above (n. 55), p. 8.
[65] Ibid., p. 9; Rabel, op. cit. above (n. 55), pp. 453–4.
[66] Ibid., p. 453.

was followed by the courts until 1952.[67] The Swiss Federal Act of International Private Law, which came into force on 1 January 1989, makes no
provision for split proper law or dépeçage.[68] As one leading commentator
observed: 'Dépeçage increases the danger of contradictory solutions resulting from references of different aspects of the question to different laws'.[69]
The French had taken a similar approach, arguing that dépeçage runs
counter to the fundamental purpose of choice of law in contract, to unite
the various provisions of the contract under a single system.[70]

In the United States, the Beale approach, discredited in the courts, has
now been replaced by a form of dépeçage, developed under the influence of
those writers who have contributed to the 'American Revolution in the
Conflict of Laws',[71] which refers to the law governing a particular issue,
rather than the contractual relationship as a whole. The *Second Restatement* accepts that parties may, by express choice, choose the law to govern
all of the obligations under their contract.[72] While the liberty of the parties
to choose different laws to govern different obligations within a contract
was said to be uncertain in the original edition of the *Second Restatement*, a
revision promulgated in 1988, referring *inter alia* to the Rome Convention,
makes it clear that parties may elect to have different laws govern different
issues in the contract.[73] The approach to be taken by the courts, in the
absence of express choice, is said to be directed towards selecting the local
law of the State most appropriate to determine the particular *issue* before the
court.[74] Reese has argued that 'amidst the chaos and tumult of choice of
law'[75] this is at least one point on which there seems to be general agreement
in the United States. Whatever the relevance of 'issue selection' approaches
in the law of contract (as opposed to the law governing other forms of obligation, which in general have proved more fruitful subjects for the American
debates[76]), this form of dépeçage has had limited influence on choice of law
in contract elsewhere, and has received short shrift in international fora.[77]

Dépeçage received a cautious reception in the Rome Convention on the

---

[67] It was rejected by the Swiss Federal Tribunal in the *Chevalley* case, (1952) BGE 78 II 74.

[68] Articles 116 and 117 prescribe the general rules on choice of law in contract.

[69] Vischer, 'Drafting National Legislation and Conflict of Laws: the Swiss Experience', *Law and
Contemporary Problems*, 41 (1977), p. 131 at p. 138.

[70] See, e.g., Loussouarn and Bourel, *Droit international privé* (3rd edn., 1980), p. 258. Batiffol and
Lagarde, *Droit international privé* (7th edn., 1983), vol. 2, p. 274, express a more equivocal view. As of
1 April 1991, the Rome Convention is in force in France.

[71] See, e.g., Reese, 'Dépeçage: A Common Phenomenon in Choice of Law', *Columbia Law Review*,
73 (1973), p. 58. Cavers, however, considers that: 'Multiple issue contract cases are likely to remain
infrequent. The risk of having to resort to "an amalgam" of laws from two or more jurisdictions . . .
seems a much less serious hazard in the field of contracts': op. cit. above (n. 4), at p. 199.

[72] Section 187.

[73] p. 570.

[74] Section 188.

[75] Loc. cit. above (n. 71), p. 58.

[76] Reese devotes most of his discussion of dépeçage to tort, and see Juenger's critique, loc. cit. above
(n. 4).

[77] See the discussion below of the Hague Convention on the Law Applicable to Contracts for the
International Sale of Goods 1985.

Law Applicable to Contractual Obligations 1980, now in force in the United Kingdom by virtue of the Contracts (Applicable Law) Act 1990.[78] Article 3, entitled 'Freedom of Choice', provides *inter alia* that: 'By their choice the parties can select the law applicable to the whole or part only of the contract'. Article 4, which prescribes the applicable law in the absence of choice, allows that ' . . . a severable part of the contract which has a closer connection with another country may by way of exception be governed by the law of that other country'. The explanatory report of Giuliano and Lagarde suggests that this was a hotly contested issue in the drafting of the Convention.[79] Some experts argued that the contract should in principle be governed by one law, unless that contract consisted in reality of several contracts or parts which were separable and independent of each other, from legal and economic points of view. Those experts opposed any direct reference to severability in the Convention. Others had argued that severability was directly linked to the freedom of contract and so would be difficult to prohibit. Giuliano and Lagarde venture the view that:[80]

. . . when the contract is severable the choice must be logically consistent, i.e. it must relate to elements in the contract which can be governed by different laws without giving rise to contradictions. For example, an 'index-linked clause' may be made subject to a different law; on the other hand it is unlikely that repudiation of the contract for non-performance would be subjected to two different laws, one for the vendor and the other for the purchaser.

They refer to the stabilizing effect of Article 7 in preventing the use of a split proper law technique to avoid mandatory rules. As to the provision in Article 4 for judical dépeçage, the explanatory report reveals that there was little enthusiasm for such a provision, but that it was felt that a residual discretion should be maintained.[81] Examples of where it might be used are suggested to be contracts for joint ventures and complex contracts.[82] This is valuable guidance on provisions which in themselves provide little indication as to what is involved in splitting the proper law or when it should be done.

A more limited view of dépeçage was taken in the Hague Convention on the Law Applicable to Contracts for the International Sale of Goods 1985.[83] Article 7 of the Convention, which deals with choice of law by the parties, allows that 'such a choice may be limited to a part of the contract'. However, there is no parallel provision in Article 8 allowing for a severance of the proper law by the courts. Pelichet, in his preliminary report, had

---

[78] *Official Journal of the European Communities*, 1980, L. 266. The convention entered into force on 1 April 1991 in France, Italy, Denmark, Luxembourg, Greece, Germany, Belgium and the UK: ibid. 1991, C. 52/1.

[79] *Official Journal of the European Communities*, 1980, C. 282: Article 3, para. 4; Article 4, para. 8.

[80] Ibid., Article 3, para. 4.

[81] Ibid., Article 4, para. 8.

[82] Ibid.

[83] Hague Conference on Private International Law, *Recueil des conventions* (1988), p. 326; *Actes et documents* (1985). See generally McLachlan, loc. cit. above (n. 6).

doubted whether, in a Convention limited solely to a particular type of contract, there was any need for dépeçage.[84] However, the Special Commission appointed to produce the initial draft of the Convention did see merit in allowing the parties to nominate a law governing part only of their contract.[85] A more radical proposal was made by the United States during the debates.[86] Mr Reese for the USA had proposed an amendment inserting a provision that 'The parties may choose to have different laws govern different issues'.[87] This would have admitted into the Convention a form of issue selection. The American proposal was rejected, but in the event, the Convention leaves the matter of dépeçage unresolved. The language of Article 7 expressly permits a choice of law relating to a part only of the contract but says nothing as to the choice of two separate laws to govern two separate aspects of the contract. Aware of this difficulty, the Reporter, Professor von Mehren, asked the meeting whether it was their intention, though not specifically allowing for this possibility in this Convention, by not expressly prohibiting it, to leave parties with such an option.[88] This was indeed the Commission's view.

Reference to the comparative experience thus confirms a sceptical view of the value of dépeçage techniques. How, then, has the doctrine come to receive renewed attention in England? The contexts of the two recent cases on the subject, reinsurance and Eurodollar automatic funds transfer arrangements, reveal some of the pressures of an increasingly internationalized market.

IV. *Vesta* v. *Butcher* and the Reinsurance Contract

The reinsurance contract presents something of a conundrum in the conflict of laws. Dicey and Morris submit that their proposed rule of choice of law in insurance contracts 'yields no solution in cases concerning reinsurance'.[89] A reinsurance policy indemnifies the insurer for claims brought by the original insured. Reinsurance will typically be effected at a major insurance centre such as London, to support original insurance effected by domestic insurers in many different countries. From a choice of law perspective, there is an apparent dichotomy between the intention of reinsurance, to indemnify fully the insurer's obligations under local law, and the centralized nature of the reinsurance market, which may, by the operation of ordinary choice of law rules, lead to the reinsurance contract

---

[84] *Actes et documents* (previous note), p. 65; see also Pelichet's discussion in *Recueil des cours*, 201 (1987–I), pp. 119–21.

[85] *Actes et documents* (above, n. 83), p. 185.

[86] Ibid., p. 381.

[87] Ibid., Proposal no. 4, p. 295.

[88] Ibid., p. 725.

[89] Dicey and Morris, op. cit. above (n. 12), p. 1295; see also Monachos, 'Reinsurance in English Private International Law', *Journal of Business Law*, 1972, p. 206; Merkin, 'The Proper Law of Insurance and Reinsurance Contracts', in Rose (ed.), *New Foundations for Insurance Law* (1987), p. 61.

being governed by a different legal system from that of the insurance contract. Despite the presumption that closely connected contracts should normally be governed by the same law, the courts have not shrunk from accepting the possibility that the reinsurance contract might be governed by a different law from that of the original insurance contract.[90] This can, however, create practical difficulties where the extent of the reinsurer's liability is differently defined by the two different systems.

This was the problem which confronted the courts in *Vesta* v. *Butcher*.[91] The plaintiff, a Norwegian insurance company, had insured the owner of a fish farm in Norway, and had reinsured its liability at Lloyds. The fish farm had been damaged in a storm and many of the fish had escaped. The fish farmer had made a claim against Vesta under the insurance contract, which had eventually been met. Vesta in turn sought to recover from its reinsurers. The reinsurers resisted liability on a number of grounds. The relevant ground for present purposes was the effect of a clause which warranted that a 24-hour watch would be kept over the fish farm, and that failure to comply with that warranty would render the policy null and void. Under Norwegian law, this clause did not preclude the insured from making a claim against his insurer because the breach was irrelevant to the loss. A 24-hour watch could not have prevented the loss of fish caused by the storm. Under English law, however, the breach of such a warranty would have rendered the policy null and void.

The courts' difficulties arose from the way in which the reinsurance policy had been constructed. Both the insurance and the reinsurance policies had been put together by London brokers. The reinsurance policy consisted of a slip to which Lloyds' standard reinsurance policy and the original policy of insurance were annexed. The reinsurance policy provided that it was 'a reinsurance of and warranted same gross rate, terms and conditions as and to follow the settlements of the company'. The insurance policy had been amended so as to refer to Vesta rather than to the fish farmer, and it was accepted in argument throughout that all of the terms of the original contract of insurance had been incorporated into the reinsurance contract.

The case was considered at first instance by Hobhouse J and then on appeal by the Court of Appeal and the House of Lords. At every stage, the judges unaminously found the reinsurers liable to indemnify Vesta for the claim. However, their reasons for this canvas a wide range of views on the split proper law doctrine. Hobhouse J approached the matter as a choice of law question. He accepted that 'it is the almost invariable rule that there is only a single proper law of a contract which governs all aspects of the contract'.[92] However, he found that 'choice of law is a matter for the actual or

---

[90] *Royal Exchange Assurance Corp.* v. *Vega*, [1902] 2 KB 384; *Armadora Occidental SA* v. *Horace Mann Insurance Co.*, [1977] 1 WLR 1098; *Citadel Insurance Co.* v. *Atlantic Union Insurance Co.*, [1982] 2 Lloyd's Rep. 543.

[91] Loc. cit. above (n. 1). For comment see Merkin, loc. cit. above (n. 89), and id., 'Reinsurance, Brokers and the Conflict of Laws', *Lloyd's Maritime and Commercial Law Quarterly*, 1988, p. 5.

[92] [1986] 2 All ER 488, 504.

imputed choice of the parties and it has been recognised for a long time that parties may chose that different parts of the contract should be governed by different laws'.[93] He referred in support of this proposition to *Dicey and Morris, Hamlyn* v. *Talisker* and *Re Helbert Wagg.*

Having already decided that the original contract of insurance was indisputably governed by Norwegian law, and that all of the ordinary factors for determining the proper law of the reinsurance contract pointed to English law, Hobhouse J had to grapple with the express provision for the reinsurance contract to be back-to-back with the original insurance. He reasoned as follows:[94]

> From this one should infer a contractual intent that the legal effect of the clauses which define and limit the scope of the cover should be the same in the reinsurance and in the original insurance. When one takes into account that the parties clearly must contemplate that the original insurance was governed by Norwegian law I infer as a matter of English law that the parties intended that construction and effect of the clauses of the Aquacultural wording shall be governed by Norwegian law. Whether one chooses to categorise this conclusion as an application of the English substantive law of construction of an English law contract or as the application of the English choice of law rules does not matter. They are in the present context essentially the same thing. The parties have on the true ascertainment of their contractual intention chosen that that part of the contract shall be governed by Norwegian, not English, law.

Hobhouse J observed that this solution was 'hybrid and admittedly somewhat unorthodox',[95] but found that to have reached any other result would have been contrary to the manifest intention of the parties to provide Vesta with reinsurance cover of an original insurance contract governed by Norwegian law.

The Court of Appeal (O'Connor and Neill LJJ and Sir Roger Ormrod) reached the same result as Hobhouse J, but for different reasons. Neill LJ saw the matter solely as one of the interpretation of an English contract. He held:[96]

> . . . as a matter of construction of the reinsurance contract and by seeking to ascertain the presumed intention of the parties the watch clause has to be given the same effect as it is given in the underlying insurance contract. In the context of the present case this solution is to my mind the only one that makes commercial sense.

Sir Roger Ormrod, criticizing the Lloyd's reinsurance market for failing to deal satisfactorily with such an obvious problem, saw an implied term as the only solution. Such a term would provide that a breach of warranty would only permit reinsurers to repudiate their policy if breach of the same

[93] Ibid.
[94] Ibid. 504–5.
[95] Ibid. 505.
[96] [1989] AC 852, 875.

warranty would permit the reinsured to avoid the original insurance policy.[97]

When the matter reached the House of Lords, the leading judgments were delivered by Lords Templeman and Lowry. Lord Templeman did not phrase his judgment as a matter of choice of law. He held that:[98]

. . . a warranty must produce the same effect in each policy. The effect of a warranty in the reinsurance policy is governed by the effect of the warranty in the insurance policy because the reinsurance policy is a contract by the underwriters to indemnify Vesta against liability under the insurance policy.

He plainly regarded any other construction as simply inconsistent with the concept of reinsurance and with the whole basis on which reinsurance work was conducted in the market.

Lord Lowry likewise stressed that 'reinsurance is prima facie a contract of indemnity'.[99] He saw the problem as 'one of construing the words in the reinsurance contract and not one involving an imputed choice of law'.[100] Approaching the matter on this basis, he held that the consequence of failure to comply with the 24-hour watch clause was the same in the English contract of reinsurance as in the original Norwegian contract of insurance:[101]

The parties to that contract are deemed to have used the same dictionary, in this case a Norwegian legal dictionary, to ascertain the meaning of the terms and conditions in wording No. V, including the conditions relating to the 24 hour watch and the words 'failure to comply'. There is, in my view, no need to treat the reinsurance contract as partly governed by Norwegian law, except in the special sense that one must resort to Norwegian law in order to interpret and understand the meaning and effect of the No. V wording in *both* contracts. That is a different concept from 'the proper law of the contract' (or of part of the contract) which is discussed in the authorities on that subject.

It is submitted, therefore, that *Vesta* v. *Butcher* lends no support to the doctrine of the split proper law. Hobhouse J had to approach the matter in this way, because he had characterized the problem as one of choice of law. In the Court of Appeal, Sir Roger Ormrod saw some attraction in Hobhouse J's approach, as an unavoidable necessity in giving effect to the intentions of the parties. He referred in support to a dictum of Evatt J in *Wanganui-Rangitikei* case which accepted that the proper law might itself refer to the law of the place of performance to determine the methods and incidents of performance. The application of that dictum in *Vesta* would have been a dangerous one, if it led to a matter going to the heart of the reinsurer's liability being categorized as one of the 'methods and incidents of performance'. In the event, however, Sir Roger Ormrod adopted an

[97] Ibid. 878.
[98] Ibid. 892.
[99] Ibid. 908.
[100] Ibid. 911.
[101] Ibid.

implied term approach, which was not followed in the House of Lords. Neill LJ and a majority in the House categorized the question as one of interpretation of an English contract. It was accepted that the reinsurance contract was governed by English law but, as a matter of English law, the content of the warranty was determined by reference to the content of the warranty in the original insurance contract, as determined by Norwegian law. There was, as Lord Lowry was at pains to point out, therefore no question of a split proper law. Rather, an English contract incorporated a reference to Norwegian law for a specific purpose.

A more radical solution to construction of the reinsurance contract was advocated by Lord Griffiths following reasoning which also had some attraction for Lords Bridge and Lowry. Lord Griffiths noted that the litigation had been conducted on the basis that the same terms were terms of both the insurance policy and the reinsurance policy. In so far as he was bound to accept this assumption, he agreed that the appeal failed for the reasons given in the speeches of Lords Templeman and Lowry. However, he noted that at the trial it had been sought to argue that the 24-hour watch clause and other clauses in the original insurance policy were not terms of the reinsurance policy. Hobhouse J had refused leave to amend the pleadings to adduce this argument.[102] Lord Griffiths regretted this, and was by no means persuaded that on its true construction the reinsurance contract did make the terms of the original policy of insurance terms of the policy of reinsurance. As he pointed out, a contract of insurance will almost inevitably contain terms that are wholly inappropriate in a contract of reinsurance:[103]

The original policy is concerned to define the risk that the insurer is prepared to accept. The contract of reinsurance is concerned with the degree of that risk as defined in the policy that the reinsurer is prepared to accept.

He referred by way of example of the absurdity to the inclusion of a stock control clause in the reinsurance contract. He asked whether it was seriously to be supposed that it was the intention of the parties that London underwriters were to have the option of discharging their liability to Vesta by delivering a load of live fish to them.[104] He referred in support to the case of *Home Insurance Co. of New York* v. *Victoria-Montreal Fire Insurance Co.*,[105] where reinsurers had argued that a clause requiring the claim to be reported within a fixed time contained in the original insurance policy was also a term of the reinsurance policy. The Privy Council rejected this notion. In their view, the insurance policy was included for the purpose of indicating the origin of the reinsured's liability. They declined to accept that the clause was part of the reinsurance contract, holding that to decide otherwise would 'be to adhere to the letter without paying due attention to

---

[102] [1986] 2 All ER 488, 496.
[103] [1989] AC 852, 896.
[104] Ibid.
[105] [1907] AC 59.

the spirit and intention of the contract'.[106] Merkin[107] demonstrates that the courts have consistently developed an approach to reinsurance which supports the fundamental obligation to indemnify the reinsured for the risks undertaken by him, and not to incorporate terms of the original policy so as to alter this fundamental obligation. If this is indeed the case, *Vesta* v. *Butcher*, so far from being a case on split proper law, ought really to have been seen as a case involving two separate contracts, one of which merely defined the nature and the extent of the risk which the reinsurer was indemnifying.

V. The *Libyan Arab Foreign Bank* Cases: Eurodollar Automatic Funds Transfer Arrangements

The second context in which the doctrine of the split proper law has received recent attention is that of the Eurodollar market. Under modern banking practice, very large sums of United States dollars are held on deposit outside the United States, where they earn a better rate of interest. In their desire to facilitate this investment, but to allow customers to meet their daily trading requirements in New York, many banks have developed a form of automatic funds transfer arrangement, whereby sums are automatically transferred between a current account in New York and a deposit account in London. In this type of arrangement, the London account acts solely as a reservoir for surplus funds, and debits are not in normal circumstances made from that account, save by way of credit to the New York account.

The vulnerability of Eurodollar deposits held with the branches of US banks in London was put in issue during the Iranian crisis, following a United States Presidential Order blocking all property of the Government of Iran in the possession or control of United States persons.[108] Only the Algiers Accord stopped the issue from being tried in England. The promulgation by the United States, therefore, of sanctions against Libya in 1986[109] provided the first opportunity for the English courts to consider the effect of foreign sanctions on London Eurodollar deposits. The Libyan Sanctions Regulations could have applied to the London account if United States law

---

[106] Ibid. 65.
[107] Merkin, loc. cit. above (n. 89).
[108] Executive Order No. 12170,44 FR 65,729 (1979); Executive Order No. 12205,45 FR 24,099 (1980); Iranian Sanctions Regulations, 31 CFR Part 535. The text of the Algiers Accord appears at *International Legal Materials*, 20 (1981), p. 223. For comment, see Carswell and Davis, 'The Economic and Financial Pressures: Freeze and Sanctions', in *American Hostages in Iran* (1985), p. 173; and Goode, op. cit. above (n. 47), pp. 119–20.
[109] Executive Order No. 12543, 51 FR 875 (1986); Executive Order No. 12544, 51 FR 1235 (1986); Libyan Sanctions Regulations, 31 CFR Part 550. For comment, see Bialos and Juster, 'Libyan Sanctions: A Rational Response to State-Sponsored Terrorism?', *Virginia Journal of International Law*, 6 (1986), p. 799.

were the proper law of the banking contract, or if there were a term of the contract requiring payment through New York, either as a result of the express agreement of the parties, or to be implied by market practice. These arguments were exhaustively tested before Staughton J in *Libyan Arab Foreign Bank* v. *Bankers Trust Co.*,[110] and subsequently before Hirst J in *Libyan Arab Foreign Bank* v. *Manufacturers Hanover Trust Co.*[111] There was a substantially similar banking arrangement in both of these cases. A major American bank had agreed with the leading Libyan State-owned foreign trading bank to establish an automatic funds transfer arrangement, supported by a current account in New York and a deposit account in London. All payments to third parties were made on a day to day basis out of the New York account, and the London account was used as an investment reservoir. Automatic transfers were made between the two accounts to keep the New York account at the level of an agreed peg, and to ensure that the maximum amount available was transferred to earn interest in London. Applying ordinary choice of law principles to this contractual arrangement, there could be little doubt that, viewed as a whole, it was governed by New York law, where the agreement was negotiated and made and where it was administered on a daily basis. The question of a split proper law thus assumed critical importance.

Staughton J commenced his reasoning from a general rule that 'The contract between a bank and its customer is governed by the law of the place where the account is kept, in the absence of agreement to the contrary'.[112] He found nothing in the parties' contractual arrangements to displace this general rule, which led to the London account being governed by English law and thus not subject to the Sanctions Regulations. He then had to choose between two separate contracts and one contract with two proper laws. He found the notion of two separate contracts 'artificial and unattractive'.[113] He observed that it had been adopted as a device by the courts on occasions to achieve justice, 'but at some cost to logic and consistency'.[114] He therefore preferred a split proper law. He referred in support to the textbook writers, and to Article 4 of the Rome Convention (not then in force in the United Kingdom). He did not regard such a solution as leading to uncertainty, adverting to the fact that for many purposes the law treated the branch of a bank as separate from its head office. Therefore he concluded that 'The rights and obligations of the parties in respect of the Lon-

---

[110] Loc. cit. above (n. 2).

[111] [1989] 1 Lloyd's Rep 608 (Hirst J).

[112] [1989] 1 QB 728, 746. While there will be many instances where this presumption will accurately reflect the intentions of the parties, it is submitted that there is no authority for elevating this guide to the status of a legal rule. The cases cited in support by Staughton J, *X AG* v. *A Bank*, [1983] 2 All ER 464, and *MacKinnon* v. *Donaldson Lufkin & Jenrette Securities*, [1986] Ch. 482, do not support his formulation. Further support was, however, given to the rule by Staughton LJ delivering the judgment of the Court of Appeal in *Attock Cement Co. Ltd.* v. *Romanian Bank for Foreign Trade*, [1989] 1 Lloyd's Rep. 572, 580–1.

[113] [1989] 1 QB 728, 747.

[114] Ibid.

don account were governed by English law'.[115] This conclusion left him free to find that the automatic funds transfer arrangement, in so far as it included a term requiring payment out of the London account only through New York, was in the nature of a mandate which could be, and had been, unilaterally terminated by Libyan Arab Foreign Bank ('LAFB'), entitling them to payment in London.[116]

When the same issue came to be considered in LAFB's case against Manufacturers Hanover Trust Co. ('MHT'), many of the difficulties with Staughton J's approach were rehearsed. LAFB did not, in that case, adopt split proper law as its primary case, preferring to rely on the existence of two separate contracts, with split proper law as only a fall-back position. MHT advanced the view that the automatic funds transfer arrangements (comprising the New York account, the London account and provisions for transfers between the two) constituted a single contractual package with a single proper law, New York law. Alternatively, it argued that, even if there were a split proper law, or two separate contracts, the law governing the relationship between the two accounts (which relationship included the term of the automatic funds transfer arrangement that all payments out of the London account should be made through New York) was New York law.

LAFB relied on the alleged presumption as to the proper law of a bank account, and on a number of matters of fact which suggested that the London account had been treated by the parties as governed by English law, and distanced from the effects of United States law. MHT argued that the presumption was inapplicable in this type of international banking contract, and that all the ordinary factors which determined the closest and most real connection of this contract pointed to New York. As to split proper law, MHT contended that there was a strong presumption in English law in favour of a single proper law in respect of a single contract. The rationale for this presumption was the need to eliminate the real conflicts of laws which would be likely to arise where issues arose concerning the interrelationship of the component parts of the contract. It was suggested that a split proper law was only workable where the contract comprised self-contained parts operating wholly independently, and that where the parts of the contract were intended to operate together as elements in a single commercial scheme there was no justification for splitting the proper law.

Hirst J found that there were sound financial and political reasons for keeping the two accounts so far as possible separate.[117] In particular, he referred to the evidence as to the need to distance the London account from any requirement to maintain federal reserves in the United States, and to concern over the possible effect of any freeze order. He therefore put his judgment primarily on the basis of two separate contracts. However if, contrary to his primary conclusion, the proper interpretation of the

[115] Ibid. 748.
[116] Ibid. 756.
[117] [1989] 1 Lloyd's Rep. 608, 619.

arrangements was that there was one single contract, he would have held that the proper law was split, the proper law in relation to the English bank account being English law, and the proper law in relation to the New York bank account being New York law.[118] He further found that 'the proper law of the interrelationship constituted by the AFT [automatic funds transfer] arrangement, to the extent that it related to payments into and out of the London account, was English law . . .'.[119]

The Libyan bank cases illustrate the difficulties of applying a split proper law. Staughton J was able to side-step these difficulties by characterizing the issue before him as one concerning the London account, and therefore governed by English law. However, to hold that the law governing the connection between the two accounts, in so far as it affected the London account, was English law is simply to beg the question. The automatic funds transfer arrangement was bilateral in operation: it did not merely affect the London account.

Almost all the questions of any importance in the Libyan bank cases were interrelationship questions. Thus, to give another example, a subsidiary issue in the *MHT* case concerned a transfer which it was alleged had been made from the New York account to the London account on the day on which the Sanctions Regulations came into force, and subsequently reversed. The question of what in law constitutes a transfer is plainly one on which legal systems could differ, and it is by no means obvious that it ought to be resolved by reference to English law. Thus the adoption of a split proper law in the Libyan bank cases lent no guide as to the crucial question in those cases, namely, which law was to govern the interrelationship between the two accounts.

It is submitted that there is an alternative approach to the contractual arrangements in the Libyan bank cases, which might reflect more accurately the parties' intentions. The relationship between the parties may be seen as constituted by an overall umbrella contract, comprising the automatic funds transfer arrangement, and two subsidiary contracts governing the London and New York accounts. This interpretation draws some support from the way in which the arrangements were in fact negotiated by the parties. An overall package was agreed, and then, subsequently, two accounts (with the usual attributes, such as statements, interest, etc.) were established to serve that overall arrangement. Viewed in this way, the automatic funds transfer arrangement itself would clearly be governed by New York law (the place of its conclusion and administration), and each of the accounts would be governed by local laws. This analysis would, however, have the same result (unattractive on policy grounds) of rendering the Sanctions Regulations applicable to the contractual arrangements for payment out of the London account.

[118] Ibid. 621.
[119] Ibid.

VI. Reassessing the Role of the Proper Law

The burden of this article has been to demonstrate that, so far from being an unchallengeable part of the English approach to choice of law in contract, the doctrine of split proper law is supported neither by the experience of decided cases nor on principle. The inconclusive state of the authorities has been remarked upon by others.[120] What this article has sought to show, by reference to actual examples of its attempted application, is that the idea of a split proper law is fundamentally at odds with the role of the proper law of a contract. The truth is that the proper law is both a unifying and a simplifying concept, whose purpose is to resolve conflicts of law by subjecting a contract to a single legal system. The notion of a split proper law makes nonsense of this. As the discussion above on the money of account cases and of the experience in other jurisdictions of attempts to split the law governing each party's obligations to perform, or to split the law governing performance from that governing formation, shows, confusion and error result from departures from the unity principle. The English courts' recent foray into the doctrine in the Libyan bank cases only underlines the point that the doctrine of the split proper law gives no guide whatsoever as to which law is to define which obligations.

The net result therefore is to reaffirm that one law only ought to govern the existence, fundamental validity, interpretation and performance of a contract. As Evatt J observed in the passage cited at the outset of this article, this theory, however difficult it may be in application, 'lies at the root of private international law'.[121] This is not merely a matter of judicial convenience or State policy. The parties to a contract view it as a single legal and economic unit, and not as capable of dismemberment, so as to subject different obligations to the uncertain application of different laws. As Lord Hewart CJ pointed out in *Jones* v. *Oceanic Steam Navigation Co.*: ' . . . it is not probable that the parties would intend that some parts of the contract should be governed by the law of one country and other parts by the law of another country'.[122]

If the thesis advanced herein is right, how, then, is one to approach the construction of a contract where there appears to be a split proper law, either as a result of the express choice of the parties, or because the nature and circumstances surrounding the contract suggest such an inference? It is submitted that the following principles may assist as a guide to construction:

---

[120] Lando, loc. cit. above (n. 55); Sykes and Pryles, *Australian Private International Law* (1987): 'The above authorities suggest that the question of whether the essential validity and discharge of different parts of a contract may be governed by different laws is not as clearly established in present Anglo-Australian law as some text writers would have us believe. This is not to say that an appellate court would not accept the technique of dépeçage in this respect but merely to acknowledge that the question is still open' (pp. 536–7).

[121] (1933–4) 50 CLR 581, 604.

[122] [1924] 2 KB 730, 733.

(1) In most cases, as reference to the authorities which have considered the possibility of a split proper law suggests, an apparent connection with the laws of more than one country will in fact be capable of resolution in favour of a single proper law.

(2) In a significant number of cases, what is apparently a single contract is in fact constituted by two or more separate contracts, each of which may be governed by its own law. Although closely connected contracts will normally be governed by the same law,[123] this need not be the case. It is widely accepted, for example, that an arbitration clause in a contract constitutes a separate contract.[124] It has been suggested that this view furnishes a better guide to the interpretation of reinsurance contracts and of Eurodollar automatic funds transfer arrangements.

(3) In all other cases, the contract will be governed by a single proper law. However, that does not preclude the proper law from allowing reference to, or incorporation of, provisions of another legal system for a specific purpose. The crucial practical difference betweeen this and the split proper law is that there is a single reference point to determine the parties' rights and obligations. When the proper law itself refers to another legal system it will do so (a) because it is necessary in order to resolve a question of interpretation which arises under the proper law, or (b) because a foreign legal system must be taken account of in carrying out the contract, or (c) because the parties have chosen to incorporate a reference to particular foreign law provisions. An example of the first situation is furnished by the speech of Lord Lowry in *Vesta* v. *Butcher*. This situation has been illuminatingly addressed by Dr Mann as 'the primary question of construction'.[125] The second situation is illustrated by the state of the law in the wake of the 'money of account' cases. There will still be questions of mode of performance, including, in that context, the money of payment, which will be referable to the place of performance. The third situation is that of the clause which expressly ties a particular term in the contract to a given legal system. Examples are an index-linking clause,[126] or the coffee quality clause in *Tamari* v. *Rothfos*.[127]

The Rome Convention's formulation is now receiving widespread acceptance, and not merely in the European States party to the Convention. In the United States, the Convention rule has been approved in the

---

[123] *The Njegos*, [1936] P 90.

[124] See authorities cited above, n. 32.

[125] Mann, 'The Primary Question of Construction and the Conflict of Laws', *Law Quarterly Review*, 79 (1963), p. 525.

[126] The example given by Giuliano and Lagarde, loc. cit. above (n. 79). See also the discussion in Delaume, *Transnational Contracts: Applicable Law and Settlement of Disputes (A Study in Conflict Avoidance)* (1985), section 1.03.

[127] Above, n. 28.

Restatement.[128] In England, Staughton J cited it with approval in the *Bankers Trust* case, even prior to its entry into force.[129] The Convention as a whole[130] now has the force of law in the United Kingdom, despite some trenchant criticism,[131] as a result of the Contracts (Applicable Law) Act 1990. However, it is doubtful whether the Convention offers any useful guidance on the question. As the *Bankers Trust* decision illustrates, there is a danger that, by apparently sanctioning a split proper law, the Convention may encourage its incorrect application. The explanatory report[132] goes some way towards a solution similar to that proposed here, but stops short of the fundamental distinction between splitting the proper law and incorporation. The answer to the problem of an express or implied reference to a multiplicity of legal systems in a contractual arrangement, with or without the Rome Convention, as now, will only be found by a careful construction, in accordance with the approach suggested above, of the parties' intentions in the light of the necessary function of the proper law.

---

[128] See text at n. 73, above.

[129] See text at n. 115, above.

[130] Save for Articles 7(1) and 10(1)(e), which are expressly excluded under Section 2(2) of the Act. The Act entered into force (save in respect of those provisions relating to the Brussels Protocol on the Interpretation of the Convention by the European Court) on 1 April 1991: Contracts (Applicable Law) Act 1990 (Commencement No. 1) Order 1991, SI 1991/707.

[131] See, e.g., Mann, *International and Comparative Law Quarterly*, 32 (1983), p. 265: ' . . . this is one of the most unnecessary, useless and indeed, unfortunate attempts at unification or harmonisation of the law that has ever been undertaken.' See also Mann's letter to *The Times*, 19 December 1989.

[132] See text at nn. 79–82, above.

NOTE

TOWARDS THE ELIMINATION OF INTERNATIONAL LAW: SOME RADICAL SCEPTICISM ABOUT SCEPTICAL RADICALISM*

By IAIN SCOBBIE‡

From Apology to Utopia: The Structure of International Legal Argument. By M. KOSKENNIEMI. Helsinki: Finnish Lawyers' Publishing Company, 1989. xxvi + 501 pp. + bibliography and index. FIM 275.

Rules, Norms and Decisions: On the Conditions of Practical and Legal Reasoning in International Relations and Domestic Affairs. By F. V. KRATOCHWIL. Cambridge: Cambridge University Press, 1989. 312 pp. + index. £35; $49.50.

Both these books are to be welcomed: skilled legal theorists, as opposed to international lawyers as such in search of some jurisprudential tinsel with which to decorate their theses, have turned their attention to international law as an area worthy of serious philosophical analysis in its own right. Both Mr Koskenniemi and Professor Kratochwil argue against both the use of domestic analogies and the facile translation of the Hobbesian state of nature as the archetypes for the analysis of the international legal order. Furthermore, both employ varieties of argumentation theory as their principal mode of analysis, although they adhere to opposed conclusions, Professor Kratochwil being broadly constructivist in approach whereas Mr Koskenniemi is avowedly deconstructionist. Their theses represent the opposed poles of a current theoretical debate,[1] and accordingly comparison of their views proves to be instructive. Both books are relatively long and complex works, and although it could be argued that neither is for the jurisprudentially illiterate, both should be accessible to the careful reader.

To start with Mr Koskenniemi's *From Apology to Utopia*: flicking through the pages of a recent issue of the *American Journal*, one might well be struck by the sudden profusion of the term 'deconstruction',[2] a term well known in contemporary literary theory, borrowed from the further reaches of the 'scorched-earth radicalism'[3] of modern French philosophy, but until relatively recently little heard in

---

* © Dr Iain Scobbie, 1991.

‡ LL B (Hons.) (Edin.), LL B (Cantab.), Dip. Int. Law (ANU), Ph. D (Cantab.); Lecturer in Law, University of Dundee.

[1] This is the opposition between the deconstruction and ordinary language/speech act schools. For an account of this debate (between Derrida and Searle), see Norris, *Deconstruction: Theory and Practice* (Methuen, London, 1982), at pp. 108 ff.

[2] For instance, see *American Journal of International Law*, 84 (1990), at pp. 504 n. 4 (Farer); 521 (D'Amato); 599 (Carty); 634 (Carnahan).

[3] Kenner, *A Colder Eye: The Modern Irish Writers* (Allen Lane, London, 1983), p. 288.

scholarly discussion of international law. This is no longer the case, as a number of scholars, associated with the Critical Legal Studies (CLS) movement, have turned their attention to international law.[4] Mr Koskenniemi's book attempts to combine a deconstructivist account of, and a critical CLS approach to, international law. The former is expounded in the introduction and Chapters One to Seven and the latter in Chapter Eight of *From Apology to Utopia*. The problem is that Mr Koskenniemi appears to be pursuing incompatible objectives: his deconstructivist views would appear to leave no room for his critical reading. Accordingly, to do justice to a complex argument, both these aspects will be considered separately before its overall success is assessed.

Deconstruction[5] was originally a method for the analysis of philosophical texts which has also become a technique of literary criticism. Very broadly, deconstruction argues that language has indeterminate meaning: meaning is part of a system, thus the determination of the meaning of any one term involves unravelling the whole system, and accordingly the complete meaning of any word or term, or ultimately text, can never be attained because there will always be some further nuance to pursue. The deconstructive reading of a text can involve various techniques —in particular the exploration of internal contradictions (*aporia*, or self-engendered paradoxes)—in order to turn the text against itself and thus disrupt its claim to meaning. Internal contradictions are seen as inevitable because a tenet (or dogma) of deconstruction is that concepts are constituted through the opposition of contrasting ideas—for instance, in relation to international law, Koskenniemi argues that internal contradictions arise through the opposition of natural law and positivism, world community and State sovereignty, and apology and utopia (of which, more anon). In trying to define or describe concepts, argument attempts to establish the priority of one or other term of the contrasting pair in issue,[6] but deconstruction maintains that such priority cannot be definitively established because the terms of the pair are not fundamentally in opposition to but are dependent upon one another—very simply, ideas are defined in terms of what they are not, in terms of their apparent opposition or contradiction. As Koskenniemi says:

> In a sense, expressions are like holes in a net. Each is empty in itself and has identity only through the strings which separate it from the neighbouring holes . . . Meaning is *relational*. Knowing a language—understanding the meaning of words—is to be capable of operating these differentiations. A deconstructive study . . . sees each discursive topic (eg . . . 'nature of international law') to be constituted by a conceptual opposition . . . The

---

[4] One of the most active writers in this area is David Kennedy: see, for instance, his 'Theses about International Law Discourse', *German Yearbook of International Law*, 23 (1980), p. 353—of whom Mr Koskenniemi is an avowed admirer.

[5] Useful introductions to deconstruction in general are Eagleton, *Literary Theory: An Introduction* (Basil Blackwell, Oxford, 1983), pp. 127–50, and Norris, *Deconstruction: Theory and Practice* (Methuen, London, 1982). See also D'Amato, 'The Invasion of Panama was a Lawful Response to Tyranny', *American Journal of International Law*, 84 (1990), p. 516 at pp. 520–2, for a succinct account of deconstruction and international law.

[6] It should be noted that the importance of the use of contrasting pairs in (philosophical) argument is recognized by theorists who are not deconstructivists. Perhaps the most apposite for the purposes of this review is the Belgian legal philosopher Chaïm Perelman, who stressed the argumentative importance of 'philosophical pairs' in his collaborative work with Mme L. Olbrechts-Tyteca entitled *The New Rhetoric: A Treatise on Argumentation* (University of Notre Dame Press, Notre Dame, 1969, translation), at pp. 411 ff., originally published as *La Nouvelle Rhétorique: traité de l'argumentation* (Presses Universitaires de France, 1958).

opposition is what the topic (*problématique*) is about. The participants in the discourse proceed by attempting to establish the priority of one or other of the opposing terms . . . [but] disagreement persists because it is impossible to prioritize one term over the other. For although the participants believe that the terms are fundamentally opposing (that is, that their meanings are non-identical), they turn out to depend on each other.[7]

In deconstructive analysis, the analyst turns the text in issue against itself, by seizing on such contradictions and insisting on the necessary ambiguity of language. In some cases, the analyst may also exploit metaphors and analogies used by the author, or material contained in footnotes, to overturn the apparent certainty, or objectivity, of the text.

Koskenniemi's analysis of international law relies on the exploration of alleged contradictory concepts:

> I shall derive the sense of particular doctrines, arguments, positions or rules exhaustively from the way in which they *differentiate* themselves from other, competing doctrines, arguments etc. This involves envisaging that legal argument proceeds by establishing a *system of conceptual differentiations* and using it in order to justify whatever doctrine, position or rule (ie whatever argument) one needs to justify. And I shall then attempt to show that the fact that discourse stops at points of familiar disagreement follows from its inability to uphold these differentiations consistently. We cannot make a preference between alternative arguments because they are not alternative at all; they rely on the correctness of each other.[8]

He argues that international law is built on contestable and arguable assumptions—in particular, apology/utopia in describing the nature of international legal order, normativity/concreteness as the requirements of legal norms, and the ascending/descending modes of international legal argument.

Koskenniemi's central argument is that international law is irredeemably indeterminate because it is predicated on the conceptual opposition of apology and utopia. This opposition is simple—apologism is the view that State behaviour determines the content of international law, whereas utopianism is the assumption that a normative code overrides State behaviour, will or interest. Koskenniemi argues that either the normative code (i.e. international law) is superior to the State or the State superior to the code—'A middle position seems excluded' (at p. 41).

Related to this is Koskenniemi's argument that international law has classically assumed that international legal norms are both normative and concrete:

> The requirement of concreteness related to the need to verify the law's content not against some political principles but by reference to the concrete behaviour, will and interest of States. The requirement of normativity related to the capacity of the law to be opposable to State policy. But these requirements tended to overrule each other. A doctrine with much concreteness seemed to lose its normative nature and end up in descriptive apology. A truly normative doctrine created a gap between itself and State practice in a manner which made doubtful the objectivity of the method of verifying its norms. It ended up in undemonstrable utopias.[9]

These two conceptual oppositions cohere in Koskenniemi's hypothesis (at p. 49) that the international legal argumentation employed by the International Court does not provide a material justification for its decisions, but 'is there only' to avoid openly political rhetoric, and leads only to the constant opposition, dissociation

---

[7] Koskenniemi, pp. xx–xxi, emphasis in original, notes omitted, paragraph break suppressed.

[8] Koskenniemi, p. xxi, emphasis in original.

[9] Koskenniemi, p. 40.

and association of points about the concreteness and normativity of law. Its pronouncements are only a form of making arguments, but not for reaching conclusions—to be defensible, each argument employed would have to appear to be both normative and concrete, but as these notions conflict each argument can be challenged as being only coherent on one of these bases, as being either utopian or apologist. This process of challenge Koskenniemi sees as inevitable:

> To defend one's view on the normative character of a practice so as to avoid apologetics one needs to discuss justice. To defend one's theory of justice without lapsing into utopias one needs to show that one's rule accords with some relevant practice. In both cases one's defence will remain vulnerable to the reverse objection. And so on, *ad infinitum*.[10]

Koskenniemi maintains that the point of the technique of conceptual oppositions is quite simple: if a doctrine or argument is utopian or apologist only in relation to some other doctrine or argument, then the attempt to create a law which is simultaneously normative and concrete can only be successful if there is a shared perspective from which these classifications may be made coherently which is beyond the dichotomy of apologist/utopian, but this is not provided by modern theories of international law.[11]

The third opposition in Koskenniemi's structural triad is that of ascending and descending argumentation. This serves as a bridge between his apology/utopia dichotomy and his view that international law is predicated on a liberal account of politics. However, Koskenniemi argues that liberalism itself entails a paradox because to preserve freedom, order must be created which restricts freedom;[12] this is a fundamental contradiction because it assumes a tension between individual freedom and communal order but fails to reconcile the two.[13] A similar strategy characterizes international law because it describes international relations alternatively in terms of community and autonomy, in terms of conflicting demands of freedom and order. Neither can be exclusive goals because to think of community as the ultimate goal is utopian whereas so to conceive State autonomy is apologist—but these are the controlling conditions for international legal argument.[14]

Accordingly, Koskenniemi argues that liberalism gives rise to two opposed types of argument—the ascending individualist argument that social order is only legitimate in so far as it provides for individual freedom, and the descending communitarian argument that individual freedom depends on a normatively compelling social order. Koskenniemi's thesis is that reconciliation of these two arguments depends on the rule of law, and thus on formally neutral and objectively ascertainable rules;[15] Koskenniemi takes the position that the rule of law is premised on the idea that theories of justice are neither objective nor neutral (because of the liberal denial of a natural hierarchy of values) and thus must be excluded from specifically legal argumentation,[16] but if the objective nature of the rule of law is an illusion, then this reconciliation and the justification of liberalism collapses.[17]

---

[10] Koskenniemi, p. 117.
[11] Koskenniemi, p. 137.
[12] Koskenniemi, p. 52.
[13] Koskenniemi, p. 423.
[14] Koskenniemi, p. 424.
[15] Koskenniemi, p. 52.
[16] Koskenniemi, pp. 456–7.
[17] Koskenniemi, p. 52.

Koskenniemi sees the 'objectivity' of international law as comprising two elements:

i. international law is delimited from descriptions of international relations because it is normative, i.e. it does not simply describe but prescribes behaviour; and
ii. international law is delimited from politics because it is assumed to be less dependent on subjective (political) belief regarding what international order should be like.

Not only do these two delimitations give international law its 'objectivity', but Koskenniemi continues that inasmuch as international law has an identity, it must differ from descriptive and normative accounts of politics in both these senses. This he sees as impossible: these delimitations leave no room for any specifically legal discourse, because the distinctions they entail cannot be simultaneously maintained. International legal discourse continually lapses into either factual description (apologism) or political prescription (utopianism), and further, every resultant argument is vulnerable to a justifiable counter–argument based on the tendency which it has discounted—thus an argument stressing utopianism is open to an apologist response, and vice versa.[18] Given Koskenniemi's adherence to the deconstructivist tenet that neither element of the pair may be consistently preferred, he argues that no objective legal resolution may occur of international disputes and thus he doubts whether any meaningful distinction may be drawn between international law, politics and morality because:

[the] normativity [of international law entails] our duty to exclude everything that is not contained in verified rules from the justification we give for our solution [to a given problem].[19]

This view of international law arises from its liberal underpinnings which assume both that States differentiate between their subjective political opinions and the law, and that legal rules must be neutral, uniformly applicable and their content capable of verification. Koskenniemi denies the possibility of ensuring that all three requirements are met—principally because of the indeterminate nature of language and the need for rules, cast in natural language,[20] to be interpreted. Koskenniemi denies that law can fulfil its aim of providing 'determinate outcomes to normative problems' as the need for interpretation threatens the assumption that international law may be distinguished from international politics by virtue of being more objective;[21]

. . . rules are not automatically applicable. They need interpretation and interpretation seems subjective. This is not merely a 'practical' difficulty of interpretation. The doctrine of sovereign equality makes it impossible to decide between competing interpretations . . . there is no other basis to make the [interpretative] choice than . . . either by referring to a theory of justice or to the identities of the States involved: one interpretation is better either because it is more just or because it is produced by this, and not that, State. And the former solution is utopian, the latter violates sovereign equality. Both seem purely political.[22]

[18] Koskenniemi, p. 1.
[19] Koskenniemi, p. 9.
[20] 'Natural' language, as opposed to the 'artificial' languages of logic and mathematics.
[21] Koskenniemi, p. 24.
[22] Koskenniemi, p. 245.

Here Koskenniemi's approach is that of Unger, one of the major figures in the Critical Legal Studies movement, adopting the view that law embodies a set of authoritative concepts and categories which can be used to settle social conflict without recourse to political ideas. This implies that law itself sustains some defensible and coherent scheme of human association: if conflict solution cannot coherently be undertaken without going beyond available legal concepts and categories, then the 'legal project' is faulted or incomplete.[23]

For Koskenniemi, a legal system must be fully determinate; he denies the possibility of judicial choice between competing interpretations because this would involve recourse to 'subjective' political views rather than be a decision on the basis of 'objective' law:

> No discretion seems allowed. *Legal systems* are absolutely determinant. If the [International] Court cannot reach decision, this is not due to any indeterminacy in law. It is because no legal standards exist.[24]

Koskenniemi's conclusion is that a rule-based approach to international law must concede that law is relatively indeterminate (ambiguous and in need of interpretation) and accordingly there is a margin of political discretion in legal activity. But this margin of discretion is uncertain and conflicting views on the correct norms are only capable of decision if a position is taken on rival theories of justice. Because rules cannot be applied automatically, the rule-approach lawyer is constantly faced with the objection that his interpretations are only political constructions and unless he can explain why his interpretation is non-political, the emphasis on the law/politics distinction is misplaced:

> Interpretation creates meaning rather than discovers it. But conventional theories have regarded this as a marginal problem, existing in law's penumbral areas. The analysis here suggests, however, that it affects every disagreement within international law, from the definition of *that* expression to the finding of the sense of contested rules. Far from being marginal, it is the very core of law—the generator of there being a possibility to disagree. In this sense, the finding that there is no objective meaning to legal concepts, no extratextual referent which could be pointed at when disagreements arise provides the most serious threat we have hereto encountered to the possibility of delimiting law from arguments within 'essentially contested' political concepts.[25]

And the inability of natural language to embody 'objective', i.e. fully determined, meaning Koskenniemi argues makes a nonsense of the liberal concept of the rule of law.

The indeterminacy of language, Koskenniemi claims, has another consequence as it denies an epistemology, an account of specifically legal knowledge, to law: language is ambiguous, thus rules are not fully determinate and require interpretation—but this involves reliance on concepts of value which are political:

> whether we think of law as a set of rules or some constellation of behaviour we seem unable to grasp it through a specifically legal method which would not involve a discussion of . . . contested ideas about the political good. The lawyer could only record that whatever difference of view about the *correct* law there existed, these disagreements were not capable of being dealt with by a legal method which would have secured the *objectivity* and impartiality of the result. Any suggested method only seemed to involve the lawyer in further discussion

---

[23] Koskenniemi, pp. 422–3.

[24] Koskenniemi, p. 16, emphasis added.

[25] Koskenniemi, p. 475, note omitted, emphasis in original.

about principles, purposes and systemic justice which were themselves subject of political dispute.[26]

Accordingly, according to Koskenniemi, there can be no specifically and peculiarly legal discourse which may be delimited from political ideas:

> if 'all' is interpretation, and interpretation has no solid epistemological foundation, what basis is there to embark on any specifically legal enterprise at all?[27]

Thus Koskenniemi eliminates international law as a separate conceptual category because he alleges it is indistinguishable from politics, but this deconstructivist conclusion is jettisoned in his Chapter Eight adoption of a CLS approach as the appropriate method to evaluate international law—in this, Koskenniemi apparently assumes the existence of law as separate from politics. He argues that the elimination of law does not entail a freedom of State action, but rather that expectations of legal certainty should be down-played and that international actors and lawyers should take seriously and take responsibility for the moral and political choices with which they are faced 'even when arguing "within the law" '. This assumes the existence of specifically legal discourse; otherwise, how can one adopt a critical approach to law?

Further, although he recognizes that his deconstructive argument could be taken to mean that all discourse will end in an unending play of conceptual oppositions in which there is no basis to prefer one conflicting idea over another, Koskenniemi argues that despite the inevitable movement to politics in legal argument, politics (viz., justice and morality) is not subjective and arbitrary, as political views may be held without belief that these are objective and may be discussed without assuming that everyone should agree.[28] Politics is simply a continual critical discourse on societal conditions.[29] Koskenniemi concludes that he has only shown that standard legal discourse is vulnerable to well-known criticisms which result from the arbitrary restriction of the argumentative possibilities open to lawyers: the critical (CLS) position for which he argues lies in showing that it is possible to escape the weaknesses of legal discourse by extending the range of possible legitimate argumentative styles—for instance, by including discussion of justice and politics.[30]

It might be that Koskenniemi's critical thesis boils down to the idea that when discussing international law, those involved should be aware of the issues lying behind the norms and take a critical (or questioning) view of the substantive content of the law. But it should also be remembered that the CLS movement is one of the most influential and fashionable contemporary 'schools' of legal theory. If, indeed, the central tenet of this school may be reduced to the idea that law has such a political dimension, then one would be well justified in a retort of 'So what?', as this is hardly a novel insight into the legal process. If the CLS movement adopts a 'critical' stance in order to stimulate law reform then, leaving utilitarianism to one side, it bears obvious similarities to a Benthamite programme. The affinities with Bentham lie also in the underlying linguistic theory that meaning is 'relational': the

---

[26] Koskenniemi, pp. 476–7; quotation at p. 477, emphasis supplied.
[27] Koskenniemi, p. 478.
[28] Koskenniemi, p. 479.
[29] Koskenniemi, p. 480.
[30] Koskenniemi, pp. 484–5.

'holes in the net' analogy bears some similarity to Bentham's doctrine of paraphra-sis.[31] Moreover, the elimination of judicial discretion, the need for any legal system to be fully determinate, recalls Bentham's strictures on 'dog law'.[32] Accordingly a quiet chorus of 'Come in Jeremy Bentham, someone is infringing your copyright' might not be an inappropriate response to the CLS enterprise.

However, as may be apparent from this brief account, Koskenniemi's argument is very complex, and furthermore, it is a well-written and persuasive read, but in hands less well-read and expert than Mr Koskenniemi's, deconstruction might simply prove to be a pitfall gift-wrapped for the intellectually pretentious in that it seems to be a new and powerful method of analysis. It is this reviewer's opinion that deconstruction, in so far as law is concerned, is only a rehashing of established analytical methods, dressed up in modern linguistics, and predicated on a naïve truth-theory, which ultimately would appear to be self-defeating. Mr Koskennie-mi's thesis, although interesting and thought-provoking, is flawed at its roots—partly because of the consequences deconstruction must hold for his own thesis; partly because of the emphasis he places on, and the version he employs of, liberal-ism; and partly because of the materials on which he relies to construct his argu-ment.

The first problem Mr Koskenniemi's work shares with all deconstructive texts is a simple *tu quoque* riposte: if the indeterminacy of language is inevitable, 'objec-tivity' lacking, and meaning a mirage,[33] then how are such texts privileged, in the sense that they are not meaningless or hopelessly indeterminate? On his own lights, how can we 'understand' Mr Koskenniemi's book 'if "all" is interpretation' and 'interpretation creates meaning rather than discovers it'? On this basis, *From Apo-logy to Utopia* is simply rather a long performative inconsistency,[34] but Kosken-niemi himself has to concede that behind all communication, including discussion about norms, is the presupposition that rational argument is possible because otherwise the discussion is pointless.[35] This concession undermines Koskenniemi's claim of inevitable indeterminacy; all *cannot* be interpretation but some shared or settled meaning must exist. Whether expressions have an 'objective' meaning is one issue, but it is apparent that inter-subjective meaning is possible: even assuming the impossibility of objective meaning, this does not entail that the only option

---

[31] On Bentham and language, see Hart, *Essays on Bentham* (Clarendon Press, Oxford, 1982), pp. 9–10, 42–3; Waldron, *Nonsense upon Stilts: Bentham, Burke and Marx in the Rights of Man* (Methuen, London, 1987), at pp. 34 ff.

[32] See Postema, *Bentham and the Common Law Tradition* (Clarendon Press, Oxford, 1986), at pp. 275 ff.

[33] 'By interpretation we can only attain new expressions and texts which are just as indeterminate as the original texts were. There remains no extralinguistic, non-textual method of checking the objective correctness of the interpretation arrived at . . . The problem is that in case somebody disagrees with our interpretation, we are left with very little means to convince him . . . the world of "pure ideas" recedes always to the background and remains incapable of being grasped without the mediation of the prison-house of language . . . There is, then, no "objective" meaning to the linguistic expressions of rules': Koskenniemi, pp. 474–5; notes omitted.

[34] A performative inconsistency is an 'inconsistency between what is asserted by a statement and facts that are given in and by the *making* of the statement': see Finnis, 'Scepticism, Self-Refutation, and the Good of Truth', in Hacker and Raz (eds.), *Law, Morality and Society: Essays in Honour of H.L.A. Hart* (Clarendon Press, Oxford, 1977), p. 247 at p. 251. See also Passmore, *Philosophical Reasoning* (Basic Books, New York, 1969), at pp. 58–64, with reference to pragmatic self-refutation.

[35] Koskenniemi, p. 487 n. 67.

open is subjective (and thus indeterminate) meaning.[36] Koskenniemi simply goes too far—but this arises from his adherence to the deconstructivist view that language is a net of meaning, with meaning being constructed from the differences between terms, and thus ambiguity is always available by pursuing an unpursued nuance.

The desire to backtrack from deconstruction's conclusions is also apparent in Koskenniemi's argument for critical reflection in his final chapter: despite his claim that international law cannot be distinguished from international politics, he denies that this leaves him open to the charge of legal nihilism[37] or that the elimination of international law entails a freedom of State action, because although the move to politics in legal argument is inevitable, politics is not subjective and arbitrary. There are two inter-related points here worth exploring; the first concerns the truth theory underlying Koskenniemi's analysis; and the second concerns Koskenniemi's view of law and legal argument.

Underlying Koskenniemi's thesis is rather an odd conception of the nature and aims of a legal system which arises from his claim that international law is predicated on a liberal political doctrine and from his adherence to a bivalent truth theory. By the latter is meant that, with the apparent exception of political discourse, Koskenniemi sees propositions as being either true or false, either objective or subjective—indeed, this latter dichotomy dominates his work.

This bivalent distribution of worth is inadequate, falling into the logical trap of the excluded middle, and calling into question Koskenniemi's (and the deconstructive project's) dogma that all concepts are constructed in terms of bipolar oppositions. A pertinent question here is how one chooses which terms to oppose—for instance, State sovereignty may be opposed not only to world community, but also to self-determination, or even regional organization. A bipolar approach is accordingly question-begging, especially in the light of the covert ontology which Koskenniemi's analysis appears to entail. As for the excluded middle, a rigid categorization of propositions into either true or false ignores the possibility of there being probable or plausible or, importantly, undecidable propositions, whereas an inflexible objective/subjective division leaves out matters which have inter-subjective status—a status which Koskenniemi appears to accord only to political discourse, which is neither objective nor subjective nor arbitrary, and which accordingly achieves a privileged status which he denies to all other uses of inherently indeterminate language.

Despite protests that there is 'no extralinguistic, non-textual method of checking the objective correctness of the interpretation arrived at', Koskenniemi's analysis is predicated on the existence of such 'objective' concepts—'The "idea" or the "rule" seems unattainable in its objective true sense'; 'the correspondence between our interpretation and the expression's "real" extraconceptual meaning'; 'the world of "pure ideas" recedes always to the background and remains incapable of being grasped without the mediation of the prison-house of language'.[38] This is a somewhat bizarre ontological position to adopt in relation to law, akin to Platonic essentialism—the view that somewhere, somehow there exists a perfect idea of every entity against which we can assess the success of the correspondence of those of

---

[36] See below for further discussion of Koskenniemi's underlying truth-theory.

[37] See Koskenniemi, p. 478.

[38] All quotations, Koskenniemi, pp. 474–5.

which we have experience. Legal terms do not correspond to brute facts which have a material reality,[39] but are, as Koskenniemi accepts,[40] institutional facts:[41] thus legal concepts and terms do not correspond to an ontological sphere external to the legal system—there can be no ' "real" extraconceptual' 'objective' reference which Koskenniemi appears to demand. But such objectivity is the predicate of Koskenniemi's deconstruction: his argument from indeterminacy appears to entail an existential commitment to objectivity. Moreover this covert ontological programme is at odds with Koskenniemi's adoption of the deconstructive tenet of inevitable conceptual contradiction as his underlying quest is for a 'world of "pure ideas" ', of 'objective' concepts untainted by that very contradiction.

It is perhaps not too crudely reductive to conclude that Koskenniemi postulates that language is indeterminate, but then criticizes law, which is language-based, for exhibiting this indeterminacy, maintaining that this subverts the very idea of law because it fails to fulfil Koskenniemi's self-imposed ideal of objectivity. But he fails to indicate how such objectivity may be attained.

The model legal system which underlies Koskenniemi's analysis is similarly odd: it is a flawed conceptual construction arising from his assumption that international law is predicated on a liberal doctrine of politics, and from the version of liberalism which he adopts. He argues that in a legal system no discretion is allowed as legal systems must be absolutely determinant[42] because:

Inasmuch as law has the function of guiding problem-solution . . . it must be envisaged as a set of directives, standards, rules etc which have 'binding force' in that they claim to determine a preference between competing solutions (rival meanings).[43]

For a legal system to meet this requirement, it would have to be fully-interpreted and complete, containing no lacunae or ambiguities and covering all possible activities, either expressly or by virtue of a closing rule which provided that what was not expressly regulated was either prohibited or allowed. Moreover, such a system would have to be free of all norm-conflicts and be composed entirely of rules. These requirements reduce Koskenniemi's view of law to an oracular or purely declaratory system which contains an unequivocal, pre-determined answer to all normative problems which might arise. It reduces the role of the judge to the Montesquieuan ideal of 'la bouche de la loi':

the judges of the nation are . . . only the mouth that pronounces the words of the law, inanimate beings who can moderate neither its force nor its rigor . . . [44]

This equates a legal system with a logical system—but a logical system must meet the requirements of univocity of terms, non-contradiction and completeness. Gödel demonstrated that any formal (logical) system of relative complexity is

---

[39] A point apparent to Bentham: see Hart, op. cit. above (n. 31), at p. 43.

[40] Koskenniemi, p. 470.

[41] For accounts of this doctrine, see MacCormick, 'Law as Institutional Fact', *Law Quarterly Review*, 90 (1974), p. 102; MacCormick and Weinberger, *An Institutional Theory of Law* (Reidel, Dordrecht, 1986); and Kratochwil, *Rules, Norms and Decisions*—below.

[42] Koskenniemi, p. 16.

[43] Koskenniemi, pp. 11–12, note omitted.

[44] Montesquieu, *The Spirit of the Laws* (1748); edition used translated and edited by Cohler, Miller and Stone (Cambridge University Press, Cambridge, 1989); quotation at p. 163.

necessarily incomplete as it will contain propositions which are undecidable.[45] Given the necessary complexity of any legal system, Koskenniemi's underlying model cannot be fulfilled as, assuming the possibility of its translation into a formal system, some legal questions will be undecidable or 'intractable'.[46] The underlying problem here is Koskenniemi's quest for 'objectivity', which is dependent on his bivalent truth theory which presupposes that a given proposition is either true or false: if bivalence is inadequate even for relatively simple logics which manipulate univocal terms, a *fortiori* it is an inadequate array for law. If one adopts the closing rule approach to provide for the formal completeness of a legal system, then one simply teeters off into the crude deontic logics of Stone and Tammelo, which does take account of undecidability, but which cannot account for the interrelationship of rules within a system as it can only assign deontic value to rules in isolation.[47]

Indeed, the postulate of complete rules, each viewed in isolation, would appear to dog Koskenniemi's deconstruction of 'liberal' international law: his model is not that of an interrelated legal system but of a set of atomized propositions which do not affect the incidence and interpretation of one another. Moreover it is a system of *rules*—the judicial manipulation of principles and standards in any legal system, regardless of its underlying political ideology, necessarily requires interpretation. Here again his truth theory proves to be inadequate: in giving content to standards such as those embodied in the *Caroline* Note ('a necessity of self-defence, instant, overwhelming, leaving no choice of means, and no moment for deliberation'), the judge surely does not rely on some objective or subjective meaning; rather, an inter-subjective assessment will be made in much the same way as a municipal judge determines the requirements of standards such as 'the reasonable man' or 'the officious bystander'. This may leave room for disagreement, but it is not subjective and arbitrary. Accordingly, Koskenniemi's reference-group of municipal law, against which he measures international law and finds it wanting, exhibits the same tendency to indeterminacy.[48] One may well think that Koskenniemi, in his desire for determinist law, himself exhibits the Oedipal repression of conflict to which he adverts:

The ambivalence between desire (for mother) and fear (of castration) is solved by the

---

[45] See Carnap, *Introduction to Symbolic Logic and its Applications* (Dover, New York, 1958, translation), at pp. 173–4; Mates, *Elementary Logic* (Oxford University Press, New York, 1972), at p. 229. A non-technical account of Gödel's incompleteness theorem may be found in Hofstadter, *Gödel, Escher, Bach: An Eternal Golden Braid* (Penguin, Harmondsworth, 1980), at pp. 15 ff.

[46] On intractability see Farago, 'Intractable Cases: the Role of Uncertainty in the Concept of Law', *New York University Law Review*, 55 (1980), p. 195. To assume that legal systems may be translated into formal systems is at least controversial, if not untenable.

[47] See, for instance, Stone, *Legal Controls of International Conflict* (Stevens, London, 2nd edn., 1959), at pp. 153–64; *Legal System and Lawyers' Reasonings* (Stevens, London, 1964), at pp. 185–98; Tammelo, 'Sketch for a Symbolic Juristic Logic', *Journal of Legal Education*, 8 (1955), p. 277. 'On the Logical Openness of Legal Orders', *American Journal of Comparative Law*, 8 (1959), p. 187. 'Syntactic Ambiguity, Conceptual Vagueness, and the Lawyer's Hard Thinking', *Journal of Legal Education*, 15 (1962), p. 56. Both subsequently recanted from excessive reliance on deontic analysis; Stone's eventual view was to reject its relevance completely: see 'Comments on Chaïm Perelman: "Legal Ontology and Legal Reasoning" ', *Bulletin of the Australian Society for Legal Philosophy*, 1981 (Special Issue), p. 68, whereas Tammelo came to view logical and rhetorical reasoning as complementary: see 'The Law of Nations and the Rhetorical Tradition of Legal Reasoning', *Indian Yearbook of International Affairs*, 13–II (1964), p. 277, and *Modern Logic in the Service of Law* (Springer-Verlag, Vienna, 1978), at pp. 2–4.

[48] See Koskenniemi, p. 143.

introjection of the father, that is, the all-powerful normative order . . . The law makes conflict go away. It takes on the appearance of the external third, the solver of the conflict, a
father in possession of 'truth'.[49]

Koskenniemi's father-figure is a straw man: a model of a legal system so flawed and
improbable that it cannot but 'prove' his argument—but that straw man is required
by the terms of his argument, by the terms of his attack on liberalism, and in particular 'the liberal ideal of the objectivity of law-ascertainment'.[50] He argues that
the problems of, for instance, treaty interpretation lie deeper than linguistic indeterminacy, in the contradictions between the legal principles used to arrive at an
interpretation, which themselves arise from the contradiction between the subjective and objective positions on matters of value. Neither liberal law nor politics can
cope with the assessment of values and, in particular, the use of evaluation within a
liberal legal system predicated on the subjective nature of values means either
recourse to arbitrary choice or a radical departure from the system itself. If the
latter, then the distinctions law/politics, legislation/adjudication become meaningless and a move is made beyond the conceptual system of liberal politics.[51]

What Koskenniemi forgets here is that a legal system, even one based on
liberalism, embodies values. Interpretation may therefore have recourse to values
already embodied within the system to determine which interpretation best makes
sense systemically in terms of producing a consistent and coherent result.[52]
Again, although the result may not be 'objective' or 'correct', it is arguably inter-
subjective.

Moreover, while stressing one aspect of the law/politics relationship, Koskenniemi forgets another—that the construction of a legal system is an historical process. Legal systems do not drop ready-made from the skies. Koskenniemi appears
to presuppose that legal systems should be based on a unified and consistent political theory rather than laws being the segmental expression of policy which underlies discrete areas of the legal system. The issue here is whether politics provides a
full or partial underpinning of the legal system: given that law results from a political process through time, and that political ideals change, only partial segmental
underpinning may be expected as ideals embodied in law at one time may sit ill
with ideals enacted at another. This tendency is magnified if we assume that political manifestoes do not guarantee a logically consistent legislative programme and
further recognize that the outcome of the political process may well be a compromise which masks the underlying dispute but provides some regulation of the
matter in hand—for instance, consider the definition of mercenaries embodied in
Article 47 of 1977 Geneva Protocol I, or in Article 1 of the 1989 UN Mercenaries
Convention. These factors combine to preclude the pure objectivism which Koskenniemi appears to desire, and also open his thesis up to the charge of incurable
utopianism.

Koskenniemi[53] also argues that the rule-approach international lawyer must concede that the use of discretion in interpretative decisions entails that interpretations

---

[49] Koskenniemi, p. 490 n. 76.
[50] Koskenniemi, p. 298 n. 111.
[51] Koskenniemi, pp. 298–9.
[52] Compare MacCormick, *Legal Reasoning and Legal Theory* (Clarendon Press, Oxford, 1978).
[53] Koskenniemi, p. 166.

are only political constructions. He repeatedly argues that if a given legal issue is decided against the arguments proffered by a State, then this either infringes that State's sovereign equality (because the decision-maker gives preference to the other State's arguments), or the decision maker must employ a theory of justice in making his choice which Koskenniemi claims cannot be justified under the rule of law.[54]

To deal first with the sovereign equality point: simply to participate in legal argument before someone empowered to make a decision is to commit oneself in advance to that decision, whatever it may be. To hold otherwise would be to make the process meaningless.[55] It has long been established that to undertake international engagements is an attribute of sovereign equality; accordingly Koskenniemi's claim is self-contradictory.

As for the recourse to justice argument, here Koskenniemi would appear to misconstrue the nature of legal argument, which is not a metaphysical speculation in search of some absolute Platonic truth but is an instrumental enterprise which attempts to justify action. Accordingly, to some extent, interpretations are tailored to a predetermined end. He fails to recognize that legal argumentation is structured dialogue which assigns a burden of proof in relation to facts, and in relation to norms a burden of persuasion: States must persuade judges of the worth of their argument. Consequently the decision-maker need only endorse the argument he thinks more plausible, which need not entail judicial recourse to justice, but simply an assessment of relative weight. As the Permanent Court noted in *Eastern Greenland*:

> It is impossible to read the records of the decisions in cases as to territorial sovereignty without observing that in many cases the tribunal has been satisfied with very little in the way of actual exercise of sovereign rights, provided that the other State could not make out a superior claim.[56]

Further, in his attack on liberalism, Koskenniemi may prove too much: he argues that there is a fundamental contradiction in the liberal doctrine of politics because it assumes a tension between individual freedom and communal order, but fails to reconcile the two.[57] But if liberalism did reconcile the two, then surely the resultant answer would eliminate politics—which assuredly is about the relationship between the interests of the individual and the wider community and where the balance is to be drawn. Accordingly, Koskenniemi's search for a position beyond this contradiction is the search for a meta-position which eliminates political discourse—the search for the 'true' 'objective' nature or essence of social relations. But by Koskenniemi's own lights, how can a scale of meta-political value be 'objective'. Unless he accepts that this is innate and simply known (although how do such 'pure ideas' escape 'the prison house of language'?), then he must concede that values are constructed and interpreted (finding the balance of freedom versus

---

[54] For instance, at pp. 450, 453–4: Koskenniemi sees the rule of law as premised on the idea that theories of justice are neither objective nor neutral and thus must be excluded from specifically legal argument: Koskenniemi, p. 456.

[55] See Kelsen, *Principles of International Law* (Rinehart, New York, 1952), at p. 395; Rosenne, *The Law and Practice of the International Court* (Sijthoff, Leyden, 1965), p. 127.

[56] *PCIJ Reports*, Series A/B, No. 53 (1933), at p. 46.

[57] Koskenniemi, p. 423.

order).[58] Either way, Koskenniemi loses: either he falls foul of the indeterminacy of meaning or he must embrace the liberal contradiction.

Moreover, even assuming that Koskenniemi's desired meta-position were available, his book sets out neither the epistemic nor the ontological aspects of that position, and so his thesis begs more questions than it can attempt to answer because it can give no basis for the conclusions it offers. Consequently these conclusions are detached and fundamentally acritical, because Koskenniemi fails to establish the critical position from which they arise: he cannot claim that his theory should be privileged and be less stringently established than that which he opposes.

Finally Koskenniemi betrays the philosophical and linguistic roots of deconstruction in the sources he uses: these are solely textual, and in particular he reconstructs from doctrinal writings, using these to demonstrate the contradictions he claims bedevil the discipline of international law. His principal source is general textbooks which cannot bear the significance Koskenniemi assigns, as introductory works for undergraduates cannot be seen as detailed expositions of legal or political theory: conceptual infelicity is accordingly to be expected. If nothing else, textbook writers do not have the space to write complex theoretical argument— Koskenniemi takes 500+ pages to criticize their attempts, but fails to provide a coherent alternative.

In the *Namibia* advisory opinion, Sir Gerald Fitzmaurice commented that law was not 'an interesting parlour game'.[59] Mr Koskenniemi has invested too much effort in *From Apology to Utopia* to be accused of such a frivolous intention, and furthermore it is a stimulating book, but the motivations of those who are not as well-read or as thoughtful as he is but who jump upon the deconstructivist bandwagon must be open to question. Following intellectual fashions can too easily be an end in itself. The deconstructivist writings of Jacques Derrida contain a device which might be useful to recall at this point, the device of *sous rature*:

or 'under erasure', signified by crossing [words] through in the text and thus warning the reader not to accept them at philosophical face value.[60]

In legal theory there is one prime candidate for this treatment: ~~deconstruction~~

*   *   *

Turning now to Professor Kratochwil's *Rules, Norms, and Decisions*, this assumes some knowledge of speech act and games theory on the part of the reader and its ambit embraces philosophy (principally the linguistic theory of speech/communication acts), legal theory and international relations. Again we are faced with a thesis which emphasizes the linguistic basis of international law but which, unlike Koskenniemi, concentrates on the institutional nature of legal concepts and endorses a theory of non-compelling legal argumentation (rhetorical or topical reasoning), rather than a quest for an objectively 'correct' answer.

---

[58] And even if Koskenniemi were to argue that such political values were innate, this would not solve the problem of how they were to be ranked—which is an interpretative task. This point has been captured metaphorically by Eco:

' " . . . laughter is proper to man, it is a sign of his rationality," William said.

"Speech is also a sign of human rationality, and with speech a man can blaspheme against God. Not everything that is proper to man is necessarily good . . . " ': *The Name of the Rose* (Picador, London, 1984), p. 131.

[59] *ICJ Reports*, 1971, dissenting opinion of Sir Gerald Fitzmaurice, p. 299 at p. 303 paragraph 12.

[60] Quotation, Norris, op. cit. above (n. 5), p. 69.

The thrust of Professor Kratochwil's thesis is relatively simple: he claims that the conventional understanding of social action and the governing role of norms is inadequate because the social function of language has been fundamentally misunderstood.[61] Because the use of language is governed by rules, it may be used to analyse the function of norms:

> Conventional analysis focused solely on the propositional content of an utterance and its reference. It held that effective communication takes place when the propositional content of the message matched empirical reality. All other messages were either metaphysical or nonsense. Consequently, since normative statements containing such words as 'ought', 'must', etc, provided no match with objects of the outer world, they could only refer to certain mental or emotional states of the speaker, such as to his/her preference or values. On this basis language could be neatly divided into two mutually exclusive sets of 'is' and 'ought' statements. Debates about normative concerns outside of the goal-means context of instrumental rationality, therefore, had to be considered useless because of their lack of 'reference'.[62]

To explain normative statements, Kratochwil employs speech act theory which distinguishes between three aspects of a statement:

its locutionary dimension:	simply saying something
its illocutory force:	doing something by saying something (for instance, promising) and
its perlocutionary effects:	the impact it has on hearers (the audience)[63]

The difference between Koskenniemi's and Kratochwil's linguistic approaches to international law should be apparent: Kratochwil does not presuppose some extra-textual universe of pure objective concepts, some 'real' world of material referents, as the bench-mark for his analysis. He also rejects the bivalent truth function of logic as an appropriate model for assessing the success of communication because this cannot account for the illocutory and perlocutionary aspects of speech acts.[64]

Nor does Kratochwil reduce the question of meaning to the analysis of individual terms, and then build from the postulate of relational meaning to a denial of meaning, but emphasizes the context in which a statement is made.[65] Koskenniemi misses not only the point that language is rule-governed but also that meaning does not purely lie in the analysis of terms detached from the context of their utterance. He concentrates on dead and inanimate texts in contextual isolation—but context,

---

[61] Kratochwil, p. 5.

[62] Kratochwil, pp. 6 ff., quotation at pp. 7–8. Here Kratochwil is endorsing J.L. Austin's theory of speech acts; this ought to be familiar to all, or at least some, lawyers to an extent because it is the linguistic theory which influenced H.L.A. Hart's *The Concept of Law* (Clarendon Press, Oxford, 1961): on this, see MacCormick, *HLA Hart* (Edward Arnold, London, 1981), at pp.12 ff.

[63] Kratochwil, p. 8. The term 'audience' has been inserted here, borrowed from Perelman's 'new rhetoric' which stresses the importance of the audience addressed, and its beliefs, for the success of an argument: see Perelman and Olbrechts-Tyteca, op. cit. above (n. 6), pp. 17–35, 65–6, 99–110, and also Perelman, *Logique juridique: nouvelle rhétorique* (Dalloz, Paris, 1976), paras. 52–4 at pp. 107 ff.

[64] Kratochwil, p. 29.

[65] Kratochwil, pp. 29–30.

excoriated by Koskenniemi,[66] is surely the inarticulate premise of the deconstruc-tive identification of *aporia*: to know which pair of oppositions to employ (for instance, sovereignty as against community or self-determination or regional organization) one needs to know the context—the reason why the chosen pair, and not others, is being opposed.

As noted, Kratochwil argues that it is impossible to reduce obligations to state-ments about fact or value, but nor may they be reduced to psychological statements about the speaker's state of mind because, for instance, insincere promises are obligatory. This last point would appear to put paid to Koskenniemi's attempt to exclude contextuality. He notes that 'modern theories about social explanation' hold that to:

> understand the meaning of social behaviour, we must include the behaving person's self-understanding of that meaning into our account. But it will lead normatively into simple apologism. The State can always say its activity was such and thus escape criticism . . . If the act's contextual meaning is constructed without reference to what the State(s) involved believed its meaning was, then we face the difficulty of justifying our construction. Why should a State which disagrees with our contextual evaluation be bound by it?[67]

The difficulties here again lie in the elimination of intersubjectivity in Koskennie-mi's truth-theory: the institutional theory which Kratochwil defends provides a framework for the interpretation of State action. This does not occur in a vacuum, nor is it unidirectional: one pertinent aspect is the reaction of other States.[68] Regardless of the subjective explanation of the acting State, it must realize that others will categorize and interpret its action. Thus the perlocutionary effects of an utterance give a framework for interpreting action: such conventions (or legal insti-tutions or rules) accordingly have a communicative function, by indicating the prima facie intention of the actor to others.[69]

In a further rejection of logical systems as the relevant model for the analysis of law, and in common with a number of theorists (e.g. Alexy, MacCormick, Perelman), Kratochwil sees legal reasoning as a specialized (or restricted) form of practical reasoning—reasoning which is aimed at making a decision. In particular, Kratochwil maintains that legal reasoning is rhetorical, which means that it aims at persuading the judge or other decision-maker to adopt a given decision from a range of possible alternatives, but which does not compel that decision as, unlike a logical argument, the conclusion of a legal argument is not determinant.[70]

---

[66] See in particular Koskenniemi, pp. 147–8, 319–20. Koskenniemi's exclusion of context, and thus the shared expectations attendant on the use of speech acts, bears some affinity to the fallacy which Lang terms 'the fallacy of misplaced concreteness': see Lang, *The Anatomy of Philosophical Style* (Blackwell, Oxford, 1990), at pp. 5–7; his discussion of Hamlet's grandmothers is of oblique relevance here: see pp. 159–67. See also below, nn. 100–2 and accompanying text, for a consideration of the con-sequences of Koskenniemi's approach.

[67] Koskenniemi, pp. 147–8, notes omitted, paragraph breaks suppressed.

[68] See Kratochwil, p. 56.

[69] Kratochwil, p. 11: this point is further considered below.

[70] Kratochwil, pp. 32–3, 40 ff: at pp. 41–2, he argues that the widespread rhetorical orientation of legal systems calls into question the view that legal orders are closed systems susceptible to complete mapping and logical formalization, although this does not preclude legal reasoning from following logi-cal canons. On the difference between persuasion and logical compulsion, see also Perelman and Olbrechts-Tyteca, op. cit. above (n. 6), pp. 13–14. Perelman pithily encapsulates his view that legal argument is rhetorical and not determinative in his metaphor that the judge is not a calculating machine: the best account of this is in Perelman, *The Idea of Justice and the Problem of Argument* (Routledge and Kegan Paul, London, 1963), at pp. 62–3, 146–7.

The justification of authoritative decisions in law is based on certain topics (bases of argument)[71] which are specific to legal orders, whose function is largely to justify conclusions and also to limit the range of facts and proofs relevant to the argument and resultant decision.[72] Kratochwil views the main characteristics of legal reasoning as being concerned with finding and interpreting applicable norms and procedures, and presenting and evaluating the relevant facts: both turn on whether a given proposition is acceptable rather than true. Thus Kratochwil emphasizes pragmatics, rather than objectivity:[73]

ultimately our substantive determinations cannot be grounded in an absolute Archimedean point. They depend for their validity on the assent they can marshal.[74]

However, like Koskenniemi, Kratochwil argues that law cannot easily be distinguished from other normative disciplines because he rejects the 'fundamental assumption' of varieties of legal positivism that the question of the legal validity of a norm can be reduced to a cognitive question of how one is to recognize a legal norm. He argues that there are two basic varieties of positivism—that legal rules share some characteristic, such as an attached sanction, or that they 'are part of a particular system of rules'. Kratochwil argues that both views fundamentally misconstrue the problem of decision-making through the use of rules and norms, as not all legal rules are characterized by sanctions or 'form part of a deductive hierarchical system of norms'. Accordingly, legal rules and norms cannot be conceptualized as possessing a common characteristic, or being treated merely as institutional rules. Kratochwil's view is that by emphasizing the style of reasoning with rules a more realistic account of law can be given.[75]

---

[71] Possibly the most elaborate modern theory of topical reasoning is that of Perelman—see Perelman and Olbrechts-Tyteca, op. cit. above (n. 6), for his general theory, and Perelman, *Logique juridique: nouvelle rhétorique*, for the application of his 'new rhetoric' to law specifically. Perelman defines a topic as a premise of argument, holding that:

'[t]he unfolding as well as the starting point of the argumentation presuppose . . . the agreement of the audience . . . analysis of argumentation is concerned with what is supposed to be accepted by the hearers. On the other hand, the actual choice of premises and their formulation, together with the adjustments involved, are rarely without argumentative value . . . When a speaker selects and puts forward the premises that are to serve as foundation for his argument, he relies on his hearers' adherence to the propositions from which he will start. His hearers may, however, refuse their adherence . . .':

Perelman and Olbrechts-Tyteca, op. cit. above (n. 6), p. 65. Kratochwil adheres to this view that a topic is an initial and presumptive point of agreement between the arguer and his audience (see pp. 219–20, and below), and as he notes, the theory of topical reasoning may be traced back to Aristotle: see Kratochwil, p. 41.

[72] Kratochwil, p. 39.

[73] Kratochwil, p. 42.

[74] Kratochwil, p. 138.

[75] Kratochwil, pp. 186–7. Necessarily, to some extent, this is a simplification of Kratochwil's thesis that legal rules cannot be easily distinguished from other types of rules and norms by virtue of some property which delineates them as legal. He also reaches this conclusion through an analysis of promises, arguing that to claim that promises (and thus contracts) are obligatory because of the expectations they generate fails to distinguish adequately between promises and threats. As there is no obligation to execute one's threats, this implies that there is no obligation to keep one's promises—more generally, the issue may be reduced to the question why expectations attendant on promises are so different from those which attend unilateral declarations of intent by an actor where it is recognized that the actor might change his mind. Although speech act theory appeared to solve this problem by arguing that the use of the institution (promising) created the obligation, it does not provide a satisfactory explanation by itself as expectation cannot be the sole reason for the obligation incurred. Threats differ from promises because the success of a threat is necessarily connected with the perlocutionary effect of the

Kratochwil rejects the possibility of law being demarcated from other normative disciplines because imperative theories which hold that sanctions are a necessary requirement of laws are inadequate. On demarcation by reference to a systemic membership requirement, Kratochwil analyses Hart's rule of recognition[76] as the paradigm of such theses and finds it wanting.[77] His criticism of the rule of recognition is rooted in the indeterminacy of language: because judges have to go beyond established rules and use discretion in interpretative decisions and the like, he thinks it problematic to take institutional practices as the model of law in general. Further, Hart appears to view it as a power-conferring rule but, because *inter alia* it indicates sources of law and norm-hierarchies, Kratochwil holds that it must be duty-imposing.[78] Kratochwil concludes that because of these problems, the Hartian analysis of law as a system of rules is inadequate, and thinks that there are two ways of dealing with the resultant difficulties—either the Hartian programme of the systemic nature of law must be elaborated to eliminate the problems, or a 'clear demarcation criterion of law' may be omitted and law be seen in terms of the degree of influence various norms have on decision-making.[79]

Kratochwil continues that according to the Hartian account of law as a system of rules, the set of primary duty-imposing and secondary power-conferring rules is exhaustive of the law, but unless it is assumed that law is 'a deductive system of norms' the process of deciding between two possible but contradictory claims cannot be decided in terms of purely logical operations. He further objects that not all devices used by courts function like rules—for instance, principles.[80] Rejection of the system-of-rules explanation leads Kratochwil to his central thesis:

from the fact that not all rules that have legal import are of the same character it does *not* follow that anything goes. If the constraints for legal decision-making do not lie in the type of norms, such constraints can still lie in the way norms are *used*, ie, in the decision-making *style* which distinguishes legal from other modes of decision-making . . . the unity of law consists less in the special character of the norms involved, or in their systemic character, than in the norm-use.[81]

Thus, for Kratochwil, law is distinguished from other normative disciplines by virtue of the way it is used; however, he cautions against identifying legal reasoning with judicial rule-handling because this is misleading. Judicial activity is significantly influenced by the role-expectations directed at the judge which go beyond

speech act—a threat is ineffective if the addressee is not moved by it whereas a promise is not invalid simply because the promisee does not pay much credence to it: the illocutory effect of a promise, not its perlocutionary effect, is crucial. Because important legal institutions (for instance, contracts) are parasitic on promises, Kratochwil concludes that legal rules cannot easily be distinguished from other types of rules—see Kratochwil, p. 146, and at pp. 146–8. This would appear to be a *non sequitur*: even assuming that basic legal institutions are parasitic on morals, it does not follow that law cannot be distinguished from morals. The matter is one of identity, not derivation.

[76] See Hart, *The Concept of Law*, in particular at chapter 6 and pp. 144 ff.

[77] See Kratochwil, pp. 192–3.

[78] As MacCormick notes, there are 'serious ambiguities' in the central passage in Hart's account of primary and secondary rules (*The Concept of Law* at p. 79)—see MacCormick, *HLA Hart*, p. 103.

[79] Kratochwil, p. 193.

[80] Kratochwil, pp. 193–4: here Kratochwil employs the norm-type distinction of Ronald Dworkin—that rules are mandatory and apply in an 'all or nothing' fashion, whereas principles have a discretionary application as they have a dimension of weight or importance, and so their relevance must be considered in cases. For criticism of Dworkin's demarcation, see MacCormick, *Legal Reasoning and Legal Theory* (Clarendon Press, Oxford, 1978), pp. 155–6 and chapter 9.

[81] Kratochwil, p. 205, emphasis in original.

merely technical criteria of competency in reasoning with rules. Kratochwil thinks this a particularly important point for international lawyers where adjudication is the exception rather than the normal way in which rules are applied to resolve disputes.[82]

Kratochwil sees law as a specialized form of practical reasoning, which is fundamentally topical rather than systemic-deductive in character and which is path-dependent, that is, influenced by the sequence of pleadings and rebuttals. Topics are starting-places for arguments, which locate the issues within a network of shared understandings. Kratochwil sees the typical form of topical reasoning being the Aristotlean enthymeme (or practical syllogism), which aims at establishing probabilities by:

express[ing] some shared interpretation of actions on the basis of certain practical experiences. Such a topos is therefore a *shared judgment* in a society that enables the respective actors to back their choices by means of accepted beliefs, rules of preference, or general classification schemes . . .[83]

The adoption of topical theory, Kratochwil argues, casts further doubt on the Hartian system of rules model of law because it demonstrates that principles exist in law and function in a different way from rules; because law is topically orientated, this makes the image of a deductive system inappropriate; and because legal argument is path-dependent, the importance of procedural norms in admitting or rebutting proofs demonstrates that questions of evidence do not fit easily into the Hartian distinction of primary and secondary rules, because evidential rules aim at regulating the appropriateness of the characterization of an action which may be interpreted in diverse ways.[84]

Rules, Norms, and Decisions is a significant work in that it places institutional theories of law and argumentation theory firmly on the international legal map, but although it expounds a clear and penetrating institutional theory, unfortunately Kratochwil's treatment of argumentation theory is fairly cursory—at most it is an introduction for international lawyers to an expanding area. He constructs his argument by going back to the historical roots of this discipline—to the practical syllogism of Aristotle—but pays insufficient attention to modern writers who have made significant contributions to the fields of legal and practical reasoning. Accordingly his discussion of the techniques of rhetoric (or topical reasoning) is a bit thin but, on the other hand, the linkage he establishes between topical reasoning and speech acts is an important contribution to understanding the mechanics of rhetoric.

However, the central core of his thesis—that law may be distinguished from other normative disciplines by virtue of its decision-making style—would appear to be question-begging. Kratochwil adopts this position because he thinks that other positivist demarcation theories are inadequate. He rightly rejects imperative (sanctions-based) theories as these fail to provide a realistic demarcation criterion,[85] but in rejecting Hart's argument for system membership Kratochwil would appear to

---

[82] Kratochwil, pp. 205–11.

[83] Quotation, Kratochwil, p. 218, emphasis in original: see pp. 212–20.

[84] Kratochwil, pp. 236–7.

[85] Apart from Hart's powerful argument that the nullity of a transaction cannot be a sanction (see *The Concept of Law* at pp. 33–8), see also for instance Oberdiek, 'The Role of Sanctions and Coercion in Understanding Law and Legal Systems', *American Journal of Jurisprudence*, 21 (1976), p. 71; and Finnis, *Natural Law and Natural Rights* (Clarendon Press, Oxford, 1980), pp. 7–8.

be on less firm ground. He correctly points out that to view Hart's rule of recognition as power-conferring is untenable—'correctly' because it is a duty-imposing rule and this would appear always to have been Hart's own view.[86] Nor is Hart's universe of legal concepts limited to rules—as MacCormick points out, in *The Concept of Law* Hart adverts to, but fails to develop, the distinctions between rules, principles and standards.[87] This could give rise to the objection that the rule of recognition cannot capture principles, although it can account for rules, and accordingly should be rejected as inadequate, but if one adopts MacCormick's account of principles as being parasitic general norms which summarize (or rationalize) rules or sets of rules, then principles may be captured by the rule of recognition indirectly by virtue of their relationship to rules.[88] By rejecting system-membership as the delimitation criterion, Kratochwil would appear to have made a significant conceptual error which undermines his thesis. If legal norms are not different

---

[86] See Raz, *The Concept of a Legal System* (Clarendon Press, Oxford, 2nd edn., 1980), at p. 199, and generally pp. 197–200. Raz states (at p. 199):
'Hart often contrasts the rule of recognition and other secondary rules with primary rules which are rules of obligation. So presumably rules of recognition do not impose obligations but confer powers . . . But it is quite clear that this is not Hart's intention, as he himself confirmed to me . . .'
For a sympathetic revisionist commentary on Hart's theory of secondary rules see MacCormick, *HLA Hart*, chapter 9.

[87] See MacCormick, *HLA Hart*, pp. 40–3.

[88] See MacCormick *Legal Reasoning and Legal Theory*, pp. 232 ff. (for principles and the rule of recognition) and chapter 7 (for the relationship between rules and principles).
It must be noted, or better stressed, that international lawyers, and crucially the International Court, toss around norm-descriptors indiscriminately—for instance, in the *North Sea Continental Shelf* cases the Court summarized the thrust of the Denmark/Netherlands pleadings as being that 'the whole matter is governed by a mandatory rule of law . . . which was designated by them as the "equidistance-special circumstances" *rule*' (*ICJ Reports*, 1969, pp. 19–20, para. 13, emphasis supplied), but in considering this argument stated 'does the equidistance-special circumstances *principle* constitute a mandatory *rule*' (ibid., p. 23, para. 21; see also p. 24, para. 24, emphasis supplied). If often appears that the rules-principles dichotomy refers primarily to the generality of the normative proposition in issue rather than the nature of its application. If MacCormick's thesis is adopted then it is obvious that principles do not have the existential autonomy this view implies because principles are parasitic on rules rather than possessing an independent content. This view gains some support from Fitzmaurice:
'By a principle, or general principle, as opposed to a rule, even a general rule, of law is meant chiefly something which is not itself a rule, but which underlies a rule, and explains or provides the reason for it. A rule answers the question "what": a principle in effect answers the question "why". In the event of any dispute as to what the correct rule is, the solution will often depend on what principle is regarded as underlying the rule':
Fitzmaurice, 'The General Principles of Law considered from the Standpoint of the Rule of Law', *Recueil des cours*, 92 (1957–II), p. 1 at p. 7.
Principles cannot be distinguished from rules by reference to the generality of content because rules may have a wide reference if they embody standards. Kratochwil is correct in arguing that principles are distinguished from rules by virtue of the way in which they are manipulated in argument. Principles do not fall for mandatory application whereas rules have presumptive mandatory application in the absence of countervailing reasons which defeat its application by creating an exception to the rule, or by showing that its operative conditions have not been met. However, such defeasive arguments must be established by the party which claims that an apparently relevant rule is legally irrelevant to the decision—see below on Perelman's doctrine of inertia.
If specificity of substantive content were the feature which distinguished rules from principles and accordingly which determined the modality of the application of a given norm, then a normative proposition could not be both general in reference and have (presumptively) mandatory application. The consequence of such a position is apparent if one again considers the classic formulation of self-defence embodied in the Caroline Note: because of the generality of the standards it embodies, the conclusion that it is a principle which does not have mandatory application is as inexorable as it is absurd.

from other norms by some intrinsic characteristic but only become so through the process of their application,[89] and this process is rhetorical reasoning dependent on topics, then how can Kratochwil identify the topics proper for legal reasoning (the 'topoi that are *specific to legal orders*')?[90] His argument that a demarcation criterion may be foregone if law is seen as a matter of degrees of influence which various norms have in decision-making[91] simply shoves the question one step back—how is this influence to be calibrated and distributed? How may, for instance, a right be differentiated from a mere interest—a distinction important in Kratochwil's thesis?[92] Kratochwil's argument that the unity of law lies in the transmission of argumentation techniques through the socialization of those who become rule-handlers (viz. lawyers and judges)[93] would appear to be equivalent to Hart's internal aspect of the rule of recognition.[94] The point is simply that an argumentation which is specifically legal presupposes institutional concepts which indicate and categorize material as legally relevant, that is which identify legal material, and this requires a pre-existent membership criterion.

Kratochwil's failure adequately to explain how topics may be identified, and the matters which may be used as topics, causes his thesis to fall into the trap, which Perelman does not escape,[95] of not indicating how his thesis may be used: he provides no guidelines for the determination of the relevance and strength of arguments, apart from the *ex post facto* assessment that endorsement by the decision-maker meant that the argument was successful. Simply to hold that questions of identification, relevance and strength would be apparent to those socialized in the discipline is less than candid.

Such a lack of evaluative standards may open Kratochwil's thesis to criticisms made of other topical theories—that they present law as being asystemic, dealing with disputes episodically and instrumentally and failing to make sense of the available legal material as an integrated whole. This is an objection which may apply acutely to Kratochwil's theory because he denies law a delimitation criterion apart from argumentative practice—but how may legal and non-legal topics be distinguished in order that they might be seen to be relevant or irrelevant to a legal argument? Moreover, how can he distinguish between rules and principles in a systematic, as opposed to an *ad hoc* and situational, manner? If norm-type distinction

---

[89] For instance, Kratochwil, p. 251.

[90] Quotation, Kratochwil, p. 39.

[91] Kratochwil, p. 193.

[92] See Kratochwil, chapter 6, *passim*. Kratochwil's analysis of rights (see especially chapter 6 at pp. 155 ff.) is penetrating; however, he pays insufficient attention to Hohfeldian rights analysis and thus to the idea of conceptual legal primitives: see Hohfeld, *Fundamental Legal Conceptions as applied in Judicial Reasoning* (Yale University Press, New Haven, 1919), *passim*, but especially at pp. 35–64. This appears to lead him to the conclusion that powers are legal resources available only to officials: see Kratochwil, p. 165.

[93] Kratochwil, p. 205.

[94] Kratochwil must be committed to the view that rule-handlers feel that there is a duty to employ the techniques validated by their socialization process, otherwise his thesis collapses because there would be no basis either to expect or identify a community of technique, thus raising the spectre of a resurgence of the Magnaud phenomenon (below). Consequently his argument seems similar to Hart's 'internal aspect'—on which, see Hart, *The Concept of Law*, pp. 54–6, 102, 111 ff.; MacCormick *HLA Hart*, pp. 65–7; and MacCormick *Legal Reasoning and Legal Theory*, appendix. Compare Perelman and Olbrechts-Tyteca, op. cit. above (n. 6), pp. 99–100, on socialization in specialized groups (or élite audiences).

[95] See Horovitz, *Law and Logic: A Critical Account of Legal Argument* (Springer-Verlag, Vienna, New York, 1972), at p. 108.

is not established prior to argument, then how may the degrees of influence to be attributed to the propositions invoked be assessed—for instance, in order to advise the client or construct the argument—before the outcome is reached? If rules have mandatory application but principles a dimension of weight then this demarcation must exist prior to the joining of argument, in which they will play a different role. Simply to hold that questions of relevance and degree of influence may be assessed from argumentative practice would appear to be hopelessly self-referential and ultimately episodic.[96]

Further, although Kratochwil is correct in emphasizing the importance of procedural rules, which in Hartian terms would presumably fall within the secondary rules of adjudication,[97] his emphasis on these as disrupting Hartian analysis isolates the distortion in his own: law is wider than adjudication and restrictive procedural or evidentiary rules play little part in various non-adjudicative manipulations of law, such as bargaining in the shadow of the law. Moreover the reduction of law to argumentative techniques ignores constitutive and planning functions of law where norm-manipulative argument is a contingent future possibility—for instance, consider the conclusion of a marriage where future legal argument is presumably not envisaged or consider the conclusion of a treaty where the intent is to provide norms for future argumentation should some dispute arise.[98] Indeed, given Kratochwil's delimitation of law through argumentative techniques, and his failure to provide criteria for topic identification and relative strength, arguably he comes close to committing Gray's great fallacy, if we replace 'judicial organs' with 'argumentation':

the rules for conduct laid down by the persons acting as judicial organs of the State, are the Law of the State, and . . . no rules not so laid down are the Law of the State.[99]

Further, perhaps Kratochwil does not deal sufficiently with the problem of the insincere user of an institution—for instance, the false promiser. This general question may be reconceptualized to illustrate an escape from Koskenniemi's strictures on why a State which disagrees with the contextual evaluation of an act should be bound by that evaluation. Consonant with Kratochwil's endorsement of practical reasoning in the understanding of international legal argument, the prob-

---

[96] For criticisms of topical theories of legal reasoning, see Alexy, *A Theory of Legal Argumentation* (Clarendon Press, Oxford, 1989, translation of *Theorie der juristischen Argumentation* (1978) by Adler and MacCormick), at pp. 20–4; Stoljar, 'System and Topoi', *Rechtstheorie*, 12 (1981), p. 385 at pp. 385, 392–3, and *passim*; and Stoljar, 'Paradigms and Borderlines', ibid. 13 (1982), p. 133 (also published in *Bulletin of the Australian Society for Legal Philosophy*, 1981 (Special Issue), p. 26).

[97] See Hart, *The Concept of Law*, pp. 94–6.

[98] Further, in common with a number of legal theorists, Kratochwil appears to give an inadequate array of norm-types:

'all rules and norms are problem-solving devices for dealing with the recurrent issues of social life: conflict and cooperation':

Kratochwil, p. 69: see also p. 70 for his argument that norms have three distinct ordering functions.

Kratochwil would appear to restrict the ambit of law to issues which might best be termed private law, ignoring the structural and administrative functions of rules, such as Hart's 'rules of adjudication' and rules which regulate taxation or succession—for instance, Kelsen also cannot account for taxation and other administrative functions within his pure theory: see Harris, *Legal Philosophies* (Butterworths, London, 1980), at pp. 65–7 for an account of this criticism of Kelsen. It would be procrustean to encompass these aspects of rules within the ambit of 'conflict and cooperation'.

[99] Gray, *The Nature and Sources of the Law* (MacMillan, New York, 2nd edn., 1948), quotation at p. 95; see chapter 4 generally. Gray argued that legislative acts were not part of the law as such, but only sources of the law: see pp. 124–5. Compare Hart, *The Concept of Law*, pp. 141–4.

lem of the false promiser may be solved by reference to Perelman's principle of inertia:

> When a given social arrangement has been accepted—either explicitly or, as is more frequent, implicitly—and when people have conformed to it long enough to have made it customary or traditional, then it is regarded as normal and just to adhere to this arrangement and unjust to deviate from it . . . The principle of inertia transforms every habitual way of doing things into a norm . . . A customary form of behaviour, one which conforms to the expectations of the members of the group, needs no justification . . . This does not mean that what is must remain forever, but rather that there should be no change without reason. *Change only must be justified.*[100]

As Alexy points out, the importance of this is that it allocates the burden of argumentation (or the burden of proof). Further, and this reinforces Kratochwil's view that speech act theory allows for the interpretation of acts, Perelman's principle of inertia makes argument possible, because '[a]rgumentation cannot start without presuppositions'.[101] Consequently the burden of proving that an apparent promise was not a promise lies on the false promiser, and so, for Koskenniemi's maverick State, it is up to that State to show why the normal contextual interpretation should not be applied to its actions.

This aspect of argumentation—the distribution of shifting burdens of justification, or more generally the procedural aspects of argumentation—which is rightly emphasized by Kratochwil is completely discounted by Koskenniemi, possibly because he fails to grasp the significance of the perlocutionary effects of acts. But the omission of perlocutionary effects, when relocated within the framework of Perelman's principle of inertia, makes Koskenniemi's deconstructive programme meaningless because it denies any basis to argument: if the interpretation of an action cannot start from how third parties understand this act (because that cannot be imposed on the acting State), nor from the understanding of the acting State (because this is simple apologism), then how can it start at all?[102] The result is the paradox of an interpretative theory which forestalls interpretation.

It is perhaps an oddity that both these books maintain that international law somehow isn't: Mr Koskenniemi eliminates it as a category whereas Professor Kratochwil reduces it to a style of argument. Both these conclusions would appear to be wildly reductive, and perhaps this is rooted in a tendency in both authors to overestimate the extent of indeterminacy in international law. The archetypical international legal issue they address is the 'hard case' where matters are unsettled, but as Judge Cardozo elegantly noted:

> In countless litigations, the law is so clear that judges have no discretion . . . often there are no gaps. We shall have a false view of the landscape if we look at the waste spaces only, and refuse to see the acres already sown and fruitful.[103]

If international law is eliminated then international disputes can only be settled by

---

[100] Perelman, *Justice, Law and Argument: Essays on Moral and Legal Reasoning* (Reidel, Dordrecht, 1980), at pp. 27–8, emphasis in original; see also pp. 169 ff., and Perelman and Olbrechts-Tyteca, op. cit. above (n. 6), at pp. 105 ff.

[101] See Alexy, op. cit. above (n. 96), at pp. 171–3, 196; quotation at p. 172.

[102] Compare Finnis on the irrationality of utilitarianism: see Finnis, *Natural Law and Natural Rights*, at pp. 112 ff., especially at p. 117.

[103] Cardozo, *The Nature of the Judicial Process* (Yale University Press, New Haven, 1921), at p. 129.

'the *ipse dixit* of an interested party'[104] or, should third party resolution be sought, by the 'sorte d'anarchie juridique' employed by President Magnaud of the Tribunal of First Instance of Château-Thierry at the turn of the century. He disregarded law and doctrine and decided as if he were the incarnation of justice on the basis of his subjective appreciation of the merits of the case and of the parties.[105] With reference to the latter option, to eliminate an indeterminate rule of law is simply to consecrate a judicial rule of thumb.

*　　*　　*

In conclusion, both books are well worth reading for those with an interest in theoretical aspects of the international legal order. *Rules, Norms, and Decisions* not only makes a substantial contribution to institutional theories of law and emphasizes the importance of rhetorical argument, but contains insights on issues of wider philosophical interest.[106] *From Apology to Utopia* is a meticulously researched and scholarly example, which constantly stimulates and provokes, of a contemporary school of legal theory. It is to be hoped that both Professor Kratochwil and Mr Koskenniemi will enrich us in the future with further theoretical thoughts.

---

[104] Lauterpacht, *The Development of International Law by the International Court* (Stevens, London, 1958), at p. 1.

[105] Quotation, Perelman, *Logique juridique: nouvelle rhétorique*, para. 38 at p. 71: see also Cardozo, op. cit. above (n. 103), at p. 138, and Gény, *Methode d'interprétation et sources en droit privé positif* (Louisiana State Law Institute. 1954, translation of 2nd edn., 1919), at pp. 494 ff.

[106] For instance, Kratochwil gives an excellent and lucid account of the problems with the Kantian categorical imperative: see pp. 133 ff.

REVIEWS OF BOOKS

The IAEA Notification and Assistance Conventions in Case of Nuclear Accident. By A. O. ADEDE. Dordrecht: Martinus Nijhoff/Graham and Trotman, 1987. xxii + 208 pp.

As the fifth anniversary of the accident at the Chernobyl nuclear power plant, on 26 April 1986, approaches, the accident is increasingly coming to be seen as an event at which great international change was unleashed. Some have suggested that the event will come to be seen as the moment at which the new Soviet policy of *glasnost*, or openness, first produced a tangible result, even if it was a few days late. Others, including Dr Adede, take the view that intergovernmental co-operation at the IAEA which immediately followed the accident marked an 'unprecedented event' in such co-operation.

Dr Adede's book is concerned with that aspect of international co-operation which led to the negotiation, drafting and signature of the IAEA Notification and Assistance Conventions. As he points out, these two conventions were negotiated in just four weeks and adopted within five months of the accident. Within ten months both had entered into force—undoubtedly a most speedy process, described by the author as a 'success', 'a successful working out', and even an 'unprecedented event in the history of the multilateral treaty making process . . . Never before has it been possible to conclude a multilateral treaty, let alone two, in so short a negotiating time' (p. xix) (not quite correct, since as described by John Maynard Keynes the Articles of Agreement of the International Monetary Fund were drafted and adopted in *three* weeks).

Dr Adede has written an important and useful guide to the international legislative and negotiating process leading to these two conventions. Being essentially descriptive of a process, the book fulfils its task clearly and concisely and will contribute to a greater understanding of the objects and purposes of the two conventions. The book will also serve as an excellent case study of how international agreements are reached, illustrating the multilateral negotiating process, as well as the role of the various parties, including the important role of the Secretariat of the IAEA in that process.

Where the book is to be faulted, however, is in the manner in which it is so uncritically based upon the assumptions that the endeavour which it describes, as well as the end result, are necessarily good things in themselves. Certainly, most of the nuclear power governments will be satisfied with the outcome (Italy is an example of an exception), and there is no reason to suspect the *bona fides* or intensity of the co-operation attained. But, fundamentally, certain issues remain unanswered. Are we actually better off with these conventions? Are bad conventions better than no conventions at all? Has the public been duped?

One must of course be sympathetic to the fact that Dr Adede participated in the negotiation of these conventions as a member of the IAEA Secretariat, and thus as an international civil servant. Nevertheless, in that capacity his principle obligation was not to the member States of the IAEA, but to the international community as a whole. And it is not clear that these two conventions, which may serve the interests of a minority of nuclear power States, necessarily serve the interests of the international community as a whole.

The author himself correctly reminds us that 'the negotiations were on notice that the international community expected concrete positive results from their meeting as part of an effective response to some of the problems revealed by the Chernobyl accident' (p. 131). The expectations of the world community are frequently referred to (see pp. xi and 36). By this criterion, the author's enthusiasm for the end result seems somewhat misguided.

In at least two respects, the public is likely to be disappointed by the Notification and Assistance Conventions. First, the Notification Convention does not, as the Dutch

Ambassador and Chairman of the Group of Governmental Experts writes, establish 'the legal obligation to notify and to give detailed information on all accidents within the broad framework of the nuclear fuel cycle' (p. xiv). It only requires notification of an accident 'from which a release of radioactive material occurs or is likely to occur and which has resulted or may result in an international transboundary release that could be of radiological safety significance to another State' (Article 1). In the absence of any agreed definition of the words 'radiological safety significance', and given the requirement of 'an international transboundary release', it can easily be argued that Article 1 would not have required the Soviet Union to inform the world of the Chernobyl accident within the first two days, the period during which information was most needed in order to take appropriate precautionary measures. If one objective is to reassure the public and ensure that information is made available in order that *preventative* steps may be taken, then an effective Notification Convention would have made the reporting of *all* accidents mandatory. Nearly five years after Chernobyl and the adoption of the Notification Convention, and despite the many incidents we read about in our newspapers, not a single incident appears to have been formally notified under the Convention.

From the perspective of public confidence, a second major flaw of the Notification Convention is that, unlike the IAEA Reporting Guidelines of 1984 (see paragraph 4.5.1), on which the Notification Convention was largely based, the latter does not deal with the need for dissemination of information to the public. Thus the Convention establishes no obligation on the part of a State which receives information under the Convention to pass it on, in any form, to its own citizens. Such an obligation might have helped to avoid the discrepancies which followed Chernobyl when, judging by the differences in information provided to citizens, the Chernobyl radiation clouds appeared mysteriously to pass over certain States without depositing any fallout. Finally, of course, there is the gross failure of the Soviet authorities to provide adequate, if any, information to their own citizens within a reasonable period of time. The Notification Convention would not affect this obligation, or failure, in any way.

The Assistance Convention establishes some important basic rules which might provide some help next time the international community is faced with a serious nuclear incident with transboundary consequences. But, as with the Notification Convention, the loopholes are wider than they needed to be, and one is left with the feeling that the Convention will not be as effective as it might have been. In negotiating these two conventions the IAEA and its membership, especially its nuclear membership, missed an important opportunity to show the international community that it was committed to adopting effective and meaningful legislation. On a slightly more positive note, the fact that these two conventions, flawed as they are, were negotiated in such a short period of time provides useful ammunition to those who seek to challenge the view that the negotiation of any international convention will *necessarily* take many years. Dr Adede is to be thanked for showing us how it can be done.

PHILIPPE SANDS

Free Movement in European Community Law. By F. BURROWS Oxford: Clarendon Press, 1987. xxx + 346 pp. £35.

European law is well blessed with texts written by those with an intimate knowledge of the daily workings of that bold and imaginative legal system. The importance of such texts to those teaching and studying the subject can scarcely be overstated. The manner in which the European Court uses subtle modifications in the language of its often delphic judgments to signal major developments in its approach makes it unusually difficult to progress from rote learning of the rules to a clear understanding of the dynamics of the system. The book here reviewed, written by a former Legal Adviser in the Office of the British Permanent Representative to the European Communities, is another fine example of a text illuminated by the insights flowing from actual involvement in the life of Community law.

The book has the merit of covering the fields of free movement of goods, capital, services and persons, and the related issue of sex discrimination. By bringing the discussion of the various freedoms together in a single text, the author is able to build up a picture of the basic conception of freedom of movement within the Community, which is the mainspring driving the decisions in particular cases. The book is written with great clarity and precision, breaking down each topic into its component parts in a comprehensive and logical fashion. It is written, with a welcome dry wit, in the style of a scholarly monograph, rather than a quick reference practitioner text; but both academics and practitioners will value the incisiveness with which Mr Burrows analyses, and frequently criticizes, the Court's decisions. This is, without doubt, a standard text on the subject, and one which should be held in every European law collection.

Sadly, all that is said above could better have been said five years ago. The manuscript was completed on 1 January 1985, and the book published in 1987. A similar delay has attended publication of this review. In consequence, the text and the helpful references to the secondary literature are now rather dated, and many important cases, such as *Marshall*, *Patricia* and *Factortame*, are not covered. None the less, the book is a model treatment of a complex subject, and the critical analysis of the development of the law which it presents is of lasting value. Any library which does not yet have this book should buy it.

A. V. Lowe

The Wehrmacht War Crimes Bureau, 1939–1945. By Alfred M. de Zayat in collaboration with Walter Rabus. Foreword by Howard Levie. Lincoln and London: University of Nebraska Press, 1989. xix+ 364 pp.

The author of this book, originally published in German, seems to have assigned himself a twofold purpose: first, to examine the organization and work of the German Army Bureau that was responsible for investigating allegations of German and Allied war crimes during the Second World War, and secondly, to offer a 'study into the crimes of the Allies' in that war (p. 272). Accordingly, the book is divided into Part I, which deals with the history and methods of the War Crimes Bureau, as well as the various uses made of its investigations, and Part II, devoted to specific cases of reported Allied violations. Both parts testify to an intense scholarly effort by the author to find out whether or to what extent the investigations of the Bureau were objective and reliable and, consequently, whether the alleged crimes had indeed been committed.

In the first part, the author examines, *inter alia*, the functioning of German State organs engaged in the investigation of alleged Allied war crimes during the First World War; the mandate and the membership of the War Crimes Bureau; the role of German military judges; the methods of the War Crimes Bureau for obtaining evidence, such as verification through multiple witnesses; and the use of the Bureau's investigations in the formulation of German 'white books' dealing with alleged breaches of the law of war by Allied forces, as well as their use in the matter of diplomatic protection, in the preparation of war crimes trials against Allied prisoners-of-war and in the preparation of reprisals against the Allies.

Chapter 11 of Part I is devoted to investigations of alleged German war crimes. The role of the Bureau, as reflected in this chapter, is confined to assisting the German Foreign Office in answering a British protest on the killing by German soldiers of three British prisoners-of-war in North Africa. No investigation was pursued in this case (pp. 113–14). The author explains the paucity of material on the investigation of alleged German crimes by the fact that the surviving 226 volumes of Bureau records include only one thin volume dealing with alleged German war crimes (in North Africa). It is not known whether other relevant records were lost or deliberately destroyed, or whether the Bureau 'for whatever reason' failed to investigate other alleged German war crimes. More importantly, in the view of the author, the available records give no indication whether the members of the Bureau received any official or unofficial communications regarding the mass murder of Jews in German concentration camps. Indeed, there was a fundamental Order No. 1 of Hitler on the keeping of official secrets, including the top State secret of the Final Solution of the Jewish question, but, as an historian, the author finds it unsatisfactory to explain 'the apparent inaction' of members of the Bureau by that Order. He concedes that the moral question remains unanswered, pending the discovery of additional files which might shed light on the 'uncertainties' about this aspect of the Bureau's work (pp. 109–12).

In Part II the author describes the Bureau's investigations into allegations of specific war crimes committed by the Allies, e.g., massive killings of German prisoners-of-war by Soviet soldiers; the murder of over four thousand Polish officers by the Soviet secret service in the Katyn Forest in the Soviet Union; the killing of German prisoners-of-war by the French Forces of the Interior (FFI), following the refusal of Germany to grant the FFI combatant status and POW rights in captivity; killings of German wounded by British soldiers in Crete; and British attacks on German shipwrecked soldiers and hospital ships.

The author reaches the conclusion that the War Crimes Bureau was not established for the purpose of fabricating documents on Allied war crimes, that its records are genuine, and that its investigations were carried out methodically, in a judicial manner (p. 270). In his final comments Dr de Zayat stresses that no comparison is possible between Nazi and Allied crimes and that the book does not diminish the guilt of the Nazi war criminals condemned in Nuremberg and elsewhere. At the same time, he urges the reader to consider that all soldiers, including enemy soldiers, have certain human rights, regardless of the criminality of their governments.

This original book is based on comprehensive research in many archives, supplemented by over three hundred interviews with former German military judges, victims and witnesses. The presentation is clear and systematic. Students of the law of war will find the book useful for the historical data contained therein, bearing in mind that what is missing is of significant importance for the appraisal of the Bureau's work. The lack of evidence of any inquiry into alleged German crimes may be explained by reference to Professor Levie's view, expressed in the Foreword, that the Bureau could not have eluded the grasp of Hitler, von Ribbentrop, Goebbels and Himmler.

NISSIM BAR-YAACOV

Joint Ventures in the Soviet Union. By KAJ HOBER. New York: Transnational Publishers Inc., 1989. Loose-leaf; US $125.

This is a manual of considerable utility, written by a practising partner of White and Case. It has a brief introduction on the Soviet legal system, and a somewhat fuller description of the organization of foreign trade in the USSR. It then gives a translation of the 1987 Soviet Decree on Joint Ventures, with a commentary on each provision, and, in Section V, proceeds to a lucid and detailed discussion of the legal structure of joint ventures.

It is here that the author displays his knowledge. This text proceeds to deal with each issue arising in the creation of a joint venture: the notion of a separate legal entity, ownership, management, relationship to the planning system, personnel, protection of industrial property, financing and accounting, insurance, taxation, dispute resolution, and the intital problems of negotiating a joint venture agreement.

The work is supplemented by some twenty-one appendices, including standard forms for joint venture agreements, and it represents a model of what a good manual should be.

D. W. BOWETT

The Theory and History of Ocean Boundary-Making. By DOUGLAS M. JOHNSTON. Kingston and Montreal: McGill—Queen's University Press, 1989. 488 pp. £37.95.

This monograph has two purposes: first, to trace the history of all modes of boundary-making in the ocean; and, second, to provide a conceptual framework for the analysis and evaluation of all ocean boundary claims.

The first purpose is achieved well. Part Two of the book—on the history of boundary-making—surveys the evolution of the rules on outer limits, baselines and closing lines, and 'lateral' boundaries in a clear, concise manner. Chapter 11, in particular, gives a very clear account of the cases and concludes (at pp. 210–13) with a series of sensible propositions.

But Part Three—the Functionalist Approach to Ocean Boundary-Making—which is intended to achieve the second purpose, is disappointing. Much of it is rather a statement of the obvious, such as the eleven diplomatic options in 'direct bilateral diplomacy'. The discussion of the adjudicative process is surprisingly brief, and addresses none of the real problems. For example, if the use of the equidistance method is adopted, is there any rational basis for opting for a reduced effect for certain features—be it half-effect, quarter-effect or whatever? Is it to be related to the areas accruing to a State by reason of full-effect, as compared to the area of the feature itself; or distance from the main directional line of the coast, or what? Or, to take another example, if third-State claims effectively confine the area to be delimited, as did the Italian claims in *Malta/Libya*, how should one proceed? Is it possible to envisage *trilateral* adjudication? Or can an appropriately drafted *compromis* preclude an arbitral tribunal from considering third-party claims?

D. W. BOWETT

Mediterranean Continental Shelf Delimitations and Regimes, International and National Legal Sources. Edited by U. LEANZA and L. SICO. Dobbs Ferry NY: Oceana Publications Inc., 1988. 4 Volumes. 2003 pp. + maps.

This is a remarkable publication, testifying to the vitality of the contemporary Italian activity in international law. Edited by Professors Leanza and Sico, with the assistance of a group of young scholars, it brings together in four volumes a collection of materials on State practice with regard to delimitation in the Mediterranean which is unique in its comprehensiveness.

Volume I is in two parts, covering delimitation agreements and domestic legislation respectively (with English translations). Volume II contains court decisions, both international and national, but with the ICJ judgments reduced to a citation of the judgment and the separate and dissenting opinions on each issue; and with national decisions being confined to those of higher courts.

In the same volume one also finds diplomatic notes, records and working papers from the First and Third UN Conferences on the Law of the Sea describing the views of Mediterranean States on a wide variety of delimitation issues. The diplomatic notes, minutes of meetings, etc., are particularly valuable because they begin to show *why* a particular method of delimitation was adopted. This is often a matter of pure surmise, if the only evidence available is the text of the agreement itself. Then, in the concluding volume, one has an exceedingly thorough bibliography, broken down into specialized topics, plus a useful chronological index, and finally indexes of documents, countries and authors.

But there is a feature of this publication which calls for particular comment. Too often collections of materials are just that, with the reader being left to make such sense of them as his native wit or previous knowledge allows. However, here we have a 'foreword' by the two editors, some thirty pages long, in which the reader is guided through the whole evolution of the law on maritime delimitation. It is naturally focused on the Mediterranean and, as the editors point out, it is the special feature of the Mediterranean that delimitation issues arise throughout its length and breadth because of its restricted size. Nevertheless, this 'foreword' also takes the reader through the evolution of the law in general in a quite masterly way.

D. W. BOWETT

Common Law Aboriginal Title. By KENT McNEIL. Oxford: Clarendon Press, 1989. xiv + 357 pp. including index and bibliography.

Until recently the international community has been slow to respond to the claims of aboriginal minority tribal populations such as the Indians of the American continent, Australian Aborigine and Scandinavian Saami. For many years the sole international instrument remained ILO Convention 107 (1957), recently updated into the new Convention 169. The 1957 instrument largely concerned conditions of labour but also touched upon issues of language, treaty, land and cultural rights, although in a manner which envisaged the eventual assimilation of tribal populations into a Western capitalist lifestyle. That approach has not prevailed in the new Convention 169 nor the draft Declaration produced by a United Nations Working Group on the rights of indigenous tribal populations (whose status as 'peoples' remains contentious). Rights to language, political autonomy and land are amongst those recognized in the draft instrument. These issues are of great interest to Commonwealth lawyers as aboriginal claims in Canada and Australasia assume a sharper profile in national political and legal life.

Kent McNeil's scholarly *Common Law Aboriginal Title* analyses the legal status of tribal property rights subsequent to the British Crown's claim to the territorial sovereignty over their land. The legality of any such claim under international law does not worry McNeil. As a common lawyer he accepts the unchallengeability of the Crown's sovereign title in its own courts. Instead, his concern is with the extent to which the original tribal title can be recognized by these courts. His basic conclusion is obvious from the book's title. He shows that this 'aboriginal title' is legally recognizable and enforceable under common law doctrine. The book explores and explains this doctrine.

McNeil's argument is that the doctrine of aboriginal title 'is based on the presumptions arising in English law from occupation of land'. Factual occupation provides a presumption of possession which, in turn, presumes seisin, which further leads to the presumption of a fee simple estate. Possession not shown as wrongful by common law is taken as rightful, so that an occupier of land 'is therefore presumed to have not only a fee simple estate, but a valid title as well'.

Since McNeil's argument rests upon the common law's response to the fact of tribal occupation, he spends much effort explaining the history of English land law on questions of title and occupation. After a dense chapter on those points he looks more closely at the feudal doctrine of tenures. Feudalism—the legal fiction that the Crown is the paramount owner of all its lands—has on occasions conspired against the judicial recognition of original tribal title, such title not deriving from any Crown grant. McNeil shows that the sole purpose of the feudal doctrine of tenures was simply to explain the relationship of lord and vassal. The doctrine of tenures, 'though capable at common law of giving the Crown a title to land in the event an estate held of it expires, cannot be used otherwise to claim lands which subjects possess' (p. 107).

This argument occupies a third of the book. The remainder looks at the common law principle governing the Crown's acquisition of new territory and the status of aboriginal property rights in its new colonial possessions. Previously McNeil tended to dwell rather laboriously and painstakingly over propositions and points which might have been made less strenuously. From the fourth chapter the discussion becomes more readable, the style and exposition fleeter-footed. This portion of the book explores the case law from which derives the common law doctrine of aboriginal title. The author stresses the fundamental distinction between sovereignty (*imperium*) and title to land (*dominium*). Throughout, as one would expect from his opening chapters, the emphasis is upon the common law's response to the fact of tribal occupation of ancestral land. This leads him rather to downplay the role of the tribal customary law. Whilst he observes that upon the Crown's acquisition of sovereignty 'private property rights under local laws or customs would be presumed to continue' (at p. 192), he immediately qualifies that. The important juridical aspect is always 'the fact of their presence on and use of lands at the time the Crown acquired sovereignty', not any system of property rights which the tribe might have 'under their own laws' (p. 195). So it is that McNeil claims that definition of the aboriginal title through the customary law has 'limitations' (ibid). It is preferable, he argues, that the doctrine can be seen as no more than a legal response to the fact of tribal occupation. This conclusion appears to stem from the author's reluctance to condone any judicial approach other than a response to the provable fact of tribal presence on ancestral land. He cites *Milirrpum* v. *Nabalco Pty.* (1971), 17 FLR 141 (at 270-1, *per* Blackburn J), an Australian judgment since discredited in the New Zealand and Canadian jurisdictions, as justification.

Here McNeil's description of common law aboriginal title veers towards characterization as a passive doctrine responsive simply and only to tribal occupation. He fails to consider the role of tribal customary law in defining the content of any aboriginal title. How else, one might ask, is the character of any such title to be defined other than by reference to the customary law which breathes life and coherence into the tribal occupation and use of traditional land resources? McNeil is concerned with the legal starting point of the common law doctrine—the recognition as opposed to consequential questions about the incidents of that title. For instance, there is growing controversy over the extent to which an aboriginal title can include a right to exploit the tribal resource for commercial purposes using non-traditional technology. If one takes the McNeil approach too far then, arguably, tribal exploitation might be restricted to uses and means as of the time of British sovereignty. Such a view must be rejected as taking a static view of property ownership. It is inconceivable that any ordinary landowner could be legally restricted to developing his property according to his own needs and technology as of the moment of purchase. Yet that view has been seriously advocated by those who would limit the aboriginal title to subsistence and ceremonial purposes. There is nothing in McNeil's book even to hint at his agreement with such a view; however, his emphasis upon occupation at the time of sovereignty has that tendentious aspect. Property rights no less under a tribal customary tenure than under Western systems are inherently dynamic. Incorporation of tribal customary law into the common law aboriginal title recognizes that dynamic character. It also permits a measure of legal pluralism into the municipal legal system responsive to the means by which the subject tribal societies define and manage their property rights. This, of course, requires forensic judicial inquiry into tribal customary law, the kind of exercise which McNeil is reluctant to condone given the dismal result in *Milirrpum* (1971). However, legal scholarship and judicial experience have advanced considerably since then, and the author's reluctance to place too great a weight on the role of tribal customary law may well be seen as too cautionary.

Such conservatism is symptomatic of the author's scholarly determination to unravel exhaustively the rudiments of the doctrine. He carefully avoids speculation as to what were once (but are increasingly less) seen as the more radical possibilities of the doctrine. The relationship of the doctrine to Crown 'ownership' of such resources as coal and the sea-bed, the effect of Torrens systems of land registration upon any unextinguished aboriginal title and the role of the developing doctrine of Crown fiduciary duty to subject tribes—these are contemporary issues arising from the common law doctrine which are ignored by the book although they are becoming the fronts on which litigation is proceeding in Commonwealth jurisdictions.

This book, then, illuminates the basis of the common law aboriginal title but it does not follow the legal debate into the newer, less certain, reaches of the doctrine. It sheds strong, indispensable light on the established, if often murkily grasped, fundamentals. The book does not, however, aspire to give the reader guidance as to the future directions which Commonwealth courts (particularly the Canadian courts) may take with the common law doctrine. To some extent this dates the book already, but in another sense it establishes its worth as a vital and erudite landmark.

P. G. McHugh

Human Rights and Humanitarian Norms as Customary Law. By THEODOR
MERON. Oxford: Clarendon Press, 1989. 263 pp. £30.

As the author states in his 'Concluding Remarks', this study examines 'a wide range of
related yet discrete questions'. The range is indeed impressive, but the relationship between
the questions addressed is not always apparent. While many passages in the book contain
interesting insights into particular points, the book as a whole lacks coherence.

There are three chapters, each divided into a number of sections. The first two chapters
deal with the subject-matter indicated in the book's title, while the third deals with quite
separate questions of State responsibility. Chapter I is entitled 'Humanitarian Instruments
as Customary Law'. Introductory sections deal with the importance of knowing whether a
treaty rule is also a rule of customary international law, the significance of reservations to a
treaty's value as evidence of customary international law, and the *Nicaragua* judgment and
its 'antecedents'. The author then proceeds to consider to what extent the rules set forth in
the Geneva Conventions on the Laws of War and the 1977 Additional Protocols are, or
might be, rules of customary international law. Chapter II, entitled 'Human Rights Instruments and Customary Law', is divided into three sections dealing respectively with 'the
question of universality'; the International Court of Justice and 'customary human rights';
and customary human rights in selected national courts (England, India, Australia, the
USA and the Federal Republic of Germany).

Chapter III is entitled 'Responsibility of States for Violations of Human Rights and
Humanitarian Norms'. Unlike the earlier chapters, it is not specifically concerned with
human rights and humanitarian norms as customary international law, but deals rather with
a series of issues relating to State responsibility (including imputability, exhaustion of local
remedies, obligations *erga omnes*, judicial and non-judicial remedies, international crimes,
necessity). Much of this chapter is concerned with the International Law Commission's
work on State responsibility.

The first two chapters are essays on what are traditionally termed 'the sources of international law'. The author applies traditional methods for the formulation of rules of international law, while allowing for special conditions that may be said to apply to the
development of customary international law in the fields of human rights and humanitarian
law (in particular, greater emphasis on what States say rather than what they do). The third
chapter is largely concerned with certain fundamental aspects of the theory of State responsibility: in the author's own words, in this chapter '[d]ue to the scarcity of practice dehors
human rights treaties, our discussion will frequently be largely theoretical'. One of the
author's conclusions may be summarized by saying that both those whom he terms 'human
rights lawyers' and those whom he terms 'generalist international lawyers' should accept that
human rights are a respectable branch of international law, in which the basic principles of
international law apply. He calls for the utilization of 'irreproachable methods'. These are
sentiments with which most readers will agree.

MICHAEL C. WOOD

*UNO-Pakt über bürgerliche und politische Rechte und Fakultativprotokoll:
CCPR – Kommentar.* By MANFRED NOWAK. Kehl am Rhein, Strasbourg;
Arlington: N.P. Engel Verlag, 1989. xxvi + 946 pp. DM 262.

Dr Nowak's book is a detailed article-by-article commentary on the International Covenant on Civil and Political Rights and its Optional Protocol. It states the law as of 1 January
1989. It is in German, but an English translation is promised shortly. The volume is a first
rate piece of work, which fills an important gap, and is likely to prove invaluable to all
those—practitioners, academics and others—who have to interpret the Covenant.

Following a brief introduction, the author deals in turn with the preamble and each article
of the Covenant and the Optional Protocol. The negotiating history of each article is set out,
following by an analysis of the text. Emphasis is placed—rightly—on the practice of the

Human Rights Committee (case law, general comments, consideration of State reports); and there are also helpful references to the position under other human rights instruments, in particular to the case law of the European Convention on Human Rights, and to selected academic writings. The Appendices include a Secretariat document of 12 May 1989 (with corrections by the author) containing the texts of the reservations, declarations, notifications and objections made by States to the Covenant and Protocol, the Provisional Rules of Procedure of the Human Rights Committee, all the general comments under Article 40(4), as well as lists of ratifications, State reports, individual communications and Covenant documents. There is a useful select bibliography and index.

The book follows the same pattern as the excellent Frowein/Peukert commentary on the European Convention on Human Rights (to which the author acknowledges his debt). Whereas Frowein/Peukert condensed their analysis of the Convention (with its vast case law) into some 500 pages, Nowak's analysis of the Covenant (with its comparatively sparse practice) extends to about 800 pages. The present commentary is, in fact, considerably more comprehensive than that of Frowein/Peukert. So detailed a commentary on the European Convention would risk becoming unwieldy, but in the case of the Covenant the detail is extremely valuable. As practice under the Covenant expands, future editions—and it is hoped that the author plans future editions—may need to be more selective.

The writer of such a commentary should resist the temptation to inject too many of his own views if the end result is to be useful as a general work of reference rather than a particular view of the law under the instrument in question. Where personal views are included, they should be carefully identified as such if the work is not to be misleading: what appears to be neutral analysis may be no more than one person's point of view. Nevertheless, some personal comment or speculation is inevitable, particularly where practice is as yet unsettled, as is the case with many provisions of the Covenant. By these criteria Nowak has done a good job. One may not always agree with his views. (Perhaps too little account is taken of the legitimate needs of governments; dare one suggest that the balance is weighted just a little too often on the side of the individual. But the same could be said of certain utterances of the Human Rights Committee and of its members.) In general, the author's analyses are clear, illuminating and, above all, full of useful information; they offer a sound basis for forming one's own view as to the interpretation of the Covenant in the knowledge that no significant point of negotiating history or practice has been overlooked.

This book is likely to become a standard work of reference on the Covenant. It is a most useful companion to Marc Bossuyt's Guide to the *travaux préparatoires*. Nowak states in his preface that neither his own book nor Bossuyt's can be a substitute for reading the original documents; true no doubt, but for the busy practitioner I wonder. In any event, the task of those who do go on to the original documents has been significantly lightened.

Finally, the publishers are to be congratulated not only for the excellent presentation of this book (which one has come to take for granted from Engel) but especially for having encouraged the author to undertake this task. Their contribution to the publication of materials in the field of human rights is second to none.

MICHAEL C. WOOD

Judging the World: Law and Politics in the World's Leading Courts. By G. STURGESS and P. CHUBB. Sydney: Butterworths (Australia), 1988. xiv + 562 pp.+ index. £45.

In their preface Sturgess and Chubb stoutly declare that their book 'is an analysis of the interrelation of law and politics . . . a book intended for a general audience rather than a narrow professional audience . . . [it is] essentially a work of journalism' (pp. ix–x). The general reader should pause before paying out £45 for this essentially slight volume—pause indefinitely.

The book lacks one of two things: it requires either a set of easily assembled legs to facilitate its conversion into an unusual coffee table or, in the alternative, an articulated and coherent theoretical structure—an explicit framework into which the argument of the book may be fitted. As it stands, it is simply a large-format glossy book, replete with a surfeit of official judicial portraiture—how could there be so many photographs of judges in and out of uniform?—with a text tending towards a mere linkage of quotations drawn from the authors' interviews of various judges, edited extracts of which form the second part of the volume.

This book simply reports what judges said to the authors: it does not grapple with the issues raised to any extent. For instance, the impression is given that entrenched bills of rights are a 'Good Thing', but Sturgess and Chubb never address the question of the extent to which, in a democracy, it is legitimate for the judiciary to exercise the broad interpretative—if not creative—powers these entail. This is a function which, moreover, may nullify legislation. Similarly, Sturgess and Chubb ignore the problems inherent in the enforcement of morality by law, simply adopting the view that in contentious matters where public opinion is divided, the government should do something, failing which resolution of the issue may be left to the wisdom of the judiciary.

One may also consider how this work can be an account of 'law and politics in the world's leading courts' when it ignores civilian systems completely, casts but a blind eye at various international courts (the International and European Courts of Justice, and European and Inter-American Courts of Human Rights), and concentrates to an undue degree on one incident in recent Australian judicial history. The last appears to be the point of the work—a vindication of the late Lionel Murphy, Judge of the Australian High Court, ostensibly set within a wider, global and theoretical framework of the proper relationship between the judiciary and the legislature. But this incident concerned criminal allegations made against Murphy, and not the interrelationship of law and politics as such. If this truly is the aim of the book, then its 'analysis' of law, politics and the judicial function is not only inept, but superfluous.

In so much as the work concerns international law, Sturgess and Chubb simply beg the question—they assume (p.x) that international judges may be assimilated to municipal judges with reference to the political dimension of their judicial role. Simply to state this is to expose the fallacy at the heart of this part of Sturgess and Chubb's endeavour: had they thought about the relationship between adjudication and the political process, such assimilation would have become demonstrably untenable. Their municipal sample deals only with judges in democracies. The justification of 'legislative' judicial action in such a setting is one thing—what is the proper relationship between an unelected judiciary and elected legislature; how international judges face and address political aspects of their role is another. Simply to postulate some immutable judicial function which transcends the structural differences between international and municipal law is to miss the point of 'analysis', a point driven home by the fact that the authors throughout speak blithely of 'judicial independence' without considering, far less analysing, what this means, and without realizing that in different legal systems the broad concept may have a different content'.[1]

For the international lawyer, a further idiosyncrasy is that the authors use Judge Manfred Lachs as the exemplar of the proper discharge of the judicial function in the International Court. This is not as uncontroversial as they seem to think. Without wishing to denigrate Judge Lachs in any way, it can be argued that his view of the judicial function is not as unassailable as Sturgess and Chubb assume.[2]

The explanation for this unsatisfactory book would appear to be that Sturgess and Chubb have not done the basic research necessary to mount a proper argument: there is more to

---

[1] That 'judicial independence' means different things in different legal systems is made abundantly clear in the 'country studies' which form Part I of Shetreet and Deschênes (eds.), *Judicial Independence: The Contemporary Debate* (Nijhoff, Dordrecht, 1985).

[2] For instance, as President of the Court, he must take primary responsibility for the collegiate judgment in *Nuclear Tests*, the underlying judicial philosophy of which was ferociously criticized in the joint dissent: *ICJ Reports*, 1974, p. 253 (*Australia* v. *France*); see the joint dissent at paras. 1–29, pp. 312–26, especially.

legal reasoning than Stone's categories of illusory reference,[3] and more to the sociolegal analysis of the judicial role than the work of Griffith.[4] If this is a book intended for the general public, then there must be an increased duty of care on the authors to indulge in sufficient basic research to ensure that their exposition is built on solid foundations. Sturgess and Chubb rest content with the assertion of vague views and banal prejudices as a substitute for serious thought.

In short, this work simply skates over the issues, without analysis and without an examination of the underlying questions regarding the relationship of the judiciary to the legislature in a democracy, leaving to one side their assimilation of international law to the common law writ large and global. It is completely detached from any serious analysis of the judicial process, and although, as the authors intended, it is essentially a work of journalism, it is extremely thin journalism at that, gliding from assertion to assertion without pausing for thought or critique or even, at times, justification—'judges, generally, do not go to hotels' (p. 165): why not, what grounds are there for this claim, and why is it important?.

The second part of this book comprises the edited texts of the interviews which Sturgess and Chubb conducted in assembling the book. Although no solid conclusions concerning the judicial function may be founded on the texts of these interviews, they do contain interesting anecdotal material, giving a flavour of diverse judicial philosophies.[5] There is the slight drawback that the interviews do not follow a standard format: to have had the judicial answers to the same questions would have been more useful. But the utility to be gained from this section does not detract from the fact that the text is marginal.

In conclusion, this is not a book to buy for either one's collection or library: my considered advice would be to obtain it on inter-library loan from a copyright library should one wish to examine the material culled from interviews.

IAIN SCOBBIE

International Navigation: Rocks and Shoals Ahead? Edited by JON M. VAN DYKE, LEWIS M. ALEXANDER and JOSEPH R. MORGAN. Honolulu: Law of the Sea Institute, University of Hawaii, 1988. 430 pp.

This is a useful set of papers, and records of discussions, of a Workshop held in 1986. There are seven substantive chapters covering: freedom of navigation; baselines, the territorial sea and innocent passage; international straits and transit passage; archipelagoes and archipelagic sea lanes passage; environmental issues and national security interests. The final chapter is one of conclusions.

Whilst there is considerable variation in the quality of the thirty or more papers, they have in common the virtue that they all address current, and controversial, problems. By and large, the problems covered relate to some aspect of State security, and it is significant that it is here that the problems are anticipated, rather than in issues arising from access to resources.

[3] For instance, see MacCormick, *Legal Reasoning and Legal Theory* (Clarendon Press, Oxford, 1978) and 'On Legal Decisions and their Consequences: from Dewey to Dworkin', *New York University Law Review*, 58 (1983), p. 239; and also Dworkin, *Taking Rights Seriously* (Duckworth, London, 1978, rev. edn.) and *Law's Empire* (Harvard University Press, Cambridge/Fontana, London, 1986).

[4] Griffith, *The Politics of the Judiciary* (Fontana, London, 1977). Sturgess and Chubb rely on this edition: the current (third) edition was published in 1985.

There is a fair amount of work on sociological aspects of the judicial role, for instance, Paterson, *The Law Lords* (MacMillan, London, 1982); Prott, *The Latent Power of Culture and the International Judge* (Professional Books, Abingdon, 1979); and Schubert, *Judicial Policy-Making: The Political Role of the Courts* (Scott, Foresman and Company, Glenview, Illinois, 1965) and *Comparative Judicial Behaviour* (Oxford University Press, London, 1969).

[5] Interviews with the following judges of the International Court of Justice appear: Nagendra Singh (at p. 449), de Lacharrière (at p. 454), Lachs (at p. 461), Schwebel (at p. 470), Ni (at p. 475) and Tarassov (at p. 477).

Some contributions are general in character. For example, there is an excellent and comprehensive survey by Anand on 'Transit Passage and Overflight in International Staits', and another by Louis Sohn on 'International Navigation; Issues related to National Security'. Other contributions are more specialized, but very informative: of these the discussion by Choon-Ho Park on 'The Korea Strait' and that by Judge Oda on 'The Passage of Warships through Straits and Archipelagic Waters' deserve special mention.

The summary by William T. Burke highlights what is called 'creeping uniqueness', the claims by States to special interests which require protection, notwithstanding that the claim falls outside the general legal regime. He sees this as, in part, a reflection of the reality that the growth of customary law is not halted by codification, even codification on so large a scale as the 1982 convention. Of course, such new customary rules will not be rules of general application, but rather special rules applicable to particular situations, but generally recognized. The analogy with the old Scandinavian four-mile territorial sea, or the Norwegian straight baselines system, springs to mind. The suggestion is that the USA will be forced into the role of the 'persistent objector' in order to champion these traditional freedoms of the seas.

D. W. Bowett

International Crimes of State: A Critical Analysis of the ILC's Draft Article 19 on State Responsibility. Edited by Joseph Weiler, Antonio Cassese and Marina Spinedi. European University Institute, Series A—Law, volume 10. Berlin, New York: Walter de Gruyter, 1989. xii + 368 pp. DM 152.

This volume presents the results of a Conference on State Responsibility and Crimes of State which took place in Florence in 1984 under the auspices of the European University Institute and the University of Florence. Participants included the President and several members of the International Court of Justice, several members of the International Law Commission, as well as academics and diplomats from Western, Socialist and Third World countries. Among those present were the then Special Rapporteur on State Responsibility, Professor Riphagen, and his predecessor, Judge Ago.

In broad terms, the subject of the various contributions is the meaning of the notion of crimes of State as propounded for the first time in Draft Article 19 of the Draft Articles on State Responsibility formulated by the International Law Commission. This draft article, unanimously adopted on first reading in 1976, defines as an international crime any internationally wrongful act which results from the breach by a State of an international obligation so essential for the protection of fundamental interests of the international community that its breach is recognized as a crime by that community as a whole. By way of examples of international crimes, the draft article lists serious breaches of international obligations of essential importance (*a*) for the maintenance of international peace, e.g. the prohibition of aggression; (*b*) for safeguarding the right of self-determination of peoples, e.g. the prohibition of the establishment or maintenance by force of colonial domination; (*c*) for safeguarding the human being, e.g. the prohibition of slavery, genocide and *apartheid*; and (*d*) for safeguarding the human environment, e.g. the prohibition of massive pollution of the atmosphere or of the seas. The draft article also stipulates that any internationally wrongful act which is not an international crime constitutes an international delict.

The book under review is divided into eight parts. Part I consists of a background paper of some 130 pages by Marina Spinedi, which examines the legislative history and academic discussion of the concept of crimes of State. (According to Professor Ted Stein, the paper convincingly demonstrates that the debate regarding 'crimes of States' has been so confused as to be intellectually incoherent: at p. 194.) Part II comprises four papers presented to the Conference by G. Abi-Saab, G. Gaja, B. Graefrath and P.-M. Dupuy. The papers deal respectively with the concept of international crimes; the relationship between the concepts of obligations *erga omnes*, international crimes and *jus cogens*; the legal consequences of international crimes; and the implications of the institutionalization of international crimes. Part III represents an edited version of the general discussion, introduced by Judge T. O. Elias. The participants were G. Abi-Saab, R. Ago, G. Aldrich, M. Bennouna, H. Bokor-Szego, A. Cassese, L. Condorelli, B. Conforti, H. De Fiumel, C. Dominicé, B. Graefrath, E. Jiménez de Aréchaga, S. McCaffrey, T. Meron, W. Riphagen, J. Sette Camara, Sir Ian Sinclair, M. Spinedi, E. Stein and Ted L. Stein. In Parts IV S. Torres Bernandez and D. Thiam present general overviews of the debate. Part V consists of a paper by Bruno Simma on injury and countermeasures. This paper takes account of the deliberations of the International Law Commission subsequent to the Florence Conference. Part VI contains a revised version of the concluding speech of Joseph Weiler, centred on the question as to why it is that some scholars and some States espouse, even enthusiastically, the concept of crimes of State, whereas others reject it, at times as anathema. Part VII contains a bibliography for the period 1946–1984, prepared by Marina Spinedi, while Part VIII consists of two documentary annexes containing draft articles.

The issues discussed by the various contributors could be divided into two main categories: first, those relating to the notion of crimes of State *stricto sensu*, i.e., the scope of the notion as defined in Draft Article 19; and secondly, those relating to the consequences of crimes of States to be defined in Part Two of the Draft Articles on State Responsibility.[1] Various and, at times, opposing opinions are expressed throughout the volume.

With regard to the first category, the following issues were raised: Is the distinction between international delicts and international crimes in line with the international law in force and, if not, should it be provided *de lege ferenda*? Was the International Law Commission justified in making the distinction between international delicts and international crimes without regard to the legal consequences which flow from the distinction? Is it desirable to use the term 'crime' in view of its association with internal penal law? What is the relationship between international crimes of State and international crimes of the Nuremberg type? In particular, are grave breaches under the Geneva Conventions to be considered crimes of State? Should aggression and the ensuing self-defence or collective measures under the Charter of the United Nations be considered as part of the law of international responsibility? Does the notion of aggression include economic aggression? Is it appropriate to consider a serious breach of an international obligation of essential importance for the safeguarding of the environment as an international crime? What is the meaning of maintenance 'by force' of colonial domination? What is the meaning of 'international community as a whole' in regard to the recognition of the existence of an international crime? Which body of the United Nations is to determine, in case of dispute, whether an internationally wrongful act constitutes an international crime? In particular, should resort be made either to the Security Council, or to the General Assembly, or to the International Court of Justice, depending on the nature of the act?

A considerable part of the book is devoted to questions relating to the consequences of international crimes of State. The most pertinent issues are: Is the responsibility regime appropriate to international crimes to be distinguished from that appropriate to international delicts, as regards both the forms of responsibility and the subjects which are permitted to implement that responsibility? Should there be a uniform regime of responsibility applicable

---

[1] The International Law Commission decided first to establish in Part One of the Draft Articles, which includes Draft Article 19, the conditions of the existence of an internationally wrongful act of State and subsequently to deal in Part Two with the legal consequences of such acts. Part One of the project was adopted on first reading in 1980. By the time of the Florence Conference, the Commission had made only a limited study of the consequences of international crimes, based on five reports submitted by Professor Riphagen between 1980 and 1984. Ever since, the ILC has not been able to deal in earnest with that question. Following the suggestion of the present Special Rapporteur, Professor Gaetano Arangio-Ruiz, the Commission discussed in its 1989 and 1990 sessions Draft Articles relating to the legal consequences of international delicts and only after completing this subject will it deal with the legal consequences of international crimes.

to all international crimes? Except in the case of armed aggression, is the State directly injured entitled to apply peaceful countermeasures which are otherwise illegal? If so, could these countermeasures be exercised independently of any claim for reparation? Are States not directly injured entitled to claim reparation in the form of cessation of the crime and of *restitutio in integrum*? Is there a duty of States not directly injured to supply assistance to the victim of the crime, and to refrain from condoning the crime and from recognizing as valid its consequences? Except in the case of armed aggression, are States not directly injured entitled to decide individually to apply peaceful countermeasures which are otherwise illegal? If so, are such countermeasures subject to prior request by the State directly injured? Is the primary aim of countermeasures to bring about the cessation of the ongoing breach, or rather to impose some form of retribution on the guilty State, or a combination of both? Is the notion of punishment applicable in respect of States, in view of the suffering that might be inflicted on innocent individuals?

The analysis of the various issues is extensive. The uninitiated reader is provided with abundant information and insights which will enable him or her to grasp the intricacies of the problems raised by the introduction of the concept of crimes of State. In this respect, the editors have certainly achieved their purpose, as stated in the Introduction, to provide a 'Guide to the Perplexed'. As it happens, experts on the subject also find the book valuable. Thus the present Special Rapporteur, Professor Gaetano Arangio-Ruiz, testified at the 1989 session of the International Law Commission that many interesting thoughts emerged from the book in relation to the difficult problem of determining the specific consequences to be attached to international crimes of State.[2]

On the technical side, the book suffers from certain deficiencies. The organization is not systematic. There is no clear division between the main subjects under consideration, different themes interchanging throughout. In the circumstances, a concluding chapter, summarizing the main issues, would have been welcome. Unfortunately, the two 'overview' articles do not fulfil this purpose.

The editors fail to mention in their Introduction when the Florence Conference took place. (The Introduction itself has no date.) This information is 'hidden' in the Library of Congress cataloguing data and in footnotes on pages 151 and 310. Seeing that the Conference took place in 1984 and that the book was published in 1989, and bearing in mind that the subject of the book concerns the ongoing work of the International Law Commission, the mention of such detail acquires particular importance.

The above drawbacks should not detract from the valuable contribution of the book to the understanding of the notion of crimes of State.

NISSIM BAR-YAACOV

---

[2] Report of the International Law Commission on the work of its 41st Session, 2 May—21 July 1989, *General Assembly Official Records*, 44th Session Supplement No. 10 (A/44/10) (1989), para. 244.

DECISIONS OF BRITISH COURTS DURING 1990 INVOLVING QUESTIONS OF PUBLIC OR PRIVATE INTERNATIONAL LAW

A. PUBLIC INTERNATIONAL LAW*

State immunity—immunity from corporation tax—shares in British company held by foreign government—whether immunity from tax liability or from judicial proceedings only—State Immunity Act 1978

Case No. 1. R v. Inland Revenue Commissioners, ex parte Camacq Corp. and another, [1990] 1 WLR 191, [1990] 1 All ER 173, CA, affirming QBD (Kennedy J). This was an unusual case in which private litigants sought to rely on the immunity from jurisdiction of a foreign State in an application for judicial review. The first applicant, Camacq Corp., was a United States corporation which had acquired some 70 per cent of the shares of the second applicant, Cambrian and General Securities plc, a British company. Camacq wanted to acquire a further 20 per cent then held by an escrow agent for the benefit of the United States Treasury.[1] The escrow agent had not accepted Camacq's public offer for the shares, while the City Code on Take-overs and Mergers prevented Camacq from simply increasing its offer. Camacq therefore proposed a more complex transaction which involved the payment by Cambrian of a dividend out of capital profits prior to the sale. Normally where a British company declares a dividend, it is paid to the shareholder net of the prevailing level of corporation tax. A payee who is tax exempt can then claim the amount withheld from the Revenue.[2] The long standing practice of the Revenue has been to allow foreign governments holding shares in British companies to recover these amounts on account of their sovereign immunity. The point of the proposed arrangement was that the tax credit that the escrow agent would be paid would effectively increase the amount he would receive for the shares.

In cases where it is clear that the payee is tax exempt, the Revenue can authorize the company to pay the dividend without deduction for corporation tax, avoiding the need for a claim from the Revenue. The escrow agent's acceptance of the arrangement with Camacq was conditional on such authorization being given. At first it was, but the authorization was subsequently revoked when Revenue officers, in light of new information, came to the view that the proposed arrangement was similar to the tax avoidance practice of 'dividend stripping'[3] and that in the

---

* © Christopher Staker, 1991.

[1] The shares had been acquired as part of a civil penalty imposed on an American by a United States court. It was accepted by Kennedy J that 'the shares held by the escrow agent can be treated as held by the United States government': [1990] 1 All ER at 176.

[2] The relevant provisions of the Income and Corporation Taxes Act 1988, which are slightly more complex than this, are set out in the judgment of Lloyd LJ, [1990] 1 All ER at 186–7.

[3] i.e., the practice of transferring shares to tax exempt owners shortly before a large dividend is paid. Measures to prevent this practice are found in s. 235 of the Income and Corporation Taxes Act 1988 and in Article 10 (1) and (7) of the 1975 double taxation agreement between the United Kingdom and the United States: see the Double Taxation Relief (Taxes on Income) (The United States of America) Order 1980, SI 1980/568. It was assumed that the provisions of this agreement, which apply to persons

circumstances there was some doubt whether the United States was entitled to, or would wish to claim, sovereign immunity. The applicants sought judicial review of this decision to revoke the authorization.

The applicants argued that a mere doubt as to whether the United States had the benefit of sovereign immunity was insufficient reason for revoking the authorization, and that the Revenue was required to express a view one way or the other. Both Kennedy J and the Court of Appeal unanimously agreed that if the Revenue had a reasonable doubt, it was entitled to require the United States Government, if it so chose, to claim the tax credit so that the matter could be determined if necessary in accordance with the statutory procedure for taxation appeals. The court was not prepared to allow that procedure to be preempted by this application for judicial review.[4] Clearly the Revenue was under no obligation to authorize payment of the gross amount of the dividend directly to the escrow agent, and here there had been sufficient reason for revoking the authorization previously given. It was thus unnecessary for the court in this case to decide any more than that the precise extent of sovereign immunity in the circumstances could reasonably be considered uncertain. However, the judgments in this case do highlight two important issues.

First, it was noted that by virtue of sections 11 and 16(5) of the State Immunity Act 1978, the immunity of a foreign State from the jurisdiction of the courts in proceedings relating to taxation (other than proceedings relating to VAT, customs and excise duties, agricultural levies or rates in respect of commercial premises) is still governed by common law.[5] Precisely what the common law position is in relation to corporation tax is uncertain, especially if it is accepted that the common law rules of State immunity are not static, but will evolve to reflect changes in customary international law.[6] As a matter of customary international law, foreign States are not required to be accorded immunity in proceedings relating to income tax and similar taxes in respect of their commercial activities conducted in the forum.[7] On the other hand, the Crown in this case appeared to assume that the immunity still subsists as a matter of English law.

Secondly, however, as counsel for the Crown pointed out, sovereign immunity is

---

'resident' in the United States, do not apply to the United States Government itself: [1990] 1 All ER at 176–7. However, the Revenue officers considered that the proposed arrangement was analogous, because the profits out of which dividends were to be paid were earned largely before the escrow agent acquired the shares, and because the arrangement seemed to be structured to net the escrow agent a higher price for the shares at virtually no additional cost to Camacq. One Revenue officer suggested that the arrangement could be 'an abuse of sovereign immunity': ibid. at 188.

[4] [1990] 1 All ER at 179, 183 (Kennedy J), 189 (Dillon LJ), 191 (Lloyd LJ). Farquharson LJ agreed, at 192.

[5] To similar effect, see the State Immunity Act 1979 (Singapore), ss. 13 and 19 (2)(c), and the State Immunity Ordinance 1981 (Pakistan), ss. 12 and 17 (2)(c). See also the Foreign States Immunity Act 1981 (South Africa), s. 12. By contrast, the Foreign States Immunities Act 1985 (Australia), s. 20, provides that a foreign State is immune from all proceedings relating to taxation other than those prescribed by regulation. By virtue of the Foreign States Immunities Regulations made under that Act, foreign States are not immune in respect of proceedings concerning Australian income tax.

[6] *Trendtex Trading Corp.* v. *Central Bank of Nigeria*, [1977] 1 QB 529, *per* Lord Denning MR and Shaw LJ.

[7] See the commentary to Article 17 of the International Law Commission's Draft Articles on the Jurisdictional Immunity of States and their Property, *Yearbook of the International Law Commission*, 1984, vol. 2, part 2, pp. 69–70.

normally considered to be immunity from *suit*, not from *liability*.[8] Because the United States Government was not a party to the proceedings in this case, its immunity from suit was irrelevant. The applicants had to rely instead on the argument that a foreign government has no *liability* to pay corporation tax, so that the Revenue had no good reason for preventing payment of the full amount of the dividend direct to the escrow agent. The applicants referred to a passage in the Canadian case of *Municipality of St John* v. *Fraser-Brace Overseas Corp.*[9] to the effect that statutes imposing taxation on property are prima facie presumed inapplicable to foreign States.[10] The submission of the Crown was to the contrary: that statutes imposing taxation will always apply to a foreign State in the absence of some specific exemption.[11] There was no such exemption in the Income and Corporation Taxes Act 1988. Counsel for the Crown argued that because of the foreign State's immunity from judicial proceedings, it might not be possible to enforce this tax liability through the courts, but that it could be enforced by the Crown by any other available means, such as a set-off. Hence, it was argued, the established practice of the Revenue in meeting claims by foreign governments for tax credits was not one which it was bound to follow, and there were good reasons in this case for wishing to depart from it.[12] Without deciding between these competing views, Kennedy J noted that the court in the *Fraser-Brace* case was concerned with property acquired by the foreign State for a public purpose, and suggested that 'More general observations may well have represented the law of Canada in 1958, but it does not follow that they reflect the law of the United Kingdom 30 years later'.[13] On the other hand, Dillon LJ seemed more inclined to the position taken in *Fraser-Brace*, and saw an analogy in the presumption that statutes imposing taxation do not apply to the Crown.[14] He considered that the argument put by counsel for the Crown constituted 'a revolutionary reversal of previous practice',[15] and said that

---

[8] The State Immunity Act 1978, like the equivalent legislation in the United States, Singapore, Pakistan, South Africa, Canada and Australia, as well as, for instance, the European Convention on State Immunity 1972, the International Law Commission's Draft Articles on the Jurisdictional Immunities of States and their Property and the International Law Association's Montreal Draft Convention on State Immunity 1982, are all concerned only with the immunity of foreign States from the jurisdiction *of the courts*, and immunity from execution of judgments. The immunity of foreign States from the *operation of the substantive law* of the forum is an issue which is usually paid little attention. Of course, to the extent that the forum can exercise judicial jurisdiction over a foreign State, it must be assumed that the substantive law of the forum can apply.

[9] [1958] SCR 263, 281–2, referring to *Re Ottawa City Corp. and Rockcliffe Park Village Corp.*, [1943] SCR 208, 231.

[10] The applicants also referred to a statement by the Paymaster General in the House of Commons in 1988 that 'the income, profits and gains of sovereigns, foreign states and integral parts of foreign Governments arising in the United Kingdom are immune from United Kingdom tax': see HC Official Report, Standing Committee A (Finance (No. 2) Bill), 21 June 1988, col. 578.

[11] An example given of such an exemption was the immunity of foreign States and their ambassadors from dues and taxes in respect of the premises of diplomatic missions: see Diplomatic Privileges Act 1964, implementing the Vienna Convention on Diplomatic Relations 1961, Article 23(1).

[12] See especially [1990] 1 All ER at 180–1 (Kennedy J), 189 (Dillon LJ).

[13] [1990] 1 All ER at 182. Lloyd LJ considered that the terms of s. 232(3) of the Income and Corporation Taxes Act 1988 might in any case have destroyed any presumption that the statute was not intended to apply to foreign States: ibid. 191.

[14] *Madras Electric Supply Corp. Ltd. (in liq.)* v. *Boardland (Inspector of Taxes)*, [1955] AC 667, [1955] 1 All ER 753. See [1990] 1 All ER at 190.

[15] [1990] 1 All ER at 189.

his view, 'without full development in argument, would be that the Crown's original practice was correct and the new thoughts are misconceived'.[16]

Thus there is uncertainty both as to the liability of foreign States to pay United Kingdom corporation tax and as to the immunity of foreign States from judicial proceedings relating to such taxation. It is most desirable that this uncertainty be resolved by legislation, given the number of States and sums of money affected by it.[17] If it is the case that foreign States are *liable* to pay United Kingdom corporation tax (whether or not they are immune from judicial proceedings to enforce that liability), it would not only mean that the Revenue could at any time reverse its existing practice and withhold large sums of money which at present are payed to the foreign States concerned. Given that the Revenue has no discretion to forgive taxes, it would also appear to mean that the Revenue's existing practice is unauthorized by law.[18] This would indeed be startling.

International organization—Arab Monetary Fund—personality in international law—capacity to sue and be sued in England—Arab Monetary Fund Agreement 1976

Case No. 2. Arab Monetary Fund v. Hashim and others (No. 3), [1990] 3 WLR 139, [1990] 2 All ER 769, CA. The decision of Hoffmann J at first instance in this case was noted in the previous volume of this *Year Book*.[19] The Arab Monetary Fund (the AMF) is an international organization which has its headquarters in Abu Dhabi, one of the seven emirates forming the United Arab Emirates. The AMF commenced an action in the Chancery Division against its former director general, Dr Hashim, and several other defendants based on an allegation that while in office Dr Hashim had misappropriated some US$ 70 million of the AMF's assets. The defendants applied to have the proceedings struck out on the grounds that English law did not recognize the AMF as a legal person with capacity to be party to proceedings before the English courts.

The Arab Monetary Fund Agreement 1976, which established the organization, provided that it was to have 'independent juridical personality and . . . in particular, the right to own, contract and litigate'. The provisions of this international agreement had been incorporated into the municipal law of the United Arab Emirates by a Federal Decree, and accordingly the AMF had independent legal personality and the capacity to sue and be sued in the law of that country. However, in the United Kingdom, no Order in Council had been made in respect of it under the International Organizations Act 1968—indeed, no such Order in Council could be made, since neither was the United Kingdom a member of the organization, nor did the organization maintain or intend to maintain any establishment in the United Kingdom.[20] The AMF's first argument before Hoffmann J was that even in the absence of legislation, English law recognizes the existence of a legal entity constituted under international law, just as it recognizes one constituted under the law of a foreign State. This argument was abandoned in light of the decision of the

[16] Ibid. 190.
[17] See ibid. (Dillon LJ). In the year to 31 March 1988, £119 million in tax was refunded by the Crown to bodies considered to enjoy sovereign immunity: ibid. 188.
[18] Although Lloyd LJ was 'not persuaded' that this was the case: ibid. 191.
[19] This *Year Book*, 60 (1989), pp. 475–6.
[20] See ss. 1 and 4 of that Act.

House of Lords in the *International Tin Council* case[21] and was not pursued further on appeal. The second argument was that as the AMF had been constituted under the domestic law of Abu Dhabi, it should be recognized as an ordinary foreign juridical entity under English conflict of laws rules.[22] This proposition was accepted by Hoffmann J, but rejected by a majority in the Court of Appeal.

Hoffmann J saw it a consequence of the *International Tin Council* case that the international agreement establishing the AMF had to be simply ignored, so that it could not be a barrier to recognition of what was plainly a legal entity under the law of the United Arab Emirates.[23] In the Court of Appeal, Lord Donaldson MR (with whom Nourse LJ in a separate opinion agreed) said that this was a 'basic fallacy'.[24] Lord Donaldson pointed out that while Lord Oliver in the *International Tin Council* case had said that a treaty could not create rights and obligations in English law (and hence could not confer on an international organization the capacity to be a party to proceedings before the English courts), he had also said in that case that it was a 'statement of the obvious' that 'a treaty may be referred to where it is necessary to do so as part of the factual background against which a particular issue arises'.[25] The AMF had legal personality under the law of the United Arab Emirates by virtue by a Federal Decree which ratified the AMF Agreement. That this decree had been enacted pursuant to a treaty obligation of the United Arab Emirates to recognize in its domestic law the legal personality of an international organization of which it was a member was a fact that the English courts could not ignore. Lord Donaldson concluded that the decree did not constitute the AMF a domestic corporation of the United Arab Emirates, any more than the International Tin Council had been converted into a domestic United Kingdom corporation by the 1972 Order in Council under the International Organizations Act.

In his dissenting judgment, Bingham LJ accepted this, but said that nevertheless

the evidence is clear and uncontradicted that the decree (not, be it noted, the Arab Monetary Fund Agreement) conferred on the fund legal personality and the capacity to sue and be sued in the law of the United Arab Emirates . . . On the evidence, the fund had no legal existence in the law of the United Arab Emirates without the decree . . . [I]n suing as a juridical person the fund does not depend on a status derived from a non-justiciable treaty but on a status conferred by the law of a friendly foreign sovereign. Comity would seem to require that the United Kingdom recognize the fund by virtue of Decree No 35 as the United Kingdom would doubtless wish the United Arab Emirates to recognize the International Tin Council by virtue of the 1972 order (as, it appears the Supreme Court of the State of New York did, although the United States was not a party to the Sixth Tin Agreement . . .).[26]

With respect, however, if it is the case that the legal capacity of an international organization cannot be recognized in domestic law in the absence of legislation, it is difficult to see that the fact it has been recognized in the municipal law of any other

---

[21] *J.H. Rayner (Mincing Lane) Ltd.* v. *Department of Trade and Industry*, [1989] 3 WLR 969, [1989] 3 All ER 523, this *Year Book*, 60 (1989), pp. 461–73.

[22] See Dicey and Morris, *Conflict of Laws* (11th edn., 1987), vol. 2, pp. 1134–5: 'Rule 171. The existence or dissolution of a foreign corporation duly created or dissolved under the law of a foreign country is recognized in England.'

[23] [1990] 3 WLR at 147.

[24] Ibid. at 158.

[25] [1989] 3 WLR at 1003.

[26] [1990] 2 All ER at 781–3, [1990] 3 WLR at 164–6.

State should make any difference.[27] Lord Donaldson MR noted that under the law of some States, such as Switzerland, the legal personality of an international organization is recognized automatically or *de plano*, without the need for further action. It was common ground that the fact that the legal personality of the AMF had been automatically recognized in Swiss law was no basis for recognizing it in English law as a foreign corporation created under the law of Switzerland. Lord Donaldson said:

> I can see no reason why the English courts should adopt a different attitude towards the Abu Dhabi and United Arab Emirates manifestation of the fund and a 'manifestation' is what it is: a persona ficta designed solely to give tangibility and visibility to something which would otherwise be intangible and invisible in the eyes of the law. This is wholly different from a foreign municipal juridical person whose existence is fully recognized under English law.[28]

He added that:

> I am fortified in this conclusion by the considerations which Hoffmann J characterized as 'unappetizing'. If the fund has a separate existence under the laws of each of the member states and also has a separate international existence under the laws of, for example, Switzerland, not only could they sue each other in the English courts, which is a somewhat unlikely eventuality, but it would be necessary to specify which fund was suing or being sued in litigation with strangers and very difficult questions could arise whether the cause of action was vested in one national fund or another. With all respect to Hoffmann J, one cannot simply dismiss 'the questions of trinitarian subtlety' to which he refers. They have to be addressed and confronted. If they are, it becomes apparent that something is amiss. The solution is that which he attributes to the argument of counsel for the banks, namely that the legislation conferring personality under the law of a member state should, as a matter of English private international law, be regarded as purely territorial in scope.[29]

Accordingly, the appeal was allowed, and the AMF's action against Dr Hashim was struck out. Lord Donaldson reached his conclusion 'with the greatest possible reluctance' (and Nourse LJ agreed 'without enthusiasm'[30]) because he regarded the result 'as wholly without merit from the point of view of doing justice between the parties'.[31] However, he considered this conclusion inescapable given the decision in the *International Tin Council* case. Those who were critical of the decision of the House of Lords in that case will no doubt consider the attitude of the majority of the Court of Appeal in this case to reinforce their view.

One possibility which was not considered by the court and which appears not to have been raised by counsel is that even if the AMF could not be recognized as having all the capacities of a body corporate under English law,[32] the effects of specific transactions entered into by the AMF under the law of other countries could still be recognized pursuant to the rules of private international law applicable to such transactions. On this view, the AMF would have no capacity to acquire property

---

[27] Thus Nourse LJ took the view that considerations of public policy overrode the principle of comity to which Bingham LJ referred, saying 'It would be inconsistent with what the House of Lords has held to be the policy of our law if we were to recognize an international organization constituted as a persona ficta under some other municipal law when, without such a constitution, we cannot recognize it for itself': [1990] 3 WLR at 160, [1990] 2 All ER at 778.

[28] [1990] 2 All ER at 777, [1990] 3 WLR at 158–9.

[29] Ibid.

[30] [1990] 3 WLR at 160, [1990] 2 All ER at 778.

[31] [1990] 3 WLR at 159, [1990] 2 All ER at 777.

[32] i.e., pursuant to rule 171 of Dicey and Morris (above, n. 22).

under English law, but could be recognized as owner of property acquired under the law of another State. Suppose (to simplify the facts alleged in this case) that the AMF acquired an item of tangible movable property in the United Arab Emirates and that this property was stolen and brought to England. Under the ordinary principles of private international law, English law would recognize as owner of the property the person who had good title to it in United Arab Emirates law, namely the AMF. In this case the law of the United Arab Emirates under which title was acquired would be a genuine municipal law, not one which merely gave domestic recognition to something transacted on the international plane, and recognition of the property title could not realistically be said to amount to allowing an unincorporated treaty to produce effects in domestic law. If the capacity of the AMF to bring proceedings in the English courts to recover the property were not recognized, presumably its member States could not sue instead as members of an unincorporated association, since under the law of the United Arab Emirates they did not own the property.[33] Thus, the AMF and its member States through no action of their own effectively would be deprived of any means of recovering the property by virtue of United Kingdom law, a situation which could amount to a *de facto* expropriation contrary to international law. On the other hand, if the AMF was recognized as owner of the property, it should also be recognized as having limited capacity to sue in English courts in respect of that property.[34]

Of course, even if this approach could be adopted, it would not assist an international organization in respect of which an Order in Council cannot be made under the International Organizations Act 1968, but which wished to enter into legal transactions in the United Kingdom. Given the importance of London as a major commercial and financial centre, no doubt such organizations do exist which enter into engagements in Britain. Not only can such organizations not sue in respect of these engagements, but they cannot be made liable upon them.[35] As both Nourse LJ and Bingham LJ pointed out, prior to the decision in the *International Tin Council* case at least, the Government appears to have assumed that the legal capacity of any international organization would be recognized without the need for legislation, which is why the International Organizations Act deals only with those international organizations which may enjoy privileges and immunities under United Kingdom law.[36] Following the decision of the House of Lords in that case, it is now evident that there is a gap in the law in relation to other types of international organizations. The immediate enactment of legislation to fill this gap, as recommended by Nourse LJ,[37] seems the only sensible solution.

Judicial review—unimplemented treaty—statutory interpretation—whether legislation presumed consistent with treaty obligations—human rights—European Convention for the Protection of Human Rights and Fundamental Freedoms 1950

Case No. 3. R v. Secretary of State for the Home Department, ex parte Brind

[33] Cf. Bingham LJ, [1990] 3 WLR at 165, [1990] 2 All ER at 782.

[34] Here too, the 'unappetizing' considerations referred to above would not arise: the only manifestation of the AMF that could be suing in this situation would be that which existed under the law of the United Arab Emirates.

[35] As Nourse LJ notes, [1990] 3 WLR at 161, [1990] 2 All ER at 779. See also [1990] 3 WLR at 144 (Hoffmann J).

[36] [1990] 3 WLR at 162–3, [1990] 2 All ER at 180–1 (Bingham LJ).

[37] [1990] 3 WLR at 161, [1990] 2 All ER at 778–9.

and others, [1990] 2 WLR 787, [1990] 1 All ER 469, CA. In the United Kingdom it is a fundamental principle of constitutional law that treaties to which the United Kingdom is a party cannot alter domestic law without the intervention of Parliament,[38] and that the courts must give effect to statutes in accordance with the intention of Parliament, even where the statute is inconsistent with the treaty obligations of the United Kingdom.[39] This does not mean that the provisions of treaties are wholly irrelevant to statutory interpretation, but rather that the courts only give effect to treaty obligations to the extent that Parliament intends. Since *Salomon,*[40] it has never been disputed that where there is cogent extrinsic evidence that a statute was enacted in order to fulfil obligations under a particular convention, the courts will in interpreting the statute consider the provisions of that convention to resolve ambiguities or obscurities.[41] Less clear is the extent to which the United Kingdom's treaty obligations may be relevant in interpreting other statutes. The law reports are replete with examples of cases where the courts have referred to unincorporated treaties in this situation. The majority of these cases, like the present case, concern the European Convention for the Protection of Human Rights and Fundamental Freedoms 1950,[42] and in these cases the Convention has often been used merely to illustrate or confirm general principles already established as a part of English law, such as the presumption that penal statutes do not have retrospective effect.[43] In other cases there were special reasons why an unincorporated treaty was relevant.[44] The general rule for determining the significance of an unincorporated treaty in this situation is normally not spelled out by the courts.

The applicants in the present case were journalists who sought judicial review of directives issued by the Secretary of State to the British Broadcasting Corporation (BBC) and the Independent Broadcasting Authority (IBA), requiring the addressees to refrain from broadcasting on radio or television statements spoken by representatives of certain specified organizations or by any person speaking in support of such organizations.[45] The directive addressed to the IBA was given pursuant to

[38] The House of Lords recently had occasion to reaffirm it in the *International Tin Council* case, above, n. 21, at 1002 (Lord Oliver). See also Case No. 2, above.

[39] *Salomon* v. *Commissioners of Customs and Excise,* [1967] 2 QB 116, *per* Lord Diplock at 143. As Lord Donaldson MR said in the present case, 'the duty of the English courts is to decide disputes in accordance with English domestic law as it is, and not as it would be if full effect were given to this country's obligations under the Treaty, assuming that there is any difference between the two': [1990] 2 WLR at 798.

[40] Above, n. 39.

[41] See also, e.g., the judgment of Lord Oliver, above n. 38, at 1002–3.

[42] TS 71 (1953), Cmd. 8969. For a survey of the cases to 1980, see P.J. Duffy, 'English Law and the European Convention on Human Rights', *International and Comparative Law Quarterly,* 29 (1980), p. 585. For subsequent examples, see the notes in this section of previous volumes of this *Year Book.*

[43] *Waddington* v. *Miah,* [1974] 1 WLR 692. As Lord Donaldson said in this case, in most of the earlier cases reference to the Convention 'has been fleeting and usually consisted of an assertion, in which I would concur, that you have to look long and hard before you can detect any difference between the English common law and the principles set out in the Convention, at least if the Convention is viewed through English judicial eyes': [1990] 2 WLR at 797.

[44] e.g. *R* v. *Secretary of State for Transport, ex parte Philippine Airways Ltd.,* [1984] TLR 273 and 570, this *Year Book,* 56 (1985), pp. 320–4.

[45] The directives applied to any proscribed organization under the Prevention of Terrorism (Temporary Provisions) Act 1984 or the Northern Ireland (Emergency Provisions) Act 1978, Sinn Fein, Republican Sinn Fein and the Ulster Defence Association. The directives were subject to certain exceptions relating to Parliamentary proceedings and elections.

section 29(3) of the Broadcasting Act 1981, and that addressed to the BBC pursuant to clause 13(4) of the licence and agreement of 1981 between the Secretary of State and the BBC.[46] The applicants argued that the directives were *ultra vires* because they were inconsistent with the guarantee of freedom of expression in Article 10 of the European Convention, and because section 29(3) of the Broadcasting Act (and by parity of reasoning clause 13(4) of the BBC licence and agreement) must be interpreted as not authorizing the discretion conferred to be exercised in a manner inconsistent with Article 10.

Lord Donaldson MR approached this argument with a very general statement about the relevance of unincorporated treaties in statutory interpretation. He said:

> [I]n most cases the English courts will be wholly unconcerned with the terms of the Convention. The sole exception is when the terms of primary legislation are fairly capable of bearing two or more meanings and the court, in pursuance of its duty to apply domestic law, is concerned to divine and define its true and only meaning. In that situation various prima facie rules of construction have to be applied, such as that, in the absence of very clear words indicating the contrary, legislation is not retrospective or penal in effect. To these can be added, in appropriate cases, a presumption that Parliament has legislated in a manner consistent, rather than inconsistent, with the United Kingdom's treaty obligations.[47]

It seems, therefore, that where there is any ambiguity in *any* statute, the courts will endeavour to construe the provision in a manner not inconsistent with *any* of the United Kingdom's treaty obligations. This is a significant extension of the principle stated in *Salomon*, which only contemplated reference being made to the particular treaty to which the legislation under consideration is intended to give effect.[47A] The full significance of this extension will depend, however, on how readily the courts will find that there is an ambiguity in a statute. In the case of legislation which is intended to implement the provisions of a particular treaty, the ambiguity need not appear on the face of the legislation: the mere fact that the statute appears inconsistent with the treaty it seeks to implement can give rise to an ambiguity.[48] Thus the rule could more accurately be stated to be that where legislation seeks to implement a particular treaty, the courts will wherever possible construe it as consistent with that treaty.[49] The applicants argued that there was an ambiguity in this case, in the sense that the discretion conferred on the Secretary of

[46] The relevant part of s. 29(3) of the Broadcasting Act 1981 provides that 'the Secretary of State may at any time by notice in writing require the Authority to refrain from broadcasting any matter or classes of matter specified in the notice; and it shall be the duty of the Authority to comply with the notice'. Clause 13(4) of the BBC licence and agreement contains substantially similar terms.

[47] [1990] 2 WLR at 798. See also at 806 (Ralph Gibson LJ).

[47A] At the same time, the judgment in this case significantly restricts the suggestion found in some of the earlier cases that the provisions of an unincorporated treaty may be relevant in statutory interpretation as evidence of a general policy, in the absence of any ambiguity at all (see below, n. 56 and accompanying text). In cases not involving the interpretation of a statute, the provisions of an unincorporated treaty may be considered in other contexts, for instance, in determining the public policy of the forum or in determining whether the court will exercise a particular discretion (see, e.g., *Cheall* v. *APEX*, [1983] 1 QB 126, 136–7 (*per* Lord Denning MR); *Trawnik* v. *Lennox*, [1985] 1 WLR 532, 541 (*per* Sir Robert Megarry VC), this *Year Book*, 57 (1986), at pp. 311–15). In such cases, of course, there can be no prerequisite of a legislative ambiguity.

[48] Brownlie, *Principles of Public International Law* (4th edn., 1990), p. 49.

[49] *Garland* v. *British Rail Engineering Ltd.*, [1983] 2 AC 751, 771 (Lord Diplock): 'it is a principle of construction of United Kingdom statutes, now too well established to call for citation of authority, that the words of a statute passed after the Treaty has been signed and dealing with the subject matter of the international obligation of the United Kingdom, are to be construed, if they are reasonably capable of bearing such a meaning, as intended to carry out the obligation, and not to be inconsistent with it.'

State was expressed to be unrestricted whereas it was clearly subject to some restriction, including for instance the requirement that it not be exercised unreasonably.[50] This argument was accepted by Watkins LJ in the Divisional Court,[51] but unanimously rejected by the Court of Appeal, which found that nothing in either section 29(3) or clause 13(4) required the Secretary of State to have regard to the Convention, and that accordingly there was no ambiguity.[52] Lord Donaldson MR added that to construe legislation which delegates power to legislate or to take executive action as subject to the limitation that it not be exercised inconsistently with the Convention involved 'imputing to Parliament an intention to import the Convention into domestic law by the back door, when it has quite clearly refrained from doing so by the front door'.[53]

Thus, the general rule, at least, is that there must be some ambiguity on the face of a statute before the provisions of unincorporated treaties can be used as an aid in its interpretation.[54] Nevertheless, as it remains the overriding duty of the courts to give effect to the intention of Parliament in every case, it surely ought still to be possible that in some situations an intention of Parliament to legislate in a manner consistent with unincorporated treaty obligations could be inferred from other circumstances. In this case it was argued by the applicants that the provisions of the Convention had not been incorporated into domestic law because successive Governments had assumed that all United Kingdom law was compatible with it, and that it must therefore have been the intention of Parliament when subsequently enacting legislation that it not be inconsistent with the Convention.[55] This argument is not illogical, and is supported by some *dicta* in earlier cases,[56] although the weight of authority is against it. The difficulty with the argument, given that it must always be presumed that the Government intends to observe the treaties it enters into, is that it would effectively mean that all statutes are to be interpreted in light of all of the United Kingdom's unincorporated treaty obligations except where the language of the statute makes this impossible. Such a proposition may be attractive from the point of view of preventing inadvertent breaches of treaty obligations without undermining the ultimate authority of Parliament, but it is also completely unsupported by authority. On the other hand, in

---

[50] *Associated Provincial Picture Houses Ltd* v. *Wednesbury Corporation*, [1948] 1 KB 223.

[51] The relevant part of the judgment is quoted at [1990] 2 WLR at 807: 'In our judgment, where Parliament has created for a minister a statutory power in terms which place no limitation on that power but where it is accepted, as in this case, that there must be and are limitations upon that power, then reference may be made to article 10 by a court when deciding what are the limitations to be placed on the use of that power.'

[52] Ibid. at 798 (Lord Donaldson MR), 806 (Ralph Gibson LJ), 807–9 (McCowan LJ).

[53] [1990] 2 WLR at 798. A similar conclusion was reached in *R* v. *Chief Immigration Officer, Heathrow Airport, ex parte Salamat Bibi*, [1976] 1 WLR 979, and *Chundawadra* v. *Immigration Appeal Tribunal*, [1988] Imm AR 161, which were cited in the judgments. See also, e.g., *R* v. *Secretary of State for the Home Department, ex parte Kirkwood*, [1984] 1 WLR 913, [1984] 2 All ER 390, this *Year Book*, 55 (1984), p. 338; *Malone* v. *Metropolitan Police Commissioner*, [1979] Ch 344, 354, [1979] 2 All ER 620, 628. See, however, *R* v. *Secretary of State for the Home Department, ex parte Bhajan Singh*, [1976] QB 198, [1975] 2 All ER 1081, 1083 (Lord Denning MR); *R* v. *Secretary of State for the Home Department, ex parte Phansopkar*, [1976] QB 606, [1975] 3 All ER 497, 511 (Scarman LJ).

[54] This confirms what Duffy considered to be the position, above, n. 42, at 589–90. See also *Bibi*, above, n. 53 at 984 (Lord Denning MR).

[55] [1990] 2 WLR at 804–5.

[56] *Attorney-General* v. *British Broadcasting Corporation*, [1981] AC 303, 354 (Scarman LJ); *Ahmad* v. *Inner London Education Authority*, [1978] 1 QB 36, 41 (Lord Denning MR) and 48 (Scarman LJ); *Singh*, above, n. 53 at 1083 (Lord Denning MR).

certain situations, such as where a provision of a statute deals with a very specific subject-matter that is also the subject-matter of an unincorporated treaty, there may be more scope for arguing that the statute was intended to comply with the convention, and Lord Diplock's statement in *Garland* [57] maybe applicable. [58]

Extradition—fugitive convicted in another State—whether prosecution barred by lapse of time—whether extradition an abuse of process—Extradition Act 1870

Case No. 4. R v. *Governor of Pentonville Prison, ex parte Sinclair,* [1990] 2 QB 112, [1990] 2 WLR 1248, [1990] 2 All ER 789, [1990] Crim LR 584, QBD (Watkins LJ and Nolan J). This case highlighted once again the limited powers of the magistrate under the Extradition Act 1870, in cases where extradition is sought of a person convicted of an offence under the law of the requesting State. [59] Section 10 of that Act provides that subject to the Act, if such evidence is produced as would, according to the law of England, prove that the prisoner was convicted of the crime, the magistrate shall commit him to prison to await surrender, and otherwise shall order him to be discharged. There was no doubt in this case that the applicant had in 1976 been convicted by a United States court of various offences and sentenced to four years' imprisonment. However, before beginning to serve his sentence, he had left the United States, apparently with the consent of the United States authorities, and had never returned. He claimed that he had sought to reenter the United States to serve the sentence, but had been denied a visa. The United States authorities were aware that he had moved to the United Kingdom in 1983, but did not formally seek his extradition until 1987. Although some of his claims were contested by the United States authorities, Watkins LJ considered it incontrovertible that the extradition had been 'badly delayed in respect of offences committed as long as 17 years ago'. [60]

In this application for habeas corpus, the applicant argued that the magistrate should not have ordered his committal because of Article V(1)(b) of the extradition treaty between the United States and the United Kingdom, [61] which provides that extradition shall not be granted if 'prosecution for the offence for which extradition is requested has become barred by lapse of time according to the law of the requesting or requested Party'. The time bar was said to arise by virtue of the doctrine of 'credit for time at liberty' which exists in United States law. According to this doctrine, where a prisoner is released prior to service of sentence and no attempt is made over a long period of time to regain custody of him or her, he or she may be given credit for the time involved, and not have to serve the remainder or the whole

---

[57] Above n. 49.

[58] See, e.g., *Ahmad* v. *ILEA*, above, n. 56, in which all judges appeared to assume that s. 30 of the Education Act 1944 (which prohibited discrimination against teachers on the grounds of religion) was to be construed in light of Article 9 of the Convention, although the majority considered that the Convention was of no assistance to the teacher concerned. See also, e.g., *R* v. *McCormick*, [1977] NI 105, in which the words 'torture or inhuman or degrading treatment' when used in a statute were presumed to have the same meaning as in Article 3 of the Covention.

[59] The Extradition Act 1870 has now been repealed and replaced by the Extradition Act 1989.

[60] [1990] 2 QB at 117.

[61] The treaty is contained in Schedule 1 to the United States of America (Extradition) Order 1976, SI 1976/2144.

of the sentence.[62] This argument was rejected, on the grounds that Article V(1)(b), which refers to a *prosecution* being time barred, had no application in conviction cases. The court was not persuaded by the applicant (who called expert evidence on the point) that under United States law the prosecution of an offence continues until the defendant begins to serve the sentence, and preferred the view that prosecution ends when sentence is passed and that the extradition process does not form part of the prosecution. The court also considered that even if this were incorrect, the doctrines on which the applicant relied did not operate automatically in United States law but were in the discretion of the courts, and the English courts were clearly not competent to grant a discretionary remedy under United States law. Given the very limited extent to which the magistrate in extradition proceedings can examine questions of foreign law,[63] it may be doubted whether the magistrate could have refused extradition on this ground even if the doctrines did apply automatically.[64]

The applicant's second argument was that in the circumstances his extradition amounted to an abuse of process. In a succession of recent cases the courts have confirmed that a magistrate has the power in exceptional circumstances to stop a prosecution on the grounds of an abuse of process, *inter alia* where the defendant has been prejudiced in the preparation or conduct of his or her defence by unjustifiable delay on the part of the prosecution.[65] The question was whether the magistrate may exercise such a power in proceedings under the Extradition Act 1870. A number of recent cases have left this question open,[66] although the authority of *Atkinson's* case[67] appeared to preclude the exercise of such a discretion in extradition cases. Watkins LJ considered that the correct position was that stated by Hutchinson J in *Brij Parekh*,[68] namely that the House of Lords in *Atkinson* was merely emphasizing that section 9 of the Act requires the magistrate in extradition proceedings to determine the matter 'as near as may be' as if he or she were dealing with domestic committal proceedings, and that as it has since been established that a magistrate in domestic proceedings has a discretion to stop a prosecution on grounds of an abuse of process, the discretion must likewise be exercisable in cases where the extradition of an *accused* person is sought. However, Watkins LJ considered that there was no precedent for applying this doctrine in *conviction* cases,

---

[62] [1990] 2 QB at 121, referring to *Smith* v. *Swope*, 91 F 2d 260 (1937). The applicant also relied on a related doctrine that a prisoner will not be required to serve a sentence after a lapse of time 'if the government's action or inaction is so affirmatively wrong or grossly negligent that service of the sentence would be inconsistent with fundamental principles of liberty and justice': [1990] 2 QB at 121–2, referring to *Shelton* v. *Ciccone*, 578 F 2d 1241 (1978).

[63] See the speech by Lord Diplock in *In re Nielsen*, [1984] AC 606, 621–2, [1984] 2 WLR 737, 746, [1984] 2 All ER 81, 89, this *Year Book*, 55 (1984), pp. 343–5.

[64] If a magistrate is not entitled to enquire whether a conviction is a nullity owing to a failure to observe the rules of natural justice (*Royal Government of Greece* v. *Governor of Brixton Prison*, [1969] 3 WLR 1107, [1969] 3 All ER 1337), the magistrate would presumably also be unable to enquire whether service of a sentence is time barred, in a case where the conviction itself is undoubtedly valid. Watkins LJ did consider, however, that the magistrate was entitled to consider evidence relating to a time bar in United States law specifically applicable to a request for extradition: [1990] 2 QB at 123.

[65] [1990] 2 QB at 126, quoting *R* v. *Derby Crown Court, ex parte Brooks*, (1985) 80 Cr App R 164, 168–9. The applicant claimed to have been prejudiced in a number of ways by the delay.

[66] *R* v. *Bow Street Magistrates Court, ex parte Van Der Holst*, (1985) 83 Cr App R 114, 124, *In re Rees*, [1986] AC 937, 964, *In re Brij Parekh* (unreported), 17 May 1988: see [1990] 2 QB at 127.

[67] *Atkinson* v. *United States Government*, [1971] AC 197, 232–3, [1969] 3 All ER 1317, 1322–3.

[68] Above, n. 66.

and that the applicant had in any case suffered no prejudice arising out of the delay.[69]

This refusal to extend the doctrine of abuse of process to conviction cases under the 1870 Act is unfortunate in that it denies what would otherwise be an important guarantee to the person whose extradition is sought. The applicant claimed in this case that he had been prevented by the United States authorities from serving his sentence some 14 years earlier, and if this were true, it would be manifestly unjust that he should have to live for the rest of his life 'under the shadow' of the possibility of extradition proceedings being brought at any time.[70] The answer to this given in *Atkinson* is that under section 11 of the Act the Secretary of State has power to refuse the surrender of a person committed, where in his or her view this would be wrong, unjust or oppressive. This does not overcome the problem, however, that the fate of the person concerned is left to be determined by executive authority, rather than the courts. Section 8 (3) of the Fugitive Offenders Act 1967 contained a provision enabling the High Court on an application for habeas corpus to order a person committed to be discharged if in all the circumstances it was unjust or oppressive to return him, by reason of the trivial nature of the offence, the passage of time since conviction or the fact that extradition was not sought in good faith or in the interests of justice. It is to be welcomed that a similar provision now applies to all extradition proceedings by virtue of section 11 (3) of the Extradition Act 1989.[71, 72]

Hague Convention on the Civil Aspects of International Child Abduction 1980— whether child wrongfully removed—whether child wrongfully retained

Case No. 5 C v. *S (minor: abduction: illegitimate child)*, [1990] 3 WLR 492, [1990] 2 All ER 961, [1990] 2 FLR 450, HL, affirming [1990] 2 All ER 449, [1990] 2 FLR 442, CA. This case involved a short point of interpretation of the Hague Convention on the Civil Aspects of International Child Abduction 1980.[73]

---

[69] [1990] 2 QB at 127–8.

[70] See the passage quoted by Watkins LJ from *Smith* v. *Swope*, above, n. 62.

[71] See n. 59, above. The 1989 Act also repeals and replaces the Fugitive Offenders Act 1967.

[72] In two other extradition cases decided in 1990, the United States Government had sought the extradition of persons accused of offences against United States law committed outside United States territory. The court was concerned in both cases with whether the acts constituting the offences would also amount to extra-territorial crimes under the law of the forum, so that the rule of double criminality was satisfied: see *R* v. *Governor of Pentonville Prison, ex parte Naghdi*, [1990] 1 All ER 257, QBD (Woolf LJ and Saville J), and *Liangsiriprasert* v. *United States Government and another*, [1990] 3 WLR 606, [1990] 2 All ER 866, PC. In the latter case the applicant had been lured from Thailand (where the offences were committed) to Hong Kong by United States undercover agents because extradition was not available from Thailand. The court rejected the argument that this had been in breach of 'international comity', since the authorities of Thailand had participated in the operation. In *R* v. *Governor of Pentonville Prison, ex parte Osman (No. 3)*, [1990] 1 WLR 878, [1990] 1 All ER 999, QBD (Parker LJ and Tudor Evans J), the court noted that it is not a requirement for the issue of a provisional warrant of arrest under the Fugitive Offenders Act 1967 that a warrant of arrest has been issued in the requesting country, although this is a requirement for a lawful authority to proceed. The court also held that an otherwise valid committal pursuant to a valid authority to proceed will not be vitiated by the fact that the provisional warrant under which the person concerned was originally arrested was invalid.

[73] TS 66 (1986), Cm. 33. The provisions of the Convention are given force in the law of the United Kingdom by the Child Abduction and Custody Act 1985. In another case decided in 1990, the Court of Appeal said that the Convention gave effect to the general principle, also recognized in English law, that

The child, who had been living with his parents, both United Kingdom citizens, in Western Australia, was taken by his mother without the consent of his father to live in the United Kingdom. The father subsequently obtained from the Family Court of Western Australia an order giving him sole guardianship and custody of the child, and a declaration that the removal of the child had been wrongful. He then instituted proceedings in the English courts, seeking the return of the child pursuant to the Convention.

The issue before the English courts was whether the child had been 'wrongfully removed' or 'wrongfully retained' within the meaning of Article 3 of the Convention.[74] Despite the decision of the Australian court to the contrary, the House of Lords affirmed that the removal of the child from Australia was not 'wrongful', since at the relevant time the parents were not married, so that the mother had sole custody and guardianship of the child by virtue of section 35 of the Family Court Act 1975 (Western Australia).[75] It was pointed out that while English courts are bound by the decisions of the Western Australian courts on questions of Western Australian law, the English courts are entitled to form their own view on the application of Article 3 of the Convention.[76] Both the Court of Appeal and the House of Lords also agreed that the mother's retention of the child immediately after the making of the order by the Western Australian court was not wrongful for the purposes of Article 3, since at the time of the making of the order the child was not 'habitually resident' in Australia. Lord Brandon said that the words 'habitually resident' were not a term of art, and were to be given their ordinary meaning. He added:

there is a significant difference between a person ceasing to be habitually resident in country A, and his subsequently becoming habitually resident in country B. A person may cease to be habitually resident in country A in a single day if he or she leaves it with a settled intention not to return to it but to take up long-term residence in country B instead. Such a person cannot, however, become habitually resident in country B in a single day. An appreciable period of time and a settled intention will be necessary to enable him or her to become so. During that appreciable period of time the person will have ceased to be habitually resident in country A but not yet have become habitually resident in country B.[77]

Thus, whether or not the child was now habitually resident in the United Kingdom, he had ceased to be habitually resident in Australia when his mother left there with the settled intention that neither she nor the child should return. This does, however, seem to leave an unusual gap in the Convention, since it would mean that if a child changed residence from country A to country B, and before

---

the welfare of the child is paramount, so that a similar outcome will be achieved whether or not the country from which the child was abducted is a party to the Convention: *Re F (minor: abduction: jurisdiction)*, [1990] 3 All ER 97.

[74] Article 3 provides: 'The removal or the retention of a child is to be considered wrongful where— *(a)* it is in breach of rights of custody attributed to a person, an institution or any other body, either jointly or alone, under the law of the State in which the child was habitually resident immediately before the removal or retention; and *(b)* at the time of removal or retention those rights were actually exercised, either jointly or alone, or would have been so exercised but for the removal or retention.'

[75] Which provides that where the parents of a child are not married at the time of the birth of a child or subsequently, the mother has the custody and guardianship of the child until a court order is made under that Act.

[76] [1990] 2 All ER at 452 *(per* Lord Donaldson) and 964 *(per* Lord Brandon).

[77] Ibid. at 965. Similar comments were made by Lord Donaldson at 454. It was also stated by both judges that the habitual residence of a child of two was necessarily that of his mother in whose custody he was.

becoming 'habitually resident' in the latter was abducted to country C, the Convention would not apply, even if countries A, B and C were all parties to it.[78, 79]

Diplomatic privileges and immunities—time of commencement—appointment of member of mission not notified to receiving State—whether immune from immigration control—Vienna Convention on Diplomatic Relations 1961, Article 39— Diplomatic Privileges Act 1964—Immigration Act 1971, section 8(3)

Case No. 6. R v. *Secretary of State for the Home Department, ex parte Bagga and others*, [1990] 3 WLR 1013, [1991] 1 All ER 777, CA. Given that the immunities of members of diplomatic missions and their families constitute a significant limitation on the territorial jurisdiction of the receiving State, the question of how and when such immunities commence is undoubtedly an important one. Article 39 (1) of the Vienna Convention on Diplomatic Relations 1961[80] provides that

> Every person entitled to privileges and immunities shall enjoy them from the moment he enters the territory of the receiving State on proceeding to take up his post or, if already in its territory, from the moment when his appointment is notified to the Ministry for Foreign Affairs or such other ministry as may be agreed.

From this it is clear that where a person already in the territory of the receiving State is appointed to a position in a diplomatic mission, the person will enjoy no privileges and immunities until the receiving State is notified. It is also clear that

---

[78] The *travaux préparatoires* provide no assistance on this point: see Hague Conference on Private International Law, *Actes et documents de la 14ème session* (1980), vol. 3 (Child Abduction), pp. 449–50, paras. 75–8.

[79] Several other cases decided during the period under review involved the interpretation and application of particular treaty provisions. *The Bowbelle*, [1990] 1 WLR 1330, [1990] 3 All ER 476, [1990] 1 Lloyd's LR 532, concerned the Convention on Limitation of Liability for Maritime Claims 1976 (TS 13 (1990), Cm. 955), which has effect in British law since 1 December 1986 by virtue of s. 17 of the Merchant Shipping Act 1979. Sheen J held that the combined effect of Articles 2 and 13 of that Convention is that a shipowner can only be compelled to constitute one limitation fund under Article 11 in respect of one incident, and that where such a fund has been constituted, a person claiming in respect of the incident may not arrest any ships belonging to the shipowner, even if it is alleged that the shipowner is guilty of conduct barring limitation of liability under Article 4 of the Convention. In *R. G. Mayor (T/A Granville Coaches)* v. *P & O Ferries Ltd. and others (The Lion)*, [1990] 2 Lloyd's LR 144, QBD, Hobhouse J held that Article 12(1) of the International Convention on the Carriage of Passengers and their Luggage 1974 (the Athens Convention) (which disentitles a carrier from the benefit of limitation of liability where damage results from an intentional or reckless 'act or omission of the carrier') does not apply to acts of servants or agents who are not an *alter ego* of the carrier. It was further held that the carrier is entitled to rely on the Convention, notwithstanding a failure to give adequate notice to the passenger that the Convention was applicable (in contravention of Statutory Instrument 1980/1125, made pursuant to the Merchant Shipping Act 1979). In *Inland Revenue Commissioners* v. *Commerzbank AG*, [1990] Simon's Tax Cases 285, Ch D (Mummery J), it was held to be the effect of Article XV of the double taxation agreement between the United States of America and the United Kingdom (above, n. 3) that all dividends and interest paid by United States corporations is tax exempt in the United Kingdom except where the recipient is a United Kingdom citizen, resident or corporation, so that interest and dividends paid by United States corporations to German and Brazilian banks maintaining branches in London was not taxable. See also *Ashai Kasei Kogyo KK's Application*, [1990] Fleet Street Reports 546, CA, concerning the application of the European Patent Convention; and *Newtherapeutics Ltd.* v. *Katz and another*, [1990] BCLC 700, [1990] BCC 362, Ch D (Knox J), and *Arkwright Mutual Insurance Co.* v. *Bryanstone Insurance Co. Ltd. and others*, [1990] 3 WLR 705, [1990] 2 All ER 335, [1990] 2 Lloyd's LR 70, QBD (Potter J), concerning the EEC Convention on Jurisdiction and the Enforcement of Judgments in Civil and Commercial Matters 1968.

[80] *UN Treaty Series*, vol. 500, p. 95. The provisions of the Convention are given effect in United Kingdom law by the Diplomatic Privileges Act 1964.

where the receiving State is given prior notification that a person is to enter its territory to take up a post at the mission, privileges and immunities will commence from the moment of arrival. Whatever the position may have been under general international law,[81] it also seems clear that under the Vienna Convention a person who enters the territory of the receiving State to take up an appointment at a diplomatic mission will enjoy privileges and immunities from the time of arrival, even if notification has not at that time been given to the receiving State. The duty of the sending State to notify the receiving State of the appointment, arrival and departure of members of the mission is contained in Article 10(1). Article 10(2) then provides that '*Where possible*, prior notification . . . shall also be given'. *Prior* notification, then, is desirable, but not essential. At general international law, prior notification appears to have been necessary on the basis that a person could not enjoy diplomatic status until the receiving State had consented to the appointment. However, under the Vienna Convention, Article 7 establishes the general principle that the sending State may freely appoint the members of the staff of the mission. This general principle is expressed to be subject to certain other provisions of the Convention, such as the requirement of *agrément* for the appointment of the head of mission (Article 4 (1)) and the requirement that nationals of the receiving State not be appointed members of the diplomatic staff without the consent of the receiving State (Article 8), and to the possible requirement that the receiving State give prior approval in the case of the appointment of service attachés (Article 7). Otherwise the approval of the receiving State is not required, and Article 7 is not expressed to be subject to the requirement of notification in Article 10. Notification to the sending State is thus not a prerequisite for the enjoyment of privileges and immunities under the Vienna Convention.[82]

Nevertheless, in *R* v. *Governor of Pentonville Prison, ex parte Teja*,[83] Parker LJ (with whom the other two members of the court agreed) said:

> I confess that at the very outset this argument [that a foreign diplomatic agent enjoys privileges and immunities from the moment of arrival, even in the absence of notification], simple as it was, seemed to me to produce a frightening result in that any foreign country could claim immunity for representatives sent to this country unilaterally whether this country agreed or not. As I see it, it is fundamental to the claiming of immunity by reason of being a diplomatic agent that that diplomatic agent should have been in some form accepted or received by this country . . . In other words, immunity depends on mutual agreement on the person entitled to the immunity.[84]

That case admittedly concerned a person who claimed to be a member of an *ad hoc* mission, and who therefore fell outside the provisions of the Vienna Convention, although it has been relied on in subsequent cases which have involved members of diplomatic missions.[85] In the instant case, the court had an opportunity to re-

---

[81] As to which, see the *Vitianu* case (1949), *Annual Digest*, vol. 16, p. 281, No. 94; H. Lauterpacht, *Collected Papers*, vol. 3 (1977), pp. 433–57; Whiteman, *Digest of International Law*, vol. 7, pp. 108–26.

[82] See further O'Connell, *International Law* (2nd edn., 1970), vol. 2, pp. 906–7, Brownlie, this *Year Book*, 45 (1971), at p. 399, and Crawford, this *Year Book*, 56 (1985), at p. 330; Dembinski, *The Modern Law of Diplomacy* (1988), p. 187. Of course, the receiving State remains free to declare a member of the mission *persona non grata* under Article 9.

[83] [1971] 2 QB 274, this *Year Book*, 45 (1971), pp. 398–9.

[84] Ibid. at 282.

[85] *R* v. *Lambeth Justices, ex parte Yusufu*, [1985] Crim LR 510, [1985] TLR 114, this *Year Book*, 56 (1985), pp. 328–31; *In re Osman* (unreported), 21 December 1988, QBD.

examine the issue, although it arose in a very unusual way. Four of the appellants in this case sought judicial review of a decision that they were not entitled to remain indefinitely in the United Kingdom. Each of them had come to the United Kingdom to take up employment at a diplomatic mission,[85a] and had since ceased such employment. In each case, the Foreign and Commonwealth Office had not been notified of the appointment at the time of their arrival. On arrival each had been given an open date-stamp in his or her passport. These appellants now maintained that these stamps amounted to an indefinite leave to enter and remain in the United Kingdom pursuant to the Immigration Act 1971. The Secretary of State relied on section 8(3) of that Act, which provides that the Act does not apply:

to any person so long as he is a member of a mission (within the meaning of the Diplomatic Privileges Act 1964), a person who is a member of the family and forms part of the household of such a member, or a person otherwise entitled to like immunity from jurisdiction as is conferred by that Act on a diplomatic agent.

The appellants argued that under Article 39 of the Vienna Convention, they enjoyed no privileges and immunities until their appointments were notified to the Foreign and Commonwealth Office, and that consequently when they originally entered the United Kingdom, they did so subject to the Immigration Act.

In deciding the case, the court found it sufficient to refer to the precise wording of section 8(3) of the Immigration Act, without needing to apply Article 39. Parker LJ said:

We are, however, not concerned with enjoyment of diplomatic immunities, but with exemption from immigration control. This is dependent [under section 8(3)], and dependent only, on whether the person concerned '*is* a member of a mission . . . or *is* a member of the family and forms part of the household of such a member . . . ' Under article 1 (*a*) and (*b*) of the Convention, the 'head of the mission' is a 'member of the mission' and is 'the person charged by the sending state with the duty of acting in that capacity'. Whatever may be said about other persons, it therefore seems clear that if a person who has in fact been so charged arrives in this country, he is a 'member of the mission' notwithstanding that he has arrived to take up but has not yet taken up his appointment, and that there is at the time no notification to the Foreign and Commonwealth Office.

I can see no valid reason why any other person arriving to take up a post within the definition should be in any different position so far as immigration control, which operates on entry, is concerned . . .

The truth is that, so far as immigration is concerned, the Home Office are not in any way involved in what may be the diplomatic niceties as to when a head of mission or other diplomat begins to enjoy the benefits conferred by the Act of 1964, but only with the question whether a person *is* a member of a mission, be it the head of a mission, a member of the diplomatic staff of the mission, or of the technical, administrative or service staff of the mission.

That question appears to me to involve only the determination of the question whether the person has in fact been appointed to some post in the mission, be it a diplomatic, administrative, technical or service appointment, or is in fact employed by the mission in one or other of such categories.[86]

Thus, in the court's view, for the purposes of section 8(3) of the Immigration Act the question whether a person is a member of a mission is one of fact, and is independent of the question whether the person enjoys privileges and immunities

[85a] Or were members of the family of such persons.
[86] [1990] 3 WLR at 1020–1. Glidewell LJ (at 1030) and Leggatt LJ (at 1032–3) agreed.

under the Diplomatic Privileges Act 1964. With respect, it is difficult to follow this reasoning, since the words in section 8(3) 'or [is] a person *otherwise* entitled to the like immunity' surely indicate that the only persons excluded from the operation of that Act are those who actually enjoy privileges and immunities under the 1964 Act. The result of the court's approach, as Parker LJ acknowledged, is that a person appointed to a position in a diplomatic mission when already in this country, but whose appointment was not notified to the Foreign and Commonwealth Office, would have no privileges and immunities under Article 39 of the Vienna Convention or the 1964 Act, but would be exempt from immigration control.[87]

Accordingly, the court found that the appellants had not been subject to the Immigration Act at the time of arrival, and could not have been given indefinite leave to enter and remain under that Act.[88] It was thus strictly speaking unnecessary for the court to decide whether a person who enters the country as a member of a mission but whose appointment has not yet been notified enjoys privileges and immunities from the moment of entry. However, Parker LJ was clearly of the view that the person does, saying that 'In my judgment save, possibly, in the case of a head of mission or other person of diplomatic rank, *Teja, Yusufu* and *Osman*,[89] although plainly right on the facts, were wrong on the point that immunity under the Act of 1964 depends on notification and acceptance'.[90] Glidewell LJ[91] and Leggatt LJ[92] appeared to agree with Parker LJ, although the latter suggested that different considerations may arise depending on the context in which immunity is claimed,[93] and considered *Teja* to be wrongly decided '*in so far as* the ratio decidendi of [that case] would preclude a member of a mission from enjoying exemption *from immigration control* on entry into this country'.[94] Given the importance of this question, it is unfortunate that the court did not take better advantage of the opportunity to examine it in more detail.

CHRISTOPHER STAKER

---

[87] [1990] 3 WLR at 1020. However, this result is now avoided by an amendment to the legislation. The Immigration Act 1988, s. 4, inserted a new subsection (3A) into s. 8 of the 1971 Act, which provides that in the case of a member of a mission other than a diplomatic agent, the exemption from immigration control under s. 8(3) applies only if the person enters the United Kingdom as a member of the mission or in order to take up a post at the mission offered to the person prior to arrival.

[88] One of the appellants had, after ceasing employment at the mission, left the United Kingdom and subsequently returned, at which time he was clearly subject to the Immigration Act. On return his passport was date-stamped by an immigration officer in the belief that he was still a member of the mission. The court found that in the circumstances he had not been given indefinite leave to enter, and if he had, that the decision of an immigration officer that the leave was obtained by deception would not be quashed. Another appellant in this case was a member of the service staff of an embassy whose employment had been terminated by the embassy, but who sought an extension of his leave to enter to accept an offer of employment by the commercial attaché in his personal capacity. The court upheld the refusal to grant such leave.

[89] Above, nn. 83–5.

[90] [1990] 3 WLR at 1023. See also at 1019H, 1020D and G, 1023-A-B. It is unclear, though, precisely what Parker LJ means by 'other person of diplomatic rank'. He could be suggesting that only administrative, technical and service staff have immunities prior to notification, but this would appear to contradict his earlier comments at 1019H.

[91] Ibid. at 1030B-D.

[92] Ibid. at 1032E-F.

[93] Ibid. at 1032B.

[94] Ibid. at 1033 (emphasis added).

B. Private International Law*

Jurisdiction: (1) service of process upon an absent defendant; (2) submission

Case No. 1. Order 11, rule 1(1), of the Rules of the Supreme Court lists the prin-cipal cases in which, with leave of the court, service of a writ out of the jurisdiction is permissible. Two of these cases relate specifically to claims in contract. Service is permissible in certain specified circumstances under rule 1(1)(d) if 'the claim is brought to enforce, rescind, dissolve, annul or otherwise affect a contract, . . .'; it is permissible under rule 1(1)(e) if 'the claim is brought in respect of a breach com-mitted within the jurisdiction of a contract made within or out of the jurisdic-tion . . .'. One of the issues before Adrian Hamilton QC (sitting as a deputy High Court judge) in the recent case of *Finnish Marine Insurance Co. Ltd.* v. *Protective National Insurance Co.*[1] was as to the meaning of the term 'contract' in these con-texts. The learned deputy judge said:

. . . the arguments before me raise two points as to the 'contract' on which the plaintiffs rely: (1) Does the contract have to between the plaintiffs and the defendants? (2) Can a plaintiff base a claim for service out of the jurisdiction on a claim that no contract has ever come into existence?[2]

The first of these points was dealt with quite shortly. Rejecting the argument that it is sufficient to show that a contract between the plaintiff and a third party is 'affec-ted' as being 'clearly wrong', his Lordship said:

It is probably sufficient to construe the rule alone. It seems to me clear that all the earlier grounds ('enforce, rescind, dissolve annul') can only relate to a contract between plaintiff and defendant. There is nothing to indicate that a different type of contract becomes avail-able when the claim is to 'affect' a contract. In each case 'contract' means a contract between plaintiff and defendant.[3]

The second point as to the meaning of 'contract' was material in the instant case because the plaintiffs were seeking a declaration that in fact no contract had ever existed between them and the defendants. The learned deputy High Court judge recognized that a claim for a declaration that a contract had been rescinded for mis-representation,[4] or a claim that it had been discharged by frustration,[5] would be a claim 'otherwise affecting a contract'; but he saw a clear distinction between such cases and those (such as the present) in which the plaintiffs' case was that there had never been a contract. The distinction would appear as a matter of construction, and in the particular circumstances as a matter of common sense, to be warranted. It is, however, to be noted that doctrinal considerations could indicate that a corre-sponding distinction would lead to rejection of a plaintiff's claim that a contract was void *ab initio* for, e.g., mistake. Or would focus then be upon the word 'annul'?

At a more general level it may be noted that (as is twice mentioned in the course of the judgment), jurisdiction under Order 11 often being 'exorbitant' and

---

* © P.B. Carter, 1991.
[1] [1990] 1 QB 1078.
[2] Ibid. 1082–3.
[3] Ibid. 1083.
[4] See *Insurance Corporation of Ireland* v. *Strombus International Insurance Co.*, [1985] 2 Lloyd's Rep. 138, 142.
[5] See *per* Kerr J in *BP Exploration Co. (Libya) Ltd.* v. *Hunt*, [1976]1 WLR 788 at p. 795.

'extraordinary',[6] any doubts as to its reach should be resolved in favour of the foreigner. With regard to the two limitations considered by the court in the instant case there may have been little room for such doubt. However, that sight is not lost of this general approach to Order 11 is eminently consistent with contemporary emphasis upon restraint in the exercise of jurisdiction in inappropriate circumstances.

In *Finnish Marine Insurance Co. Ltd.* v. *Protective National Insurance Co.* the plaintiffs had contended in the alternative, and regardless of Order 11, that the defendants had in any event voluntarily submitted to the jurisdiction by virtue of their issue of a summons to stay under section 1 of the Arbitration Act 1975. Of this his Lordship drily observed: 'For those not familiar with *Henry* v. *Geopresco International Ltd.* [1976] Q.B. 726, this would appear a startling conclusion. The summons seeks to stop the English action, so that the arbitration can proceed. It does not indicate any wish to have the English courts try the merits of the dispute—quite the contrary.'[7] In the controversial *Geopresco* case the Court of Appeal, following a general approach laid down in the earlier and also controversial case of *Harris* v. *Taylor*,[8] had held that an application to a foreign court for a stay of proceedings on the ground of an arbitration clause constituted submission to the jurisdiction of that foreign court for the purpose of the recognition in England of the ultimate judgment of that court. An effect of section 33 of the Civil Jurisdiction and Judgments Act of 1982 was to reverse the *Geopresco* decision. That section is, however, concerned with voluntary submission to the jurisdiction of a foreign court for recognition purposes, and not with voluntary submission to the jurisdiction of an English court for its own purposes. However, Adrian Hamilton QC said: 'Now that the direct effect of the *Geopresco* case has been reversed by statute, I see no basis for extending the principles applied to issues of voluntary submission to the English courts. What is a voluntary submission depends upon the facts.'[9] What then is the factual criterion? The learned acting High Court judge found guidance in the words of Goff LJ in *Astro Exito Navegacion SA* v. *Hsu (The Messiniaki Tolmi)*[10]:

Now a person voluntarily submits to the jurisdiction of the court if he voluntarily recognises, or has recognised, that the court has jurisdiction to hear and determine the claim which is the subject matter of the relevant proceedings. In particular, he makes a voluntary submission to the jurisdiction if he takes a step in proceedings which in all the circumstances amounts to a recognition of the court's jurisdiction in respect of the claim which is the subject matter of those proceedings.[11]

What is crucial is that, as is twice emphasized, for a submission to be voluntary it must be directed to determination of the claim which is the subject-matter of the proceedings. It is not enough that it is directed simply to the issue of jurisdiction. Moreover, it is immaterial that determination of the issue of jurisdiction may involve provisional determination of an issue as to the merits. In *Finnish Marine Insurance Co. Ltd.* v. *Protective National Insurance Co.* itself it had been contended that dealing with the application for a stay necessarily involved the court in

[6] *Per* Lord Goff of Chieveley in *Spiliada Maritime Corporation* v. *Cansulex Ltd.*, [1987] AC 460, 481, and referred to by Adrian Hamilton QC, at p. 918.
[7] [1990] 1 QB 1078, 1086.
[8] [1915] 2 KB 580.
[9] [1990] 1 QB 1078, 1087.
[10] [1984] 1 Lloyd's Rep. 266.
[11] Ibid. 270.

deciding whether there was a contract which was one of the very issues going to the merits of the plaintiffs' claim. Adrian Hamilton QC rejected this contention:

I do not, however, consider that that fact changes the nature of the jurisdiction invoked by the application to stay. It remains the invocation of the court's jurisdiction to decide if it has jurisdiction; not the jurisdiction to decide the merits.[12]

The finding that there was no submission to the jurisdiction of the English court was, like the restrictive interpretation placed upon Order 11, r. 1(1)(e) and (f), consistent with present day attitudes of judicial restraint over the assumption of jurisdiction. Moreover, the holding of no submission also manifests a developing and welcome correspondence between the extent of a court's own jurisdiction and that of the jurisdiction of a foreign court in the recognition context. It can perhaps be seen as another sign that the philosophy of the Brussels Convention is beginning to permeate English private international law more generally.

Jurisdiction: (1) exclusive jurisdiction under Article 16(2) of the Brussels Convention; (2) RSC, Order 11, rule 1(1)(d)

Case No. 2. In the recent case of *Newtherapeutics* v. *Katz*[1] a writ had been served out of the jurisdiction on two directors of an English registered company. One of the directors was domiciled in France; the other was domiciled in New York. Each director disputed service. Knox J set aside the service of the writ on each defendant but on different grounds.

The management, control and business of the company was conducted exclusively outside the United Kingdom and mostly in France. The company's main income-producing asset at the material time was a contract with a French pharmaceutical company (Debat) under which the company was to proceed with clinical experimentation needed to develop one of its products in return for very substantial payments. Disagreements had arisen between those in charge of the company's affairs. The director who was domiciled in France had resigned and had executed an agreement with the company whereby the company waived all claims against him in respect of any act on his part as a director or in any other capacity. The New York director had refused to resign but was removed from office. Subsequently the company had issued a writ with a statement of claim in which breaches of duty by the directors were alleged, but there was no plea of any breach of any other contractual relationship between the company and the defendants. In the statement of claim it was alleged *inter alia* that the defendants had at a meeting with representatives of Debat signed certain documents, although no board meeting had been called for that purpose at which the validity and contents of the documents could have been discussed, and that they had failed to heed the protests of a fellow director.

The company had applied to the Master for leave under RSC, Order 11, to serve the writ on the defendants out of the jurisdiction. Leave had been granted to serve the New York defendant, but the Master had concluded that leave was unnecessary in relation to the French defendant by virtue of the Civil Jurisdiction and Judgments Act 1982.

Both defendants applied to Knox J for a declaration that the court lacked jurisdiction in respect of the subject-matter of the claim or the relief sought, and for an

[12] [1990] 1 QB 1078, 1088.
[1] [1990] 3 WLR 1183.

order discharging the master's order granting leave to serve the New York defendant *ex juris*.

The two main grounds advanced on behalf of Dr Lablanchy, the French domiciled defendant, were, first, that under the Brussels Convention he could be sued
only in France in respect of the matters in issue; and, secondly, that in any event
the action against him was bound to fail having regard to the waiver agreement and
that accordingly the action should be struck out under the inherent jurisdiction of
the court to prevent its process being abused.

The Brussels Convention deals with 'civil and commercial matters'. There are
exceptions, but it was common ground that the matters in issue in the instant case
fell within the category 'civil and commercial' and did not fall within any exception.
Article 2 of the Convention provides that generally in such cases 'persons domiciled
in a contracting state shall, whatever their nationality, be sued in the courts of that
state'. However, this general rule is qualified by *inter alia* Article 16. It provides:

The following courts shall have exclusive jurisdiction, regardless of domicile: . . . (2) in
proceedings which have as their object the validity of the constitution, the nullity or the dissolution of companies or other legal persons or associations of natural or legal persons, or the
decisions of their organs, the courts of the contracting state in which the company, legal person or association has its seat.

The critical question was as to whether, notwithstanding the fact that this director
was domiciled in France, the English court had jurisdiction by virtue of this latter
article. Knox J answered the question in the affirmative. His Lordship therefore
held that the court had jurisdiction. However, he accepted the second ground
advanced on behalf of Dr Lablanchy, namely that the action against him 'was so
hopeless because of the waiver document that it should be struck out'.[2] In this context Knox J rejected *inter alia* the argument that the waiver agreement had been
obtained under duress, and concluded 'that the action against Dr Lablanchy is
bound to fail and accordingly I shall set aside the service of the writ as against
him'.[3]

The main interest of the judgment with regard to this defendant lies, however,
in the learned judge's meticulous analysis of several aspects of Article 16(2).

First, his Lordship noted that the reference to the 'object' of the proceedings
must be seen, not as a reference to their purpose, but rather as a reference to their
'subject-matter'. Secondly he addressed himself to a more difficult question of construction. Is the phrase 'the decisions of their organs' governed only by the words
'in proceedings which have as their object' or is it (more restrictively) governed by
the phrase 'in proceedings which have as their object the validity of'? The English
text is not free from ambiguity but might suggest the former construction. His
Lordship, however, after exploring the corresponding French and German texts,
was able to conclude that the latter construction is the correct one. He accordingly
held that it is to the *validity* of the decisions of the organs of companies that Article
16(2) refers.

The question in the instant case was, therefore, as to whether the subject-matter
of the instant proceedings was as to the validity of a decision or decisions of an
organ of the company. His Lordship noted that virtually the only material to assist
him in answering this question was the statement of claim itself. He continued:

[2] Ibid. 1200.
[3] Ibid. 1202.

The statement of claim alleges breaches of duty by the defendants as directors of the company. There is no plea of any breach of any other contractual relationship between the plaintiff and the defendants. The particulars given of the breaches of duty complained of fall into two classes. First, there is a class of claims that the variation documents were signed in the absence of a board meeting and that it was beyond the defendants' powers as directors to sign the variation documents. Secondly, there is the claim put in various ways that the transaction contained in the variation documents was so detrimental to the company that no reasonable board of directors or directors could properly have entered into it.[4]

His Lordship saw the latter claim as falling outside Article 16(2) because it essentially concerned simply the propriety of individual directors' actions. On the other hand, the former claim was within Article 16(2) because the substance of the issue raised there was as to whether a board meeting was necessary and, if so, as to whether one (or its equivalent) had been held. In reaching this conclusion his Lordship made reference to what the European Court of Justice had intimated in *Sanders* v. *Van der Putte*[5] to the effect that 'it is clear that the courts which are given exclusive jurisdiction are those which are the best placed to deal with the disputes in question'.[6] Viewed, both as a matter of construction of Article 16(2), and from the standpoint of the overall purpose of Article 16 more generally, the decision is unassailable. However, his Lordship saw himself as being left with a further question, namely 'which of the two types of claims of breach of duty made by the company against the defendants raises the principal issue?'.[7] In response to this 'conundrum', Knox J, having suggested that the issue upon which the defendants are most likely to lose is the principal one because they only have to lose one to lose the action, concluded: 'It must be a matter of judgment which is the principal issue even with the assistance of that test, and my judgment, which I do not propose to elaborate, is that the issue regarding the absence of a board resolution and the need for it is the principal issue in the case'.[8] It may perhaps be respectively queried whether the question need have been asked. It is true that Article 19 does refer to 'a claim which is *principally* concerned with a matter over which the courts of another contracting state have exclusive jurisdiction by virtue of Article 16' (italics supplied). But it is to be observed that there 'principally' refers, not to a comparison of one claim with another, but to the nature of a particular claim. May it not be that once a claim has been held to be within (or at least clearly within) Article 16, this should suffice to ground exclusive jurisdiction, even if an alternative (and perhaps substantial) claim has been found to be outside that article?

For Dr Katz, the defendant who was domiciled in New York, it was contended that leave had been wrongly granted to serve him out of the jurisdiction under Order 11, rule 1, of the Rules of the Supreme Court. Two questions arose: first as to whether the facts fell within any of the situations in which the granting of such leave is permissible; secondly, whether, if so, the court should have granted leave.

The ground relied upon as a basis for the court's power to grant leave was apparently that set out in Order 11, rule 1(1)(d). That paragraph runs as follows:

The claim is brought to enforce, rescind, dissolve, annul or otherwise affect a contract, or to recover damages or obtain other relief in respect of the breach of a contract, being (in either

---

[4] Ibid. 1199.
[5] (Case 73/77) [1977] ECR 2383.
[6] Ibid. 2390.
[7] [1990] 3 WLR 1183, 1200.
[8] Ibid.

case) a contract which (i) was made within the jurisdiction, or . . . . (iii) is by its terms, or by implication, governed by English law . . .

It was accepted that the only relationship between the company and Dr Katz was one of company and director, there being no contract of employment between them. It was argued, however, that the scope of Order 11, rule 1(1)(d), is not restricted to contracts in a strict sense but extends to the relationship created by the appointment of a company director, this being closely analogous to a contractual relationship. Although his Lordship was disposed to see some force in the argument, he rejected it in accordance with the general and well settled principle that Order 11 should not be liberally construed in favour of a plaintiff and against a foreigner. He cited[9] Lord Diplock in *Siskina (Owners of Cargo Lately Laden on Board)* v. *Distos Compania Naviera SA*,[10] who was himself citing Farwell LJ in *The Hagen*,[11] when he said: 'It has long been held that where there is any room for doubt as to their meaning the provisions of the sub-rules [of Order 11] are to be strictly construed in favour of the foreigner'.[12]

Knox J further indicated that even if the case had fallen within the ambit of Order 11, rule 1, he would still have set aside leave to serve Dr Katz out of the jurisdiction in the light of the plaintiffs' failure, when seeking leave, to make a full and frank disclosure of the fact that Dr Katz's only co-defendant had (by virtue of the waiver agreement) at least an arguable complete defence.

Foreign copyright laws not justiciable

Case No. 3. The facts giving rise to the recent case of *Tyburn Productions Ltd*. v. *Conan Doyle*[1] were as follows. The plaintiffs had produced, and wished to distribute commercially in the United States of America, a television film which was original in all respects except that it featured the characters 'Sherlock Holmes' and 'Dr Watson'. The defendant had made assertions that this would be a breach of copyright vested in her. The plaintiffs, believing that repetition of these assertions would inhibit or prevent effective distribution of the film, sought a declaration that the defendant had no rights under the copyright, unfair competition or trademark laws of the United States which would entitle her to prevent distribution, and they sought an injunction restraining the defendant from asserting the contrary. Vinelott J held that the action was not justiciable in England and that accordingly the claims for a declaration and for an injunction must fail.

His Lordship said:

The central issue in this case is whether the distinction between transitory and local actions, which was considered by the House of Lords in *British South Africa Co*. v. *Companhia de Mocambique*,[2] was funamental to that decision and, if it was, whether an action raising questions as to the validity or infringement of patent rights, copyrights, rights of trademark and other intellectual property rights are properly to be considered actions of a local nature; or whether that distinction was, as it were, an historical prologue setting out the basis of the narrower rule that English courts will not entertain proceedings raising questions as to the title to, or for damages for trespass to, land.[3]

[9] Ibid. 1207.
[10] [1979] AC 210.
[11] [1908] P 189, 201.
[12] [1979] AC 201, 254–5.
[1] [1990] 3 WLR 167.
[2] [1893] AC 602.
[3] [1990] 3 WLR 167, 170.

His Lordship appears to have concluded that the distinction between transitory and local actions was fundamental to the House of Lords holding in the *Mocambique* case. He then went on to hold that the operation of the distinction does extend to rights in intellectual property. In reaching this latter conclusion Vinelott J placed considerable reliance upon the 1906 decision of the High Court of Australia in *Potter* v. *Broken Hill Proprietary Co. Ltd.*,[4] where the High Court had held that the validity of a New South Wales patent right was not justiciable in the courts of the State of Victoria. In *Tyburn Productions Ltd.* v. *Conan Doyle* it was accepted that no distinction could be drawn for the purpose in hand between patent rights, copyright, rights of trade marks and other intellectual property rights.

The decision in *Tyburn Productions* v. *Conan Doyle* would, therefore, seem to stand for the broad and general proposition that, in the light of the distinction between transitory and local actions, an English court is precluded from adjudicating upon title to, or rights relating to, foreign intellectual property.

The first enquiry which such a proposition may provoke is as to the actual meaning of the distinction between 'transitory' and 'local' actions. This elusive distinction has historically been the subject of much inconclusive debate. In 1792 Buller J in *Doulson* v. *Matthews*,[5] having drily observed that it 'is now too late for us to inquire whether it were wise or politic to make a distinction between transitory and local actions',[6] concluded: 'We may try actions here which are in their nature transitory, though arising out of a transaction abroad, but not such as are in their nature local'.[7] These words were cited with approval in the *Mocambique* case by Lord Herschell LC, who took them to be indicative of 'the fact that our courts did not exercise jurisdiction in matters arising abroad "which were in their nature local".'[8] But how is one to discover whether a matter is 'in its nature' local? Why, for example, is a breach abroad of a foreign copyright to be seen as being in its nature local, but the commission abroad of a tort or other civil wrong is not usually designated local in its nature? The distinction would in fact appear to turn, not on the intrinsic 'nature' of a matter, but rather upon the willingness of the courts of other countries to adjudicate upon it. There is here an element of circular reasoning. A legitimate enquiry is not as to whether the matter has some mystical quality which compels the courts of other countries to refrain from adjudication, but rather as to whether there are policy grounds indicating the desirability of such restraint by other countries. The response to this enquiry should be pragmatic not *a priori*.

It was held in the *Mocambique* case that English courts will not adjudicate upon title to foreign land. It was further held that the courts will not entertain actions for trespass to foreign land. In *Hesperides Hotels* v. *Aegean Holidays*[9] Lord Fraser of Tullybelton said that he had serious doubts as to whether this latter rule was 'either logical or satisfactory in its result',[10] and the rule has now been very largely abrogated by statute.[11] Even the former and more basic rule is consistently disregarded

[4] (1906) 3 CLR 479.
[5] (1792) 4 Durn. and E 503.
[6] Ibid. 504.
[7] Ibid. 504, cited by Vinelott J in *Tyburn Productions Ltd.* v. *Conan Doyle* at p. 171.
[8] [1893] AC 602, 621.
[9] [1979] AC 508.
[10] Ibid. 544.
[11] Civil Jurisdiction and Judgments Act 1982, s. 30.

when the issue of title has to be decided for the purpose of the administration of an estate or trust of property, some of which is situated in England.[12] Moreover its practical effect will often be negatived by virtue of the doctrine of *Penn* v. *Baltimore*.[13] This overall pattern of development would appear to smack of pragmatism rather than adherence to any supposedly valid doctrinal distinction.

One is therefore tempted to wonder whether this supposed doctrinal distinction is happily to be injected into the private international law of intellectual property. Are there no circumstances in which it would be seemly and perhaps positively desirable for an English court to entertain an action for breach of a foreign copyright? For choice of law purposes, an analogue with the tort rule in *Phillips* v. *Eyre*[14] might perhaps be apt. Or, alternatively, independent choice of law rules specifically tailored to suit the needs of intellectual property (or particular types of intellectual property) might be developed. Such choice of law rules might be fairly restrictive, but they could reflect appropriateness in sophisticated detail. Such development is precluded by a rigid rule of non-justiciability.

However, there is certainly room for the view that, especially in the light of the increasing complexity of national intellectual property law, a court should have reserve power to decline to give a *declaratory judgment* involving the determination of foreign law in this area. The exercise of such power would mean that the actual result in *Tyburn Productions Ltd.* v. *Conan Doyle* would, of course, have been the same: the claims for a declaration and for an associated injunction would have failed. Such failure would, however, not have involved the invocation of the outmoded and analytically dubious distinction between transitory and local actions; nor would it have involved resort to any analogy with *British South Africa Co.* v. *Companhia de Mocambique*, a case decided nearly a century ago, and the scope of which has been limited by statute[15] and partially eroded by judicial decision,[16] and which is often circumvented by equity.[17] On the contrary, a precisely limited ratio would have contributed to the construction of a much needed private international law of intellectual property.

Foreign judgments: (1) jurisdiction of the foreign court; (2) natural justice

Case No. 4. In the recent case of *Adams* v. *Cape Industries plc*[1] the plaintiffs in 205 consolidated actions sought to enforce a default judgment given against the defendants in a United States Federal District Court sitting in the State of Texas. The first defendant, Cape, was an English company which presided over a group of subsidiary companies engaged in the mining in South Africa, and the marketing, of asbestos. The company's marketing subsidiary in the United States of America was a wholly owned subsidiary, NAAC, incorporated in the State of Illinois in 1953. The company's worldwide marketing subsidiary was the second defendant, Capasco, a wholly owned English company. Neither defendant had a place of business anywhere in the United States; but NAAC did have a place of business there until 31 January 1978, when it was wound up. Cape then promoted a new Illinois Corporation, CPC, whose shares were all owned by the former chief executive of

---

[12] See, e.g., *Re Duke of Wellington*, [1948] Ch. 118.
[13] (1750) 1 Ves. Sen. 144.
[14] (1870) LR 6 QB 1.
[15] See footnote 11, above.
[16] See footnote 12, above.
[17] See footnote 13, above.
[1] [1990] Ch. 433.

NAAC. When marketing asbestos in the United States neither NAAC nor CPC sold it for Cape or Capasco; they themselves bought the asbestos from Cape's South African subsidiaries and then resold it in the United States.

In a Federal District Court in Texas the plaintiffs had claimed and been awarded damages for personal injuries and consequential loss allegedly suffered as a result of their exposure to asbestos fibres emitted from a factory in Texas. The basis of the liability of the defendants, Cape and Capasco, was alleged to be negligent acts and omissions and breaches of warranties. The plaintiffs' contention had been that the defendants had been responsible for the supply of fibres directly or indirectly without giving proper warning of the dangers thereof. The plaintiffs sought to enforce the unsatisfied Texas judgment in English proceedings. Their action was dismissed by Scott J. This was affirmed by the Court of Appeal, where the very full judgment of the whole court was delivered by Slade LJ.

The central issue was as to the jurisdictional competence of the Texas court. A further issue considered by the Court of Appeal was as to whether the Texas judgment comported with the requirements of natural justice.

It is, of course, accepted and was indeed reaffirmed in the case[2] that, in an action upon a foreign judgment, the burden of proving that the foreign court had jurisdiction upon a recognized ground rests upon the plaintiff. One such recognized ground is presence. In the case of an individual defendant his physical presence in the foreign country at the time when the foreign action was commenced will itself ground the jurisdiction of the foreign court. Indeed the Court of Appeal confirmed that even temporary and casual presence suffices.[3] It also held that an action is to be regarded as commencing for this purpose when the defendant is served with process and not when it is issued.[4]

The concept of presence must clearly cause difficulty in the case of a corporate defendant. Resort must be had to a fiction. The substantive issue is as to the circumstances in which 'presence' will be ascribed to a corporation in this context. Slade LJ considered at some length and in some detail the authorities bearing upon the determination of this issue, and his Lordship felt able to derive three propositions from his survey. First,

The English courts will be likely to treat a trading corporation incorporated under the law of one country ('an overseas corporation') as present within the jurisdiction of the courts of another country only if either (i) it has established and maintained at its own expense (whether as owner or lessee) a fixed place of business of its own in the other country and for more than a minimal period of a time has carried on its own business at or from such premises by its servants or agents (a 'branch office' case), or (ii) a representative of the overseas corporation has for more than a minimal period of time been carrying out *the overseas corporation's* business in the other country at or from some fixed place of business.[5]

Secondly his Lordship emphasized that particularly in the latter case

the question whether the representative has been carrying on the overseas corporation's business or has been doing no more than carry on his own business will necessitate an

---

[2] Ibid. 550.

[3] Ibid. 518–59. See, too, the recent decision of the Supreme Court of the United States in *Burnham* v. *Superior Court of California*, (1990) US 110 S Ct. 2105. In *Adams* v. *Cape Industries plc* the Court of Appeal deliberately left open the question as to whether residence without presence will suffice ([1990] Ch. 433, 518).

[4] Ibid. 518.

[5] Ibid. 530 (original emphasis).

investigation of the functions which he has been performing and all aspects of the relationship between him and the overseas corporation.[6]

Thirdly, Slade LJ gave a detailed catalogue of questions likely to be relevant to such an investigation. This catalogue, although lengthy, was not intended to be exhaustive; moreover Slade LJ singled out as an important factor in the case of agency, the presence or absence of authority in the agent to enter into contracts on behalf of the corporation without submitting them to the corporation for approval.[7]

In *Adams* v. *Cape Industries plc* it was argued that Cape and Capasco were present in the United States through NAAC and then through CPC. The argument was rejected. Neither company had authority to contract so as to bind the defendants. Although this was not decisive, it was highly relevant. What was crucial was that their businesses were their own, not the defendants'. The Court of Appeal also rejected any suggestion that they could 'lift the corporate veil', the principle of *Salomon* v. *A. Salomon & Co. Ltd.* being applied 'in the ordinary way'.[8] Rejected, too, was the notion that when a group of companies forms an 'economic unit' it can be treated in law as if it was all one company.[9]

The Court of Appeal concluded that the defendants had not been present in the United States and that, therefore, the Texas court lacked jurisdiction. The Court did, however, consider what the position would have been if it had found that the defendants were present in the United States but not in the State of Texas. Indeed, if Cape had been found to be present anywhere in the United States it would have been in Illinois, NAAC and CPC being Illinois corporations. Texas and Illinois are, of course, separate law districts, and had the Texas court been a State (as distinct from Federal) court, the defendants' presence in Illinois would have been irrelevant. However, the Court of Appeal appears to have inclined to the view that as the Texas court was a Federal District court its jurisdiction could be based upon the presence of the defendants anywhere in the United States. This would, with all respect, appear to be misconceived. A Federal court (unless dealing with a Federal matter) will apply the law of the State in which it is sitting.[10] In the United States such a judgment of a Federal court sitting in one State is for recognition and enforcement purposes regarded (like the judgment of a State court) as a 'foreign judgment' by another State of the Union. Acceptance of the view which the Court of Appeal was inclined to espouse could therefore lead to a situation in which the judgment of a Federal court sitting in Texas could be enforced in England although it would not be recognized or enforced in any State of the Union outside Texas.

The Court of Appeal also gave consideration to the defendants' contention that the Texas judgment should in any event be denied recognition on the ground that the method by which the Court assessed the amount of damages was contrary to the requirements of natural justice. Natural justice relates to procedural standards and its impact is not confined to cases of complete absence of notice or of the opportunity to be heard. The court saw it as extending to more complex situations. In the instant case the method suggested by the plaintiffs and adopted by the Texas

---

[6] Ibid. 530.
[7] Ibid. 530–1.
[8] Ibid. 539–44.
[9] Ibid. 532–9.
[10] *Erie RR* v. *Tompkins*, 304 US 64; 58 S Ct. 817; 82 L Ed. 1188 (1938).

judge for the assessment of damages was gravely irregular, and the defendants had received no notice of it. Nor was its nature revealed in the judgment. The defendants had, therefore, had no opportunity to get the matter corrected.

However, the main long term importance of the Court of Appeal's judgment in *Adams* v. *Cape Industries plc* is likely to lie in the principles laid down for the determination of the 'presence' of a foreign corporation so as to ground jurisdiction. Previous authority on this, although considerable, had been diverse and uncoordinated. The three propositions now formulated by the Court[11] constitute an ordered framework—albeit a framework with some unavoidable and indeed desirable built-in flexibility. On the score of certainty at least this framework bears favourable comparison with the famous words of Chief Justice Stone delivering the judgment of the Supreme Court of the United States in the landmark case of *International Shoe Co.* v. *State of Washington*:

> . . . due process requires only that in order to subject a defendant to a judgment in personam, if he is not present within the territory of the forum, he have certain minimum contacts with it such that the maintenance of the suit does not offend 'traditional notions of fair play and substantial justice'.[12]

Foreign judgments: the defence of fraud

Case No. 5. It was first laid down in 1882 by the Court of Appeal in *Abouloff* v. *Oppenheimer*[1] that at common law a foreign judgment can be impeached for fraud even though no newly discovered evidence is produced and even though the allegation of fraud had been made in the foreign proceedings. Eight years later in the case of *Vadala* v. *Lawes*,[2] where the evidence of fraud offered in the English proceedings was identical with that which had been offered and rejected in the foreign court, Lindley LJ refused to 'fritter away' the doctrine of *Abouloff* v. *Oppenheimer*, saying: ' . . . if the fraud upon the foreign court consists in the fact that the plaintiff has induced that court by fraud to come to a wrong conclusion, you can reopen the whole case even although you will have in this court to go into the very facts which were investigated and which were in issue in the foreign court'.[3] This clearly does not lie easily with the doctrine that a recognized foreign judgment is conclusive in the sense that the merits cannot be reopened, and over the years it has been the subject of considerable, if largely ineffectual, academic criticism. However, in the course of his judgment in the Court of Appeal in the recent case of *House of Spring Gardens Ltd.* v. *Waite and others*[4] Stuart-Smith LJ has adverted to the fact that *Abouloff* v. *Oppenheimer* and *Vadala* v. *Lawes* 'were decided at a time when our courts paid scant regard to the jurisprudence of other countries'.[5] Although he nevertheless felt bound by them and noted that they had been recently followed by the Court in *Jet Holdings Inc.* v. *Patel*,[6] his Lordship went on to say: 'But in my judgment the scope of these decisions should not be extended . . .'.[7] There are three ways in which the decision of the Court of Appeal in *House of Spring Gardens Ltd.*

---

[11] See pp. 403–4, above.
[12] 326 US 310; 66 S Ct. 154; 90 L Ed. 95 (1945).
[1] (1882) 10 QBD 295.
[2] (1890) 25 QBD 310.
[3] At pp. 316–17.
[4] [1990] 3 WLR 347.
[5] Ibid. 355.
[6] [1990] QB 335.
[7] [1990] 3 WLR 347, 355.

v. *Waite and others* would seem to manifest this welcome reluctance to extend their scope.

The factual background of the case was as follows. The plaintiffs, in an action brought in the High Court of Ireland before Costello J against three defendants for misuse of confidential information and breach of copyright, had obtained judgment for some £3,000,000 damages. Following the dismissal of the defendants' appeal by the Supreme Court of Ireland, the first and second defendants had brought a separate action seeking to have the judgment set aside alleging that it had been obtained by fraud. This second action in the High Court of Ireland was dismissed by Egan J. The plaintiffs then sought to enforce their judgment in England. Sir Peter Pain (sitting as a High Court judge) held that in the absence of any new evidence the defendants were estopped from alleging in the present proceedings that the judgment in question was obtained by fraud. Sir Peter Pain held that Mr McLeod, the third defendant, although in a different position from the first and second defendants because he had not been a party to the proceedings before Egan J, was nevertheless also bound by the estoppel on account of the privity of interest between him and the first and second defendants. In the light of these holdings Sir Peter Pain found it unnecessary to consider the alternative argument put forward by the plaintiffs to the effect that it would be an abuse of the process of the court for the defendants to be allowed to re-litigate the fraud allegation. Mr McLeod, the third defendant, appealed from Sir Peter Pain's judgment to the Court of Appeal.

The Court of Appeal considered three issues, the first of which was as to whether the first and second defendants were estopped by the judgment of Egan J from contending that the original judgment, that of Costello J, was obtained by fraud. The Court held that they were so estopped. It was acknowledged by Stuart-Smith LJ that, but for the judgment of Egan J, Costello J's judgment could have been impeached for fraud. This would, of course, have been in accord with the doctrine of *Abouloff* v. *Oppenheimer*[8] and *Vadala* v. *Lawes*.[9] But, as his Lordship pointed out, 'the plaintiffs contend that the judgment of Egan J is final and conclusive on the issue whether or not the prior judgment was obtained by fraud, and cannot itself be impeached'.[10] This contention was accepted: 'Unless Egan J's decision is itself impeached for fraud, it is conclusive of the matter thereby adjudicated upon, namely, whether Costello J's judgment was obtained by fraud'.[11] The Court found no acceptable evidence that Egan J's judgment was itself impeachable for fraud.

The second issue considered by the Court of Appeal was as to whether the appellant, Mr McLeod, was bound by Egan J's decision. He was not a party to that action, but an estoppel will bind those who are privy to the parties bound. Such privity may derive from sufficient common interest. These propositions can be confidently stated, but as Stuart-Smith LJ drily observed, 'It is not easy to detect from the authorities what amounts to a sufficient interest'.[12] Having conceded that 'A mere interest in the outcome of the litigation is not sufficient',[13] his Lordship relied on two considerations or circumstances in reaching the conclusion that Mr McLeod was bound by Egan J's decision. He first cited the words of Sir Robert

[8]   Above.
[9]   Above.
[10]   [1990] 3 WLR 347, 355.
[11]   Ibid. 355.
[12]   Ibid. 356.
[13]   Ibid. 356.

Megarry V-C in *Gleeson* v. *Wippell & Co. Ltd.*[14] that 'having due regard to the subject matter of the dispute, there must be a sufficient degree of identification between the two to make it just to hold that the decision to which one was party should be binding in proceedings to which the other is party. It is in that sense that I would regard the phrase "privity of interest".'[15] Stuart-Smith LJ referred, too, to the relevance of a situation, such as that mentioned by Lord Denning giving the judgment of the Privy Council in *Nana Ofori Atta II* v. *Nana Abu Bonsra II*,[16] 'which is not one of active participation in the previous proceedings or actual benefit from them, but of standing by and watching them fought out or at most giving evidence in support of one side or the other'. In the present case all three defendants were joint tortfeasors. The judgment against them was joint and several. If the action to set aside Costello J's judgment had succeeded, that judgment would have been set aside *in toto*, not just as against the first and second defendants. Mr McLeod was well aware of the proceedings before Egan J. He could have applied to join them. It would only involve going to Dublin, not to a distant country. He was content to sit back and let others fight his battle at no expense to himself. Stuart-Smith LJ concluded that such considerations and circumstances were sufficient to make the third defendant privy to the estoppel: 'it is just to hold that he is bound by the decision of Egan J'.[17]

The third matter upon which the Court of Appeal pronounced concerned the plaintiffs' alternative submission namely that to allow-re-litigation of the issue of fraud would be an abuse of the process of the court. Of this Stuart-Smith LJ said: 'In my opinion the same result can equally well be reached by this route, which is untrammelled by the technicalities of estoppel'.[18] In this context another member of the Court, McCowan LJ, addressed himself to the particular facts of the instant case. He saw Mr McLeod's non-participation in the proceedings before Egan J as 'a very clever tactic' because

If the judgment of Costello J were set aside as against the Waites [the first and second defendants], he would certainly have benefitted because in practical terms it could never have been enforced against him. If, on the other hand, the Waites failed in their Irish action, he could do what he has in fact now done, which is to say that he is not bound by the decision in that action since he was not a party to it, and have another bite at the cherry of alleging fraud against the plaintiffs.[19]

The response of Stuart-Smith LJ was more general and is perhaps making new law. After stating that the categories of abuse of process are not closed His Lordship continued:

The question is whether it would be in the interests of justice and public policy to allow the issue of fraud to be litigated again in this court, it having been tried and determined by Egan J in Ireland. In my judgment it would not; indeed I think that it would be a travesty of justice. Not only would the plaintiffs be required to re-litigate matters which have twice been extensively investigated and decided in their natural forum, but it would run the risk of inconsistent verdicts being reached, not only as between the English and Irish courts, but as

---

[14] [1977] 1 WLR 510.
[15] At p. 515 (italics supplied).
[16] [1958] AC 95, 102.
[17] [1990] 3 WLR 347, 358.
[18] Ibid.
[19] Ibid. 361–2.

between the defendants themselves . . . Public policy requires that there should be an end of litigation and that a litigant should not be vexed more than once in the same cause.[20]

The implications of the Court of Appeal's holding in *House of Spring Gardens Ltd.* v. *Waite and others* are perhaps threefold. Two of these are fairly specific; the third is more general but may turn out to be the most far-reaching. Each in its separate way may be seen as a manifestation of a new judicial willingness to contain or mitigate resort to the defence of fraud in actions concerned with the recognition and enforcement of foreign judgments.

First and most obviously it has been made clear that, if the issue of fraud has already been re-litigated in separate proceedings in the country of original rendition, the issue cannot be re-opened in England in the absence of fresh evidence. One may perhaps optimistically conjecture that considerations of finality would similarly prevail if the earlier separate proceedings had been in a third country. Suppose, for example, that there had been no proceedings before Egan J, but the plaintiffs had sought to enforce Costello J's judgment in, say, Scotland or France, and the Scots or French court had after investigation found no fraud. If, the defendants having failed to satisfy the Scots or French judgment, the plaintiffs had then sought to bring an action on that judgment in England, surely it should not be open to the defendants to raise the issue of fraud. Again one may conjecture, although less optimistically, about a different type of variant on the situation in the *House of Spring Gardens* case. Would it have made any difference there if the issue of fraud had not been raised before Costello J, but had been raised for the first time before Egan J? In other words, is an English court to require that the issue has been litigated twice before it will decline itself to investigate fraud? Or would even then the argument that it would not be Egan J's judgment which was being impeached prevail?

The second implication of the Court of Appeal's decision is to be seen in its willingness to find the necessary relationship of privity between Mr McLeod and the first and second defendants so as to preclude him from reopening the issue of fraud.

The third implication of the Court's decision derives from its willingness to invoke the doctrine of abuse of process. The availability of this 'route' is put in emphatic terms by Stuart-Smith LJ.[21] The facts of the instant case were, of course, strong: as his Lordship pointed out, the matters had 'twice been extensively investigated . . . in their natural forum'.[22] But this route may perhaps now have been opened for the purposes of more frequent escape from the legacy of *Abouloff* v. *Oppenheimer* and *Vadala* v. *Lawes*.

It is interesting to remember that, had the Civil Jurisdiction and Judgments Act 1982 been applicable to the Irish judgment, there could have been no question as to the issue of fraud as such. The defendants could then only have sought to show that its recognition and enforcement would be contrary to English public policy.[23]

P.B. CARTER

---

[20] Ibid. 358–9.
[21] Ibid. See p. 407, above.
[22] Ibid. 359.
[23] Civil Jurisdiction and Judgments Act 1982, Schedule 1; Convention on Jurisdiction and the Enforcement of Judgments in Civil and Commercial Matters, Article 27(1).

DECISIONS ON THE EUROPEAN CONVENTION ON HUMAN RIGHTS DURING 1990*

Right to a fair trial (Article 6(1))—the presumption of innocence (Article 6(2))—rights of the defence (Article 6(3))—discrimination (Article 14)—just satisfaction (Article 50)

Case No. 1. *Kamasinski* case.[1] The Court held unanimously that there had been a breach of Article 6(1) of the Convention, occasioned by the unilateral character of an inquiry carried out by the Austrian Supreme Court, when examining a plea of nullity which the applicant had lodged against a criminal conviction for fraud. However, the Court rejected numerous other complaints concerning the right to a fair trial, the presumption of innocence, the rights of the defence and discrimination. As just satisfaction under Article 50, the Court ordered the Government to pay the applicant the sum of 5,000 US dollars in respect of his costs and expenses.

The applicant in this case was an American who at the material time was living in Austria. In October 1980 he was arrested on charges of fraud and misappropriation arising out of several unpaid bills. As Mr Kamasinski could not speak or understand German, interpretation was provided during the pre-trial investigations. However, he did not receive written English translations of the records of the police interrogations, the records of his examination by the investigating judges, or the indictment. Dr S, a lawyer who was a registered interpreter, was appointed to be the applicant's defence counsel. Dr S did not attend the hearing at which the indictment was served on the applicant, but visited him several times in prison and submitted a number of written motions on his behalf.

Mr Kamasinski's trial took place before the Innsbruck Regional Court in April 1981. Interpretation was provided at the trial, though the applicant and the Government subsequently disagreed about its scope. The applicant was found guilty of aggravated fraud and misappropriation and sentenced to eighteen months' imprisonment. He was also ordered to pay more than 80,000 Austrian schillings to two private 'civil parties', who had appeared as witnesses for the prosecution and had claimed compensation. He was not supplied by the authorities with an English translation of the judgment. After the trial and at Mr Kamasinski's request a new official defence counsel was appointed. On behalf of the applicant he filed a plea of nullity and an appeal against sentence and against the compensation order.

In the nullity proceedings the Austrian Supreme Court conducted an inquiry into the scope of the interpretation provided at the trial. Neither the applicant nor his counsel was given notice of this inquiry, or advised of its results. The Supreme Court, sitting in chambers, rejected the plea of nullity in September 1981. In its decision it held that as a matter of law incomplete translation did not in itself constitute a ground for nullity, but that in any event the inquiry had shown that the

* © Professor J. G. Merrills, 1991. My thanks are due to the Registrar of the Court for his co-operation in the preparation of these notes. Cases decided in the latter part of 1990 which appeared too late for inclusion in the present survey will be covered in the next issue of the *Year Book*.

[1] European Court of Human Rights (ECHR), judgment of 19 December 1989, Series A, No. 168. The Court consisted of the following Chamber of Judges: Ryssdal (President); Matscher, Pinheiro Farinha, Sir Vincent Evans, Macdonald, De Meyer, Carrillo Salcedo (Judges).

interpretation provided was adequate. Because he was in custody, Mr Kamasinski had to seek permission to attend the public hearing of his appeal. However, his request was rejected by the Supreme Court in November 1981. His appeal was then dismissed by the Supreme Court after a hearing at which the applicant was represented by defence counsel. Mr Kamasinski was released from prison in the following month and deported to the United States in January 1982.

In his application to the Commission in November 1981 Mr Kamasinski complained of a large number of violations of the Convention. In its report in May 1988 the Commission expressed the opinion that as regards the proceedings before the Regional Court there had been no violation of the applicant's rights under Articles 6(1), 6(2) or 6(3) of the Convention. However, as regards the two sets of proceedings before the Supreme Court, the Commission found that there had been a violation of Article 6(1) in the nullity proceedings and a violation of Article 14, read in conjunction with Articles 6(1) and 6(3)(c), in the appeal proceedings. As regards the case as a whole, the Commission decided that no separate issue arose under Article 13 (right to an effective remedy before a national authority). The Commission then referred the case to the Court.

Article 6 of the Convention provides:

1. In the determination . . . of any criminal charge against him, everyone is entitled to a fair and public hearing within a reasonable time by an independent and impartial tribunal established by law. . . .
2. Everyone charged with a criminal offence shall be presumed innocent until proved guilty according to law.
3. Everyone charged with a criminal offence has the following minimum rights:
(a) to be informed promptly, in a language which he understands and in detail, of the nature and cause of the accusation against him;
(b) to have adequate time and facilities for the preparation of his defence;
(c) to defend himself in person or through legal assistance of his own choosing or, if he has not sufficient means to pay for legal assistance, to be given it free when the interests of justice so require;
(d) to examine or have examined witnesses against him and to obtain the attendance and examination of witnesses on his behalf under the same conditions as witnesses against him;
(e) to have the free assistance of an interpreter if he cannot understand or speak the language used in court.

One of the applicant's main contentions was that his first lawyer, Dr S, had not provided him with effective assistance in preparing and conducting his case and that as a result he had been denied a fair trial and the right to legal assistance which is guaranteed by Article 6(3)(c). The Court recognized that 'in itself the appointment of a legal aid defence counsel does not necessarily settle the issue of compliance with the requirements of Article 6(3)(c)',[2] because in its decision in the *Artico* case[3] in 1980 it had held that the Convention requires the provision of legal assistance which is effective. Nevertheless, it pointed out that 'a State cannot be held responsible for every shortcoming on the part of a lawyer appointed for legal aid purposes'.[4] It therefore agreed with the Commission that 'the competent national authorities are required . . . to intervene only if a failure by legal aid counsel to provide effective representation is manifest or sufficiently brought to their

---

[2] Judgment, para. 65.
[3] ECHR, judgment of 13 May 1980, Series A, No. 37, and this *Year Book*, 51 (1980), p. 332.
[4] Judgment, para. 65, quoting the judgment in the *Artico* case.

attention in some other way'.[5] Finding that this had not been shown to be the situation here, the Court held that there had been no violation of the applicant's specific rights under Article 6(3)(c), nor of the general safeguard in Article 6(1).

The applicant's other principal source of grievance derived from his inability to speak or understand German, which was, of course, the language in which the proceedings against him had been conducted. He alleged inadequate interpretation of oral statements and complained of a lack of written translation of official documents, which in his view had given rise to violations of Articles 6(3)(a) and 6(3)(e).

Dealing first with the applicant's right to the free assistance of an interpreter, the Court recalled that in its previous case law it has held that this entitlement applies not only to oral statements made at the hearing, but also to documentary material and pre-trial proceedings.[6] It explained, however, that Article 6(3)(e) does not require written translation of all items of written evidence or official documents. Rather, the assistance provided 'should be such as to enable the defendant to have knowledge of the case against him and to defend himself'.[7] Having regard to the interpretation facilities provided, the Court was not satisfied that Mr Kamasinski had been unable to comprehend the case against him, to make his replies understood, or to defend himself. It therefore rejected the claim based on Article 6(3)(e).

Turning to the defendant's right to be informed of the accusation in a language which he understood, the Court observed that whilst Article 6(3)(a) does not specify that a foreigner must be given the relevant information in writing, it does demonstrate that special attention must be paid to the notification of the accusation against such defendants. In particular, the Court stated, 'a defendant not conversant with the court's language may in fact be put at a disadvantage if he is not also provided with a written translation of the indictment in a language he understands'.[8] Although Mr Kamasinski had not in fact received a written translation of the indictment, the Court inferred from the evidence, including the applicant's behaviour, that as a result of the oral explanations which he had been given, he had been sufficiently informed of the accusations against him. There had therefore been no violation of Article 6(3)(a).

A number of other complaints relating to the proceedings before the Regional Court were also rejected. Thus the rule of Austrian law which restricts access to the court file to the lawyer of a represented defendant was held not to be incompatible with a defendant's right under Article 6(3)(b) to have adequate time and facilities for preparing his defence. Similarly, as regards the non-attendance of three witnesses at the trial, the Court held that there was no violation of Article 6(3)(d) because the applicant was in effect complaining about tactical decisions taken by his lawyer and the complaint about Dr S's competence had already been rejected. The provisions which allowed prosecution witnesses to be joined to criminal proceedings as 'civil parties' were held to be not inconsistent with the guarantee of a fair trial in Article 6(1) and to involve no unjustifiable discrimination contrary to Article 14. Finally, the questions which had been put to the applicant by the presiding judge after the reading out of the indictment were found to have involved no violation of the presumption of innocence in Article 6(2). The Court therefore

[5] Ibid.
[6] See the *Luedicke, Belkacem and Koç* case, Series A, No. 29, and this *Year Book*, 49 (1978), p. 315.
[7] Ibid., para. 74.
[8] Ibid., para. 79.

concluded that, whether taken individually or cumulatively, the alleged deficiencies in the proceedings at first instance did not give rise to any violations of the Convention.

As regards the subsequent proceedings before the Supreme Court, Mr Kamasinski's first complaint concerned the inquiry into the scope of interpretation at his trial. As he had not been able to participate in the inquiry, the applicant claimed that his rights under Article 6(1) had not been respected. The European Court upheld this complaint. When examining this point, the Court declared that 'it is an inherent part of a "fair hearing" in criminal proceedings as guaranteed by Article 6(1) that the defendant should be given an opportunity to comment on evidence obtained in regard to disputed facts even if the facts relate to a point of procedure rather than the alleged offence as such'.[9] In conducting its factual inquiry the Supreme Court had failed to observe the principle that contending parties should be heard, although this is one of the principal guarantees of a judicial procedure. Consequently, even though the information obtained as a result of the inquiry was not the primary reason for the rejection of the applicant's nullity plea, the Court decided that in this respect there had been a violation of Article 6(1).

The applicant's other complaint concerned the appeal proceedings and raised an issue under Article 14, which provides:

> The enjoyment of the rights and freedoms set forth in this Convention shall be secured without discrimination on any ground such as sex, race, colour, language, religion, political or other opinion, national or social origin, association with a national minority, property, birth or other status.

Mr Kamasinski alleged that the refusal to allow him to be present at the hearing of his appeal involved discrimination as between appellants in custody, such as himself, and appellants at liberty and the 'civil parties' in his own case, who were under no such disability.

Unlike many of the other points raised by the applicant, this was an argument with some substance, but as with most of his earlier points, the Court rejected it. The Court's starting point was that 'the personal attendance of the defendant does not take on the same crucial significance for an appeal hearing . . . as it does for the trial hearing'.[10] This is therefore an area where the national authorities enjoy a margin of appreciation. The Court stated that the special features of the appeal procedure before the Austrian Supreme Court and the particular circumstances of Mr Kamasinski's appeal were both factors which must be taken into account. On the facts, the Court held that even if the applicant were assumed to be in a comparable position to appellants at liberty and 'civil parties', the national authorities 'had good reason for believing that there existed an objective and reasonable justification for any difference of treatment in regard to attendance at the appeal hearing'.[11] Accordingly, the Court held by 6 votes to 1 that no discrimination contrary to Article 14, in conjunction with Articles 6(1) and 6(3)(c), had occurred.[12]

The Court, like the Commission, decided that no separate issue arose under Article 13. The only remaining issue was therefore the 'just satisfaction' due to the applicant under Article 50, which provides:

---

[9] Ibid., para. 102.
[10] Ibid., para. 106.
[11] Ibid., para. 108.
[12] Judge De Meyer delivered a short separate opinion on this point.

If the Court finds that a decision or a measure taken by a legal authority or any other authority of a High Contracting Party is completely or partially in conflict with the obligations arising from the present Convention, and if the internal law of the said Party allows only partial reparation to be made for the consequences of this decision or measure, the decision of the Court shall, if necessary, afford just satisfaction to the injured party.

As only one of Mr Kamasinski's many complaints had been upheld, the question of compensation was not a difficult one. The applicant asked the Court to award him 1,000 dollars for each day of his incarceration in Austria, making a total of 435,000 dollars. The Court, however decided that in view of the nature and limited extent of the breach found, the judgment itself constituted adequate just satisfaction. The applicant's claim for costs and expenses was also substantial, although it included nothing for his American counsel who had agreed to accept a contingency fee.[13] The Court expressed doubt as to the necessity and reasonableness of a number of the applicant's claims and again recalled that he had succeeded on only one of the 'plethora of issues' he had raised. It therefore decided that in all the circumstances only a small proportion of the costs which he had claimed should be reimbursed.

Right to be informed of the nature and cause of an accusation (Article 6(3)(a))— right to a fair trial (Article 6(1))—exhaustion of domestic remedies (Article 26)— just satisfaction (Article 50)—jurisdiction of the Court (Article 45)

Case No. 2. Brozicek case.[14] In this case, which concerned Italy, the Court held by 15 votes to 5 that there had been violations of Articles 6(3)(a) and 6(1) of the Convention because the applicant was not informed of the charge against him in a language he could understand and because he had not been given a fair trial. It also decided unanimously that the respondent State must pay the applicant 4,027.27 Deutschmarks and 1,900 Swiss francs in respect of his costs and expenses.

In 1981 the applicant, who was a national of and resident in Germany, was convicted by an Italian court and given a suspended sentence of five months' imprisonment for having resisted the police and committed an assault causing bodily harm in 1975. He had been notified of the charge in 1976 when the authorities sent him a letter in Italian, which he had returned with a request that they write to him in a language he could understand. The authorities did not respond to this request, but in 1978 sent a second notification which had to be returned to the sender because Mr Brozicek claimed that he had changed his address. In the absence of any reply from the applicant, the prosecution had declared him untraceable. His trial and conviction had consequently taken place in his absence.

Mr Brozicek learned of his conviction in 1984 when he received a letter from the German authorities informing him that it had been entered in their criminal records in accordance with German law. When Mr Brozicek wrote to the Italian Ministry of Justice for information, he was told that he could lodge a 'late appeal' against the judgment if its notification to him had not been lawful. He did not, however, make use of this opportunity.

---

[13] The applicant was represented by Professor A. D'Amato of Northwestern University. Under the contingency arrangement, which the Court recognized as lawful, Professor D'Amato would have received twenty-five per cent of any amount awarded to Mr Kamasinski as financial compensation.

[14] ECHR, judgment of 19 December 1989, Series A, No. 167. This case was decided by the plenary Court.

In his application to the Commission in May 1984 Mr Brozicek alleged that he was the victim of violations of Articles 6(1) and 6(3)(a) of the Convention. In its report in March 1988 the Commission expressed the opinion that there had been a violation of both provisions. The Commission then referred the case to the Court.

It will be recalled from Case No. 1 that Article 6(1) guarantees the right to a fair trial, and Article 6(3)(a) provides that everyone charged with a criminal offence has the right 'to be informed promptly, in a language which he understands and in detail, of the nature and cause of the accusation against him'. Dealing first with the alleged violation of Article 6(3)(a), the Court observed that the judicial notification sent to the applicant in 1976 constituted an 'accusation' within the meaning of the Convention. Consequently, the Italian judicial authorities should have taken steps to comply with his request to receive the notification in German, or, as he had also suggested, in one of the official languages of the United Nations. As they had not demonstrated that in fact the applicant had sufficient knowledge of Italian to understand the notification, there had been a violation of the Convention. Mr Brozicek also maintained that the notification lacked the detail required by Article 6(3)(a) and in this respect too had resulted in a violation. However, the Court unanimously rejected this point on the facts.

The applicant's complaint that he had not received a fair trial was based on the argument that he had been tried *in absentia* and had not been given an opportunity to participate in the trial and to defend himself. The Court agreed. Pointing out that there was no evidence that Mr Brozicek intended to waive his right to participate in the trial, the Court explained that the first notification had just been found to violate Article 6(3)(a), whilst it was not satisfied that the second had been received. Furthermore, the President of the Italian court had not sought to notify the applicant in person of the summons to appear. Accordingly, the Court concluded that there had also been a violation of Article 6(1).

There remained the question of 'just satisfaction' for the applicant under Article 50 of the Convention. Mr Brozicek first asked the Court to declare the judgment against him void and to order it to be struck out of his record. However, the Court, following its established practice, observed that it did not have the power to do this and so rejected the request. The applicant also sought compensation for pecuniary and non-pecuniary damage, but these too were rejected; the first because the alleged loss was not related to the violation of the Convention, and the second because the Court found that its ruling constituted sufficient just satisfaction. The applicant was, however, awarded a modest sum on an equitable basis to cover his costs and expenses.

The five judges who dissented did so not because they disagreed with the Court's application of Article 6, but because they considered that the applicant had failed to exhaust his domestic remedies, with the result that his claim was inadmissible.[15] Article 26 of the Convention provides:

The Commission may only deal with the matter after all domestic remedies have been exhausted, according to the generally recognized rules of international law.

In the dissenting judges' view the applicant's failure to lodge a 'late appeal' meant this requirement had not been satisfied. This argument was examined at some length by the Court, but ultimately rejected on the ground that the remedy in question might not have been effective and in the particular circumstances was not suf-

[15] Joint dissenting opinion of Judges Thór Vilhjálmsson, Pettiti, Russo, De Meyer and Valticos.

ficiently available. The disagreement on this point, which appears to have caused the Court much more difficulty than the main issue, prompted one judge to suggest that it was time for the Court to overrule its decision in the *Vagrancy* cases[16] and leave questions of admissibility entirely to the Commission. Although this would be a radical step, what Judge Martens called 'the continuing and rather alarming increase in the Court's case-load'[17] may, as he suggested, call for a fresh look at accepted doctrine.

Right to the peaceful enjoyment of possessions (Article 1 of Protocol No. 1)—application to legislation imposing rent control—the margin of appreciation

Case No. 3. Mellacher and others case.[18] The Court decided that rent deductions granted to certain tenants under Austrian legislation introduced in 1981 had not infringed their landlords' property rights under Article 1 of Protocol No. 1.

The applicants in this case owned blocks of apartments in Graz, Innsbruck and Vienna. Three apartments, A, B and C, of different sizes were let to tenants under freely negotiated leases at monthly rents of ATS (Austrian Schillings) 1870, ATS 800 and ATS 3,800 respectively. The rents for apartments B and C were linked to the consumer price index and were periodically increased. In 1981 the Austrian Government introduced a Rent Act, which came into force in 1982, and which laid down a maximum rent which could be charged under new leases, according to the size and facilities of the premises. In the case of existing leases tenants could apply to have their rents reduced to 150 per cent of the statutory amount. The tenants of the apartments in question took advantage of the new legislation and successfully applied to have their rents reduced. The new rents ordered by the courts were: apartment A, ATS 300, apartment B, ATS 561 and apartment C, ATS 3,300. The landlords were also ordered to refund the overpayments which they had received after the date of the applications for a reduction.

In their applications to the Commission in 1983 and 1984 the landlords claimed that the rent reductions amounted to an unjustified interference with their right to the peaceful enjoyment of their possessions, as guaranteed by Article 1 of Protocol No. 1 to the Convention. It was also alleged in relation to apartment B that the reduction was discriminatory and contrary to Article 14, read in conjunction with Article 1. In its report in July 1988 the Commission expressed the opinion that there had been a violation of Article 1 in the case of apartments A and B, but not in the case of apartment C. It also considered that no separate issue arose under Article 14 in the application concerning apartment B. The Commission then referred the case to the Court.

Article 1 of the Protocol No. 1 is worded as follows:

Every natural or legal person is entitled to the peaceful enjoyment of his possessions. No one shall be deprived of his possessions except in the public interest and subject to the conditions provided for by law and by the general principles of international law.

The preceding provisions shall not, however, in any way impair the right of a State to

[16] ECHR, judgment of 18 June 1971, Series A, No. 12, and this *Year Book*, 46 (1972–3), p. 463.

[17] Separate opinion of Judge Martens, para. 4.4. For discussion of the significance of the Court's ruling in the *Vagrancy* cases, see Merrills, *The Development of International Law by the European Court of Human Rights* (1988), p. 44.

[18] ECHR, judgment of 19 December 1989, Series A, No. 169. This case was decided by the plenary Court.

enforce such laws as it deems necessary to control the use of property in accordance with the general interest or to secure the payment of taxes or other contributions or penalties.

It was agreed that the rent reductions complained of constituted an interference with the enjoyment of the applicants' rights as owners of the rented properties. However, the Court pointed out that even if they deprived the applicants of part of their income from the property, they did not amount to either a formal or a *de facto* expropriation, but rather constituted merely a control of the use of property. Accordingly, the case had to be considered under the second paragraph of Article 1. In this regard the Court recalled that in its previous case law it had held that in order to implement its social and economic policies in the field of housing, 'the legislature must have a wide margin of appreciation both with regard to the existence of a problem of public concern warranting measures of control and as to the choice of the detailed rules for the implementation of such measures'.[19] The legislature's judgment as to what is in the general interest must therefore be respected unless that judgment is 'manifestly without reasonable foundation'.[20] To determine this issue the Court had to consider both the aim of the interference and the question of proportionality.

The Court found that the 1981 Rent Act was intended to reduce excessive and unjustified disparities between rents for equivalent apartments and to combat property speculation. It was also intended to make accommodation more readily available at reasonable prices to less affluent members of the population, and at the same time to provide landlords with an incentive to improve substandard properties. Therefore, although the applicants claimed that the legislation was not intended to redress a social injustice, but to effect a redistribution of property, the Court, after reviewing the new law, was satisfied that it pursued a legitimate aim in the general interest.

The proportionality of the interference was a more complex question. In answer to the applicants' complaint that the legislation violated the principle of freedom of contract, the Court held that, 'in remedial social legislation and in particular in the field of rent control, which is the subject of the present case, it must be open to the legislature to take measures affecting the future execution of previously concluded contracts in order to attain the aim of the policy adopted'.[21] It also rejected the claim that the legislation was indiscriminate. Explaining that legislation which sought to establish an appropriate standard of rents for equivalent apartments must inevitably be general in its scope, the Court found that the various exceptions and exclusions provided for could not be said to be inappropriate or disproportionate. Recalling again the significance of the margin of appreciation, it stated that, 'Provided that the legislature remains within the bounds of its margin of appreciation, it is not for the Court to say whether the legislation represented the best solution for dealing with the problem or whether the legislative discretion should have been exercised in another way'.[22]

Finding that the rents laid down in the Act were intended to cover the cost of maintaining apartments at their existing standard, the Court held that account also had to be taken of other relevant provisions and in particular of the fact that under their existing contracts the landlords were entitled to charge a rent for each prop-

---

[19] Judgment, para. 45.
[20] Ibid.
[21] Ibid., para. 51.
[22] Ibid., para. 53.

erty 50 per cent higher than would be allowed under a new lease. Although it was true that the rent reductions were striking, especially in the case of apartment A, the Court decided that it did not follow that they constituted a disproportionate burden, or that the legislature could not reasonably decide that the original rents 'were unacceptable from the point of view of social justice'.[23] The Court therefore concluded that there had been no violation of Article 1 of Protocol No. 1 and, like the Commission, decided that it was unnecessary to examine the case under Article 14.

As regards apartment C the Court's decision was unanimous. As regards apartments A and B, however, it reached its decision by 12 votes to 5. The dissenting judges agreed with the view of the Commission that in these cases the reductions in rent were so drastic as to constitute a disproportionate interference with the applicants' rights. At first sight the question on which the Court was divided is one of degree; on closer consideration, however, it can be seen to have significant implications. The view that it is permissible to reduce the monthly rent of an apartment in a large city to 'the price of a simple meal for two persons in a cheap restaurant'[24] is plainly one which attaches no weight to market forces. More generally, to regard such matters as falling within the respondent's margin of appreciation is virtually to relinquish supervision of a major aspect of States' regulation of the use of property. The scope for rent control under the Convention is thus the kind of question which raises fundamental issues of economic and social policy and, as a corollary, invites reflection on the purpose and function of the Strasbourg system.

Right to liberty (Article 5(1))—application to detention of a psychiatric patient— the meaning of 'arrest' in Article 5(2)—right to have the lawfulness of detention decided 'speedily' (Article 5(4))—just satisfaction (Article 50)

Case No. 4. Van der Leer case.[25] The Court held unanimously that the circumstances in which the applicant was detained in a psychiatric hospital in the Netherlands had involved breaches of Articles 5(1), 5(2) and 5(4) of the Convention. The respondent State was ordered to pay the applicant 15,000 guilders by way of just satisfaction.

In November 1983 the applicant, Mrs Van der Leer, was admitted as a voluntary patient to a psychiatric hospital in the Netherlands. A week later, on the application of her husband, a local judge ordered her to be compulsorily confined in the same hospital for a period of six months. Mrs Van der Leer was given no opportunity to appear before the judge prior to this decision, nor was she immediately informed of it. In December 1983, having learned of the order, the applicant requested the hospital authorities to release her. When they refused, she at once applied to the District Court. The Court lifted the committal order in May 1984. In the meantime, however, Mrs Van der Leer had left hospital in January without authorization and later in that month the hospital had granted her probationary leave.

---

[23] Ibid., para. 56.
[24] Joint dissenting opinion of Judges Cremona, Bindschedler-Robert, Gölcüklü, Bernhardt and Spielmann.
[25] ECHR, judgment of 21 February 1990, Series A, No. 170. The Court consisted of the following Chamber of Judges: Ryssdal (President); Cremona, Spielmann, De Meyer, Carrillo Salcedo, Valticos, Martens (Judges).

In her application to the Commission in May 1984 Mrs Van der Leer alleged that she was the victim of violations of Articles 5(1), 5(2) and 5(4) of the Convention and also of Article 6(1). In its report in July 1988 the Commission expressed the unanimous view that the violations of Article 5 had been established, but that there had been no violation of Article 6(1). The Commission then referred the case to the Court.

The relevant parts of Article 5 provide:

1. Everyone has the right to liberty and security of person. No one shall be deprived of his liberty save in the following cases and in accordance with a procedure prescribed by law:

. . .

   (e) the lawful detention of persons for the prevention of the spreading of infectious diseases, of persons of unsound mind, alcoholics or drug addicts or vagrants;

. . .

2. Everyone who is arrested shall be informed promptly, in a language which he understands, of the reasons for his arrest and of any charge against him.

. . .

4. Everyone who is deprived of his liberty by arrest or detention shall be entitled to take proceedings by which the lawfulness of his detention shall be decided speedily by a court and his release ordered if the detention is not lawful.

As regards Article 5(1) Mrs Van der Leer claimed that the order authorizing her confinement had not been made 'in accordance with a procedure prescribed by law', because she was denied the hearing which it was clear that she was entitled to under the law of the Netherlands. To satisfy Article 5(1) it is, of course, not always sufficient to show that domestic law has been complied with, but this is certainly a necessary condition and the Government accepted that when making its decision the local court had failed to act properly. The Court therefore concluded that there had been a violation of Article 5(1).

The complaint under Article 5(2) raised an interesting point of interpretation. The Government argued that this provision had no bearing on the case because the words 'arrest' and 'charge' showed that it was only relevant to cases arising under the criminal law. The Court, however, rejected the Government's argument and agreed with the Commission that the words in question:

. . . should be interpreted 'autonomously', in particular in accordance with the aim and purpose of Article 5, which are to protect everyone from arbitrary deprivations of liberty. Thus the 'arrest' referred to in paragraph 2 of Article 5 extends beyond the realm of criminal law measures. Similarly, in using the words '*any* charge' ('*toute* accusation') in this provision, the intention of the drafters was not to lay down a condition for its applicability, but to indicate an eventuality of which it takes account.[26]

Having established that Article 5(2) was applicable, the Court pointed out that neither the manner in which Mrs Van der Leer had been informed of the measure depriving her of her liberty, nor the time it had taken to communicate this information to her, corresponded to the Convention's requirements. It followed therefore that there had been a breach of Article 5(2).

In relation to Article 5(4) the applicant complained of a two-fold violation. First, she argued that she should have been informed promptly of the grounds on which her detention was based in order to enable her to institute proceedings to challenge

---

[26] Judgment, para. 27.

its lawfulness. However the Court, having dealt with the information Mrs Van der Leer should have been given in the context of Article 5(2), held that it was unnecessary to discuss this matter again. The applicant's second argument was that the lawfulness of her detention had not been decided 'speedily', and here she was more successful. Although there was some argument over the period to be taken into consideration, the Court decided that neither the fact that the applicant absconded, nor that she was granted probationary leave, was relevant to the delay in dealing with her case, which began in December 1983 and ended in May of the following year with the judicial order for her release. Deciding that this period of five months was excessive, the Court ruled that consequently there had been a breach of Article 5(4).

Since the applicant's complaint concerning Article 6(1) was withdrawn in the course of the proceedings, the only other issue was just satisfaction for the various violations of Article 5. Mrs Van der Leer claimed 10,000 guilders in respect of pecuniary and non-pecuniary loss and more than three times that amount in costs and expenses. She was, however, in receipt of legal aid and had also rejected an offer from the Government to pay her 15,000 guilders by way of a friendly settlement. Making an equitable assessment, the Court concluded that it would be appropriate to award Mrs Van der Leer a total of 15,000 guilders in respect of all her claims under Article 50.

Right to the peaceful enjoyment of possessions (Article 1 of Protocol No. 1)—right of access to the courts and to a public hearing (Article 6(1))—waiver—just satisfaction (Article 50)

Case No. 5. Håkansson and Sturesson case.[27] The Court held unanimously that the authorities' handling of an application to retain land which had been bought by private purchasers in Sweden had involved a violation of Article 6(1) of the Convention, but no violation of Article 1 of Protocol No. 1. A claim by the applicants that further proceedings concerning the validity of a compulsory auction had also violated Article 6(1) was rejected by a majority of 6 votes to 1. As just satisfaction under Article 50, the Government was ordered to pay the applicants 60,000 Swedish crowns (SEK) in respect of their costs and expenses.

In 1979 the applicants, Mr Håkansson and Mr Sturesson, jointly bought an agricultural estate at an auction for 240,000 SEK. Under the Land Acquisition Act 1979 they were obliged to resell the estate within two years unless they obtained a permit to retain it from the County Agricultural Board. They applied to the Board for a permit, but their applications were rejected on the ground that the land was needed to rationalize agriculture in the area. On appeal the Board's decisions were upheld, in the final instance by the Government, whose decisions were not subject to review by the courts. An action in the Swedish courts to have the estate redeemed by the State was also unsuccessful.

At the request of the Board, a compulsory auction of the property was arranged for June 1985. Prior to the auction the Board rejected four of the five requests which various persons had made to buy the property. However, at the auction the

[27] ECHR, judgment of 21 February 1990, Series A, No. 171. The Court consisted of the following Chamber of Judges: Ryssdal (President); Thór Vilhjálmsson, Pettiti, Walsh, Russo, Bernhardt, Palm (Judges).

farmers whose request had been accepted by the Board made no bid. The Board therefore bought the property itself for 172,000 SEK, this being the minimum price fixed for the property by two special valuers appointed by the Board, as required by legislation. The applicants appealed to the Göta Court of Appeal to challenge the validity of the auction, but their appeal was rejected without an oral hearing. The Supreme Court subsequently refused their application for leave to appeal.

In their application to the Commission in April 1984 Mr Håkansson and Mr Sturesson complained of various violations of the Convention. In its report in October 1988 the Commission expressed the opinion that there had been violations of Article 6(1) arising out of the applicants' inability to challenge the administrative decisions not to grant them a permit to retain the estate and the absence of a public hearing before the Göta Court of Appeal. However, it also found that there had been no violation of Article 1 of Protocol No. 1 and decided that it was unnecessary to consider the case under Article 13. The Commission and the Government then referred the case to the Court.

Article 1 of Protocol No. 1, which has been quoted in Case No. 3, guarantees the right to the peaceful enjoyment of one's possessions and provides that 'no one shall be deprived of his possessions except in the public interest and subject to the conditions provided for by law . . . '. Since it was clear that the applicants' right to the peaceful enjoyment of their possessions had been interfered with, and that this interference amounted to a deprivation of property, the only question was whether the authorities' action could be justified. This depended on the lawfulness and purpose of the interference and the proportionality of the disputed measures.

The Court observed that the stated aim of the interference was the rationalization of agriculture, which was undoubtedly a legitimate 'public interest' for the purposes of Article 1. As the case originated in an individual application, the Court next pointed out that it was not called upon to examine whether the system established by the Land Acquisition Act, as such, complied with the rule of law, but rather to determine whether the manner in which it had affected the applicants had given rise to any violation of the Convention. In this regard the Court recalled that its power to review compliance with domestic law is limited and decided that, as the evidence did not show that the authorities' real concern was not the stated one, the impugned measures were in accordance with Swedish law. The Court also rejected the applicants' argument that the authorities had been inconsistent in dealing with the matter of permits and that the valuers had failed to act impartially. The Court therefore concluded that the measures in question had pursued a legitimate aim and were lawful.

On the issue of proportionality the Court found that the applicants had not been made to carry an individual and excessive burden as a result of the disputed measures. When buying the estate they had been aware that they might have to sell it on the conditions laid down in the 1979 Act; the resale had been effected in conformity with the Act and the price they had received, 'having regard to the margin of appreciation enjoyed by the national authorities',[28] could be regarded as reasonably related to the estate's value. The Court therefore held that there had been no violation of Article 1 of Protocol No. 1.

---

[28] Judgment, para. 54.

The other main issue concerned Article 6(1).[29] The Court decided that it was clear that the applicants considered that they were entitled to a permit to retain the estate. In the light of the Court's case law this meant that 'civil rights and obligations' were at stake in the ensuing disputes before the administrative authorities and the Göta Court of Appeal. Article 6(1) was therefore applicable to both sets of proceedings. Under Swedish law the dispute regarding the lawfulness of the refusal of a permit could be determined only by the Government in the final instance. Since its decisions were not open to review by any organ which could be considered a 'tribunal' for the purposes of Article 6(1), it followed that there had been a violation of that provision.

The absence of a public hearing before the Göta Court of Appeal raised a more difficult issue. That court was the only body to deal with all aspects of the applicants' complaints against the compulsory auction. Accordingly, the applicants were entitled to a public hearing there, as laid down by Article 6(1), and such a hearing could have been held under Swedish law. The applicants had not expressly waived their right to such a hearing, but the Court concluded they they had tacitly, but unequivocally, done so by failing to ask for a public hearing and accepting the Swedish court's normal procedure. The Court added that it did not appear that the litigation involved any questions of public interest which could have made a public hearing necessary. The Court therefore held by 6 votes to 1 that in this respect there had been no violation of Article 6(1).

As just satisfaction under Article 50 the applicants claimed a large sum, together with interest, as compensation for pecuniary damage. The Court, however, agreed with the Government that no causal link existed between the alleged damage and the violation of Article 6(1). This claim was therefore rejected, although the Court held on an equitable basis that the applicants were entitled to reimbursement of a proportion of their costs and expenses.

The most significant feature of this case is the Court's recognition that a right can be waived tacitly. From the case law on waiver it is clear that only certain of the rights protected by the Convention are subject to waiver and that when it is claimed that the doctrine applies, any waiver must be unequivocal.[30] While this requirement need not, perhaps, exclude the concept of a tacit waiver of rights altogether, there is force in the view of Judge Walsh that in rejecting part of the applicants' claim in this case the Court was in error because:

. . . only where both parties agree to a hearing other than in public can the mandatory provisions of Article 6(1) be waived. Any such waiver of a guaranteed right must be manifested by clear and unambiguous words from which the only reasonable inference to be drawn is that both parties were so agreed . . . silence cannot amount to such waiver, particularly, as in this case, where there is no evidence that the applicants ever contemplated a joint or several waiver.[31]

---

[29] For the text of Article 6(1) see Case No. 1. Like the Commission, the Court rejected a claim that there had been a violation of Article 1 of Protocol No. 1, taken in conjunction with Article 14, and decided that it was unnecessary to consider the issue of Article 13.

[30] See, for example, the *Colozza* case, Series A, No. 89, and this *Year Book*, 56 (1985), p. 339. For a survey of the evolution of the Court's jurisprudence on waiver and its significance, see Merrills, *The Development of International Law by the European Court of Human Rights* (1988), pp. 160–6.

[31] Partly dissenting opinion of Judge Walsh, para. 4.

Right to an effective remedy before a national authority (Article 13)—jurisdiction of the Court and the Commission

Case No. 6. Powell and Rayner case.[32] In this case, which concerned disturbance from aircraft noise to people living near Heathrow Airport, the Court held unanimously that there had been no violation of Article 13 of the Convention. In relation to certain other complaints which were raised by the applicants the Court held that it had no jurisdiction.

The two applicants lived near Heathrow Airport. Mr Powell lived in Esher which is several miles away. Since 1972, however, his house had been situated under a flight departure route which was in use for about four months each year. According to the Noise and Number Index (NNI), which is the official method of measuring disturbance, his property fell within a contour considered to be a low noise-annoyance rating. About half a million other people live within this contour area. Mr Rayner was a farmer and lived much closer. His home was situated just over a mile from the airport in direct line with the northern runway. It was frequently overflown and had a high NNI rating. Only about 6,500 people in the vicinity of Heathrow are exposed to noise levels equal to or greater than that suffered by Mr Rayner.

In English law the liability of aircraft operators in respect of damage caused to third parties on the ground is limited by the Civil Aviation Act 1982, section 76 of which has the effect of conferring exemption from liability in respect of noise emanating from aircraft flying at a reasonable height and observing the relevant air navigation and noise certification regulations. A certain number of noise abatement measures have been implemented at Heathrow Airport, which has grown steadily since its opening in 1946 to become the busiest international airport in the world. These include restrictions on night jet movements, approach procedures, noise monitoring and noise insulation grant schemes, as well as noise certification. The main forum for aircraft noise certification is the International Civil Aviation Organization. The standards set by this Organization are implemented in the United Kingdom by means of Air Navigation (Noise Certification) Orders.

The application in this case was first lodged with the Commission in December 1980 by a body called the Federation of Heathrow Anti-Noise Groups. In March 1984 the Commission rejected the Federation's complaint, but the application was then continued by Mr Powell and Mr Rayner, together with a third applicant whose claim was subsequently settled. The application complained of excessive noise levels resulting from the operation of Heathrow Airport and relied on Article 1 of Protocol No. 1 and Articles 6(1), 8 and 13 of the Convention. In 1985 and 1986 the claims of Mr Powell and Mr Rayner were declared admissible as regards Article 13, but inadmissible for the rest. In its report in January 1989 the Commission expressed the opinion that there had been a violation of Article 13 in relation to Mr Rayner's claim under Article 8, but not in relation to any of the other claims. The Commission then referred the case to the Court.

The first question was the scope of the case before the Court. The applicants sought to revive their complaints under Article 6 and Article 8, but were unsuccessful. Pointing out that these complaints had been rejected by the Commission at the admissibility stage, the Court held that it had no jurisdiction to rule on these

---

[32] ECHR, judgment of 21 February 1990, Series A, No. 172. The Court consisted of the following Chamber of Judges: Ryssdal (President); Thór Vilhjálmsson, Pettiti, Sir Vincent Evans, Spielmann, Palm, Foighel (Judges).

complaints except in the context of Article 13. Consequently, the only issue in the case was whether in respect of these complaints the applicants had an effective national remedy available.

Article 13 of the Convention provides:

Everyone whose rights and freedoms as set forth in this Convention are violated shall have an effective remedy before a national authority notwithstanding that the violation has been committed by persons acting in an official capacity.

There is a considerable amount of case law on this provision, and its effect is to establish that Article 13 requires a domestic remedy to be available only in respect of grievances which can be regarded as 'arguable' in terms of the Convention.[33] Thus the question in each case under Article 13 is whether the applicant's complaints in respect of the substantive articles concerned raise an arguable issue. This requires the Court to examine the particular facts and the legal issues in a way analogous to, but not identical with, the approach it would adopt if it were applying the main provision.

The applicants' claim under Article 6(1) was that they had been denied a right of access to the courts. Here the Court noted that the grievance was in essence directed against the terms of section 76(1) of the Civil Aviation Act because this limited their right to pursue a civil remedy. In the Court's view such a complaint did not bring into play either Article 6(1) or Article 13. To the extent that section 76(1) excluded liability in nuisance in certain circumstances there was no 'civil right' recognized in domestic law to attract the application of Article 6. 'In any event', the Court added, 'Article 13 does not go so far as to guarantee a remedy allowing a Contracting State's laws as such to be challenged before a national authority'.[34]

The claim under Article 8, which concerned the applicants' right to respect for their private life and home,[35] raised a more difficult question. The Court agreed that this provision was relevant to both applicants, since in each case, albeit to differing degrees, the quality of the applicant's private life and the scope for enjoying the amenities of his home had been adversely affected by aircraft noise. It pointed out, however, that the applicants had conceded that the operation of a major international airport pursues a legitimate aim, and that its negative impact on the environment cannot be entirely eliminated. Moreover, the Court noted that a number of measures had been introduced to control, abate and compensate for noise around the airport. These measures, progressively adopted as a result of consulting those concerned, had taken due account of established international standards, developments in aircraft technology and the varying levels of disturbance suffered by those living near Heathrow.

As regards the exclusion of liability in nuisance contained in section 76(1) of the Civil Aviation Act, the Court explained that successive Governments had taken the view that the problems posed by aircraft noise were better dealt with by specific regulatory measures than by actions under the common law. In the Court's view this was a matter which fell within the national authorities' margin of appreciation. In the light of the evidence there was 'no serious ground for maintaining that either

[33] See, for example, the *Boyle and Rice* case, Series A, No. 131, and this *Year Book*, 59 (1988), p. 383, and the *Plattform 'Ärzte für das Leben'* case, Series A, No. 139, and ibid., p. 401.
[34] Judgment, para. 36. A subsidiary assertion that the limited entitlement to sue permitted by section 76(1) was illusory was also rejected.
[35] For the text of Article 8 see Cases Nos. 12 and 13 below.

the policy approach to the problem or the content of the particular regulatory measures adopted by the United Kingdom authorities [gave] rise to violation of Article 8, whether under its positive or negative head'.[36] This was so even in the case of Mr Rayner, who had suffered a high level of disturbance and whose case had been carefully considered and, as regards Article 13, had been upheld by the Commission. The Court's conclusion was therefore that in relation to both applicants no arguable claim of violation of Article 8 had been made out, and accordingly there was no entitlement to a domestic remedy.

This case is discussed in detail in Ms Hampson's article elsewhere in this *Year Book*.[37] It is therefore unnecessary to comment further on it here, other than to say that it confirms that when a claim under one of the substantive provisions of the Convention has been rejected, it will normally be difficult to develop an alternative line of argument on the basis of deficiencies in domestic law. Moreover, although the Court is not applying the relevant substantive provisions directly in such cases, they give a good indication of the approach it is likely to adopt if it is called upon to do so. In this respect the treatment of Article 8 in the present case, and in particular the Court's emphasis on the respondent's margin of appreciation, suggests that those affected by aircraft noise have little protection at Strasbourg.

Right to a hearing before an 'impartial' tribunal (Article 6(1))—friendly settlement (Rule 49(2))

Case No. 7. Jón Kristinsson case.[38] Following a friendly settlement between the Icelandic Government and the applicant, the Court decided unanimously to strike this case out of its list.

In 1984 the applicant, who was an Icelandic citizen, was convicted by the Akureyri District Criminal Court of two traffic offences and sentenced to a fine. The trial took place before Mr S.J., representing the town magistrate, who is also chief of police, in his capacity as district court judge. Mr S.J. had previously dealt with the case as deputy to the chief of police. On appeal the Icelandic Supreme Court rejected the applicant's plea that since Mr S.J. had acted as both chief of police and judge, his case had not been heard by an impartial judge.

In his application to the Commission in April 1986 Mr Jón Kristinsson alleged that there had been a violation of Article 6(1) of the Convention. In its report in March 1989 the Commission expressed the unanimous opinion that this article had been violated. The Commission then referred the case to the Court.

In December 1989 the Court was informed that the Government and the applicant had concluded an agreement relating to the case. The agreement referred to an Act recently adopted by the Icelandic Parliament and due to come into force in 1992, which assigns the administration of the police to executive agents, to be known as magistrates, and criminal cases to district court judges, who will be independent of the executive. The terms of the agreement were as follows:

1. That the Icelandic State Treasury reimburse Mr Jón Kristinsson for his fine and the costs of the case he has paid, Icel. Kr. 26,650, with interest as from 12 May 1986, Icel. Kr. 53, 353, or a total of Icel. Kr. 80,003.

---

[36] Judgment, para. 45.
[37] See p. 279 above.
[38] ECHR, judgment of 1 March 1990, Series A, No. 171 B. The Court consisted of the following Chamber of Judges: Ryssdal (President); Cremona, Thór Vilhjálmsson, Matscher, Valticos, Martens, Palm (Judges). This was the first case involving Iceland to be referred to the Court.

2. That the Icelandic State Treasury pay Mr Jón Kristinsson the costs incurred by him for legal assistance on account of his application to the European Commission of Human Rights, totalling Icel. Kr. 461,130 when the financial assistance received by Mr Kristinsson from the European Commission of Human Rights has been taken into account.

3. That Mr Jón Kristinsson undertakes, following the payment of the above amounts and without receiving damages or any further payments from the Icelandic State Treasury, not to prosecute the case now before the European Court of Human Rights any further, and not to take any other legal action against the Government of Iceland before Icelandic or international courts on account of the facts described above.

4. That Mr Kristinsson accepts that the Icelandic State Treasury pays the above payments immediately, provided the European Court of Human Rights agrees to strike the case, referred to it by the European Commission of Human Rights, against the Government of Iceland out of its list in accordance with Rule 49 para 2 of the Rules of Court.

5. That the Icelandic Minister of Justice will request the Public Prosecutor of Iceland to have a note entered into the State Criminal Register relating to Jón Kristinsson, stating that the Government of Iceland have today, on account of the stand taken by the European Commission of Human Rights with regard to his application, concluded a settlement with him providing for refund of the amounts he was ordered to pay to the Icelandic State Treasury by the judgment of the Supreme Court of Iceland of 25 November 1985.

6. That the obligations here undertaken by the Government of Iceland, on the one hand, and Mr Jón Kristinsson, on the other, be automatically cancelled in case the European Court of Human Rights withholds its approval as referred to under (4) above.

In view of the settlement the Government requested the Court to strike the case off the list in accordance with Rule 49(2) of the Rules of the Court which provides:

When the Chamber is informed of a friendly settlement, arrangement or other fact of a kind to provide a solution of the matter, it may, after consulting, if necessary, the Parties, the Delegates of the Commission and the applicant, strike the case out of the list.

Since the applicant and the Commission had no objection, the only question was whether considerations of public policy required a continuation of the proceedings. Having regard to the modification of Icelandic law, to subsequent changes in domestic case law and practice, and to its own extensive case law on the issue of impartiality, the Court saw no reason to proceed with consideration of the case. It therefore unanimously decided to strike the case from the list.

Freedom of expression (Article 10)—the scope for national licensing of broadcasting in Article 10(1)—the meaning of 'prescribed by law' and 'necessary in a democratic society' in Article 10(2)—the concept of 'victim' in Article 25

Case No. 8. Groppera Radio AG and others case.[39] In this case, which concerned Switzerland, the Court held by 16 votes to 3 that a ban on cable retransmission in Switzerland of programmes broadcast from Italy had not infringed the applicants' right to impart information and ideas regardless of frontiers. Accordingly, there had been no violation of Article 10 of the Convention.

The applicants in this case were a Swiss limited company, Groppera Radio AG, and three Swiss citizens: M, the director and legal representative of the company, and F and C, two journalists who were employees. In October 1983 Groppera

---

[39] ECHR, judgment of 28 March 1990, Series A, No. 173. This case was decided by the plenary Court.

Radio AG, acting through an Italian subsidiary, began using a powerful transmitter in Italy to broadcast radio programmes to audiences in Switzerland. The transmitter was very close to the border and the programmes were not only received by individuals directly, but also picked up and retransmitted by Swiss cable network companies which are widely used in Switzerland owing to the mountainous nature of the country.

In January 1984 an Order entered into force which prohibited Swiss cable network companies from broadcasting radio programmes emanating from transmitters which did not satisfy the requirements of international conventions and agreements on radio and telecommunications. As a result, most Swiss companies ceased to broadcast the programmes in question. However, one company, the M co-operative, continued to do so and was consequently the subject of proceedings instituted by the Swiss postal and telecommunications authorities. Subsequently, the M co-operative brought an administrative law appeal in the Swiss Federal Court and Groppera Radio AG joined those proceedings. In June 1985 the appeal was dismissed, mainly on the ground that as the transmitter in Italy had been destroyed by lightning in August 1984, the appellants no longer had any legal standing.

In their applications to the Commission in February 1984 the applicants complained of violations of Articles 10 and 13 of the Convention. In its report in October 1988 the Commission expressed the opinion by 7 votes to 6 that there had been a breach of Article 10, but unanimously rejected the claim based on Article 13. The Commission and the Government then referred the case to the Court.

Before it could address the merits of the case, the Court had to deal with a preliminary objection from the Government based on Article 25(1). This provides that:

The Commission may receive petitions . . . from any person . . . claiming to be the victim of a violation by one of the High Contracting Parties of the rights set forth in this Convention . . .

The Government argued that by reason of their situation, the various applicants could not claim to be 'victims' within the meaning of this provision. The Court, however, rejected the submission. It explained that according to its case law a 'victim' is the person directly affected by the act or omission in question, whether or not there is detriment suffered. It found that the applicants had all been affected by the Order complained of, and the decisions of the postal and telecommunications authorities, even though these were not formally directed at the applicants, who had continued to broadcast over the air freely. It also held that there was no ground for distinguishing between the different applicants, as they all had a direct interest in the continued transmission of the programmes by cable. Finally, it attached no importance to the fact that the applicants were not subscribers to the cable network. The Government's preliminary objection was therefore dismissed.

The main issue concerned the scope and application of Article 10 of the Convention, which provides:

1. Everyone has the right to freedom of expression. This right shall include freedom to hold opinions and to receive and impart information and ideas without interference by public authority and regardless of frontiers. This Article shall not prevent States from requiring the licensing of broadcasting, television or cinema enterprises.
2. The exercise of these freedoms, since it carries with it duties and responsibilities, may be

subject to such formalities, conditions, restrictions or penalties as are prescribed by law and are necessary in a democratic society, in the interests of national security, territorial integrity or public safety, for the prevention of disorder or crime, for the protection of health or morals, for the protection of the reputation or rights of others, for preventing the disclosure of information received in confidence, or for maintaining the authority and impartiality of the judiciary.

To establish the applicability of this provision the Court stated that it was unnecessary to give a precise definition of what the Convention means by 'information' and 'ideas'. Instead it simply observed that 'both broadcasting of programmes over the air and cable retransmissions of such programmes are covered by the right enshrined in the first two sentences of Article 10(1), without there being any need to make distinctions according to the content of the programmes'.[40] The authorities' decisions had prevented the subscribers in the relevant area from receiving Groppera Radio AG's programmes by retransmission. They therefore amounted to 'interference by public authority' with the exercise of freedom of expression.

The next question was whether the interference could be justified by virtue of the reference to the licensing of broadcasting in Article 10(1). The Court agreed with the Government that this sentence was applicable, but pointed out that its scope had to be assessed in the context of the article as a whole and in particular in relation to the requirements of Article 10(2). A comparison with neighbouring provisions suggested that the reference to licensing was not intended to be a major limitation on freedom of expression:

There is no equivalent of the sentence under consideration in the first paragraph of Articles 8, 9 and 11, although their structure is in general very similar to that of Article 10. Its wording is not unlike that of the last sentence of Article 11(2). In this respect, however, the two Articles differ in their structure. Article 10 sets out some of the permitted restrictions even in paragraph 1. Article 11, on the other hand, provides only in paragraph 2 for the possibility of special restrictions on the exercise of the freedom of association by members of the armed forces, the police and the administration of the State, and it could be inferred from this that those restrictions are not covered by the requirements in the first sentence of paragraph 2, except for that of lawfulness ('lawful'/'légitimes'). A comparison of the two Articles thus indicates that the third sentence of Article 10(1), in so far as it amounts to an exception to the principle set forth in the first and second sentences, is of limited scope.[41]

This conclusion was also supported by the omission of an equivalent reference from Article 19 of the International Covenant on Civil and Political Rights. The Court therefore concluded that the reference to licensing in Article 10(1) was included to make it clear that States are permitted to control the way in which broadcasting is organized in their territories, particularly in its technical aspects, but not to remove any licensing arrangements which might be adopted from the requirements of Article 10(2). It was therefore necessary for the Court to determine whether the interference complained of here was 'prescribed by law', had a legitimate aim or aims and was 'necessary in a democratic society' in order to achieve them.

It is clear that in order to be 'prescribed by law' it is not enough for an interference with an applicant's rights to have a basis in domestic law; it is also necessary for the law in question to be sufficiently precise and accessible for the applicant to

[40] Judgment, para. 55.
[41] Ibid., para. 61.

be able to regulate his conduct thereby. The interesting question in this case was whether these criteria could be satisfied by an Order which made only a very general reference to certain rules of international law. The Government maintained that it could. The applicants, on the other hand, while acknowledging the relevance of international law in this context, submitted that the relevant rules of telecommunications law were not sufficiently accessible or precise for a citizen to be able to adapt his behaviour to them.

The Court observed that 'the scope of the concepts of foreseeability and accessibility depends to a considerable degree on the content of the instrument in issue, the field it is designed to cover and the number and status of those to whom it is addressed'.[42] In the present case the relevant provisions of international telecommunications law were highly technical and complex and were intended primarily for specialists. The Official Collection of Federal Statutes gave such specialists information as to how they could be obtained and it was reasonable to expect a company engaged in broadcasting across a frontier to seek the necessary information. Moreover, the various instruments containing the rules were themselves not lacking in clarity or precision. The Court therefore concluded that the disputed measures were 'prescribed by law'.

The Court also ruled that the interference complained of had a legitimate purpose because it pursued two aims which were fully compatible with the Convention, namely the maintenance of orderly international telecommunications and the protection of the rights of others. Thus the only remaining issue was whether the interference could be regarded as 'necessary in a democratic society', for the achievement of these aims. To answer this question the Court took a number of factors into account. It noted that once the Order came into force most Swiss cable companies ceased transmitting Groppera Radio AG's programmes, and the Swiss authorities never tried to jam the broadcasts in question. The disputed ban was imposed on the M co-operative, which was a Swiss company, and whose subscribers all lived in Switzerland and continued to receive the programmes of several other stations. Lastly and above all:

. . . the procedure chosen could well appear necessary in order to prevent evasion of the law; it was not a form of censorship directed against the content or tendencies of the programmes concerned, but a measure taken against a station which the authorities of the respondent State could reasonably hold to be in reality a Swiss station operating from the other side of the border in order to circumvent the statutory telecommunications system in force in Switzerland.[43]

The Court therefore decided the national authorities did not overstep the margin of appreciation left to them under the Convention. As the Court found that the disputed measure was in accordance with Article 10(1) and satisfied the requirements of Article 10(2), it concluded that there had been no breach of the Convention.[44]

Several members of the Court delivered separate opinions. Judge Pinheiro Farinha agreed with the decision, but considered that as the Convention permits licensing, it was unnecessary to apply Article 10(2). Judge Valticos also concurred, but held that as the broadcasts of Groppera Radio AG consisted mainly of light entertainment, its activities lay outside the ambit of Article 10. Judges Matscher

[42] Ibid., para. 68.
[43] Ibid., para. 73.
[44] Since the applicants had not pursued the issue of Article 13, the Court held that it had no need to consider this provision.

and Bindschedler-Robert rejected that view, but also said that they could easily imagine programmes which in no way involved the communication of 'information and ideas' and which would therefore not be protected. Judge Pettiti dissented and explained in some detail why he considered that the Court had paid insufficient attention to the jurisdictional aspects of the case. Judges Bernhardt and De Meyer, on the other hand, dissented because they considered that the international illegality of the broadcasting activities of Groppera Radio AG, on which the decision seemed to hinge, had never been properly established.

Although this is not the first case in which the Court has had to consider the relation between the Convention and other international obligations,[45] it is the first in which it has examined the incorporation into domestic law of restrictions permitted or required by international law. It is also the first occasion on which the question of broadcasting has arisen in the context of Article 10. In the *Autronic AG* case (Case No. 16), which also involved Switzerland, both of these matters were considered again.

Right to legal assistance (Article 6(3)(c))—application to unsuccessful criminal appeal—just satisfaction (Article 50)

Case No. 9. Granger case.[46] The Court held unanimously that the refusal of legal aid for representation at the hearing of a criminal appeal in Scotland had given rise to a violation of Article 6(3)(c), taken together with Article 6(1) of the Convention. As regards just satisfaction under Article 50, the Court held by 4 votes to 3 that the United Kingdom must pay the applicant £1,000 for non-pecuniary damage, and unanimously that it must pay him £7,000 in respect of his costs and expenses.

In 1984 Mr Granger appeared as a principal witness for the Crown at the trial in Glasgow of a number of persons accused of arson and murder. Earlier, in signed statements, he had given the police details of how the crimes had been committed and named the perpetrators. When in the witness box, however, he denied all knowledge of the crimes and claimed that the statements had been made up by the police, who had forced him to sign them.

Mr Granger was then arrested and prosecuted for perjury. After a trial which lasted four weeks he was convicted on three charges relating to his evidence at the murder trial, but acquitted on two others. He was sentenced to five years' imprisonment. At his trial Mr Granger received legal aid, but when he appealed against his conviction the Supreme Court Legal Aid Committee refused his application for legal aid for representation at the hearing because it was not satisfied that he had substantial grounds for his appeal. Mr Granger's counsel had previously advised against an appeal, but his solicitor disagreed with this opinion.

The appeal was heard by the High Court of Justiciary in two stages, an adjournment being necessary when the court decided that it could not determine one of the grounds of appeal without considering a transcript of the evidence at the perjury trial. Mr Granger presented his case in person, reading out submissions which had

[45] For discussion of other situations in which the relation between the Convention and international law has been considered, see Merrills, *The Development of International Law by the European Court of Human Rights* (1988), chapter 9.

[46] ECHR, judgment of 28 March 1990, Series A, No. 174. The Court consisted of the following Chamber of Judges: Ryssdal (President); Matscher, Pettiti, Sir Vincent Evans, Russo, De Meyer, Martens (Judges).

been prepared by his solicitor. The Crown was represented by the Solicitor-General for Scotland, accompanied by junior counsel and a member of the Crown Office. The appeal was refused unanimously, the court having concluded that none of the grounds of appeal had substance and that there had been no miscarriage of justice at the applicant's trial.

In his application to the Commission in December 1985 Mr Granger claimed to be the victim of a violation of a number of articles of the Convention. In its report in December 1988 the Commission expressed the unanimous opinion that there had been a violation of Article 6(3)(c), but rejected, or decided that it was unnecessary to consider, his other complaints. The Government and the Commission then referred the case to the Court.

The main issue in this case concerned the application of Article 6(3)(c) which, it will be recalled, provides that everyone charged with a criminal offence is entitled to free legal assistance 'when the interests of justice so require'.[47] In previous cases involving Article 6(3) the Court has held that the guarantees in this paragraph are specific aspects of the right to a fair trial guaranteed by Article 6(1) and so has considered the two provisions together.[48] It adopted the same approach in this case. Since it was common ground that the applicant did not have sufficient means to pay for legal assistance, the only question was whether 'the interests of justice' required that he should be given it free. In this regard the Court explained that it would not be appropriate for it to consider the prospects of success of the applicant's appeal, or to express a view as to the correctness of the Legal Aid Committee's conclusion. Whether the interests of justice required a grant of legal aid had to be determined in the light of the case as a whole, and for this purpose 'not only the situation obtaining at the time the decision on the application for legal aid was handed down, but also that obtaining at the time the appeal was heard',[49] was material.

As the applicant had been convicted of perjury and sentenced to five years' imprisonment, the Court pointed out that there was no doubt as to the importance of what was at stake. At the appeal hearing the Solicitor General had addressed the court at length, whereas Mr Granger, 'who was unable to comprehend the legal niceties',[50] had not fully understood the speeches prepared for him, or the opposing arguments, and had the occasion arisen, would not have been able to reply effectively. The Court considered that these factors were of particular weight in view of the fact that one of the grounds of appeal was complex and had required the Scottish court to adjourn its hearing. When it became clear that this ground raised an important issue, the authorities, including the appeal court with its responsibility for the fair conduct of proceedings, should have had some means available whereby the refusal of legal aid could have been reconsidered.[51] In fact no such review took place. In all the circumstances the Court found that it would have been in the interests of justice for free legal assistance to be given to Mr Granger 'at least

---

[47] For the full text see Case No. 1.
[48] See, for example, the *Kostovski* case, Series A, No. 166, and this *Year Book*, 60 (1989), p. 564.
[49] Judgment, para. 46.
[50] Ibid., para. 20.
[51] The view that such a procedure was in fact available was the basis of a preliminary objection by the Government, claiming that the applicant had failed to exhaust his domestic remedies. However, the Court rejected this submission on the ground that the Government had failed to show that the remedy in question was sufficiently available.

at that stage for the ensuing proceedings'.[52] In this way he would have been able to make an effective contribution and the appeal court would have had the benefit of expert argument from both sides on a complex issue. The Court therefore concluded that there had been a violation of Article 6(3)(c), taken together with Article 6(1).

As claims involving Articles 5, 8 and 13 which the Commission had rejected had not been pursued before the Court, there remained only the question of just satisfaction under Article 50. Mr Granger claimed £10,000 for damage suffered as a result of his imprisonment and stress arising out of the case. The Court, however, agreed with the Government that no causal link had been established between the violation of Article 6 and the alleged pecuniary damage. On the other hand, a majority was prepared to accept that the applicant 'must have been left with a certain sense of isolation and confusion',[53] and on this account decided to award him £1,000 for non-pecuniary damage. As regards costs and expenses, the Court accepted in part a submission from the Government that the applicant's claim was excessive and, considering the matter on an equitable basis, awarded a reduced sum under this head.

Although the Court was unanimous on the substantive issue, this has all the appearance of a borderline case. The decisive factor was almost certainly the issue which prevented Mr Granger's appeal from being dealt with in a single hearing. It does not, of course, follow from the decision in this case that there is now an obligation to provide legal aid in every criminal appeal, for, as the Court emphasized, everything depends on an assessment of the particular facts. In relation to Article 6(3)(c), then, as elsewhere, the application of the Convention can often prove as troublesome as its interpretation.

Pre-trial detention (Article 5(3))—trial within a reasonable time (Article 6(1))— just satisfaction (Article 50)

Case No. 10. B v. *Austria.*[54] The Court held unanimously that the excessive length of criminal proceedings involving the applicant had resulted in a breach of Article 6(1) of the Convention. However, it held that there had been no breach of Article 5(3) because the duration of the applicant's detention on remand had not exceeded a reasonable time. As just satisfaction for the violation of Article 6(1) the Government was ordered to pay the applicant 150,000 Austrian schillings in respect of his costs and expenses.

B, an insurance broker and financial consultant, set up and acquired several companies in Austria, Liechtenstein and Switzerland. In 1979 he succeeded in persuading a number of persons to entrust him with large sums of money for investment. He then transferred a considerable proportion of these funds to the Federal Republic of Germany and Switzerland and used them for his own companies. In July 1980 B was arrested and criminal proceedings were begun against him by the Austrian authorities. In November 1982 the Salzburg Regional Court sentenced B to eight years' imprisonment on various counts of fraud and infringement of the exchange control legislation. However, the text of the judgment took nearly three

---

[52] Judgment, para. 47.
[53] Judgment, para. 52.
[54] ECHR, judgment of 28 March 1990, Series A, No. 175. The Court consisted of the following Chamber of Judges: Cremona (President); Thór Vilhjálmsson, Matscher, Walsh, Sir Vincent Evans, Russo, Palm (Judges).

years to prepare and was not served on B until August 1985. In November 1985 the Supreme Court dismissed his application for a declaration of nullity, but in the following month it allowed his appeal against his sentence, which was reduced to six years' imprisonment.

While awaiting the judgment, B had applied for his release on two occasions. He withdrew his first application in June 1985 because he was unable to meet the bail requirements. He immediately submitted a new application and offered to put up bail of 250,000 Austrian schillings. The Review Chamber of the Regional Court allowed his application, but set bail at two million schillings. As B was unable to find this amount, he remained in prison.

In his application to the Commission in January 1986 B complained that the length of the criminal proceedings had violated his rights under Article 6(1)[55] and that his detention on remand had violated Article 5(3). In its report in December 1988 the Commission upheld the first claim unanimously, but by a majority rejected the second claim. The Commission then referred the case to the Court.

Article 5(3) of the Convention provides:

> Everyone arrested or detained in accordance with the provisions of paragraph 1(c) of this Article shall be brought promptly before a judge or other officer authorized by law to exercise judicial power and shall be entitled to trial within a reasonable time or to release pending trial. Release may be conditioned by guarantees to appear for trial.

In order to decide whether the applicant's detention on remand had been unreasonably prolonged, the Court first had to establish the period to be taken into consideration. There was no doubt that this began in July 1980 when B was arrested; however the date at which it ended was a matter of dispute. The Government maintained that the relevant time was November 1982, when B was convicted. The applicant, on the other hand, claimed that it was December 1985, the date of the Supreme Court's judgment and therefore of his final sentencing.

In support of his argument B could point to the fact that in Austrian law if a conviction at first instance is followed by further proceedings, detention on remand is deemed to last until the Supreme Court's final decision. As against this, however, the Government could cite the decision in the *Wemhoff* case[56] where the Court held that as soon as a person has been convicted, his detention is no longer based on Article 5(1)(c), but on Article 5(1)(a), which authorizes 'the lawful detention of a person after conviction by a competent court'. The applicant invited the Court to review the decision in *Wemhoff* in the light of observations in its subsequent case law, but the Court declined to do so. Pointing out that the position of an individual after conviction is the subject of important differences among the Contracting States, the Court said that, like the Commission, it found it 'reasonable that the important guarantees of Article 5(3) of the Convention should not be made dependent on any one particular situation'.[57] It therefore concluded that the period of detention on remand ended in November 1982, having lasted just over two years and four months.

In deciding whether this period was unreasonable the Court recalled that according to its case law the persistence of reasonable suspicion that the person arrested has committed an offence is an essential condition for the validity of continued

---

[55] For the text of Article 6(1) see Case No. 1.
[56] ECHR, judgment of 27 June 1968, Series A, No. 7.
[57] Judgment, para. 39.

detention. After a certain time, however, more than this is needed and the Court must then examine the grounds for the judicial authorities' decision. When such grounds are relevant and sufficient, it must further determine whether the authorities displayed the necessary 'special diligence'.[58]

Applying the above principles to the facts, the Court found that the reasons given to justify B's continued detention were: the gravity of the offences, the risk of his absconding, the possibility of collusion and the danger that he might commit other offences. In the circumstances it accepted that all these reasons appeared to be relevant. Moreover, the judge had shown the necessary diligence during the investigation. An accused held in detention on remand was entitled to have his case given priority and conducted with particular expedition. However, the Court stated that this could not stand in the way of the efforts of judges to clarify the facts, to give both defence and prosecution the necessary facilities and to pronounce judgment only after adequate reflection. Since it did not appear that the Austrian courts had failed to act with the necessary despatch, the Court decided that there had been no breach of Article 5(3).

The claim that the criminal proceedings had exceeded a reasonable time, as in most cases where this aspect of Article 6(1) is in issue, simply required the application of well-established principles to the facts. The period to be taken into consideration ran from July 1980, when B was arrested, to December 1985, when the Supreme Court gave its final decision, a total of five years, five months and eighteen days. The Court noted the difficulties encountered during the preliminary investigation and others which derived from the nature of the accusations. However, by November 1982 the decision had been made and the main grounds for it outlined. It only remained for the judgment to be prepared, but owing to the judge's ineptitude, this had taken 33 months. The Government had taken certain steps in an attempt to speed up the process, but the Court ruled that these were inadequate. Therefore although it found that there were no shortcomings before the trial, and that the final stages before the Supreme Court were also satisfactory, the Court decided that the unreasonable delay in drawing up the judgment had occasioned a breach of the applicant's rights under Article 6(1).

As just satisfaction B claimed a large sum for loss of earnings and a further sum for non-pecuniary damage. However, the Court ruled that there was no causal connection between the breach of the Convention and the applicant's loss of earnings and held that as regards non-pecuniary damage, the judgment itself constituted adequate just satisfaction. The award in respect of the applicant's costs and expenses was just under half the sum B claimed.

The length of legal proceedings was also in issue in *Obermeier* (Case No. 17).

Just satisfaction (Article 50)—friendly settlement (Rule 53(4))

Case No. 11. Kostovski case.[59] In view of the friendly settlement between the Netherlands Government and the applicant in respect of the latter's claim for just satisfaction under Article 50 of the Convention, the Court unanimously decided to strike this case out of its list.

---

[58] See the *Matznetter* judgment, Series A, No. 10, at para. 12.

[59] ECHR, judgment of 29 March 1990, Series A, No. 170 B. This case was decided by the plenary Court.

In its judgment on the merits in 1989[60] the Court found that the applicant's conviction for armed robbery, which had been based to a substantial extent on the reports of statements by two anonymous witnesses, had given rise to a violation of Article 6(3)(d) of the Convention, taken together with Article 6(1). The question of just satisfaction under Article 50 was reserved.

In February 1990, soon after the decision on the merits, the Government notified the Court that it was willing to pay Mr Kostovski the sum of 150,000 Dutch guilders which he had claimed as compensation for the non-pecuniary damage resulting from his detention in the Netherlands. The applicant subsequently made known his agreement to this arrangement and the Delegate of the Commission indicated that he had no objection to it.

In cases of this kind the Court's function is defined by Rule 53(4) of the Rules of the Court which provides:

> If the Court is informed that an agreement has been reached between the injured party and the party liable, it shall verify the equitable nature of such agreement and, where it finds the agreement to be equitable, strike the case out of the list by means of a judgment . . .

In a short judgment the Court found that the agreement was equitable and therefore decided to strike the case from its list.

Right to respect for correspondence and private life (Article 8)—application to telephone tapping—the meaning of 'in accordance with the law' in Article 8(2)—just satisfaction (Article 50)

Cases Nos. 12 and 13. Kruslin case.[61] *Huvig case.*[62] In these cases, which concerned France, the Court held unanimously that there had been violations of Article 8 of the Convention because the interception of the applicants' telephone conversations had infringed their right to respect for their private life and correspondence. As just satisfaction under Article 50, France was ordered to pay the first applicant 20,000 French francs in respect of his costs and expenses.

These cases originated in applications lodged with the Commission in August 1984 by two French citizens, Mr and Mrs Huvig, and in October 1985 by Mr Kruslin, who was also French. In 1973 Mr Huvig, who ran a fruit and vegetable business with his wife's assistance, was the subject of a complaint alleging tax evasion and false accounting. The investigating judge in the case issued a warrant to the local gendarmerie requiring them to monitor all the Huvigs' telephone calls, and as a consequence in April 1974 their telephone was tapped for a period of 28 hours. Subsequently charges were brought against Mr and Mrs Huvig and in 1982 they were convicted on nearly all of them. On appeal their convictions were upheld and their sentences of imprisonment were increased. In 1984 an appeal by the applicants to the Court of Cassation was dismissed.

Mr Kruslin was committed for trial in 1985 on charges of aiding and abetting a murder, aggravated theft and attempted theft. One item of evidence was a record-

---

[60] ECHR, judgment of 20 November 1989, Series A, No. 166, and this *Year Book*, 60 (1989), p. 564.

[61] ECHR, judgment of 24 April 1990, Series A, No. 176 A. The Court consisted of the following Chamber of Judges: Ryssdal (President); Bindschedler-Robert, Gölcüklü, Matscher, Pettiti, Walsh, Sir Vincent Evans (Judges).

[62] ECHR, judgment of 24 April 1990, Series A, No. 176 B. This case was decided by the same Chamber as the previous case.

ing of a telephone conversation which the applicant had had on a line belonging to a third party. This recording had been made at the request of an investigating judge in connection with other proceedings. An attempt to challenge the admissibility of the recording before the Court of Cassation was unsuccessful and Mr Kruslin was eventually convicted of armed robbery.

In their applications to the Commission all the applicants complained that they were victims of violations of Article 8 of the Convention. In its reports in December 1988 the Commission expressed the opinion that this provision had been violated. The Commission then referred both cases to the Court.

Article 8 of the Convention provides:

1. Everyone has the right to respect for his private and family life, his home and his correspondence.
2. There shall be no interference by a public authority with the exercise of this right except such as is in accordance with the law and is necessary in a democratic society in the interests of national security, public safety or the economic well-being of the country, for the prevention of disorder or crime, for the protection of health or morals, or for the protection of the rights and freedoms of others.

There was no doubt that in both cases the interceptions complained of amounted to interferences by a public authority with the exercise of the applicants' right to respect for their correspondence and private life. The question was therefore whether such interferences were justified under Article 8(2). Here the first issue was whether they were 'in accordance with the law'.

In its previous case law, including its earlier decisions on telephone tapping,[63] the Court has established that this expression requires that the impugned measure should have some basis in domestic law, but also relates to the quality of the law in question, which must be accessible to the person concerned, foreseeable in its application and compatible with the rule of law. Whether the first condition had been satisfied in this case was a matter of disagreement, with the Government maintaining that case law, as well as legislation, could be taken into account, and the Commission and the applicant taking the opposite view. On this point the Court agreed with the Government. Explaining that it was primarily for the national authorities, and in particular for the courts, to interpret and apply domestic law, the Court said that it was not its function to express an opinion contrary to theirs as to whether the ordering of telephone tapping by investigating judges was compatible with the Criminal Code. For many years the French courts had regarded the Code as providing a legal basis for telephone tapping and settled case law of this kind could not be disregarded. Adding that in relation to Article 8(2) and similar clauses the Court had 'always understood the term "law" in its "substantive" sense, not its "formal" one',[64] it concluded that in view of the domestic jurisprudence the interferences complained of had the necessary basis in French law.

There was no doubt that the law in question was sufficiently accessible. The issue of foreseeability, however, the Court found to be less straightforward. Although the Court was concerned with the particular facts and not with the merits

---

[63] See the *Malone* case, Series A, No. 82, and this *Year Book*, 55 (1984), p. 387, and the *Klass* case, Series A, No. 28, and this *Year Book*, 49 (1978), p. 310.

[64] *Kruslin* judgment, para. 29.

of the law in the abstract, it held that it had to assess the relevant law by reference
to the fundamental principle of the rule of law. More specifically, it held that:

> Tapping and other forms of interception of telephone conversations represent a serious
> interference with private life and correspondence and must accordingly be based on a 'law'
> that is particularly precise. It is essential to have clear, detailed rules on the subject,
> especially as the technology available for use is continually becoming more sophisticated.[65]

The Government had listed seventeen safeguards which they said were provided
in French law and which related either to the way in which telephone tapping was
carried out, the use which was made of the results, or the means of correcting irre-
gularities. The Court stated that it did not minimize the value of several of the safeguards, but noted that only some of them were expressly set out in the Criminal
Code. Others had been laid down piecemeal in judgments, while some had not yet
been incorporated in case law at all. In general the Court was not satisfied that the
system provided adequate safeguards against possible abuses:

> For example the categories of people liable to have their telephones tapped by judicial
> order and the nature of the offences which may give rise to such an order are nowhere
> defined. Nothing obliges a judge to set a limit on the duration of telephone tapping. Simi-
> larly unspecified are the procedure for drawing up the summary reports containing inter-
> cepted conversations; the precautions to be taken in order to communicate the recordings
> intact and in their entirety for possible inspection by the judge . . . and by the defence; and
> the circumstances in which recordings may or must be erased or the tapes be destroyed, in
> particular where an accused has been discharged by an investigating judge or acquitted by a
> court.[66]

Pointing out that 'the information provided by the Government on these various
points shows at best the existence of a practice, but a practice lacking the necessary
regulatory control in the absence of legislation or case-law',[67] the Court decided
that 'French law, written and unwritten, does not indicate with reasonable clarity
the scope and manner of exercise of the relevant discretion conferred on the public
authorities'.[68] It therefore concluded that in both cases there had been a breach of
Article 8.

In view of its decision that the interference with the applicants' rights was not 'in
accordance with the law', the Court held that it was unnecessary to consider the
other requirements of Article 8(2), namely the purpose and necessity of the interference. The only remaining issue was therefore the question of just satisfaction
under Article 50.

Mr Kruslin claimed a large sum by way of compensation in respect of the fifteen-
year prison sentence he had received, together with reimbursement of his lawyer's
fees and expenses in two sets of national proceedings. In relation to the former
claim, however, the Court considered that the finding that there had been a breach
of Article 8 afforded him sufficient just satisfaction and that it was consequently
unnecessary to grant pecuniary compensation. As regards his costs and expenses,
the Court disallowed the claim with respect to proceedings which were not the subject of the application, but allowed the remainder. Mr and Mrs Huvig had asked

---

[65] Ibid., para. 33.
[66] Ibid., para. 35.
[67] Ibid.
[68] Ibid., para. 36.

the Commission to award them 'just compensation', but before the Court had not sought either compensation or reimbursement of their costs and expenses. As these are not matters which the Court is required to examine on its own motion, it found that it was unnecessary to apply Article 50 in their case.

Trial within a reasonable time (Article 6(1))—friendly settlement (Rule 49(2))

Case No. 14. Clerc case.[69] Following a friendly settlement between the French Government and the applicant, the Court decided unanimously that this case should be struck out of its list.

The applicant in this case was the manager of a French company. After an administrative inquiry an investigating judge started an investigation in 1974 into the criminal liability of officials associated with companies which were suspected of having taken concerted action inimical to free competition. The applicant was one of the officials investigated. Following a complex set of interrelated proceedings, the defendants were eventually acquitted of the charges against them in April 1987.

In his application to the Commission in August 1986 Mr Clerc claimed that the length of the proceedings against him had exceeded a reasonable time and had consequently violated Article 6(1) of the Convention. In its report in July 1989 the Commission expressed the unanimous opinion that there had indeed been a violation. The Commission then referred the case to the Court.

In April 1990 the Court was informed that a friendly settlement had been concluded under which the Government was to pay the applicant the sum of 100,000 French francs in respect of all his claims.

As we have seen in Case No. 7, the Court's function in situations of this kind is to consider whether it is appropriate to strike a case out of its list in accordance with Rule 49(2) of the Rules. Accordingly, the Court took formal note of the friendly settlement. It then observed that there were no reasons of public policy to justify retaining the case, since the nature and scope of the Contracting States' obligations in relation to this aspect of Article 6(1) had been examined in several previous decisions, including most recently B v. Austria (Case No. 10). The Court therefore decided to strike the case out of the list.

Right to a public hearing on a 'criminal' charge (Article 6(1))—validity of a reservation (Article 64)—freedom of expression (Article 10)—just satisfaction (Article 50)

Case No. 15. Weber case.[70] The Court held that Switzerland had violated Article 6(1) of the Convention when the applicant was fined for a breach of the Vaud Code of Criminal Procedure without a public hearing. It also held that the applicant's conviction and sentence involved a violation of Article 10 because they constituted an interference with the exercise of his right to freedom of expression for which

---

[69] ECHR, judgment of 26 April 1990, Series A, No. 176 C. The Court consisted of the following Chamber of Judges: Ryssdal (President); Thór Vilhjálmsson, Matscher, Pettiti, Sir Vincent Evans, Macdonald, Martens (Judges).

[70] ECHR, judgment of 22 May 1990, Series A, No. 177. The Court consisted of the following Chamber of Judges: Ryssdal (President); Bindschedler-Robert, Walsh, Macdonald, Russo, De Meyer, Foighel (Judges).

there was no justification. The Government was ordered to pay the applicant 8,482.5 Swiss francs in respect of his costs and expenses.

The applicant in this case was a Swiss journalist who lived in the Canton of Vaud. In 1980 he brought an action for defamation against the author of a letter which had appeared in a local newspaper. In March 1982, while these proceedings were pending, he gave a press conference at which he described the proceedings and also indicated that he had lodged a criminal complaint against an investigating judge who had ordered the production of the accounts of certain associations run by Mr Weber. Some of this information had already been disclosed by the applicant at an earlier press conference. In April 1982 the President of the Criminal Cassation Division of the Vaud Cantonal Court, in summary proceedings, imposed a fine of 300 Swiss francs on the applicant for breaching the secrecy of the investigation at the March press conference, contrary to the Code of Criminal Procedure. Appeals by Mr Weber against this decision to the Divisional Court and the Federal Court were unsuccessful.

In his application to the Commission in 1984 Mr Weber complained that the summary proceedings had been conducted in private and without the parties and witnesses being questioned and argued that this constituted a breach of Article 6(1) of the Convention. He also claimed that the imposition of the fine constituted an unjustified interference with his right to freedom of expression, contrary to Article 10. In its report in March 1989 the Commission expressed the opinion that Article 6(1) was not applicable to the proceedings in question, but upheld the claim on the basis of Article 10. The Commission and the Government then referred the case to the Court.

The text of Article 6(1) has been quoted in Case No. 1 above and the present case called for the Court to consider its scope. In the Government's submission the dispute fell outside Article 6(1) because in Vaud law the proceedings taken against the applicant were not 'criminal' but disciplinary. The Commission had accepted this argument, but the Court rejected it. It is clear from the Court's case law that the concept of a criminal charge is an autonomous one[71] and that to decide whether a given situation is covered by the Convention it is necessary to have regard both to the nature of the particular offence and the nature and degree of severity of the penalty incurred. Applying these criteria to the present facts, the Court found that the offence in question was one which potentially affected the whole population and was thus distinct from a disciplinary sanction applicable only to the members of a particular group or profession. Likewise, the penalty was a fine which could lead to imprisonment and was accordingly not insignificant. In the light of these considerations the Court concluded that the proceedings of which the applicant complained were criminal proceedings and were therefore covered by Article 6(1).

When Switzerland ratified the Convention in 1974 it made a reservation to Article 6(1) in the following terms:

The rule contained in Article 6(1) of the Convention that hearings shall be in public shall not apply to proceedings relating to the determination of civil rights and obligations or of any criminal charge which, in accordance with cantonal legislation, are heard before an administrative authority.

---

[71] See, for example, the *Öztürk* case, Series A, No. 73, and this *Year Book*, 55 (1984), p. 370, and the *Campbell and Fell* case, Series A, No. 80, and ibid., p. 381.

The rule that judgment must be pronounced publicly shall not affect the operation of cantonal legislation on civil or criminal procedure providing that judgment shall not be delivered in public but notified to the parties in writing.

The Government's alternative argument was that even if Article 6(1) was applicable, the reservation prevented Mr Weber from arguing that the proceedings before the Cantonal courts must be public.

The weakness in the Government's argument was that although Article 64 of the Convention permits reservations, Article 64(2) provides that:

Any reservation made under this Article shall contain a brief statement of the law concerned.

In the *Belilos* case[72] case in 1988 the Court rejected another Swiss reservation to Article 6(1) for failure to comply with this provision and in the present case it came to the same conclusion. Explaining that the requirement in Article 64(2) is not formal, but substantive, the Court decided that as the Government had not appended 'a brief statement of the law concerned', the reservation was invalid and consequently could not be relied on.

Turning to the question of compliance with Article 6(1), the Court pointed out that although the proceedings before the Federal Court had been public, that court could only satisfy itself that there had been no arbitrariness and was not empowered to retry the case. Accordingly, this final stage of the proceedings could not cure the defects in the proceedings below. As the proceedings before the President of the Criminal Cassation Division and the Division itself had not been public, there had been a violation of Article 6(1).

The other issue in the case concerned Article 10, which has been quoted in Case No. 8. The applicant's conviction and sentence clearly constituted an interference by a public authority with his freedom of expression. Since it was 'prescribed by law', the crucial question was whether it was 'necessary in a democratic society' for attaining one of the aims recognized in Article 10(2). The aim of the proceedings against Mr Weber was to ensure the proper conduct of the investigation. They were therefore designed to protect 'the authority and impartiality of the judiciary'. The Court decided, however, that they could not be regarded as necessary in the light of the facts. At the second press conference the applicant essentially repeated what he had said earlier. Thus the interest in maintaining the confidentiality of information already made public no longer existed. In addition, the investigation disclosed by Mr Weber was almost complete. Having regard to the particular circumstances of the case, the Court therefore concluded that there had been an interference with the applicant's right to freedom of expression which could not be justified under Article 10(2).

As just satisfaction under Article 50, the Court awarded the applicant the sum mentioned earlier in respect of costs and expenses relating to the national proceedings and the proceedings before the Convention organs.

[72] ECHR, judgment of 29 April 1988, Series A, No. 132, and this *Year Book*, 59 (1988), p. 386.

Freedom to receive information (Article 10)—application to satellite broadcasting—the meaning of 'prescribed by law' and 'necessary in a democratic society' in Article 10(2)—just satisfaction (Article 50)

Case No. 16. Autronic AG case.[73] In this case, which concerned Switzerland, the Court decided by 16 votes to 2 that there had been a violation of Article 10 of the Convention because the authorities refused the applicant company permission to receive uncoded television programmes from a Soviet telecommunications satellite, thereby infringing its freedom to receive information and ideas regardless of frontiers. As just satisfaction under Article 50, the Government was ordered to pay the applicant 25,000 Swiss francs in respect of its costs and expenses.

The applicant in this case was a Swiss limited company which specialized in home electronics, including dish aerials. In 1982 it asked the Swiss Post and Telecommunications Authority to allow it to show a Soviet public television programme at an exhibition in Zürich, the programme in question being received directly from a Soviet telecommunications satellite, G-Horizont, by means of a private dish aerial. The Authority replied that it could not authorize this without the express agreement of the Soviet authorities.

In January 1983 Autronic AG applied to the Authority for a declaratory ruling that the right to receive uncoded broadcasts from telecommunications satellites for private use could not depend on the consent of the broadcasting State. The Authority, however, rejected the application and held that such reception could not be authorized without the State's consent in view of various provisions of the 1973 International Telecommunication Convention and the Radio Regulations and in particular the provisions relating to secrecy of telecommunications. In July 1986 the Federal Court refused to rule on a public law appeal lodged by Autronic AG on the ground that the company had no direct economic interest worthy of protection. At that time the only satellite television programmes which could be received in Switzerland by means of a dish aerial were those from G-Horizont.

In its application to the Commission in January 1987 Autronic AG complained of a violation of its right to receive information as secured by Article 10 of the Convention. In its report in March 1989 the Commission expressed the opinion by 11 votes to 2 that there had been a violation of this provision. The Commission and the Government then referred the case to the Court.

Article 10 of the Convention, which has been quoted in Case No. 8, protects freedom 'to receive . . . information and ideas without interference by public authority and regardless of frontiers'. The first question which had to be considered in the present case was whether this provision was applicable. The Court ruled that it was, stating that neither the applicant's status as a limited company, nor the commercial character of its activities could deprive it of the protection of Article 10. The intrinsic nature of freedom of expression was likewise no obstacle. The article applied to 'everyone', whether natural or legal persons and concerned not only the content of information, but also the means of transmission or reception, since any restriction on the latter interfered with the right to receive and impart information. The reception of television programmes by means of a dish or other aerial thus came within the right laid down in Article 10(1) without any need to go into the purpose for which the right was claimed. Since the administrative and judicial

---

[73] ECHR, judgment of 22 May 1990, Series A, No. 178. This case was decided by the plenary Court.

decisions complained of had prevented Autronic AG from lawfully receiving G-Horizont's transmissions, they amounted to 'interference by public authority' with the exercise of the applicant's freedom of expression.

Having established that Article 10 was applicable, the next task was to decide whether the restriction imposed by the authorities could be justified under Article 10(2); specifically whether it was 'prescribed by law' and 'necessary in a democratic society' for achieving a legitimate aim. On the first of these issues the Court adopted the same general approach as in the *Groppera Radio AG* case (Case No. 8). It found that the legal basis for the interference was to be found in the relevant domestic legislation, together with several provisions of international telecommunications law. Given the public for which they were intended, the Court found that these instruments were sufficiently accessible. On the other hand, it recognized that there might be room for doubt as regards their clarity and precision, but held that it was unnecessary to resolve this question, as it had found that the interference was not justified.

The aims of the interference were, the Court found, the prevention of disorder in telecommunications and the need to prevent the disclosure of confidential information. As both aims were fully compatible with the Convention, the crucial question was whether the interference complained of was 'necessary in a democratic society' for achieving these aims. The Court decided that it was not and that the national authorities' action lay outside their margin of appreciation. This was firstly because the nature of the broadcasts in question prevented them from being regarded as programmes which were not intended for the general public, and secondly because, as the Government had conceded, there was actually no risk of obtaining secret information by means of dish aerials which received broadcasts from telecommunications satellites.

In support of its decision the Court referred to two recent developments which it regarded as highly significant. In the technical field a number of other telecommunications satellites broadcasting television programmes had come into service, while in the legal field the European Convention on Transfrontier Television had been signed and several States had authorized the reception of uncoded broadcasts from satellites, without requiring the consent of the broadcasting State and apparently without arousing protests from either the signatories to the International Telecommunication Convention or the international authorities. In the Court's view such developments could be taken into account in so far as they contributed to a proper understanding and interpretation of the relevant rules and reinforced the conclusion that there had been a violation of Article 10.

As just satisfaction under Article 50 Autronic AG had not sought compensation for damage but had claimed more than 42,000 Swiss francs as reimbursement for its costs and expenses. The Court, however, considered this claim to be excessive and, making an equitable assessment, awarded the reduced sum mentioned earlier.

There has been relatively little case law dealing with the right to receive information[74] and so the present decision is a useful addition to the jurisprudence on this aspect of Article 10. This is, of course, also the first case to deal with the issue of satellite broadcasting and so, like the *Groppera Radio* case, required the Court to apply the Convention to a situation involving both commercial interests and modern means of communication.

[74] See, however, the *Leander* case, Series A, No. 116, and this *Year Book*, 58 (1987), p. 476, and the *Gaskin* case, Series A, No. 160, and this *Year Book*, 60 (1989), p. 549.

Right of access to the courts (Article 6(1))—trial within a reasonable time (Article 6(1))—just satisfaction (Article 50)

Case No. 17. Obermeier case.[75] The Court decided unanimously that there had been a breach of Article 6(1) because the applicant, when dismissed from his job, was unable to have the validity of his dismissal decided by the courts in Austria. It also decided that a further breach of Article 6(1) had occurred because the applicant had not had a question concerning his civil rights determined within a reasonable time. As just satisfaction under Article 50, the Government was ordered to pay the applicant 100,000 Austrian schillings as compensation and a similar sum in respect of his costs and expenses.

The applicant, who was disabled, was the director of the regional branch of an Austrian insurance company. In 1978, following a dispute with the company, he was suspended from his duties. In March 1981 he began legal proceedings to contest his suspension, but shortly afterwards was dismissed by his employer. Mr Obermeier's initial action to contest his suspension was unsuccessful because the courts took the view that once he had been dismissed, he no longer had an interest in having his suspension revoked. The applicant then sought to challenge his dismissal before the relevant administrative authorities and his dismissal and suspension in the courts. However, the Austrian courts held that only the administrative authorities were competent to determine the question of dismissal, and stayed the action against suspension until this question had been determined. At the time the case was decided by the European Court these proceedings had still to be concluded.

In his application to the Commission in September 1985 Mr Obermeier claimed that he had been deprived of his right of access to the courts, contrary to Article 6(1), and that the issue of his suspension had not been settled in a reasonable time, contrary to the same article. In its report in December 1988 the Commission expressed the unanimous opinion that Article 6(1) had been violated on both counts. The Commission and the Government then referred the case to the Court.

It will be recalled that in *Håkansson and Sturesson* (Case No. 5) the Court held that Article 6(1) had been violated because the applicants were unable to have a claim relating to their 'civil rights and obligations' determined by a court. The first aspect of Mr Obermeier's claim raised a similar issue. His suspension and dismissal were clearly matters which involved his civil rights. Thus the question was whether he was able to raise before a court the lawfulness of his suspension and, since this was a crucial preliminary issue, the dispute as to his dismissal.

The Court found that in Austrian law the dismissal of disabled persons required authorization from an administrative board. Since the labour courts treated the board's rulings as conclusive, the applicant's right to a court would only be respected if the decisions of the board satisfied the Convention's requirements. The Court noted, however, that it was agreed that the board itself could not be regarded as an independent tribunal for Convention purposes. Moreover, although an appeal from the board lay to the administrative courts, their power to review the board's decisions was limited. Observing that such restricted powers could not be regarded as effective judicial review in the present context, the Court concluded that the applicant had been deprived of his right to a court. In this respect, therefore, there had been a breach of Article 6(1).

[75] ECHR, judgment of 28 June 1990, Series A, No. 179. The Court consisted of the following Chamber of Judges: Ryssdal (President); Matscher, Macdonald, Bernhardt, De Meyer, Martens, Foighel (Judges).

The applicant's second complaint concerned the length of the proceedings relating to his suspension. These had already lasted for nine years and had not yet produced a final decision. The Court recalled the criteria which it applies in such cases, but decided that it was unnecessary to examine the situation in detail. Emphasizing that 'an employee who considers that he has been wrongly suspended by his employer has an important personal interest in securing a judicial decision on the lawfulness of that measure promptly',[76] it held that despite its undoubted complexity, the case had been unreasonably prolonged. In this respect also, therefore, there had been a breach of Article 6(1).

As just satisfaction Mr Obermeier claimed over two million schillings as compensation for non-pecuniary damage and another large sum in respect of his costs and expenses. The Court, however, agreed with the Government that both claims were excessive and, applying the principles to be found in its case law, awarded the sums mentioned earlier.

Right of access to the courts (Article 6(1))—the meaning of 'contestation' *in Article 6(1)—jurisdiction of the Court—just satisfaction (Article 50)*

Case No. 18. Skärby case.[77] In this case, which involved Sweden, the Court held by 5 votes to 2 that there had been a violation of Article 6(1) of the Convention because the applicants were denied access to a court on an issue which concerned their civil rights and obligations. The Court also decided by 6 votes to 1 that the Government must pay the applicants 30,000 Swedish crowns in respect of non-pecuniary damage, and unanimously that it must pay them 77,408 Swedish crowns, in respect of their costs and expenses.

In 1913 the late Mr and Mrs Skärby bought a property on the shore of Skälder-viken bay in southern Sweden, which is an area of outstanding natural beauty. The property, which became the home of the Skärby family, was subject to a number of planning restrictions. In 1986 Mr B. Skärby applied to the local Building Committee for a permit to erect a house and two garages on the property, but his application was rejected on the ground that the proposed buildings would not comply with the building plan for the area. This decision also meant that the Committee found that there was no reason to grant his accompanying request for an exemption from the plan. No appeal was possible on this point.

In their application to the Commission in June 1986 Mr Skärby and other members of the family complained that the rejection of the request for a building permit had involved breaches of Articles 6(1), 8, 17 and 18 of the Convention and of Article 1 of Protocol No. 1. The Commission ruled that only the first of these complaints was admissible and in its report in March 1989 expressed the opinion that there had been a violation of Article 6(1). The Commission and the Government then referred the case to the Court.

Before the Court the applicants sought to raise again their complaints under Articles 8, 17 and 18 of the Convention and Article 1 of Protocol No. 1. The Court, however, pointed out that as these complaints had been rejected by the Commission, it lacked jurisdiction to examine them, in the same way as in *Powell and Rayner* (Case No. 6). Thus the only question was whether the applicants had

---

[76] Judgment, para. 72.
[77] ECHR, judgment of 28 June 1990, Series A, No. 180 B. The Court consisted of the following Chamber of Judges: Ryssdal (President); Cremona, Bindschedler-Robert, Pinheiro Farinha, Russo, Spielmann, Palm (Judges).

been denied the right of access to courts which is guaranteed by Article 6(1) and which had recently been considered in *Håkannson and Sturesson* (Case No. 5) and *Obermeier* (Case No. 17). This depended on whether that provision was applicable, and specifically whether the applicants had shown that the question of their building permit involved a 'dispute' over 'civil rights and obligations'.

In its extensive case law on the scope of Article 6(1) the Court has established that for the Convention to be applicable 'the dispute must be genuine and serious; it may relate not only to the actual existence of a right but also to the scope and the manner of its exercise; and, finally, the result of the proceedings must be directly decisive for the right in question'.[78] The Government argued that Swedish legislation did not recognize a right to build without a permit and that the applicants were not contesting the lawfulness of the decision, but seeking to challenge the Building Committee's exercise of its discretion. These arguments persuaded two members of the Court,[79] but were rejected by the majority. In the Court's view the crucial factor was that the Building Committee did not enjoy unfettered discretion, but was bound by generally recognized legal principles. Moreover, the applicants claimed to have been discriminated against and complained that the authorities had been guided by extraneous considerations and improper motives. In these circumstances the Court was satisfied that there was a genuine and serious dispute concerning a right.

There was no doubt that the right in question was a 'civil' right and the Government had recognized that no judicial procedure was available to challenge the Building Committee's decision. The Court therefore concluded that the applicants had been deprived of their right to a court and that there had been a violation of Article 6(1).

The applicants' claim for compensation for pecuniary damage was rejected on the ground that no causal connection had been established between the violation and the alleged loss. On the other hand, the Court accepted that the applicants had suffered some non-pecuniary damage and awarded them compensation under this head. Their claim in respect of costs and expenses, though queried by the Government, was accepted by the Court in full.

Right to liberty (Article 5(1))—application to arrest on suspicion of involvement in terrorist offences—right to be informed promptly of the reasons for arrest (Article 5(2))—right to have the lawfulness of detention decided 'speedily' (Article 5(4))— right to compensation for unlawful arrest or detention (Article 5(5))

Case No. 19. Fox, Campbell and Hartley case.[80] In this case, which concerned the arrest and detention of suspected terrorists in Northern Ireland, the Court held by 4 votes to 3 that there had been violations of Articles 5(1) and 5(5) of the Convention. However, it decided unanimously that there had been no breach of Article 5(2) and that it was unnecessary to examine the applicants' complaints under Article 5(4) and Article 13. The issue of just satisfaction under Article 50 was reserved.

The three applicants in this case lived in Northern Ireland and in 1986 were

[78] Judgment, para. 27. For recent discussion of this issue see the *Pudas* case, Series A, No. 125, and this *Year Book*, 59 (1988), p. 365.

[79] See the short dissenting opinions of Judge Ryssdal and Judge Pinheiro Farinha.

[80] ECHR, judgment of 30 August 1990, Series A, No. 182. The Court consisted of the following Chamber of Judges: Ryssdal (President); Cremona, Pinheiro Farinha, Sir Vincent Evans, Bernhardt, Martens, Palm (Judges).

arrested on suspicion of involvement in terrorist offences. Mr Fox and Ms Campbell were arrested together in February and detained for a period of 44 hours, during which they were questioned about their activities and about the Provisional IRA. They were then released without charge. Mr Hartley was arrested in August and questioned about a kidnapping. He was released after 30 hours in detention and was also not charged. Mr Fox and Ms Campbell each had a previous conviction for a terrorist offence; Mr Hartley had no criminal record.

In their applications to the Commission in 1986 all three applicants claimed that their arrest and detention had involved several violations of Article 5 of the Convention and that the absence of a domestic remedy meant that there had also been a violation of Article 13. In its report in May 1989 the Commission expressed the opinion that there had been violations of Articles 5(1), 5(2) and 5(5), but not of Article 5(4). It also concluded that no separate issue arose under Article 13. The Commission then referred the case to the Court.

The main issue in this case concerned the scope of Article 5(1) of the Convention, the relevant part of which provides:

1. Everyone has the right to liberty and security of person. No one shall be deprived of his liberty save in the following cases and in accordance with a procedure prescribed by law:

. . .

(c) the lawful arrest or detention of a person effected for the purpose of bringing him before the competent legal authority on reasonable suspicion of having committed an offence.

In the present case the applicants were arrested and detained under section 11(1) of the Northern Ireland (Emergency Provisions) Act 1978, which provided that 'any constable may arrest without warrant any person whom he suspects of being a terrorist'.[81] As interpreted by the House of Lords,[82] this section imposed a subjective test of honest belief, rather than an objective requirement of reasonable suspicion. The applicants therefore argued that the Act itself was in conflict with Article 5(1)(c), and furthermore that on the facts their arrests had not been shown to have been based on reasonable suspicion.

The Court began by noting that the requirement of 'reasonableness' in this section of the Convention forms an essential part of the safeguard against arbitrary arrest and detention. It agreed with the Commission and the Government that having a 'reasonable suspicion' presupposes the existence of facts or information which would satisfy an objective observer that the person concerned might have committed the offence. It added, however, that what might be regarded as 'reasonable' must depend on all the circumstances, and explained that:

In this respect, terrorist crime falls into a special category. Because of the attendant risk of loss of life and human suffering, the police are obliged to act with utmost urgency in following up all information, including information from secret sources. Further, the police may frequently have to arrest a suspected terrorist on the basis of information which is reliable but which cannot, without putting in jeopardy the source of the information, be revealed to the suspect or produced in court to support a charge.[83]

In view of the special problems posed by terrorism, the Court was prepared to recognize that the 'reasonableness' of the suspicion justifying such arrests 'cannot

---

[81] This provision has now been replaced by section 6 of the Northern Ireland (Emergency Provisions) Act 1987. See para. 22 of the judgment.

[82] See *McKee* v. *Chief Constable for Northern Ireland*, [1985] 1 All ER 1.

[83] Judgment, para. 32.

always be judged according to the same standards as are applied in dealing with conventional crime'.[84] However, referring to its recent decision in the *Brogan* case,[85] it held that these exigencies 'cannot justify stretching the notion of "reasonableness" to the point where the essence of the safeguard secured by Article 5(1)(c) is impaired'.[86] In the present case the Commission had concluded that the Government had not provided information from which it could find that the suspicions against the applicants were objectively grounded, and the Court agreed. Neither the criminal records of Mr Fox and Ms Campbell, nor the Government's assurances that in all three cases the arrests were based on information which could not be disclosed, were enough to prove the reasonable suspicion which the Convention required. The Court therefore concluded that there had been a breach of Article 5(1).

The applicants' second claim involved Article 5(2). It will be recalled from *Van der Leer* (Case No. 4) that this provides for everyone who is arrested to be 'informed promptly . . . of the reasons for his arrest and of any charge against him'. The Court observed that this is an important provision, but explained that in deciding whether it has been complied with it is essential to consider the particular features of each case. In the present case the applicants were initially told only that they were being arrested under section 11(1) of the 1978 Act. In itself this would not have been enough to comply with Article 5(2), but after their arrest the applicants were interrogated about their suspected involvement in specific crimes. In the Court's view this was enough to enable them to understand why they had been arrested. It therefore concluded that there had been no violation of Article 5(2).

Article 5(4) of the Convention, which has been quoted in Case No. 4, entitles everyone who is deprived of his liberty to take proceedings by which the lawfulness of his detention 'shall be decided speedily by a court'. The majority of the Commission concluded that in the present case there had been no violation of this provision because the applicants were released before a speedy determination of the lawfulness of their detention could take place. The Court adopted a slightly different approach. Agreeing that they had been released speedily, it stated that it was not required to rule *in abstracto* as to whether, if their release had been delayed, the remedies available to them would have satisfied the requirements of the Convention. It therefore concluded that it was not called upon to examine the merits of the applicants' complaint under Article 5(4).

The final provision to be considered[87] was Article 5(5) which reads:

Everyone who has been the victim of arrest or detention in contravention of the provisions of this Article shall have an enforceable right to compensation.

It was clear that under the law of Northern Ireland the applicants had no possibility of bringing a claim for compensation in respect of the violation of Article 5(1)

---

[84] Ibid.

[85] ECHR, judgment of 29 November 1988, Series A, No. 145 B, and this *Year Book*, 60 (1989), p. 514.

[86] Judgment, para. 32.

[87] The Court, like the Commission, held that it was unnecessary to consider the case under Article 13 and, as indicated earlier, reserved the issue of Article 50.

identified earlier in the judgment. The Court therefore concluded that there had also been a violation of this provision.

Three judges dissented from the decision on Article 5(1) and the consequential ruling on Article 5(5).[88] In essence their argument was that in cases such as this the authorities should be given the benefit of the doubt. This is certainly a tenable position. There is, as they pointed out, an element of artificiality in drawing a sharp distinction between genuine suspicion, which it was conceded existed in this case, and reasonable suspicion which had not been established to the Court's satisfaction. Although the Court was at pains to indicate that it was aware of the need 'for a proper balance between the defence of the institutions of democracy in the common interest and the protection of individual rights',[89] here, as in previous cases posing this dilemma, not everyone will find its answer convincing.

Right to respect for correspondence (Article 8)—just satisfaction (Article 50)

Case No. 20. McCallum case.[90] The Court held unanimously that there had been a breach of Article 8 of the Convention on account of the measures which the authorities in the United Kingdom had taken with regard to the applicant's correspondence while he was in prison. As just satisfaction under Article 50, the Court ordered the Government to pay the applicant £3,000 in respect of his costs and expenses.

This case originated in an application lodged with the Commission in August 1981 by a man who was serving a sentence of six years' imprisonment for assault and robbery. In the course of his sentence the applicant, Mr McCallum, spent two periods in the segregation unit at Inverness prison following assaults on staff. He also attempted to send various letters which were stopped or delayed by the authorities on the ground that they contravened Standing Orders which, together with Rule 74 of the Prison Rules, are the provisions which govern the issue of prisoners' correspondence in the United Kingdom.

In his application Mr McCallum raised various complaints concerning the conditions and circumstances of his imprisonment. In July 1984 the Commission declared inadmissible as manifestly ill-founded a complaint that the conditions of the applicant's detention had constituted 'inhuman or degrading treatment or punishment', contrary to Article 3, and that there had been unnecessary interference with his right to respect for family life as guaranteed by Article 8. However, several other complaints were subsequently found to be admissible. In its report in May 1989 the Commission unanimously expressed the opinion that there had been violations of Article 8 in respect of the stopping of certain letters, but no violation in respect of the delaying of two other letters; that there had been a violation of Article 13 (right to an effective remedy) in relation to two of the applicant's letters, but not as regards the others; and that it was unnecessary to examine the case under Article 10. By 9 votes to 6 the Commission also expressed the opinion that there had been a violation of Article 13 in conjunction with Article 3. The Government then referred the case to the Court.

Article 8 of the Convention, which has been quoted in Cases Nos. 12 and 13,

[88] See the joint dissenting opinion of Judges Sir Vincent Evans, Bernhardt and Palm.
[89] Judgment, para. 28.
[90] ECHR, judgment of 30 August 1990, Series A, No. 183. The Court consisted of the following Chamber of Judges: Ryssdal (President); Thór Vilhjálmsson, Bindschedler-Robert, Sir Vincent Evans, De Meyer, Palm, Foighel (Judges).

guarantees 'the right to respect for . . . correspondence'. The application of this provision to the specific issue of prisoners' correspondence has been considered in a number of previous cases.[91] These establish that while a wide measure of control can be exercised by the authorities under Article 8(2), the grounds for restricting correspondence and the way in which such restrictions are applied must both be in accordance with the Convention. In the present case the Commission had found that in most of the incidents complained of the restrictions imposed could not be justified. These included the stopping of letters from the applicant to the press, to his solicitor, to his MP and to the Procurator Fiscal and the withholding from the applicant of two letters from his legal representative. On the other hand, a delay in passing on two letters from the applicant to his representative was found to be justified in view of doubts about whether the latter was prepared to respect the Commission's rules of confidentiality. Before the Court neither the applicant nor the Government contested the Commission's opinion on the various allegations relating to Article 8. The Court therefore confirmed the Commission's conclusions and held that, except in the two cases indicated, there had been a violation of this provision.

As the applicant did not pursue his claim under Article 10, and abandoned his claims under Article 13 at the hearing, the only remaining issue was the question of just satisfaction under Article 50. The applicant claimed the sum of £3,000 as compensation for the 'distress and increased sense of isolation'[92] occasioned by the unjustified interference with his correspondence. The Government contested the claim, pointing out that no evidence of the alleged damage had been produced. The Court agreed that no compensation was necessary and rejected this part of the claim. As reimbursement for his costs and expenses the applicant claimed nearly £15,000, a sum which the Government described as 'excessive in the extreme'.[93] Again the Court agreed with the Government and, noting that the majority of the applicant's claims had been rejected, decided that only a proportion of his costs and expenses were recoverable. The Court therefore decided to award him only £3,000 under this head, together with any value-added tax that might be chargeable.

Right to respect for family life (Article 8)—friendly settlement (Rule 49(2))

Case No. 21. Nyberg case.[94] Following a friendly settlement between the Swedish Government and the applicants, the Court decided unanimously to strike this case out of its list.

The applicants in this case were a married couple who at the material time were living in Sweden. In 1981 they had a son, Björn, who shortly after his birth was taken into public care and subsequently placed in a foster home. In 1986 the Nybergs were successful in having the public care of Björn terminated; however,

---

[91] See the *Golder* case, Series A, No. 18, and this *Year Book*, 47 (1973–4), p. 391; the *Silver* case, Series A, No. 61, and this *Year Book*, 54 (1983), p. 326; the *Campbell and Fell* case, Series A, No. 80, and this *Year Book*, 55 (1984), p. 381; and the *Boyle and Rice* case, Series A, No. 131, and this *Year Book*, 59 (1988), p. 383.

[92] Series A, No. 183, para. 36.

[93] Ibid., para. 38.

[94] ECHR, judgment of 31 August 1990, Series A, No. 181 B. The Court consisted of the following Chamber of Judges: Ryssdal (President); Cremona, Thór Vilhjálmsson, Bindschedler-Robert, Pettiti, Walsh, Macdonald, Martens, Palm (Judges). Under the amendment to Article 43 of the Convention, introduced by Article 11 of Protocol No. 8, Chambers of the Court now consist of nine, instead of seven, Judges. This was the first case to be decided by an enlarged Chamber.

they were prohibited from removing him from his foster home. After further proceedings they eventually succeeded in getting this prohibition removed and in 1987 Björn was returned to his natural parents, with whom he now lives in Germany.

In their application to the Commission in June 1986 the Nybergs complained of violations of Articles 3, 6(1), 8 and 13 of the Convention. In its report in March 1990 the Commission expressed the unanimous opinion that there had been a violation of Article 8 (right to respect for family life), but rejected the other complaints. The Commission then referred the case to the Court.

In July 1990 the Court was informed that the Government and the applicants had concluded an agreement relating to the case. The agreement was in the following terms:

(*a*) The Government accepts the conclusions to which the Commission has arrived and which to a large extent are in line with the opinions expressed by the Swedish Parliamentary Ombudsman after her examination of the matter.

(*b*) The Government will pay the sum of 225,000 Swedish crowns to Mr and Mrs Nyberg.

(*c*) The Government will pay the applicants' legal costs in the amount of 160,000 Swedish crowns.

Mr and Mrs Nyberg declare that they have no further claims in the matter.

In view of the settlement the Government requested the Court to strike the case off the list in accordance with Rule 49(2) of the Rules of the Court, which has been quoted in Case No. 7. The Court therefore took formal note of the friendly settlement. It then observed that there were no reasons of public policy to justify continuation of the proceedings as the family was now reunited and the scope of the Contracting States' obligations in relation to this aspect of Article 8 has been examined in a number of previous decisions.[95] It therefore decided to strike the case out of the list.

J. G. MERRILLS

---

[95] See the *Olsson* case, Series A, No. 130, and this *Year Book*, 59 (1988), p. 380, and the *Eriksson* case, Series A, No. 156, and this *Year Book*, 60 (1989), p. 539.

DECISIONS OF THE COURT OF JUSTICE OF THE EUROPEAN COMMUNITIES DURING 1990*

I. *Rights derived from provisions of Community Law—protection by national courts—relationship between rights under Community law and remedies under national law—interim relief*

I.I. *Case C-213/89, R v. Secretary of State for Transport, ex parte Factortame Ltd. and others*, 19 June 1990. The applicants in the main proceedings were companies incorporated in the United Kingdom and also the directors and shareholders of those companies, most of whom were Spanish nationals. They were owners or operators of fishing vessels registered as British vessels under the Merchant Shipping Act 1894. Most of the vessels had originally been registered in Spain and flew the Spanish flag but were transferred to the British register after 1980. The rest were purchased by Spanish interests, mainly after 1983. By the Merchant Shipping Act 1988 and the Merchant Shipping Act (Registration of Fishing Vessels) Regulations 1988, SI No. 1926, the United Kingdom amended the previous legislation in order to stop the practice of 'quota hopping' whereby fishing quotas reserved under EEC legislation for the United Kingdom are fished by vessels flying the British flag but having no genuine link with the UK.

In August 1989 the Commission brought proceedings against the UK pursuant to Article 169 of the EEC Treaty contending that by imposing nationality requirements under the Act of 1988 the UK had failed to fulfil its obligations under the Treaty. The Commission also sought an interim order requiring the UK to suspend application of those nationality requirements as regards nationals of other Member States. By Order of 10 October 1989 the President of the Court granted that application.[1] Accordingly the Secretary of State made an Order in Council amending the 1988 Act.

Before that Order in Council was made, the applicants in the main proceedings applied for judicial review of part of the 1988 Act, on the ground of its incompatibility with Community law, and applied for interim relief. On 10 March 1989 the Divisional Court granted interim relief suspending the application to the applicants of the relevant parts of the 1988 Act and the Regulations. The Court of Appeal set aside the order of the Divisional Court, holding that courts have no power to suspend Acts of Parliament. On further appeal, the House of Lords referred questions to the European Court.

Responding to those questions, the European Court relied on its judgment of 9 March 1978 in Case 106/77, *Amministrazione delle Finanze dello Stato v. Simmenthal*.[2] There the Court had stated that directly applicable rules of Community law

---

* © Dr Richard Plender, 1991.
[1] Case 246/89R, *Commission v. United Kingdom*.
[2] [1978] ECR 629; [1978] 3 CMLR 263.

'must be fully and uniformly applied in all Member States'. Accordingly, it ruled that a national court which, in a case before it concerning Community law, considers that the sole obstacle which precludes it from granting interim relief is a rule of national law must set aside that rule.

I.2. *Case C-195/90 R, Commission v. Germany*, 12 July 1990. A German Law of 30 April 1990, which was to enter into force on 1 July 1990, imposed a new tax on the use of roads by heavy goods vehicles whose total authorized load exceeded 18 tons. The Commission brought proceedings in the European Court under Article 169 of the EEC Treaty, seeking a declaration that Germany had failed to fulfil its obligations under the Treaty by enacting the Law of 30 April 1990. The Commission requested the Court to order Germany to suspend the operation of the Law pending judgment.

Making that order in accordance with the Commission's request, the Court noted that the Commission had put forward serious reasons to support its argument that the imposition of the tax would violate the Treaty; that the need for relief was urgent; and that any losses suffered in consequence of a breach of Community law by Germany would not be rectified by an award of damages.

The Commission's argument on the substance was that Article 76 of the EEC Treaty prohibits national measures which alter, to the detriment of other Member States, the conditions on which international transport may be effected between or across Member States. The urgency arose from the fact that the Law was due to enter into force seven days after the initiation of the Commission's action. Losses to transporters were liable to be irreparable since the tax would force many of them to give up their businesses and to cause irremediable alterations in the division of the market between German transporters and those from other Member States.

II. *Interpretation of domestic legal provisions in the light of Community law—jurisdiction—jurisdiction of European Court to rule on such interpretation*

II.1. *Joined Cases C-297/88 and C-197/88, Dzodzi v. Belgian State*, 18 October 1990. Mme Dzodzi, of Togolese nationality, was the widow of a Belgian national. She claimed the right to return to Belgium and reside there, following the death of her husband. Under Article 40 of a Belgian Law of 15 December 1980, the foreign spouse of a Belgian national, whatever his or her nationality, was treated as a Community national. The Belgian law did not extend to widows of Belgian nationals the rights conferred by Community legislation on widows of Community nationals. The Belgian authorities maintained that Mme Dzodzi was not entitled to enter and reside in Belgium. They contended, moreover, that there was no factor linking her case to any of the situations governed by Community law.[3] In particular she had never resided or worked in any Member State other than Belgium.

---

[3] Case 175/78, *R v. Saunders*, [1979] ECR 1129; [1979] 2 CMLR 216; Joined Cases 35 and 36/82, *Morson and Jhanjan*, [1982] ECR 3723; [1983] 2 CMLR 221.

Accordingly, Belgium asked the Court to decline to answer certain questions referred under Article 177 of the EEC Treaty by the *Tribunal de première instance*, Brussels. The Court nevertheless answered the questions. The Court stated that neither the wording of Article 177 nor the purpose of the procedure instituted by that article indicated that the authors of the Treaty had intended to exclude from the jurisdiction of the Court references for preliminary rulings concerning a Community provision in the particular case where a Member State's national legislation referred to the content of that provision for the purpose of determining the rules applicable to a situation that was purely internal to that State. The novelty of the judgment lies in the fact that the Court appears to assert jurisdiction to rule on the meanings to be attributed to provisions of national law when the latter refer to Community law. This appears from the sequel, Case C-231/89.

II.2. *Case C-231/89, Galerie Gmurzynska v. Oberfinanzdirektion, Cologne*, 8 November 1990. The plaintiff in the main proceedings purchased in the Netherlands a work of art consisting of a steel plate coated in enamel-glaze colours. Intending to import it into Germany, the plaintiff applied to the German authorities for a binding customs tariff ruling. The German authorities referred to the Common Customs Nomenclature, which contains in Headings 9701 and 9703 provisions for the application of a reduced rate of tax. The German authorities, however, ruled that the work fell under Heading 8306. The applicant challenged the German authorities' ruling before the *Bundesfinanzhof*, which referred questions to the European Court on the meaning to be given to the German legal provisions incorporating the Customs Nomenclature.

The Court stated first of all that the interpretation which the Court was requested to give of the relevant provisions of the Common Customs Tariff was intended to enable the national court to rule on the application which referred to the Nomenclature of the Common Customs Tariff. Consequently, the first question to be decided was whether the procedure laid down in Article 177 of the Treaty was applicable and therefore whether the Court had jurisdiction to rule on the questions submitted to it by the *Bundesfinanzhof*.

In this regard the Court stated that it did not follow from the terms of Article 177 of the Treaty or from the purpose of the procedure laid down in that article that the authors of the Treaty had intended to exclude from the Court's jurisdiction preliminary references on a provision of Community law in the particular case in which the national law of a Member State referred to the content of that provision in order to determine the rules applicable to a situation which related solely to that State. On the contrary, in such a case it was necessary to ensure that Community law had the same effect in all the Member States in the Community in order to prevent disparities in the interpretation of Community law in cases in which its application was directly at issue. Consequently, the Court had jurisdiction to rule on the questions submitted to it by the *Bundesfinanzhof*.

On the merits, the Court ruled that Heading 9701 applied.

II.3. *Case C-106/89, Marleasing SA v. La Comercial Internacional de Alimentación SA*, 13 November 1990. Council Directive 68/151 of 9 March 1968,[4]

---

[4] *Official Journal*, 1968, p. 41.

known as 'the First Council Directive on Company Law', governs among other matters the nullity of companies. Article 11 provides that the laws of the Member States may not provide for the nullity of companies otherwise than by a decision of a court of law ordered on any of six grounds specified therein. Spain was under an obligation to implement this Directive in conformity with Article 395 of the Spanish and Portuguese Act of Accession to the European Communities.[5] By 1989, however, Spain had failed to do so.

Marleasing SA, a Spanish company, instituted proceedings in a court in Oviedo to annul the articles of association of La Comercial Internacional de Alimentación. The action was based on Articles 1261 and 1275 of the Spanish Civil Code, which authorizes the annulment of companies on grounds other than those listed in Article 11 of the First Council Directive on Company Law. La Comercial applied to have the action struck out, contending that the grounds for annulment invoked by Marleasing were not among those listed in Article 11. The court in Oviedo therefore referred to the European Court for preliminary ruling a question enquiring whether Article 11 of the First Council Directive on Company Law is directly applicable so as to protect a company against being annulled on grounds other than those specified therein.

The European Court first re-stated the well-established principle that a Directive, even when directly applicable, can be invoked only against Member States and not against a person such as Marleasing.[6] It considered, however, that the real question was whether a national judge is bound to interpret national law in the light of the Directive, when the national law governs a matter falling within the scope of the Directive.

The Court ruled that a national court, when seised of a matter falling within the field of application of the First Council Directive on Company Law, is required to construe national law in the light of the text and purposes of the Directive, so as to refrain from annulling a company other than on the grounds listed in Article 11 of that Directive.

This decision appears to reverse the effect of the judgment of the House of Lords in *Duke* v. *GEC Reliance Ltd.*,[7] where it was held that the construction of an Act of Parliament, even one passed for the purpose of giving effect to an obligation imposed by Community law, was a matter of judgment to be determined by British courts and to be derived from the language of the legislation considered in the light of the circumstances prevailing at the date of enactment.

III. *Privileges and immunities—jurisdiction of the Court—Protocol on Privileges and Immunities—Article 5 of the EEC Treaty—duty to abstain from measures liable to impede the functioning of the Community institutions*

III.1. *Case C-201/89, Jean-Marie Le Pen and Parti Front National* v. *Puhl and*

---

[5] *Ibid.*, 1985, No. L 302/23.
[6] Case 152/84, *Marshall* v. *Southampton and South West Hampshire Area Health Authority*, [1986] ECR 723; [1986] 1 CMLR 688.
[7] [1988] 1 All ER 626.

others, 22 March 1990. The first plaintiff in the main proceedings was a Member of the European Parliament and leader of a political party established in France, 'Le Front National', the second plaintiff. The first defendant was a journalist who was commissioned by the Socialist Group of the European Parliament to write a pamphlet which was entitled *Gegen Faschimus und Rassismus in Europa*. The English version of the pamphlet, *Against Fascism and Racism in Europe*, was written jointly by the first defendant and the second defendant, A. Bell. By an action initiated in the *Tribunal de grande instance* of Strasbourg the plaintiffs claimed damages for defamation. That court dismissed the action. On appeal, the *Cour d'appel* of Colmar asked the European Court whether it had jurisdiction, in view of the fact that the acts were committed on the premises of the European Parliament in Strasbourg.

The European Court was familiar with the circumstances giving rise to this case; for in a judgment of 4 June 1986 it had dismissed an application made by the Group of the European Right, represented by M Le Pen, for annulment of the European Parliament's decision to set up a committee of enquiry into the rise of fascism and racism in Europe.[8] The Court held that it was not open to the defendants to rely on Article 1 of the Protocol on Privileges and Immunities of the European Parliament. That article preserves the premises of the Parliament against measures of constraint but does not concern the division of jurisdiction as between the Court of Justice and national courts regarding non-contractual liability. Accordingly the Court had no jurisdiction to hear an action for non-contractual liability simply because the act took place on the premises of the European Parliament. Moreover, no rule of Community law implied that acts of a political group might be attributed to the European Parliament as a whole. Accordingly, the Communities are not liable for the distribution by a political group of a pamphlet considered to be defamatory.

III.2. *Case C-333/88, P.J. Krier Tither* v. *Commissioners of Inland Revenue*, 22 March 1990. The applicant in the main proceedings, known to the Court as a previous litigant in questions involving the rights of Community officials,[9] appealed to the Special Commissioners of Income Tax against the refusal of his tax inspector to grant the notice necessary to enable him to benefit from the MIRAS (Mortgage Interest Relief at Source) system, established by the Finance Act 1982. The inspector's decision was based on provisions of the 1982 Act whereby the scheme extended only to a 'qualifying borrower', and this expression did not extend to persons, like Mr Tither, who held an office in respect of which they were not liable to tax by reason of a special immunity.

The Special Commissioners referred to the European Court a question on the interpretation of Article 13 of the Protocol on Privileges and Immunities, designed to determine whether the obligation imposed on Member States to refrain from taxing officials' salaries included an obligation to ignore such salaries for the purpose of applying the MIRAS scheme.

---

[8] Case 78/85, *Group of the European Right* v. *Parliament*, [1986] ECR 1753; [1988] 3 CMLR 645.

[9] Case 175/80, *P. J. Krier Tither* v. *Commission*, [1980] ECR 2345.

The Court ruled that Article 13 does not require Member States to grant officials and other servants of the Communities the same treatment as is given in that State to persons having no taxable income, in respect of a subsidy on interest paid by such persons on loans for the acquisition or improvement of housing.

Mr Tither relied in the alternative on Article 5 of the EEC Treaty, which requires Member States to take appropriate measures to achieve the Community's tasks. The Court had previously ruled that this article prohibits Member States from adopting measures in respect of taxation likely to impede the functioning of the Community institutions.[10] The Court ruled that although a system such as the MIRAS scheme might have the effect of depriving officials and servants of the Communities of a financial advantage which they might enjoy if they did not have that status, the scheme was not likely to dissuade persons from entering the service of the Communities or to induce them to quit that service. Consequently it was not of such a nature as to impede the functioning of the Community institutions.

III.3. *Case C-6/89, Commission v. Belgium*, 5 April 1990. In Case 44/84, *Hurd v. Jones*,[11] the European Court ruled *inter alia* that Article 5 of the EEC Treaty, read with Article 24(2) of the Regulations for Members of the Teaching Staff of the European School, prohibits Member States from taxing the remuneration and allowances paid by the European School to its teachers in accordance with those Regulations. However, it added that this obligation does not produce direct effects capable of being relied upon in relations between the Member States and their subjects.

The Court's judgment of 5 April 1990 is the sequel to *Hurd v. Jones*. In the later case, the proceedings were initiated by the Commission, so no issue of direct effect arose. The Court ruled that by adopting Article 2 of Royal Decree No. 471 of 24 October 1986, reducing by 50 per cent the secondment pay or the salary allowance granted to members of the teaching staff seconded to European Schools, the Kingdom of Belgium had failed to fulfil its obligations under Article 5 of the EEC Treaty. Taken together with *Hurd v. Jones*, the decision establishes an implied obligation on Member States to afford certain privileges for the benefit of teachers at the European Schools, notwithstanding their exclusion from the Protocol on Privileges and Immunities of the European Communities.

III.4. *Case C-2/88, Criminal Proceedings against J.J. Zwartveld and others*, 13 July 1990. The *Rechter-commissaris* (or examining judge) of the Arondisse-nentsrechtsbank, Groningen, when conducting an enquiry into allegations of false accounting alleged to have been committed by the directors and managers of the fish market of Lauwersoog, requested the Court to order the Commission

---

[10] Case 208/80, *Lord Bruce of Donington v. Aspden*, [1981] ECR 2205; [1981] 3 CMLR 506.
[11] [1986] ECR 29; [1986] 2 CMLR 1.

to provide him with the reports drawn up by the Commission's inspectors who had carried out inspections of the Dutch sea fishing industry since 1983, and to allow those inspectors to be examined as witnesses. The *Rechter-commissaris* based his request on Articles 1 and 2 of the Protocol on the Privileges and Immunities of the European Communities and on European conventions on judicial co-operation.

The Commission contended that the request was wholly inadmissible: the Court had no jurisdiction to respond to requests from national courts, save on the basis of Article 177 of the EEC Treaty; and by common consent that Article did not apply since no request was made for the interpretation of a Treaty provision or for a ruling on the meaning or validity of Community legislation.

The Court ruled, however, that it had jurisdiction. Recalling that it had previously emphasized that the Community was based on the rule of law,[12] and observing that pursuant to Article 5 of the EEC Treaty, the relationship between Member States and Community institutions is based on the principle of reasonable co-operation, the Court concluded that it was competent in the matter. Moreover, the privileges and immunities which the Protocol granted to the Communities had a purely functional character, inasmuch as they were intended to avoid any hindrance to the functioning and independence of the Communities. Accordingly, the Commission was ordered to draw up a list of the relevant reports of its officials, for transmission to the *Rechter-commissaris*, and to authorize its officials to be examined as witnesses; alternatively, to submit to the Court a statement of imperative reasons relating to the need to avoid any hindrance to the functioning and independence of the Communities justifying the refusal to transmit any particular item or to submit to examination any particular official.

The decision marks a significant extension in the Court's known jurisdiction: the relationship between the European Court and national courts can no longer be described on the basis of Article 177 of the EEC Treaty alone.

IV. *Law governing the institutions—capacity of the European Parliament to bring an action for annulment of a measure adopted by the Council*

Case C-70/88, European Parliament v. Council, 'Chernobyl', 22 May 1990. By its judgment of 27 September 1988 in Case 302/97, *European Parliament v. Council, 'Comitology'*,[13] the Court had held that 'the European Parliament . . . was not . . . accorded the possibility of bringing actions for annulment' under Article 173 of the EEC Treaty. Nevertheless, in a further action, initiated in 1988, the Parliament instituted proceedings under Article 173 for the annulment of a Regulation, made in the aftermath of the nuclear accident at Chernobyl, laying down maximum permitted levels of radioactive contamination of foodstuffs in the event of a radiological emergency.

---

[12] Case 294/83, *Partie Ecologiste 'Les Verts' v. Parliament*, [1986] ECR 1339; [1987] 2 CMLR 343.
[13] [1988] ECR 5616 at 5644, paragraph 26.

The Parliament submitted that the action challenging the Regulation on radio-active contamination differed from the action instituted in the *Comitology* case. In the *Comitology* case it had been open to the Commission to defend the Parliament's prerogatives (so that the Court's judgment in that case did not create a jurisdictional vacuum). In the *Chernobyl* case, on the other hand, the Commission and the Council had been in agreement. The Commission had failed to comply with the Parliament's request to base the draft Regulation on Article 100A of the EEC Treaty; and this refusal had led the Council to base the Regulation on Article 31 of the Euratom Treaty.

The Court concluded that the action was admissible. Were it otherwise, the absence in the treaties of a provision giving the Parliament a right to bring an action for annulment might constitute a procedural gap. Consequently an action for annulment brought by the Parliament against an act of the Council or of the Commission was admissible, provided that the action in question sought only to safeguard its prerogatives and that it was founded on submissions based on the infringement of those prerogatives.

The decision appears to mark a retreat from the position apparently taken in the *Comitology* case. It assures for the Parliament a limited right of initiation of proceedings even though Article 173 of the EEC Treaty gives the Court jurisdiction only in the case of 'actions brought by a Member State, the Council or the Commission . . . '.

V. *Interpretation of treaties other than EEC Treaty—Treaty of Association with Turkey—General Agreement on Tariffs and Trade—European Convention on Service Abroad of Documents*

V.1. *Case C-192/89, Sevince* v. *Staatssecretaris van Justitie*, 20 September 1990. It is well established that the European Court has jurisdiction to construe an agreement concluded between the EEC and a third State, pursuant to Articles 228 and 238 of the EEC Treaty, since such an agreement is, as far as the Community is concerned, an act of one of the institutions.[14] Consequently the Court has held that it does have jurisdiction to interpret the provisions of the EEC–Turkey Association Agreement, and of the Protocol thereto, governing freedom of movement for workers; and that direct effects[15] are not produced by Article 12 of that Agreement, which states that the parties will secure freedom of movement progressively.

In 1980 a Turkish national, Mr Sevince, was refused an extension of the residence permit issued to him by the Dutch authorities in 1979. However, he obtained a work permit while the outcome of his appeal against the refusal of the extension was pending. In 1987, claiming that he had been employed in the Netherlands for a certain number of years, he applied for a residence permit. In support of this application he relied on Decisions 2/76 and 1/80 of the Council of

---

[14] Case 181/73, *Haegemann* v. *Belgium*, [1974] ECR 449; [1975] 1 CMLR 515.
[15] Case 12/86, *Demirel* v. *Stadt Schwäbisch Gmünd*, [1987] ECR 3747; [1989] 1 CMLR 421.

Association set up under the EEC–Turkey Association Agreement. Those Decisions provide that after four and/or five years of legal employment in a Member State a Turkish worker is to enjoy free access to any paid work of his choice.

On a reference for preliminary ruling from the Raad van State, the European Court ruled that it had jurisdiction to interpret Decisions 2/76 and 1/80; that Article 2(1)(b) of Decision 2/76 and/or Article 6(1) of Decision 1/80 produce direct effects; and that the expression 'legal employment', used in those articles, does not cover the situation of a Turkish worker authorized to engage in employment for such time as the effect of a decision refusing him a right of residence, against which he has lodged an appeal which has been dismissed, is suspended.

The Court's assertion of jurisdiction to interpret the Decisions of the Association Council is not surprising, although it marks an extension of the jurisdiction established by the *Haegemann* case. What is, perhaps, surprising is that the relevant parts of the Decisions produced direct effect within the European Community, even though there could be no guarantee at all that the Turkish authorities would attribute direct effects to them.

V.2. *Case C-331/88, R* v. *Minister of Agriculture, Fisheries and Food and Secretary of State for Health, ex parte FEDESA and others*, 13 November 1990. The prohibition by the European Communities of the marketing of beef reared with the use of hormonal growth promoters has provoked a formal complaint by the United States pursuant to the General Agreement on Tariffs and Trade, the imposition of retaliatory sanctions by the United States and several rounds of litigation in the European Court.[16]

In Case 68/86, *United Kingdom* v. *Council*,[17] the United Kingdom succeeded in its action challenging the validity of a Directive imposing the prohibition; but since it won on procedural grounds, rather than on the basis of its substantive argument relating to the choice of the legal basis, the Council was able to adopt a new Directive having the same effect as the measure annulled by the Court.

FEDESA, an association of manufacturers, producers or distributors of veterinary medicinal products, brought proceedings in the Divisional Court for a declaration that the measure challenged by the United Kingdom was invalid. Although Henry J decided to refer the questions to the European Court, it transpired that the reference was premature, for the Directive was annulled. Those proceedings were withdrawn. When a new Directive was made, a new action was initiated and again questions were referred to the European Court.

The Court replied that its examination of the questions had disclosed no factor such as to affect the validity of the Directive. Responding to the argument that there was no scientific evidence at all to warrant the prohibition of the use of the

---

[16] See Meng, 'Hormonstreit Zwichen der EG und den USA in Rahmen des GATT' *Recht der Internationalen Wirtschaft*, 35(1989), pp. 544–51.
[17] [1988] ECR 855; [1988] 2 CMLR 543.

substances in question, the Court held that faced with different appraisals by the national authorities of the Member States, reflected in the differences between existing national legislation, the Council remained within the limits of its discretionary power in deciding to adopt the solution of prohibiting the hormones in question.

The dispute will now form the basis of further proceedings under GATT arrangements.

V.3. *Case C-305/88, Isabelle Lancray v. Peters und Sickert KG*, 3 July 1990. In proceedings before the *Bundesgerichtshof* between Lancray and Peters, companies established in Neuilly-sur-Seine (France) and Essen (Germany) respectively, the former sought to rely upon a judgment obtained in a French court in default of the latter's appearance. Lancray placed reliance on Article 27 of the Brussels Convention on Jurisdiction and the Recognition and Enforcement of Judgments in Civil and Commercial Matters.[18] Paragraph (2) of that article provides that a judgment shall not be recognized, where it is given in default of appearance, if the defendant was not duly served with the document which instituted the proceedings or with an equivalent document in sufficient time to arrange for his defence.

The *Bundesgerichtshof* referred questions on the interpretation of Article 27. In responding to those questions, the European Court took great care to avoid expressing any opinion on the proper construction of relevant provisions in the Convention on the Service Abroad of Judicial and Extrajudicial Documents in Civil or Commercial Matters[19] to which France and Germany were parties. The European Court ruled, however, that in applying Article 27 of the Brussels Convention the national court must take account of conventions on the service of documents applicable in that State.

The European Court answered the *Bundesgerichtshof*'s questions as follows:

1. Article 27(2) of the Brussels Convention precludes a court in one Contracting State from recognizing a judgment given by a court in another Contracting State in default of appearance by the defendant where the document instituting the proceedings or an equivalent document was not duly served on the defendant, even where that document was received by the defendant in good time for it to arrange its defence.

2. In deciding whether the document instituting the proceedings or an equivalent document was duly served on the defendant for the purposes of Article 27(2) of the Brussels Convention, a court of a Contracting State which is asked to recognize a judgment given by a court in another Contracting State must apply the provisions of the internal law of the second State and those of any international conventions on the service of documents abroad which are applicable in that State. A court in the first State may cure defects of service only if permitted by those provisions to do so.

---

[18] 27 September 1968, Cmnd. 7345; *Official Journal*, 1978, No. L304/77; *International Legal Materials*, 8 (1969), p. 229.

[19] November 1965, Cmnd. 3986; *United Nations Treaty Series*, vol. 658, p. 163; *United States Treaties and Other International Agreements*, vol. 20, p. 361.

The Court's careful abstention from interpreting Conventions other than the Brussels Convention is to be welcomed, but may be contrasted with its attitude to the interpretation of national legal provisions in Case C-106/89, *Marleasing SA v. La Comercial Internacional de Alimentación SA*.[20]

RICHARD PLENDER

[20] Above, p. 453.

UNITED KINGDOM MATERIALS ON INTERNATIONAL LAW 1990*

Edited by GEOFFREY MARSTON[1]

[*Editorial note:* Attention is drawn to the editorial note in UKMIL 1983, p. 361. The publication schedule of the present edition of UKMIL has permitted the citation of the definitive column references in the bound volumes of the Parliamentary Debates.

Some amendments have been made to Parts Thirteen and Fourteen in order to classify more satisfactorily the material relating to coercion and the use of force. These amendments will be retained in future issues of UKMIL.]

INDEX[2]

---

* Editorial arrangement and comments © Geoffrey Marston, 1991. Copyright in the materials cited is in the original copyright holders.

[1] LL M, Ph.D (Lond.): Lecturer in Law, University of Cambridge; Fellow of Sidney Sussex College. The assistance of Mr M.C. Wood, Legal Counsellor, Mr J.J. Rankin, Assistant Legal Adviser, and the News Department, Foreign and Commonwealth Office, and the staff of the Official Publications Department, University Library, Cambridge, is gratefully acknowledged.

[2] Based on the *Model Plan for the Classification of Documents concerning State Practice in the field of Public International Law* adopted by the Committee of Ministers of the Council of Europe in Resolution (68) 17 of 28 June 1968. For a more detailed index of subject-matter, readers are referred to the general index to this volume.

Abbreviations

HC Debs *Hansard*, House of Commons Debates (6th series)
HL Debs *Hansard*, House of Lords Debates (5th series)
Cmnd.   Command Paper (5th series)
Cm.   Command Paper (6th series)
UKMIL *United Kingdom Materials on International Law*
TS   *United Kingdom Treaty Series*

EC   European Community
FCO   Foreign and Commonwealth Office

Part One: II. C. *International law in general—relationship between international law and municipal law—municipal remedies for violations of international law*

In reply to a question on the subject of possible prosecutions for breach of the Geneva humanitarian law conventions, the Parliamentary Under-Secretary of State, FCO, wrote:

States party to the Geneva conventions are well aware of their legal duties since they have an obligation to ensure that grave breaches of the conventions are an offence under their national legislation.

(HC Debs., vol. 183, Written Answers, col. *281*: 20 December 1990)

Part One: II. D. 1. *International law in general—relationship between international law and municipal law—implementation of international law in municipal law—treaties*

(See also Part Eight: II.D. (item of 22 January 1990), below)

Introducing before the UN Human Rights Committee the UK's second periodic report under Article 40 of the International Covenant on Civil and Political Rights, 1966, the UK representative, Mr. P.R. Fearn, stated on 3 November 1988:

. . . as the Committee was aware, the Covenant did not itself form part of the domestic law of the dependent territories. Although there were no examples of judicial decisions directly relating to the Covenant, if a conflict were alleged, the courts would be entitled, in accordance with common law rules of statutory interpretation, to look at the Covenant to resolve any ambiguity in domestic legislation relating to the rights and freedoms guaranteed by the Covenant. Furthermore, in Bermuda, the Falkland Islands, Gibraltar and the Turks and Caicos Islands, the fundamental rights provisions of their respective Constitutions, which reflected the Covenant, took precedence over other domestic laws in force in those territories. If a conflict between the Covenant and domestic law were established and not remedied in the courts, the law could be amended either by local legislation in the territory or by United Kingdom legislation.

With regard to proposed new legislation in the dependent territories, harmony with the Covenant was achieved through the awareness of the legal advisers to the local Governments of the provisions of the Covenant and by the process of debate in local legislatures. Furthermore, Governors were constitutionally required to withhold assent—and thus enactment into law—of new legislation where they considered it might conflict with treaty obligations binding on the United Kingdom, until authorized to do so by the United Kingdom Government. In addition, laws enacted in dependent territories were examined by the United Kingdom Government, which had powers to require their amendment or to disallow them if they were found to conflict with the United Kingdom's treaty obligations.

His delegation had no further information to add to that given in the second report on activities relating to the promotion of greater public awareness of the provisions of the Covenant. Since the Covenant did not have the force of law in the dependent territories, its provisions were given effect through various legal instruments. They included chapters which provided for the protection of fundamental rights and freedoms in some constitutions, local legislation, applicable British legislation and case law. Important human rights provisions were often referred to in debates in the Legislative Councils and Assemblies of those territories and those debates were reported in the press and mass media.

(CCPR/C/SR. 855, pp. 6–7)

In the course of the second reading debate on the Aviation and Maritime Security Bill, the Secretary of State for Transport, Mr Cecil Parkinson, said:

Part II enables the Government to give effect to the International Maritime Organisation's convention on terrorism at sea and its linked protocol on fixed platforms. The Bill makes it an offence to hijack any ship or unlawfully to seize or exercise control of a fixed platform.

(HC Debs., vol. 164, col. 960: 10 January 1990)

In the course of the Committee stage of the House of Lords debate on the Criminal Justice (International Co-operation) Bill, the Minister of State, Home Office, Earl Ferrers, said:

. . . one of the main advantages we hope to obtain from the Bill is that it will enable us to participate with other countries in Europe in the full range of mutual legal assistance arrangements provided for in the European Convention on Mutual Assistance in Criminal Matters. Part I of the Bill is intended to make it possible for us to co-operate with other countries in relation to any kind of criminal offence, subject to the Secretary of State's general discretion to refuse to act upon any particular request from overseas where it appears to him right to do so. The Bill does not specifically refer to fiscal offences, . . . but it is the Government's intention to accede to Chapter 1 of the additional protocol to the European convention, the effect of which will be to require us to provide assistance to other European convention countries in relation to fiscal offences just as with any other criminal offences.

(HL Debs., vol. 514, cols. 881–2: 22 January 1990)

Later in the same debate, Earl Ferrers, in moving certain amendments to the Bill, stated:

I explained on Second Reading that we were endeavouring to put into statute the requirements of the Vienna Convention [UN Convention against Illicit Traffic in Narcotic Drugs and Psychotropic Substances, signed in Vienna on 20 December 1988] which was signed only 12 months ago. The Bill provided a wonderful legislative opportunity for immediate implementation of that convention. As my noble and learned friend rightly said, the Bill contains technical matters. It was not possible to have all those technical matters resolved by the time the Bill was introduced. I explained the dilemma that the Government then faced: either we introduced the Bill without the terms of the Vienna Convention or we asked the indulgence of this place to introduce a Bill which was inadequate and incomplete so that the requirements of the Vienna Convention could be immediately introduced. We can take some pride in that, even though it might irk my noble and learned friend. It is only one year since the convention was signed. That is pretty recent to enact enabling legislation. I do not say this with any great pride, but it took 17 years to ratify the 1971 convention.

(Ibid., cols. 887–8; see also ibid., vol. 515, col. 1472: 15 February 1990)

In the course of the HC Standing Committee debate on the Aviation and Maritime Security Bill, the Minister for Public Transport, Mr Michael Portillo, stated:

I take this opportunity to outline the intention behind part II. It enables the Government to ratify and implement the International Maritime Organisation's 1988 Rome convention and protocol dealing with the apprehension, prosecution or extradition of offenders following terrorist attacks against ships or fixed platforms. The United Kingdom signed the convention and protocol in September 1988 and neither instrument has yet entered into force internationally.

Part II deals with terrorist attacks against ships or fixed platforms and the offences are drafted—as were those discussed under clause 1 of the Bill in relation to the 1988 Montreal protocol—to apply anywhere in the world, irrespective of the nationality of the perpetrator. They derive directly from the offences specified in the Rome convention and protocol. All the states who wish to become parties to the convention and protocol will be defining the offences in the same way in their national legislation. International uniformity in defining the offences is essential if the prosecution or extradition of offenders is to work properly. The convention and protocol specify that the penalties for the offences should reflect their serious nature. This we have done in part II.

. . .

Clause 7 creates the totally new offence under United Kingdom law of hijacking a ship anywhere in the world. This meets the requirement of the Rome convention and a recommendation of the Law Commission that such an offence should be created.

(HC Debs., 1989–90, Standing Committee A, Aviation and Maritime Security Bill, cols. 98–9; 13 February 1990)

In the course of the Committee stage of the House of Lords debate on the Contracts (Applicable Law) Bill, the Lord Chancellor, Lord McKay of Clashfern, referred to the 1980 Rome Convention on the Law applicable to Contractual Obligations and said:

As I understand it, it is quite impossible in good faith to ratify a convention and give it the force of law in the United Kingdom unless one is in a position to make it the law.

. . .

The purpose of the Bill is to enable us properly to bring the law of the United Kingdom into line with the convention—to give the convention the force of law in the United Kingdom.

(HL Debs., vol. 515, col. 1483: 15 February 1990; see also item of 20 June 1990, below)

In reply to the question

in what manner the rights and freedoms guaranteed by the European Convention on Human Rights and by the international covenant on civil and political rights are directly secured by domestic law to everyone within the jurisdiction of the United Kingdom,

the Parliamentary Under-Secretary of State, Home Office, wrote:

The provisions of our common and statute law have always recognised basic human rights and freedoms. New laws are drafted in the light of international conventions and covenants; and, where necessary, existing laws are amended in the light of international judgments to meet our obligations.

In reply to a further question, the same Parliamentary Under-Secretary wrote in part:

The United Kingdom fully meets its obligations under the various international instruments dealing with civil and political rights to which it is party.

(HC Debs., vol. 167, Written Answers, cols. *591–2:* 19 February 1990)

The following passage appeared in the UK's third periodic report under Article 40 of the International Covenant on Civil and Political Rights:

Some legislation is introduced with the intention or the effect of enabling the United Kingdom to subscribe to international agreements or to incorporate their provisions on a statutory basis. For example, the Criminal Justice Act 1988 contained provisions on compensation for wrongful conviction, which secures the United Kingdom's compliance with article 14, paragraph 6, of the Covenant, and on the proscription of torture, following which the United Kingdom ratified the United Nations Convention against Torture and Other Cruel, Inhuman or Degrading Treatment or Punishment.

(CCPR/C/58/Add. 6, p. 1: March 1990)

In reply to a question, the Parliamentary Under-Secretary of State, Home Office, wrote:

Both Jersey and the Isle of Man have been made aware of the need to amend their current legislation in order to enable the United Kingdom to conform with its international obligations under the European Convention on Human Rights. The Island authorities are also aware that the United Kingdom would need to legislate on their behalf, if necessary.

(HC Debs., vol. 170, Written Answers, col. *1002:* 19 April 1990)

In reply to a question, the Parliamentary Under-Secretary of State, Department of Transport, wrote:

Annex V of the MARPOL convention 73/78 came into force internationally on 31 December 1988. The Merchant Shipping (Prevention of Pollution by Garbage) Regulations, 1988 (statutory instrument 1988/2292) which came into force on the same day apply the provisions of this annex to United Kingdom ships, and to other ships when they are within the United Kingdom or its territorial waters. The Merchant Shipping (Reception Facilities for Garbage) Regulations 1988 (statutory instrument 1988/2293) requires harbour authorities and terminal operators to provide reception facilities for garbage adequate to meet the needs of ships using the harbour or terminal.

(HC Debs., vol. 171, Written Answers, col. *54*: 23 April 1990; see also ibid., col. *154*: 24 April 1990)

In a debate in the HC Second Reading Committee examining the Contracts (Applicable Law) Bill, the Solicitor-General, Sir Nicholas Lyell, stated:

The Bill relates to a technical area of law, the conflict of laws, otherwise known as private international law, which deals with cases having a foreign element. Into this frequently complex area the Bill brings a valuable measure of harmony, with the incorporation into United Kingdom law of the 1980 Rome Convention on the law applicable to contractual obligations, a convention between the member states of the European Community.

(HC Debs., 1989–90, Second Reading Committee: 20 June 1990, col. 3).

In reply to a question on the subject of the judicial implications of the ruling of the European Court of Justice in *Factortame*, the Attorney-General wrote:

The Context

Owners and operators of certain fishing vessels formerly registered as British have claimed that some of the registration conditions contained in Part II of the Merchant Shipping Act 1988 are incompatible with Community law. They have applied to the High Court for judicial review.

The divisional court has referred the relevant questions of Community law to the European Court of Justice for a ruling. But the applicants also asked the divisional court for interim relief to protect their claimed rights in the meantime, by disapplying the relevant provisions of the Act pending final judgment.

The Secretary of State for Transport has opposed this application strongly.

The Divisional Court decided to grant the interim relief that was asked for. It ordered that the relevant part of the 1988 Act should be disapplied, so as to allow all previous registrations to remain in effect pending the European Court's ruling.

The Secretary of State appealed. The Court of Appeal reversed that order, and the House of Lords upheld the Court of Appeal. It held that, as a matter of national law, the divisional court had no jurisdiction to make any such order.

The House of Lords itself, however, referred to the European Court the separate question whether in the circumstances of the case Community law either obliged the national court to grant interim relief by suspending the application of a national measure, or alternatively gave it power to grant such interim protection of the rights claimed; and, if so, upon the application of what criteria.

The immediate effect

The United Kingdom argued before the European Court that Community law neither obliged nor enabled a national court to grant interim relief suspending the application of a national measure where the national court was debarred by national law from doing so. The court has, however, ruled that, where a national court would have granted such interim relief in order to protect directly effective Community law rights had it not been for a rule of its national law prohibiting it from so doing, it must as a matter of Community law set aside that rule.

In consequence the application for judicial review now returns to the English courts for decision as to whether interim relief should now be granted and, if so, on what terms. The Secretary of State will make submissions as to the general criteria to be applied and will argue strongly that interim relief ought not to be granted in the present case; but since the matter is sub judice it would be wrong to say more. Meanwhile, the practical position as regards fishing rights remains unchanged pending resolution of this issue.

The juridical significance

When a country joins the Community it is obliged to reconcile its constitution, whether written or unwritten, with Community membership. It has to provide for the application of Community law within its territory, which means providing for Community law to have supremacy over any conflicting provisions of its own national law.

Community law requires that directly effective Community law rights must be fully and uniformly applied in all the member states. If the provisions of any national law might prevent, even temporarily, Community rules from having such force and effect as Community law requires, then national courts shall be able to set them aside. This requirement derives from article 5 of the treaty of Rome. It is Parliament that has given effect to requirements such as this, by means of the provisions of section 2(1) of the European Communities Act 1972:

'All such rights, powers, liabilities, obligations and restrictions from time to time created or arising by or under the Treaties, and all such remedies and procedures from time to time provided for by or under the Treaties, as in accordance with the Treaties are without further enactment to be given legal effect or used in the United Kingdom shall be recognised and available in law, and be enforced, allowed and followed accordingly; . . . '

In Factortame the Court of Justice held that the full effectiveness of Community law would be impaired if a jurisdictional rule in the law of a member state prevented its national courts from granting interim relief so as to preserve directly effective rights claimed under Community law, where the national courts would otherwise consider it appropriate to do so. The House of Lords is accordingly now under a Community law obligation to give effect to the ruling, because that ruling is automatically brought into English law by the operation of section 2(1) of the 1972 Act. Moreover, by virtue of section 2(4) of the Act, Parliament has provided that an Act of Parliament such as the 1988 Act is to be construed and have effect subject to the obligations and powers which arise under section S2(1):

'[S2(4)] . . . and any enactment passed or to be passed, other than one contained in this Part of this Act, shall be construed and have effect subject to the foregoing provisions of this section . . . '

Finally, it is important to note that the ruling of the Court of Justice applies equally to the national courts of every member state.

(HC Debs., vol. 175, Written Answers, cols. *141–3*: 26 June 1990)

In reply to the question to what extent, under UK legislation, Article 227 of the Treaty of Rome had been invoked, the Minister of State, FCO, wrote:

Article 227 of the treaty of Rome is fully incorporated into United Kingdom law and the question of invocation does not arise.

(HC Debs., vol. 176, Written Answers, col. *260*: 11 July 1990)

In moving the consideration in HC Standing Committee of the draft Merchant Shipping (Prevention and Control of Pollution) Order 1990, the Minister for Aviation, Shipping and Public Transport, Mr Patrick McLoughlin, stated:

The Order amends the Merchant Shipping (Prevention and Control of Pollution) Order 1987, which enables regulations to be made to give effect to annex II of the International Convention for the Prevention of Pollution from Ships, 1973. The order will empower the Secretary of State to amend the regulations to incorporate updated requirements that have been adopted by the International Maritime Organisation. It will also empower the Secretary of State to make regulations to give effect to annex II of the Convention.

(HC Sixth Standing Committee on Statutory Instruments, etc.: 27 November 1990, col. 3)

In moving the approval in the House of Commons of the draft Civil Jurisdiction and Judgments Act 1982 (Amendment) Order 1990, the Solicitor-General, Sir Nicholas Lyell, stated in part:

The purpose of this Order in Council is to enable the United Kingdom to ratify the convention by which Spain and Portugal acceded to the 1968 Brussels convention on jurisdiction and the enforcement of judgments in civil and commercial matters as well as to the 1971 protocol.

The Brussels convention established a scheme to determine the international jurisdiction of the courts of the member states, to facilitate recognition and to introduce an expeditious procedure for securing the enforcement of judgments within the Community. The 1971 protocol confers jurisdiction on the Court of Justice of the Community to interpret the convention.

On becoming a member of the Community each state undertakes to accede to the Brussels convention and the protocol. The United Kingdom, Denmark and Ireland acceded by a convention signed on 9 October 1978, and the Brussels convention is now in force in each of those states. Greece acceded by a convention signed on 25 October 1982. That convention was ratified by the United Kingdom last year and came into force on 1 October 1989. The convention on the accession of Spain and Portugal, the two final states, was signed on 26 May 1989.

Section 14 of the Civil Jurisdiction and Judgments Act 1982 provides that Her Majesty may by Order in Council make such modifications of the Act as she considers appropriate in consequence of any revision of the Brussels convention or the protocol. The greater part of the printed order consists of schedules replacing those presently in the 1982 Act.

. . . .

There are just a few changes of substance to the effect of the Brussels convention. The Civil Jurisdiction and Judgments Bill was introduced in another place on 15 November. The object of that Bill is to enable the United Kingdom to ratify the Lugano convention on jurisdiction and the enforcement of judgments. That convention was drawn up between the member states of the European Community and the member states of the European Free Trade Association, and creates a régime between the states of those two organisations parallel to that of the Brussels convention. Although the provisions of the Lugano convention follow, so far as is appropriate, those of the Brussels convention, the opportunity was taken to incorporate some changes deemed to be necessary in the light of 20 years' experience of the practical operation of the Brussels régime.

Given the parallel nature of these two conventions, it was considered desirable by the working party negotiating the Spanish and Portuguese accession convention to take that opportunity to reflect—if I might call them this—the Lugano improvements back into the 1968 Brussels convention.

(HC Debs., vol. 181, cols. 712–13: 26 November 1990; see also HL Debs., vol. 523, cols. 954–6: 27 November 1990)

In the course of a debate in the House of Lords on a motion to call attention to the case for the incorporation of the European Convention on Human Rights, 1950, into United Kingdom law as a Bill of Rights, the Government spokesman, Lord Reay, stated:

The Government are firm believers in and supporters of the European Convention on Human Rights. Let there be no doubt about that. Now that we have just celebrated the 40th anniversary of the opening for signature of the convention, we see that these basic rights have stood the test of time.

Since the UK ratified the convention, there has been debate over the years as to whether we should incorporate its provisions in our domestic law. The Select Committee on a Bill of Rights of your Lordships' House which sat in 1977 and 1978 concluded that in any country, whatever its constitution, the existence or absence of legislation in the nature of a Bill of Rights can in practice play only a minor part in the protection of human rights. The committee also concluded that it had received no evidence that human rights were better protected in countries which had a code of basic rights embodied in their law than they were in the United Kingdom. I see no reason to think that matters have changed in the interim.

Nevertheless, we must recognise that there is criticism of the fact that we have not incorporated the European convention on the grounds that there have been a number of unfavourable judgments against us in Strasbourg. However, that needs to be put in context.

We have heard it said that we compare unfavourably with other countries when the ECHR league table, as it were, is consulted. Statistics in this field can give a false impression; for example, of the 26 court findings of violations by the UK, five of these concerned similar child care cases heard simultaneously. Moreover, there is no distinction between major and minor violations and there have been cases in which the UK has been vindicated in respect of the major issue, although a finding is recorded against us on a minor subsidiary point. I should add also that our record in providing a remedy is a good one and violations have been recorded against us even though we have subsequently changed the law.

In relation to decisions of the court, one has to recognise that the statistics take no account of when a country accepted the right of individual petition. The UK accepted the right of individual petition since 1966, whereas a number of other countries have accepted it much more recently; for example, France and Spain in 1981 and Turkey in 1986. Since, in addition, it can take five or six years for an application to be decided by the court or Committee of Ministers, it is not surprising that fewer violations have been found in the case of those countries. We regard as fallacious, therefore, the argument that breaches against the United Kingdom demonstrate the need for incorporation and would argue that we have a good record overall.

It has been suggested that Parliament can no longer adequately protect our citizens and that as government activity increases in complexity, the need for protection is all the greater, but afforded all the less. But we consider incorporation of the convention into domestic law would not bring the advantages claimed.

It is the Government's firm view that imposing on the judges a duty to interpret the convention would add a new and undesirable dimension to their current role. That new role would be to decide broad issues of policy. The more we draw judges into political matters, the more shall we impinge on the constitutional concept of the political neutrality of the judges in terms of the general public's reception of them.

It is worth reminding ourselves that in respect of judicial review . . . the grounds of challenge do not extend to the merits of the action under challenge. In judicial review the courts do not seek to substitute their view for that of the Government on such matters as national security and the public interest. The courts are concerned with the procedure whereby the act in question was taken, not the action itself.

I mentioned the judges' role in judicial review simply to emphasise that those who say that requiring them to interpret the convention would introduce no radical change are, in our view, being unduly optimistic.

I do not doubt for one moment that British judges would be far better placed than those in Strasbourg to decide what does and does not comply with the convention in the British context. But that is not the point. The point is that at present judges are charged with interpreting and applying the will of Parliament as set down in precisely drafted statute law. Interpreting the principles set down in the convention would be an entirely different matter, and would involve the weighing of policy issues and conclusions being reached on the basis of the judge's perceptions of the public interest.

As the noble Lord, Lord Allen of Abbeydale, said . . . judges would tend to become embroiled in political issues, and, like the noble Lord, I should find it hard to take the judicial encroachment on our traditional procedures.

The commission and court have tended to construe the various articles in the light of political, social and ethical developments in Europe. This approach has meant that the court and Committee of Ministers have, on occasion, reached decisions which would have been quite unforeseen at the time of our signature and ratification. For example, it was determined in Strasbourg that not only did prisoners have a right to marry provided for in the UK, but that they also had a right to marry within prison itself. To meet this judgment, an amendment to our marriage law was necessary and enacted. We have to ask ourselves whether the judiciary in the United Kingdom might not also adopt a similarly dynamic approach, based on political and other considerations, if faced with interpretation of such broadly defined principles.

Another disadvantage of the proposal to incorporate the convention into domestic law is that it would introduce a significant element of uncertainty into the law. Strasbourg, in finding against us, cannot strike down our law. The court and Committee of Ministers create no vacuum and time is given to reflect and make changes, if Parliament agrees.

Incorporation of the convention would be a recipe for muddle and confusion.

We might well find ourselves facing a scenario such as this: Parliament passes a law, without reserved provision, which it fully believed to conform to the convention. Next day, or next year, this law could be struck down by a judge who, acting in good faith, took a different view according to his perceptions of the public interest. The judgment would have immediate effect which in turn could have urgent and significant administrative implications. I suggest this would impose an unpredictable burden on Parliament. If, for example, the law concerned entry to the UK, there would be enormous problems attendant thereafter on the operation of entry control procedures while a new law was being prepared.

A number of points were raised to which I should like to refer. . . .

The noble Lord, Lord Holme, made the point that most other countries have incorporated the provisions of the convention without difficulty. He asked, therefore, why we could not do that. The answer is that we do not have a written constitution although unlike the noble Lord, Lord Holme, I do not find that to be an embarrassment. Rights exist under common law in this country unless taken away by statute. Thus, an Englishman's home is his castle unless Parliament gives power to the police or others to enter it. To introduce conferred rights into our present system by way of a written constitution could have effects which are not readily apparent. The same problems do not necessarily arise in other countries which have written constitutions and the need to confer rights. Therefore, for them it is far less of a departure from tradition to incorporate the convention.

As regards doing something different from that which other Eastern countries may be about to do, Czechoslovakia, Hungary and Poland would be amazed if they were told that we in this country wished to adapt our traditional practices to fit in with whatever they choose to do now. Surely they are in the position of wanting to learn from us and to select what they want from our constitutional arrangements rather than the other way round, now that they have emerged from the dark night of communist tyranny.

My noble friend Lord Campbell of Alloway suggested that it may be possible to establish a commission to deal specifically with complaints regarding breaches of human rights. I wonder if we really need that in addition to our domestic courts— leading up to the House of Lords—and the European Commission—leading up to the European Court. All those remedies are available whether or not we incorporate the convention.

I agree with the basic tenor of the speech of the noble Lord, Lord Allen of Abbeydale. He referred to the exceptions set out in Article 8 of the convention. I agree that it should not be for the courts to determine matters of public policy or the public interest. As I indicated earlier, I agree that the political arena is not the place for judges.

The noble Lord, Lord Hutchinson, said that in his view the independent selection and training of judges is the best guarantee that they will continue to command public respect and confidence, even if we incorporate the convention. I suggest that one only needs to look to the United States to realise that a time may soon come when a judge's political neutrality is something that may be called into question. It is apparent that in the United States the most important criteria for appointment to the Supreme Court are the candidate's social and political views.

. . .

My noble friend Lord Beloff pointed out that incorporation would not be a panacea, and that as the right of individual petition would remain, litigating matters in British courts first would only add to the length of time it would take for an eventual decision to be reached in Strasbourg.

That brings me to the point raised by the noble Lord, Lord Harris, and others relating to the length of time, which they deplored, before decisions in Strasbourg can be heard. The noble Lord, Lord Hutchinson, also referred to the long five-year trek, as he put it, to Strasbourg. I assure noble Lords that discussions are currently taking place in the Council of Europe regarding the splitting up of the Strasbourg machinery. That is something in which we are very much involved.

However, it should not be thought that incorporation will obviate the necessity of providing for the individual right of petition to Strasbourg if applicants are not satisfied by the interpretation which judges in the United Kingdom place on the incorporation provisions. They would still have the right to apply to the Commission and that would lengthen the procedure which exists rather than shorten it.

The noble Lord, Lord Harris, referred to the case of the closed shop. I do not want to comment in any detail on specific cases that he raised, save to say that the Government have further extended individual freedom by giving ordinary trade union members the right to be balloted before industrial action.

The noble Lord, Lord McGregor of Durris, argued that if we accepted the Treaty of Rome provisions as part of our law, we should also accept the provisions of the European Convention on Human Rights. My answer is that the Treaty of Rome contains specific provisions. Those which have direct application are drafted in specific terms which would leave limited scope for different interpretation. On the other hand, the European convention sets out a set of principles in general terms. That leaves much scope for interpretation, as illustrated by the differences that arise even between the Commission and the court.

I do not agree with the noble Lord, Lord Harris, that I and others who argued in the same way are making a last ditch effort to prevent incorporation. I do not believe it is as imminent as the use of that term implies. There is no evidence that the public seek a written constitution. There is no great clamour for change, as my noble friend Lord Beloff pointed out. Over the years and centuries we have evolved a stable constitutional system second to none. It depends on delicate checks and balances. If the price of incorporation is a threat to the impartial independence of the judiciary and the ordinary working of the legislature, then I submit that that price is too high.

(HL Debs., vol. 524, cols. 209–13: 5 December 1990)

In an explanation of vote in the UN General Assembly on 14 December 1990, on the subject of the law of the sea, the UK representative, Mr A. Aust, stated:

. . . we have implemented the Vienna Convention Against Illicit Traffic in Narcotic Drugs by means of the Criminal Justice (International Cooperation) Act 1990.

(Text provided by the FCO; see also A/45/PV. 68, p. 61)

Part Two: I. *Sources of international law—treaties*

In the course of a debate on the subject of the judgment of the Supreme
Court of the Irish Republic in *McGimpsey*, the Parliamentary Under-
Secretary of State for Northern Ireland, Dr Brian Mawhinney, stated:

Article 1 of the Anglo-Irish Agreement, which is an internationally binding
treaty, is not and cannot be affected by a judgment of the Irish Court.

(HC Debs., vol. 169, col. 647: 14 March 1990)

In reply to the question what significant differences exist between the
1961 Social Charter of the Council of Europe and the 1989 EC Social
Charter, the Parliamentary Under-Secretary of State, Department of
Employment, wrote:

There are a number of important differences between the two social charters.
These are differences in content, the nature of the instrument and whether or not
member states have flexibility to adopt selected parts of them.

The Council of Europe's European social charter addresses economic and social
rights for all sections of society. Once ratified by a member state it becomes a binding international treaty. In order to ratify the charter a member state must undertake to accept 10 or more of the 19 articles contained in it. Five of these must be
taken from a list of seven specified articles, otherwise states are free to decide which
parts of the charter they will accept.

There is scope for a contracting state subsequently to denounce articles which it
no longer wishes to ratify, subject to continuing acceptance of the minimum of 10.

The European Community social charter, on the other hand, is essentially concerned with the rights of workers. It is a political statement of intent agreed by 11
of the EC member states; it is not a legally binding document. It has to be accepted
as a whole or not at all. It includes an invitation to the European Commission to
propose an action programme of measures to implement the rights contained in it.

The Commission action programme, published in November 1989, contains
nearly 50 separate measures, around half of which are for measures which would be
legally binding on member states. Once a measure has been adopted a member
state cannot subsequently denounce it; and changes can only be made to an agreed
Community instrument where there is general agreement that that is necessary.

(HL Debs., vol. 520, col. 1720: 27 June 1990)

Following the report of the HC Foreign Affairs Committee on the unification of Germany, the Government presented to Parliament, in October
1990, written observations in which the following passage appeared:

25. The Treaty on the Final Settlement with respect to Germany is a treaty under
international law between the five parties thereto. As between the parties it settles

definitively matters arising out of the Second World War. Certain other issues are covered in a letter from the two German Foreign Ministers, which is not part of the Treaty: this quotes part of the FRG-GDR Joint Declaration of 15 June 1990 on the settlement of outstanding property matters; states that monuments to victims of war and tyranny in Germany, and war graves, will be respected and protected; states that the German constitution provides the basis for prohibiting parties that seek to impair or abolish the free democratic order, which applies to parties with National Socialist aims; and cites Article 12 of the FRG-GDR Unification Treaty on the future of the GDR's treaties.

(Cm. 1246, p. 7)

Part Two: II. *Sources of international law—custom*

(See Part Eleven: II. D. (item of 4 June 1990) and Part Fourteen: I. B. 1., below)

Part Two: VIII. *Sources of international law—restatement by formal processes of codification and progressive development*

(See Part Nine: XIV. (second item) and Part Twelve: II. (reference to Vienna Conventions), below)

Part Two: IX. *Sources of international law—comity*

(See Part Eight: II. D. (*amicus curiae* Briefs of 16 November 1989 and 6 August 1990), below)

Part Two: X. *Sources of international law—acquisition, retention and loss of rights*

(See also Part Three: I.E. (item of 3 November 1988), and Part Six: II. E. and Part Eight: II. A. (item of 6 December 1990), below)

The following passage appeared in a Joint Statement issued by the delegations of the British and Argentine Governments following a meeting in Madrid on 17–19 October 1989:

Each government undertook not to pursue any claim against the other, including nationals of the other, in respect of loss or damage arising from the hostilities and all other actions in and around the Falkland Islands, South Georgia and the South Sandwich Islands before 1989.

(Text provided by the FCO)

The FCO Press Release No. 240 of 1990 (see Part Nine: IX., below) of 27 November 1990 covering the arrangements for fisheries cooperation in the South Atlantic stated that these arrangements were concluded under the 'sovereignty umbrella' agreed by the UK and Argentina at Madrid in October 1989 (for the text of this 'sovereignty umbrella', see UKMIL 1989, p. 583).

Part Two: XI. *Sources of international law*—jus cogens

(See Part Three: I. A. 3. (item of 5 April 1990 referring to the Molotov-Ribbentrop pact), below)

Part Three: I. A. 1. *Subjects of international law*—*States*—*international status*—*sovereignty and independence*

(See also Part Eight: II. A. (items on Kuwait), below)

In reply to a question, the Minister of State, FCO, wrote:

We cannot establish diplomatic relations with Lithuania, which is not a sovereign independent state. It was unlawfully incorporated into the Soviet Union in 1940.
(HC Debs., vol. 166, Written Answers, col. 697 : 7 February 1990)

In the course of a debate in the HC Second Reading Committee on the Brunei (Appeals) Bill, the Parliamentary Under-Secretary of State, FCO, Mr Tim Eggar, stated:

For over a century our two countries have enjoyed special treaty relations, Brunei being a British protected state until 1971. On achieving full independence on 31 December 1983, Brunei chose to maintain her legal link with the Privy Council.
The Bill allows for an adjustment of the arrangements for appeals from the Supreme Court of Brunei to the Judicial Committee. This is considered appropriate because the existing arrangements, which date from when Brunei was a British protected state, do not adequately take account of her independent status.
(HL Debs., 1989–90, Second Reading Committee, col. 3: 6 July 1990)

In the course of an interview on 2 August 1990 with the Minister of State, FCO, Mr William Waldegrave, on the subject of the Iraqi invasion of Kuwait, it was suggested to the Minister that Iraq might claim that Kuwait 'was a natural part of its territory, being part of the old Mesopotamia'. The Minister replied:

Those arguments have come up from time to time since 1913, but Kuwait is a member of the United Nations internationally recognised with diplomatic relations with the world's leading countries, and these matters cannot be settled in this way.
(Text provided by the FCO)

Opening an emergency debate in the House of Lords on the subject of the situation in the Gulf, the Minister of State, FCO, the Earl of Caithness, stated:

Your Lordships will recall that in July Iraq and Kuwait became involved in a dispute over oil pricing and production levels, and over mutual obligations resulting from the production and sale of oil during the Iraq-Iran war. Saddam Hussein also introduced the question of Iraqi territorial claim on Kuwait. The claims by successive Iraqi governments that Kuwait, as part of the former Ottoman province of Basra, was an integral part of Iraq are without legal basis. Kuwait has enjoyed full and recognised independence since 1961 and is a full member of the United Nations.

(HL Debs., vol. 521, col. 1795: 6 September 1990)

In a reply to a question from the British Bankers Association about the legal status of Kuwait business enterprises in the UK following the invasion of Kuwait by Iraq, the Secretary of State for Foreign and Commonwealth Affairs, Mr Douglas Hurd, wrote on 24 October 1990 in part:

Her Majesty's Government, in accordance with United Nations Security Council Resolution 662, considers that the annexation of Kuwait by Iraq has no legal validity, and is therefore null and void. We continue to accept the legitimacy of the Kuwait Government and to have normal dealings with its Embassy in London. Your members will wish to be guided by the above in considering the question of the legal personality of companies established under the law of Kuwait as it applied there before the Iraqi invasion. They will also need to take their own legal advice on a case by case basis.

(Text provided by the FCO)

In moving the second reading in the House of Lords of the Namibia Bill, the Minister of State, FCO, the Earl of Caithness, stated:

Namibia's attainment of independence and entry into the Commonwealth on 21st March this year were a great source of satisfaction to Britain. As a co-author of the UN plan for Namibian independence adopted in 1978 and a major contributor to the UN Transition Group (UNTAG), we played an important role in the independence process.

. . .

The purpose of the Bill before us today is to modify existing legislation to place Namibia on an equal footing with other Commonwealth countries for the purposes of UK law. The Bill follows earlier precedents, the most recent being the Pakistan Act 1990. It involves purely technical amendments to a number of Acts to apply them to Namibia. The Bill covers Namibia's relationship with the Commonwealth Institute. It provides for Namibian forces to be included in the definition of Commonwealth forces with implications for their legal status when visiting the UK, for example for training. It makes provision for the exercise of command and discipline when British and Commonwealth forces are serving together and for attachments of members of one force to another. The Bill also ensures that regulatory powers applying to the whaling industry will not apply to ships registered in Namibia as it is not appropriate for these powers to extend to the shipping of independent members of the Commonwealth.

Clause 2(2) of the Bill deems the Act to have come into force on 21st March 1990, the day Namibia achieved independence and became a member of the Commonwealth. There is no technical reason for this, but clearly there is a strong symbolic value in deeming the provisions of the Act to come into effect on Namibia's independence day.

I should remind your Lordships that the immigration and electoral implications of Namibia's admission to the Commonwealth have been dealt with separately by an Order in Council which came into effect on 25th August 1990. This added

Namibia to the list of Commonwealth countries in Schedule 3 to the British Nationality Act 1981.

(HL Debs., vol. 523, cols. 1091–2: 29 November 1990)

Part Three: I. A. 2. *Subjects of international law—States—international status—non-intervention and non-use of force*

(See also Part Eight: II.D. (item of 6 August 1990))

Interviewed immediately after the invasion of Kuwait by Iraq on 2 August 1990, the Minister of State, FCO, Mr William Waldegrave, stated:

It is a very serious act which we unreservedly condemn as a breach of the United Nations Charter.

(Text provided by the FCO)

Interviewed on the same day, the Secretary of State, for Foreign and Commonwealth Affairs, Mr Douglas Hurd, stated:

This is as clear a case of aggression as anyone could imagine.

(Text provided by the FCO)

The following passage appeared in the report of a press conference held by the FCO on 2 August 1990:

Spokesman drew attention to the statements made earlier today by Mr Waldegrave in which he unreservedly condemned the invasion as a breach of the United Nations Charter.

. . .

Spokesman said that the Iraqi Ambassador had been summoned in this morning by Mr Roger Tomkys, Deputy Under Secretary, to protest at the invasion and repeated the demands for Iraq to withdraw its forces. These views had also been expressed to the Iraqi government at a meeting in Baghdad this morning by our Chargé d' Affaires, Mr Robin Kealy.

(Text provided by the FCO)

Speaking in the UN Security Council on 2 August 1990 on a draft resolution which was then passed as Resolution 660 (1990), the UK Permanent Representative, Sir Crispin Tickell, stated:

We strongly condemn a clear breach of the Charter of the United Nations, as indeed of the Charter of the Arab League. The Security Council must today take its responsibilities.

. . .

We have co-sponsored a strong draft resolution to condemn an unquestionable act of aggression. We welcome the invocation of articles 39 and 40. Iraqi forces must now withdraw unconditionally to where they were only yesterday.

(S/PV. 2932, pp. 19-21, *passim*)

On 3 August 1990, the Twelve Member States of the EC issued a statement which read in part:

Following the break down of talks held in Jeddah under Arab auspices, the Community and its member states are now gravely concerned at the latest developments in the dispute and in particular at the military aggression carried out by Iraq against Kuwait, not only a hostile action to a neighbour country, but also a dangerous threat to peace and stability in the region.

The Community and its member states strongly condemn the use of force by a member state of the UN against the territorial integrity of another state. This constitutes a breach of the UN charter and an unacceptable means to solve international difference. They therefore fully support the resolution adopted today by the Security Council. The Community and its member states call upon all governments to condemn this unjustified use of force and to work for an early re-establishment of the conditions for the immediate resumption of peaceful negotiations: in this light they ask for an immediate withdrawal of Iraqi forces from Kuwait territory.

(Text provided by the FCO)

On 4 August 1990, the Twelve Member States of the EC issued a statement about Kuwait of which a passage read as follows:

The Community and its member states reiterate their unreserved condemnation of the brutal Iraqi invasion of Kuwait and their demand for an immediate and unconditional withdrawal of Iraqi forces from the territory of Kuwait, already expressed in their statement of August 2.

(Text provided by the FCO)

Speaking at Aspen, Colorado, USA, on 5 August 1990 on the same matter, and repeated on BBC radio, the Prime Minister, Mrs Margaret Thatcher, stated in part:

Iraq's invasion of Kuwait defies every principle for which the United Nations stands.

(Text provided by the FCO)

In the case of *In re Insurance Antitrust Litigation* in the US Court of Appeals for the Ninth Circuit, on appeal from the US District Court for the Northern District of California (723 F Supp. 464), the UK Government was permitted to file an *amicus curiae* Brief in support of the dismissal of the claims against British defendants for lack of subject-matter jurisdiction. The Brief, dated 6 August 1990, contained the following passages:

A conflict between U.S. and U.K. law and policy arises in this case because Appellants ask the United States courts to restrict certain conduct in the London reinsurance market, which is for the British Government to regulate, and to subject British nationals to substantial legal liability for conduct the District Court properly found was 'conducted in conformity with English law . . . [for] a legitimate business purpose.' 723 F. Supp. at 490. In these circumstances, an assertion of jurisdiction by the U.S. courts would constitute an interference with the sovereign rights and interests of the British Government which would be inconsistent with international law and comity. Consequently, the District Court properly held that, under the *Timberlane* test, it should not exercise subject matter jurisdiction over the claims against the British Defendants.

. . .

The competition rules of the European Community are part of the framework of competition law in which British insurance operates. The District Court considered and doubted the applicability of Article 85 of the Treaty of Rome in this case. The Court properly drew attention to limitations in that Article. Article 85 only applies to agreements which may affect trade between member States and which have as their object or effect the prevention, restriction or distortion of competition within the Common Market. 723 F. Supp. at 488.

Given this framework and the British Government's obvious legitimate interest in the stability and reliability of the reinsurance market in its territory, the conflict in this case arises because Appellants ask this Court to place restrictions on the British industry which is operating under the British regulatory and competition regime and also to subject British nationals to substantial legal liability for conduct the District Court properly found was 'conducted in conformity with English law . . . [for] a legitimate business purpose.' 723 F. Supp. at 488, 490. Appellants' request that this Court enforce divergent state insurance laws vis à vis the London market gives rise to even more inconsistency and conflict. In these circumstances, an assertion of jurisdiction by the U.S. courts here would constitute an offensive interference with the sovereign rights and interests of the British Government. Consequently, such an assertion of jurisdiction would trigger the provisions of the Protection of Trading Interests Act 1980, ch. 11 described by the District Court. 723 F. Supp. at 488–89.

The District Court correctly found that the challenged practices were 'openly conducted in conformity with English law.' 723 F. Supp. at 488. In any event, Appellant States' argument based on U.K. and EC competition law misconstrues the basis of the conflict with U.K. law and policy. The reason that the British Government objects to Appellants' request that this Court assert extra-territorial jurisdiction over the British defendants is that such an assertion of jurisdiction would constitute an inappropriate interference with the regulatory and competition regime established by the British Government.

That system of regulation, including the competition policy aspects, has its origins in the history of the British insurance industry and of British competition policy, and the way in which the British Parliament has thought fit to legislate on both aspects over the years. It is for the British Parliament in the light of developments, *e.g.*, in the U.K. insurance industry, to decide whether to change the system.[16] It would be inappropriate for a U.S. District Court to do so.

---

[16] Some changes flow from British membership of the European Community. That is quite different from the order of a U.S. District Court applying extraterritorially acts of Congress in whose formulation the British Government played no part, and to whose jurisdiction it has not assented.

(Text provided by Dr A. V. Lowe)

In a statement dated 10 August 1990 the Twelve Member States of the EC declared:

The invasion of Kuwait by Iraqi forces has already provoked an unreserved condemnation by the Community and its member states, which have not only called for the immediate and unconditional withdrawal of Iraqi forces from the territory of Kuwait, but also clearly stated the unacceptability of the situation created by Iraqi military aggression against Kuwait.

Accordingly they reject the announced annexation of Kuwait which is contrary to international law and therefore null and void, as stated in UN Security Council Resolution 662. The same applies to the announced removal of Diplomatic Missions from Kuwait and to any attempt by the Iraqi authorities to exert powers of government within the territory of Kuwait.

(UN Documents A/45/409; S/21502)

In a Communiqué dated 21 August 1990, issued by the Western Economic Union, it was stated:

The Foreign and Defence Ministers of WEU met on 21 August 1990 to discuss the situation in the Gulf caused by the Iraqi invasion and then the annexation of Kuwait. The meeting was held pursuant to Article VIII, Paragraph 3, of the WEU Treaty, the Rome Declaration of October 1984 and the Platform of European Security Interests of October 1987, which provides for member countries to concert their policies on crises outside Europe in so far as they may affect European Security interests.

The Ministers of the WEU member states repeat their unreserved condemnation of the invasion and annexation of Kuwait by Iraq and call on Iraq to comply immediately and unconditionally with UN Security Council Resolutions 660 and 662. They restate their firm determination to continue to take all necessary steps to comply with the embargo of Iraq in accordance with UN Security Council Resolution 661 and to render it effective. They call on the Security Council to take any further useful measures to this end.

Ministers declare that the determination their countries intend to display in upholding the law is for the sole purpose of ending aggression and its consequences. The action they have initiated is aimed to uphold respect of the principles, which must obtain in relations among states, that concerns the whole international community and serves as a safeguard for all its members.

(Text provided by the FCO)

In a television interview on 1 September 1990, the Prime Minister, Mrs Margaret Thatcher, stated with reference to the sending of armed forces to Saudi Arabia:

. . . the real reason we went in was to make it quite clear that in this end of this 20th century you cannot sit back when someone invades another country and takes it by force. If you do that there is no international law, no country is safe. That was the fundamental point of principle.

(Text provided by the FCO)

Later in the interview she stated:

. . . we are showing up Saddam Hussein for what he is, we are making it quite clear that what he is doing is totally contrary to international law as well as totally contrary to civilised behaviour.

(Text provided by the FCO)

In the course of an emergency debate in the House of Commons, on the subject of the situation in the Gulf, the Prime Minister, Mrs Margaret Thatcher, stated:

To return to recent events, despite having assured other Arab Governments and leaders that he had no aggressive intent, Saddam Hussein ordered Iraqi forces to invade Kuwait in the early hours of 2 August. They did so under the pretext of responding to a request for assistance from a non-existent revolutionary government, which they alleged had overthrown the Government of Kuwait.

Saddam Hussein then established a puppet regime consisting of Iraqi officers. That so-called government have now disappeared without trace, and Saddam Hussein claims to have annexed Kuwait, which he now describes as a province of Iraq. History has many examples of perfidy and deceit. This ranks high among them and shows that nothing Saddam Hussein says can be trusted. Moreover, it is an outrageous breach of international law.

Iraq's actions raise very important issues of principle as well as of law. There can be no conceivable justification for one country to march in and seize another, simply because it covets its neighbour's wealth and resources. If Iraq's aggression were allowed to succeed, no small state could ever feel safe again. At the very time when at last we can see the prospect of a world governed by the rule of law, a world in which the United Nations and the Security Council can play the role envisaged for them when they were founded, Iraq's actions go back to the law of the jungle.

(HC Debs., vol. 177, col. 735: 6 September 1990)

In the emergency debate in the House of Lords, the Minister of State, FCO, the Earl of Caithness, stated:

As the dispute developed, Iraq deployed troops in forward positions near the border with Kuwait. Following active Arab diplomacy, notably by President Mubarak of Egypt, Iraq and Kuwait agreed to bilateral talks in Jedda on 1st August with the prospect of a further round in Baghdad. The Iraqi Government gave explicit assurances to Egypt and Saudi Arabia that they had no intention of invading Kuwait. Despite his assurances to other Arab governments and leaders, Saddam Hussein ordered Iraqi forces to invade Kuwait in the early hours of 2nd August. They did so under the pretext of responding to a request for assistance from a non-existent revolutionary government, which they alleged had overthrown the government of Kuwait. Saddam Hussein then established a puppet regime consisting entirely of Iraqi officers. He later claimed to have annexed Kuwait, which he now describes as a province of Iraq.

The invasion was a flagrant breach of faith. It shows that Saddam Hussein cannot be taken at his word. It is equally a flagrant and indefensible breach of international law.

(HL Debs., vol. 521, cols. 1795–6: 6 September 1990)

On 10 September 1990 a joint press statement was issued following a meeting between the Foreign Minister of Japan, Mr Taroi Nakayama, and the Secretary of State for Foreign and Commonwealth Affairs, Mr Douglas Hurd. It read in part:

The Ministers agreed that Iraq's actions were contrary to all norms of international behaviour and clearly contravened the Charter of the United Nations, of which Iraq is a member, as well as established international law.

(FCO Press Release No. 192 of 1990)

On 18 September 1990, the Twelve Member States of the EC issued a declaration which began as follows:

The European Community and its member states reiterate their utter condemnation of the policy of brutal aggression of the Iraqi Government, the increasing persecution of the citizens of Kuwait as well as of the foreign nationals in that country and in Iraq, the taking of hostages and the unacceptable violation of diplomatic premises in Kuwait. They welcome the unanimous adoption by the Security Council of Resolution 667, condemning Iraq for its actions which constitute a flagrant violation of international law and confronting this country with its responsibilities.

(Text provided by the FCO)

On 26 September 1990, the EC and its Member States and the Soviet Union adopted a statement which in part read as follows:

The Gulf crisis has to be urgently resolved. The invasion and military occupation of Kuwait, a sovereign and independent State, by Iraq have been condemned by the whole international community. These acts must not be tolerated since they violate fundamental principles of the UN Charter and international law and create a new, dangerous source of tension in the region.

Proceeding from the principles of inadmissibility of the use of force to settle disputes between States and of the respect for the right of every State to safeguard its national independence and territorial integrity, the European Community and its member States and the Soviet Union demand that Iraq strictly comply with the resolutions of the UN Security Council and immediately and unconditionally withdraw its forces from Kuwait.

They express satisfaction at the high degree of consensus among all members of the UN Security Council and the international community as a whole concerning the need to put an end as soon as possible to the invasion and to restore international legality.

(Text provided by the FCO)

In a statement issued in September 1990, the Heads of State or Government of the States, including the UK, participating in the Conference on Security and Co-operation in Europe, held in Paris, declared:

In accordance with our obligations under the Charter of the United Nations and commitments under the Helsinki Final Act, we renew our pledge to refrain from the threat or use of force against the territorial integrity or political independence of any State, or from acting in any other manner inconsistent with the principles or purposes of those documents. We recall that non-compliance with obligations under the Charter of the United Nations constitutes a violation of international law.

(Text provided by the FCO)

In a statement made on 8 November 1990 in the Sixth Committee of the UN General Assembly, the UK representative, Sir Arthur Watts, remarked:

The work of the International Law Commission, and of our annual debates here in the Sixth Committee on the Report of the Commission, may sometimes appear rather abstract. This year, however, events in the Gulf demonstrate all too clearly the continuing relevance of the topic of the Draft Code of Crimes against the Peace and Security of Mankind.

We are all aware of the blatant aggression against a Member State and its purported annexation, and of a whole series of very serious breaches of international law associated with those events. The catalogue of the international law obligations which have been violated is endless: the Charter, the Geneva Conventions, the Vienna Conventions on Diplomatic and Consular Relations, as well as basic humanitarian principles.

(Text provided by the FCO; see also A/C.6/45/SR.35, p.7)

In the course of a reply to a question, the Secretary of State for Foreign and Commonwealth Affairs wrote in part:

We utterly reject Iraq's illegal occupation and annexation of Kuwait.

(HC Debs., vol. 182, Written Answers, col. *483*: 13 December 1990)

In reply to a question, the Secretary of State for Foreign and Commonwealth Affairs wrote:

Our Chargé d'Affaires in Tehran has expressed to the Iranian Ministry of Foreign Affairs our concern about certain recent statements made in Iran about Mr Rushdie. We continue to understand that the Iranian Government respects international law and would not interfere in the internal affairs of any other country any more than the UK would.

(HC Debs., vol. 183, Written Answers, col. *279*: 20 December 1990)

Part Three: I. A. 3. *Subjects of international law—States—international status—domestic jurisdiction*

(See also Part Three: I. A. 2. (item of 26 November 1990), above)

In reply to a question on the subject of the treatment in Brazil of the Yanomami Indians, the Minister of State, FCO, wrote in part:

I believe the Government's views about the treatment of indigenous minority groups are well known to other Governments, including Brazil. We shall take all suitable opportunities to express our legitimate concern about the plight of the Yanomami indians. However, we must respect the rights of sovereign countries to conduct their own affairs in accordance with their laws. In this case, we must await the outcome of the due legal processes in Brazil.

(HC Debs., vol. 166, Written Answers, col. *189*: 31 January 1990)

In the course of a debate on the subject of the Baltic States, the Minister of State, FCO, Mr William Waldegrave, stated:

Britain does not regard the matter as an internal one for the Soviet Union. Our position, like that of most of the principal western countries, is that the Molotov-Ribbentrop pact was illegal and that there has never been a legal incorporation of the Baltic states into the Soviet Union. Therefore, it is not pari passu with events in other parts of the Soviet Union; it is important to make that distinction.

(HC Debs., vol. 170, col. 1360: 5 April 1990)

Speaking on 26 November 1990 in the Third Committee of the UN General Assembly, the Permanent Representative of Italy, on behalf of the EC and its Member States, stated:

Human rights inherently belong to all human beings and are not granted by governments nor bestowed by States. Unless we all scrupulously and constantly uphold our obligations, we undermine the very foundations of the United Nations. The violation of human rights in any part of the world is a legitimate concern of States, the UN and the world public at large. Such concern and its concomitant activity cannot be construed as constituting an unwarranted interference in the internal affairs of States. This point has been made very clear by the International Court of Justice.

(Text provided by the FCO; see also A/C.3/45/SR.52, p.9)

Part Three: I. B. 1. *Subjects of international law—States—recognition of States*

(See also Part Three: I. B. 5. (item of 1 May 1990), and Part Eight: II. C. (Memorandum of March 1990, paragraph 9), below)

In the course of answering an oral question on the subject of Tibet, the Minister of State, FCO, Mrs Lynda Chalker, stated:

Successive British Governments have regarded Tibet as autonomous, although recognising the special position of the Chinese authorities. That continues to be the Government's view, but we sincerely hope that China will give the people of Tibet their rightful stance.

(HC Debs., vol. 167, col. 658: 19 February 1990; see also HL Debs., vol. 523, Written Answers, col. *35*: 27 November 1990)

In reply to the question whether Her Majesty's Government recognize the declaration of political independence by the new Parliament in Lithuania, the Minister of State, FCO, wrote:

The well-established criteria which we have applied to the recognition of a state are that it should have, and seem likely to continue to have, a clearly defined territory with a population, a government who are able of themselves to exercise control of that territory, and independence in their external relations. We will therefore continue to watch the situation closely as it develops.

(HC Debs., vol. 169, Written Answers, cols. *449–50*: 19 March 1990)

In reply to the question

What steps [Her Majesty's Government] will take to assist the people of Lithuania, Latvia and Estonia in the exercise of their rights of self-determination and in particular whether they will now entertain claims by the governments of those territories for the return of assets which belonged to their predecessors, as foreshadowed by the then Under-Secretary of State for Foreign and Commonwealth Affairs in 1969,

the Government Minister wrote:

If independence is restored to the Baltic States, it would be open to the governments of those states to submit claims. The well established criteria which we have applied to recognition of a state are that it should have, and seem likely to continue to have, a clearly defined territory with a population, a government who are able of themselves to exercise control of that territory, and independence in their external relations.

(HL Debs., vol. 517, col. 721: 26 March 1990)

The FCO presented to the HC Foreign Affairs Committee a memorandum, dated March 1990, entitled 'The Status of the Two German States' in which the following passage appeared:

16. As explained above, HMG recognises both the Federal Republic of Germany and the German Democratic Republic as having the full authority of sovereign States over their external and internal affairs, subject only to Allied rights and responsibilities. Germany as a whole continues to exist as a State in international law, and the special Berlin area remains subject to a special quadripartite status.

(*Parliamentary Papers*, 1989-90, HC, Paper 335-i, p.3)

The following oral question was asked of the Minister of State, FCO, Mr William Waldegrave:

As it is clear that we have never recognised the annexation of the Baltic states by the Soviet Union and, therefore, that we still recognise those nations as independent states, may we have an assurance that the Foreign Office will apply without bias its usual criteria in recognising democratically elected Governments in those countries and will deal normally with them?

Mr Waldegrave replied:

My hon. Friend conflates two things. We recognise states, not Governments. It is perfectly clear at present that there is no independent state of Lithuania to recognise. We wish to encourage the processes which could lead to that rightful outcome.

(HC Debs., vol. 172, col. 180: 9 May 1990)

In reply to the question what conditions have to be fulfilled to enable Her Majesty's Government to establish full diplomatic relations with Lithuania, Latvia and Estonia, the Minister of State, FCO, wrote:

Before we can establish full diplomatic relations with Lithuania, Latvia and Estonia, these republics would need to fulfil our criteria for the recognition of an independent state, which were set out in the answer which I gave . . . on 19 March.

(HC Debs., vol. 173, Written Answers, col. *464*: 5 June 1990)

In reply to the question whether the relationship between the USSR and the Baltic republics is comparable to that between China and Tibet, the Minister of State, FCO, Lord Brabazon of Tara, stated:

. . . the relationships are not comparable. The Government have never recognised the legality of the incorporation of the Baltic states into the Soviet Union in 1940.

Successive governments have regarded Tibet as autonomous, while recognising the special position of the Chinese authorities there.

(HL Debs., vol. 520, col. 2011: 3 July 1990)

In the course of a debate on the subject of Tibet, the Parliamentary Under-Secretary of State, FCO, Mr Tim Sainsbury, reiterated the view set out in the Minister of State's reply of 19 February 1990 and continued:

As the House will be aware, self-determination is an extremely difficult concept to define and there are many different interpretations of its meaning. I accept that, under the United Nations covenant, all people have the right to self-determination, but, as I have said, we do not believe that independence for Tibet is realistic; nor do we believe that United Nations' involvement would lead to a solution of the problem. Tibet has never been internationally recognised as an independent country.

(HC Debs., vol. 177, col. 192: 23 July 1990)

In the course of a debate in the UN Security Council on 9 August 1990, the UK Permanent Representative, Sir Crispin Tickell, stated:

The Iraqi Government is now trying to invoke arguments to justify its actions by harking back to the time of the Ottoman sultans to demonstrate a right to engulf Kuwait. I would just remind the council that on 4 October 1963 Iraq formally recognized Kuwait's sovereignty and independence. Iraq should stand by that undertaking now.

(S/PV. 2934, p. 17)

In reply to the question

what discussions her Majesty's Government, or representatives of alliances of which the United Kingdom is a member, had with Kuwait to Iraq prior to 2 August, concerning adjustment or delineation of the border between Iraq and Kuwait,

the Minister of State, FCO, wrote:

The United Kingdom has not been involved in such discussions since before 1961 when the British Government terminated the exclusive agreement of 1899 with the Kuwaiti Government and recognised Kuwait as a sovereign independent state.

(HC Debs., vol. 183, Written Answers, col. 71: 17 December 1990)

Part Three: I. B. 2. *Subjects of international law—States—recognition— recognition of governments*

In reply to a question on the subject of the recognition of the regime of Mr Endara in Panama, the Parliamentary Under-Secretary of State, FCO, wrote in part:

It is the practice of the United Kingdom and other EC countries to recognise states rather than Governments, so the question of formal recognition does not arise.

(HC Debs., vol. 164, Written Answers, col. *510*: 8 January 1990)

In reply to a question on the subject of the withdrawal of the staff from the British Embassy in Kuwait, the Secretary of State for Foreign and Commonwealth Affairs wrote in part:

We continue to recognise the legitimate Government of Kuwait, who have been informed of our decision to withdraw the embassy staff.

(HC Debs., vol. 182, Written Answers, col. *483*: 13 December 1990)

Part Three: I. B. 5. *Subjects of international law—States—recognition— non-recognition*

Speaking in the UN Commission on Human Rights on 16 February 1990, the UK representative, Mr H. Steel, stated:

. . . the United Kingdom had not recognized the State of Palestine proclaimed on 15 November 1988, and considered that Palestine's present accession to the four Geneva Conventions of 1949 had no legal effect.

(E/CN. 4/1990/SR. 28, p. 7)

In reply to a question, the Minister of State, FCO, wrote:

Since we do not recognise North Korea as a state, and accordingly have no relations with any authorities in North Korea, we can offer no consular protection there. British travellers to North Korea who seek advice from the Foreign and Commonwealth Office are warned of this difficulty.

(HC Debs., vol. 169, Written Answers, col. *330*: 15 March 1990; see also ibid., vol. 168, Written Answers, col. *697*: 7 March 1990)

In reply to an oral question, the Prime Minister, Mrs Margaret Thatcher, stated in part:

. . . we have never recognised the legal annexation of Estonia, Latvia and Lithuania. We recognise especially that Lithuania has expressed the wish to determine her own future.

(HC Debs., vol. 169, col. 1010: 20 March 1990)

In reply to an oral question, the Prime Minister, Mrs Margaret Thatcher, stated in part:

. . . we have never recognised the annexation of Lithuania by the Soviet Union as legal, although it was recognised in fact in the Helsinki accords.

(HC Debs., vol. 170, col. 205: 27 March 1990)

In reply to a question, the Minister of State, FCO, wrote:

We have never recognised de jure the incorporation of Estonia, Latvia and Lithuania into the Soviet Union in 1940. We recognise the right of the Baltic peoples to say what their own future should be.

(HC Debs., vol. 170, Written Answers, col. *189*: 28 March 1990)

In the course of an oral question on the subject of the Baltic States, the Prime Minister, Mrs Margaret Thatcher, stated in part:

I have indicated before in the House that this country never recognized the legality of the annexation of Lithuania, Latvia and Estonia into the Soviet Union. Thus, we have never had any representation in those states and we do not recognize the legality of their annexation now. The Helsinki accord recognized the boundaries in fact but not in law.

(HC Debs., vol. 170, col. 1030: 3 April 1990; see also ibid., col. 1360: 5 April 1990, and HL Debs., vol. 518, col. 1028: 1 May 1990)

In the course of an oral question on the subject of Cyprus, the Minister of State, FCO, Mr Francis Maude, stated in part:

. . . there is certainly no intention to recognise the proclaimed so-called republic of Turkish northern Cyprus. It was illegally declared and we shall not recognise it.

(HC Debs., vol. 170, col. 1181: 3 April 1990)

In reply to a question, the Minister of State, FCO, wrote:

. . . in 1950 we ceased to recognise the nationalist authorities as the Government of China; since that date it has been our policy to have no formal dealings with the authorities in Taiwan.

(HC Debs., vol. 170, Written Answers, col. 705: 4 April 1990)

In reply to the question

Whether annexation of the Baltic States by the Soviet Union in 1940 affected their right to recognition as independent nations; and whether they recognise the recently freely elected President and Government of Lithuania,

the Minister of State, FCO, Lord Brabazon of Tara, stated:

. . . we have never recognised the legality of the incorporation of the Baltic States into the Soviet Union in 1940. The question of the recognition of Lithuania as a state is, however, a separate issue. Lithuania does not at present satisfy the long-standing criteria which we apply to the recognition of a state.

(HL Debs., vol. 518, col. 895: 1 May 1990)

In reply to a further question, the Minister stated:

. . . I was referring to the criteria for the recognition of states. As I said, that applies to the recognition of Lithuania as an independent state. Those criteria are that a state should have and should seem likely to continue to have clearly defined territory with a population, a government who are able to exercise control over that territory and independence in their external relations.

(Ibid., col. 896)

In reply to a question, the Prime Minister wrote:

The Dalai Lama is a distinguished spiritual leader, who is welcome to visit the United Kingdom at any time. But he is also regarded by many of his followers as the leader of a government in exile, which is not recognised by any Government, and with which successive British Governments have had no dealings. I believe that a meeting with him would therefore be open to misinterpretation.

(HC Debs., vol. 172, Written Answers, col. 126; 9 May 1990)

In reply to a question, the Minister of State, FCO, wrote:

The only party to the non-proliferation treaty—the NPT—which has significant nuclear facilities and has not concluded a safeguards agreement with the IAEA is North Korea. We do not recognise North Korea as a state, but we have made clear our concern about the absence of a safeguards agreement, as required under article III of the NPT, at the International Atomic Energy Agency.

(HC Debs., vol. 173, Written Answers, col. *619*: 6 June 1990)

In reply to a question, the Minister of State, FCO, wrote in part:

Five states have acceded to the nuclear non-proliferation treaty since the 1985 review conference, and four others have ratified the treaty. In addition, North Korea, which we do not recognise as a state, acceded in 1985.

(HC Debs., vol. 174, Written Answers, col. *683*: 21 June 1990)

In reply to a question, the Minister of State, FCO, wrote:

Our policy of non-recognition of the so-called 'Turkish Republic of Northern Cyprus' does not preclude operational contracts between British police forces and the Turkish Cypriot police. These are working effectively. The question of extra-dition has not arisen.

(HC Debs., vol. 175, Written Answers, cols. *15–16*: 25 June 1990)

In reply to a question, the Parliamentary Under-Secretary of State, FCO, wrote in part:

We have no plans to recognise North Korea as a state.

(HC Debs., vol. 176, Written Answers, col. *306*: 12 July 1990)

In the course of a table setting out the parties to the Nuclear Non-Proliferation Treaty, the Government Minister in the House of Lords wrote that Taiwan was 'not recognised as a State by Her Majesty's Government' and that North Korea was 'not recognised as a State by Her Majesty's Government'.

(HL Debs., vol. 521, col. 1786: 26 July 1990)

In the course of a statement dated 4 August 1990 on the Iraqi invasion of Kuwait, the Twelve Member States of the EC observed:

They consider groundless and unacceptable the reasons provided by the Iraqi Government to justify the military aggression against Kuwait, and they will refrain from any act which may be considered as implicit recognition of authorities imposed in Kuwait by the invaders.

(Text provided by the FCO)

In reply to a question, the Minister of State, FCO, wrote in part:

While we and other countries, with the exception of South Africa itself, do not recognise Bophuthatswana as an independent state, assistance has been approved since April 1989 for 12 community development projects located within that territory.

(HC Debs., vol. 177, Written Answers, col. 628: 15 October 1990)

In reply to a question, the Minister of State, FCO, wrote:

We welcomed the decision of the French Government to invite representatives of the Baltic states to attend the CSCE summit as 'distinguished guests'. We look forward to a time when it will be possible for the Baltic states to participate in the CSCE process as full members. However, membership and observer status are open only to states internationally recognised as such. The Baltic states are not recognised as independent states.

(HC Debs., vol. 181, Written Answers, col. 200: 22 November 1990)

In reply to a question about the visit of Mr Lennart Meri, Foreign Secretary of Estonia, the Minister of State, FCO, wrote in part:

My right hon. Friend the Secretary of State for Foreign and Commonwealth Affairs and I held separate talks with Mr. Meri on 5 and 6 November. We emphasised that we had never recognised de jure the incorporation of the Baltic States into the USSR and that we continued to support the right of the Estonian people to decide their own future.

(HC Debs., vol. 181, Written Answers, cols. 255-6: 26 November 1990)

In reply to a question about the visit of Mr Landsbergis, President of Lithuania, the same Minister of State wrote in part:

My right hon. Friend the Prime Minister had talks with Professor Landsbergis on 13 November. She emphasised that we had never recognised de jure the incorporation of the Baltic States into the USSR and that we continued to support the right of the Lithuanian people to decide their own future.

(Ibid., col. 256)

In the course of reply, the Minister of State, FCO, wrote:

We do not recognise an independent Kurdish state. The frontiers of states in the region are set by international treaty.

(HC Debs., vol. 182, Written Answers, col. 64: 4 December 1990)

The following certificate, dated 7 December 1990, was issued in respect of the action in the Chancery Division of the High Court of Justice *In the Matter of 167 Queen's Gate, [London] S.W. 7* and *In the Matter of the Trustee Act 1925* (Reference CH 1988 J No. 9745):

I, the Rt Hon Douglas Richard Hurd, Her Majesty's Principal Secretary of State for Foreign and Commonwealth Affairs, refer to the application made under the Trustee Act 1925 by Mr Ernst Jaakson and Dr Aarand Roos in the matter of 167 Queen's Gate, London SW7, and hereby certify as follows:
1. The position of Her Majesty's Government regarding the status of Estonia was set out in a certificate supplied to the Court in the case of the *A/S Tallinna Laevau-*

hisus v *Estonian State Steamship Line (THE VAPPER)* (1946) 79 Lloyd's List
Law Reports page 245. This certificate stated, in part, as follows:–

  '2. His Majesty's Government recognise that Estonia has *de facto* entered the
  Union of Soviet Socialist Republics, but have not recognised this *de jure*.
  3. His Majesty's Government recognise that the republic of Estonia as constituted prior to June, 1940, has ceased *de facto* to have any effective existence.'

The position of Her Majesty's Government remains as stated in such paragraphs of
the above Certificate.

2. Her Majesty's Government do not have dealings with Mr Ernst Jaakson or Dr
Aarand Roos as the representatives of Estonia or the Government thereof.

The following affidavit, dated 10 December 1990, was sworn in respect
of the same action:

I, RODERIC MICHAEL JOHN LYNE of King Charles Street, London, Civil
Servant MAKE OATH AND SAY as follows:

1. I am the head of the Soviet Department of the Foreign and Commonwealth
Office and am authorised to swear this affidavit on behalf of the Crown. I have held
my present post since November 1990. Prior to this I was a Counsellor (Head of
Chancery) in the British Embassy in Moscow. I first served in the Embassy in
Moscow from 1972 to 1974 and in the Eastern European and Soviet Department of
the Foreign and Commonwealth Office from 1976 to 1979.

2. It may assist the Court if I provide a brief account of relevant events in Estonia
and in particular recent events during the course of the present year.

3. The State of Estonia, together with the States of Latvia and Lithuania, came
into existence at the end of the First World War by establishing an effective
national government in its territory and proclaiming its independence. These three
Baltic States were accorded *de jure* recognition by the United Kingdom, together
with other European States, in 1921. They became members of the League of
Nations in 1921. The previous year Estonia and the other two States had concluded treaties with the fledgling Soviet State in which Russian claims to sovereignty were renounced in perpetuity.

4. The Baltic States were incorporated into the Soviet Union in 1940 after secret
Soviet/German agreements delimiting spheres of interest. Her Majesty's Government have never recognised this incorporation *de jure*. Her Majesty's Government
have however recognised that Estonia together with the other Baltic States became
part of the Soviet Union *de facto*. My attention has been drawn to the Certificate
issued in this case, a copy of which is now produced and shown to me marked
'RMJL 1' [see above]. Paragraph 1 of this Certificate repeats the position of Her
Majesty's Government which has been held since 1940 and is in all material
respects the same as that issued on behalf of His Majesty's Government in the case
of *A/S Tallinna Laevauhisus* v *Estonian State Steamship Line: The Vapper* (1946)
79 Lloyd's List Law Reports 245, 251 and 80 id. 101. in the following terms:

  '1. His Majesty's Government recognise the Government of the Estonian Soviet
  Socialist Republic to be the *de facto* Government of Estonia, but do not recognise it as the *de jure* Government of Estonia.
  2. His Majesty's Government recognise that Estonia has *de facto* entered the
  Union of Soviet Socialist Republics, but have not recognised this *de jure*.

3. His Majesty's Government recognise that the Republic of Estonia as constituted prior to June 1940, has ceased *de facto* to have any effective existence.'

5. I should, however, state that it is no longer appropriate to repeat paragraph 1 of the Certificate supplied to the Court in the *Vapper*, because since 1980 Her Majesty's Government have no longer accorded recognition to Governments. That change of practice is set out in the settlement made in the House of Commons by the Lord Privy Seal on 25 April 1980, a true copy of which is now shown and produced to me marked 'RMJL 2' [not reproduced; see UKMIL 1980, p. 367].

6. The position, as it remains to day, was expressed by the then Minister of State at the Foreign and Commonwealth Office, Lord Belstead, on 28 March 1983:

'In 1940 HMG ceased to recognise any authorities as constituting the Governments of the Baltic States and they still take a similar position. Thus, there is no authority which can appoint diplomatic representatives for Latvia, Estonia and Lithuania. Therefore, no persons who did not hold diplomatic rank in the legations of those countries in 1940 can be accorded diplomatic courtesies.' (1983 440 HL Debs., 1449) [see UKMIL 1983, p. 384].

7. Mention should be made at this stage of the Agreement between the Government of the United Kingdom of Great Britain and Northern Ireland and the Government of the Union of Soviet Socialist Republics concerning the settlement of mutual financial and property claims made in London on 5 January 1968. This Agreement is referred to in paragraph 4 of the Affidavit of John Stowell Allan dated 20 December 1988 and extracts from which are exhibited as exhibit 'JSA 2' [not reproduced]. The purpose of the Agreement is set out in its preamble which reads 'The Government of the United Kingdom of Great Britain and Northern Ireland and the Government of the Union of Soviet Socialist Republics; in formulation of the agreement concerning the final settlement of mutual property and financial claims arising after 1 January 1939 reached between the parties and set out in the joint declaration of 12 February 1967; have agreed as follows:-'. I need not set out the rest of the Agreement which is now produced and shown to me marked 'RMJL 3' [not reproduced; see TS No. 12 (1968) (Cmnd. 3517)]. This Agreement did not affect the position of Her Majesty's Government with regard to recognition.

8. Throughout the decades from 1945 through to the 1980s the Soviet Government was in *de facto* control of Estonia and there was nothing apparent to an observer to suggest that this position might change. However, in the late 1980s, the new policies of democratisation and *glasnost* allowed long-suppressed national aspirations to be articulated and increasing demands for sovereignty to be expressed, in Estonia as elsewhere.

9. On 30 March 1990, the Estonian Supreme Soviet passed a decree asserting that the Soviet occupation of 1940 did not *de jure* curtail the existence of the Estonian Republic and that Estonian territory remained under occupation.
The decree also:

a. asserted Soviet power to have been illegal since its inception and proclaimed the start of the restoration of the Estonian State; and

b. announced a transitional period leading to the formation of the constitutional authorities of the Estonian Republic.

10. On 7 April 1990 the USSR Supreme Soviet adopted a law on secession. The main points are that:
  - a referendum must take place in the republic concerned, not less than six months after the decision to begin secession procedures;
  - at least two thirds of the permanent residents of the republic must vote in favour of secession;
  - the USSR Congress of People's Deputies must set a term (of up to five years) for a transition period of negotiation between the republic and Moscow (which covers a number of potentially very difficult areas);
  - after this period the Congress is required to confirm that the process has been properly carried out before the republic finally secedes;
  - in republics (such as Estonia) where there are places densely populated by non-indigenous groups, the latter have the right to decide whether to remain within the USSR or the seceding republic.

11. A new draft Union treaty being discussed by the Supreme Soviet of the USSR includes the following points: under the terms of the draft, the Union of Sovereign Soviet Republics is a Sovereign federal state composed of a free association of sovereign states. Membership of the Union is voluntary. The treaty also outlines areas of Union and republican competence and sets out new state and government structures. Many important areas remain under central control (defence, security, major foreign policy and economic policy decisions). The Estonian authorities have made it clear that they are unwilling to sign a new treaty or to participate in its elaboration.

12. Successive Governments of Her Majesty have not recognised *de jure* the forcible incorporation of the three Baltic States into the Soviet Union. They support the right of the Baltic peoples to determine their own future. There is now a viable constitutional route open by which the Estonians and the other Baltic States could obtain independence. But they would have to pass through all the hoops of the secession legislation before achieving independence. The position of the Estonian authorities, however, is that Estonia has never formed part of the Soviet Union and is therefore not bound by Soviet legislation. The process of negotiation between Moscow and Tallinn has therefore been difficult. Her Majesty's Government has urged both sides to continue negotiation as the only way satisfactorily to resolve their differences. Talks broke down in early September after only 3 meetings; they resumed in early November.

13. If events develop to a point where Her Majesty's Government has dealings with a Government of Estonia on a normal government-to-government basis, there will be questions to be resolved—including that of property rights. These are, however, unlikely to be resolved as questions of pure law and they will probably be a matter for political negotiations. Her Majesty's Government would have to consider at this point whether Estonia is regarded as a continuation of the old state, or its successor or something in between. Her Majesty's Government have not adopted any position or made any public announcements on whether the pre-1940 Baltic States can in some sense be said to still be in existence. It is difficult at this stage to speculate what might happen. Much would depend on the form in which the State is established and the nature of its relationship with the Union of Soviet Socialist Republics, or whatever it is ultimately styled.

(Texts provided by the FCO)

Part Three: I. C. 4. *Subjects of international law—States—types of States—dependent States and territories*

(See also Part One: II. D. 1. (items of 3 November 1988 and 19 April 1990), above, and Part Three: I. E. (items of 3 November 1988, March 1990, 16 February, 20 November, 6 December 1990), below)

On 15 January 1990 the Secretary of State for Foreign and Commonwealth Affairs, Mr Douglas Hurd, sent a message to the Pitcairn Islanders to commemorate their 200th anniversary. The territory of Pitcairn comprises Pitcairn, Oeno, Henderson and Ducie Islands, of which only Pitcairn, with a population of about 56, is inhabited. The Governor, who is also British High Commissioner to New Zealand, resides in Wellington and his Commissioner resides in Auckland. In a background paper accompanying the FCO Press release, it was stated:

CONSTITUTION

3. In November [1838], Pitcairn was annexed as a British Colony when Captain Russell Elliott of HMS 'Fly' drew up a simple constitution and code of laws for the Pitcairners and in 1893 Captain Rooke of HMS 'Champion' introduced parliamentary government to Pitcairn. In 1904 the British Consul in Tahiti drew up a constitution which lasted until 1940 when the present system of government was introduced.

4. Management of internal affairs is now in the charge of an 11-member Island Council, meeting under the chairmanship of the Island Magistrate. The Council is composed of the Magistrate, two Councillors, the Chairman of the Internal Committee, the Island Secretary, three nominated members and two advisory members. The Island Education Officer also acts as Government adviser but has no vote on the Council.

(FCO Press Release No. 15 of 1990)

On 1 February 1990, a Memorandum of Understanding on co-operation in the field of maritime narcotics interdiction operations ('Shiprider' Memorandum) was signed in Tortola, British Virgin Islands, by the Governor of the British Virgin Islands for the UK (on behalf of the British Virgin Islands) and the Commander of the 7th US Coastguard District for the US. In a background paper released at the time of signature it was stated that the Memorandum 'covers areas of co-operation between the US Coastguard and the BVI forces of law and order and will enable representatives of the two forces to travel on each other's vessels on the seas in and around the British and US Virgin Islands'. (FCO Press Release No. 37 of 1990)

In an explanation of vote in the UN General Assembly on 25 October 1990 on the subject of information from non-self-governing territories, the UK representative stated:

My delegation as usual abstained on the draft resolution just adopted. We have always made clear that we will continue to comply with our obligations under

Article 73e of the United Nations Charter in respect of the British Dependent Territories. But we do not agree with the assertion, contained in operative paragraph 2 of the draft resolution, that it is for the General Assembly to decide when a non-self-governing territory has reached a level of self-government sufficient to relieve the administering power of the obligation to submit information under Article 73e. Such decisions must be left to the government of the territory concerned and the administering power.

(Text provided by the FCO)

Part Three: I. D. 2. *Subjects of international law—States—formation, continuity and succession of States—identity, continuity and succession*

(See also Part Three: I. B. 5. (affidavit of 10 December 1990, paragraph 13), above, and Part Eight: II. A. (item of 25 September 1990), below)

In the course of a debate on the subject of gold and other items deposited in London for safe keeping in the early 1920s by Latvia, Lithuania and Estonia at a time when these entities were independent sovereign States, the Minister of State, FCO, Mr William Waldegrave, first referred to the Foreign Compensation Bill which became the Foreign Compensation Act 1969. He continued:

Mr. Whitlock, who was the junior Minister responsible for the legislation, repeated in column 608 of the *Official Report* for 22 January 1969 what he had said in Committee:
'nothing contained in or done under the Bill would preclude any independent Baltic republic at some time in the future from submitting a claim to the British Government of the day in respect of the property in question if it considered that it had such a claim'—[*Official Report, Standing Committee A*, 19th November 1968, c. 23.]
Therein lies the heart of the matter.
My hon. Friend correctly said that we had never recognised de jure the incorporation of the states into the Soviet Union. We believe that independence now can be achieved only by a process of negotiation. Doubtless that is the course of action which my right hon. Friend the Prime Minister will discuss with the elected Prime Minister of Lithuania at their meeting tomorrow. Doubtless she will wish to urge and explore the possibility of a route to successful negotiation.
If such negotiations were successful, if independent statehood was achieved and if recognition could be accorded, there would be nothing to preclude that state, or any of the other Baltic states, bringing action if they believed they had a claim and could prove title in succession to the original Governments. They would then have to accept that if they were in a position to make claims they would also be in a position to accept their obligations. That would be a matter for the courts at the time.
My hon. Friend referred to the know-how funds for eastern European countries. If the happy outcome which I have described were to be achieved, we and, I am sure, other western countries would not be backward in bringing help and know-how to independent Baltic states. Sadly, we are some way from that, although Baltic independence is now a real possibility which would have seemed inconceivable in 1968.

If there is a happy outcome, and if the Baltic states win back their legal right to independence, the matters may come before the courts again. Nothing in the action of the Government in 1968 could prevent that from happening. The outcome would be a matter for the legal jurisdiction at that time.

(HC Debs., vol. 172, col. 172: 8 May 1990)

Part Three: I. E. *Subjects of international law—States—self-determination*

(See also Part Three: I. B. 1. (item of 23 July 1990), above, and Part Eight: II. A. (items of 14 March, 20 June and 22 November 1990), below)

Introducing before the UN Human Rights Committee the UK's second periodic report under Article 40 of the International Covenant on Civil and Political Rights, 1966, the UK representative, Mr P. R. Fearn, stated on 3 November 1988:

One of the territories examined during the Committee's consideration of the initial report—Belize—was absent from the second report because its people had acquired their independence in 1981. In the light of the United Kingdom's commitment to self-determination and its resolve to fulfil its obligations under the Charter of the United Nations and the Covenant to the best of its ability, the United Kingdom Government had, in 1987, reviewed its policy towards its Caribbean dependent territories and Bermuda, and had concluded that it should not seek to influence opinion in the territories on the question of independence but would remain ready to respond favourably when the people clearly and constitutionally expressed their wish for such independence. That policy, which had been announced in Parliament on 16 December 1987, had been given widespread publicity in the territories concerned. The United Kingdom's aim was to ensure the good administration and economic and social development of all its dependent territories, whose reasonable needs would continue to be a first charge on its aid funds. It remained determined to discharge its obligations under the Covenant in full, even when that meant the temporary suspension of ministerial government, as had been necessary in the Turks and Caicos Islands in 1986.

(CCPR/C/SR. 855, p. 4)

Mr Fearn later observed:

. . . self-determination did not inevitably lead to independence; that would be a contradiction in terms. [He described the various options which existed in that regard in the 10 dependent territories referred to in the report of the United Kingdom.]

Firstly, in Gibraltar, independence was excluded under the provisions of the 1713 Treaty of Utrecht, which stated that, if the United Kingdom gave up its sovereignty over those territories, Spain would exercise its rights. In 1967, a referendum on the future of Gibraltar had produced clear-cut results: 99 per cent of the voters had chosen to maintain the current constitutional relationship with the United Kingdom. Independence was therefore not an option for Gibraltar: the choice was between the present constitutional relationship and becoming part of Spain.

(Ibid., p. 8)

The third periodic report of the UK under Article 40 of the above Covenant contained the following passage, referring to its Article 1:

Successive British Governments have since 1945 consistently promoted self-government and independence in the dependent territories of the United Kingdom in accordance with the wishes of the inhabitants and the provisions of the United Nations Charter. The United Kingdom's policy towards the dependent territories for which the United Kingdom is still responsible continues to be founded on respect for the inalienable right of peoples to determine their own future. The vast majority of the dependent territories for which the United Kingdom was previously responsible have chosen, and now enjoy, independence. A small number, however, prefer to remain in close association with the United Kingdom, although they are able to modify their choice at any time.

As regards paragraph 3 of article 1, the United Kingdom's support for the right of self-determination is well known. The United Kingdom regularly supports resolutions in United Nations bodies calling for the realization of that right.

The right to self-determination in the United Kingdom itself is exercised primarily through the electoral system. British citizens and citizens of other Commonwealth countries, together with citizens of the Republic of Ireland, are entitled to vote at Parliamentary elections provided they are aged 18 or over, resident in the United Kingdom and not subject to any legal incapacity to vote; most British citizens living abroad are also eligible to register as electors.

(CCPR/C/58 Add. 6, pp. 3–4: March 1990)

Speaking on 1 February 1990 in the UN Commission on Human Rights, the UK representative, Mr H. Steel, stated in respect of the situation in the Middle East:

No solution to the problems of that region could be regarded as realistic unless it was based on full respect for all the human rights of the Palestinians, including their right to self-determination, as well as the right of Israel to exist within secure and recognized boundaries.

(E/CN. 4/1990/SR. 5, p. 15)

Later in his speech, Mr Steel observed:

. . . the right to self-determination was a right of peoples, not of the State or the Government of a State. Indeed, it was a right which peoples often had to assert against the encroachments of their Governments. The right to self-determination therefore always entailed the option of choosing a new social or political order in response to new demands.

(Ibid., p. 16)

In reply to a question, the Minister of State, FCO, wrote:

We support Palestinian self-determination and are closely involved in current efforts to promote a dialogue between Israel and representative Palestinians, as an important step towards a settlement.

(HC Debs., vol. 166, Written Answers, col. *684*: 7 February 1990)

In reply to a question on the subject of relations with Argentina in respect of the Falkland Islands, the Parliamentary Under-Secretary of State, FCO, wrote in part:

The normalisation of relations with Argentina has been achieved without discussion of sovereignty over the Falklands. The Government's determination to defend the islanders' right to determine their own future remains firm.

(HC Debs., vol. 167, Written Answers, col. *452*: 16 February 1990)

In reply to a question, the Secretary of State for Foreign and Commonwealth Affairs, Mr Douglas Hurd, stated in part:

We have made clear our long-standing support for German unity on the basis of free self-determination.

(HC Debs., vol. 172, col. 177: 9 May 1990)

In reply to a question about her discussions with the Prime Minister of Lithuania, the Prime Minister wrote in part:

We stressed that the Lithuanian people have the right to self-determination.

(HC Debs., vol. 172, Written Answers, col. *283*: 14 May 1990)

In the course of a debate on the subject of India and Kashmir, the Parliamentary Under-Secretary of State, FCO, Mr Tim Sainsbury, stated:

. . . there have been a number of United Nations resolutions on Kashmir. In 1948 and 1949, the issue was whether Kashmir should accede to Pakistan or to India, and not independence; that was not on the table. Self-determination was always understood to mean the freedom of the Kashmiri people to choose between India and Pakistan. Britain voted in favour of the resolutions, the texts of which represented agreement between India and Pakistan at the time.

(HC Debs., vol. 177, col. 210: 23 July 1990)

In the course of a letter, dated 1 August 1990, to Sir Peter Blaker MP, the Secretary of State for Foreign and Commonwealth Affairs, Mr Douglas Hurd, wrote:

We continue to work for peace and justice in the Middle East, where there is an urgent need for progress towards a settlement which will permit the Palestinians to exercise their right to self-determination while guaranteeing Israel's security.

(Text provided by the FCO)

In a statement issued in September 1990, the Heads of State or Government of the States, including the UK, participating in the Conference on Security and Co-operation in Europe, held in Paris, declared:

We reaffirm the equal rights of peoples and their right to self-determination in conformity with the Charter of the United Nations and with the relevant norms of international law, including those relating to territorial integrity of States.

(Text provided by the FCO)

Speaking on 8 October 1990 in the Third Committee of the UN General Assembly on behalf of the EC and its Member States, the Permanent Representative of Italy stated:

A further item on our agenda is the right to self-determination, a subject which is, in our view, one of the most important on the agenda of the United Nations.

The Principles laid down in the Charter and the first article of the International Covenants, which is common to both, proclaim the right to self-determination. It is important to underscore that, under these instruments, self-determination is the right of all peoples and not the right of States. All human beings have the right to self-determination and they are entitled to exercise it, wherever and under whichever conditions.

The European Community and its member States fully support this fundamental right and consistently strive for its universal respect and implementation. We are therefore deeply concerned at the too many instances in which the right to self-determination is denied to people, or they are deprived of it.

The speaker then continued:

The European Community and its member States have strongly condemned, therefore, the brutal invasion, occupation and annexation of Kuwait by Iraq. It constitutes a flagrant breach of the U.N. Charter and has been condemned, as such, by the Security Council. The international community has been united in its denunciation of this violation of fundamental principles and norms of international law.

(Text provided by the FCO; see also A/C. 3/45/SR. 3, p. 11)

Speaking on 16 October 1990 in the same Committee, the UK representative, Mr M. Raven, stated:

Our commitment to self-determination is well-known. And our decolonisation record amply demonstrates the importance we attach to the principle of self-determination. Of course self-determination is an on-going process. But since this Assembly last met there has been a blatant example of one country refusing to accept the right of self-determination. I refer of course to the situation in the Gulf, where Iraq so brutally invaded and purported to annex its neighbour Kuwait—a most intolerable act of aggression. The Security Council has demonstrated the resolve of the international community to reverse Iraq's actions. We call once again for the immediate and unconditional withdrawal of foreign troops from Kuwait and for the restoration of Kuwait's territorial integrity and sovereignty, under the authority of its legitimate government. Iraq's blatant disregard for the principle of self-determination cannot be tolerated.

(Text provided by the FCO; see also A/C. 3/45/SR. 9, p. 3)

On 17 October 1990 the FCO issued a statement which it had released earlier in Jerusalem. The statement read in part:

The British Foreign Secretary was misreported this morning in the local media. He did not say that Britain was opposed to a Palestinian State. The British position is well-known—it favours self-determination for the Palestinian people. Whether or not that leads to a Palestinian State is a matter for them and for negotiation.

(Text provided by the FCO)

In the course of a statement on the subject of developments in the Middle East, the Secretary of State for Foreign and Commonwealth Affairs, Mr Douglas Hurd, remarked:

The policy of the British Government is clear. It has been restated today and was restated during my recent visit. It involves self-determination for the Palestinian people and the right of Israel to live in peace behind secure borders.

(HC Debs., vol. 178, col. 336: 24 October 1990)

Having repeated in the House of Lords the above statement, the Government spokesman, Lord Reay, observed in the course of the following debate:

Self-determination may or may not result in an independent Palestinian state. That is the Government's view.

(HL Debs., vol. 522, col. 1355: 24 October 1990)

In reply to a question, the Parliamentary Under-Secretary of State, FCO, wrote:

We have always supported the Palestinians' legitimate right to self-determination. We also support Israel's right to exist within secure borders. A settlement of the Palestinian problem should be on this basis. Whether it will include a Palestinian state is a matter for resolution between the parties.

(HC Debs., vol. 178, Written Answers, col. *386*: 29 October 1990; see also ibid., vol. 181, col. 856: 28 November 1990)

Reporting on a meeting held on 6 November 1990 between Mr Lennart Meri, the Estonian Minister of Foreign Affairs, and the Secretary of State for Foreign and Commonwealth Affairs, Mr Douglas Hurd, the FCO press spokesman said:

Mr Hurd had reaffirmed the British Government's support for the right of the Baltic peoples to determine their own future.

(Text provided by the FCO)

Speaking on 20 November 1990 in the UN General Assembly, the UK representative, Mr T. L. Richardson, stated:

We remind the Assembly once again that the right to self-determination does not necessarily mean full independence. The peoples of our remaining dependent territories exercise their right to self-determination every time they go to the polls. Whether they decide to assume the responsibilities of full independence is entirely a matter for them. We respect their decisions.

(Text provided by the FCO; see also A/45/PV. 44, p. 72)

In the course of a reply, the Minister of State, FCO, wrote:

Britain's commitment to the people of Gibraltar, enshrined in the 1969 constitution, is well known. This Government will not enter into arrangements under which the people of Gibraltar would pass under the sovereignty of another state against their freely and democratically expressed wishes. The 1969 constitution also sets out the division of powers between the elected Government of Gibraltar and the British Government. It bestows an appropriate level of self-government for domestic matters while preserving British sovereignty and reserving necessary powers to Britain.

. . .

The British Government are fully committed to the negotiating process with Spain (the Brussels process) aimed at overcoming all the differences between the British and Spanish Governments over Gibraltar. It covers the question of sovereignty, as well as mutually beneficial co-operation. Spanish sovereignty over Gibraltar would be possible only if acceptable to the Gibraltarians. Under the treaty of Utrecht independence is not an option, unless Spain is prepared to agree.

(HC Debs., vol. 182, Written Answers, col. *189* : 6 December 1990)

Part Three: II. A. 1. *Subjects of international law—international organizations—in general—legal status*

In response to a suggestion to incorporate a 'European flag' on the number-plates of vehicles registered in the UK, the Minister of State, FCO, Lord Brabazon of Tara, wrote in part that '[t]he object of the European flag proposal is to foster in all member States a sense of identity with the European Community' (HL Debs., vol. 521, col. 1444: 24 July 1990).

In reply to the question

Following the answer of Lord Brabazon of Tara on 24th July, whether they now perceive the European Community as a state rather than a group of co-operating sovereign nations,

the Minister of State, FCO, wrote:

No. The status of the European Community is set out in the Treaties, from which it is clear that the EC does not constitute a state.

(HL Debs., vol. 522, col. 135: 8 October 1990)

Part Three: II. A. 1. (c). *Subjects of international law—international organizations—in general—legal status—privileges and immunities*

In moving the consideration in HC Standing Committee of the draft European Communities (Privileges of the European School) Order 1989 and the draft European Communities (Definition of Treaties) (European School) Order 1989, the Parliamentary Under-Secretary of State, FCO, Mr Tim Sainsbury, stated:

The United Kingdom acceded to the statute of the European school and protocol on 30 August 1972. The European school at Culham in Oxfordshire was set up in 1978 to provide a school for the children of Community staff working at the Joint European Torus, known normally as JET. A substantial number of scientists and officials working at JET are members of the staff of the European Commission and may at any time be required to return to other Community centres or to their own member states.

Article 28 of the statute of the European school provides for the conclusion by the board of governors of the school of agreements governing the treatment of the schools. It is in accordance with this provision that the headquarters agreement between the United Kingdom and the board of governors concerning the European school at Culham was concluded. This headquarters agreement is designed to ensure, in accordance with article 28 of the statute, that the school can operate 'in a favourable atmosphere under the best possible physical conditions.'

The agreement serves the purpose of applying in detail the general provisions on the establishment and government of European schools which are included in the statute and the protocol. It is, therefore, ancillary to the statute and protocol, which are themselves regarded as pre-accession treaties, and therefore comes within the terms of section 1(3) of the European Communities Act 1972.

It is, therefore, proposed that the first draft order before the Committee, that relating to the definition of treaties, should be made under section 1(3) of the 1972 Act specifying the headquarters agreement as a Community treaty. That order provides the basis for the second order, that relating to the privileges of the European school provided by the headquarters agreement, which will be made under section 2(2) of the European Communities Act.

The headquarters agreement specifies the privileges which the European School is to enjoy in the UK. The principal privileges to be conferred are, first, for the European school itself, legal capacity, exemption from taxes on income and capital gains, relief from VAT, exemption from import duties; secondly, for teachers seconded to the school by member states, exemption from social security legislation, first arrival customs privileges, exemption from income tax on earnings, limited in the case of staff seconded by the United Kingdom to the European supplement paid by the school. Similar privileges have been granted by all other host Governments. The UK is in any event required to provide exemption of the European supplement by judgment of the European Court. The locally recruited staff at the school do not benefit from these privileges, and the Committee will note that no one is given any immunity.

The draft Orders in Council will, when made, enable the Government to give effect to the agreement between the United Kingdom and the board of governors of the European school. We are satisfied that the privileges accorded under the draft orders are necessary both to fulfil our obligations and to enable the school at Culham to function effectively.

(*Parliamentary Papers*, 1989–90, HC, Third Standing Committee on Statutory Instruments, etc.: 23 January 1990, cols. 3–4. See also UKMIL 1989, pp. 600–1 and 603)

In moving the approval of the draft European Bank for Reconstruction and Development (Immunities and Privileges) Order 1990, the Minister for Overseas Development, Mrs Lynda Chalker, stated in part:

As a member of the bank, we shall, of course, need to grant it certain immunities and privileges. The draft order will give effect to the immunities and privileges set out in chapter VIII of the articles of agreement, and attested to by all signatories as necessary to enable the bank to fulfil its purpose and functions. All member states will grant the bank these immunities and privileges. The order will confer legal status upon the bank and gives it certain exemptions from duties and taxation; its property will also enjoy certain immunities from seizure.

The officers and employees of the bank will be exempt from taxation on the salaries paid to them by the bank, although they will pay an internal tax for the benefit of the bank, and they will be immune from suit and legal process in respect of their official acts.

While the order cannot come into force until the date on which the agreement establishing the bank comes into force—that is, after ratification by members with two thirds of the total voting power—it is important that the draft order be approved now so that the United Kingdom can ratify as proposed.

We shall also need to negotiate a headquarters agreement with the bank, as an international organisation to be established in this country. This headquarters agreement will set out in detail the immunities and privileges of the bank and its employees, within the limits imposed by the International Organisations Act 1968, and will require a further order to be approved by the House when negotiations are completed.

The headquarters agreement, once approved by Parliament, will not have effect until the bank comes into existence, but as host nation, we would of course wish matters to be settled before entry into force of the articles of agreement. We would therefore expect to return to the House with the second order as soon as possible in the autumn.

The United Kingdom is already home to several important international organisations, but this is the first multilateral development bank to be established here.

(HC Debs., vol. 177, cols. 401–2: 24 July 1990)

In moving the approval of the same draft Order in the House of Lords, the Government spokesman, Lord Reay, stated:

. . . the order, when made, will give effect to the immunities and privileges set out in chapter VIII of the articles of agreement and attested to by all signatories as necessary to enable the bank to fulfil its purposes and functions. All signatories are required to give effect to these basic immunities and privileges.

. . .

The principal privileges and immunities to be conferred on the bank by this order, under the provisions of the International Organisations Act 1968, as amended, are legal capacity, certain immunities from seizure of its property and assets, inviolability of its archives, exemptions from taxes on income, capital gains and other direct taxes, certain exceptions from Customs and Excise duties and restrictions on goods imported for official use, and relief from VAT. Officers and employees of the bank will be exempted from taxation on salaries paid to them by the bank, although there will be an internal tax for the benefit of the bank, as well as immunity from suit and legal process in respect of their official acts.

. . . a headquarters agreement is to be negotiated with the bank which will set out in detail the immunities and privileges of the bank and its employees within the limits imposed by the International Organisations Act 1968, as amended. Approval by your Lordships of a further order will be sought later when negotiations are completed. This process must be finalised before the bank is ready to commence full operations here.

(HL Debs., vol. 521, cols. 1544–5: 25 July 1990)

In moving the consideration by the HC First Standing Committee on Statutory Instruments of the draft European Commission and Court of Human Rights (Immunities and Privileges) (Amendment) Order 1990, the Parliamentary Under-Secretary of State, FCO, Mr Mark Lennox-Boyd, stated:

The order arises from the fifth protocol to the general agreement on the privileges and immunities of the Council of Europe.

. . .

The draft statutory instrument which has been laid in accordance with section 10 of the International Organisations Act 1968 will enable the Government to give effect to the United Kingdom's obligations under the protocol by conferring an exemption from income tax on the emoluments paid by the Council of Europe to members of the Commission and judges of the court. It is usual for the emoluments of officials of international organisations to be exempted from national tax. Exemption of the emoluments of members of the Commission and judges of the court will ensure equality of treatment with emoluments paid to judges of the European Court of Justice, and the International Court of Justice.

(HC Debs., 1989–90, First Standing Committee on Statutory Instruments, etc.: 23 October 1990, cols. 3–4. See Statutory Instruments 1990 No. 2290 made on 20 November 1990)

Speaking on 1 November 1990 in the Fifth Committee of the UN General Assembly on behalf of the Member States of the EC, the Permanent Representative of Italy stated:

The Twelve believe that the subject of respect for the privileges and immunities of officials of the U.N. System is worthy of particular attention especially now.

The Twelve want first of all to express their support for action by the Secretary-General in cases of arrest, detention or any other matters relating to that respect which is due to U.N. staff in the exercise of their functions in connection with and on behalf of the Organizations as spelled out in article 105 of the Charter.

They appeal to all governments and other groups responsible for the illegal detention of U.N. staff members immediately to release them. As in previous years, . . . The Twelve wish to remember the case of Alec Collett who has been missing without news since 1985.

The Twelve are concerned about all such violations. They deem unacceptable the disregard for article 105 of the Charter that has been displayed by some Member States. The Twelve strongly urge all Member States to scrupulously respect the privileges and immunities of all officials of the United Nations and the specialized Agencies and related organizations.

. . .

The Twelve Member States of the European Community renew their appeal to all Governments for their utmost solidarity in exercising any possible pressure for obtaining the respect of international law, including the Charter, the Convention of 1946 and other relevant international instruments and several bilateral agreements. The Twelve reiterate their support to the Secretary-General and the Executive Heads of the Agencies for obtaining that respect.

(Text provided by the FCO; see also A/C. 5/45/SR. 19, p. 4)

Part Three: II. A. 2. (a). *Subjects of international law—international organizations—in general—legal status—participation of States in international organizations—admission*

In moving the second reading in the House of Commons of the Pakistan Bill, the Parliamentary Under-Secretary of State, FCO, Mr Tim Sainsbury, stated:

The Bill's purpose is, I hope, welcome, It is to modify existing domestic legislation in order to place Pakistan on the same footing as other Commonwealth countries, following its return to the Commonwealth on 1 October of last year, after a decision by consensus of the other member countries of the Commonwealth.

. . .

To return to the contents of the Bill, it is intended to amend a number of Acts in order to extend to Pakistan the provisions applying to other Commonwealth countries. It deals with Pakistan's relationship with the Commonwealth Institute. It reinstates the right of the Government of Pakistan to appoint a trustee to the board of the Imperial War Museum. It makes amendments to our legislation relating to the armed forces in order to define the legal status of Pakistan forces when, for example, training in this country. It provides for the exercise of command and discipline when British forces and Commonwealth forces are serving together, and for attachment of members of one force to another. It ensures that arrangements for the reciprocal enforcement of judgments with Pakistan remain in force.

The immigration and electoral implications of Pakistan's renewed membership of the Commonwealth were dealt with separately by an Order in Council made on 2 August last year. That added Pakistan to the list of Commonwealth countries given in schedule 3 to the British Nationality Act 1981. It is a technical Bill. I hope it is a welcome Bill, and I commend it to the House.

(HC Debs., vol. 172, cols. 692–3: 14 May 1990)

Part Three: II. B. 2. *Subjects of international law—international organizations—particular types of organizations—regional organizations*

In the course of a debate on the subject of the North Atlantic Salmon Conservation Organization, the Minister of State, Scottish Office, Lord Sanderson of Bowden, stated:

It might be helpful if I were to explain to your Lordships that the North Atlantic Salmon Conservation Organisation (NASCO) was set up in 1984 and that its objective is to promote the conservation, restoration, enhancement and rational management of north Atlantic salmon stocks. At present, there are nine contracting parties to NASCO covering all the 'home water' coastal states for salmon throughout their range in the north Atlantic from the USA to the USSR. The European Community is a contracting party represented by the Commission, and so too, separately, is Denmark in respect of its special relationship with the Faroe Islands and Greenland.

(HL Debs., vol. 519, col. 1500: 6 June 1990)

Part Three: III. D. *Subjects of international law—subjects of international law other than States and organizations—mandated and trust territories, Namibia*

(See Part Three: I. A. 1. (item of 29 November 1990), above, and Part Eight: III. B. (item of 5 April 1990), below)

Part Three: III. F. *Subjects of international law—subjects of international law other than States and organizations—miscellaneous—national liberation movements*

In an explanation of vote in the Sixth Committee of the UN General Assembly on 20 November 1990, the representative of Italy, on behalf of the Twelve Member States of the EC, stated:

The Twelve will not vote in favour of Draft Resolution L.12 on the 'observer status of national liberation movements recognized by the Organization of African Unity and/or by the League of Arab States'.

The negative votes and the abstentions of the Twelve member States of the European Community are due to purely legal considerations.

None of the Twelve has signed or ratified the 1975 Vienna Convention on the Representation of States in their relations with International Organizations. None of them has either acceded to it. We wish to recall that that Convention was not adopted by consensus and that in the fifteen years that have elapsed since its opening to signature the Convention has obtained only 25 ratifications or accessions and just a few more signatures. Consequently in fifteen years the Convention has not entered in force.

We do not think it appropriate for a resolution of the United Nations General Assembly to try to enhance the status of such an unsuccessful Convention. This holds particularly true if one considers that the principal States which host international organizations—among which are several States member of the European Community—have maintained that they cannot agree with a number of provisions in the Convention.

(Text provided by the FCO; see also A/C. 6/45/SR. 45, pp. 5–6)

Part Four: I. *The individual (including the corporation) in international law—nationality*

In the UK's third periodic report under Article 40 of the International Covenant on Civil and Political Rights, 1966, the following passage appeared:

The position at the time of the second periodic report [1984] was as follows. The British Nationality Act 1981 had replaced the status of citizen of the United Kingdom and Colonies (CUKC), created by the British Nationality Act 1948, by three separate citizenships:
  (a) *British citizenship*: for those closely connected with the United Kingdom; acquired mainly by birth in the United Kingdom of a parent who is a British citizen or settled there;

(b) *British Dependent Territories citizenship (BDTC)*: for persons connected with the dependencies;
(c) *British Overseas citizenship (BOC)*: for those CUKC's not having the above connections with the United Kingdom or dependencies;

the 1981 Act had also preserved the status of:
(d) *British subject*: mainly persons born before 1949 who did not subsequently become a CUKC or a citizen of a Commonwealth country; and
(e) *British Protected Person (BPP)*: persons connected with former protectorates or former trust territories;

subsequently, however, a new category of citizenship was created on 1 July 1987 by the Hong Kong (British Nationality) Order 1986:
(f) *British Nationals (Overseas) (BNO)*: persons who are BDTCs solely by connection with Hong Kong, who may then apply to register as BNOs before 1 July 1997.

(SCPR/C/58/Add. 6, p. 39: March 1990)

In the course of the HC Standing Committee debate on the War Crimes Bill, the Minister of State, Home Office, Mr John Patten, stated:

All British citizens have absolute right of residence in the United Kingdom and other categories do not. After the passage of the [British Nationality Act 1981], all citizens of the United Kingdom and colonies with the right of abode in the United Kingdom automatically became British citizens.

(HC Debs., 1989–90, Standing Committee A: War Crimes Bill, col. 75; 3 April 1990)

In reply to a question, the Prime Minister wrote:

The question of who are to be regarded as its nationals for the purposes of enjoyment of the rights of free movement given in the treaty of Rome, by reason of a connection either with its metropolitan or its overseas territories, is determined by each member state in accordance with its nationality law.

(HC Debs., vol. 171, Written Answers, col. 623: 3 May 1990)

Part Four: III. *The individual (including the corporation) in international law—aliens or non-nationals*

Speaking in the UN Security Council on 18 August 1990 on the subject of the situation in Kuwait and Iraq, the UK Permanent Representative, Sir Crispin Tickell, stated:

Since [yesterday] there have been two acts which outrage international law and international opinion. The first was the use of innocent civilians, justified by nauseating rhetoric about their status as 'guests', to act as a human shield to protect strategic sites. The second was the punishment of the hundreds of thousands of civilians caught in Kuwait and Iraq—a sort of act of retaliation against the Security Council for having adopted resolution 661(1990) imposing economic sanctions upon Iraq.

(S/PV. 2937, p. 21)

At a press conference given by the FCO on 20 August 1990, the FCO spokesman stated:

. . . late Friday night, 17 August, a speaker at the Iraqi National Assembly said that Westerners would be detained and held at key military and civilian installations in Kuwait and Iraq. The FCO protested to the Iraqi authorities on Saturday morning and the Secretary of State issued a written statement as follows:

'We are deeply concerned by the recent statement by the Speaker of the Iraqi Parliament. The detention of foreign nationals in Iraq and Kuwait is clearly contrary to international law. Our Ambassador in Baghdad is urgently pressing the Iraqi government for an explanation. We need to know whether this is an authoritative statement of the Iraqi government's position. The Iraqi Ambassador in London was summoned this morning to underline our grave concern and to relay to his authorities the need for immediate clarification. . . .'

(Text provided by the FCO)

The Twelve Member States of the EC issued a statement on 21 August 1990 which read in part as follows:

The Community and its member states, deeply concerned at the situation of foreigners in Iraq and Kuwait, renew their condemnation of the Iraqi decision to detain them against their will as contrary to international law and fully support the Security Council Resolution 664 which requires Iraq to permit and facilitate their immediate departure from Iraq and Kuwait. They denounce that the Iraqi Government has reacted up to now negatively to many representations of the Community and its member states.

As members of the International Community, which is founded not only on law but also on clear ethical standards, the European Community and its member states express their indignation at Iraq's publicized intention to group such foreigners in the vicinity of military bases and objectives, a measure they consider particularly heinous as well as taken in contempt of the law and of basic humanitarian principles. In this context the fact that some foreigners have been prevented from contacting their consular or diplomatic missions or have been forcibly moved to unknown destination is a source of further deep concern and indignation. In this connection, they attach the greatest importance to the mission of two envoys of the Secretary-General of the United Nations which is now taking place. They warn the Iraqi Government that any attempt to harm or jeapordize the safety of any EC citizen will be considered as a most grave offence directed against the Community and all its member states and will provoke a united response from the entire community.

They confirm their commitment to do all in their power to ensure the protection of the foreigners in Iraq and Kuwait and reiterate that they hold the Iraqi Government fully responsible for the safety of their nationals.

(Text provided by the FCO)

At a press conference given by the FCO on 24 August 1990, the FCO spokesman stated:

The United Kingdom will continue to hold Iraq responsible for the protection of British nationals and for their treatment in accordance with international law.

(Text provided by the FCO)

Speaking in an emergency debate in the House of Commons on the subject of the situation in the Gulf, the Prime Minister, Mrs Margaret Thatcher, stated:

The plight of British and other foreign nationals in Iraq and Kuwait has shocked everyone. Every norm of law, of diplomatic convention and of civilised behaviour has been offended by the way in which those citizens have been rounded up, treated as hostages, and used as a human shield. It is strange for someone who claims to be the leader of the Arab world, a latter-day Saladin, to hide behind women and children. Through the United Nations and bilaterally we have done everything possible to press Iraq to let our people go, just as theirs are free to go from Britain. There has been particularly good co-operation with other European countries on this matter. The International Committee of the Red Cross is seeking but has not yet obtained the right of access to all hostages held in Iraq and Kuwait, which they are entitled to under the Geneva convention.

(HC Debs., vol. 177, col. 739: 6 September 1990)

Speaking in the emergency debate in the House of Lords, the Minister of State, FCO, the Earl of Caithness, stated:

We are all shocked by the Iraqi Government's action in rounding up foreign nationals for use as a human shield. It is abhorrent and a further breach of humanitarian law.

(HL Debs., vol. 521, col. 1798: 6 September 1990)

On 10 September 1990 a joint press statement was issued following a meeting between the Foreign Minister of Japan, Mr Taroi Nakayama, and the Secretary of State for Foreign and Commonwealth Affairs, Mr Douglas Hurd. It read in part:

The Ministers strongly condemned Iraq's mistreatment of foreign nationals in Kuwait and Iraq as contravening international law and humanitarian requirements.

(FCO Press Release No. 192 of 1990)

The following passage appeared in the account of a press conference given by the FCO on 28 September 1990:

Spokesman said that the British Ambassador in Baghdad had been attempting to obtain clarification from the Iraqi authorities concerning reports that foreigners in Iraq would not be allowed to purchase food from 1 October. So far these attempts had not yielded any clarification. We were in touch with our partners and allies as well as the ICRC on the subject.

Spokesman pointed out that Iraq's obligations towards foreign nationals in Iraq under international humanitarian law was quite clear. These obligations included ensuring that foreign nationals were not denied access to food.

Spokesman also pointed out that Iraq was in contravention of the International Covenant on Civil and Political Rights to which it is a signatory. The Covenant provided for the right of foreign nationals to leave other countries at will.

(Text provided by the FCO)

The following extract appeared in the report of a press conference given by the FCO on 5 October 1990:

Spokesman also announced that the Iraqi Ambassador Mr Azmi Al-Salihi had been summoned to the Foreign Office this morning by Assistant Under-Secretary of State, Mr David Gore-Booth, to receive two British Notes in response to decrees issued by the Iraqi Revolutionary Command Council. The first Note concerned the Iraqi decision to seize all real and personal estate belonging to the Emir of Kuwait, his family and Kuwaiti Cabinet members. The British Government rejected this decision which it regarded as null and void.

The second Note concerned the British Government's response to a decree issued by the Revolutionary Command Council last month excusing Iraqi organizations from a range of contractual and financial obligations and sequestering the assets of companies of certain foreign states. The British Government's Note of protest had reserved the UK's rights and those of UK nationals and companies in respect of this matter.

(Text provided by the FCO)

Speaking on 8 October 1990 in the Third Committee of the UN General Assembly on behalf of the EC and its Member States, the Permanent Representative of Italy stated:

The Iraqi Government must respect its obligations and allow all foreign nationals, who wish to go, to leave Iraq and Kuwait. Its decision to use certain foreign nationals as a human shield is illegal and morally repugnant.

(Text provided by the FCO; see also A/C. 3/45/SR. 3, p. 11)

In the course of a debate, the Parliamentary Under-Secretary of State, FCO, Mr Mark Lennox-Boyd, stated:

The Iraqi authorities' refusal to allow foreign men to leave the country—and, even worse, to hold them against their will at strategic sites, denying them consular access—is a flagrant and inhumane breach of international law.

(HC Debs., vol. 178, col. 480: 24 October 1990)

In reply to a question, the Minister of State for the Armed Forces wrote:

The members of the British liaison team who have been moved to Iraq are being illegally detained. We continue to press for the immediate release of all hostages being held by Iraq, in accordance with international law and United Nations Security Council resolutions.

(HC Debs., vol. 178, Written Answers, col. 763: 1 November 1990)

Speaking on 26 November 1990 in the Third Committee of the UN General Assembly, the Permanent Representative of Italy, on behalf of the EC and its Member States, stated in respect of the position in Iraq and Kuwait:

The Twelve also strongly deplore the ongoing violations of the basic principles for the protection of the civilian population during armed conflicts, the forced relocation of the civilian population or individuals and especially the taking of foreign hostages in order, in some cases, to attempt to shield military installations.

(Text provided by the FCO; see also A/C. 3/45/SR. 52, p. 12)

Speaking in the UN Security Council on 29 November 1990 in a debate on a draft resolution which was then adopted as Resolution 677 (1990), the UK Permanent Representative, Sir David Hannay, stated:

The principal victims of Iraqi atrocities have of course been the Kuwaitis. But we should not forget the numerous foreigners who have lost their livelihoods as a result of the Iraqi invasion. These range from Indian and Palestinian businessmen and entrepreneurs to Sri Lankan housemaids, whose losses have had a devastating effect on their home economies and whose human tragedy is incalculable. The Iraqis have also abused foreigners in Kuwait in another way. In breach of international law, and in defiance of resolution 664 (1990) of the Council, large numbers have been taken hostage in a bid to dissuade the international community from taking action to restore the independence and sovereignty of Kuwait.

(S/PV. 2962, p. 7)

Part Four: V. *The individual (including the corporation) in international law—statelessness, refugees*

In reply to a question, the Parliamentary Under-Secretary of State, Home Office, wrote:

Applications for asylum on arrival at United Kingdom ports are considered under the criteria of the 1951 United Nations convention and 1967 protocol relating to the status of refugees. Article 1 of the convention defines a refugee as inter alia someone who 'owing to well-founded fear of being persecuted for reasons of race, religion, nationality, membership of a particular social group or political opinion, is outside the country of his nationality and is unable or, owing to such fear, is unwilling to avail himself of the protection of that country'.

If the person has arrived from a safe third country he or she may be returned to that country to pursue an application there. A refugee who has already found protection in another country may be admitted to the United Kingdom if this is a more appropriate country of refuge.

(HC Debs., vol. 164, Written Answers, col. *465*: 8 January 1990; see also ibid., vol., 166, Written Answers, col. *115*: 30 January 1990)

During the debate in HC Standing Committee on the British Nationality (Hong Kong) Bill, the Minister of State, FCO, Mr Francis Maude, stated:

I gladly accept the invitation of the hon. Member . . . to clarify our firm commitment to the 1951 Convention. That commitment will remain for those in Hong Kong after 1997. There has never been any doubt about that and I do not believe that there will be in future.

(HC Debs., 1989–90, Standing Committee A: British Nationality (Hong Kong) Bill, col. 210; 22 May 1990)

Speaking on 15 November 1990 in the Third Committee of the UN

General Assembly on the subject of the office of the UN High Commissioner for Refugees, the representative of Italy, on behalf of the Member States of the EC, stated:

The European Community and its Member States have always considered UNHCR's mandate and activities of paramount importance and have lived up to their obligations under the Geneva Convention of 1951 and the Protocol of 1967. Over the years, the Twelve have consistently been a major source of financial assistance to the Office. The Twelve wish to take this opportunity to reaffirm their commitment.

(Text provided by the FCO; see also A/C. 3/45/SR. 43, p. 4)

Part Four: VI. *The individual (including the corporation) in international law—immigration and emigration, extradition, expulsion and asylum*

In the course of the Committee stage of the House of Lords' debate on the amendments dealing with drug control sought to be introduced into the Criminal Justice (International Cooperation) Bill, the Minister of State, Home Office, Earl Ferrers, stated:

United Kingdom extradition law is now largely contained in the Extradition Act 1989. This defines an extradition crime as one which carries imprisonment for a term of 12 months or more. The fresh offences created by the Bill are punishable on trial on indictment with terms of over 12 months, and so no additional provision is required in respect of Commonwealth countries. Nor need we be concerned about states which are parties to the European Convention on Extradition which we intend to ratify shortly and other foreign states with which we establish new treaties under the 1989 Act. But for the time being extradition with the remaining foreign countries with which we have arrangements will continue to be governed by treaties made under the Extradition Act 1870. It is therefore, necessary in respect of the latter to make provision so that new offences are treated as extraditable for the purposes of an Order in Council under Section 2 of the 1870 Act.

(HL Debs., vol. 514, col. 896: 22 January 1990)

In the course of the HC Standing Committee debate on the Aviation and Maritime Security Bill, the Minister for Public Transport, Mr. Michael Portillo, stated:

Under the Extradition Act 1989, an offence is extraditable if it attracts a minimum sentence on indictment of 12 months' imprisonment in both countries. That definition applies now to all extraditions involving Commonwealth countries and will apply from a date yet to be fixed later this year to extraditions involving countries which have ratified the European convention on extradition. As for other foreign countries, extradition will continue to depend on the terms of bilateral treaties drawn up under the Extradition Act 1870, until such time as new treaties have been negotiated. Those treaties rely on the list system for their definition of extradition crimes. The Extradition Act 1870 has been repealed, but its key features are preserved, as schedule 1 to the 1989 Act.

(HC Debs., 1989–90, Standing Committee A: Aviation and Maritime Security Bill, cols. 37–8; 6 February 1990)

In reply to a question, the Minister of State, FCO, Lord Brabazon of Tara, stated in part:

So far as concerns the granting of asylum to Kurds in this country, we are fully committed to the United Nations 1951 refugee convention and its protocol. There is no question of turning away any genuine refugees.

(HL Debs., vol. 516, col. 729: 28 February 1990)

The following passages appeared in the UK's third periodic report under Article 40 of the International Covenant on Civil and Political Rights, 1966:

Asylum

196. The United Kingdom fully meets its obligations under the 1951 United Nations Convention relating to the Status of Refugees and the 1967 Protocol relating to the Status of Refugees and gives asylum to those with a well-founded fear of persecution. The number of applicants has increased fivefold in the last 10 years, although the proportion of successful applicants decreased from 60 per cent in 1981 to 25 per cent in 1988. This is not because criteria are now more stringent, but because increasing numbers of refugees are not fleeing political persecution, but are in reality economic migrants with a (perfectly understandable) desire to improve their conditions. It would however be unfair to allow economic migrants to settle as though they were refugees and it would cause delay and frustration to genuine refugees and to the majority of immigrants who follow the normal procedures (50,000 in 1988).

197. There is no full right of appeal exercisable while in the United Kingdom for those who seek asylum at the port of entry. There is no such right for the majority of passengers refused leave to enter on other grounds, and to single out asylum seekers for special treatment would encourage applications for asylum. The lesson from other countries, particularly in Europe, which have such a system, is that delays soon run into years as appeals go from lower to higher courts. While waiting for a hearing, asylum-seekers establish themselves and start families and, if they fear they will not be successful, cannot be traced. This again is inequitable both to genuine political refugees and to normal immigrants.

Extradition

198. The United Kingdom has to engage in two types of extradition, foreign and Commonwealth. In addition, a simplified form of extradition, the backing of warrants procedure, operates between the Republic of Ireland and Scotland, Northern Ireland, and England and Wales. Each type is subject to legislation: the Extradition Act 1870, the Fugitive Offenders Act 1967 and the Backing of Warrants (Republic of Ireland) Act 1965. The 1870 and 1967 Acts have now been consolidated in the Extradition Act 1989. Avenues of appeal are set out in the extradition legislation, and in foreign and Commonwealth cases there is also a discretion available to the Home Secretary to refuse to surrender a fugitive. Additionally, it is a long-standing principle enshrined in United Kingdom legislation that persons should not be extradited if they are accused or convicted of crimes of a political character. It is also illegal for deportation powers to be used as a form of disguised extradition.

199. Extradition law also embodies the principle that fugitives should be surrendered only for acts which are offences not only against the law of the requesting State but which, if committed within the jurisdiction of the requested State, would also constitute offences against its own law. In addition, the offence for which the fugitive is sought must be extraditable under the law of both States. It is a generally accepted feature of extradition practice that the requesting State should specify the crimes for which the fugitive is sought and that the requested States should exercise some control over the prosecution of the surrendered fugitive for other crimes committed before his surrender.

200. A foreigner would not be extradited to a country where he or she might be in danger of persecution or torture. The Home Secretary has unfettered discretion not to surrender a fugitive if he considers that the standard of justice that the fugitive might receive in the requesting country is not adequate.

201. The Extradition Act 1989 has recently introduced important reforms in extradition law. As a means of simplifying and expediting extradition proceedings against serious international criminals, the Act provides for the United Kingdom to enter into extradition arrangements which do not require the requesting State to establish in United Kingdom courts that there is a *prima facie* case against the fugitive, and defining an extradition crime as any offence punishable with 12 months' imprisonment or more (provided the conduct of which the fugitive is accused would also be an offence so punishable in the United Kingdom). The existing safeguards mentioned above are however preserved or enhanced. For example, specific provision is made for a fugitive to submit representations against the Home Secretary's decision to surrender and to seek judicial review of such a decision.

(CCPR/C/58/Add. 6, pp. 46–8: March 1990)

In reply to a question, the Minister of State, Home Office, wrote in part:

The United Kingdom, which has very limited extra-territorial jurisdiction, is prepared (subject to the circumstances of the case and our treaty arrangements with the country concerned) to extradite United Kingdom nationals to stand trial in the place where the offence was committed. This contrasts with the position in many civil law countries, which have wide extra-territorial powers to prosecute for offences committed outside their territory, but which are restricted constitutionally from extraditing their own nationals. The United Kingdom's extradition arrangements with the member countries of the European Community reflect this difference of approach.

Under the treaties with Belgium, France, the Federal Republic of Germany, Portugal and Spain, the United Kingdom may extradite nationals to stand trial abroad, but those countries have discretion to refuse the extradition of their nationals here. The Netherlands are in a broadly similar position, although an amendment to their domestic law in 1981 now permits the extradition of a Dutch national here if the Dutch authorities are satisfied that there is sufficient guarantee that the offender would be returned to serve any prison sentence in the Netherlands. The Luxembourg treaty expressly prohibits the extradition of their nationals, while allowing United Kingdom nationals to be extradited there. Three further treaties, with Denmark, Greece and Italy, prohibit the extradition of nationals in either direction, so that the United Kingdom cannot at present extradite United Kingdom nationals to those countries. (This limitation on United

Kingdom freedom of action will be removed later this year when the United Kingdom ratifies the European convention on extradition, which will take the place of existing extradition treaties with convention countries.) There are no restrictions on the extradition of nationals in either direction between the United Kingdom and the Republic of Ireland.

(HC Debs., vol. 170, Written Answers, cols. 908–9: 18 April 1990)

In reply to a question, the Parliamentary Under-Secretary of State, Home Office, wrote:

Any applications for asylum in this country from Albanian nationals would be considered in accordance with our obligations under the 1951 United Nations convention relating to the status of refugees.

(HC Debs., vol. 176, Written Answers, col. 683: 19 July 1990)

In reply to a question, the Secretary of State for the Home Department wrote:

The United Kingdom is committed to its obligations under the 1951 United Nations convention relating to the status of refugees. In accordance with this convention, no refugee will be moved by the United Kingdom to a territory in which his life or freedom would be threatened on account of his race, religion, nationality, membership of a particular social group or political opinion.

It is an internationally accepted concept that a person fleeing persecution, who cannot avail himself of the protection of the authorities of a country of which he is a national, should normally seek refuge in the first safe country reached. I agree entirely with the concept. The convention's primary function is to give refugees who cannot turn to their own authorities the protection of the international community. It is an instrument of last resort—not a licence for refugees to travel the world in search of an ideal place of residence. Where protection issues do not arise, an application should therefore be dealt with in accordance with normal immigration criteria.

Accordingly, an application for asylum from a passenger who has arrived in the United Kingdom from a country other than the country in which he fears persecution, will not normally be considered substantively. The passenger will be returned to the country from which he embarked, or to another country in which he has been since he left the country of feared persecution or, if appropriate, to his country of nationality, unless I am satisfied that the country is one in which his life or freedom would be threatened on account of his race, religion, nationality, membership of a particular social group or political opinion, or that it would return him to such a country. However, in considering any individual case I shall take into account any evidence of substantial links with the United Kingdom which in my view would make it reasonable for the claim for asylum exceptionally to be considered here.

All western European countries which are signatories to the United Nations convention operate safe third-country procedures and the approach is consistent with the convention determining the state responsible for examining applications for asylum lodged in one of the member states of the European Communities signed in Dublin on 15 June 1990, but not as yet in force.

(HC Debs., vol. 177, Written Answers, cols. 262–3: 25 July 1990)

In reply to a question, the Parliamentary Under-Secretary of State, Home Office, wrote in part:

We do not record separately the entry to the United Kingdom of minors from Ethiopia or other countries. Their entry is governed by the immigration rules. Under the rules, minors with no support or accommodation to go to would be liable to refusal. If such minors sought asylum it would be necessary to consider their claims to refugee status under the 1951 United Nations convention before a refusal decision could be taken.

(HC Debs., vol. 178, Written Answers, col. *446* : 30 October 1990)

In reply to a question, the Parliamentary Under-Secretary of State, Home Office, wrote:

I am satisfied that asylum procedures in my Department meet the United Kingdom's obligations under the 1951 United Nations convention relating to the status of refugees.

(HC Debs., vol. 182, Written Answers, col. *403*: 12 December 1990)

Part Four: VII. *The individual (including the corporation) in international law—protection of human rights and fundamental freedoms*

(See also Part One: II. D. 1. (items of 3 November 1989, 19 February, 19 April, 9 December 1990) and Part Three: I. A. 3. (item of 26 November 1990), above, and Part Five: VIII. A. (item of 5 July 1990), below)

In the course of a debate on the subject of Hong Kong, the Secretary of State for Foreign and Commonwealth Affairs, Mr Douglas Hurd, stated:

With regard to what will happen after 1997, the two United Nations covenants on human rights will, as the joint declaration makes clear, continue to apply to Hong Kong after 1997. There is no dispute about that, and that provision is fully reflected in the current draft of the Basic Law.

(HC Debs., vol. 165, col. 294: 17 January 1990)

In reply to the question whether Her Majesty's Government will introduce legislation to incorporate the European Convention on Human Rights, the Parliamentary Under-Secretary of State, Home Office, wrote:

We have no plans to do so.

(HC Debs., vol. 167, Written Answers, col. *5*: 12 February 1990)

In the course of a statement issued on 20 February 1990 by the Twelve Member States of the EC concerning the extension of Jewish settlements in the Occupied Territories, it was observed:

. . . the Twelve warmly welcome the liberalisation of Soviet emigration controls, including the freedom of Soviet Jews to emigrate to Israel and elsewhere. They believe that this sentiment is very widely shared in the international community, on the basis that the right of everyone to leave any country, including his own, is enshrined in the International Covenant on Civil and Political Rights. The attainment by Soviet Jews of this right must not, however, be at the expense of the rights of the Palestinians in the Occupied Territories.

(Text provided by the FCO)

The following passages appeared in the UK's third periodic report under Article 40 of the International Covenant on Civil and Political Rights:

1. The first and second reports on Hong Kong (CCPR/C/1/Add. 37 and CCPR/C/32/Add. 14 and 15) set out the general framework within which the rights recognized by the International Covenant on Civil and Political Rights are currently protected in Hong Kong.

2. At the meetings of the Human Rights Committee which discussed the second report in November 1988, the Committee expressed a special interest in knowing how the protection of human rights would be provided for in Hong Kong after the reversion of the territory to China in 1997. Given the Committee's concern, and the growing importance of the issue to the Hong Kong people, it may be useful in this, the third report, to supplement the information already provided with a general explanation of the safeguards now in place and those being prepared for the future protection of human rights in Hong Kong.

3. The Sino-British Joint Declaration on the Question of Hong Kong (the Joint Declaration) made by the British Government and the Government of the People's Republic of China in 1984 contains the following provision on basic rights (para. 3(5)):

'Rights and freedoms, including those of the person, of speech, of the press, of assembly, of association, of travel, of movement, of correspondence, of strike, of choice of occupation, of academic research and of religious belief will be ensured by law in the Hong Kong Special Administrative Region. Private property, ownership of enterprises, legitimate right of inheritance and foreign investment will be protected by law.'

4. This provision is further elaborated in various sections of annex I to the Joint Declaration, and in particular Section XIII, the full text of which is attached (see annex below). *Inter alia*, it stipulates that:

'The provisions of the International Covenant on Civil and Political Rights and the International Covenant on Economic, Social and Cultural Rights as applied to Hong Kong shall remain in force.'

5. The provisions of the Joint Declaration will be reflected and stipulated in the Basic Law of the Hong Kong Special Administrative Region of the People's Republic of China, and they will remain unchanged for 50 years. While the preparation of the Basic Law is a matter for the Chinese Government, the British Government has the right and responsibility to satisfy itself that the Basic Law faithfully reflects the provisions of the Joint Declaration.

6. The Basic Law Drafting Committee is holding consultations with the people of Hong Kong, through the medium of the Basic Law Consultative Committee, to seek views on the content of the Basic Law. A consultation exercise was carried out following the release of the first draft of the Basic Law in April 1988, and the views then expressed were taken into account to a large extent in preparing the second draft, which was released in February 1989 for another round of consultation. Before the promulgation of the Basic Law by the National People's Congress of

China in spring 1990, the second draft will undergo further revision in the light of comments on it.

7. A major concern in Hong Kong is the protection of human rights after 1997, in particular the continued application and implementation of the two International Covenants on Human Rights in the Hong Kong Special Administrative Region as provided for in the Joint Declaration. Under section 4 of annex II to the Joint Declaration, the means by which the British and Chinese Governments will ensure the continued application of the international rights and obligations affecting Hong Kong is a matter for consideration in the Sino-British Joint Liaison Group and its sub-group on international rights and obligations. It is essentially a question of how best the People's Republic of China can succeed in 1997 to the treaty rights and obligations which the United Kingdom has at present in respect of Hong Kong, under the Covenants.

8. In addition, article 39 of the second draft of the Basic Law states:
   'The provisions of the International Covenant on Civil and Political Rights, and the International Covenant on Economic, Social and Cultural Rights . . . as applied to Hong Kong shall remain in force and shall be implemented through the laws of the Hong Kong Special Administrative Region.
   'The rights and freedoms enjoyed by Hong Kong residents shall not be restricted unless prescribed by law. Such restrictions shall not contravene the provisions of the preceding paragraph of this article.'

9. Section XIII of annex I to the Joint Declaration also specifies *inter alia*: 'The Hong Kong Special Administrative Region Government shall maintain the rights and freedoms as provided for by the laws previously in force in Hong Kong, including freedom of the person, of speech, of the press, of assembly, of association, to form and join trade unions, of correspondence, of travel, of movement, of strike, of demonstration of choice of occupation, of academic research, of belief, inviolability of the home, the freedom to marry and the right to raise a family freely.' Chapter III of the second draft of the Basic Law contains relevant provisions.

(CCPR/C/58/Add. 6, pp. 111–12: March 1990)

In the course of a debate on the subject of the British Nationality (Hong Kong) Bill, the Secretary of State for Foreign and Commonwealth Affairs, Mr Douglas Hurd, stated:

The joint declaration and the Basic Law provide that people in the SAR after 1997 will have the full protection of the law, including basic human rights as enshrined in the international covenant on civil and political rights and the international covenant on economic, social and cultural rights.

(HC Debs., vol. 170, col. 1645: 19 April 1990)

In the course of a debate on the subject of civil liberties, the Government spokesman in the House of Lords, Viscount Ullswater, stated:

Civil rights are already protected in our legal systems and by statute and are in far more precise terms than, for example, in the European convention, which most proponents of a Bill of Rights would like to incorporate in our domestic law.

Incorporating the European convention would mean that the courts rather than Parliament would determine society's needs. That is no reflection on the impartiality of the judiciary. Rather, it is a re-affirmation that it is for Parliament in the exercise of its sovereignty to decide. We do not doubt the ability of the judges, but we believe that requiring them to undertake such tasks would propel them into the political arena. One has only to look to the United States to see that the two most important criteria for appointment to the Supreme Court are the candidate's social views and his or her political opinions. There is no evidence that the general public favours either a written constitution or a new Bill of Rights. The Government therefore believe that until consensus as to such a need emerges, the present adequate safeguards should remain.

(HL Debs., vol. 519, col. 934: 23 May 1990)

In the course of a statement issued on 16 July 1990 on the situation in Somalia, the Twelve Member States of the EC observed:

The expectations of governments and of international public opinion are set at naught by repressive measures, violating fundamental human rights.

(Text provided by the FCO)

On 13 September 1990, the Twelve Member States of the EC issued a statement in which they declared:

The Community and its member states are following with concern developments in the situation in Somalia. They condemn the continuing human rights violations in that country and in particular the killings in Berbera by Somali military forces of 20 members of the Issaq ethnic group. They call on the Somali Government to ensure more effective protection of the life and property of foreign citizens as well as of diplomatic missions in Somalia.

(Text provided by the FCO)

Speaking on 8 October 1990 in the Third Committee of the UN General Assembly on behalf of the EC and its Member States, the Permanent Representative of Italy stated:

The Charter of the United Nations commits the Organization to be at the forefront of the battle against racism and racial discrimination. From its establishment the United Nations has striven to raise public awareness of this phenomenon and has promoted the adoption of international instruments aimed at its elimination. The Universal Declaration, the Covenants and, most particularly, the Convention on the Elimination of all Forms of Racial Discrimination all make clear the absolute unacceptability of such practices.

We celebrate this year the 25th anniversary of the adoption by the General Assembly of the Convention on the Elimination of all Forms of Racial Discrimination. The Convention, with 130 States parties, has the largest number of ratifications or accessions ever reached by any instrument adopted by the General Assembly in the field of human rights. Monitoring of the implementation of the provisions of the Convention is made by the Committee on the Elimination of Racial Discrimination.

(Text provided by the FCO; see also A/C.3/45/SR. 3, pp. 10–11)

In reply to the question what representations have been made to the Soviet Government to allow the wife and daughters of Mr Oleg Gordievski to join him in the UK, the Minister of State, FCO, the Earl of Caithness, stated:

. . . we have repeatedly pressed the Soviet authorities to allow Mr. Gordievski's family to join him in the United Kingdom. My right honourable friend the Secretary of State for Foreign and Commonwealth Affairs raised this matter again when he saw Mr. Shevardnadze in New York on 24th September. There is no justification for Mrs. Gordievski being kept apart from her husband. Such reunifications are explicitly covered in the Helsinki Final Act and we shall continue to press the Soviet authorities to honour their obligations.

(HL Debs., vol. 522, col. 890: 17 October 1990)

In reply to a question, the Parliamentary Under-Secretary of State, FCO, wrote in part:

We have . . . told the Chinese authorities on every possible occasion of our concern about the human rights situation in Tibet.

(HC Debs., vol. 177, Written Answers, col. 905: 10 October 1990)

On 19 October 1990, the Twelve Member States of the EC made a statement about the situation in Rwanda. It read in part:

The European Community and its Member States are following with concern the development of the situation in Rwanda. They express their disquiet on the subject of respect for human rights.

(Text provided by the FCO)

On 22 October 1990, the Twelve Member States of the EC issued a statement on the subject of the situation in Sri Lanka in which it was stated:

The Community and its member states have regularly conveyed to the Sri Lankan Government their serious concern about continuing threats to human rights. . . . They . . . hope that the sub-Commission on disappearances of the UN Commission on human rights will visit Sri Lanka soon. Meanwhile, the Community and its member states note that obstruction of citizens intending to testify to the said sub-commission is contrary to Resolution 1990/76 of the UN Commission for Human Rights, which calls on all Governments to allow unhindered contact between private individuals and UN human rights bodies, and condemns all acts of intimidation and reprisal.

The Community and its member states strongly support the efforts of the democratically elected Sri Lankan Government to overcome the challenge posed by terrorist activities. But in doing so, the Community and its member states urge the Government to observe its international obligations in the field of human rights. The Community and its member states wish to draw attention to the fact that member states will be considering their future assistance for the development of Sri Lanka's economy with reference, among other factors, to the Government's performance in regard to human rights.

(Text provided by the FCO)

In moving the consideration by the HC First Standing Committee on Statutory Instruments of the draft European Commission and Court of Human Rights (Immunities and Privileges) (Amendment) Order 1990, the

Parliamentary Under-Secretary of State, FCO, Mr Mark Lennox-Boyd, stated:

Under the European convention on human rights, the task of protecting human rights is shared by the European Commission of Human Rights and the European Court of Human Rights. The role of the members of the Commission is to examine complaints of alleged breaches of the convention, to establish the facts and to try to obtain a friendly settlement of cases, failing which they express their opinion as to whether there has been a violation of the convention. There is one member for each state that has ratified the convention. In 1989, the Commission delivered 1,338 decisions concerning applications from individuals, of which 1,190 were declared inadmissible, 53 were struck off the list and 95 were declared admissible.

The role of the judges of the court is to give judgment in cases referred to it by the commission or any state concerned. The number of judges is equal to the number of members of the Council of Europe. The judges must either possess qualifications for appointment to high judicial office or be jurists of recognised competence. The court does not sit permanently but is becoming increasingly busy. Thirty cases were referred to it in 1989.

(HC Debs., 1989–90, First Standing Committee on Statutory Instruments, etc.: 23 October 1990, col. 3)

In the course of a debate on the subject of the Council of Europe, the Government spokesman in the House of Lords, Lord Reay, stated:

Before going on to the future, let me say something about the Council of Europe's achievements. The Council's work in the field of human rights is uniquely valuable and Britain has contributed significantly to it. Britain was the first country to ratify the European Convention on Human Rights in 1951. This preceded the creation of the European Commission of Human Rights in 1954 and the establishment of the European Court of Human Rights in 1959. The European Convention on Human Rights was a landmark in the development of international law and sets a standard of law and behaviour by which modern democracies can be and have been judged. If a country fails to meet that standard, it runs the risk of being expelled.

(HL Debs., vol. 522, col. 1756: 29 October 1990)

Later in his speech, Lord Reay said:

Of course . . . the Council of Europe is not the only body which has a role to play in the field of human rights in Europe. The CSCE, through the 1975 Helsinki Final Act, affords the West an unrivalled opportunity to monitor the human rights performance of all European states. The CSCE of course includes the Soviet Union, Canada and the United States, in addition to the 23 Members of the Council of Europe and the Eastern European countries. We believe that their close involvement in multilateral human rights work in Europe is desirable. . . .

The Council of Europe and the CSCE have developed their respective instruments and practices along distinctive lines. While the European Convention on Human Rights is based upon legally enforceable obligations, the human rights commitments of the Helsinki Final Act are exclusively of a political rather than a legal nature. Both the CSCE and the Council of Europe in their different ways have been of enormous value as benchmarks and as a means of encouraging the development of human rights and of democracy.

(Ibid., col. 1757)

In reply to a question, the Minister of State, FCO, wrote in part:

We have made our own views on Iraq's current human rights abuses in Kuwait entirely clear in UN Security Council resolutions including resolutions 664 and 674.

(HC Debs., vol. 178, Written Answers, col. 700: 1 November 1990)

In reply to a question on the subject of human rights abuses in the Punjab, the Parliamentary Under-Secretary of State, FCO, wrote in part:

We have repeatedly made clear our concern to the Indian Government that human rights must be respected and have also urged them to exercise the greatest restraint in dealing with the violent challenge to law and order from military groups.

(Ibid., cols. 699–700)

Speaking on 7 November 1990 in the Third Committee of the UN General Assembly on behalf of the EC and its Member States, the Permanent Representative of Italy stated:

In the opinion of the European Community and its member States the promotion and protection of human rights is one of the highest priorities of the United Nations. Building on the foundation laid by the Universal Declaration, the Organization has established through the International Covenant on Civil and Political Rights and its Optional Protocols, the International Covenant on Economic, Social and Cultural Rights, the International Convention on the Elimination of all Forms of Racial Discrimination and the Convention against Torture as well as other instruments an impressive framework of international legal obligations in the human rights area. The adoption by the General Assembly at its Forty-fourth Session of the Convention on the Rights of the Child and of the Second Optional Protocol to the International Covenant on Civil and Political Rights aiming at the abolition of the death penalty were an important extension of this framework.

It is, of course, only when States abide by their international obligations and effectively implement the provisions of instruments to which they are party that the potential of these instruments can be fully realized. This is why the European Community and its member States believe that for the future particular attention should be given to securing universal adherence to, and monitoring compliance with, existing instruments. This, of course, does not exclude consideration of further instruments, provided that the need for them be clearly established and the guidelines approved by the General Assembly at its forty-first session with resolution 41/120 on setting international standards in the field of human rights are applied.

In this connection we like to recall that these guidelines establish that the subject matter of any new international standards should be of a fundamental character, that it should be consistent with the existing body of international human rights and drafted in such a way as to define clearly recognizable rights and provide for their effective implementation. Resolution 41/120 calls also upon member States to accord priority to the implementation of the existing standards giving, among them, primacy to the Universal Declaration of Human Rights and the International Covenants.

. . .

. . . we would like to acknowledge, with satisfaction, the number of ratifications or accessions reached by the International Covenants and the Convention on the Elimination of all forms of Racial Discrimination. The legally binding nature of their norms has certainly contributed, and will contribute even more now that it is applied in more countries, towards the fulfillment of our obligation to promote human rights. The European Community and its member States hope that this trend to ratify, or accede to international instruments on human rights will be soon confirmed by an increasing number of ratifications of, or accessions to the existing instruments.

(Text provided by the FCO; see also A/C.3/45/SR. 35, pp.15–16)

Speaking on 26 November 1990 in the same Committee, the same spokesman observed:

The establishment of the standards—by international agreement or custom—which require States to ensure and promote the respect for human rights, both civil and political as well as economic, social and cultural, represents only the first stage in the attainment of a universal regime of human rights. In this regard, the respect for such rights must be clearly guaranteed and, in the final analysis, systematically assured, taking into account standard setting and monitoring and the enrichment of the notion of human rights in harmony with social and technological evolution.

(Text provided by the FCO; see also A/C.3/45/C.3/SR. 52, p.10)

In reply to a question, the Minister of State, FCO, wrote:

The Saudi Government are well aware of the importance we attach to the observance of human rights standards.

(HC Debs., vol. 182, Written Answers, col. 64: 4 December 1990)

In reply to a question, the Minister of State, FCO, wrote:

We and our EC partners have regularly made clear to the Guatemalan Government our serious concern about human rights abuses. In the past years, British Ministers have raised human rights three times with Guatemalan Ministers, and our ambassador has raised the plight of street children. He and his EC colleagues have also made representations about the shootings at Santiago de Atitlan on 2 December.

(HC Debs., vol. 182, Written Answers, col. 282: 10 December 1990)

In reply to a question, the Parliamentary Under-Secretary of State, Home Office, wrote:

We have decided to renew for a period of five years from 14 January 1991 our acceptance of the right of individual petition to the European Commission of Human Rights and of the jurisdiction of the European Court of Human Rights.

(HC Debs., vol. 183, Written Answers, col. 111: 18 December 1990)

In the course of a debate on the subject of religious freedom in education the Minister of State, Department of Education and Science, Mr Tim Eggar, stated:

My hon. Friend referred to article 2 of the first protocol to the European convention on human rights. The Government's view is that the article does not require the state to provide education in accordance with the particular religious or philosophical convictions of parents. Nor does it prevent the state from including in the school curriculum matters that do not accord with some parents' convictions, provided—this is a big proviso—that the material is presented in an objective, critical and pluralistic manner. We believe that the requirements of the national curriculum are compatible with article 2.

(HC Debs., vol. 183, col. 594: 20 December 1990)

Part Five: IV. *Organs of the State—diplomatic agents and missions*

(See also Part Three: I.B.5. (material of 7 and 10 December 1990), above)

By an Exchange of Notes, dated 29 January 1990 and 3 April 1990, the Governments of the UK and Zambia concluded an agreement by which members of the family of career members of the UK diplomatic mission in Zambia are enabled to engage in gainful employment in Zambia, on the same basis as members of the family of the Zambian diplomatic mission in the UK are enabled to engage in gainful employment. An Annex to the agreement reads in material respects as follows:

1. Authorisation to engage in a gainful occupation

(a) The members of the family forming part of the household of a member of a diplomatic mission or consular post of the sending State will be authorised, on a reciprocal basis, to engage in a gainful occupation in the receiving State in accordance with the provisions of the law of the receiving State.

(b) For the purposes of this arrangement:

(i) 'a member of a diplomatic mission or consular post' means any employee of the sending State who is not a national of the receiving State in a diplomatic mission, consular post or mission to an international organisation;
(ii) 'a member of the family' means the spouse of a member of a diplomatic mission or consular post and any minor child who forms part of the household of a member of a diplomatic mission or consular post;

(c) Any authorisation to engage in a gainful occupation in the receiving State will, in principle, be terminated at the end of the assignment of the member of the diplomatic mission or consular post.

. . .

3. Civil and administrative privileges and immunities

In the case of members of the family who enjoy immunity from the civil and administrative jurisdiction of the receiving State in accordance with the Vienna Convention on Diplomatic Relations or under any other applicable international instrument such immunity will not apply in respect of any act carried out in the course of the gainful occupation and falling within the civil or administrative law of the receiving State.

4. Criminal immunity

In the case of members of the family who enjoy immunity from the criminal jurisdiction of the receiving State in accordance with the Vienna Convention on Diplomatic Relations or under any other applicable international instrument:

(a) the provisions concerning immunity from the criminal jurisdiction of the receiving State will continue to apply in respect of any act carried out in the course of the gainful occupation. However, the sending State will give serious consideration to waiving the immunity of the member of the family concerned from the criminal jurisdiction of the receiving State.
(b) In such circumstances, the sending State will give serious consideration to waiving the immunity of the member of the family from the execution of a sentence.

5. Fiscal and social security regimes

In accordance with the Vienna Convention on Diplomatic Relations or under any other applicable international instrument members of the family will be subject to the fiscal and social security regimes of the receiving State for all matters connected with their gainful occupation in that State.

(Text provided by the FCO)

In reply to a question, the Parliamentary Under-Secretary of State, FCO, wrote in part:

In accordance with Article 41 of the Vienna Convention on Diplomatic Relations, staff of missions overseas are expected to respect the laws and regulations of the receiving State.

(HC Debs., vol. 168, Written Answers, col. *372*: 2 March 1990)

In reply to a question about break of diplomatic relations with members of the United Nations, the Parliamentary Under-Secretary of State, FCO, presented the following tables:

Cases in which the United Kingdom has initiated a break in
diplomatic relations with the United Kingdom since 1946

	Country	Dates	
1.	Albania	1946	—
2.	Uganda	28 July 1976	21 April 1979
3.	Argentina	2 April 1982	19 February 1990
4.	Libya	30 April 1984	—
5.	Syria	31 October 1986	—
6.	Cambodia	6 December 1979	—

Cases in which other countries initiated a break in diplomatic
relations with the United Kingdom since 1946

	Country	Dates	
1.	Iran	1951 7 March 1989	December 1952 —
2.	Saudi Arabia	17 November 1956	28 July 1963
3.	Yemen	16 February 1963	December 1967
4.	Somali Republic	18 March 1963	4 January 1968
5.	Guatemala	Reduced to consular level 31 July 1963 Consular relations broken September 1981 Resumed August 1986 Full diplomatic relations resumed December 1986	
6.	Algeria	18 December 1965	10 April 1968
7.	Congo (Brazzaville)	16 December 1965	10 April 1968
8.	Ghana	16 December 1965	5 March 1966
9.	Guinea	15 December 1965	20 February 1968
10.	Mali	16 December 1965	10 April 1968
11.	Mauritania	17 December 1965	10 April 1968
12.	Sudan	18 December 1965 6 June 1967	16 April 1966 25 January 1968
13.	Tanzania	15 December 1965	4 July 1968
14.	UAR	17 December 1965 1956	12 December 1967 1959
15.	Iraq	8 June 1967 1 December 1967 resumed by	1 May 1968 5 September 1974
16.	Syria	6 June 1967	28 May 1973
17.	Iceland	19 February 1976	2 June 1976

(HC Debs., vol. 173, Written Answers, cols. *110–11* : 22 May 1990)

Part Five: VIII. A. *Organs of the State—immunity of organs of the State—diplomatic and consular immunity*

(See also Part Three: I.A. (item of 10 August 1990) and Part Four: VII. (item of 13 September 1990), above, and Part Eleven: II. D. (item of 1 September 1990), below)

In April 1990, the Protocol Department of the FCO issued a revised memorandum describing the practice of the UK Government in respect of diplomatic privileges and immunities. Most of the Memorandum was substantially unchanged from the text published in UKMIL 1987, pp. 549–58. The following paragraph was extensively revised to read:

EXEMPTION FROM REGULATIONS RELATING TO THE CONTROL OF FOREIGNERS

13. Any person who is a member of a mission within the meaning of the Diplomatic Privileges Act 1964, and any person who is a member of the family and forms part of the household of such a member, is exempt from immigration control under the Immigration Act 1971, except that in the case of a member of a mission other than a diplomatic agent (within the meaning of the said Act of 1964) the exception applies only if he has entered the United Kingdom as a member of that mission; or in order to take up a post as such a member which was offered to him before his arrival.

(Text provided by the FCO)

In reply to a question, the Parliamentary Under-Secretary of State, FCO, wrote:

Forty alleged serious offences by persons entitled to immunity were drawn to the attention of the Foreign and Commonwealth Office in 1989 (four fewer than in 1988). 'Serious offences' are defined in accordance with the report to the Foreign Affairs Committee 'The abuse of diplomatic immunities and privileges (1985)' as offences falling into a category which could in certain circumstances attract a penalty of six months or more; we are advised that very few of the alleged offences would have been likely to attract a custodial sentence. The majority involved drinking and driving and shoplifting.

Fourteen diplomats were withdrawn from their posts in Britain in 1989 following alleged offences (the same number as in 1988).

(HC Debs., vol. 171, Written Answers, col. 305: 26 April 1990)

In reply to a further question, the same Minister wrote:

We have fully implemented the guidelines set out in the 1985 White Paper [Cmnd. 9497], with the objective of reducing the abuse of diplomatic immunity and privileges, while fulfilling our obligations under the Vienna conventions on diplomatic relations and on consular relations.

We have applied stricter standards to the size of diplomatic missions and the notification of staff. New legislation was introduced in 1988 to prevent the abuse of United Kingdom immigration laws by persons employed as locally engaged members of mission staff. The legislation ensures that locally engaged members of the staff of a mission who have no pre-existing legal or immigration entitlement to work in the United Kingdom are no longer exempt from the United Kingdom immigration laws. Such staff fall to be refused leave to remain for employment with a mission unless there has been prior notification to, and acceptance by, the Foreign and Commonwealth Office. The FCO continues to monitor closely all new appointments to diplomatic missions in London and elsewhere in the United Kingdom. Arrangements are being made to clarify the status of staff whose term of service in the United Kingdom exceeds 10 years. There has been little growth in the size of individual diplomatic missions.

We withdrew recognition of diplomatic status from 17 national tourist offices in 1985. In 1987 the Diplomatic and Consular Premises Act was introduced to enable the Foreign and Commonwealth Secretary to control the acquisition and disposal of diplomatic premises in London. This Act also provides for the acquisition by the Secretary of State of premises formerly used for the purposes of a diplomatic mission. The Secretary of State has so far used these powers once in relation to the premises of the former Cambodian embassy in London which were occupied by squatters.

We continue to play a full part in United Nations discussions on the regulation of the use of the diplomatic bag. Procedures for the scanning of diplomatic bags in certain circumstances have been notified to the diplomatic corps in London.

The guidelines set out in paragraphs 57 to 73 of the 1985 White Paper on the handling of alleged serious offences by diplomats have been followed fully. Statistics on such alleged offences are made available to Parliament annually. We have repeatedly made clear to members of the diplomatic corps the standards of behaviour we expect and the way in which any alleged offences committed by persons entitled to diplomatic immunity will be handled. The Foreign and Commonwealth Office takes action with the appropriate diplomatic mission in the case of every alleged offence by an entitled person notified to the Foreign and Commonwealth Office by the police. The Foreign and Commonwealth Office also continues to intervene on behalf of individuals who are precluded by diplomatic immunity from pursuing through normal legal channels valid claims against members of diplomatic missions in London.

The Foreign and Commonwealth Office has dealt firmly with the problem of unpaid parking fines by diplomatic missions in London. With the assistance of a computerised system, the Foreign and Commonwealth Office monitors all such fines left unpaid by members of diplomatic missions in London and by official cars owned by diplomatic missions. In 1984, there were 108,845 unpaid fines outstanding; in 1989 this figure had fallen to 7,831 representing a drop of 93 per cent. between 1984 and 1989. Detailed statistics on unpaid parking fines are published in Parliament every six months.

(HC Debs., vol. 171, Written Answers, cols. 305–6 : 26 April 1990)

The following statement was issued on 5 July 1990 by the Twelve Member States of the EC:

The Community and its member states are deeply concerned by the gravity of the situation in Albania where human rights and the fundamental principles of international law are being violated.

They strongly urge the Albanian Government, first, to take the necessary measures to ensure the physical safety of the persons who have taken refuge in embassies, to refrain from reprisals against their families, to allow them to receive such assistance as is necessary and to guarantee their free departure from Albanian territory, and secondly, to respect international law and the provisions of the Vienna Convention on diplomatic relations as regards the inviolability of diplomatic missions.

Moreover, they express the hope that the Albanian authorities will rapidly adopt the reforms and measures necessary for Albania to become engaged in a process of democratisation bringing about a situation in which human rights are fully respected.

The European Community and its member states recall that respect for human rights and the principles of international law is an essential condition for the establishment of normal relations with the Community.

(Text provided by the FCO)

The Twelve Member States of the EC issued a statement on 3 August 1990 on the subject of the conflict in Liberia. It read in part:

In particular, the Community and its member states call upon the parties in the conflict, in conformity with international law and the most basic humanitarian principles, to safeguard from violence embassies and other places of refuge such as churches, hospitals, etc where defenceless civilians have sought shelter.

(Text provided by the FCO)

In a statement issued on 21 August 1990, the Twelve Member States of the EC declared:

The Community and its member states, in the light of their condemnation of the Iraqi aggression against Kuwait as well as of their refusal to recognise the annexation of that state to Iraq, firmly reject the unlawful Iraqi demand to close the diplomatic missions in Kuwait and reiterate their resolve to keep those missions open in view also of the task of protecting their nationals.

(Text provided by the FCO)

At a press conference given by the FCO on 24 August 1990, the FCO spokesman stated:

The United Kingdom will also continue to hold Iraq responsible for ensuring respect for and observance of the special status and immunities to which the British Embassy and its staff in Iraq are entitled under international law.

(Text provided by the FCO)

On 10 September 1990 a joint press statement was issued following a meeting between the Foreign Minister of Japan, Mr Taroi Nakayama, and the Secretary of State for Foreign and Commonwealth Affairs, Mr Douglas Hurd. It read in part:

The Ministers demanded that Iraq cease to interfere with the functioning of the diplomatic and consular missions in Kuwait and refrain from actions contrary to the status and inviolability of their members.

(FCO Press Release No. 192 of 1990)

At a FCO press conference given on 14 September 1990, the FCO spokesman stated:

. . . the Iraqi Ambassador had been summoned to the Foreign Office yesterday afternoon to see Mr David Gore-Booth, Assistant Under-Secretary of State responsible for the Middle East. The purpose of the meeting had been to protest at the entirely unacceptable and illegal violation of the Dutch and French residences in Kuwait . . .

(Text provided by the FCO)

The Twelve Member States of the EC issued the following statement on 14 September 1990:

The Community and its member states denounce the very grave violation of the provisions of the 1961 Vienna Convention, which Iraq has subscribed to, perpetrated by the Iraqi occupying forces in Kuwait when they broke into the premises of the French and Dutch Embassies and took away French nationals, one of them a diplomat.

The Community and its member states similarly denounce those acts committed against other Embassies and their nationals.

This represents an intolerable affront to international law and to the rights of the individual.

The Community and its member states demand the immediate release of the captured foreign nationals and invite the Iraqi authorities to urgently respect the provisions of international law.

A Community *démarche* to this end will be made to the Iraqi authorities.

(Text provided by the FCO)

In the course of a speech in the Sixth Committee of the UN General Assembly on 26 September 1990, the Italian delegate, on behalf of the Twelve Member States of the EC, stated:

We would also like to underline our concern for other violations of the obligations regarding diplomatic and consular privileges and immunities. We consider it essential that all States observe scrupulously all obligations concerning the immunities, protection, security and safety of diplomatic and consular missions and representatives incumbent on them by virtue of general international law as well as the relevant international conventions.

The Twelve remain strongly committed to the resort to all lawful means for preventing crimes against diplomatic and consular representatives and violations of their immunities. They are ready to strengthen international cooperation to this end by all possible means.

International law grants privileges and immunities to missions and representatives not for their personal benefit, but in order to ensure the smooth and efficient exercise of their functions, to the benefit of international relations as a whole. While sending States have a right to expect that their diplomatic and consular representatives be adequately protected and their immunities strictly observed, abuses by missions or representatives of their privileges and immunities must be avoided. Respect for the laws of the receiving State is essential. The Twelve will continue to cooperate in measures to deal with abuses, which only undermine the public's understanding of the need for privileges and immunities and, ultimately, jeopardize the safe conduct of international relations.

There is no lack of international instruments on the obligations of States in the field of the protection of diplomatic and consular representatives and missions. General international law contains also a wealth of principles and rules on the subject. While the Twelve wish that States which have not yet become parties to the relevant conventions will soon do so, they would like to underline that what is essential is the full observance of existing obligations. Consequently, efforts should be concentrated on strengthening the determination of States to abide fully by their international obligations.

In discussing this item at previous sessions of the General Assembly the Twelve refrained from commenting upon specific cases of violations. At the present session we feel compelled to make an exception: the violations of obligations under international law concerning the protection of diplomatic and consular representatives and missions which occurred in Kuwait after its invasion and purported annexation by Iraq in August are so grave that they cannot be passed over in silence or merely alluded to obliquely.

The Twelve reiterate their strong and unequivocal condemnation of Iraq for the orders for closure of diplomatic and consular missions and the withdrawal of the immunity of their personnel. In its resolution 664 of 18 August, the Security Council has demanded that such orders be rescinded. As stated by the Twelve in the Declaration issued at the Extraordinary Ministerial Meeting held in Brussels on the 10th of August (U.N. document A/45/409–S/21502), the orders for closure of diplomatic and consular missions and the withdrawal of the immunities of their personnel, are serious violations of international law.

During the last few weeks, Iraq has persisted in its flouting of the basic principles and rules of international law on the protection and status of diplomats, in resorting to acts of violence against diplomatic missions, violating diplomatic premises and abducting personnel enjoying diplomatic immunity and foreign nationals present in these premises. This behaviour represents an intolerable affront to international law and to the rights of the individual. The Twelve therefore share the outrage and condemnation expressed by the Security Council in its Resolution n. 667 of the 16th of September.

In comparison with the magnitude of the wilful violations by Iraq, most of the violations considered in the Report by the Secretary General might appear of lesser gravity. We wish nonetheless to reiterate the importance we attach to the faithful and scrupulous observance of all obligations under international law for the protection of diplomatic and consular representatives and missions, and the view that the reporting procedures established more than ten years ago with resolution 35/168 perform a useful, even though modest, function in the prevention of violations.

(Text provided by the FCO; see also A/C. 6/45/SR. 6, pp. 3–4)

The following material appeared in the report of a press conference given by the FCO on 27 September 1990:

Spokesman also said that the Iraqis had sent diplomatic Notes to foreign embassies in Baghdad about the Revolutionary Command Council decree issued last month which said that harbouring a foreigner with the intent of hiding him from the authorities was a crime in the category of espionage punishable by death. The note had gone on to ask missions to state whether any of their or other nationals were residing in Embassy properties.

We totally rejected the Iraqi Note as a further example of blatant Iraqi disregard for international law.

Under the Vienna Convention on Diplomatic Relations our diplomats enjoyed total immunity from Iraqi criminal law. Embassy buildings were inviolable: Iraqi authorities could not enter them without the Ambassador's explicit agreement.

(Text provided by the FCO)

The following statement was made at a FCO press conference given on 17 October 1990:

Spokesman said that Mr Gore-Booth had also taken the opportunity to register with the Iraqi Ambassador our concern at the refusal of the Foreign Ministry in Baghdad to accept the accreditation of 8 diplomatic service personnel (whose service in Kuwait had come to an end), as members of the diplomatic staff of our Embassy in Baghdad.

Spokesman explained that these staff were members of HM Embassy Kuwait whose postings had been brought to an end when they were unable to fulfil their proper functions as a result of Iraq's illegal action in occupying Kuwait. It had been decided that they should be given new assignments in Baghdad. The Iraqi authorities had been notified by our Ambassador of their appointment as members of our diplomatic staff but we were informed on 12 October that Iraq could not accept them as members of the Diplomatic Corps, and considered them for the duration of their stay in Iraq simply as ordinary British citizens (whom the Iraqis have refused to allow to leave).

Spokesman said that this incident was a further example of Iraq's flagrant disregard for international law. Article 40 of the Vienna Convention required Iraq to accord diplomats passing through or in their territory inviolability and other such immunities as may be required to ensure their transit or return. Under Article 44 the Iraqis were required, even in the case of armed conflict, to grant facilities to enable persons enjoying privileges and immunities to leave at the earliest possible moment. In neither case had they fulfilled their obligations.

(Text provided by the FCO)

In a statement made on 19 November 1990 in the Sixth Committee of the UN General Assembly considering the report of the Committee on Relations with the Host Country, the Italian delegate, on behalf of the Twelve Member States of the EC, remarked:

Concerning in particular the question of transport and the application of traffic laws, the Twelve wish to recall the importance that they attach to the respect of article IV of the Headquarters Agreement and of article 31 of the Vienna Convention of 1961 under which diplomatic agents enjoy immunity from criminal, civil and administrative jurisdiction in the receiving State. They expect the Host Country to take appropriate steps to comply fully with these obligations.

It is true that for such delicate matters related to the implementation of the said Agreement, continuous vigilance combined with the necessary courtesy are indispensable. For our delegations it is very important that questions of principle as well as of practical consequence in this field be dealt with in full respect for international law.

(Text provided by the FCO; see also A/C. 6/45/SR. 44, p. 3)

In a statement made on 20 November 1990 in the Sixth Committee of the UN General Assembly concerning draft resolution L.15 on 'Consideration of effective measures to enhance the protection, security and safety of diplomatic and consular missions and representatives', the representative of

Italy, on behalf of the Twelve Member States of the EC, having recalled the EC's statement on 28 September 1990, observed:

. . . we can indicate our satisfaction in seeing that the draft resolution submitted to our approval does not, indeed, pass over in silence the grave violations committed by Iraq of its obligations under international law concerning the protection of diplomatic and consular representatives and missions.

We consider particularly appropriate the inclusion in the resolution of the fifth preambular paragraph recalling Security Council resolutions 664, 667 and 674 which concern the above mentioned violations and of the third operative paragraph calling for the immediate cessation of these violations.

(Text provided by the FCO; see also A/C. 6/45/SR. 45, p. 8)

Speaking on 26 November 1990 in the Third Committee of the UN General Assembly, the Permanent Representative of Italy, on behalf of the EC and its Member States, stated:

The basic principles and rules of international law governing treatment of foreign nationals as well as the protection of diplomats and their missions have been violated by the Iraqi authorities, including the continuing attempts to force closure of embassies accredited to the State of Kuwait.

(Text provided by the FCO; see also A/C. 3/45/SR. 52, p. 12)

Part Five: VIII. B. *Organs of the State—immunity of organs of the State— immunity other than diplomatic and consular*

In the course of a debate on 31 October 1990 in the Sixth Committee of the UN General Assembly considering the draft articles of the International Law Commission on the subject of the jurisdictional immunities of States and their property, the UK representative, Sir Arthur Watts, stated:

As to this year's work, Mr Chairman, the British Government welcome the progress that has been made on a significant number of the draft articles. The underlying doctrinal and legal bases for this subject still seem, however, to be matters on which views in the Commission are divided. In previous years my delegation has set out our views on this matter, and it may be helpful if I mention them again. In short, international law has developed in such a way that the old rule of absolute immunity is now obsolete. We believe that a substantial body of State practice, as well as a number of developments in international law, support the principle that those who find themselves involved in a dispute with the Government of a foreign State, acting in a non-sovereign capacity, should be able to have that dispute determined by the ordinary processes of law.

Mr Chairman, I wish to mention briefly in this statement only three specific points, to which my delegation attaches particular importance. The first concerns the question whether or not a transaction is a 'commercial transaction'. We note, Mr Chairman, that the text of draft Article 2 still refers to the 'purpose' of a transaction in determining the answer to that question. We have on previous occasions made clear our view that factors such as purpose should not be introduced into that definition, and that remains our view.

(Text provided by the FCO; see also A/C. 6/45/SR. 26, pp. 3–4)

Later in his speech, Sir Arthur Watts observed:

I would refer to the rules on immunity of States from measures of constraint, which is the subject of draft Articles 21 and 22. We share the views of those States which favour limiting the immunity from measures of constraint. We cannot support the grant of absolute immunity from such measures. As pointed out by the Special Rapporteur, the recent tendency in State practice has been to restrict State immunity in this respect, not to enlarge it.

(Ibid., p. 4)

In an Annex to the above speech, the UK made the following comment:

ARTICLE 2

Use of terms

Para (b): Definition of a 'State'

We are disappointed that the formulation in paragraph 1(b)(iii) (political subdivisions) has been adopted by the Drafting Committee on second reading. As indicated in the United Kingdom's earlier written observations, the correct proposition is that 'political subdivisions' only enjoy immunity *ratione materiae*. We note that paragraph 1(b)(iii) *bis* has not been adopted by the Drafting Committee pending decision on Article 11 *bis*. The suggestion by the Special Rapporteur to exclude entities, established by the State for the purposes of performing commercial transactions and which have an independent legal personality, does not of course address the point raised by us that such entities should only enjoy immunity *ratione materiae*.

(Text provided by the FCO)

Part Five: IX. *Organs of the State—protecting powers*

The following is an example of a treaty between the UK and Argentina concluded by Exchange of Notes between their Protecting Powers, the Swiss Confederation and Brazil respectively. It concerned certain commercial debts. The note, dated 24 October 1989, from the Minister in the Swiss Embassy at Paris, on behalf of the UK Government, to the Ambassador of Brazil at Paris, read as follows:

I have the honour to refer to the Conference held in Paris on 19 and 20 May 1987, regarding the Consolidation of Argentine Debts, at which the Government of the United Kingdom of Great Britain and Northern Ireland, the Government of the Republic of Argentina, certain other Governments, the International Monetary Fund, the International Bank for Reconstruction and Development, the Inter-American Development Bank, the Secretariat of the United Nations Conference on Trade and Development, the Organisation for Economic Co-operation and Development and the Commission of the European Communities were represented. On behalf of the Government of the United Kingdom I have the honour to inform Your Excellency that the terms and conditions set out in the Annex to this Note, which have been agreed between British and Argentine technical representatives, are acceptable to the Government of the United Kingdom.

If the terms and conditions are acceptable to the Government of the Republic of Argentina, I have the honour further to propose, for and on behalf of the Government of the United Kingdom of Great Britain and Northern Ireland, that this Note together with its Annex and your reply to that effect shall constitute an Agreement in this matter between the Government of the United Kingdom of Great Britain and Northern Ireland and the Government of the Republic of Argentina, which shall be known as the 'United Kingdom/Argentina Debt Agreement No. 2 (1987)' and which shall enter into force on the date of your reply.

(TS No. 50 (1990); Cm. 1139. See also TS No. 50 (1989); Cm. 839)

Part Six: I. A. *Treaties—conclusion and entry into force—conclusion, signature, ratification and accession*

(See also Part Six: I.B., below)

In reply to the question when would the UN Convention on the Rights of the Child be ratified, the Parliamentary Under-Secretary of State, FCO, Mr Tim Sainsbury, stated in part:

The Government take our obligations under such conventions extremely seriously and we will not ratify until we are sure that our domestic legislation is entirely in harmony with our commitments under the convention.

. . .

. . . the legislation is wide ranging and complex. Many aspects of the convention are already dealt with in our domestic legislation. We want to make sure that our domestic legislation is entirely in harmony with our commitments under the convention, because we take these matters seriously and we are determined to get them right. There are nine Government Departments involved and—inevitably, I am afraid—the consultations involve many lawyers because there are legal aspects to the matter. I am afraid that at this stage I cannot give a timetable; I can only confirm that we shall complete the work as soon as we possibly can so that we can ratify the convention.

(HC Debs., vol. 176, cols. 291–2: 11 July 1990)

The following item appeared in the report of a FCO press conference given on 19 September 1990:

Spokesman confirmed that we had seen reports concerning the reciprocal impounding of assets by Iraq. We were seeking further clarification. Spokesman added that the only British Government asset in Iraq was the Embassy, which was protected by the Vienna Convention on diplomatic relations.

(Text provided by the FCO)

Part Six: I. B. *Treaties—conclusion and entry into force—reservations and declarations to multilateral treaties*

In acceding to the International Convention on the Elimination of All Forms of Racial Discrimination, 1966, the Yemen Arab Republic made reservations to Article 5(c) and (d)(iv), (vi) and (vii). On 4 August 1989, the Secretary-General of the United Nations, as depositary, received from the UK Government the following objection with regard to these reservations:

The Government of the United Kingdom of Great Britain and Northern Ireland do not accept the reservations made by the Yemen Arab Republic to Article 5(c) and (d)(iv), (vi) and (vii) of the International Convention on the Elimination of All Forms of Racial Discrimination.

(TS No. 64 (1989); Cm. 1076, p. 10)

In acceding to the Vienna Convention on the Law of Treaties, 1969, Algeria made the following reservation:

The Government of the People's Democratic Republic of Algeria considers that the competence of the International Court of Justice cannot be exercised with respect to a dispute such as that envisaged in Article 66(a) at the request of one of the parties alone.

It declares that, in each case, the prior agreement of all the parties concerned is necessary for a dispute to be submitted to the said Court.

(TS No. 61 (1989); Cm. 949, p. 16)

On 11 October 1989, the Secretary-General of the United Nations, as depositary, received from the UK Government the following objection with regard to the above reservation:

The Government of the United Kingdom wish in this context to recall their declaration of 5 June 1987 (in respect of the accession of the Union of Soviet Socialist Republics) (*see* Treaty Series No. 61 (1987), Cm 286, p. 20) which in accordance with its terms applies to the reservations mentioned above, and will similarly apply to any like reservations which any other State may formulate.

(TS No. 64 (1989); Cm. 1076, p. 20 (for the text of the 1987 declaration, see UKMIL 1987, pp. 578–9))

In the course of a statement made on 26 January 1990 to the UN Committee on the Elimination of Discrimination against Women, the UK representative, Mrs P. Denham, referred to the UK's ratification of the UN Convention on the Elimination of All Forms of Discrimination against Women, 1979. She went on:

Madam Chairman, you yourself and almost every member of the Committee were concerned at the number of reservations, particularly when viewed against the United Kingdom's good record in promoting equality.

I can assure you that the United Kingdom supports the basic objectives of the Convention and that the number of the declarations and reservations should not be taken to suppose lack of commitment on our part.

First of all I should stress that the statements made when we ratified the Convention were not only reservations; many were declarations as to our understanding of the purpose of the Convention and its provisions. For example, paragraph (b) to which Ms Tallawy and others referred is intended to make clear that we regard existing legislation such as the Equal Pay Act 1970 and the Sex Discrimination Act

1975 as appropriate measures for the implementation of the Convention. We made these (often very detailed) declarations and reservations because the United Kingdom takes its international obligations very seriously. We do not ratify a convention until we are in a position to implement it in our domestic law. And where in certain respects that may not be possible we are scrupulous (some might say over-scrupulous) in making the necessary reservations.

In the case of the Convention the main reason for the length and complexity of the reservations and declarations was that, because of the desire to adopt the Convention by the deadline in 1979, we felt that some of the provisions had been rather hastily drafted and imprecise. It is clear that the drafters envisaged a progressive implementation of its provisions where these could not be complied with immediately. But unless a State made declarations or reservations upon ratification, it would be fully bound by all provisions of the Convention. We are therefore bound to enter reservations or declarations on those provisions we could not implement immediately upon ratification, even if we intended to rectify the position shortly.

Our declarations and reservations were designed to cover various exceptions provided for in UK law which largely relate to matters of propriety, privacy or common sense, or to provisions of the Convention which would be too expensive to implement immediately. I should like to repeat that we keep them all under review.

(Text provided by the FCO)

On 6 April 1988, the Government of Vietnam acceded to the Convention on the Privileges and Immunities of the United Nations, 1946, with the following reservation:

Reservation in respect of article VIII, section 30:
1. Disputes concerning the interpretation or application of the Convention shall be referred to the International Court of Justice for settlement only with the consent of all parties concerned.
2. The opinion of the International Court of Justice referred to in article VIII, section 30, shall be merely advisory and shall not be considered decisive without the consent of all parties concerned.

(C.N. 87. 1988. TREATIES–1)

On 29 January 1990, the UK Permanent Representative to the UN in New York communicated to the UN Secretary-General, as depositary, the following statement with reference to the above reservation:

The instrument of accession deposited by the Government of Vietnam contains a reservation relating to Article VIII, Section 30, of the Convention concerning the settlement of disputes over the interpretation or application of the Convention. The Government of the United Kingdom of Great Britain and Northern Ireland have consistently stated that they are unable to accept reservations in respect of Article VIII, Section 30. In their view, these are not the kind of reservations which intending parties to the Convention have the right to make.

Accordingly, the Government of the United Kingdom do not accept the reservation entered by the Government of Vietnam against Article VIII, Section 30, of the Convention.

(Text provided by the FCO)

Part Six: II. A. *Treaties—observance, application and interpretation—observance*

In reply to a question, the Government Minister in the House of Lords wrote:

We attach great importance to the Nuclear Non-Proliferation Treaty (NPT) and we value our well-established reputation as a strict upholder of all our international obligations.

(HL Debs., vol. 521, col. 1787: 26 July 1990)

Part Six: II. B. *Treaties—observance, application and interpretation—application*

Article 1 of the Agreement between the Governments of the UK and the Czech and Slovak Federal Republic for the Promotion and Protection of Investments, signed on 10 July 1990, is illustrative of the content of similar agreements concluded or signed by the UK in 1990. It reads in part as follows:

ARTICLE 1

Definitions

For the purposes of this Agreement:

. . .

(d) the term 'territory' means:
    (i) in respect of the Czech and Slovak Federal Republic: the territory of the Czech and Slovak Federal Republic;
    (ii) in respect of the United Kingdom: Great Britain and Northern Ireland, including the territorial sea and any maritime area situated beyond the territorial sea of the United Kingdom which has been or might in the future be designated under the national law of the United Kingdom in accordance with international law as an area within which the United Kingdom may exercise rights with regard to the seabed and subsoil and the natural resources and any territory to which this Agreement is extended in accordance with the provisions of Article 12.

Article 12 reads:

ARTICLE 12

Territorial Extension

At the time of entry into force of this Agreement, or at any time thereafter, the provisions of this Agreement may be extended to such territories for whose international relations the Government of the United Kingdom are responsible as may be agreed between the Contracting Parties in an Exchange of Notes.

(Cm. 1306)

Part Six: II. E. *Treaties—observance, application and interpretation—treaty succession*

In reply to a question, the Minister of State, FCO, Lord Brabazon of Tara, stated:

. . . it is certainly true that when India obtained its independence in 1947 Her Majesty's Government relinquished all rights and responsibilities in Tibet as set out in the treaties between China and Tibet. The new government of India assumed those rights and responsibilities.

(HL Debs., vol. 520, col. 2014: 3 July 1990)

Part Six: III. *Treaties—amendment and modification*

The following question was put to the Secretary of State for Foreign and Commonwealth Affairs:

What opinions [has he] received as to whether other member states of the European Economic Community would be in breach of their Community obligations if they sought to make a new European Community treaty for economic and monetary union or political union exclusive of the United Kingdom?

In reply, the Minister of State, FCO, wrote:

. . . intergovernmental conferences on economic and monetary union and political union have been called under article 236 of the Treaty, which states that the conference must determine by common accord the amendments to be made to the treaty. This precludes amendment of the treaty of Rome by less than all member states.

(HC Debs., vol. 178, Written Answers, col. *694*: 1 November 1990)

Part Six: IV. C. *Treaties—invalidity, termination and suspension of operation—termination, suspension of operation, denunciation and withdrawal*

In a Note dated 12 October 1988, the UK Government gave notice to the Government of Finland of the termination of the Agreement of 18 November 1925 for the Reciprocal Exemption from Income Tax in certain cases of Profits accruing from the Business of Shipping. In accordance with the provisions of Article 5 of the above Agreement, the effective date of the termination was 12 October 1988.

(TS No. 89 (1990); Cm. 1388, p. 10)

In a Note dated 12 October 1988, the UK Government gave notice to the Government of Finland of the termination of the Agreement of 21 February 1935 for Reciprocal Exemption from Income Tax on Profits or Gains arising through an Agency. In accordance with the provisions of Article 4 of the above Agreement, the effective date of the termination was 12 April 1989.

(Ibid.)

In a Note dated 23 October 1989, the UK Government gave notice to the Government of Iceland of its intention to denounce with immediate effect Articles 1, 2, 3, 4 (paragraph 2) of the Agreement of 19 May 1933 relating to Trade and Commerce, and its Protocol, in so far as they apply to the UK, the Isle of Man and the Channel Islands, as these provisions were now governed by the terms of the EC/Iceland Agreement of 22 July 1972. These Articles will continue to apply to any other dependent territories to which the 1933 Agreement now applies.

(Ibid., p. 18)

In a Note dated 23 February 1990, the UK Government gave notice to the Government of Morocco of the termination of the Exchange of Notes of 1 October 1958 for the Mutual Abolition of Visas on Passports. In accordance with the provisions of paragraph 7 of the Agreement, the effective date of the termination was 1 April 1990.

(Ibid., p. 20)

By an Exchange of Notes on 31 July 1990 between the Executive Chairman of the International Tin Council and the Secretary of State for Foreign and Commonwealth Affairs, it was agreed that the Headquarters Agreement, 1972, between the Government of UK and the International Tin Council (TS No. 38 (1972); Cmnd. 4938), as amended by an Exchange of Notes of 1974 (TS No. 145 (1975); Cmnd. 6293), shall terminate with effect from the dissolution of the International Tin Council on 31 July 1990.

(TS No. 71 (1990); Cm. 1239)

Part Six: VI. *Treaties—breach*

In reply to a question, the Minister of State for the Armed Forced wrote:

The Soviet Union declared in 1987 that it had ceased production of chemical weapons. We are, however, not aware of any change in Soviet capacity to produce them since then. The Soviet Union is a signatory of the 1972 biological warfare convention and has stated it is in compliance with its obligations. Any production of biological weapons would be in breach of the convention.

(HC Debs., vol. 170, Written Answers, col. *329* : 30 March 1990)

Part Six: VII. *Treaties—consensual arrangements other than treaties*

(See Part Two: I. (item of 27 June 1990 referring to EC Social Charter) and Part Four: VII. (item of 29 October 1990 referring to Helsinki Final Act), above, and Part Nine: XV. D. (Memorandum of Understanding of 28 June 1988), below)

Part Eight: I.A. *State territory and territorial jurisdiction—parts of territory, delimitation—frontiers, boundaries*

(See also Part Three: I.B.5. (items of 3 April and 4 December 1990), above, and Part Eight: II.A. (items on Kuwait), below)

The FCO presented to the HC Foreign Affairs Committee a memorandum, dated March 1990, entitled 'The Status of the Two German States' in which the following passage appeared:

17. As Article 7.1 of the Relations Convention states, the final determination of the boundaries of Germany must await a peace settlement (paragraph 12 above). At Potsdam in 1945 it was agreed in principle to transfer to the Soviet Union the part of the Soviet zone which was placed under Soviet administration (the City of Königsberg and the adjacent area). In Article 1 of their Treaty of 7 December 1970 the FRG and Poland concurred that the existing border-line established at Potsdam (the Oder-Neisse line) was the Western State frontier of Poland, affirmed the inviolability of their existing borders now and in the future, and declared that they had no territorial claims against one another and would not raise such claims in the future. HMG welcomed the provisions of this Treaty, including those relating to Poland's western frontier (see Cmd 6201, pp 226–229). Further, in the Helsinki CSCE Final Act, the participating States stated that they regarded as inviolable 'all one another's frontiers as well as the frontiers of all States of Europe'.

(*Parliamentary Papers*, 1989–90, HC, Paper 335–i, p. 3)

The following map was attached to the memorandum:

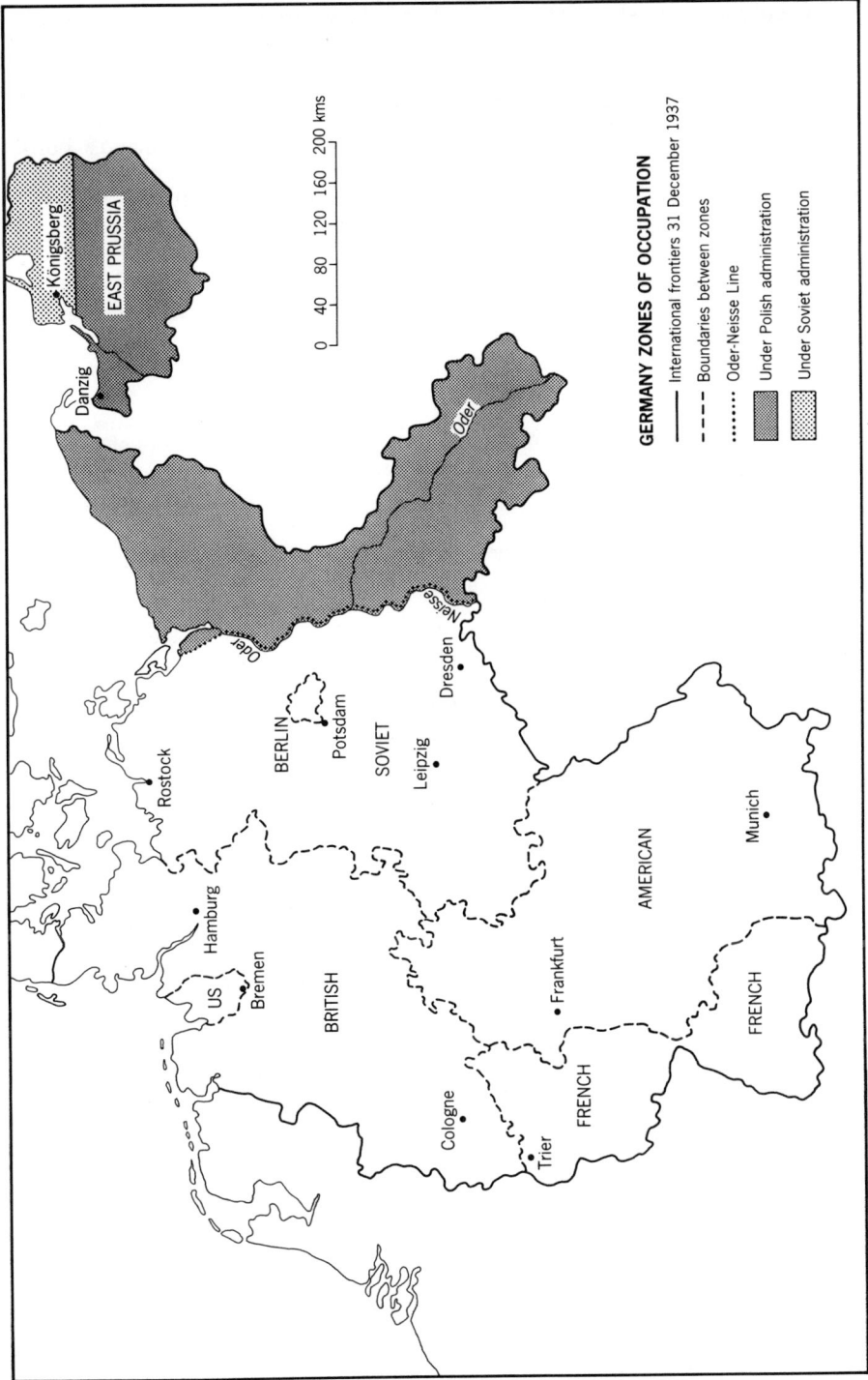

GERMANY ZONES OF OCCUPATION

International frontiers 31 December 1937
Boundaries between zones
Oder-Neisse Line
Under Polish administration
Under Soviet administration

0   40   80   120   160   200 kms

EAST PRUSSIA

Königsberg

Danzig

Oder

Neisse

Oder

Rostock

BERLIN

Potsdam

Dresden

Leipzig

SOVIET

Hamburg

US   Bremen

BRITISH

Cologne

Trier

FRENCH

Frankfurt

AMERICAN

Munich

FRENCH

In reply to a question, the Prime Minister wrote in part:

We are committed to fulfil Britain's collective defence obligations arising from the North Atlantic and modified Brussels treaties within the areas covered by these treaties. We are also committed to the principles set out in the 1975 Helsinki Final Act, including the inviolability of frontiers. The question of Poland's borders needs to be finally settled by a binding treaty instrument. We welcome the Federal German Government's intention to reaffirm the inviolability of Poland's borders.

(HC Debs., vol. 169, Written Answers, col. *156*: 13 March 1990)

In reply to the question 'which section of the Helsinki Accord recognises, de facto, the existing borders in the Soviet Union; and which section of the Accord states that any boundary changes should be conducted by negotiation', the Minister of State, FCO, wrote:

The first of the principles guiding relations between participating states, the first substantive section of the Helsinki Final Act, states that the frontiers of participating states
'can be changed, in accordance with international law, by peaceful means and by agreement'.
Principle III covers the inviolability of frontiers.

(HC Debs., vol. 172, Written Answers, col. *312*: 14 May 1990)

In reply to a question on the subject of the status of Memel and the Memel Statute of 8 May 1924, the Minister of State, FCO, wrote:

Memel (today Klaipeda) has, subject to certain provisions, formally belonged to Lithuania since 1924 (except for a brief period in 1939 when it was ceded to Germany). Following the annexation of Lithuania by the Soviet Union in 1940, we considered Memel, with the rest of Lithuania to be *de facto*, but not *de jure*, part of the Soviet Union. Our position has not changed since then. We have had no recent discussion on this matter with the co-signatories of the Memel Statute.

(HL Debs., vol. 519, col. 1364: 5 June 1990)

Following the report of the HC Foreign Affairs Committee on the unification of Germany, the Government presented to Parliament, in October 1990, written observations in which the following passages appeared:

Borders

17. Article 1 of the Treaty provides that Germany shall comprise the territory of the Federal Republic of Germany, the GDR and the whole of Berlin, and that Germany has no territorial claims whatsoever against other states and shall not assert any in the future. Germany's Basic Law is amended as from 3 October so that it contains no provisions incompatible with these provisions. Article 1 further states that Germany's borders shall be definitive from the date the Treaty comes into force, and that Germany and Poland shall confirm the existing border between them in a treaty.

(Cm. 1246, p. 6)

26. The proposed German-Polish treaty confirming the existing border has been referred to above. Germany's borders, including the Oder-Neisse border, will be

definitive with the entry into force of the Treaty on the Final Settlement with respect to Germany.

(Ibid., p. 7; see also HC Debs., vol. 178, Written Answers, col. 54: 22 October 1990)

On 11 October 1990, the Governments of UK and France concluded an Exchange of Notes relating to the Channel Tunnel. This read in part as follows:

1 (a) The date of effective connection mentioned in Article 3, paragraph 3, of the Treaty [of 12 February 1986] shall be fixed by the Intergovernmental Commission, taking account of the state of completion of the civil engineering work and the installation of the permanent systems and equipment.

(b) The date shall not be later than 31 December 1992, without prejudice to the provisions of paragraph 3 of the present Note.

2 (a) If any works carried out from one of the two States extend beyond the line of the frontier defined by paragraph 1 of Article 3 of the Treaty, the law that applies in that part shall, in relation to matters occurring before that part is effectively connected, be the law of the State from which the works on that part of the Channel Fixed Link have been carried out, up to the point, in each part of the Channel Fixed Link, where such works extending from one State have connected with those extending from the other State.

(b) The Concessionaires shall inform the Intergovernmental Commission where the works connect in each part of the Fixed Link. These boundaries shall be fixed by the Commission and shall be marked on the spot.

3. The Intergovernmental Commission shall examine no later than 30 September 1992 whether new circumstances require that the date of effective connection be postponed beyond 31 December 1992.

(Text provided by the FCO)

Part Eight: II. A. *State territory and territorial jurisdiction—territorial jurisdiction—territorial sovereignty*

On 4 April 1989, the UN Secretary-General, as depositary, received the following objection from the Argentine Republic:

The Argentine Republic rejects the extension of the territorial application of the Convention on the Elimination of all Forms of Discrimination against Women, adopted by the United Nations General Assembly on 18 December 1979, to the Malvinas (Falkland) Islands, South Georgia and the South Sandwich Islands, notified by the Government of the United Kingdom of Great Britain and Northern Ireland upon its ratification of that instrument on 7 April 1986. [*See* Treaty Series No. 2 (1989), Cm 643, page 28].

The Argentine Republic reaffirms its sovereignty over the aforementioned archipelagos, which are an integral part of its national territory, and recalls that the United Nations General Assembly has adopted resolutions 2065 (XX), 3160 (XXVIII), 31/49, 37/9, 38/12 and 39/6, in which a sovereignty dispute is recognized and the Governments of Argentina and the United Kingdom are urged to resume negotiations in order to find as soon as possible a peaceful and lasting solution to the dispute and their remaining differences relating to this question, through the good offices of the Secretary-General. The General Assembly has also adopted resolutions 40/21, 41/40, 42/19 and 43/25, which reiterate its request to the parties to resume such negotiations.

(TS No. 62 (1989); Cm. 988, p. 12)

On 27 November 1989, the Secretary-General received in response to the above the following communication from the UK Government:

The Government of the United Kingdom of Great Britain and Northern Ireland reject the statement made by the Government of Argentina on 4 April 1989 regarding the Falkland Islands and South Georgia and the South Sandwich Islands. The Government of the United Kingdom of Great Britain and Northern Ireland have no doubt as to British sovereignty over the Falkland Islands and South Georgia and the South Sandwich Islands, and their consequent right to extend treaties to those Territories.

(TS No. 89 (1990); Cm. 1388, p. 18)

In the course of a debate on the subject of the judgment in the Supreme Court of the Irish Republic in the case of *McGimpsey*, the Parliamentary Under-Secretary of State for Northern Ireland, Dr Brian Mawhinney, referred to Articles 2 and 3 of the Constitution of the Republic and stated with respect to the argument that these constituted a claim to sovereignty over Northern Ireland:

As far as we are concerned, Northern Ireland is part of the United Kingdom and is clearly so in international law.

. . .

The people of Northern Ireland and the United Kingdom have lived with this territorial claim for over 50 years. The United Kingdom Government have never accepted it, do not accept it and have said so, as I do again tonight. We regard it as having no validity in international law. It has never had any practical effect on Northern Ireland's position as part of the United Kingdom.

(HC Debs., vol. 169, col. 648: 14 March 1990; see also ibid., vol. 170, col. 286: 27 March 1990)

In reply to a question on the same subject, the Secretary of State for Foreign and Commonwealth Affairs wrote in part:

A judgment of the Irish Supreme Court cannot effect Northern Ireland's position within the United Kingdom in international law. Irrespective of articles 2 and 3 of the Irish constitution, both Governments are agreed that any change in the status of Northern Ireland would come about only with the consent of a majority of the people of Northern Ireland.

(HC Debs., vol. 170, Written Answers, cols. 706–7 : 4 April 1990)

In reply to a question asking what is the United Kingdom's current relationship with Greenland, the Minister of State, FCO, wrote in part:

Greenland is an autonomous region of Denmark, with which the United Kingdom enjoys good relations.

(HC Debs., vol. 171, Written Answers, col. 693: 4 May 1990)

In reply to a question, the Government spokesman in the House of Lords, Lord Reay, stated in part:

Under the 1960 Treaty of Establishment we retained indefinitely two Sovereign base areas in Cyprus. We have no intention of giving up those bases; nor have the Government of Cyprus ever asked us to do so.

(HL Debs., vol. 518, col. 1466: 10 May 1990)

In reply to a question, the Prime Minister wrote:

In terms of the Island of Rockall Act 1972 as read with the Local Government (Scotland) Act 1973, Rockall is part of the Western Isles Islands area. It forms part of the Crown Estates. The responsibilities of my right hon. and learned Friend the Secretary of State [for Scotland] extend to Rockall as to the rest of Scotland.

(HC Debs., vol. 174, Written Answers, col. 9 : 11 June 1990)

In reply to a question, the Secretary of State for Foreign and Commonwealth Affairs wrote:

I am not aware of any occasions in the last five years where the Government of the Republic of Ireland have raised a territorial claim over the United Kingdom at an international conference or meeting.

United Kingdom sovereignty over Northern Ireland, as a matter of international law, is clear. Our sovereignty is manifested, day by day, by acts of legislation, Government and the courts. Further, in article 1 of the Anglo-Irish Agreement, both Governments affirmed
'that any change in the status of Northern Ireland would only come about with the consent of a majority of the people of Northern Ireland'.

(HC Debs., vol. 174, Written Answers, col. 560 : 20 June 1990)

On 18 January 1990, the Secretary-General of the UN, as depositary, received from the Argentine Republic its instrument of ratification of the Vienna Convention for the Protection of the Ozone Layer, 1985. The instrument contained the following reservation:

The Argentine Republic rejects the ratification on 15 May 1987 of the 'Convention for the Protection of the Ozone Layer' by the Government of the United Kingdom of Great Britain and Northern Ireland, communicated by the Secretary-General of the United Nations in note C.N.112.187.TREATIES-1 (Depositary Notification), in respect of the Malvinas Islands, South Georgia and South Sandwich Islands and reaffirms its sovereignty over the said islands, which form an integral part of its national territory.

The United Nations General Assembly has adopted resolutions 2065 (XX), 3160 (XXVIII), 31/49, 37/9, 38/12 and 39/6, which recognize the existence of a sovereignty dispute relating to the question of the Malvinas Islands and request the Argentine Republic and the United Kingdom of Great Britain and Northern Ireland to resume negotiations in order to find as soon as possible a peaceful and definitive solution to the dispute and their remaining differences relating to the question, with the intercession of the good offices of the Secretary-General, who is to report to the General Assembly on the progress made. The United Nations

General Assembly has also adopted resolutions 40/21 and 41/40, which again request both parties to resume negotiations.

The Argentine Republic also rejects the ratification of the Convention by the Government of the United Kingdom of Great Britain and Northern Ireland in respect of what is termed by the United Kingdom the 'British Antarctic Territory'.

(C.N. 13. 1990. TREATIES–1/1)

On 6 July 1990, the Secretary-General received from the UK Government the following objection to the above reservation:

The instrument contained a reservation rejecting the ratification of the Convention by the United Kingdom of Great Britain and Northern Ireland in respect of the Falkland Islands, South Georgia and the South Sandwich Islands and the British Antarctic Territory.

The Government of the United Kingdom of Great Britain and Northern Ireland wishes to state that they have no doubt as to British sovereignty over the Falkland Islands, South Georgia and the South Sandwich Islands and the British Antarctic Territory, and their consequent right to extend treaties to those territories. In respect of the British Antarctic Territory, the Government of the United Kingdom would draw attention to the provisions of Article IV of the Antarctic Treaty of 1 December 1959, to which both Argentina and the United Kingdom are parties.

For the above reasons the Government of the United Kingdom rejects the Argentine reservation.

(C.N. 197. 1990. TREATIES–6)

The instrument of ratification of the UK, dated 16 December 1988, of the Montreal Protocol on Substances that Deplete the Ozone Layer, 1987, applied, *inter alia*, to the British Antarctic Territory. On 26 March 1990, the Secretary-General of the UN, as depositary, received from the Government of Chile its instrument of ratification of the Montreal Protocol. The instrument contained the following declaration:

[Chile] rejects the declaration made by the United Kingdom of Great Britain and Northern Ireland upon ratification, as it concerns the Chilean Antarctic Territory, including the corresponding maritime zones; [Chile] reaffirms once more its sovereignty over the said territory including its maritime areas, as defined by Supreme Decree No. 1747 of 6 November 1940.

(C.N. 77. 1990. TREATIES–3/3)

On 2 August 1990, the Secretary-General received from the UK Government the following objection to the above reservation:

The Government of the United Kingdom of Great Britain and Northern Ireland have no doubt as to British sovereignty over the British Antarctic Territory. In this respect, the Government of the United Kingdom would draw attention to the provisions of Article IV of the Antarctic Treaty of 1 December 1959, to which both Chile and the United Kingdom are parties.

(C.N. 239. 1990. TREATIES–8)

In the course of an emergency debate in the House of Commons on the subject of the situation in the Gulf, the Prime Minister, Mrs Margaret

Thatcher, referred to past differences between Iraq and Kuwait and went on:

Saddam Hussein introduced into this dispute the further question of Iraqi territorial claims on Kuwait. These claims are without legal foundation. The Al-Sabah family has ruled Kuwait since the 18th century, long before Iraq itself was created in the break-up of the Ottoman empire following the first world war.

Kuwait's borders with the newly created Iraq were drawn in 1923. They were accepted by Iraq when it became an independent state in 1932. None the less, Iraq resuscitated its territorial claim against Kuwait in 1961, when British protection of Kuwait came to an end. British forces were despatched at the request of the ruler to protect Kuwait's independence and sovereignty. They were subsequently replaced by an Arab League force. The existing border was then finally reaffirmed between Iraq and Kuwait in 1963.

(HC Debs., vol. 177, col. 735: 6 September 1990)

The FCO submitted a memorandum, dated 25 September 1990, to the Foreign Affairs Committee of the House of Commons examining the Gulf crisis. Annex 3 to the memorandum read as follows:

The Iraqi claim to Kuwait
The basis of the Iraqi claim to Kuwait is that Kuwait formed part of the Ottoman Vilayet of Basra before the First World War, and that Iraq, as successor to the Ottoman Government in the area, has assumed sovereignty over Kuwait. The Iraqis allege (wrongly) that Kuwait was subject to Ottoman administrative laws, that the Ottoman Sultan refused to accept the British Kuwaiti Agreement of 1899, that the British Ottoman Agreement of 1913 was not signed (rather than not ratified) and that Kuwait first came into existence as a result of the Sykes Picot Agreement.

The Iraqis carefully avoid mention of points which do not tell in their favour such as Iraqi recognition of Kuwait frontiers and independence in 1932 and 1963. The Iraqi claim also ignores the fact that Kuwait had been under Turkish suzerainty rather than sovereignty; that Turkish control was at best nominal, and that when the Ottoman Empire was dissolved after the First World War, the disposition of its dependent territories was decided by the international treaties of Sèvres and Lausanne. Kuwait's sovereignty, independence and international frontiers have since been recognized by the international community and by successive Iraqi governments, not only formally but also by the practice of normal bilateral relations.

(*Parliamentary Papers*, 1989–90, HC, Paper 655–ii, p. 34)

In reply to a question, the Parliamentary Under-Secretary of State, FCO, wrote in part:

Successive British Governments have always regarded Tibet as autonomous while recognising the special position of the Chinese authorities there. This remains our view.

(HC Debs., vol. 177, Written Answers, col. 905: 18 October 1990)

In reply to the question what steps have been taken to encourage signatories to the Treaty of Rome and the Helsinki Agreement to disavow territorial claims over their co-signatories, the Prime Minister wrote:

None. No machinery has been established for considering such questions under the Helsinki final act. The European Communities have no competence in this area.

(HC Debs., vol. 178, Written Answers, col. *421* : 30 October 1990)

In the course of replying to oral questions on the subject of the Anglo-Irish Agreement, the Secretary of State for Northern Ireland, Mr Peter Brooke, stated:

My views on articles 2 and 3 of the Irish constitution are already on record in the House, but the provisions of the constitution make no difference to the fact that in United Kingdom domestic law and in international law Northern Ireland is part of the United Kingdom. Successive Irish Governments have acknowledged the words of article 1 of the agreement that any change in the status of Northern Ireland would come about only with the consent of a majority of the people of Northern Ireland.

(HC Debs., vol. 181, col. 408: 22 November 1990)

In the course of a reply, the Minister of State, FCO, wrote:

The treaty of Utrecht established British title to Gibraltar and it remains under British sovereignty. The same treaty also gave Spain the right of 'first refusal' if Gibraltar ceased to be British. None of this is or has been in dispute between the United Kingdom and Spain.

(HC Debs., vol. 182, Written Answers, col. *189* : 6 December 1990)

Part Eight: II. C. *State territory and territorial jurisdiction—territorial jurisdiction—concurrent territorial jurisidiction*

The FCO presented to the HC Foreign Affairs Committee a Memorandum, dated March 1990, entitled 'The Status of the Two German States' in which the following passages appeared:

INTRODUCTION

    1. Before turning to the specific issues listed by the Committee it may be helpful to set out briefly the legal and historical background to the present status of Germany. Further detail is to be found in *Selected Documents on Germany and the Question of Berlin 1944–1961* (Cmd 1552) and *Selected Documents on Germany and the Question of Berlin 1961–1973* (Cmd 6201).

    2. Following the unconditional surrender of the German High Command in May 1945, the Governments of the United Kingdom, the United States of America and the Union of Soviet Socialist Republics and the Provisional Government of the French Republic issued on 5 June 1945 a Declaration regarding the defeat of Germany by which they assumed supreme authority with respect to Germany (Cmd 1552, p 38).

    3. For the purposes of occupation, Germany was divided into four zones, one of which was allotted to each of the occupying Powers, and a special Berlin area, in accordance with the London Protocol of 12 September 1944 on the zones of occupation in Germany and the administration of 'Greater Berlin', as amended on 14

November 1944 and 26 July 1945 (Cmd 1552, p 45). The Berlin area was jointly occupied by the armed forces of the four Powers, and was divided into four Sectors.

4. Under the London Protocol the Soviet zone comprised all of Germany east of a line running from Lübeck Bay to the 1937 Czechoslovak frontier (including East Prussia), with the exception of the special Berlin area. It was subsequently agreed at the Potsdam Conference in August 1945 (Cmd 1552, p 49) that the northern part of East Prussia (the City of Königsberg and the adjacent area) should be placed under Soviet administration and that the rest of Germany lying east of the Oder-Neisse line should be placed under Polish administration (see map).

5. Thus by August 1945 Germany within its frontiers of 31 December 1937 was divided into the following areas:

   (i)   the British zone of occupation;
   (ii) the American zone of occupation;
   (iii) the Soviet zone of occupation less the areas listed at (vi) and (vii) below;
   (iv) the French zone of occupation;
   (v)   the special Berlin area, which did not form part of any zone;
   (vi) that part of the Soviet zone of occupation which was placed under Soviet administration, that is to say, the northern part of East Prussia (the City of Königsberg and the adjacent area);
   (vii) that part of the Soviet zone of occupation which was placed under Polish administration, that is to say, the territory of Germany east of the Oder-Neisse line, except for the northern part of East Prussia.

6. Article 1 of the Agreement of 14 November 1944 on Control Machinery in Germany as amended by an Agreement of 1 May 1945 (Cmd 1522, pp 31, 35) provided that supreme authority in Germany would be exercised on instructions from their respective Governments, by the Commanders-in-Chief of the Armed Forces of the four Powers:

'each in his own zone of occupation, and also jointly, in matters affecting Germany as a whole in their capacity as members of the supreme organ of control constituted under the present Agreement'.

In 1949 this authority was transferred to the three Allied High Commissioners in Bonn; and parallel developments took place in the Soviet zone.

7. The Convention on Relations between the Three Powers (UK, US and France) and the Federal Republic of Germany (the 'Relations Convention'), entered into force on 5 May 1955 (*Germany No 1* (1955) Cmd 9368). In accordance with Article 1 the three Powers terminated the Occupation régime in the Federal Republic and abolished the Allied High Commission. The Federal Republic accordingly had 'the full authority of a sovereign State over its external and internal affairs.' By Article 2, the three Powers retained—

'the rights and the responsibilities, heretofore exercised or held by them, relating to Berlin and to Germany as a whole, including the re-unification of Germany and a peace settlement'.

Articles 6 and 7 of the Relations Convention provide for consultation and co-operation between the three Powers and the Federal Republic concerning Berlin and Germany as a whole. Upon the entry into force of the Relations Convention and the abolition of the Allied High Commission, the three Allied High Commissioners in Bonn, in accordance with the Tripartite Agreement on the Exercise of Retained Rights in Germany of 23 October 1954, became the Chiefs of Mission (Ambassadors) of the three Western Powers in Bonn.

8. The Soviet Government abolished the post of High Commissioner of the Soviet Union in Germany and established an Embassy in the Soviet (Eastern) Sector of Berlin in connection with the conclusion of the Treaty of 20 September 1955 between the Soviet Union and the GDR. The rights retained by the Soviet Union have, since 1955, been exercised by the Soviet Ambassador in the Soviet Sector of Berlin.

9. In 1973 the United Kingdom recognised the German Democratic Republic in the same terms as had been used in the Relations Convention with regard to the Federal Republic of Germany, as having the full authority of a sovereign State over its internal and external affairs, but subject to the rights and responsibilities of the Four Powers in respect of Berlin and Germany as a whole.

THE RIGHTS AND RESPONSIBILITIES OF THE UK AS ONE OF THE FOUR ALLIED POWERS

10. Quadripartite rights and responsibilities exist independently of any treaties, agreements and other arrangements. They result from the joint assumption of supreme authority by the Allies (paragraph 2 above). Their precise scope has not been defined: thus Article 2 of the Relations Convention refers in general terms to 'the rights and the responsibilities . . . relating to Berlin and to Germany as a whole, including the re-unification of Germany and a peace settlement' (paragraph 7 above). Quadripartite rights and responsibilities include those mentioned below.

(i) Berlin

11. The quadripartite status of Berlin derives from the original rights of the four wartime Allies. Based upon these original rights are a complex series of quadripartite agreements, decisions and practices.

(ii) Re-unification and a peace settlement

12. The wartime and post-war agreements of the four Powers envisaged that a peace settlement would be concluded with Germany when a German government suitable for that purpose was in place. In Article 7 of the Relations Convention the three Western Allies and the Federal Republic of Germany set out their policy towards the German question as follows:

'1. The Signatory States are agreed that an essential aim of their common policy is a peace settlement for the whole of Germany, freely negotiated between Germany and her former enemies, which should lay the foundation for a lasting peace. They further agree that the final determination of the boundaries of Germany must await such a settlement.

2. Pending the peace settlement, the Signatory States will co-operate to achieve, by peaceful means, their common aim of a re-unified Germany enjoying a liberal-democratic constitution, like that of the Federal Republic, and integrated within the European community.

3. Deleted.

4. The Three Powers will consult with the Federal Republic on all matters involving the exercise of their rights relating to Germany as a whole.'

(iii) Questions relating to borders

13. Any change in the frontiers of Germany falls within the field of quadripartite rights and responsibilities (see paragraph 17 below).

(iv) The stationing of armed forces

14. The stationing of British, American and French armed forces in the Federal Republic of Germany is now in practice governed by treaties with the Federal Republic. Nevertheless, the three Powers have retained original rights in respect of the stationing of armed forces in Germany under Article 4.2 of the Relations Convention. This expressly confirmed that the rights of the three Powers, heretofore exercised or held by them, which related to the stationing of armed forces in Germany and which were retained, were not affected insofar as they were required for the exercise of their rights and responsibilities relating to Berlin and to Germany as a whole. The Treaty of 20 September 1955 between the Soviet Union and GDR provided for Soviet troops to remain in accordance with the existing international agreements.

(v) Aviation

15. The Allies retain original rights relating to aviation in Germany. Article 6 of Chapter Twelve (Civil Aviation) of the Convention on the Settlement of Matters arising out of the War and the Occupation (Cmd 9368) provides:

'In the exercise of their responsibilities relating to Germany as a whole, the Three Powers will continue to exercise control with respect to aircraft of the Union of Soviet Socialist Republics utilising the air-space of the Federal Republic.'

(Parliamentary Papers, 1989–90, HC, Paper 335–i, pp. 2–4)

On 2 October 1990, the following press release was issued by the British Military Government in Berlin:

The final meeting of the Allied Kommandatura will be held on the morning of 2 October at the Allied Kommandatura building in Dahlem. The Allied Kommandatura will be formally abolished when the Quadripartite rights and responsibilities are terminated on the entry in force of the Treaty on the final settlement with respect to Germany which was signed by the six Foreign Ministers in Moscow on 12 September.

The Allied Kommandatura was established in accordance with the agreement of 14 November 1944 on control machinery in Germany which provided for the establishment of an Inter-Allied Governing Authority to direct jointly the administration of Greater Berlin and comprising four Commandants, one from each Power.

The Allied Kommandatura began its work on 11 July 1945. It issued a large volume of legislation which set the framework for the governance of Berlin.

After the withdrawal of the Soviet Commandant in June 1948, the Western Commandants continued to exercise the powers of the Allied Kommandatura, aware that its decisions could only be carried out in the Western Sectors.

Since 1979 there has been a monthly meeting of the Allied Kommandatura involving Western Commandants and the Allied Ministers. The administrative and legislative work of the Allied Kommandatura was supervised and directed by the three Allied Ministers who were empowered to sign Berlin Kommandatura Orders (BK/Os) and letters (BK/Ls).

The detailed work of the Allied Kommandatura was conducted in Committees: the Civil Affairs Committee (political and aviation questions), the Legal Committee (legal matters, particularly legislation), the Economic Committee (particularly demilitarisation provisions) and Public Safety Committee (Security, including supervision of the Berlin Police). The Allied Missions provided officials to staff these Committees and the Tripartite Allied Kommandatura Secretariat. The Chairmanship of the Allied Kommandatura, including its Committees, rotated monthly between the three Allies. The United Kingdom is in the chair on 1–2 October.

Communication with the Senat was conducted day by day through the Senat Liaison Officers at Rathaus Schöneberg. Their main point of contact was the Senat Chancellery.

For several years, the meetings of the Allied Kommandatura have been preceded by a military co-ordination meeting in the same building. At that meeting, the Commandants, Ministers and Chiefs of Staff are briefed on current military issues by Allied Staff Berlin.

At the Allied Kommandatura meeting on 2 October, the Commandants and Ministers will hear final reports from the Committees, all members of which will be present together with the Secretariat. A letter to the Governing Mayor of Berlin will be signed and will be delivered to him later in the morning.

(Text provided by the FCO)

Following the report of the HC Foreign Affairs Committee on the unification of Germany, the Government presented to Parliament, in October 1990, written observations in which the following passages appeared:

(IV) **The Rights and Responsibilities of the Four Powers**
13. The so-called 'Two plus Four' talks between the two German states and the Four Powers on the external aspects of German unification were completed at a meeting of the six Foreign Ministers in Moscow on 12 September, following Ministerial meetings in Bonn on 5 May, in Berlin on 11 June, and Paris on 17 July (at which the Polish Foreign Minister was present). The six Foreign Ministers signed the Treaty on the Final Settlement with respect to Germany at the Moscow meeting. In the preamble to the Treaty, the six signatories recall the Charter of the United Nations and the Helsinki Final Act, and welcome the fact that the German people, freely exercising their right of self-determination, have expressed their will to bring about the unity of Germany as a state so that they will be able to serve the peace of the world as an equal and sovereign partner in a united Europe.

Ending of Quadripartite Rights and Responsibilities

14. By Article 7 of the Treaty the Four Powers terminate their rights and responsibilities relating to Berlin and to Germany as a whole upon the coming into force of the Treaty. The Article further provides that, as a result, the corresponding, related quadripartite agreements, decisions and practices are terminated and all related Four Power institutions are dissolved. This language is comprehensive, and covers any quadripartite agreements, arrangements, decisions and practices (by

whatever name they are known and whatever form they may take) that may subsist, and any Four Power institutions that continue in being. Among the agreements, decisions and practices referred to are the London Protocol of 12 September 1944, the Agreement of 14 November 1944 on Control Machinery, the Declaration of Berlin of 5 June 1945, the Potsdam Agreement of 2 August 1945, the various agreements, arrangements and practices relating to access to Berlin (Cmnd. 1552), the Quadripartite Agreement of 3 September 1971 (Cmnd. 5135), and the Quadripartite Declaration of 9 November 1972 (Cmnd. 6201). Among the Four Power institutions referred to are the Allied Control Council, the Allied Kommandatura Berlin, the Berlin Air Safety Center and all subordinate and related institutions.

15. Pending the entry into force of the Treaty, the operation of quadripartite rights and responsibilities has been suspended, from the moment of German unity, pursuant to a Declaration of the Four Powers signed by Foreign Ministers at New York on 1 October 1990 (text at Annex 2). From 3 October quadripartite rights and responsibilities cease to have effect, and the united Germany from the outset has in practice full sovereignty over its internal and external affairs.

Berlin

16. Four Power rights and responsibilities relating to Berlin are covered by the provisions concerning quadripartite rights and responsibilities in general, which have been described above. An agreement was signed on 25 September 1990 by Germany, the United Kingdom, France and the United States of America on the settlement of certain matters arising out of the occupation of Berlin. Technical details, such as the taking over by Germany of air traffic control, are being resolved in separate negotiations. As described at paragraph 23 below, armed forces of the United Kingdom, France and the United States will remain stationed in Berlin, at German request and on a new legal footing, while Soviet troops remain in Germany.

(Cm.1246, pp. 5–6)

Annex 2 referred to in paragraph 15 of the above extract reads as follows:

DECLARATION SUSPENDING THE OPERATION OF QUADRIPARTITE RIGHTS AND RESPONSIBILITIES

The Governments of the French Republic, the Union of Soviet Republics, the United Kingdom of Great Britain and Northern Ireland and the United States of America,

Represented by their Ministers for Foreign Affairs meeting at New York on 1 October 1990,

Having regard to the Treaty on the Final Settlement with respect to Germany signed at Moscow on 12 September 1990, which provides for the termination of their rights and responsibilities relating to Berlin and to Germany as a whole,

Declare that the operation of their rights and responsibilities relating to Berlin and to Germany as a whole shall be suspended upon the unification of Germany, pending the entry into force of the Treaty on the Final Settlement with respect to Germany. As a result, the operation of the corresponding, related quadripartite agreements, decisions and practices and all related Four Power institutions shall likewise be suspended upon the unification of Germany.

The Government of the Federal Republic of Germany, represented by its Minister for Foreign Affairs, and the Government of the German Democratic Republic, represented by its Minister for Education and Science, take note of this declaration.

[Here follow the signatures:

> French Republic
> Union of Soviet Socialist Republics
> United Kingdom of Great Britain and Northern Ireland
> United States of America
> Federal Republic of Germany
> German Democratic Republic]

(Ibid., p. 14)

Part Eight: II. D. *State territory and territorial jurisdiction—territorial jurisdiction—extra-territoriality*

(See also Part One: II. D. 1. (items of 10 January and 13 February 1990), Part Three: I. A. 2. (item of 6 August 1990), and Part Four: VI. (item of 18 April 1990), above, and Part Nine: VII. H., below)

The UK Government was permitted to file an *amicus curiae* Brief relating to British defendants in a case brought before the US District Court, District of Arizona, alleging violations of ss. 1 and 2 of the Sherman Act, and of the Uniform State Antitrust Act, and seeking treble damages, compensatory and punitive damages as well as injunctions to prohibit the defendants from banning the use of a certain make of golf club by amateur and professional golfers anywhere in the world. The British defendants comprised certain individuals together with the Royal and Ancient Golf Club of St. Andrews, an unincorporated association located in Scotland.

The Brief, which was dated 16 November 1989, read in part as follows:

In this Brief, amicus respectfully urges that it would be unreasonable, under the standard for international cases laid down by the United States Supreme Court in *Asahi Metal Industry Co.* v. *Superior Court of Solano County*, 480 U.S. 102 (1987), for the Court to assert personal jurisdiction over the British Defendants here.[1] While this amicus curiae brief is limited to the issue of personal jurisdiction, which the Motion for the British Defendants has placed before the Court, the British Government wishes to reserve its right to seek participation as an amicus on other questions that may subsequently be presented to this honorable Court, including (1) whether the Court lacks subject matter jurisdiction over the Plaintiff's antitrust claims insofar as they are asserted against the British Defendants and whether, even if such subject matter jurisdiction were to exist, the Court should

---

[1] In noting and relying upon United States jurisprudence before this Court, the British Government should not be understood as necessarily accepting it for purposes of international law.

. . .

decline to exercise it as a matter of international comity and fairness[3], and (2) whether the granting of the preliminary and permanent injunctions sought by Plaintiff, prohibiting the defendants from banning the use of PING EYE2 golf clubs by amateur and professional golfers anywhere in the world, would be in excess of jurisdiction and inconsistent with international law and comity if applied to the British Defendants.

In explaining its 'statement of interest', the Brief continued:

Plaintiff's First Amended Complaint, while making no allegations that any of the British Defendants have carried out the alleged pertinent conduct within the United States or that they exercise any control over the rules of golf in the United States, yet seeks to enjoin their conduct anywhere in the world, as well as to hold them liable for treble damages under the U.S. antitrust and other U.S. laws. Successive British Governments have made clear their objections on grounds of international law to such unwarranted assertions of jurisdiction by the United States over activities of British nationals conducted outside the territory of the United States, and to unwarranted attempts by the United States to compel or prohibit conduct by such persons in territories under the sovereignty of the United Kingdom.

The Court of Appeals for the Ninth Circuit and the Supreme Court have both cited the laws and policies of other affected nations as relevant factors to be considered by the U.S. courts in cases such as this one. *See Asahi*, 480 U.S. at 115; *Sinatra v. National Enquirer, Inc.*, 854 F.2d 1191, 1199 (9th Cir. 1988); *Timberlane III*, 749 F.2d at 1384. Accordingly, it is in the sovereign interest of amicus to bring to this Court's attention its view that, under the applicable law and giving due weight to the constraints of international comity, this honorable Court should not here assert personal jurisdiction as to the British Defendants.[4]

The Brief continued:

ARGUMENT

The Motion to Dismiss filed on behalf of the R&A, Michael Bonallack and Alastair Cochran urges that this Court does not have personal jurisdiction over the British Defendants. This argument is made on a number of grounds, including the 'minimum contacts' prerequisite for such jurisdiction and under the 'reasonableness' test articulated by the Court of Appeals for the Ninth Circuit as a further due process protection. The British Government supports this analysis and the conclusion that this honorable Court lacks personal jurisdiction over the British Defendants.

In *Asahi Metal Industry Co. v. Superior Court of Solano County*, 480 U.S. 102 (1987), the United States Supreme Court discussed in detail the question of the personal jurisdiction of U.S. courts over foreign defendants. The Court's opinion

[3] *See Timberlane Lumber Co. v. Bank of America N.T. & S.A.*, 549 F.2d 597 (9th Cir. 1976) (*Timberlane I*), *on remand*, 574 F. Supp. 1453 (N.D. Cal. 1983) (*Timberlane II*), *aff'd*, 749 F.2d 1378 (9th Cir. 1984) (*Timberlane III*), *cert. denied*, 105 S. Ct. 3514 (1985).

[4] In 1978, the Department of State, at the suggestion of the Clerk of the U.S. Supreme Court, encouraged foreign governments to present their views directly to U.S. courts. Dept. of State, Circular Diplomatic Note to Chiefs of Mission in Washington, D.C. (Aug. 17, 1978), *printed in* 1978 Dept. of State *Digest of United States Practice in International Law* 560, *reprinted in part in* 73 Am. J. Int'l L.

stressed that, '[t]he unique burdens placed upon one who must defend oneself in a foreign legal system should have significant weight in assessing the reasonableness of stretching the long arm of personal jurisdiction over national borders.' 480 U.S. at 114. The Court offered further caution as follows, before holding that the exercise of personal jurisdiction by a California court over the foreign defendant in that instance would be unreasonable and unfair (480 U.S. at 115):

> In the present case, this advice calls for a court to consider the procedural and substantive policies of other *nations* whose interests are affected by the assertion of jurisdiction by the California court. The procedural and substantive interests of other nations in a state court's assertion of jurisdiction over an alien defendant will differ from case to case. In every case, however, those interests, as well as the federal interest in its foreign relations policies, will be best served by a careful inquiry into the reasonableness of the assertion of jurisdiction in the particular case, and an unwillingness to find the serious burdens on an alien defendant outweighed by minimal interests on the part of the plaintiff or the forum State. 'Great care and reserve should be exercised when extending our notions of personal jurisdiction into the international field.' (Emphasis in original citations omitted).

While the Court's language is addressed to the actions of a state court, the reasoning applies equally, of course, to the assertion of personal jurisdiction over foreign defendants by federal courts. Moreover, the Court of Appeals for the Ninth Circuit has observed this jurisprudence, both before and since *Asahi*. 'The reasonableness of jurisdiction depends also in part upon the seriousness of the potential affront to the sovereignty of the defendants' state. A foreign nation presents a higher sovereignty barrier than that between two states within our union.' *Gates Learjet Corp.* v. *Jensen*, 743 F.2d 1325, 1333 (9th Cir. 1984), *cert. denied*, 471 U.S. 1066 (1985); *FDIC* v. *British-American Ins. Co. Ltd.*, 828 F.2d 1439, 1444 (9th Cir. 1987); *Sinatra* v. *National Enquirer Inc.*, 854 F.2d 1191 (9th Cir. 1988).

The British Government submits that this Court's assertion of personal jurisdiction over the British Defendants to entertain the Plaintiff's claims would be wholly unreasonable under the standard of *Asahi* and the related case law. The British Government has a considerable procedural and substantive interest which militates against such an assertion. Procedurally, it would be highly inappropriate for this Court to require British subjects who have no reasonable expectation that they will be drawn into litigation in the United States to sustain the heavy cost and inconvenience of defending themselves there against charges based upon their activity in clarifying the rules of golf for the United Kingdom.

Substantively, the British Government, as a matter of policy, disagrees with the treble damage antitrust remedy which the Plaintiff is seeking to obtain against the British Defendants. As this amicus curiae brief itself demonstrates, there is considerable conflict between British law and policy, on the one hand, and, on the other hand, the effort to apply the United States antitrust laws to conduct carried on by British citizens within the United Kingdom. The British view opposing such an extraterritorial application of U.S. treble damage antitrust law has been repeatedly expressed by the British Government and courts and is reflected in the provisions of the Protection of Trading Interests Act, 1980 ('PTIA'). The PTIA, among other things, includes a 'clawback' provision enabling a British antitrust

122, 124 (1979). *See also* Letter from Deputy Legal Adviser Marks (June 15, 1979), *described in* 73 Am. J. Int'l L. 669, 678-79 (1979).

. . .

defendant to recover in certain cases from a successful plaintiff the punitive portion of a foreign multiple damage award in the plaintiff's favor.[6]

The setting of the rules of golf is not an unlawful activity in the United Kingdom. This Court should not undertake jurisdiction over British parties for the purposes of rearranging, at Plaintiff's behest, the rules of golf in the United Kingdom and elsewhere outside the United States. Accordingly, it is respectfully submitted that the Court should grant the British Defendants' Motion to Dismiss.

---

[6] *See also In re Westinghouse Uranium Contract*, 1978 A.C. 547, 591 (counsel for the government), 616 (Judgment of Lord Wilberforce), 639 (Judgment of Lord Diplock), 650 (Judgment of Lord Fraser of Tullybelton) cited in *In re Insurance Antitrust Litigation* [723 F Supp. 464 (N.D. Cal. Sept. 20, 1989, revised Oct. 10, 1989)].

(Brief of the Government of the UK as *amicus curiae* in *Karsten Manufacturing Corporation* v. *United States Golf Association et al.*, US District Court, District of Arizona. Text provided by the FCO (some footnotes omitted)).

The following question was asked of Her Majesty's Government:

Whether they have informed themselves of the Opinions issued by the US Justice Department's Office of Legal Counsel on 21st June, which concluded that US law enforcement agents could seize fugitives from US justice overseas without obtaining the consent of the country involved and on 3rd November, that US military forces have the legal authority to arrest drug traffickers, terrorists and other fugitives overseas without the consent of the host country, whether they consider these official 'opinions' compatible with international law and with British interests, and whether it is their view that any other government may claim such rights?

In reply, the Minister of State, Home Office, wrote:

Her Majesty's Government do not accept that any foreign country has the right or the need to exercise extra-territorial jurisdiction in the United Kingdom, since we are already taking firm steps to deal with the problems of drug trafficking, terrorism and other international crime. We understand that the Opinion to which the noble Lord refers is directed to circumstances in which normal arrangements for extradition do not apply, either because there is no effective system of law and order in the country concerned, or because of corruption.

(HL Debs., vol. 514, cols. 733–4: 17 January 1990)

In the course of the Committee stage of the House of Lords debate on the Criminal Justice (International Co-operation) Bill, the Minister of State, Home Office, Earl Ferrers, referred to the UN Convention against Illicit Traffic in Narcotic Drugs and Psychotropic Substances, signed in Vienna on 20 December 1988, in moving certain amendments to the Bill. He continued:

Taken together these maritime provisions are designed to give effect to the requirements in the Vienna Convention which require parties to 'co-operate' to the fullest extent possible to suppress illicit drugs traffic by sea. To that end each party is thus required to establish jurisdiction over offences of illicit trafficking on its own registered vessels.

Article 17(2) of the convention identifies the form which such international co-operation is expected to take. With the Committee's permission I will read the following passage from that article:

'A Party which has reasonable grounds to suspect that a vessel flying its flag or not displaying a flag or marks of registry is engaged in illicit traffic may request the assistance of other Parties in suppressing its use for that purpose. The Parties so requested shall render such assistance within the means available to them'.

Article 17(3) enables a party which suspects that a ship registered in another convention state is engaged in illicit traffic to request authorisation from the flag state to board and search the ship. That implies a regime in which the United Kingdom may be requested or authorised to board vessels flying the flag of another convention state and in which we may ask or authorise others to board our ships. There is, however, no point in boarding and searching a ship unless some form of criminal sanction is attached to the carriage of the illicit drugs which may be found as a result. Thus we need to ensure not only that the carriage of illicit drugs on a British ship is an offence but that the carriage of such drugs on the ship of any convention country is an offence also, triable in our courts. Thus we are proposing to extend the extra-territorial jurisdiction of the British courts in respect of the ships of other countries as well as our own whether on the high seas or in the territorial waters of another country. Any ship not registered in any country may, under the terms of the convention, be treated in the same way as a United Kingdom ship so far as jurisdiction is concerned.

(HL Debs., vol. 514, col. 890: 22 January 1990; see now Criminal Justice (International Co-operation) Act 1990, ss. 18-21)

In the course of a debate in HC Standing Committee on the Aviation and Maritime Security Bill, the Minister for Public Transport, Mr Michael Portillo, referred to the Convention for the Suppression of Unlawful Acts against the Safety of Civil Aviation, 1971, and its Protocol for the Suppression of Unlawful Acts of Violence at Airports serving International Civil Aviation, 1988. He stated:

The Convention already goes a long way beyond the normal scope of international law on dealing with offences on a state's territory that can be dealt with by that nation's law. It applies in an unusual way to airports that are inside another nation's territory.

(HC Debs., 1989–90, Standing Committee A: Aviation and Maritime Security Bill, col. 15; 1 February 1990. See now Aviation and Maritime Security Act 1990, s. 1 (3) and (4))

In reply to a question on the subject of United States law enforcement officers' power to act against non-United States nationals abroad without the permission of the host country, as considered in a judgment of the US Supreme Court on 28 February 1990, the Prime Minister wrote in part:

Her Majesty's Government have made it clear to the United States authorities that they do not accept that any foreign country has the right to exercise extra-territorial jurisdiction in the United Kingdom.

(HC Debs., vol. 169, Written Answers, col. 425: 19 March 1990)

On 18 April 1990, a US District Court in New York held (*Transnor (Bermuda) Ltd.* v. *BP North America Petroleum et al.*, 738 F. Supp. 1472 (1990)) that the forward market for North Sea Brent crude oil was a US futures market subject to the jurisdiction of the US Commodity Futures Trading Commission. *The Financial Times* of 23 June 1990 reported that '[t]he UK Government protested that this ruling was contrary to international law and implied a jurisdictional reach that was damaging to British national interests, insofar as US jurisdiction could be found to apply to deals struck between UK-based traders'.

Her Majesty's Government was asked the following question:

Whether they have now studied the opinion of the Supreme Court of the United States, announced on 28th February 1990, and whether they have since discussed with the United States Administration the apparent failure of the United States legal system to recognise either the sovereign rights in international law of other states in their own territories, or the status of the High Seas as one precluding searches and arrests otherwise than in accordance with international law; if so to what effect; and if not what steps they are taking to clarify or rebut the claim enunciated by the United States Supreme Court for Government agents of the United States to enforce that country's criminal law in other countries, to enter homes, carry out searches and arrests, including the use of armed force, 'halfway round the globe'; and whether they accept any of these claims?

In reply, the Minister of State, Home Office, wrote:

The United Kingdom is aware of the judgment of the United States Supreme Court, given on 28th February, in the case of a Mexican citizen, Verdugo-Urquidez. This case apparently involved officials of the United States Drug Enforcement Administration participating in the search of premises in Mexico with the authority and consent of the Mexican authorities, and accompanied by Mexican officials. The issue before the Supreme Court was whether the United States officials should also have the authority of a United States search warrant: the opinion of the Supreme Court was that the protections provided for in the United States constitution relating to search and seizure were not applicable in this case.

Although the judgment appears unlikely to affect the interests of this country, Her Majesty's Government have made clear to the United States authorities that they do not accept that any foreign country has the right to exercise extra-territorial jurisdiction in the United Kingdom.

(HL Debs., vol. 521, cols. 1606–7: 25 July 1990)

In the course of the case of *In re Insurance Antitrust Litigation*, before the US Court of Appeals for the Ninth Circuit on appeal from the US District Court for the Northern District of California (723 F Supp. 464), the UK Government was permitted to file an *amicus curiae* Brief in support of the Court of Appeal's affirmation of the decision of the District Court dismissing claims against British defendants, Hartford Fire Insurance Co., *et al.*, for lack of subject-matter jurisdiction. The UK Brief, dated 6 August 1990, read in part as follows:

STATEMENT OF INTEREST

The British Government has a substantial interest in expressing its views to the Court in connection with this matter. The three claims asserted by Plaintiffs relevant to this *amicus* brief focus on activity by British citizens within the London reinsurance and retrocessional reinsurance markets. The requested relief includes injunctions restricting certain conduct in London by the British Defendants and, where applicable, their U.S. parents, as well as treble damages. The District Court correctly pointed out that Plaintiffs' claims involve the London reinsurance and retrocessional reinsurance business which exists 'in a regulatory and competitive framework established by the British government' 723 F. Supp. 464, 488. British legislation contains extensive provisions regulating the conduct of the insurance business.

It has long been the policy of the British Government to cooperate with the U.S. Government and the U.S. courts in civil and commercial matters involving conduct deemed to be improper under the laws of both countries. Unfortunately, however, the assertion of certain claims of extraterritorial jurisdiction in antitrust proceedings in the United States has, from time to time, given rise to significant disagreements between the U.S. Government and courts, on the one hand, and their British counterparts, on the other.

Thus, there have been claims made in the U.S. courts, most recently asserted in treble damage suits (as here), against conduct by non-U.S. citizens outside the boundaries of the United States, based on the adverse effect which that conduct allegedly has on competition in U.S. domestic or foreign commerce (the 'effects doctrine'). The United Kingdom authorities and courts have consistently taken the view that such claims to jurisdiction are contrary to international law and an infringement of the sovereignty of other nations. Since the Second World War, successive British Governments have on many occasions expressed these views to the U.S. Executive and courts.

In 1978, the Department of State, at the suggestion of the Clerk of the U.S. Supreme Court, encouraged foreign governments to present their views directly to U.S. courts. Since then, friendly foreign governments have relied on the State Department's position and have presented their views directly to the relevant U.S. court.

.   .   .

B. Dismissal Of The Claims Pursuant To *Timberlane* Is Consistent With The Requirements Of International And U.S. Law

It is well established that rules of international law are part of the law of the United States, and that U.S. courts are bound to give effect to international law. *The Paquete Habana*, 175 U.S. 677, 700 (1900); Restatement (Third) of the Foreign Relations Law of the United States § 111 (1987) [hereinafter cited as 'Restatement (Third)']; Henkin, *International Law as Law in the United States*, 82 Mich. L. Rev. 1555, 1561-67 (1984). International law limits the authority of nations to assert jurisdiction over matters affecting the interests of other nations.

In particular, personal jurisdiction over a foreign entity by reason of business contacts with a state does not give that state general jurisdiction over the activities of that entity anywhere in the world, particularly when the exercise of jurisdiction is inconsistent with the law of the other state where the foreign entity is a citizen and is located.

In recognition of well established principles, the U.S. and U.K. Governments, as well as other Member States of the Organization for Economic Cooperation and Development ('OECD'), have agreed to avoid or minimize conflicts with foreign laws, policies or interests by following an approach of 'moderation and restraint, respecting and accommodating the interests of other Member Countries.' OECD, MINIMIZING CONFLICTING REQUIREMENTS: APPROACHES OF 'MODERATION AND RESTRAINT' 7 (1987).

Under international law and the principles of moderation and restraint as they have been applied in U.S. courts, the extraterritorial exercise of a U.S. court's jurisdiction to prescribe or to enforce must always be reasonable. A state 'may not exercise jurisdiction' when to do so would be unreasonable, after evaluating and balancing all of the relevant factors. Restatement (Third) at §§ 403, 431. In *Timberlane* this Court took the lead in adopting such a balancing-of-interests test in cases having international ramifications to determine whether the exercise of jurisdiction is reasonable. It did so on the ground that 'the effects test by itself is incomplete because it fails to consider other nations' interests. Nor does it expressly take into account the full nature of the relationship between the actors and this country.' *Timberlane I* 549 F.2d at 611-12.

In the British Government's view, if citizens of a nation find their interests damaged by commercial conduct abroad, it is inappropriate to deal with the matter through unilateral action under that nation's own laws and before its own courts; rather, the proper recourse is diplomatic negotiation with foreign governments, action in accordance with bilateral or multilateral intergovernmental agreements, or the pursuit of new agreements.

It is respectfully submitted that the District Court correctly analyzed this conflict between U.S. and U.K. law and policy and reached the correct result under *Timberlane*.

(Document provided by Dr A.V. Lowe (footnotes deleted))

For the creation of criminal offences on board ships and structures outside the United Kingdom, see the Broadcasting Act 1990, s. 171 and Schedule 16, which received the Royal Assent on 1 November 1990.

Part Eight: III. A. *State territory and territorial jurisdiction—acquisition and transfer of territory—acquisition*

(See also Part Three: I.A.2. (items of 10 and 21 August, 6 September and 13 December 1990), above)

In reply to the question what is Her Majesty's policy on the acquisition by States of territory through war, the Minister of State, FCO, wrote:

We support the principle stated in United Nations General Assembly resolution 2625 (XXV) (the friendly relations declaration) that no territorial acquisition resulting from the threat or use of force is legal.

(HC Debs., vol. 169, Written Answers, col. *38*: 12 March 1990)

Part Eight: III. B. *State territory and territorial jurisdiction—acquisition and transfer of territory—transfer*

(See also Gibraltar material in Part Three: I. E. (item of 3 November 1988, above, and Part Eight: II. A. (item of 6 December 1990), above)

In reply to a question, the Minister of State, FCO, wrote:

We remain committed to the principle of UN Security Council Resolution 432 that Walvis Bay should be reintegrated into Namibia. In the first instance we believe this issue is best resolved through negotiations between Namibia and South Africa.

(HL Debs., vol. 517, cols. 1616–7: 5 April 1990)

In reply to a question on the subject of the future of the island of Diego Garcia, the Minister of State, FCO, wrote in part:

The position remains that the territory will be ceded to Mauritius when it is no longer required for defence purposes. In present circumstances the defence facilities in British Indian Ocean territory continue to make a vital security contribution and we envisage no change in the status of the territory in the foreseeable future.

(HC Debs., vol. 178, Written Answers, col. 53: 22 October 1990)

Part Eight IV. *State territory and territorial jurisdiction—regime under the Antarctic Treaty*

(See also Part Eight: II. A. (items of 6 July and 2 August 1990), above)

In reply to a question, the Parliamentary Under-Secretary of State, FCO, wrote:

The Antarctic treaty system currently provides no formal means of protecting the Antarctic environment against mineral activities.

The Antarctic minerals convention (CRAMRA) would provide for a rigorous regulatory mechanism to control, or prevent, mineral exploration and development. Consent to proceed with any mineral activity would, under CRAMRA, only be permitted after consensus agreement by all Antarctic treaty consultative parties (numbering 22) and then only if the activity in question was judged not to have a significant impact on the environment. CRAMRA incorporates some of the strictest environmental protection provisions known in international law and its ratification would greatly enhance existing provisions for the protection of the Antarctic environment.

(HC Debs., vol. 171, Written Answers, col. 693: 4 May 1990)

In reply to a question, the Parliamentary Under-Secretary of State, FCO, Mr Tim Sainsbury, stated:

Negotiations on the minerals convention began in 1982 and were concluded in 1988 by consensus of 33 countries, 19 of which—the majority—signed the convention. That convention will give unparalleled protection from mineral prospecting in the Antarctic; without it there would be no legally binding or enforceable protection for the Antarctic environment. I hope that the hon. Gentleman will welcome its coming into force at an early date.

(HC Debs., vol. 174, col. 287: 13 June 1990)

In reply to a series of questions, the Minister of State, FCO, wrote:

Under the Antarctic treaty the following are prohibited:
any measure of a military nature, such as the establishment of military bases and fortifications, the carrying out of military manoeuvres, as well as the testing of any type of weapon;
any nuclear explosions and the disposal there of radioactive waste material.

None of the inspections carried out in accordance with article VII of the Antarctic treaty has indicated that there have been any breaches of these provisions of the treaty.

Apart from the Antarctic treaty itself, three Conventions have been concluded and form part of the Antarctic treaty system: the convention for the conservation of Antarctic seals of 1972 (Cmnd. 7209), the convention on the conservation of Antarctic marine living resources of 1980 (Cmnd. 8714), and the convention on the regulation of Antarctic mineral resource activities of 1988 (Cm. 634). In addition, in pursuance of the Antarctic treaty, the parties thereto have concluded the agreed measures for the conservation of Antarctic fauna and flora (set out in schedule 2 to the Antarctic Treaty Act 1967) as well as 186 recommendations.

The relevant statutes and statutory instruments currently in force are the following:

Antarctic Treaty Act 1967
The Antarctic Treaty Order in Council 1962 (SI 1962/401)
The Antarctic Treaty (Specially Protected Areas) Order 1968 (SI 1968/889)
The Antarctic Treaty (Specially Protected Species) Order 1968 (SI 1968/889)
The Antarctic Treaty (Specially Protected Area) Order 1971 (SI 1971/1236)
The Conservation of Antarctic Mammals and Birds (High Seas) Order 1973 (SI 1973/1755)
The Antarctic Treaty Act 1967 (Isle of Man) Order 1970 (SI 1970/1436)
The Antarctic Treaty Act 1967 (Channel Islands) Order 1974 (SI 1974/1109)
The Antarctic Treaty (Specially Protected Areas) Order 1977 (SI 1977/1235)
The Commission for the Conservation of Antarctic Marine Living Resources (Immunities and Privileges) Order 1981 (SI 1981/1108)
The Antarctic Treaty (Agreed Measures) Order 1988 (SI 1988/586)
The Antarctic Treaty (Specially Protected Areas) Order 1988 (SI 1988/587)
The Antarctic Treaty (Agreed Measures) (No. 2) Order 1988 (SI 1988/1296)

(HC Debs., vol. 177, Written Answers, cols. *738–9*, *passim*: 15 October 1990)

In reply to a question, the Minister of State, FCO, wrote:

Fishing in Antarctic waters is controlled by the convention on the conservation of Antarctic marine living resources (CCAMLR). Since 1980 CCAMLR has applied catch restrictions on certain fish stocks in Antarctica, and has closed some areas to protect depleted stocks. CCAMLR has been successful in achieving protection of the most threatened species and we shall continue to work towards reaching an agreement to limit krill catches in Antarctic waters.

(HC Debs., vol. 181, Written Answers, col. 252: 23 November 1990)

Part Nine: I. A. *Seas, waterways, ships—territorial sea—delimitation, baselines*

In the course of a reply to a question concerning the breadth of the relevant territorial seas in the Gulf, the Minister of State, FCO, wrote in part:

We recognise the right of all states to territorial seas of up to 12 miles in breadth.

(HL Debs., vol. 524, Written Answers, col. *15*: 5 December 1990)

The following notice was issued by the Hydrographic Division of the Navy on 1 January 1991:

ADMIRALTY NOTICES TO MARINERS

12. TERRITORIAL WATERS AND FISHERIES JURISDICTION CLAIMS.

Former Notice 1949/90 is cancelled.

The following list shows the breadth of sea (measured from the appropriate baselines) claimed respectively as territorial waters and as being under the state's jurisdiction for fishing. The information is compiled from various, sometimes unofficial, sources; the absence of a limit from this list indicates that the information is not held.

The claims are published for information only. Her Majesty's Government does not recognise claims to territorial waters exceeding twelve miles or to fisheries jurisdiction exceeding two hundred miles.

Country		
Albania[1]	12**	15
Algeria[8]	12**	12
Angola	20	200
Antigua and Barbuda[2]*	12**	200
Argentina	200	200
Australia[1]	3	200
Australian Antarctica	3	12
Bahamas*	3	200
Bahrain*	3	
Bangladesh[4]	12**	200
Barbados	12**	200
Belgium	12	200
Belize*	3	3
Benin	200	200
Brazil*	200**	200
Brunei	12	200
Bulgaria	12**	200
Burma[1]	12**	200
Cambodia[1]	12	200
Cameroon*	50	
Canada[1]	12	200
Cape Verde Islands[2]*	12	200
Chile[1]	12	200
Chinese People's Republic[1]	12**	
Colombia[1]	12	200
Comoros[2]	12	200
Congo	200	200
Costa Rica	12	200
Cuba[1]*	12	200
Cyprus*	12	12
Denmark[1]	3**	200
Djibouti	12	200
Dominica	12	200
Dominican Republic[1]	6	200
Ecuador[1]	200	200
Egypt[1]*	12**	200
El Salvador	200	200
Equatorial Guinea	12**	200
Ethiopia[1]	12	
Fiji[2]*	12	200
Finland[1]	4**	12
France[1]	12	200
French Antarctica	12	
Gabon	12	200
Gambia*	12	200
Germany [1 10 11]	12	200
Ghana*	12	200
Greece	6	6
Grenada	12**	200
Guatemala	12	200
Guinea[1]*	12	200
Guinea Bissau[1]*	12	200
Guyana	12**	200
Haiti	12	200
Honduras	12	200
Iceland[1]*	12	200
India	12**	200
Indonesia[2]*	12	200
Iran[1]	12**	50
Iraq*	12	
Irish Republic[1]	12	200
Israel	12	12
Italy[1]	12	12
Ivory Coast*	12	200
Jamaica*	12	12
Japan[11]	12	200

Country			Country		
Jordan	3	3	Sao Tome and Principe[2]*	12	200
			Saudi Arabia[1]	12	
Kenya[1]*	12	200	Senegal[1]*	12	200
Kiribati[2]	12	200	Seychelles	12**	200
Korea (North)	12**	200	Sierra Leone	200	200
Korea (South)[1]	12[6]**		Singapore	3	3
Kuwait*	12		Solomon Islands[2]	12	200
			Somalia*	200**	200
Lebanon	12		South Africa	12	200
Liberia	200	200	Spain[1]	12	200
Libya[5]	12**	20	Sri Lanka	12**	200
			Sudan*	12**	
Madagascar[1]	12**	200	Suriname	12	200
Malaysia[1]	12	200	Sweden[1] [11]	12**	200
Maldives[3]	12**	up to 200	Syria	35**	
Malta[1]	12**	25	Taiwan	12	200
Mauritania[1]	12	200	Tanzania[1]*	12	200
Mauritius[1]	12**	200	Thailand[1]	12	200
Mexico[1]*	12	200	Togo*	30	200
Monaco[3]	12	12	Tonga[3]	12	200
Morocco	12	200	Trinidad and Tobago[2]*	12	200
Mozambique	12	200	Tunisia[1] [9]*	12	12
			Turkey[1]	12[7]**	12[7]
Namibia	12	200	Tuvalu	12	200
Nauru	12	200			
Netherlands	12	200	UAE		up to 73
Netherlands Antilles	12	12			
New Zealand	12	200	Abu Zabi	3	
Nicaragua	200**	200	Ajman	3	
Nigeria*	30**	200	Dubayy	3	
Norway[1]	4	200	Fujayrah	12	
			Ra's al Khaymah	3	
Oman[1]*	12	200	Ash Shariqah	12	
			Umm al Qaywayn	3	
Pakistan	12**	200	UK[1]	12	200
Panama	200	200	Anguilla	3	200
Papua New Guinea[2]	12	200	Bailiwick of Guernsey	3	12
Peru	200	200	Bailiwick of Jersey	3	3
Philippines[2] [3]*	12	200	Bermuda	12	200
Poland[8]	12**	12	British Antarctic Territory	3	3
Portugal[1]	12	200	British Indian Ocean Territory	3	12
Qatar	3	to median lines	British Virgin Islands	3	200
			Cayman Islands	12	200
Romania	12**	200	Cyprus (Sovereign Base Areas)	3	3
			Falkland Islands[1]	12	200[12]
St. Kitts-Nevis	12	200	Gibraltar	3	3
St. Lucia*	12	200	Hong Kong	3	3
St. Vincent and the Grenadines[2]	12**	200	Isle of Man	3	12
			Montserrat	3	200

Pitcairn	3	200	Vanuatu[2]	12	200
St. Helena and			Venezuela[1]	12	200
Dependencies	12	200	Vietnam[1]	12**	200
South Georgia[1]	12	12			
South Sandwich Islands	12	12	Western Samoa	12	200
Turks and Caicos					
Islands[1]	12	200	Yemen*	12**	200
Uruguay	200	200	Yugoslavia[1]*	12	12
USA	12	200			
USSR[1]	12**	200	Zaire*	12	200

Limits of dependent territories have not been listed unless they differ from those of the metropolitan state.

[1] employs straight baseline systems along all or a part of the coast.

[2] claims all waters within the archipelago.

[3] claims water within limits defined by geographic co-ordinates not related to distance from coastline.

[4] claims straight baseline system between points along the 18 metre depth line.

[5] claims all water south of 32° 30'N. in Gulf or Sirte as internal waters.

[6] claims 3 miles in Korea Strait.

[7] claims 6 miles in Aegean Sea.

[8] fishery limit extends beyond 12 miles to limits to be agreed.

[9] fishery limit extends to 50 metre isobath off Gulf of Gabes.

[10] special claim extends limit to include deep water anchorage west of Heligoland.

[11] reduced limits in some straits and in the former Federal Republic (but see Note 10).

[12] Rhumb line between 52° 30'·00S, 63° 19'·25W and 54° 08'·68S and 60° 00'·00W.

* Indicates a state which has ratified the U.N. Law of the Sea Convention 1982. The Convention does not come into force until one year after 60 iunstruments of ratification or accession have been deposited.

** Indicates a state which requires prior permission or notification for entry of warships into territorial sea. The United Kingdom government does not recognise this requirement.

Hydrographic Department. (*HH. 085/012/01*).

(Annual Summary of Admiralty Notices to Mariners in Force on 1 January 1991)

Part Nine: I. B. 2. *Seas, waterways, ships—territorial sea—legal status—regime of merchant ships*

(See also Part One: II. D. 1. (item of 23 April 1990), above)

In the course of the Committee stage of the House of Lords' debate on the amendments dealing with drug control at sea sought to be introduced into the Criminal Justice (International Co-operation Bill), the Minister of State, Home Office, Earl Ferrers, stated:

If the vessel of another country were within our territorial waters then we could take action against that vessel because it was within our territorial waters. It would be the same way as taking action against an individual in our country who infringes the rules of our country.

(HL Debs., vol. 514, col. 892: 22 January 1990)

Part Nine: I. B. 5. *Seas, waterways, ships—territorial sea—legal status—bed and subsoil*

The Department of the Environment submitted a memorandum, dated October 1989, to the HC Agriculture Committee which was considering fish farming in the United Kingdom. One passage from the memorandum read:

Fish farms located in marine waters beyond the low water mark are outside the scope of planning control, although marine fish farms require a lease from the Crown Estate Commissioners. . . .

(*Parliamentary Papers*, 1989–90, HC, Paper 141–iv, p. 173)

The Crown Estate Commissioners submitted a memorandum, dated 15 February 1990, to the above Committee. One passage from the memorandum read:

The territorial seabed around the United Kingdom, out to 12 miles, and most of the foreshore area between high and low water mark, is part of the Crown Estate. The Crown Estate also administers certain rights in the United Kingdom Continental Shelf by virtue of the Continental Shelf Act 1964. Developments affecting these marine areas or interests is subject to control and management by the Crown Estate Commissioners who act under the powers of the Crown Estate Act 1961 and are accountable to both Parliament and the Sovereign.

(Ibid., Paper 141–iii, p. 148)

In reply to questions during oral evidence taken before the Agriculture Committee on 21 March 1990, the Minister of State, Scottish Office, Lord Sanderson of Bowden, stated:

The Secretary of State for Scotland has no locus in matters concerning the management of Crown Land. This is the situation with any decision taken by the [Crown Estate] Commissioners on individual cases relating to their role as the managers of the seabed on behalf of the Crown.

(Ibid., Paper 141–viii, p. 335)

The fact remains of course that the Crown owns the seabed below the low water mark and of course the Crown therefore has the right to issue or not issue a lease as the case may be.

(Ibid., p. 337)

. . . the powers of the Crown below the low water mark to the 12 mile limit are vested, for the purpose of Parliament by the passing of the 1961 Act, in the Crown Estate and they are therefore the owners of the seabed and even in the Shetland Islands, unless there is an appeal, that will be the case as well . . .

(Ibid., p. 340)

[*Editorial note*: The reference to an appeal relates to the opinion and judgment of the Court of Session in *Special Case for the Shetland Salmon Farmers Association, Trustees of the Port and Harbour of Lerwick, and the Crown Estate Commissioners*, delivered on 16 March 1990; see [1991] SLT 166]

Part Nine: III. *Seas, waterways, ships—internal waters, including ports*

In reply to the question whether Her Majesty's Government will consider introducing restrictions on oil tanker movements in the Minch in order to reduce damage caused to the environment by spillages, the Minister for Aviation and Shipping wrote:

Tankers cannot be banned from the Minch: their captains must always have the option of using the Minch route in adverse weather conditions, rather than the rougher deep water route (DWR) to the west of the Outer Hebrides.

We have considered the possibility of mandatory restrictions very carefully. The only restriction which could be imposed under international law is a traffic separation scheme. There is no evidence that this is needed, as tankers appear to use the existing recommended routes. All vessels would be obliged to use it in accordance with the collision regulations, and this would seriously inhibit the activities of fishing vessels. A scheme might also encourage tankers to use the Minch route. We have therefore concluded that restrictions are impracticable. My Department already urges shipowners and masters to use the outer routes when practicable, and will raise the use of the DWR at the International Maritime Organisation.

(HC Debs., vol. 177, Written Answers, col. *403*: 26 July 1990; see also ibid., vol. 180, Written Answers, cols. *139–40*: 14 November 1990. See also UKMIL 1981, pp. 465–6)

In reply to questions, the Parliamentary Under-Secretary of State, Northern Ireland Office, wrote:

The issuing of leases of the foreshore of Strangford Lough is a matter for the owners. The Crown Estate is the major owner of the foreshore.

. . .

The issuing of leases of the sea bed of Strangford Lough is a matter for the owners. The Crown Estate is the major owner of the sea bed.

(HC Debs., vol. 177, Written Answers, col. *561*: 26 July 1990)

Part Nine: VII. A. 1. *Seas, waterways, ships—the high seas—freedoms of the high seas—navigation*

(See Part Nine: IX. (item of 27 December 1989), below)

Part Nine: VII. F. *Seas, waterways, ships—the high seas—conservation of living resources*

In the course of a debate on the subject of the North Atlantic Salmon Conservation Convention, the Minister of State, Scottish Office, Lord Sanderson of Bowden, stated:

The convention is perfectly clear on the matter of fishing for salmon on the high seas. Under Article 2(1) of the convention, fishing for Atlantic salmon throughout the convention area is prohibited outside the fisheries limits of coastal states. Moreover, within the fisheries limits of the coastal states, the contracting parties have bound themselves to prohibit any fishing for salmon, by any method, outside the 12-mile limit from the baselines from which their territorial seas are measured. There are some variations to these limits around Greenland and the Faroe Islands so as to enable the prosecution of the traditional salmon fisheries further off their coasts. But the Greenland and Faroes salmon catches are tightly regulated . . . by quotas and set on the basis of impartial scientific advice from the International Council for the Exploration of the Sea. The quotas are supported also by a number of effort restrictions agreed in NASCO. The NASCO convention, in effect, applies the principles enshrined in United Nations treaties on the law of the sea which have consistently recognised the special position of salmon; and the rights in that regard of coastal states with home spawning rivers for the fish.

There is also Community legislation which seeks to discourage fishing for salmon in that part of the north Atlantic which lies outwith the control of the Community or its member states. In essence, it is an offence under EC Regulation 3094 of 1986 for vessels to bring into EC waters any salmon or sea trout which has been taken in the non-EEC part of the north Atlantic.

(HL Debs., vol. 519, cols. 1500–1: 6 June 1990)

Her Majesty's Government was asked the following question:

Whether they have accepted that part of the United Nations Convention on the Law of the Sea which allocates to the coastal state rights over and responsibility for migratory species of fish?

In reply, the Government Minister in the House of Lords wrote:

We have no objection to Article 64 of the UN Convention on the Law of the Sea, which provides for regional co-operation in conservation and utilisation of highly migratory species of fish, between both coastal states of the region and other states whose nationals fish those species in that region. Similarly, we have no objection to Articles 66 and 67, dealing with less highly migratory species.

(HL Debs., vol. 521, col. 1787: 26 July 1990)

Part Nine: VII. G. *Seas, waterways, ships—the high seas—pollution*

In moving the consideration by the HC Sixth Standing Committee on Statutory Instruments of the draft Merchant Shipping (Prevention and Control of Pollution) Order 1990, the Minister for Aviation, Shipping and Public Transport, Mr Patrick McLoughlin, stated:

The order amends the Merchant Shipping (Prevention and Control of Pollution) Order 1987, which enables regulations to be made to give effect to annex II of the international convention for the prevention of pollution from ships, 1973. The order will empower the Secretary of State to amend the regulations to incorporate updated requirements that have been adopted by the International Maritime Organisation. It will also empower the Secretary of State to make regulations to give effect to annex III of the convention.

The international convention for the prevention of pollution from ships—better known as the MARPOL convention—is the principal international instrument for controlling pollution from ships. It contains five annexes dealing with oil, noxious liquid substances in bulk, packaged dangerous goods, sewage and garbage. It is revised by the IMO as circumstances dictate which enables its provisions to keep up with newer practices and reflect current public concern. The convention commands wide international support and it is only through its regulations that we can improve the cleanliness of our seas.

Annex II of the MARPOL convention sets out the measures for preventing the pollution of the sea from noxious liquid substances in bulk. It categorises those substances into four groups according to their potential for pollution, prescribing for each category how it should be controlled and monitored. The list of substances is continually assessed by internationally recognised experts and, in the light of discussions in the IMO, the severity ratings of some substances are altered and new substances are added to the list.

Annex III to the convention deals with the prevention of pollution by marine pollutants carried in packaged form. It has been decided by the IMO that, for convenience and good order, annex III should be implemented by incorporation into the international maritime dangerous goods code. The code was developed for substances that are dangerous, rather than pollutants. However, the general precautions that need to be observed—whether a substance is dangerous or a pollutant—are the same and in transporting those substances on board ship, the trade does not differentiate between the two. A completely new edition of the code has therefore been developed by the IMO that incorporates pollutants and, for the first time, applies to them requirements on packaging, marking and labelling, documentation, stowage and segregation.

Annex III, though ratified by the United Kingdom as long ago as 27 May 1986, is not in force internationally because the number of ratifications by member Governments of the IMO is just short of that necessary to bring it into effect. The delay is a cause for concern and the IMO has urged member states to implement the annex in advance of it coming into force internationally. Ministers attending the North Sea conference in March of this year agreed to give effect to the new edition of the international maritime dangerous goods code by 1 January 1991.

Regulations made under this order are being prepared to give effect to annex III. They will incorporate broadly the same duties and responsibilities that are to be found in the Merchant Shipping (Dangerous Goods) Regulations and will include a variety of ancillary provisions.

(HC Debs., 1990–91, HC Sixth Standing Committee on Statutory Instruments, etc.: 27 November 1990, cols. 3–4)

Part Nine: VII. H. *Seas, waterways, ships—the high seas—jurisdiction over ships*

(See also Part Eight: II. D. (items of 22 January and 25 July 1990), above)

During consideration of the Environmental Protection Bill by HC Standing Committee, the Parliamentary Secretary, Ministry of Agriculture, Fisheries and Food, Mr David Curry, proposed an amendment and stated:

At present we cannot control a foreign vessel that loads and dumps outside our territorial waters. If it dumps at 11¾ miles, we can control it, but if it dumps at 12 miles, 100 yards, we cannot. So it can dump whatever it wants and we can do nothing.

The [proposed] clause aims to give us enforcement measures to control dumping by foreign vessels. It extends United Kingdom control to all vessels inside the continental shelf.

(HC Debs., 1989–90, Standing Committee H: Environmental Protection Bill, col. 1280; 15 March 1990. See now Environmental Protection Act 1990, s. 146)

The Criminal Justice (International Co-operation) Act 1990, which received the Royal assent on 5 April 1990, makes it a crime to commit on board a ship certain acts concerning drug trafficking, wherever the ship may be. Section 19(1) of the Act reads:

This section applies to a British ship, a ship registered in a state other than the United Kingdom which is a party to the Vienna Convention (a 'Convention State') and a ship not registered in any country or territory.

(The Convention is the Vienna Convention against Illicit Traffic in Narcotic Drugs and Psychotropic Substances, 1988)

During the second reading debate in the House of Lords on the Broadcasting Bill, attention was drawn to the provisions of the Bill dealing with jurisdiction over broadcast transmissions from vessels. The Minister of State, Home Office, Earl Ferrers, stated:

The provisions in the Bill are in accordance with international law. The United Nations Law of the Sea Convention allows states to act against ships on the high seas of any nationality, or none, if broadcasts from them can be received on their territory or cause interference. Of course, the powers will be exercised with moderation and restraint in the case of foreign flag vessels to avoid the diplomatic controversy which the noble Lord feared.

(HL Debs., vol. 519, col. 1355: 5 June 1990)

During the Committee stage of the same Bill in the House of Lords, there were further questions on the above matter. Earl Ferrers replied:

The noble Lord, Lord Annan, and others complained about Schedule 14 being incompatible with the law and being excessive. All states have a duty to co-operate in the suppression of unauthorised broadcasting from the high seas. Such broadcasting contravenes worldwide independent telecommunication union radio regulations. The Government are satisfied that the exercise of the powers provided for in the Bill relating to ships on the high seas will be in accordance with international law.

As the noble Lord, Lord Annan, rightly said, the powers we are taking are modelled on Articles 109 and 110 of the United Nations Convention on the Law of the Sea. These provide for a state to take action against broadcasters on ships of any nationality or of none which are on the high seas, if their broadcasts, which are contrary to international regulations, can either be received in that state's territory or cause interference there. We do not anticipate objection from other states, although we will normally consult the flag state.

The noble Lord, Lord Annan, said that that convention had not been ratified. It is true that Her Majesty's Government have not yet acceded to the Convention on the Law of the Sea. I have explained the justification for the schedule in international law. Our view is that the exercise of the powers will be in accordance with international law. That is not dependent on the convention. The convention is a model for the provision. This is the basis in international law for paragraph 2 of the schedule. Paragraph 1, which deals with broadcasts from structures on the UK's area of the continental shelf, is based on states' well-established jurisdiction over their adjacent continental shelf.

(HL Debs., vol. 521, cols. 1590–1: 25 July 1990)

During the report stage of the Broadcasting Bill in the House of Lords, Lord Monson moved an amendment, No. 333A, to add to Schedule 14 of the Bill the words 'Insofar as permitted under international law'. He explained the purpose of his proposed amendment as follows:

Amendment No. 333A provides that the very draconian powers conferred by Schedule 14, namely the powers to board foreign ships forcibly on the high seas, possibly employing our Armed Forces to do so, and then to search the ship and all those on it, seizing equipment, documents and the like, can be brought into play only provided that there is no conflict with international law.

In speaking to the proposed amendment, which Lord Monson subsequently withdrew, the Minister of State, Home Office, Earl Ferrers, stated:

I have some sympathy with the noble Lord's concern that the new enforcement powers should be exercised in accordance with international law. I can give him the assurance that the powers will be exercised in accordance with international law. But to require the United Kingdom courts to consider the state of international law, which is what Amendment No. 333A would do, would be unprecedented. I suggest that that is neither necessary nor in that case desirable.

Interpretation of international law is properly a matter for international courts, which already provide a remedy should enforcement action be taken which did not comply with international law.

(HL Debs., vol. 522, cols. 829–30, *passim*: 16 October 1990)

Later in the same debate, Lord Monson moved an amendment, No. 113, to add to Schedule 16 of the Bill the words:

Save that in relation to such suspected offences the Secretary of State shall not issue any authorisation under subsection (2) above for the exercise of the powers conferred by subsection (5) above until twelve months after the date on which the 1982 United Nations Convention on the Law of the Sea has been ratified by no fewer than sixty States in accordance with international law.

He explained the purpose of his proposed amendment as follows:

It is designed to prevent the possibility of the United Kingdom facing the embarrassment and possibly the obloquy of being hauled over the coals by the international court or possibly the European Court for the breach of international law that would occur if foreign registered vessels were forcibly boarded and searched—and their passengers also searched—on the high seas, without the consent of the foreign government concerned, before at least 12 months had elapsed since the date when at least 60 states have ratified the 1982 United Nations Convention on the Law of the Sea. To do so before then would be illegal.

In speaking to the proposed amendment, which Lord Monson subsequently withdrew, Earl Ferrers stated:

Amendment No. 113 would make the exercise of the enforcement powers conditional upon the ratification of the United Nations Convention on the Law of the Sea on which the noble Lord said he has taken legal advice. I venture to suggest to him that the amendment is unnecessary. I have given him the assurance that the powers will be exercised in accordance with international law. The powers do not hinge upon the convention but upon the international radio regulations of the International Telecommunications Union. These are already in force. Therefore, there is no need to delay the exercise of the powers until the convention, which is a separate matter, is ratified. With that explanation the noble Lord will see that we do not intend to operate in breach of international law.

. . .

The powers will be exercised with moderation and restraint. We intend to consult the flag state, where there is one, to ensure that it does not object before we act against a foreign flag vessel. Stateless vessels of course are not under the diplomatic protection of any government when on the high seas. Any force used will be kept to the minimum.

The powers are modelled on Articles 109 and 110 of the United Nations Convention on the Law of the Sea. The noble Lord is perfectly right that the United Kingdom has not yet become a party to that convention. However, that is for reasons totally unconnected with radio. The exercise of the powers will be in accordance with international law. That does not depend on the convention coming into force or the United Kingdom becoming a party to it.

(HL Debs., vol. 522, cols. 1203–5, *passim*: 22 October 1990)

The relevant changes made by the Broadcasting Act 1990, which received the Royal assent on 1 November 1990, are found in its Schedule 16 and consist of amendments to the Marine, etc., Broadcasting Offences Act 1967. The most significant amendments are as follows:

Insert in the 1967 Act a new section, s. 2A:

2A.—(1) Subject to subsection (4) below, it shall not be lawful to make a broadcast which—

(a) is made from a ship (other than one registered in the United Kingdom, the Isle of Man or any of the Channel Islands) while the ship is within any area of the high seas prescribed for the purposes of this section by an order made by the Secretary of State; and

(b) is capable of being received in, or causes interference with any wireless telegraphy in, the United Kingdom.

(2) If a broadcast is made from a ship in contravention of subsection (1) above, the owner of the ship, the master of the ship and every person who operates, or participates in the operation of, the apparatus by means of which the broadcast is made shall be guilty of an offence.

(3) A person who procures the making of a broadcast in contravention of subsection (1) above shall be guilty of an offence.

(4) The making of a broadcast does not contravene subsection (1) above if it is shown to have been authorised under the law of any country or territory outside the United Kindom.

(5) Any order under this section shall be made by statutory instrument subject to annulment in pursuance of a resolution of either House of Parliament.

Insert in the 1967 Act a new section, s. 7A:

.   .   .

(2) If an enforcement officer has reasonable grounds for suspecting—

(a) that an offence under this Act has been or is being committed by the making of a broadcast from any ship, structure or other object in external waters or in tidal waters in the United Kingdom or from a ship registered in the United Kingdom, the Isle of Man or any of the Channel Islands while on the high seas,

(b) that an offence under section 2 of this Act has been or is being committed by the making of a broadcast from a structure or other object in waters falling within subsection (3)(c) of that section, or

(c) that an offence under section 2A of this Act has been or is being committed by the making of a broadcast from a ship,

and the Secretary of State has issued a written authorisation for the exercise of the powers conferred by subsection (5) below in relation to that ship, structure or other object, then (subject to subsections (6) and (7) below) the officer may, with or without persons assigned to assist him in his duties, so exercise those powers.

.   .   .

(5) The powers conferred by this subsection on an enforcement officer in relation to any ship, structure or other object are—

(a) to board and search the ship, structure or other object;

(b) to seize and detain the ship, structure or other object and any apparatus or other thing found in the course of the search which appear to him to have been used, or to have been intended to be used, in connection with, or to be evidence of, the commission of the suspected offence;

(c) to arrest and search any person who he has reasonable grounds to suspect has committed or is committing an offence under this Act if—

(i) that person is on board the ship, structure or other object, or

(ii) the officer has reasonable grounds for suspecting that that person was so on board at, or shortly before, the time when the officer boarded the ship, structure or other object;

(d) to arrest any person who assaults him, or a person assigned to assist him in his duties, while exercising any of the powers conferred by this subsection or who intentionally obstructs him or any such person in the exercise of any of those powers;

(e) to require any person on board the ship, structure or other object to produce any documents or other items which are in his custody or possession and are or may be evidence of the commission of any offence under this Act;

(f) to require any such person to do anything for the purpose of facilitating the exercise of any of the powers conferred by this subsection, including enabling any apparatus or other thing to be rendered safe and, in the case of a ship, enabling the ship to be taken to a port;

(g) to use reasonable force, if necessary, in exercising any of those powers;

and references in paragraphs (a) to (c) above to the ship, structure or other object include references to any ship's boat or other vessel used from the ship, structure or other object.

Part Nine: VIII. *Seas, waterways, ships—continental shelf*

(See also Part Nine: VII. H. (item of 25 July 1990), above)

In reply to a question on whether the present condition of the former oil installation, Piper Alpha, is in keeping with international law, the Government Minister in the House of Lords wrote in part:

The remains of the Piper Alpha platform were toppled *in situ*, by explosive cutting, on 28th March 1989. The abandonment programme approved by the Secretary of State for Energy under the Petroleum Act, 1987 provided for a clearance of 75 metres between the sea surface at lowest astronomical tide and any remains. A survey undertaken since the toppling operation has established that a clearance of 86.27 metres has actually been achieved. The highest point of the remains of the installation is now 57.73 metres above the sea bed.

International law requires that any disused installation not entirely removed must not cause unjustifiable intereference with users of waters above the continental shelf. On 19th October 1989 the Assembly of the International Maritime Organisation (IMO) adopted, by Resolution A 672(16), Guidelines and Standards for the Removal of Offshore Installations on the Continental Shelf and in the Exclusive Economic Zone. The abandonment programme for Piper Alpha meets, and in some respects (e.g. clearance above remains) exceeds, the minimum standards annexed to the IMO resolution.

The remains of the installation lie within a 500 metre radius safety zone which is marked on charts. There is no requirement in the IMO guidelines and standards or in our domestic law to equip such remains with submarine warning devices. Vessels are prohibited from entering or remaining in the safety zone except with the consent of the Secretary of State or in the exceptional circumstances specified in the Offshore Installations (Safety Zones) Regulations 1987 (SI 1987/1331).

(HL Debs., vol. 515, cols. 827–8: 6 February 1990)

In explanation of vote in the UN General Assembly on 14 December 1990, on the subject of the law of the sea, the UK representative, Mr A. Aust, stated:

. . . under the Environmental Protection Act [1990], we have extended our powers of pollution control to cover dumping on to our continental shelf by ships of any flag.

(Text provided by the FCO; see also A/45/PV.68, p. 61)

Part Nine: IX. *Seas, waterways, ships—exclusive fishery zone*

(See also table in Part Nine: I. A., above)

In reply to a question, the Minister of State, FCO, wrote:

There are no agreements to fish in the south Atlantic between the United Kingdom or its dependent territories and other states. Some agreements have, however, been signed between the Governments of certain dependent territories and private fishing companies or associations.

In addition there are European Community agreements entered into on behalf of all member states, which have been signed with Angola, Cape Verde, Gambia, Guinea Bissau, Guinea Conakry, Guinea Equatorial, Ivory Coast, Sao Tomé and Principe, and Senegal.

(HC Debs., vol. 182, Written Answers, col. *481*: 13 December 1990)

The following press release was issued by the FCO on 27 November 1990:

Following meetings in Madrid on 12–14 and 23–24 November between UK and Argentine government representatives, Britain and Argentina have agreed arrangements for cooperation on fisheries conservation in the South Atlantic.

The two sides have agreed:

(*a*) to establish a UK/Argentine 'South Atlantic Fisheries Commission' (SAFC) to meet at least twice a year, to exchange information on fishing activity between 45°S and 60°S, and make recommendations relating to conservation and

(*b*) to a total ban on fishing in an area outside and contiguous with the FICZ [Falkland Islands Conservation Zone].

The ban, effective 26 December 1990, is necessary in view of the growing threat to the illex squid stocks from unregulated and irresponsible fishing. The area in which fishing is banned is indicated on the attached map and will be under Falkland Islands jurisdiction.

These arrangements, concluded under the sovereignty umbrella agreed at Madrid in October 1989, have been arrived at following intensive discussions with the Argentines and consultations with the Falkland Islands Councillors. They represent a practical step in UK-Argentine collaboration in protecting South Atlantic fisheries.

(FCO Press Release No. 240 of 1990; for the text of the 'sovereignty umbrella' see UKMIL 1989, p. 583)

The FCO published the following map to accompany the press release:

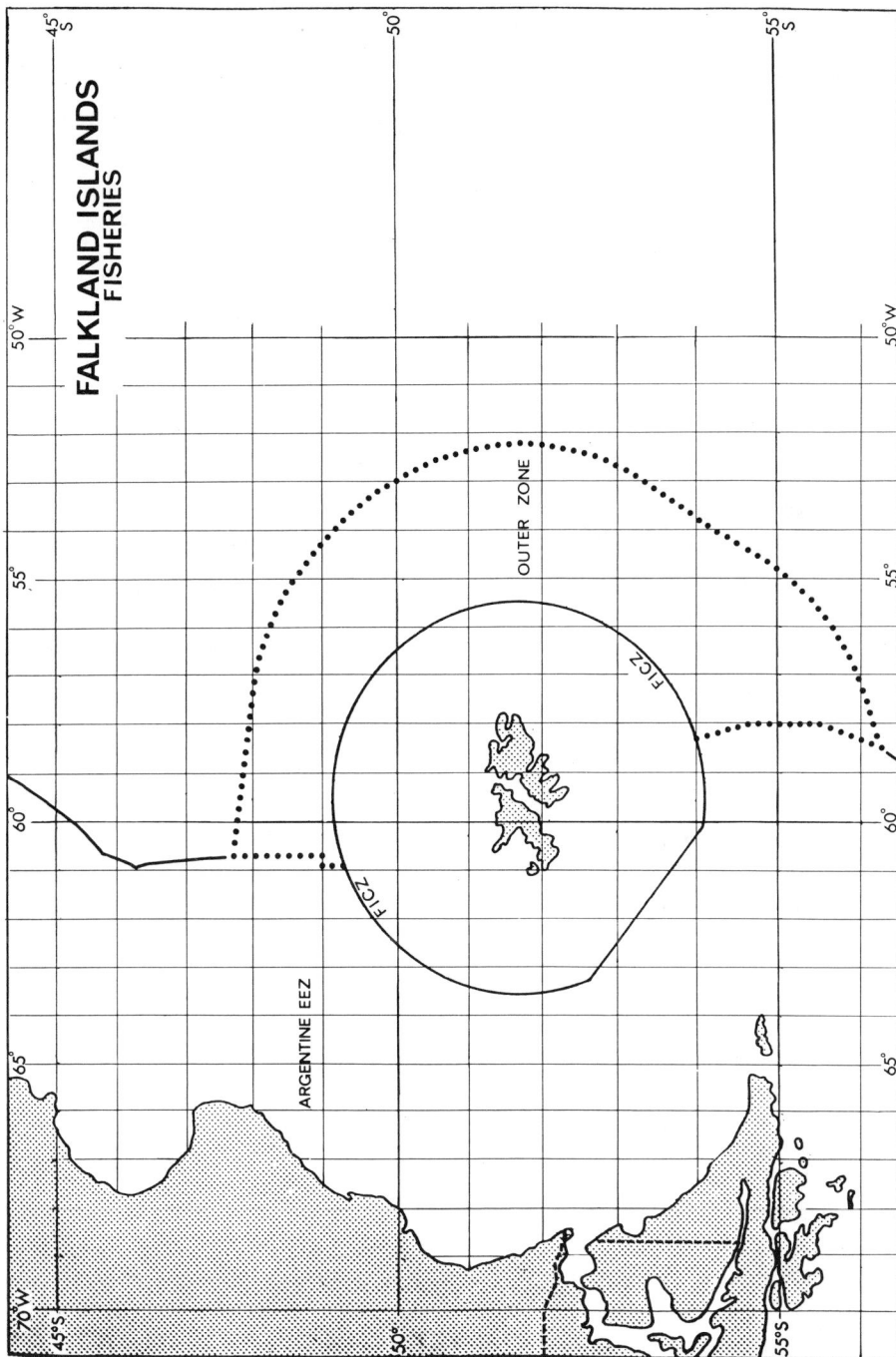

FALKLAND ISLANDS
FISHERIES

OUTER ZONE

FICZ

FICZ

ARGENTINE EEZ

Part Nine: X. *Seas, waterways, ships—exclusive economic zone*

(See also Part Nine: VIII., above)

Article 17, paragraph 11 of the UN Convention against Illicit Traffic in Narcotic Drugs and Psychotropic Substances, concluded at Vienna on 20 December 1988, reads, in the context of enforcement action at sea, as follows:

Any action taken in accordance with this article shall take due account of the need not to interfere with or affect the rights and obligations and the exercise of jurisdiction of coastal States in accordance with the international law of the sea.

On 20 December 1988, Brazil signed the Convention with the following declaration:

It is the understanding of the Brazilian Government that paragraph 11 of article 17 does not prevent a coastal State from requiring prior authorization for any action under this article by other States in the Exclusive Economic Zone.

On 27 December 1989, the Secretary-General of the UN, as depositary, received from the UK Government the following objection:

The United Kingdom of Great Britain and Northern Ireland, Member State of the European Community, attached to the principle of freedom of navigation, notably in the exclusive economic zone, considers that the declaration of Brazil concerning paragraph 11 of Article 17, of the United Nations Convention against Illicit Traffic in Narcotic Drugs and Psychotropic Substances, adopted in Vienna on 20 December 1988, goes further than the rights accorded to coastal states by international law.

(UN Doc. C.N. 359. 1989. TREATIES—16)

Part Nine: XII. *Seas, waterways, ships—bed of the sea beyond national jurisdiction*

(See also Part Nine: XIV. (second item), below)

In reply to a question, the Minister of State, FCO, wrote:

The United Kingdom has not signed the United Nations law of the sea convention because the deep sea bed mining regime for which it provides is unacceptable to us. Nevertheless, we participate in the preparatory commission in the hope that within the long period before mining can start a regime acceptable to all can be achieved. We see many of the other parts of UNLOSC as valuable and as reflecting current state practice.

(HC Debs., vol. 169, Written Answers, col. *145*: 13 March 1990)

Part Nine: XIV. *Seas, waterways, ships—international regime of the sea in general*

At the conclusion, on 1 September 1989, of the 1989 summer meeting of the UN Preparatory Commission for the International Sea-Bed Authority

and for the International Tribunal for the Law of the Sea, the representative of France, on behalf of the members of the EC, stated:

As the seventh session of the Preparatory Commission draws to a close, the
European Community and its member States would like to express their great
satisfaction at the high standard of the work which we have just carried out in New
York. This work has been characterized by a quite remarkable spirit of openness
which augurs well for the future of the efforts which we are all undertaking, jointly,
in the Preparatory Commission.

The Community and its member States take as evidence the statements which
have just been made not only by you yourself, Mr. Chairman, but also by the
Chairman of the Group of 77. We all share the same concern to open a dialogue and
to guarantee a promising future for the Convention.

The Community and its member States regard what has just happened as very
significant. Their appreciation is all the greater because of the high value they
attach to the contribution which the Convention has already made to the law of the
sea. Although it has not yet entered into force, most of its provisions constitute, in
fact, an indispensable reference for law of the sea problems. It has most certainly
strengthened co-operation among States and encouraged the harmonization of
State practice in many areas including, *inter alia*, freedom of communication and
movement on the seas. It forms an essential element in the maintenance of legal
order on the seas and oceans and, as a result, is an important contribution to international law.

However, in spite of this positive aspect, the very fact that the Convention is not
universally accepted entails a risk that, in time, diverging practices may emerge.

This risk is real. That is why conditions should be brought about immediately
which would allow the universality of the Convention to be achieved.

The Community and its member States note that a favourable atmosphere exists
at the present time for a new dialogue. They intend to contribute in a constructive
way to this dialogue. It is a matter of finding, without pre-conditions, an answer to
the deficiencies of the deep sea-bed mining regime in the Convention and, thereby,
assuring the Convention's universality.

(*Law of the Sea Bulletin*, No. 15 (May 1990), p. 59)

On the same occasion, the representative of Italy, on behalf of the
'Group of Six'—Belgium, the Federal Republic of Germany, Italy, Japan,
the Netherlands and the UK—, stated in part:

Our negotiations are entering a crucial stage. We are convinced that the United
Nations Convention on the Law of the Sea constitutes a major achievement of the
United Nations and of the process of codification and progressive development of
international law. But the States belonging to the Group of Six hold the view that
Part XI presents some serious problems which, if left unresolved, might jeopardize
this achievement. We have, therefore, tirelessly worked in this forum to find appropriate solutions to the above-mentioned difficulties, so as to pave the way for a
universally acceptable Convention. We strongly believe that the achievement of
this lofty objective might be greatly facilitated should all States agree to the launch-
ing of a dialogue, without pre-conditions and in the appropriate framework, aimed
at achieving a better understanding of those problems and solutions to them. We

would therefore welcome developments in that direction and are ready to make our contributions.

(Ibid., p. 61)

Part Nine: XV. A. 2. *Seas, waterways, ships—ships—legal status—public ships other than warships*

(See Part Nine: XV. A. 3., below)

Part Nine: XV. A. 3. *Seas, waterways, ships—ships—legal status—warships*

In the course of the HC Standing Committee debate on the Aviation and Maritime Security Bill, the Minister for Public Transport, Mr Michael Portillo, stated:

Warships, naval auxiliaries, customs and police ships are usually excluded from international conventions. However, we consider that offences should be specified in respect of such vessels in situations where the United Kingdom has jurisdiction under international law.

. . .

Warships, naval auxiliaries or ships used in customs or police service are precluded from the provisions of the Rome convention. It is considered appropriate that the hijacking of such ships should also be made an offence under United Kingdom law. This is done by subsection (2) which provides that it is not an offence to hijack a warship, or similar ship, except in specified circumstances where we have jurisdiction—that is, if the perpetrator is a United Kingdom national, or the incident occurred in the United Kingdom, or the warship or other ship involved was used by the United Kingdom armed forces, police or customs. The extradition provisions of the Rome convention will not apply to this offence.

(HC Debs., 1989–90, Standing Committee A: Aviation and Maritime Security Bill, col. 99; 13 February 1990)

Part Nine: XV. B. *Seas, waterways, ships—ships—nationality*

In reply to a question on the subject of sub-standard shipping, the Parliamentary Under-Secretary of State, Department of Transport, wrote in part:

Merchant ships belonging to other members of the European Community are regarded as foreign ships and therefore subject to port state control inspection when they enter a United Kingdom port.

(HC Debs., vol. 171, Written Answers, col. *263*: 26 April 1990)

In reply to a question, the Parliamentary Under-Secretary of State, Department of Agriculture, Fisheries and Food, wrote in part:

The action that we have taken to seek to ensure that the quota system operates for the benefit of the genuine United Kingdom fishing fleet has been on two fronts. First, we have imposed operating conditions to ensure that fishing vessels entitled to fly the United Kingdom flag have a real economic link with this country, through licence conditions imposed under powers contained in the Sea Fish (Conservation) Act 1967. Secondly, we have gone to the heart of the problem by enacting the provisions of part II of the Merchant Shipping Act 1988, as amended, where we require British-registered fishing vessels to be mainly owned, managed and controlled by people resident in Britain.

(HC Debs., vol. 174, Written Answers, cols. 746–7 : 22 June 1990)

Part Nine: XV. D. *Seas, waterways, ships—ships—jurisdiction*

(See also Part Nine: I. B. 2, and Part Nine: VII. H., above)

On 28 June 1988, the Governments of the UK and the Commonwealth of the Bahamas concluded a Memorandum of Understanding in respect of the registration in the Commonwealth of the Bahamas of ships owned by British nationals. The text of the Memorandum of Understanding, as corrected by an Exchange of Notes dated 28 November 1988, on which date it came into operation, reads in material part as follows:

Considering the preamble of British owned ships to the defence of the United Kingdom, having regard to the number of British owned ships that are entered on The Commonwealth of The Bahamas register of shipping, wishing to facilitate the making available of such ships for the defence of the United Kingdom in time of war or other hostilities or when war or hostilities are threatened.

The Government of The Commonwealth of the Bahamas and the Government of the United Kingdom have reached the following understanding:—

1. The Minister responsible for Merchant Shipping in The Commonwealth of The Bahamas will whenever requested by the owner of a Bahamian vessel, in accordance with the legislation of The Commonwealth of The Bahamas, waive the exercise of its sovereign authority over such a vessel where the following circumstances exist:

(a) the vessel is owned directly or indirectly by a person who is:
  (i) A British citizen, British Dependent Territories citizen, British Overseas citizen; British subject or British protected person, or
  (ii) A body incorporated or constituted under the law of any part of the United Kingdom; of any of the Channel Islands, of the Isle of Man or of a colony; or
(b) the vessel property in which is divided into shares whereof the greater part are owned by persons falling within sub-paragraph (a) above; and
(c) there exists a state of war or other hostilities involving the United Kingdom or the threat of such war or other hostilities.

2. The Government of The Commonwealth of The Bahamas in waiving its sovereign authority will allow the control of such a vessel to be committed to the Government of the United Kingdom in the circumstances mentioned aforesaid.

This Memorandum will come into operation on signature and will continue in operation until terminated by either Government on six months' written notice to the other.

(Text provided by the FCO. See also UKMIL 1988, p. 548; and for similar agreements in treaty form with Liberia and Vanuatu, see UKMIL 1989, pp. 676–7. For material relevant to the legal status of a Memorandum of Understanding, see UKMIL 1989, p. 581)

Part Eleven: II. A. 6. *Responsibility—responsible entities—States— reparation*

(See also Part Eleven: II. A. 7.(b)., below)

In reply to a question, the Minister of State, FCO, wrote:

When the Baltic states were incorporated into the Soviet Union in 1940, the property of a number of British nationals was seized without compensation. The Soviet authorities also did not accept responsibility for the external debts of the Baltic states, including three external loans which had been placed in London. To safeguard British interests, the British Government responded by freezing the gold reserves of the three Baltic central banks which were deposited in London, and which were claimed by the Soviet authorities.

Negotiations between the British and Soviet Governments culminated in an agreement which was signed on 5 January 1968. This provided that the British and Soviet Governments would not pursue their respective claims. It thus enabled the British Government to use most of the money realised from the sale in 1967 of the Baltic gold reserves (in addition to certain other assets of the Baltic States and ceded territories) to meet in part the claims of British creditors who had lost assets in the former Baltic states and in certain other territories incorporated into the Soviet Union. The judicial determination of these claims was carried out by the Foreign Compensation Commission in accordance with the Foreign Compensation (Union of Soviet Socialists Republics) Order 1969; claimants eventually receiving 42.6 per cent. of the assessed value of their claims.

The Baltic gold (weighing 460,220 fine ounces) realised £5.8 million when sold in 1967. Its value would be approximately £112.17 million at current prices.

(HC Debs., vol. 168, Written Answers, col. *403*: 5 March 1990)

In reply to a question, the Minister of State, FCO, wrote in part:

Our policy remains that we shall be able to agree to the Tripartite Gold Commission's releasing gold to Albania only when Albania has paid the compensation awarded to Britain by the International Court of Justice in the Corfu channel case.

(HC Debs., vol. 169, Written Answers, col. *451*: 19 March 1990)

Giving evidence on 4 April 1990 to the HC Foreign Affairs Committee examining some immediate issues of German reunification, the Secretary of State for Foreign and Commonwealth Affairs, Mr Douglas Hurd, was asked how he saw the outstanding issues on reparation being handled. He replied:

There are a wide range of outstanding issues. There are big issues between the two German States, and I have the impression these matters of law as regards property between the two Germanys are one of the most difficult which will be established. The Soviet Union has said that there should be no change to existing property arrangements in the GDR, and there they are talking about justifying, I think, the successive waves of expropriation which took place after 1945. So you are quite right that this may complicate the Two plus Four process. We have claims against the GDR.

. . .

The GDR agreed in 1973 to discuss these claims. We have been trying since then to bring those claims talks to a conclusion, but they have gone extremely slowly and they are not reaching a conclusion. The Americans and French, I am told, are in the same position.

. . .

The best guess is that we are talking about British claims in the region of £10 million or £15 million sterling. So it is a sizeable amount. We have been trying to pursue it with the East German Government, not very successfully, and therefore this is a matter which falls to be pursued by us and indeed by others.

(*Parliamentary Papers*, 1989–90, HC, Paper 335–i, pp. 8–9)

In reply to a question asking about the progress in implementing the Foreign Compensation (Union of Soviet Socialist Republics) (Distribution) Order 1987, the Parliamentary Under-Secretary of State, FCO, wrote:

The Foreign Compensation Commission . . . will on 1 June begin making final payments from the Russian fund amounting to approximately £28.2 million, representing 24.78 per cent. of the value assigned to a claim, to successful claimants against the fund. Taking into account the two previous interim payments, the total sum paid to claimants from the fund will amount to approximately £62.4 million, representing 54.78 per cent. of the assessed value of successful claims. The disbursements commencing on 1 June will exhaust the balance in the fund.

(HC Debs., vol. 173, Written Answers, cols. *187–8*: 23 May 1990)

Articles 5 and 6 of the Agreement for the Promotion and Protection of Investments between the Governments of the UK and the Czech and Slovak Federal Republic, signed on 10 July 1990, read as follows:

ARTICLE 5

Expropriation

(1) Investments of investors of either Contracting Party shall not be nationalised, expropriated or subjected to measures having effect equivalent to nationalisation or expropriation (hereinafter referred to as 'expropriation') in the territory of the other Contracting Party except for a public purpose related to the internal needs of that Party on a non-discriminatory basis and against prompt, adequate and effective compensation. Such compensation shall amount to the genuine value of the investment expropriated immediately before the expropriation or before the impending expropriation became public knowledge, whichever is the earlier, shall include interest at a normal commercial rate until the date of payment, shall be

made without delay, be effectively realisable and be freely transferable. The investor affected shall have a right, under the law of the Contracting Party making the expropriation, to prompt review, by a judicial or other independent authority of that party, of his or its case and of the valuation of his or its investment in accordance with the principles set out in this paragraph.

(2) The provisions of paragraph (1) shall also apply where a Contracting Party expropriates the assets of a company which is incorporated or constituted under the law in force in any part of its own territory, and in which investors of the other Contracting Party own shares.

ARTICLE 6

Repatriation of Investment and Returns

Each Contracting Party shall in respect of investments guarantee to investors of the other Contracting Party the unrestricted transfer of their investments and returns. Transfers shall be effected without delay in the convertible currency in which the capital was originally invested or in any other convertible currency agreed by the investor and the Contracting Party concerned. Unless otherwise agreed by the investor transfers shall be made at the rate of exchange applicable on the date of transfer pursuant to the exchange regulations in force.

(Cm. 1306)

The following statement was made at a FCO press conference given on 17 October 1990:

Notification by British nationals of loss and damage

Spokesman said that the Iraqi Ambassador Mr Azmi Al-Salihi had been summoned to the Foreign Office yesterday afternoon (16 October) by Assistant Under-Secretary of State, Mr David Gore-Booth, to receive a British Note reserving the rights of HMG and of UK nationals and companies including the right to full restitution compensation or other reparations with respect to acts or omissions attributable to the Government of Iraq or the Iraqi occupation authorities in Kuwait since the illegal occupation of Kuwait by Iraq on 2 August 1990. The meeting had lasted 11 minutes. The atmosphere was correct.

The FCO will be inviting UK companies and nationals whose property in Kuwait or Iraq has been lost, damaged, or destroyed, or who have suffered personal injury, as a result of Iraq's illegal invasion of Kuwait to notify us of the details, with a view to opening a list. Advertisements are being placed in the national press for this purpose. UK companies and nationals are not being asked to submit claims at this stage, and the notification procedure does not imply that HMG will necessarily consider any claims on behalf of UK companies and nationals in the future. The handling of claims is a matter which can only be decided once the Gulf crisis is over.

Losses resulting from compliance with or the operation of the UN embargo against Iraq are not covered by this exercise.

(Text provided by the FCO)

The following notice was placed in the UK press on 18 October 1990:

Notification of loss and damage suffered by UK nationals and companies in Kuwait and Iraq

United Kingdom nationals and companies whose property in Kuwait or Iraq has been lost, damaged, or destroyed, or who have suffered personal injury, as a consequence of the illegal invasion and occupation of Kuwait are invited to notify their losses to Her Majesty's Government, so that a list can be opened.

(This will not constitute submission of a claim.)

In the course of evidence given on 24 October 1990 to the Foreign Affairs Committee of the House of Commons examining the Gulf crisis, the Secretary of State for Foreign and Commonwealth Affairs, Mr Douglas Hurd, stated:

In international law as it is, which has already been touched on in Security Council resolutions . . . there is a responsibility which exists that does not have to be created by a Security Council resolution but it would be useful and sensible to have a Security Council resolution which deals specifically with these points. What we have in mind is a resolution which would make clear Iraqi responsibility for making restitution or compensation to individuals and companies and states as a result of the invasion of Kuwait. The wording may not correspond exactly to this but this is the idea in the British mind, that states may be invited to establish national registers of claimants. We on 17 October handed the Iraqi Ambassador here a note in which we referred to the rights of HM Government and all British nationals and companies, including the right to full restitution, compensation or other reparation with respect to acts or omissions attributable to the Government of Iraq or the Iraqi occupation authorities in Kuwait, and we are inviting British companies and nationals whose property in Kuwait or Iraq has been seriously damaged or destroyed or those who have suffered personal injuries—this is personal and companies—to notify us of the details so that we can open the kind of register which we hope the Security Council resolution will encourage all nations to do, and we will be putting advertisements in the national press for this purpose and I hope this procedure will be followed. We were talking about notification and we would put forward an international claim ourselves if it looks as if the legal remedies available to individuals or companies are insufficient. You go more widely . . . to Kuwait itself. I would certainly understand Iraqi compensation would be required to deal with that. I think a great deal of finance would be needed very quickly which Iraq, however rigorously treated, would not be able to supply quickly. So it is going to be a huge task and obviously what the Saudi Minister was referring to and thinking of, but we would certainly expect that Iraq would be responsible but the means will have to be found of obliging her to pay, presumably out of the oil revenue when the oil flow resumes, substantial sums in compensation across a very wide front.

(*Parliamentary Papers*, 1989–90, HC, Paper 655–ii, p. 46)

In the course of a statement on 5 November 1990 in the Sixth Committee of the UN General Assembly considering the International Law Commission's draft articles on State responsibility, the UK representative, Sir Arthur Watts, stated:

In his Second Report, the Special Rapporteur proposed three draft Articles, and these have now been referred to the Drafting Committee. On the first of these, concerning 'reparation by equivalent' (Article 8), we agree with the Special Rapporteur that restitution in kind is the primary mode for reparation, which should be applied where at all possible, while also recognising that there is a need for reparation by pecuniary compensation where reparation in kind cannot ensure complete reparation. We thus, in general, welcome draft Article 8.

The Special Rapporteur's second proposed draft Article concerned payment of interest (Article 9). My delegation would at this stage like to make just two points. First, we support the view that interest should be paid in cases involving loss of property. That view seems to be supported by the awards of international claims commissions. Secondly, we support the general agreement in the Commission that the provision in the draft (Article 9(2)) on compound interest be deleted. Such interest has only been awarded in the rarest of past cases.

(Text provided by the FCO; see also A/C. 6/45/SR. 30, p. 15)

In an Annex to the above statement, the UK Government made the following comments on the draft articles:

ARTICLE 8

With respect to the two alternatives proposed for paragraph 1 of Article 8, the United Kingdom sees little substantive difference between them but believes that the eventual draft should be as clear as possible. As regards paragraph 2, the discussion in the Commission on the expressions 'economically assessable damage' and 'moral damage' is noted. We agree with those members who stated that what matters in the final analysis is that compensation should be adequate, but we do not see why the need for adequacy leads to the necessity of taking into account the financial status of the offending state or requires the introduction here of the concept of 'excessive onerousness', as suggested by some members. As the United Kingdom remarked in its statement last year on this topic in the context of Article 7, we are concerned that the introduction of this concept could result in a major source of weakness in the draft articles.

With respect to paragraph 4, we are inclined to share the view of those members of the Commission who expressed some doubts about the concept of 'uninterrupted causal link'. The introduction of some notion of proximate cause or foreseeability would seem desirable from the perspective of equity and in accordance with the approach of most legal systems.

. . .

ARTICLE 24

The United Kingdom delegation has difficulties with the concept that reparation should be paid for purely environmental damage which cannot be restored, and would not wish to see Article 24(*a*) requiring States to compensate for environmental damage beyond restoration costs.

(Text provided by the FCO)

In reply to the question what representations have been received from the Government of the Soviet Republic of the Ukraine concerning the return of a barrel of gold deposited with the Bank of England in the early 18th century, the Minister of State, FCO, wrote:

None.

(HC Debs., vol. 181, Written Answers, col. *337* : 27 November 1990)

In the course of a debate on the subject of the Gulf crisis, the Minister of State, FCO, the Earl of Caithness, stated:

My noble friend Lord Boyd-Carpenter reminded me of the question he asked before regarding reparations following the removal of Iraq from Kuwait. There is provision under international law for compensation to be sought from Iraq. I remind my noble friend of Security Council Resolution 674 adopted on 29th October. That re-emphasised Iraqi responsibility to pay compensation. We shall seek ways of ensuring that the aggressor pays for his aggression.

(HL Debs., vol. 524, col. 719: 17 December 1990)

Part Eleven: II. A. 7. (a). *Responsibility—responsible entities—States—procedure—diplomatic and consular protection*

In December 1990, the Commercial Management and Exports Department of the FCO issued a Background Note on Investment Promotion and Protection Agreements (IPPAs). The text of the document was substantially identical with that of November 1987 reproduced in UKMIL 1987, p. 620. The following list of UK IPPAs was also issued:

Country	Date/Signature	Date of Entry into Force
Egypt	11 June 1975	24 February 1976
Singapore	22 July 1975	22 July 1975
Korea	4 March 1976	4 March 1976
Romania	19 March 1976	22 November 1976
Indonesia	27 April 1976	24 March 1977
Thailand	28 November 1978	11 August 1979
Jordan	10 October 1979	24 April 1980
Sri Lanka	13 February 1980	18 December 1980
Senegal	7 May 1980	9 February 1984
Bangladesh	19 June 1980	19 June 1980
Philippines	3 December 1980	2 January 1981
Lesotho	18 February 1981	18 February 1981
Papua New Guinea	14 May 1981	22 December 1981
Malaysia	21 May 1981	21 October 1988
Paraguay	4 June 1981	Not yet in force
Sierra Leone	8 December 1981	Not yet in force

Country	Date/Signature	Date of Entry into Force
Yemen Arab Rep.	25 February 1982	11 November 1983
Belize	30 April 1982	30 April 1982
Cameroon	4 June 1982	7 June 1985
Costa Rica	7 September 1982	Not yet in force
St Lucia	18 January 1983	18 January 1983
Panama	7 October 1983	7 November 1983
Haiti	18 March 1985	Not yet in force
China	15 May 1986	15 May 1986
Mauritius	20 May 1986	13 October 1986
Malta	4 October 1986	4 October 1986
Jamaica	20 January 1987	14 May 1987
Dominica	23 January 1987	23 January 1987
Hungary	9 March 1987	28 August 1987
Antigua & Barbuda	12 June 1987	12 June 1987
Benin	27 November 1987	27 November 1987
Poland	8 December 1987	14 April 1988
Grenada	25 February 1988	25 February 1988
Bolivia	24 May 1988	16 February 1990
Tunisia	14 March 1989	4 January 1990
Ghana	22 March 1989	Not yet in force
Soviet Union	6 April 1989	Not yet in force
Congo	25 May 1989	9 November 1990
Guyana	27 October 1989	11 April 1990
Czechoslovakia	10 July 1990	Not yet in force
Burundi	13 September 1990	13 September 1990
Morocco	30 October 1990	Provisionally in force
Argentina	11 December 1990	Not yet in force
Nigeria	11 December 1990	11 December 1990

(Text provided by the FCo)

Part Eleven: II. A. 7. (a). (i). *Responsibility—responsible entities— States—procedure—diplomatic and consular protection—nationality of claims*

Article 1 of the Agreement for the Promotion and Protection of Investments between the Governments of the UK and the Czech and Slovak Federal Republic, signed on 10 July 1990, is illustrative of such agreements concluded or signed by the UK in 1990. It reads in part as follows:

ARTICLE 1

Definitions

For the purposes of this Agreement:

. . .
  (c) the term 'investors' means:
     (i) in respect of the Czech and Slovak Federal Republic:
       (aa) all legal entities established under Czechoslovak law;

(bb) all natural persons who, according to Czechoslovak law, are Czecho-slovak citizens and have the right to act as investors;

(ii) in respect of the United Kingdom:

(aa) physical persons deriving their status as United Kingdom nationals from the law in force in the United Kingdom;

(bb) corporations, firms and associations incorporated or constituted under the law in force in any part of the United Kingdom or in any territory to which this Agreement is extended in accordance with the provisions of Article 12.

(Cm. 1306)

Part Eleven: II. A. 7. (a). (ii). *Responsibility—responsible entities— States—procedure—diplomatic and consular protection—exhaustion of local remedies*

The following passage appeared in the Annex to a statement made on 5 November 1990 in the Sixth Committee of the UN General Assembly by the UK representative, Sir Arthus Watts, in the course of considering the draft articles of the International Law Commission dealing with inter-national liability for injurious consequences arising out of acts not prohi-bited by international law:

Chapter V

The United Kingdom delegation is content that there should be a Chapter on civil liability in particular because, as already indicated, it believes that primary liability should fall on the operator. But it would question the usefulness of Article 28(*a*) which provides that local remedies need not be exhausted before an affected State may submit a claim under the present Articles. It is important that there should not be several actions proceeding in parallel with respect to the same damage and the UK therefore considers that injured parties should first look to, and exhaust, local remedies.

(Text provided by the FCO; see also A/C. 6/45/SR. 30, pp.15–16)

Part Eleven: II. A. 7. (b). *Responsibility—responsible entities—States— procedure—peaceful settlement*

The following press statement was issued by the FCO on 18 September 1990:

PROPERTY CLAIMS IN THE GERMAN DEMOCRATIC REPUBLIC

In a Regulation dated 11 July, published in its Official Gazette of 27 July, the Government of the German Democratic Republic (GDR) provided for the regis-tration of claims concerning property expropriated in the GDR subsequent to 3 October 1949 and foreign owned property taken into state administration as from 8 May 1945. The deadline for the filing of applications with the appropriate GDR authorities was originally 31 January 1991 but this has now been advanced to 13 October 1990.

The Foreign and Commonwealth Office have conveyed the contents of the Regulation to British nationals whose claims were registered by the Foreign Compensation (German Democratic Republic) (Registration) Order 1975. This has been done by sending letters to their last known address.

The FCO has placed advertisements in national newspapers to alert all British nationals who may have a claim.

(FCO Press Release No. 205 of 1990)

Part Eleven: II. B. *Responsibility—responsible entities—international organizations*

In reply to a question, the Secretary of State for Trade and Industry wrote:

A proposal supported by all known creditors of the International Tin Council's buffer stock operation for a settlement at £182.5 million payable on 30 March 1990 has been approved by the ITC as the basis for a settlement. A Supplementary Estimate covering a United Kingdom contribution not exceeding £31,790,000 to the settlement amount will be laid before the House in February.

(HC Debs., vol. 165, Written Answers, col. *184*: 16 January 1990)

Part Eleven: II. D. *Responsibility—responsible entities—individuals, including corporations*

During a debate on the War Crimes Bill, the Minister of State, Home Office, Mr John Patten, stated:

My hon. Friend . . . asked about Vichy France. Actions by Vichy France against Frenchmen would not be war crimes and would, therefore, be outside the scope of international law at the time; they would be acts of homicide or crimes against humanity. Actions by puppet regimes against their own citizens in their own territory would fall outside the definition of war crime at any stage since the Hague convention of 1907. They would not be war crimes by that or by any other definition in international law, as far as I am aware, although they might certainly be caught under a number of crimes against humanity.

(HC Debs., vol. 171, col. 441: 25 April 1990)

In moving the second reading in the House of Lords of the War Crimes Bill, the Minister of State, Home Office, Earl Ferrers, referred to the inquiry carried out by Sir Thomas Hetherington and Mr William Chalmers and continued:

The inquiry recommended—in the words of Section 3 of Chapter 10 of its report—that:
'legislation should be introduced to give British courts jurisdiction over acts of murder and manslaughter committed as war crimes (violations of the laws and cus-

toms of war) in Germany or German-occupied territory during the period of the Second World War by persons who are now British citizens or resident in the United Kingdom.'
That is the background to this Bill and indeed the cause of it.

. . .

In proposing a solution to the dilemma which is right for this country, the Bill which is before your Lordships today follows very closely the terms of the main recommendation which was made by the war crimes inquiry. That recommendation was framed with great care by two eminent and experienced prosecutors who were very much alive to the need to avoid the creation of retrospective offences. Sir Thomas Hetherington and Mr. Chalmers took great care to ensure that their recommendation fell fully within the bounds of customary international law as it stood at the time of the Second World War.
In paragraph 27 of Chapter 9 of their report they said:—
'In our view, to enact legislation in this country to give the British courts jurisdiction over murder and manslaughter committed as violations of the laws and customs of war would not be to create an offence retrospectively. It would be making an offence triable in British courts to an extent which international law had recognised and permitted at a time before the alleged offences in question had been committed.'
They also noted in paragraph 38 of Chapter 5 of their report that, with the question of retrospection in mind, Article 7(2) of the European Convention on Human Rights explicitly permits:
'the trial and punishment of any person for any act or omission which at the time it was committed, was criminal according to the general principles of law recognised by civilised nations'.
These are telling expositions on the matter of retrospection.

. . .

There is a point on which there has been some misunderstanding, and that is that the Bill does not apply to crimes against humanity. The concept of crimes against humanity was only developed at Nuremberg, and the Hetherington/ Chalmers Inquiry considered that to legislate on such a basis could be seen to be retrospective legislation. For that reason the Bill seeks to give the courts jurisdiction only over offences of homicide which were committed in 'violation of the laws and customs of war'. That was what the inquiry proposed on the basis that this was a concept which was already well established in customary international law by the time of the Second World War.

(HL Debs., vol. 519, cols. 1080–4, *passim*: 4 June 1990)

The Twelve Member States of the EC issued a statement on 21 August 1990 which read in part as follows:

They also warn Iraqi citizens that they will be held personally responsible in accordance with international law for their involvement in illegal actions concerning the security and life of foreign citizens.

(Text provided by the FCO)

In a television interview given on 1 September 1990, the Prime Minister, Mrs Margaret Thatcher, referred to the detention in Iraq of foreign nationals by the regime of Saddam Hussein. She continued:

May I make it quite clear—it is absolutely contrary to international law to take hostages, some of the things he is doing are absolutely contrary to it and some of the treatment in Kuwait of some of our Embassies. We are all making due note of the people who do it because in these days they cannot say: 'We were only acting under orders.' If they are doing something which is totally cold and cruel and brutal then they, later, could in fact be prosecuted.

.   .   .

If anything happened to those hostages then sooner or later when any hostilities were over we could do what we did at Nuremberg and prosecute the requisite people for their totally uncivilised and brutal behaviour. They cannot get out of it these days by just saying: 'Well we were under orders'. That was the message of Nuremberg.

(Text provided by the FCO)

In response to the question whether she meant specific international justice, the Prime Minister replied:

I mean international justice, that each of us would be in a position, as at the Nuremberg trials, to bring charges to bear and to have them heard.

(Ibid.)

Speaking in an emergency debate in the House of Lords on the subject of the situation in the Gulf, the Minister of State, FCO, the Earl of Caithness, stated:

The Government are in constant contact with Iraqi representatives in London, New York and Baghdad and have made clear that if there are illegal actions against our people we shall hold Iraqi officials individually responsible.

(HL Debs., vol. 521, col. 1798: 6 September 1990)

On 18 September 1990, the Ministerial meeting of the Western European Union issued a Communiqué which began as follows:

The Foreign Affairs and Defence Ministers of the member countries of Western European Union, at their extraordinary meeting in Paris:
—Unreservedly condemn the new breaches of international law by the Iraqi authorities and the assault on personnel arising from the violation of diplomatic premises in Kuwait City, and following Iraq's intolerable act of aggression against another Arab country: they recall that the authors of these violations will carry a personal responsibility . . .

(Text provided by the FCO)

In the course of a debate on the subject of Cambodia, the Parliamentary Under-Secretary of State, FCO, Mr Mark Lennox-Boyd, stated:

If a way could be found to bring Pol Pot and his cronies to justice for their crimes against the Cambodian people, we would certainly be the last to object. However, hon. Members should not live in a dream world. They must remember that there are formidable legal and practical problems, which I shall describe.

Under the auspices of the United Nations, a tribunal could be established. However, it would require the agreement of a majority of United Nations members, and a legitimate Government in Cambodia would have to accept its jurisdiction before it could hear cases relating to Cambodia under the genocide convention. Alternatively, Pol Pot and others could be brought to trial under the genocide convention, but the only courts with jurisdiction under that convention would be Cambodian courts.

(HC Debs., vol. 178, col. 690: 26 October 1990)

In the course of a statement made on 8 November 1990 in the Sixth Committee of the UN General Assembly discussing the draft Code of Crimes against the Peace and Security of Mankind, the UK representative, Sir Arthur Watts, observed in respect of the invasion of Kuwait by Iraq:

It must be made clear that personal responsibility attaches to individuals for crimes such as these. State responsibility, while it undoubtedly exists, is not by itself a sufficient response. Crimes, including the most serious, are committed by individuals, and individuals must be in no doubt that they cannot afterwards claim to hide behind orders from their superiors, or from the State.

I do not, however, Mr Chairman, mean to dwell on this aspect of the Gulf crisis. The Security Council is well seized of the matter and is doing all it can to put right the great wrong which has been done by Iraq not only to Kuwait but to the world community. But these serious breaches of international law by individuals have given a new impetus to the debate on the question of the possible establishment of an international criminal court.

Mr Chairman, the Commission has considered the matter in some detail this year, and I would first of all like to express my delegation's gratitude to the Commission for responding so swiftly and so helpfully to the General Assembly's request. The Commission's report sets out lucidly the issues involved and the various questions that need to be answered.

We are all well aware that the establishment of an international criminal court would be a major undertaking, raising as it would many important and difficult issues. These would be not only legal but also political and practical. While there have been examples in the past, and there may be examples in the future, of international criminal tribunals set up to deal with particular situations, the idea of a standing international criminal court would be a development of enormous significance. But as my delegation has said on previous occasions, one cannot be serious about a Code of Crimes without at the same time looking seriously at the machinery for its implementation.

There are just five points which I should like to make at this stage.

First, we consider that if an international criminal court were to be established it should not in any way affect the jurisdiction, and in particular the finality of judgments, of national criminal courts, where they already have jurisdiction under existing treaties. There are examples of this under the Geneva Conventions, and under several international conventions which provide for jurisdiction of the 'prosecute or extradite' variety.

Second, it would, we believe, be best to continue to consider the possibility of a

Court in the context of the implementation of the Code, and not as a separate matter.

Third, we should not regard the establishment of an international criminal court as the only way to deal with international crimes. As I have said, where treaties already provide for national criminal courts to have jurisdiction, that jurisdiction should not be affected by the establishment of an international criminal court. National criminal jurisdiction may well be the most appropriate—and effective—way of dealing with many international crimes. I have in mind in particular those relating to traffic in narcotic drugs. We doubt very much whether the establishment of an international criminal court would help in the drug war. Combatting it needs more effective enforcement at the national level and greater cooperation at the international level. But there may be international crimes where some form of international criminal jurisdiction will be necessary in order to deal effectively with them. As we see it, the basic justification for an international criminal jurisdiction must be that there are international crimes which cannot be dealt with effectively by any other means. Examples of these might be those high crimes, such as waging aggressive war, crimes against humanity and such like.

This brings me to my fourth point. It is often assumed that an international criminal court would be a court of first instance, such as the Nuremburg Tribunal, and not an appeal court or a court of review. As the Commission has pointed out, an international criminal court could be established which would have no more than a review or appeal function, the cases being tried in national courts. Establishing such a jurisdiction might well be easier in many respects than establishing an international criminal court which would actually conduct trials of individuals.

Fifth, as the Commission has pointed out, a prosecution of serious international crimes, whether in national courts or an international criminal court, may need some form of prior authorisation. We think this aspect merits careful consideration given the nature of some high crimes, and the status of those most likely to be accused of committing them. It may well be that a decision to prosecute them should be taken by a body representing the international community, such as the Security Council.

(Text provided by the FCO; see also A/C. 6/45/SR. 35, pp. 7–8)

Speaking in the UN Security Council on 29 November 1990, the Secretary of State for Foreign and Commonwealth Affairs, Mr Douglas Hurd, stated:

I should also like to recall the terms of paragraph 13 of resolution 670 (1990), under which individuals are held personally responsible for grave breaches of the Geneva Convention. We should also hold personally responsible those involved in violations of the laws of armed conflict, including the prohibition against initiating the use of chemicals or biological weapons contrary to the Geneva Protocol of 1925, to which Iraq is a party.

(S/PV. 2963, p. 82).

Part Twelve: II. *Pacific settlement of disputes—modes of settlement*

In a speech in the UN Sixth Committee on 13 November 1990 on the subject of the UN Decade of International Law, the UK representative, Mr A. Aust, stated:

The last ten years of the 20th century have been declared the United Nations Decade of International Law. Our century has witnessed momentous developments in international law. It got off to a good start. 1899 saw the Hague Peace Conference. For its day the Conference was large; about 100 people took part, representing 26 Powers.

Although labelled as a peace conference, the greater part of its labours was devoted to the elaboration of rules of war. But, perhaps of more importance to our present debate was the adoption of the Convention for the Pacific Settlement of International Disputes. The Convention could be said to have laid the foundation for the modern law on the peaceful settlement of disputes between States, codifying as it did methods of peaceful settlement with which we are now all too familiar: good offices, mediation, commissions of enquiry and arbitration. In particular, it established the Permanent Court of Arbitration—which is still with us—and which was soon to be put to the test. In its first five years four arbitrations were held under its auspices. Three involved Great Britain. And recourse to a commission of enquiry prevented the outbreak of war between Great Britain and Russia over the celebrated Dogger Bank affair of 1904.

The second Peace Conference of 1907 was attended by nearly double the number of delegations and produced no less than thirteen conventions. That on the Pacific Settlement of International Disputes replaced the Convention of 1899.

The first 90 years of this century have been marked by several monumental achievements of international law: the first attempt at a global international organisation, the League of Nations; the successful establishment of the Permanent Court of International Justice; the Kellogg-Briand Pact; the Geneva Conventions; the United Nations Charter; the great codifying Conventions of Vienna. Despite two devastating world wars, international law, and respect for it, has grown inexorably.

(Text provided by the FCO; see also A/C. 6/45/SR. 40, pp. 6–7)

Part Twelve: II. G.1. *Pacific settlement of disputes—modes of settlement—arbitration—arbitral tribunals and commissions*

Article 8 of the Agreement for the Promotion and Protection of Investments, signed by the Governments of the UK and the Tunisian Republic on 17 March 1989 and in force on 4 January 1990, reads as follows:

ARTICLE 8
Reference to International Centre for Settlement of Investment Disputes

(1) Each Contracting Party hereby consents to submit to the International Centre for the Settlement of Investment Disputes (hereinafter referred to as 'the Centre') for settlement by conciliation or arbitration under the Convention on the Settlement of Investment Disputes between States and Nationals of Other States opened for signature at Washington on 18 March 1965[1] any legal dispute arising between that Contracting Party and a national of the other Contracting Party concerning an investment of the latter in the territory of the former. A company which is incorporated or constituted under the law in force in the territory of one Contracting

---

[1] Treaty Series No. 25 (1967), Cmnd. 3255.

Party and in which before such a dispute arises the majority of shares are owned by nationals of the other Contracting Party shall in accordance with Article 25(2)(b) of the Convention be treated for the purposes of the Convention as a national of the other Contracting Party. If any such dispute should arise and agreement cannot be reached within six months between the parties to this dispute through pursuit of local remedies or otherwise, then, if the national affected consents in writing to submit the dispute to the Centre for settlement by conciliation or arbitration under the Convention, either party may institute proceedings by addressing a request to that effect to the Secretary-General of the Centre as provided in Articles 28 and 36 of the Convention. In the event of disagreement as to whether conciliation or arbitration is the more appropriate procedure the national affected shall have the right to choose. The Contracting Party which is a party to the dispute shall not raise as an objection at any stage of the proceedings or enforcement of an award the fact that the national which is the other party to the dispute has received in pursuance of an insurance contract an indemnity in respect of some or all of his or its losses.

(2) Neither Contracting Party shall pursue through the diplomatic channel any dispute referred to the Centre unless

  (a) the Secretary-General of the Centre, or a conciliation commission or an arbitral tribunal constituted by it, decides that the dispute is not within the jurisdiction of the Centre, or

  (b) the other Contracting Party should fail to abide by or to comply with any award rendered by an arbitral tribunal.

(TS No. 18 (1990); Cm. 976)

Article 9 of the same Agreement reads:

ARTICLE 9

Disputes between the Contracting Parties

(1) Disputes between the Contracting Parties concerning the interpretation or application of this Agreement should, if possible, be settled through the diplomatic channel.

(2) If a dispute between the Contracting Parties cannot thus be settled, it shall upon the request of either Contracting Party be submitted to an arbitral tribunal.

(3) Such an arbitral tribunal shall be constituted for each individual case in the following way. Within two months of the receipt of the request for arbitration, each Contracting Party shall appoint one member of the tribunal. Those two members shall then select a national of a third State who on approval by the two Contracting Parties shall be appointed Chairman of the tribunal. The Chairman shall be appointed within two months from the date of appointment of the other two members.

(4) If within the periods specified in paragraph (3) of this Article the necessary appointments have not been made, either Contracting Party may, in the absence of any other agreement, invite the President of the International Court of Justice to make any necessary appointments. If the President is a national of either Contracting Party or if he is otherwise prevented from discharging the said function, the Vice-President shall be invited to make the necessary appointments. If the Vice-President is a national of either Contracting Party or if he too is prevented from discharging the said function, the Member of the International Court of Justice

next in seniority who is not a national of either Contracting Party shall be invited to make the necessary appointments.

(5) The arbitral tribunal shall reach its decision by a majority of votes. Such decision shall be binding on both Contracting Parties. Each Contracting Party shall bear the cost of its own member of the tribunal and of its representation in the arbitral proceedings; the cost of the Chairman and the remaining costs shall be borne in equal parts by the Contracting Parties. The tribunal may, however, in its decision direct that a higher proportion of costs shall be borne by one of the two Contracting Parties, and this award shall be binding on both Contracting Parties. The tribunal shall determine its own procedure.

(Ibid.)

Article 8 of the Agreement for the Promotion and Protection of Investments between the Governments of the UK and the Czech and Slovak Federal Republic, signed on 10 July 1990, reads as follows:

ARTICLE 8
Settlement of Disputes between an Investor and a Host State

(1) Disputes between an investor of one Contracting Party and the other Contracting Party concerning an obligation of the latter under Articles 2(3), 4, 5 and 6 of this Agreement in relation to an investment of the former which have not been amicably settled shall, after a period of four months from written notification of a claim, be submitted to arbitration under paragraph (2) below if either party to the dispute so wishes.

(2) Where the dispute is referred to arbitration, the investor concerned in the dispute shall have the right to refer the dispute either to:
  (a) an arbitrator or *ad hoc* arbitral tribunal to be appointed by a special agreement or established and conducted under the Arbitration Rules of the United Nations Commission on International Trade Law; the parties to the dispute may agree in writing to modify these Rules, or
  (b) the Institute of Arbitration of the Chamber of Commerce of Stockholm, or
  (c) the Court of Arbitration of the Federal Chamber of Commerce and Industry in Vienna.

(3) The arbitrator or arbitral tribunal to which the dispute is referred under paragraph (2) shall, in particular, base its decision on the provisions of this Agreement.

(Cm. 1306)

Part Twelve: II. H.1. *Pacific settlement of disputes—modes of settlement—judicial settlement—the International Court of Justice*

In the course of a speech in the Sixth Committee of the UN General Assembly on 16 October 1990, the UK representative, Mr A. Aust, stated:

I have listened with interest to suggestions made during the present debate that consideration should be given to the proposal, made by the Secretary-General in his report to the General Assembly on the work of the Organisation, that he should be authorised to request Advisory Opinions of the International Court of Justice. There are already various organs of the United Nations, and other bodies within the United Nations system, who can seek such Opinions. Under Article 96, paragraph 1, of the Charter, the General Assembly or the Security Council may request one. Under paragraph 2, other organs of the United Nations and specialised agencies may also request Advisory Opinions on legal questions arising within the scope of their activities, if they are so authorised by the General Assembly. ECOSOC, the Trusteeship Council, the Committee on Applications for Review of Administrative Tribunal Judgments, as well as many specialised agencies of the United Nations and the International Atomic Energy Agency, have all been authorised, in varying degrees, to seek Advisory Opinions.

Although we are still considering the matter, there do seem to be two particular problems inherent in any proposal that the Secretary-General should himself be authorised to seek Advisory Opinions.

First, the Secretary-General is, unlike those who have already been authorised by the General Assembly to seek Advisory Opinions, not a body composed of Member States. Although the Secretariat is a principal organ of the United Nations, it is headed by a single person. The desirability of authorising him to seek Advisory Opinions direct, without having to obtain the agreement of Member States, needs to be considered most carefully.

Secondly, perhaps an even more difficult problem relates to the Secretary-General's suggestion that he should be authorised to seek Advisory Opinions on the legal aspects of a *dispute* between States. This would, in his view, greatly add to the means of peaceful solution of international crisis situations. He points to the complementary relationship between the Security Council and the Secretary-General, and the fact that almost all situations bearing upon international peace and security require the strenuous exercise of the good offices of the Secretary-General. That may be so, but our preliminary reaction to the proposal is that it might be inappropriate for the Secretary-General, on his own initiative, to seek an Advisory Opinion regarding a dispute between States. If the States in dispute are themselves unwilling to submit the matter to the Court, is it right that the Secretary-General should do so on his own initiative? Will those States—especially the one which 'loses'—be more, or less, inclined to accept the Opinion of the Court? All this needs careful thought. In this connection, there is also the question as to the extent to which it is proper for the International Court of Justice to give an Advisory Opinion regarding a dispute between States. Only one Opinion so far (the one in 1975 dealing with Western Sahara) seems to fall into that category, and the circumstances there were rather special.

But having said all that, we believe that it may well be worth studying the matter further to see if there is scope for seeking more Advisory Opinions of the Court, and the circumstances in which they might be sought.

(Text provided by the FCO; see also A/C. 6/45/SR. 16, p. 11)

Part Twelve: II.I.1. *Pacific settlement of disputes—modes of settlement— settlement within international organizations—the United Nations*

On 10 October 1990, the Twelve Member States of the EC issued a statement about the shooting of demonstrators in Jerusalem by Israeli security forces. The statement read in part:

The tragic events in Jerusalem underline once again the need for a settlement of the Palestinian problem in accordance with justice.

The Community and its member states reaffirm their commitment to a just, comprehensive and lasting solution to the Arab-Israeli conflict and to this end they support the principle of the convening of an international peace conference under the auspices of the United Nations.

(Text provided by the FCO)

Part Twelve: II.I. 2. *Pacific settlement of disputes—modes of settlement— settlement within international organizations—organizations other than the UN*

In explaining his abstention on 17 January 1990 on a UN Security Council Resolution concerning a breach of the inviolability of Nicaraguan diplomatic premises by the US, the UK Permanent Representative, Sir Crispin Tickell, stated:

The Council will recall the terms of Article 52(2) in Chapter VIII of the Charter, where members are urged to make every effort to achieve pacific settlement of disputes through regional arrangements or by regional agencies before referring them to the Security Council. This is precisely what happened over the present incident. The question it raised was well and truly dealt with in a resolution adopted by the appropriate regional agency—the Organization of American States—on 8 January.

The matter is therefore closed. We see no reason to re-open it in the Security Council. In our view, it causes no threat to international peace and security nor provides any basis for a Security Council resolution under Chapter VI of the Charter.

(S/PV. 2905, pp. 34–5)

Part Thirteen: I.A. *Coercion and counter-measures short of the use of force—unilateral acts—retorsion*

(See Part Thirteen: I. B., below)

Part Thirteen: I.B. *Coercion and counter-measures short of the use of force—unilateral acts—non-forcible reprisals*

(See also Part Eleven: II. A. 6. (item of 5 March 1990), above)

In the course of the HC Standing Committee debate on the Aviation and Maritime Security Bill, the Minister for Public Transport, Mr Michael Portillo, referred to a new clause introduced by the Government. He went on:

It provides the Secretary of State with the power to take action against foreign-registered aircraft that land in the United Kingdom from a state that has banned UK registered civil aircraft from its airspace in breach of an international agreement between that state and this country. It will enable the Secretary of State to direct that access to the aircraft should be restricted, except for access needed to prepare the aircraft for its flight out of the UK.

The clause makes it an offence to fail to comply with a direction, intentionally to obstruct any one acting under a direction or to enter an aircraft without lawful authority or reasonable excuse for some other purpose than is provided for by the direction.

.   .   .

When a foreign country, in defiance of international convention, has decided to exclude our aircraft from its air space, it is naturally assumed that that country's aircraft will be excluded from entering our air space. Therefore, the Secretary of State would allow an aircraft from a country that had taken such action against our aircraft to land here only in exceptional circumstances.

.   .   .

The hon. Member . . . asked whether we had considered carefully the implications of the international convention. We have considered that aspect most carefully and are satisfied that the provision is consistent with the Chicago convention. The hon. Gentleman must bear in mind that we are dealing here with countries that have forbidden United Kingdom-registered aircraft to enter their airspace, in contravention of international agreements.

(HC Debs., 1989–90, Standing Committee A: Aviation and Maritime Security Bill, cols. 171–3, *passim*: 20 February 1990)

Part Thirteen: I.C. *Coercion and counter-measures short of the use of force—unilateral acts—pacific blockade*

(See Part Thirteen: II. A., below)

Part Thirteen: I.D. *Coercion and counter-measures short of the use of force—unilateral acts—other unilateral acts, including self-defence*

In reply to a question, the Parliamentary Under-Secretary of State, FCO, wrote:

In the joint statement issued after the Anglo-Argentine talks in Madrid last October, a copy of which, as I stated in my reply of 20 October to my right hon. Friend, the Member for Guildford (Mr. Howell), was placed in the Library of the House, it was announced that two small changes to the Falkland Islands protection zone would be made:
(a) the limits of the protection zone would be aligned with that of the Falkland Islands Interim Conservation and Management Zone, reducing its size slightly in the South West corner;
(b) the requirement that Argentine merchant shipping should not enter the protection zone without prior agreement would be dispensed with.
These changes subsequently came into effect on 1 December and 1 January respectively.

(HC Debs., vol. 165, Written Answers, cols. 798–9: 25 January 1990)

In reply to a question, the Minister of State, FCO, wrote in part:

Our policy is to support the sale of British military equipment overseas wherever this is compatible with the UK's political, strategic and security interests. This policy is based on the right of other countries to protect their independence and to exercise their rights to self-defence as embodied in Article 51 of the UN Charter. Our stringent licensing controls on all arms exports will continue to be carefully applied.

(HL Debs., vol. 515, col. 694: 6 February 1990)

Interviewed on 2 August 1990 about Iraq's invasion of Kuwait earlier that day, the Secretary of State for Foreign and Commonwealth Affairs, Mr Douglas Hurd, stated:

There [are] . . . some immediate things which need to be done. The Bank of England and the Treasury are arranging for the immediate freezing of Kuwaiti assets in this country. Iraq has virtually no assets in this country. The urgency is to freeze the Kuwaiti assets so as to prevent any puppet regime which may be installed in Kuwait from getting hold of them and transferring them. The Kuwaiti Ambassador asked us to take this action this morning and we are doing so.

(Text provided by the FCO)

Part Thirteen: II. A. *Coercion and counter-measures short of the use of force—collective measures—regime of the UN*

In a statement dated 4 August 1990 about Iraq's invasion of Kuwait, the Twelve Member States of the EC declared:

In order to safeguard the interests of the legitimate Government of Kuwait they have decided to take steps to protect all assets belonging directly or indirectly to the state of Kuwait.

The Community and its member states confirm their full support for UN Security Council Resolution N 660 and call on Iraq to comply with the provisions of that Resolution. If the Iraqi authorities fail so to comply, the Community and its member states will work for, support and implement a Security Council Resolution to introduce mandatory and comprehensive sanctions.

As of now, they have decided to adopt the following:
- an embargo on oil imports from Iraq and Kuwait
- appropriate measures aimed at freezing Iraqi assets in the territory of member states
- an embargo on sales of arms and other military equipment to Iraq
- the suspension of any cooperation in the military sphere with Iraq
- the suspension of technical and scientific cooperation with Iraq
- the suspension of the application to Iraq of the System of Generalised Preferences

(Text provided by the FCO)

Speaking in the UN Security Council on 9 August 1990, the UK Permanent Representative, Sir Crispin Tickell, stated:

Members of the Council may wish to know that four orders to give effect to Security Council resolution 661 (1990) under British law in the United Kingdom and our dependent Territories, and as regards British nationals and companies overseas, entered into force at midnight last night. In short, we have now given legislative effect within our territories to the provisions of Security Council resolution 661 (1990).

(S/PV. 2934, p. 17)

The following FCO press release was issued on 31 August 1990:

THE IRAQ AND KUWAIT (UNITED NATIONS SANCTIONS) (AMEND-MENT) ORDER 1990
THE IRAQ AND KUWAIT (UNITED NATIONS SANCTIONS) (CHAN-NEL ISLANDS) ORDER 1990

These Orders were made under the United Nations Act 1946 by Her Majesty in Council on 29 August 1990 and come into force at midnight (00.01 BST) on 30 August 1990.

The first, 'the Amendment Order', amends the Iraq and Kuwait (United Nations Sanctions) Order 1990 ('the Sanctions Order') which imposed restrictions on exports of goods from and supplies of goods to Iraq and Kuwait, pursuant to the UN Security Council Resolution No 661. The principal amendment is the imposition of a prohibition on payments under any bond in respect of a contract the performance of which is unlawful by virtue of the Sanctions Order or the Export of Goods (Control) (Iraq and Kuwait Sanctions) Order 1990 and a prohibition on payments under certain indemnities arising under such bonds. The Amendment Order also extends certain enforcement powers conferred by the Sanctions Order (applicable to ships and aircraft) to land transport vehicles used for carriage of goods from, or destined for, Iraq or Kuwait and makes minor and clarifying amendments to the Sanctions Order.

The second order, 'the Channel Islands Order', completes the implementation of Security Council Resolution in the Channel Islands by making similar provision there as has been made for the United Kingdom. The effect is that no goods can be imported into the Channel Islands from Iraq or Kuwait, restrictions are imposed on exports from Iraq and Kuwait and on the supply of goods to Iraq and Kuwait and on dealings with goods which have been exported therefrom; carriage of goods exported from Iraq and Kuwait, or destined for either country, is restricted; and the same restrictions imposed on payments under bonds and indemnities under the Amendment Order are applied in the Channel Islands.

Provision is made for investigation and enforcement and for the imposition of penalties and obtaining of evidence for criminal proceedings. The Channel Islands Order applies to activities in Guernsey and Jersey and to activities carried on elsewhere by British citizens ordinarily resident there and companies incorporated under the law of any part of the Channel Islands; the restrictions concerning carriage of goods apply to ships registered in the Channel Islands, wherever they are, and to aircraft registered in the United Kingdom and land transport vehicles in the Channel Islands.

(FCO Press Release No. 183 of 1990)

In reply to the question what steps were being taken to ensure that sanctions against Iraq are not breached by the maintenance of air transport links, the Minister of State, FCO, wrote:

Security Council resolution 670, adopted on 25 September, is designed to ensure that the embargo against Iraq is not breached by means of air transport. The resolution confirms that Security Council resolution 661 applies to all means of transport, including aircraft; requires all States to deny take-off rights to any aircraft carrying cargo other than food in humanitarian circumstances or medical supplies; and requires all States to deny overflight to aircraft destined for Iraq or Kuwait unless such aircraft land for inspection, have been approved by the sanctions committee, or are carrying supplies intended for UN forces. A number of aircraft have already landed for inspection under the terms of the resolution.

(HC Debs., vol. 177, Written Answers, col. 744: 15 October 1990)

In reply to a question, the Minister for Trade wrote:

The restrictions introduced since 2 August on trade with Iraq agreed at international forums are as follows:

6 August
United Nations Security Council Resolution (UNSCR) 661 was adopted imposing sanctions against Iraq and Kuwait.

8 August
Council Regulation (EEC) No. 2340/90 was made preventing trade by the Community as regards Iraq and Kuwait. Equivalent provision was made as regards products covered by the ECSC Treaty.

25 August
UNSCR 665 was adopted authorising the multinational forces navies to halt shipping in order to inspect and verify cargoes.

25 September
UNSCR 670 was adopted introducing measures to tighten the air embargo, and detain or deny entry to Iraqi registered ships breaching sanctions.

The measures adopted by the United Kingdom are as follows:

2 August
The Control of Gold, Securities, Payments and Credits (Kuwait) Directions 1990 were made.

4 August
The Control of Gold, Securities, Payments and Credits (Republic of Iraq) Dirctions 1990 were made.
The United Kingdom amended the Open General Import Licence to impose restrictions on the import of crude oil and petroleum products originating in Iraq or Kuwait.

8 August
The Iraq Kuwait (United Nations Sanctions) Order 1990 was made. It prohibits activities in connection with the exportation of goods from Iraq or Kuwait and the supply of goods to Iraq or Kuwait or Iraqi or Kuwaiti controlled companies except under the authority of a licence.
The Export of Goods (Control) (Iraq and Kuwait Sanctions) Order 1990 was made. It prohibits exportation from the United Kingdom of all goods to Iraq or Kuwait or to any other destination for the purposes of any business carried on in Iraq or Kuwait, except under the authority of a licence.
An amendment was made to the open general import licence of 4 December 1987 prohibiting the importation into the United Kingdom of goods originating in Iraq or Kuwait.

29 August

The Iraq and Kuwait (United Nations Sanctions) (Amendment) Order 1990 was made. It made minor amendments to the Iraq and Kuwait (United Nations Sanctions) Order and prohibits, except under a licence, payments under bonds in respect of a contract the performance of which is unlawful as a result of the sanctions.

5 October

The Iraq and Kuwait (United Nations Sanctions) (No. 2) Order 1990 was made. It imposes restrictions on aircraft overflying the United Kingdom where their destination is Iraq or Kuwait. The Order also imposes restrictions on ships registered in Iraq entering ports in the United Kingdom.

Similar provision has been made in respect of the Channel Islands, the Isle of Man and the Dependent Territories.

(HC Debs., vol. 178, Written Answers cols. 48–9 : 22 October 1990)

In reply to a question on the subject of the Middle East, the Parliamentary Under-Secretary of State, FCO, wrote:

The Security Council has passed 11 resolutions on the middle east since 2 August. The United Kingdom voted for them all, and was closely involved with each initiative, either as a permanent member of the Security Council or as president of the Security Council for the month of October.

Resolution No.	Subject
SCR 660 (adopted 2 August)	Condemned invasion and called for immediate and unconditional Iraqi withdrawal.
SCR 661 (6 August)	Imposed sanctions.
SCR 662 (9 August)	Decided annexation of Kuwait by Iraq null and void.
SCR 664 (18 August)	Reaffirmed rights of third state nationals, including the right to leave.
SCR 665 (25 August)	Authorised measures to halt shipping in order to inspect and verify cargoes.
SCR 666 (13 September)	Established system to permit food imports to Iraq and Kuwait in humanitarian circumstances.
SCR 667 (16 September)	Condemned Iraqi attacks against diplomatic premises and personnel.
SCR 669 (24 September)	Called on Sanctions Committee to consider requests for economic assistance under Article 50 of UN Charter
SCR 670 (25 September)	Measures to tighten air embargo and detain or deny entry to Iraqi-registered ships.

Resolution No.	Subject
SCR 672 (12 October)	Condemning acts of violence by Israeli Security Forces at the Temple Mount on 8 October, calling on Israel to abide by the Fourth Geneva Convention, and requesting the Secretary-General to report to the Council on the mission he had decided to send to the region.
SCR 673 (24 October)	Calling on Israel to accept the Secretary-General's Mission.

(HC Debs., vol. 178, Written Answers, col. *386* : 29 October 1990)

The following FCO press release was issued on 1 November 1990:

THE IRAQ AND KUWAIT (UNITED NATIONS SANCTIONS) (SECOND AMENDMENT) ORDER 1990

This order was made under the United Nations Act 1946 by Her Majesty in Council on 31 October 1990 and came into force on 1 November.

The above order further amends the Iraq and Kuwait (United Nations Sanctions) Order 1990 (the principal Order) by strengthening the enforcement provisions of the principal Order. The maximum term of imprisonment for the more serious offences against the Order is increased from two to five years and some of the less serious offences against the Order are now triable summarily (ie in a Magistrate's Court with a maximum penalty of six months' imprisonment or a fine of up to £2,000, or both). All offences against the Order are now made arrestable offences. The Order also makes a few minor amendments to the principal Order designed to clarify the text and remove inconsistencies.

(FCO Press Release No. 225 of 1990)

Part Thirteen: II. B. *Coercion and counter-measures short of the use of force—collective measures—outside the UN*

In reply to a question, the Minister of State, FCO, wrote in part:

Export controls in the United Kingdom are designed to ensure that companies do not act in contravention of our international commitments, including those under the missile technology control regime. Appropriate legal action is taken against any company which is found to infringe these controls.

. . .

Controls under the regime remain the national responsibility of each participating country.

(HC Debs., vol. 165, Written Answers, col. *56* : 15 January 1990)

In reply to a question, the Minister of State, FCO, wrote:

The following measures adopted by EC partners relate to trade with South Africa:

—A rigorously controlled embargo on exports of arms and para-military equipment to South Africa.
—A rigorously controlled embargo on imports of arms and para-military equipment from South Africa.

—The cessation of oil exports to South Africa.

—The cessation of exports of sensitive equipment destined for the police and armed forces of South Africa.

—The prohibition of all new collaboration in the nuclear sector.

—A ban on imports of certain South African gold coins.

—A ban on certain new investment in South Africa.

—A ban on the import of iron and steel.

Certain of these measures were enacted by the European Communities under the Community treaties, whereas others amongst them were adopted by the member states outside the Community treaties as such.

(HC Debs., vol. 167, Written Answers, col. 327: 15 February 1990)

In reply to a further question, the same Minister wrote:

We have implemented a variety of restrictive measures on our trade and other relations with a number of countries. These include:

(a) controls through COCOM on the export of high technology equipment which could be used for military as well as civil purposes to a number of proscribed destinations, including to the Soviet Union, eastern Europe and China COCOM comprises the NATO countries, less Iceland, as well as Japan and Australia.

(b) restrictive measures against South Africa. I refer the hon. Member to the reply I gave . . . on 15 February 1990 for a list of the measures adopted by the UN in conjunction with the European Community. We have also agreed with the Commonwealth a number of measures. These are:

   (i) The strict enforcement of the mandatory arms embargo against South Africa;

   (ii) A re-affirmation of the Gleneagles declaration of 1977, which called upon Commonwealth members to take every practical step to discourage sporting contacts with South Africa;

   (iii) Agreement upon and commendation to other Governments of the adoption of the following further economic measures against South Africa:

      (a) A ban on all new Government loans to the Government of South Africa and their agencies;

      (b) A readiness to take unilaterally what action may be possible to preclude the import of Krugerrands;

      (c) No Government funding for trade missions to South Africa or for participation in exhibitions and trade fairs in South Africa;

      (d) A ban on the sale and export of computer equipment capable of use by South African military forces, police or security forces;

      (e) A ban on new contracts for the sale and export of nuclear goods, materials and technology to South Africa;

      (f) A ban on the sale and export of oil to South Africa;

      (g) A strict and rigorously controlled embargo on imports of arms, ammunition, military vehicles and paramilitary equipment from South Africa;

      (h) An embargo on all military co-operation with South Africa;

      (i) The discouragement of all cultural and scientific events except

where these contribute towards the ending of apartheid or have no
possible role in promoting it;

(*j*) A voluntary ban on the promotion of tourism to South Africa;

(*l*) The implementation of any European Community decision to ban
the import of coal, iron and steel and of gold coins from South
Africa.

(*c*) Restrictions not aimed at particular countries, such as those of the missile
technology control regime, resulting from our commitment to nuclear non-
proliferation, and controls on the export of material used in production of
chemical weapons.

(*d*) Special restrictions are applied to arms exports to certain countries, for
example, in the middle east, reflecting our wish not to fuel or prolong conflicts
in the region, and our determination to take a firm line on state-sponsored terrorism.

(HC Debs., vol. 167, Written Answers, cols, *564–5*: 19 February 1990)

At a FCO news conference given on 18 September 1990 it was stated:

In line with the decision taken by EC Foreign Ministers at their meeting on 17
September we were now imposing travel restrictions on Iraqi diplomats in London. The restrictions would take effect from 20 September, and would require
Iraqi officials to seek permission to travel beyond a 25 miles radius of Central London (Charing Cross).

(Text provided by the FCO)

The Twelve Member States of the EC issued a declaration on 18 September 1990 in which they stated:

The Community and its member states already stated clearly that they consider
all acts perpetrated against one or more among them as committed against all. In
response to new very grave illegal acts against their embassies in Kuwait, and taking into account the measures already taken by some member states, they have
decided of one accord to expel the military personnel attached to the Iraqi Embassies and to limit the freedom of movement of the other members of their staff.

(Text provided by the FCO)

Part Fourteen: I. A. 5. *Use of force—international war and armed conflict—resort to war—termination of war, treaties of peace*

In reply to a question, the Minister of State, FCO, wrote:

The treaty on the final settlement with respect to Germany settles definitively
matters arising out of the Second World War as between the parties to the treaty.
There will be no separate peace treaty.

(HC Debs., vol. 177, Written Answers, col. *899*: 18 October 1990)

Part Fourteen: I. B. 1. *Use of force—international war and armed conflict—the laws of war and armed conflict—sources and sanctions*

In the course of the HC Standing Committee debate on the War Crimes
Bill, the Minister of State, Home Office, Mr John Patten, stated:

The term 'the laws and customs of war' is not, as it might appear to new readers, a general and vague phrase. It is well known and widely accepted in international law.

(HC Debs., 1989–90, Standing Committee A: War Crimes Bill, col. 30; 29 March 1990)

Later in the debate, the Minister of State observed:

At the conclusion of last Thursday's proceedings, Hon. Members on both sides of the Committee had described what they saw as a need for a precise definition of what is meant by 'the laws and customs' of war. . . .

I shall explain why a precise definition is neither possible nor necessary. . . . at the end of our previous sitting I was attempting to describe the place of the fourth Hague convention of 1907 in the development of the concept of the 'laws and custom' of war. I said . . . that the regulations annexed to the convention, which are known as the Hague rules, set out a wide range of activities that were banned in the ordinary course of war. . . . The Hague rules provide a start for assessing what was meant by the 'laws and customs' of war, but they do not allow a conclusion to be drawn.

We cannot, through this legislation, confer on the courts the jurisdiction to try breaches of the 'laws and customs' of war as that term was understood at the time of the second world war simply by reference to the Hague rules. That is because, by the time of the outbreak of war—about which the Committee agrees that the date given in the Bill is correct—the specific regulations in the Hague rules applied only to those states that were party to the Hague convention. In the years between 1907 and September 1939, those regulations had been subsumed into a wider and unwritten set of principles. Crucially, what might be termed customary international law was at that time considered to apply to all civilised nations, whether or not they were party to the convention. I shall say more about that in a moment, but those principles had been embodied in the military manuals of both the United Kingdom and Germany. In September 1939 that set of principles was known as the 'laws and customs' of war and subsumed all the specific recommendations of the Hague rules.

(Ibid., col. 33; 3 April 1990)

The Minister later stated:

I wish to refer the Committee to paragraph 5.18 of the Hetherington-Chalmers report. It deals with the 'general participation' clause in article 2 of the 1907 convention. The report quotes that clause:
'The provisions contained in the regulations (Rules of Land Warfare) referred to in Article 1 as well as in the present Convention do not apply except between contracting powers, and then only if all the belligerents are parties to the Convention.'
Several of the belligerents during the second world war were not party to the convention. For example, Italy was not. The inquiry commented that the Nuremberg tribunal
'did not consider itself limited by the terms of the 1907 Convention since customary international law also considered the acts defined in the Charter to be 'war crimes' even though not all of the belligerent parties in the Second World War had become party to the Hague Conventions.'

It is important to note the use of the phrase 'customary international law'. I remind the Committee . . . that customary international law, as it applies to war crimes, is not unique. We have customary law of the sea and, until it was codified, we had customary law of space. Much customary international law demonstrates that these provisions are not unique. Indeed, we would have serious questions to answer if we were introducing a unique provision.

The insertion in clause 1 of a reference to the 'Hague Convention of 1907' and, therefore, to the requirements of international law in 1907 instead of those developed in 1939, could raise numerous difficult questions about the fairness of defining 'laws and customs' of war by referring to a convention that applies to wars in which all belligerents are parties to the convention. That was not the case in the second world war. Some of the allied forces—the Australians, the Canadians and the South Africans—were not party to the 1907 Hague Convention.

(Ibid., cols. 35–6)

Part Fourteen: I. B. 5. *Use of force—international war and armed conflict—the laws of war and armed conflict—distinction between combatants and non-combatants*

Speaking in an emergency debate in the House of Commons on the subject of the situation in the Gulf, the Secretary of State for Defence, Mr Tom King, referred to British nationals held against their will in Kuwait and Iraq. He went on:

. . . a considerable number of those hostages are non-combatant British service men who were part of the British liaison training team serving in Kuwait. They were not involved in the hostilities. They are properly defined under international law as non-combatants.

(HC Debs., vol. 177, col. 842: 7 September 1990)

Part Fourteen: I. B. 6. *Use of force—international war and armed conflict—the laws of war and armed conflict—humanitarian law*

(See also Part One: II.C. and Part Four: III. (items of 6 September, 10 September, 28 September 1990), above, and Part Fourteen: I. B. 7. (material on Israeli occupied territories), below)

In the course of a speech on 1 February 1990 in the UN Commission on Human Rights, the UK representative, Mr H. Steel, stated:

Before any lasting peace could be achieved it was essential to create a better climate of trust and mutual confidence between Israelis and Palestinians. A major obstacle to the creation of such a climate was Israel's continuing refusal to acknowledge that the provisions of the relevant international agreements were applicable to the occupied territories. His Government, like those of the other members of the European Community, was convinced that the Hague Convention of 1907 and the Fourth Geneva Convention of 1949 were applicable.

His delegation was therefore seriously concerned at the many Israeli practices and policies which contravened those Conventions, such as the creation of settlements in the territories in question in contravention of article 49 of the Fourth

Geneva Convention; the violation of individual rights, in contravention of article 27 of that Convention; the widespread and indiscriminate use of administrative detention; and the deportation of Palestinians from the territories and refusal to accept the return of persons previously deported.

(E/CN. 4/1990/SR. 5, p. 15)

In reply to a question on the subject of the occupied West Bank and Gaza, the Minister of State, FCO, Mr William Waldergrave, said:

We take a close interest in Israeli human rights practices in the occupied territories, in accordance with our rights as a signatory to the fourth Geneva convention.

(HC Debs., vol. 166, col. 884: 7 February 1990)

In reply to a question, the Minister of State, FCO, wrote:

We frequently remind the Israelis of our view that, pending their withdrawal, they should administer the occupied territories in accordance with international law and their human rights obligations.

(HC Debs., vol. 169, Written Answers, col. *35*: 12 March 1990; see also ibid., vol. 171, Written Answers, col. *241*: 25 April 1990)

In the course of a statement on the subject of the conflict in Liberia issued on 26 April 1990 by the Presidency of the EC, it was observed:

Killings have been committed both by members of the Liberian armed forces and those opposed to the Government. While condemning violence from whatever quarter, the Twelve believe that the armed forces have a responsibility to respect human rights and to act at all times in a disciplined manner.

(Text provided by the FCO)

Speaking in an emergency debate in the House of Lords on the subject of the Gulf, the Minister of State, FCO, the Earl of Caithness, stated:

We have also been in contact with the International Red Cross, which shares our view that Iraq's action is in contravention of the Geneva conventions on treatment of civilians.

(HL Debs., vol. 521, col. 1798: 6 September 1990)

On 10 October 1990 the Twelve Member States of the EC issued a statement on the subject of the shooting of demonstrators in Jerusalem by Israeli security forces. The statement read in part:

The Community and its member states consider unacceptable and once more strongly deplore the use of excessive force by the Israeli occupying forces in repressing Palestinian demonstrations, against a background of repeated violations of international law, in particular as regards the Geneva Convention on the protection of civilians in wartime.

(Text provided by the FCO)

In reply to a question, the Minister of State, FCO, wrote in part:

Iraq has a clear obligation under international law to allow the International Committee of the Red Cross (ICRC) to exercise its humanitarian mandate.

(HC Debs., vol. 177, Written Answers, col. 754: 15 October 1990)

The UN Security Council on 29 October 1990 adopted Resolution 674 (1990), which in its preamble reaffirmed that:

the Fourth Geneva Convention applies to Kuwait and that as a High Contracting Party to the Convention Iraq is bound to comply fully with all its terms and in particular is liable under the Convention in respect of the grave breaches committed by it, as are individuals who commit or order the commission of grave breaches . . .

Speaking in his capacity as UK Permanent Representative, the President of the Security Council, Sir Crispin Tickell, stated:

On the question of human rights, evidence of a horrific and really unpleasant kind is emerging from Kuwait. Many people have been subject to arbitrary arrest; there have been beatings and killings by the occupying forces. That alone justifies the need for States to collate all the information they have on grave breaches of the Fourth Geneva Convention and of international law, as set out in operative paragraph 2 of the resolution the Council has just adopted.

(S/PV. 2951, p. 92)

Speaking in the UN Security Council on 28 November 1990 in a debate on a draft resolution which was then adopted as Resolution 677 (1990), the UK Permanent Representative, Sir David Hannay, stated:

The Council has repeatedly reminded Iraq in recent weeks of its obligations under international humanitarian law, including the Fourth Geneva Convention. It did so most recently in resolution 674 (1990), adopted on 29 October. Yet the accounts we have heard of the murder and pillage perpetrated by the Iraqi occupation forces in Kuwait show that Iraq has persistently acted with a callous disregard of the Convention. Far from observing its responsibility under article 29 for the treatment of protected persons under its control, Iraq is engaged in a determined campaign to expunge the very identity of the State of Kuwait.

The Iraqis have made life so unbearable that half the indigenous population have left, public and private property has been looted and the Iraqis have even tried to destroy Kuwait's public records. All over Kuwait, Kuwaitis are being replaced by Iraqis. We have reports that Iraqi soldiers have stripped Kuwaitis of all documentary evidence of their nationality: birth certificates, marriage certificates, passports. This amounts to an attempt by Iraq to change the demographic structure of the country it occupies, in violation of the Fourth Geneva Convention.

The basic principle of the Geneva Conventions is that protected persons shall be protected and treated humanely in all circumstances.

Sir David then recited some accounts of incidents in Kuwait. He continued:

Article 32 of the Fourth Geneva Convention specifically prohibits murder and torture.

Having recited some further accounts, Sir David went on:

Article 147 of the Fourth Geneva Convention designates certain actions as grave breaches. These include: wilful killing, torture or inhumane treatment, wilfully causing great suffering or serious injury to body or health, the taking of hostages, the unlawful confinement of a protected person, and wilfully depriving a protected person of the right to a fair trial. These grave breaches come under the criminal jurisdiction of all the parties to the Conventions and as such have been elevated to the status of international crimes. There is evidence that all these things have happened in Kuwait since 2 August.

(S/PV. 2962, pp. 3–7, *passim*)

Part Fourteen: I. B. 7. *Use of force—international war and armed conflict—the laws of war and armed conflict—belligerent occupation*

The following statement was released on 31 January 1990 by the Twelve Member States of the EC:

The Twelve members of the European Community are seriously concerned at recent suggestions that immigrants to Israel may be settled in the Occupied Territories. In this context, the Twelve recall their long-standing view that the Jewish settlements in the Occupied Territories, including East Jerusalem, are illegal.

While the Twelve warmly welcome the liberalisation of Soviet emigration controls, including the freedom of Soviet Jews to emigrate to Israel and elsewhere, they hope that the Israeli Government will not jeopardise the prospects for bringing peace to the region by either allowing or encouraging Jewish immigrants to settle in the Occupied Territories.

(Text provided by the FCO)

In a statement made on 20 February 1990, the Twelve Member States of the EC declared in part:

The Twelve reiterate their view that Jewish settlements in the Occupied Territories, including East Jerusalem, are illegal under international law.

(Text provided by the FCO)

In reply to the question whether Her Majesty's Government will make it its policy to oppose any increase in Jewish settlement in East Jerusalem, the Minister of State, FCO, wrote:

Yes. We regard Jewish settlements in the Occupied Territories, including East Jerusalem, as illegal.

(HC Debs., vol. 169, Written Answers, col. *449*: 19 March 1990; see also ibid., vol. 172, Written Answers, col. *382*: 15 May 1990; ibid., col. *410*: 16 May 1990; ibid., vol. 174, Written Answers, col. *254*: 13 June 1990; ibid., col. *300*: 14 June 1990)

In a speech in the UN Security Council of 29 March 1990, the UK representative, Mr Richardson, stated:

My Government has long made clear its condemnation of the practice of settling Israeli citizens in the occupied territories, including East Jerusalem. Such settlements are illegal under international law. They are, in particular, a flagrant violation of article 49 of the fourth Geneva Convention relative to the Protection of

Civilian Persons in Time of War, which clearly states that an occupying Power shall not transfer parts of its own civilian population into the territory it occupies. The United Kingdom is in no doubt that that Convention applies to the territories occupied by Israel since 1967, including East Jerusalem.

The practice of establishing illegal Israeli settlements in the occupied territories has been going for nearly a quarter of a century. There are now over 65,000 Jewish settlers in the West bank, some 3,000 in the Gaza Strip and some 80,000 in East Jerusalem. A further 9,000 have settled in the Golan Heights. Israel has consistently ignored Security Council and General Assembly resolutions calling for an end to this settlement programme.

This problem is now being aggravated by the arrival of Soviet Jews in the occupied territories. Let there be no misunderstanding about my Government's views. My Government warmly welcomes the liberalization of Soviet emigration controls, including the freedom of Soviet Jews to emigrate to Israel and elsewhere. The right of everyone to leave any country, including his own, is enshrined in the International Covenant on Civil and Political Rights.

(S/PV. 2915, pp. 11–12)

In reply to a question about the funding by Israel of intrusion into the traditional Christian sector of Jerusalem, the Minister of State, FCO, wrote:

We have made clear to the Israeli Government our concern at this provocative action, and reminded them of our view that all Jewish settlements in the occupied territories, including east Jerusalem, are illegal under international law.

(HC Debs., vol. 172, Written Answers, col. *183*: 10 May 1990)

In a speech to the UN Security Council on 25 May 1990, the UK Permanent Representative, Sir Crispin Tickell, stated:

My Government hopes that the latest tragedy will bring home to Israel how damaging for any prospect of peace is the expansion of Jewish settlements beyond the 1967 borders: in other words, the West Bank, the Gaza Strip, East Jerusalem, and the Golan Heights. Such settlements are illegal. They are no less illegal when the settlers are recent Soviet Jewish immigrants. We welcome the Soviet Government's new readiness to allow its Jewish citizens to leave for Israel or elsewhere if they so wish. But it would be a gross injustice if the freedom of Soviet Jews were to be at the expense of the rights, the homes and the land of the people of the occupied territories.

(S/PV. 2923, p. 66)

Speaking on 3 June 1990 in Jedda, following talks with Saudi Arabian and Jordanian leaders, the Secretary of State for Foreign and Commonwealth Affairs, Mr Douglas Hurd, stated in part:

We welcome the Soviet Union's more liberal emigration policy, which we have long urged: but the settlement of Soviet Jews in the Occupied Territories is unjust, illegal and a real danger to stability.

(FCO Press Release No. 135 of 1990)

In reply to a question on the same subject, the Minister of State, FCO, wrote:

As my right hon. Friend the Secretary of State made clear in the House on 13 June, east Jerusalem is, in our view, occupied territory. We have urged the Israelis to cease their settlement programme in the occupied territories. Such settlements are illegal, provocative and an obstacle to peace.

(HC Debs., vol. 175, Written Answers, col. *16*: 25 June 1990; see also ibid., vol. 174, Written Answers, col. *254*: 13 June 1990)

In the course of oral questions, the following questions were asked:

Will the Secretary of State take this opportunity to confirm to the Israeli Government that the United Kingdom Government's position is that east Jerusalem is occupied territory, and therefore that the provisions of the fourth Geneva convention on the protection of civilian persons in time of war apply absolutely and without exception? Will he also confirm that Israel's purported annexation of east Jerusalem is illegal and as such has no effect on the status of east Jerusalem as occupied territory; and that any measures that Israel purports to take to change the status of east Jerusalem are null and void?

In reply, the Minister of State, FCO, Mr William Waldergrave, stated:

That is the position of the British Government, yes.

(HC Debs., vol. 178, col. 329: 24 October 1990)

Speaking on 26 November 1990 in the Third Committee of the UN General Assembly, the Permanent Representative of Italy, on behalf of the EC and its Member States, stated:

The European Community and its Member States are increasingly concerned by the situation in the territories occupied by Israel. . . . The Twelve have not hesitated to denounce Israel's failure to comply with its obligations under the Fourth Geneva Convention.

(Text provided by the FCO; see also A/C. 3/45/SR. 52, p. 3)

In a speech to the UN Security Council on 5 December 1990, the UK Permanent Representative, Sir David Hannay, stated:

It is a recurrent theme of resolutions of this Council that the Fourth Geneva Convention applies to the occupied territories and that Israel must abide by its obligations under it. This is a matter to which my Government, along with its partners in the European Community, attaches the greatest importance. The point was reiterated in the declaration on the Middle East adopted by the European Council in Rome as recently as 27 and 28 October.

(S/PV. 2965, p. 7)

At a press conference given by the FCO on 17 December 1990, the FCO spokesman remarked:

Spokesman said that the British Government strongly deplored the Israeli Government's decision on 15 December to deport 4 Palestinians from the Gaza strip. Our position was well known: such deportations were illegal under international law.

(Text provided by the FCO; see also HC Debs., vol. 183, Written Answers, col. 282: 20 December 1990)

In reply to a question, the Parliamentary Under-Secretary of State, FCO, wrote in part:

The obligations of states party to the Fourth Geneva convention were reiterated by the Security Council in its resolution 674 with reference to the Iraqi occupation of Kuwait.

(HC Debs., vol. 183, Written Answers, col. 278: 20 December 1990)

Part Fourteen: I. B. 9. *Use of force—international war and armed conflict—the laws of war and armed conflict—nuclear, bacteriological and chemical weapons*

(See also Part Three: I. B. 5. (items of 6 June and 21 June 1990) and Part Six: VI., above)

The Twelve Member States of the EC issued the following statement on 20 April 1990:

The Twelve Member States of the European Community, considering that the acquisition of weapons of mass destruction by any state in the Middle East region can only lead to heightened tensions and an increased threat to peace and stability, deplore the threat recently made by Iraq to use chemical weapons. They urge all states to strengthen compliance with the 1925 Geneva Protocol on chemical weapons. They recall the Final Declaration of the 1989 Paris Conference in which the participating states recognised the importance and continuing validity of this protocol; solemnly affirmed their commitments not to use chemical weapons and to condemn such use; and expressed their determination to prevent any recourse to chemical weapons by completely eliminating them.

The Twelve are fully committed to the goal of a global, comprehensive convention to prohibit the development, production, possession and use of chemical weapons, which is currently under negotiation in the Conference on Disarmament in Geneva. They reiterate their call to all states to become parties to this Convention as soon as it is concluded. They consider that any threat to use chemical weapons is in contradiction with the purpose and spirit of these negotiations.

(Text provided by the FCO)

In reply to a question, the Minister of State, FCO, wrote:

The territories of the Falkland Islands, South Georgia and South Sandwich Islands, Cayman Islands, Turks and Caicos Islands, British Virgin Islands, Anguilla and Montserrat lie within the zone of application of the Treaty of Tlatelolco.

Only Latin American states can be full parties to the treaty. The United Kingdom has, however, signed and ratified both the additional protocols to the treaty. Under protocol 1 the United Kingdom, in the territories above, must use exclusively for peaceful purposes the nuclear material and facilities which are under its jurisdiction and prohibit and prevent:

(a) the testing, use, manufacture, production and acquisition by any means what-soever of any nuclear weapons directly or indirectly; and

(b) the receipt, storage, installation, deployment and any form of possession of any nuclear weapons, directly or indirectly.

Under protocol 2 the United Kingdom has undertaken not to contribute in any way to the performance of acts violating article 1 of the treaty itself in the states to which the treaty applies. Article 1 essentially prohibits and prevents those acts in (a) and (b) above.

(HC Debs., vol. 174, Written Answers, col. *41*: 11 June 1990)

In reply to a question, the Minister of State for the Armed Forces wrote:

The United Kingdom at all times complies with its obligation under the treaty of Tlatelolco not to deploy nuclear weapons in territories (including territorial and internal waters) which lie within the treaty's zone of application. It remains, how-ever, our invariable practice to neither confirm nor deny the presence of nuclear weapons on board particular ships at particular times.

(HC Debs., vol. 177, Written Answers, col. *296*: 25 July 1990)

In reply to a question, the Parliamentary Under-Secretary of State, Department of Energy, wrote:

The Government's policy continues to be that all civil nuclear material held in the United Kingdom is subject to Euratom safeguards under the Euratom treaty of 1957 and to the terms of the United Kingdom—Euratom—IAEA safeguards agreement of 6 September 1976—IAEA INFCIRC 263.

(HC Debs., vol. 177, Written Answers, col. *600*: 6 September 1990)

In reply to a question, the Minister of State, FCO, the Earl of Caithness, stated in part:

I assure the noble Lord that we rigorously observe our obligations under the NPT not to transfer nuclear weapons technology to any recipient whatever.

(HL Debs., vol. 522, col. 719: 16 October 1990)

In reply to a question, the Minister of State, FCO, wrote:

As a party to the Non-Proliferation Treaty (NPT), Iraq has undertaken not to acquire or manufacture nuclear weapons. It would clearly be a cause for the gravest concern internationally if any party were to ignore its obligations under the treaty.

(HL Debs., vol. 522, col. 877: 16 October 1990)

In reply to a question, the Minister of State, FCO, wrote:

The proposals resulting from the fourth non-proliferation treaty review confer-ence are currently being considered. Our policy will continue to be that all civil nuclear material held in the United Kingdom should be subject to Euratom safe-guards under the treaty of 1957 establishing the European Atomic Energy Community and to the terms of the UK/Euratom/IAEA safeguards agreement of September 1976.

(HC Debs., vol. 177, Written Answers, col. *903*: 18 October 1990)

In reply to the question what steps have been taken to ensure that the supply of nuclear reactors to Indonesia would not lead to the development of nuclear weapons, the Secretary of State for Energy wrote:

Indonesia is a party to the non-proliferation treaty. Any export of nuclear materials, equipment or technology would have to be fully consistent within our obligations under that treaty.

(HC Debs., vol. 178, Written Answers, col. *655*: 1 November 1990)

Part Fourteen: III. *Use of force—self-defence*

In the course of a debate in the UN Security Council on 9 August 1990 on the subject of Iraq's invasion of Kuwait, the UK Permanent Representative, Sir Crispin Tickell, spoke of the 'collective defence of the territory of Saudi Arabia and other threatened States in the area'. He continued:

We will do so in accordance with Article 51 of the Charter of the United Nations, which members will recall was specifically reaffirmed in the preamble to Security Council resolution 661 (1990).

(S/PV. 2934, p. 18)

The following letter, dated 13 August 1990, was addressed to the President of the UN Security Council by the UK Permanent Representative:

In accordance with Article 51 of the Charter of the United Nations, I wish on behalf of my Government to report that the United Kingdom has deployed military forces to the Gulf. These forces have been despatched in exercise of the inherent right of individual and collective self-defence, recognized in Article 51, in response to developments and requests from Governments in the region, including requests from Kuwait, Saudi Arabia and Bahrain for assistance and by agreement with Oman.

(S/21501)

Speaking at a press conference given by the FCO on 13 August 1990, the Minister of State, FCO, Mr William Waldegrave, stated:

. . . we have received today from the government of Kuwait a request for assistance under Article 51 of the United Nations Charter. I will read the central parts of it.
'I therefore request on behalf of my government and in the exercise of the inherent right of individual and collective self-defence that the Government of the United Kingdom take such military or other steps as are necessary to ensure that economic measures designed to restore our rights are effectively implemented.'
That request was received by Her Majesty's Ambassador in Saudi Arabia and we are minded to accept it and will be taking the necessary steps.

(Text provided by the FCO)

In reply to the question whether a further resolution of the Security Council would be necessary to approve such steps, the Minister of State declared:

No, the legal position is that under Article 51 we can take steps which Kuwait asks us to take to restore its sovereignty and independence. The principal weapon being used is the economic one under the Security Council Resolution but that is a completely separate legal matter. What the Kuwaitis are asking us to do is to reinforce the economic weapon which was put in place under the Security Council Resolution.

. . .

The United Nations has imposed economic sanctions. What Kuwait has asked us to do is to make sure that economic weapon is effective and that Article 51 gives us the right to do that and we are accepting that request.

(Ibid.)

Speaking in the UN Security Council on 25 August 1990 on the subject of a draft resolution which was then adopted as Resolution 665 (1990), the UK Permanent Representative, Sir Crispin Tickell, stated:

Tonight the international community has chosen the best course for dealing with such maritime breaches of economic sanctions, but I must remind the Council that sufficient legal authority to take action already exists under Article 51 of the Charter and the request which we and others have received from the Government of Kuwait. If necessary, we will use it.

(S/PV. 2938, p. 48)

In reply to the question whether it would be in order for the UK to take unilateral action in the Gulf in the light of the UN Security Council Resolution, the Minister of State, FCO, Mr William Waldegrave, stated in a radio interview on 4 September 1990:

. . . if the legal requirements were met, under Article 51, we could take further action but that would be a decision for the time and the conditions in which that decision had to be faced, not for now.

In response to the interviewer's question whether that might not be a matter of interpretation of Article 51 of the UN Charter, the Minister of State observed:

Well, I think our legal advice is clear on this but I don't want really to get into the game of hypothetical questions.

(Text provided by the FCO)

Speaking in an emergency debate in the House of Commons on the subject of the situation in the Gulf, the Prime Minister, Mrs. Margaret Thatcher, stated:

We have acted throughout in accordance with international law, and we shall continue to do so. Resolution 661, which called for comprehensive economic sanctions, expressly affirms the inherent right of individual or collective self-defence, in response to the armed attack by Iraq against Kuwait, in accordance with article 51 of the United Nations charter. We hope that economic sanctions will prove to be sufficient. That is why they must be strictly enforced. But we are not precluded by reason of any of the Security Council resolutions from exercising the inherent right of collective self-defence in accordance with the rules of international law.

(HC Debs., vol. 177, col. 737: 6 September 1990)

The Prime Minister, in response to an intervention, then stated:

I have made my position absolutely clear. May I repeat it? To undertake now to use no military force without the further authority of the Security Council would be to deprive ourselves of a right in international law expressly affirmed by resolution 661; it would be to do injustice to the people of Kuwait, who are unable to use effective force themselves; it would be to hand an advantage to Saddam Hussein; and it could put our own forces in greater peril. I have full legal authority for everything that I say on these matters, and for those reasons I am not willing to limit our legitimate freedom of action. I have made the position clear, and there is nothing further that I can add. For the reasons that I have given, I am not prepared to limit our legitimate freedom of action. If right hon. or hon. Members think to the contrary, I am sure that they will have time to put their views. My views have been approved by the topmost legal opinions that we can get.

(Ibid., cols. 737–8)

Later in the same debate, the Minister of State, FCO, Mr William Waldegrave, stated:

. . . there are three international grounds for military action: first, article 51, after a request from Kuwait; secondly, a response to an attack . . . ; thirdly, an explicit United Nations mandate. Any of those three would do.

(Ibid., col. 829)

He then observed:

We cannot rule out any action, so long as it is based—as it would be based, as the Leader of the Opposition made clear—on article 51 after a request from Kuwait.

(Ibid., col. 829)

Opening the emergency debate in the House of Lords, the Minister of State, FCO, the Earl of Caithness, stated:

Iraq has illegally invaded, occupied and attempted to annex Kuwait; our armed forces have been deployed in response to requests for assistance to deter further aggression by Saddam Hussein and under Article 51 of the UN Charter in pursuance of decisions of the Security Council intended to bring about Iraq's unconditional withdrawal.

(HL Debs., vol. 521, col. 1795: 6 September 1990)

He later observed:

The Government have co-ordinated with our American allies in planning a collective defensive response to the military threat from Iraq in accordance with Article 51 of the UN Charter and at the request of states in the region.

(Ibid., col. 1797)

Later in the debate, the Lord Privy Seal, Lord Belstead, stated:

Resolution 661 calling for comprehensive economic sanctions expressly affirms the inherent right of individual or collective self-defence in response to the armed attack by Iraq against Kuwait in accordance with Article 51 of the charter. We hope that economic sanctions will prove sufficient. That is why they must be strictly enforced. But we are not precluded by reason of any of the Security Council resolutions from exercising the inherent right of collective self-defence in accordance with the rules of international law. I simply say to your Lordships that to undertake now to use no military force without yet further authority of the Security Council would be quite simply to deprive ourselves of a right in international law already expressly affirmed by Security Council Resolution 661.

(Ibid., col. 1890: 6 September 1990)

During oral evidence taken before the Foreign Affairs Committee of the House of Commons on 24 October 1990 examining the Gulf crisis, one of the members made the following observation to the Secretary of State for Foreign and Commonwealth Affairs, Mr Douglas Hurd:

I think the Committee understands the position you have explained to the House, that you have a request from the Kuwait Government in fact by derogation, I suppose, or delegation, to exercise rights of self-defence under Article 51 of the United Nations Charter and that, therefore, no further legal means or resolutions is needed for military action to be taken to get Iraq out of Kuwait.

In response, Mr Hurd stated:

If it were decided—which it has not been—that the military option was the only way through, the only way of obtaining the objectives, then we do not have any doubt, as you explain, about the legal position . . .

(*Parliamentary Papers*, 1989–90, HC, Paper 655–ii, p. 39)

In reply to oral questions, the Government spokesman in the House of Lords, Lord Reay, stated:

. . . the multinational force deployed in the Gulf is not a United Nations force. The question of United Nations command does not arise, therefore. British and other forces have been deployed at the request of Saudi Arabia and other countries in accordance with the inherent right of individual or collective self-defence under Article 51 of the United Nations Charter. The British forces are under ultimate UK command.
. . . the important point is that in our view Article 51 of the United Nations Charter provides legal authority for the use of force in response to the armed attack on Kuwait.

(HL Debs., vol. 523, cols. 775–6, *passim*: 22 November 1990; see also ibid., vol. 524, Written Answers, col. 15: 5 December 1990)

In the course of a debate on the subject of the Gulf, the Secretary of State for Foreign and Commonwealth Affairs, Mr Douglas Hurd, was asked the question:

Is it the Government's view that article 51, plus the resolution passed by the Security Council last Thursday, constitute authority for the use of force by the United States, Britain and others without returning to the Security Council or to the House of Commons?

Mr Hurd replied:

Yes, it is. We believed, and Opposition Front Bench spokesmen agreed, that article 51 and the original request from the Kuwaitis provided a legal basis; the argument was about whether there should be an additional political basis. That has been supplied by resolution 678.

(HC Debs., vol. 182, col. 824: 11 December 1990)

He later observed:

The latest Security Council resolution, resolution 678, is not a bluff. The legal authority to use force has been there for some time, and the political authority has now been given by the Security Council. That is the strongest possible expression of collective security.

(Ibid., col. 831)

In the course of a debate on the subject of the Gulf crisis, the Lord Privy Seal, Lord Waddington, stated:

At the Kuwaiti Government's request for help we had a legal basis to drive Saddam Hussein out of Kuwait under Article 51 of the UN Charter.

(HL Debs., vol. 524, col. 650: 17 December 1990)

Part Fourteen: IV. A. *Use of force—use of force under collective measures—regime of the UN*

(See also Part Fourteen: III. (items of 6 September (third passage) and 11 December 1990), above)

In the course of a debate on the subject of the Gulf, the Secretary of State for Foreign and Commonwealth Affairs, Mr Douglas Hurd, referred to the UN Security Council Resolution 678 and stated:

The phrase 'all necessary means' includes the use of force.

(HC Debs., vol. 182, col. 823: 11 December 1990)

In the course of a debate in the House of Lords on the same subject, the Lord Privy Seal, Lord Waddington, referred to the legal basis for armed action under Article 51 of the UN Charter. He then went on:

With the adoption of Resolution 678 on 29th November, the Security Council has now specifically authorised the use of all necessary means to uphold and implement its resolutions. These clearly include military force.

(HL Debs., vol. 524, col. 650: 17 December 1990)

Part Fourteen: V. *Use of force—use of force other than international war, civil war and self-defence*

The Secretary of State for Foreign and Commonwealth Affairs was asked 'what reasons were given by the President of the United States of America for the invasion of Panama when he sought endorsement for his actions from Her Majesty's Government?'. In reply, the Parliamentary Under-Secretary of State, FCO, wrote:

President Bush has stated that the United States military intervention in Panama had four objectives: to safeguard the lives of American citizens, to help restore democracy, to protect the integrity of the Panama canal treaties, and to bring General Noriega to justice.

(HC Debs., vol. 164, Written Answers, col. *510*: 8 January 1990)

The question was then asked 'what steps were taken by Her Majesty's Government to establish the legality of the United States invasion of Panama before endorsement of such action was given?'. In reply, the same Minister wrote:

The American action was undertaken with the agreement of the leaders who clearly won the elections held last May. We had no hesitation in welcoming the establishment of democratic government in Panama and giving full support to the action that led to this. General Noriega's arbitrary rule was maintained by force. There can be no suggestion that he represented legality.

(Ibid.)

Part Fifteen: I. *Neutrality, non-belligerency—legal nature of neutrality*

In the course of a debate on the subject of India and Kashmir, the Parliamentary Under-Secretary of State, FCO, Mr Tim Sainsbury, stated:

Our longstanding position on the dispute over the status of Kashmir has been, and remains, one of neutrality.

(HC Debs., vol. 177, col. 210: 23 July 1990)

APPENDICES

I. Multilateral Agreements Signed by the United Kingdom in 1990[1]

Title	Place and Date	UK Signature	Text[2]
Decision of the Administrative Council amending the Implementing Regulations to the European Patent Convention of 5.10.1973: Decision CA/D 2/85 amending Rule 85	Munich, 14.2.1985	10.12.1984 (entry into force)	TS No. 50 (1985) (Cmnd. 9616), p.15
Convention for the Protection of the Natural Resources and Environment of the South Pacific (SPREP) and Final Act of the High Level Conference on the Protection of the Natural Resources and Environment of the South Pacific Region	Noumea/Suva, 25/26.11.1986	16.7.1987 (on behalf of Pitcairn, Henderson, Ducie and Oeno Islands)	
Protocol concerning Co-operation in Combating Pollution Emergencies in the South Pacific Region	Noumea/Suva, 25/26.11.1986	16.7.1987 (on behalf of Pitcairn, Henderson, Ducie and Oeno Islands)	
Protocol for the Prevention of Pollution of the South Pacific Region by Dumping	Noumea/Suva, 25/26.11.1986	16.7.1987 (on behalf of Pitcairn, Henderson, Ducie and Oeno Islands)	
Protocol (1986) amending the Annex to the Agreement on Trade in Civil Aircraft	Geneva, 2.12.1986	23.12.1987 (acceptance)	Misc. No. 3 (1990) (Cm. 952)

[1] Information supplied by the Foreign and Commonwealth Office. The table includes some agreements signed by the United Kingdom before 1990, where information was not previously available. The information is correct as at January 1991, although in some cases information available since that time has been included.

[2] Publication is in various series of UK Command Papers, namely: EC = European Communities Series; Misc. = Miscellaneous Series; TS = Treaty Series; Cm. and Cmnd. = Command Paper number.

Title	Place and Date	UK Signature	Text
Decision of the Administrative Council amending the Implementing Regulations to the European Patent Convention of 5.10.1973: Decision CA/D 13/86 amending Rule 37	Munich, 5.12.1986	5.12.1986 (entry into force)	
Amendments to Articles 6 and 7 of the Convention on Wetlands of International Importance especially as Waterfowl Habitat, Ramsar, 2.2.1971, as amended by the Paris Protocol of 3.12.1982	Regina, 28.5.1987	27.6.1990 (acceptance)	Misc. No. 6 (1990) (Cm. 983)
Decision of the Administrative Council amending the Implementing Regulations to the European Patent Convention of 5.10.1973: Decision CA/D 4/87 amending Rules 90 and 102	Vienna, 5.6.1987	5.6.1987 (entry into force)	
Decision of the Administrative Council amending the Implementing Regulations to the European Patent Convention of 5.10.1973: Decision CA/D 6/87 amending Rule 85(1)	Vienna, 5.6.1987	5.6.1987 (entry into force)	
Decision of the Administrative Council amending the Implementing Regulations to the European Patent Convention of 5.10.1973: Decision CA/D 7/87 amending Rules 31 and 51	Vienna, 5.6.1987	5.6.1987 (entry into force)	
Decision of the Administrative Council amending the Implementing Regulations to the European Patent Convention of 5.10.1973: Decision CA/D 8/87 amending Rules 24 and 36	Vienna, 5.6.1987	5.6.1987 (entry into force)	
1987 Amendments to the Annex to the Convention on Facilitation of International Maritime Traffic, 1965, as amended	London, 17.9.1987	1.1.1989 (entry into force)	
Amendments to Articles 10 and 12 of the Convention on the Control and Marking of Articles of Precious Metals done at Vienna on 15.11.1972	Geneva, 18.5.1988	25.6.1990 (acceptance)	Misc. No. 11 (1990) (Cm. 1040)

Title	Place and Date	UK Signature	Text
Protocol of Amendment to the International Convention on Mutual Administrative Assistance for the Prevention, Investigation and Repression of Customs Offences signed at Nairobi on 9.6.1977	Brussels, 22.6.1988	9.3.1990 (acceptance)	Misc. No. 2 (1990) (Cm. 904)
Amendments to the International Convention for the Safety of Life at Sea, 1974, concerning Radiocommunications for the Global Maritime Distress and Safety System	London, 9.11.1988	1.2.1992 (entry into force)	
Amendments to the Protocol of 1978 relating to the International Convention for the Safety of Life at Sea, 1974, concerning Radiocommunications for the Global Maritime Distress and Safety System	London, 10.11.1988		
Decision of the Administrative Council amending the Implementing Regulations to the European Patent Convention of 5.10.1973: Decision CA/D 18/88 amending Rules 17, 35, 58, 85(a) and 85(b)	Munich, 8.12.1988	1.4.1989 (entry into force)	
Amendments to the Convention on the International Maritime Satellite Organization (INMARSAT)	London, 19.1.1989	3.11.1989 (acceptance)	
Amendments to the Operating Agreement on the International Maritime Satellite Organization (INMARSAT)	London, 19.1.1989	3.11.1989 (approval)	
1989 Amendments to the Annex of the Protocol of 1978 relating to the International Convention for the Prevention of Pollution from Ships, 1973 (Appendices II and III of Annex II of MARPOL 73/78)	London, 17.3.1989	13.10.1990 (entry into force)	
1989 Amendments to the Code for the Construction and Equipment of Ships Carrying Dangerous Chemicals in Bulk (BCH Code)	London, 17.3.1989	13.10.1990 (entry into force)	
1989 Amendments to the International Code for the Construction and Equipment of Ships Carrying Dangerous Chemicals in Bulk (IBC CODE)	London, 17.3.1989	13.10.1990 (entry into force)	

Title	Place and Date	UK Signature	Text
1989 Amendments to the International Code for the Construction and Equipment of Ships Carrying Dangerous Chemicals in Bulk (IBC Code)	London, 11.4.1989	13.10.1990 (entry into force)	
Amendments to the International Convention for the Safety of Life at Sea, 1974, as amended	London, 11.4.1989		
Additional Protocol No. 4 to the Revised Convention for Rhine Navigation of 17.10.1868, as amended on 20.11.1963, with Declaration on Signature	Strasbourg, 25.4.1989	25.4.1989	Misc. No. 7 (1990) (Cm. 987)
International Convention on Salvage, 1989, with Final Act	London, 28.4.1989	28.6.1990	
Resolution to extend the International Coffee Agreement, 1983 (Resolution No. 347 of the International Coffee Council)	London, 3.7.1989	29.9.1989 (provisional application: includes Guernsey, Jersey, St Helena)	Misc. No. 11 (1989) (Cm. 767)
Convention on the Rights of the Child	New York, 20.11.1989	19.4.1990	
Final Act of the Conference on the Community Patent	Luxembourg, 15.12.1989	15.12.1989	
Fourth ACP-EEC Convention, with Final Act	Lomé, 15.12.1989	16.7.1990	EC No. 96 (1990) (Cm. 1364)
Agreement relating to Community Patents	Luxembourg, 15/21.12.1989	15.12.1989	
Joint Declaration by the Governments of the Member States of the EEC at the time of signing the Agreement relating to Community Patents	Luxembourg, 15/21.12.1989	15.12.1989	
Protocol on a Possible Modification of the Conditions of Entry into Force of the Agreement relating to Community Patents	Luxembourg, 15/21.12.1989	15.12.1989	
Protocol relating to the Madrid Agreement concerning the International Registration of Marks	Madrid, 28.6/ 31.12.1989	28.6.1989	

Title	Place and Date	UK Signature	Text
1990 Amendments to the Annex to the Convention on Facilitation of International Maritime Traffic, 1965, as amended	London, 3.5.1990		
Agreement establishing the European Bank for Reconstruction and Development	Paris, 29.5.1990	29.5.1990	Misc. No. 14 (1990) (Cm. 1116)
Convention Determining the State Responsible for Examining Applications for Asylum Lodged in One of the Member States of the European Communities	Dublin, 15.6.1990	15.6.1990	
Fifth Protocol to the General Agreement on Privileges and Immunities of the Council of Europe	Strasbourg, 18.6.1990	18.6.1990	Misc. No. 15 (1990) (Cm. 1121)
Treaty on the Final Settlement with Respect to Germany, with Agreed Minute	Moscow, 12.9.1990	12.9.1990	Misc. No. 17 (1990) (Cm. 1230)
Agreement on the Settlement of Certain Matters relating to Berlin	Bonn, 25.9.1990	25.9.1990	Misc. No. 18 (1990) (Cm. 1242)
Exchange of Notes between the Government of the Federal Republic of Germany and the Governments of Belgium, Canada, the Netherlands, the UK and the USA concerning the Convention on the Presence of Foreign Forces in the Federal Republic of Germany of 23.10.1954	Bonn, 25.9.1990	25.9.1990	TS No. 16 (1991) (Cm. 1443)
Exchange of Notes between the Government of the Federal Republic of Germany and the Governments of the French Republic, the UK and the USA concerning the Presence in Berlin of Armed Forces of the French Republic, of the UK, and of the USA	Bonn, 25.9.1990	25.9.1990	TS No. 14 (1991) (Cm. 1442)
Exchange of Notes between the Government of the Federal Republic of Germany and the Governments of Belgium, Canada, the French Republic, the Netherlands, the UK and the USA concerning the Agreement of 19.6.1951 between the Parties to	Bonn, 25.9.1990	25.9.1990	TS No. 15 (1991) (Cm. 1441)

Title	Place and Date	UK Signature	Text
the North Atlantic Treaty regarding the Status of their Forces, the Agreement of 3.8.1959 to supplement that Agreement with respect to Foreign Forces stationed in the Federal Republic of Germany, and the Agreements related thereto			
Agreement in the form of an Exchange of Notes between the Government of the Federal Republic of Germany and the Governments of the UK, the French Republic and the USA concerning the Convention on Relations between the Three Powers and the Federal Republic of Germany of 26.5.1952 and the Convention on the Settlement of Matters arising out of the War and the Occupation of 26.5.1952	Bonn, 27/ 28.9.1990	27.9.1990	TS No. 22 (1991) (Cm. 1478)
Amendment to Article 26 of the Statute of the Council of Europe	Rome, 6.11.1990	6.11.1990 (entry into force)	
Convention on Laundering, Search, Seizure and Confiscation of the Proceeds from Crime	Strasbourg, 8.11.1990	8.11.1990	

II. BILATERAL AGREEMENTS SIGNED BY THE UNITED KINGDOM IN 1990[1]

Country and Title	Place and Date	Text[2]
ANGOLA		
Exchange of Notes concerning Certain Commercial Debts (The UK/Angola Debt Agreement No. 2 (1989))	Luanda, 11.9.1990	
ARGENTINA		
Exchange of Notes concerning the Abolition of Visas	London, 9.4.1990	TS No. 2 (1991) (Cm. 1389)
Cultural Convention	Buenos Aires, 8.10.1990	

[1] Information supplied by the Foreign and Commonwealth Office. The table includes some agreements signed by the United Kingdom before 1990, where information was not previously available. The information is correct as at January 1991, although in some cases information available since that time has been included.

[2] Publication is in various series of UK Command Papers, including Treaty Series (TS). Cm. = Command Paper number.

Country and Title	Place and Date	Text
ARGENTINA—*contd* Agreement for the Promotion and Protection of Investments	Buenos Aires, 11.12.1990	
Exchange of Notes concerning Certain Commercial Debts (The UK/Argentina Debt Agreement No. 3 (1989))	London, 18.12.1990	TS No. 26 (1991) (Cm. 1497)
AUSTRALIA Agreement concerning the Co-Production of Films	Canberra, 12.6.1990	Australia No. 1 (1990) (Cm. 1143)
Agreement providing for the Reciprocal Recognition and Enforcement of Judgments in Civil and Commercial Matters	Canberra, 23.8.1990	
Agreement on Social Security	London, 1.10.1990	
BAHRAIN Agreement concerning Mutual Assistance in relation to Drug Trafficking	Manama, 1.10.1990	Bahrain No. 1 (1990) (Cm. 1305)
BANGLADESH Exchange of Notes amending the Agreement for Air Services between and beyond their respective Territories done at London on 5.7.1978	Dhaka, 20.5.1990	TS No. 68 (1990) (Cm. 1233)
BOTSWANA Agreement concerning Air Services	London, 30.1.1990	TS No. 39 (1990) (Cm. 1094)
BRUNEI Agreement concerning Air Services	London, 23.11.1990	TS No. 23 (1991) (Cm. 1481)
BURUNDI Agreement for the Promotion and Protection of Investments	London, 13.9.1990	TS No. 11 (1991) (Cm. 1420)
CHINA Exchange of Notes amending the Agreement relating to Civil Air Transport done at London on 1.11.1979	Peking, 10.3.1990	TS No. 72 (1990) (Cm. 1240)
COSTA RICA Exchange of Notes concerning Certain Commercial Debts (The UK/Costa Rica Debt Agreement No. 3 (1989))	San José, 7.6.1990	TS No. 61 (1990) (Cm. 1210)
COTE D'IVOIRE Agreement in the form of an Exchange of Notes concerning Certain Commercial Debts (The UK/Côte d'Ivoire Debt Agreement No. 5 (1989))	Abidjan, 21.8.1990	
CZECHOSLOVAKIA Agreement on Co-operation in the Fields of Education, Science and Culture	London, 3.4.1990	TS No. 57 (1990) (Cm. 1198)

Country and Title	Place and Date	Text
CZECHOSLOVAKIA—*contd*		
Agreement for the Promotion and Protection of Investments, with Protocol	Prague, 10.7.1990	Czechoslovakia No. 1 (1990) (Cm. 1306)
Exchange of Notes concerning the Abolition of Visas	Prague, 18.9.1990	TS No. 6 (1991) (Cm. 1396)
Convention for the Avoidance of Double Taxation with respect to Taxes on Income and Capital Gains	London, 5.11.1990	
DOMINICA		
Exchange of Notes extending to Gibraltar the Agreement for the Promotion and Protection of Investments signed at Roseau on 23.1.1987	Roseau, 3.1.1990	
ECUADOR		
Exchange of Notes concerning Certain Commercial Debts (The UK/Ecuador Debt Agreement No. 4 (1989))	London, 30.5.1990	TS No. 66 (1990) (Cm. 1231)
EGYPT		
Exchange of Notes regarding the Use of British Capital Untransferable Accounts in Egypt	Cairo, 7.5.1990	
FRANCE		
Exchange of Notes further amending the Air Transport Agreement signed at London on 28.2.1946	Paris, 30.4.1990	
GAMBIA		
Agreement for Air Services between and beyond their respective Territories	Banjul, 5.2.1990	TS No. 43 (1990) (Cm. 1098)
GERMAN DEMOCRATIC REPUBLIC		
Exchange of Notes concerning the Abolition of Visas	Berlin, 25.5.1990	TS No. 64 (1990) (Cm. 1213)
(*Note*: This Exchange of Notes is considered terminated with effect from the date of the Unification of Germany, 3.10.1990)		
GERMAN FEDERAL REPUBLIC		
Exchange of Notes concerning the Storage with an Option for Reprocessing of Irradiated Nuclear Fuel by the UK Atomic Energy Authority	Bonn, 3.8.1990	TS No. 3 (1991) (Cm. 1390)
Exchange of Notes concerning Air Services to and from Berlin	Bonn, 9.10.1990	TS No. 18 (1991) (Cm. 1445)
Agreement concerning Air Navigation Services in Berlin	Bonn, 23.10.1990	
HUNGARY		
Exchange of Notes concerning the Abolition of Visas	Budapest, 18.9.1990	TS No. 19 (1991) (Cm. 1471)

Country and Title	Place and Date	Text
IRAQ Agreement between the Government of Iraq and the Governments of the UK, Canada, Australia, New Zealand and India concerning the Mosul War Cemetery	Baghdad, 30.10.1989	TS No. 5 (1991) (Cm. 1399)
IRELAND Exchange of Notes amending and prolonging the Agreement on the International Carriage of Goods by Road signed at Dublin on 9.4.1980	Dublin, 2.5.1990	TS No. 80 (1990) (Cm. 1314)
ITALY Agreement concerning Mutual Assistance in relation to Traffic in Narcotic Drugs or Psychotropic Substances and the Restraint and Confiscation of the Proceeds of Crime	Rome, 16.5.1990	Italy No. 1 (1991) (Cm. 1395)
JAPAN Exchange of Notes concerning Air Services	Tokyo, 10.9.1990	TS No. 28 (1991) (Cm. 1492)
JORDAN Exchange of Notes cancelling the UK/ Jordan Loan Agreement (No. 2) 1987	Amman, 2.11.1989	TS No. 21 (1990) (Cm. 1000)
Exchange of Notes amending the UK/ Jordan Loan 1982	Amman, 6/19.3.1990	TS No. 90 (1990) (Cm. 1419), p.16
Exchange of Notes concerning the UK/ Jordan Debt Re-scheduling Agreement 1990	Amman, 16.9/ 14.10.1990	TS No. 9 (1991) (Cm. 1418)
Exchange of Notes further amending the UK/Jordan Loan 1982, done at Amman 14.3.1982	Amman, 4.12.1990	
MALI Agreement in the form of an Exchange of Notes on Certain Commercial Debts (The UK/Mali Debt Agreement 1988)	Dakar, 29.12.1989	
Agreement in the form of an Exchange of Notes concerning Certain Commercial Debts (The UK/Mali Debt Agreement No. 2 (1989))	Dakar, 8.11.1990	
MAURITANIA Exchange of Notes on Certain Commercial Debts (The UK/Mauritania Debt Agreement No. 3 (1987))	Dakar, 13.6.1988	
MEXICO Agreement on Bilateral Co-operation in the Fight against Illicit Traffic in and Abuse of Narcotic Drugs and Psychotropic Substances	London, 29.1.1990	TS No. 7 (1991) (Cm. 1398)

Country and Title	Place and Date	Text
MEXICO—*contd*		
Agreement concerning Mutual Assistance in relation to Drug Trafficking	London, 29.1.1990	
MISCELLANEOUS		
Agreement between the Three Governments of the UK, the Federal Republic of Germany, the Kingdom of the Netherlands and the Government of the United States of America regarding Protection of Information transferred into the USA in connection with the Initial Phase of a Project for the Establishment of a Uranium Enrichment Installation in the US based upon the Gas Centrifuge Process developed within the Three European Countries	Washington, 22.4.1988	TS No. 52 (1990) (Cm. 1169)
Exchange of Notes between the Government of the UK and the Director General of the Multinational Force and Observers concerning the further Extension of the Commitment of the British Component of the Multinational Force in the Sinai	London, 23.5.1988	TS No. 69 (1990) (Cm. 1237)
Exchange of Letters between the Government of the UK and the International Maritime Organization concerning the Association of the UK with the International COSPAS-SARSAT Programme as a Ground Segment Provider	London, 29.1/ 22.2.1990	TS No. 17 (1991) (Cm. 1444)
Exchange of Notes between the Government of the UK and the Director General of the Multinational Force and Observers concerning the further Extension of the Commitment of the British Component of the Multinational Force in the Sinai	London, 11.6.1990	TS No. 79 (1990) (Cm. 1313)
MOROCCO		
Agreement for the Promotion and Protection of Investments	Rabat, 30.10.1990	
MOZAMBIQUE		
Exchange of Notes concerning Certain Commercial Debts (The UK/Mozambique Debt Agreement No. 2 (1987))	Maputo, 27.3.1990	TS No. 73 (1990) (Cm. 1249)
NIGER		
Exchange of Notes concerning Certain Commercial Debts (The UK/Niger Debt Agreement No. 6 (1988))	Abidjan, 8.12.1989	

Country and Title	*Place and Date*	*Text*
NIGERIA Agreement for the Promotion and Protection of Investments	Abuja, 11.12.1990	
NORWAY Convention on Social Security, with Protocol concerning Medical Treatment	Oslo, 19.6.1990	Norway No. 1 (1990) (Cm. 1331)
PAKISTAN Exchange of Notes further amending the Air Services Agreement between and beyond their respective Territories done at Rawalpindi on 29.5.1974, as amended	Islamabad, 2.10.1989	TS No. 56 (1990) (Cm. 1197)
Agreement for the Free Exchange of Microfilms of Archives, Books, Manuscripts, Paintings of Historical Import, Transparencies of Prints and Drawings	London, 4.7.1990	TS No. 65 (1990) (Cm. 1214)
PHILIPPINES Exchange of Notes concerning Certain Commercial Debts (The UK/Philippines Debt Agreement No. 3 (1989))	Manila, 15.3.1990	TS No. 49 (1990) (Cm. 1138)
Exchange of Notes constituting an Agreement to extend the Agreement for the Promotion and Protection of Investments signed at London on 3.12.1980 to the Bailiwicks of Jersey and Guernsey, the Isle of Man and Hong Kong	Manila, 3.4.1990	
POLAND Exchange of Notes further amending the Agreement concerning Civil Air Transport done at Warsaw on 2.7.1960	Warsaw, 8.8.1989	TS No. 67 (1990) (Cm. 1232)
PORTUGAL Agreement in the form of an Exchange of Letters concerning the Termination of Article 19 of the Treaty of Commerce and Navigation signed at Lisbon on 12.8.1914	Lisbon, 4.7.1990	
SAUDI ARABIA Agreement concerning the Investigation of Drug Trafficking and Confiscation of the Proceeds of Drug Trafficking	Jeddah, 2.6.1990	Saudi Arabia No. 1 (1990) (Cm. 1308)
SENEGAL Exchange of Notes concerning Certain Commercial Debts (The UK/Senegal Debt Agreement No. 8 (1990))	Dakar, 26.10.1990	

Country and Title	Place and Date	Text
SOVIET UNION		
Exchange of Notes prolonging the Periods of Operation of the Agreement for Co-operation in the Fields of Applied Science and Technology done at London on 19.1.1968	Moscow, 23.5/ 16.8.1978	
Agreement on Co-operation in the Field of Education, Science and Culture	Moscow, 10.4.1990	Soviet Union No. 2 (1990) (Cm. 1192)
Agreement on Early Notification of a Nuclear Accident and Exchange of Information concerning the Operation and Management of Nuclear Facilities, with Protocol	Moscow, 10.4.1990	TS No. 54 (1990) (Cm. 1171)
Agreement on the Mutual Establishment and Activities of Cultural Centres	Moscow, 8.6.1990	
Programme for the Development of Economic and Industrial Co-operation for the Period 1991-2000	Moscow, 8.6.1990	
SUDAN		
Exchange of Notes amending the Agreement concerning the Provision of Certain Technical Assistance by the UK done at Khartoum on 4.4.1970	Khartoum, 19.6.1988	TS No. 70 (1990) (Cm. 1238)
SWITZERLAND		
Exchange of Notes further amending the Air Services Agreement done at London on 5.4.1950	Berne, 29.9/ 23.11.1990	TS No. 24 (1991) (Cm. 1498)
TANZANIA		
Exchange of Notes concerning Certain Commercial Debts (The UK/Tanzania Debt Agreement No. 2 (1988))	Dar es Salaam, 26.6.1990	TS No. 21 (1991) (Cm. 1474)
THAILAND		
Agreement on the Transfer of Offenders and on Co-operation in the Enforcement of Penal Sentences	Bangkok, 22.1.1990	Thailand No. 1 (1990) (Cm. 1119)
TOGO		
Exchange of Notes concerning Certain Commercial Debts (The UK/Togo Debt Agreement No. 7 (1989))	Accra, 12.3.1990	TS No. 77 (1990) (Cm. 1309)
TRINIDAD AND TOBAGO		
Exchange of Notes concerning Certain Commercial Debts (The UK/Trinidad and Tobago Debt Agreement No. 2 (1990))	Port of Spain, 9.10.1990	

Country and Title	Place and Date	Text
TUNISIA Agreement between the Government of Tunisia and the Governments of the UK, Canada, Australia, New Zealand and India concerning War Cemeteries, Graves and Memorials in Tunisia	Tunis, 2.5.1990	
UGANDA Exchange of Notes concerning Certain Commercial Debts (The UK/Uganda Debt Agreement No. 4 (1989))	Kampala, 19.11.1989	TS No. 76 (1990) (Cm. 1252)
UNITED STATES OF AMERICA Exchange of Notes further extending the Narcotics Co-operation Agreement with respect to the Turks and Caicos Islands signed on 18.9.1986	Washington, 19.1.1990	TS No. 89 (1990) (Cm. 1388), p. 28
Exchange of Notes further extending the Narcotics Co-operation Agreement with respect to the British Virgin Islands signed at London on 14.4.1987	Washington, 9.2.1990	TS No. 89 (1990) (Cm. 1388), p. 28
Exchange of Notes further extending the Narcotics Co-operation Agreement with respect to Montserrat signed at London on 14.5.1987	Washington, 27.2.1990	TS No. 89 (1990) (Cm. 1388), p. 29
Exchange of Notes further extending the Agreement in the form of an Exchange of Letters concerning the Cayman Islands and Matters connected with, arising from, related to, or resulting from any Narcotics Activity referred to in the Single Convention on Narcotic Drugs 1961, signed at London on 26.7.1984	Washington, 27.2.1990	TS No. 89 (1990) (Cm. 1388), p. 28
Exchange of Notes further extending the Narcotics Co-operation Agreement with respect to Anguilla signed at Washington on 11.3.1987	Washington, 26.3.1990	TS No. 90 (1990) (Cm. 1419), p. 27
Exchange of Notes further extending the Narcotics Co-operation Agreement with respect to Montserrat signed at London on 14.5.1987	Washington, 29.5.1990	TS No. 90 (1990) (Cm. 1419), p. 27
Exchange of Notes further extending the Narcotics Co-operation Agreement with respect to Anguilla, signed at Washington on 11.3.1987	Washington, 27.6.1990	
Exchange of Notes further extending the Narcotics Co-operation Agreement with respect to the Turks and Caicos Islands, signed on 18.9.1986	Washington, 20.7.1990	

Country and Title	*Place and Date*	*Text*

UNITED STATES OF AMERICA—
contd

Exchange of Notes further extending the
Narcotics Co-operation Agreement with
respect to Montserrat signed at London on
14.5.1987

Washington,
30.8.1990

Exchange of Notes further extending the
Narcotics Co-operation Agreement with
respect to Anguilla signed at Washington on
11.3.1987

Washington,
26.9.1990

Exchange of Notes further extending the
Narcotics Co-operation Agreement with
respect to the Turks and Caicos Islands
signed on 18.9.1986

Washington,
17.10.1990

ZAIRE

Exchange of Notes concerning Certain
Commercial Debts (The UK/Zaire Debt
Agreement No. 9 (1989))

Kinshasa, 3.4.1990

III. United Kingdom Legislation during 1990 Concerning Matters of International Law[1]

The Aviation and Maritime Security Act (1990 c. 31) gives effect to the Montreal Protocol for the Suppression of Unlawful Acts of Violence at Airports Servicing International Civil Aviation 1988, the Rome Convention for the Suppression of Unlawful Acts against the Safety of Maritime Navigation 1988, and the Protocol for the Suppression of Unlawful Acts against the Safety of Fixed Platforms located on the Continental Shelf 1988. It makes certain other provisions with respect to aviation security, civil aviation, and the protection of ships and harbour areas against acts of violence. (See Parts One: II.D.1., Eight: II.D., Nine: XV.A.3. and Thirteen: I.B., above.)

The British Nationality (Hong Kong) Act (1990 c. 34) provides for the acquisition of British citizenship by up to 50,000 Hong Kong residents (together with their spouses and minor children) selected by the Secretary of State on the recommendation of the Governor of Hong Kong.

The Broadcasting Act (1990 c. 42) by Part VIII and Schedule 16 amends the Marine Broadcasting (Offences) Act 1967 by extending the definition of the areas to which and persons to whom that Act applies, and by providing enforcement powers in relation to offences under that Act. (See Parts Eight: II.D. and Nine: VII.H., above.)

The Contracts (Applicable Law) Act (1990 c. 36) provides that the Convention on the Law Applicable to Contractual Obligations opened for signature in Rome on 19 June 1980 and related instruments shall have the force of law in the United Kingdom. (See Part One: II.D.1., above.)

The Criminal Justice (International Co-operation) Act (1990 c. 5) makes provision to enable the United Kingdom to ratify the European Convention on Mutual Assistance 1957 and the Vienna Convention against Illicit Traffic in Narcotic Drugs and Psychotropic Substances

[1] Compiled by C. A. Hopkins.

1988. It deals with international co-operation in services of process, provision of evidence and suppression of drug-trafficking. (See Parts One: II.D.1., Four: VI., Eight: II.D. and Nine: VII.H., above.)

The Environmental Protection Act (1990 c. 43) deals in Part VIII and Schedule 14 with oil pollution from ships and amends the Prevention of Oil Pollution Act 1971. (See Part Nine: VII.H. and VIII., above.)

The Pakistan Act (1990 c. 14) provides for the amendment of certain statutes and statutory instruments in consequence of Pakistan's re-admission to the Commonwealth and repeals the Pakistan Act 1973 and 1974. (See Part Three: II.A.2.(a)., above.)

TABLE OF CASES[1]

---

[1] The figures in heavier type indicate the pages on which cases are reviewed.

INDEX